Encyclopedia of
Women's Autobiography

Encyclopedia of Women's Autobiography

VOLUME 1: A–J

Edited by Victoria Boynton and Jo Malin

Emmanuel S. Nelson, Advisory Editor

GREENWOOD PRESS
Westport, Connecticut • London

Library of Congress Cataloging-in-Publication Data

Encyclopedia of women's autobiography / edited by
   Victoria Boynton and Jo Malin.
       p.   cm.
     Includes bibliographical references and index.
     ISBN 0–313–32737–8 (set : alk. paper)—
     ISBN 0–313–32738–6 (vol. 1 : alk. paper)—
     ISBN 0–313–32739–4 (vol. 2 : alk. paper)—
     1. Women's studies—Biographical methods—
     Encyclopedias.   2. Autobiography—Women authors—
     Encyclopedias   I. Boynton, Victoria.   II. Malin, Jo, 1942–.
   HQ1185.E63   2005
   305.4'092'2—dc22   2005008526
   [B]

British Library Cataloguing in Publication Data is available.

Library of Congress Catalog Card Number: 2005008526
ISBN 0–313–32737–8 (set)
       0–313–32738–6 (Vol. 1)
       0–313–32739–4 (Vol. 2)

First published in 2005

Greenwood Press, 88 Post Road West, Westport, CT 06881
An imprint of Greenwood Publishing Group, Inc.
www.greenwood.com

Printed in the United States of America

The paper used in this book complies with the
Permanent Paper Standard issued by the National
Information Standards Organization (Z39.48-1984).

10 9 8 7 6 5 4 3 2 1

Contents

Alphabetical List of Entries

Guide to Related Topics

Authors

Addams, Jane

Alexander, Meena

Allison, Dorothy

Angelou, Maya

Anzaldúa, Gloria

Beauvoir, Simone de

Benstock, Shari

Boyce, Neith

Brodzki, Bella

Brooks, Gwendolyn Elizabeth

Burney, Frances (Fanny)

Cavendish, Margaret (Lucas), Duchess of
   Newcastle

Charke, Charlotte

Chernin, Kim

Chisholm, Shirley Anita St. Hill

Conway, Jill Ker

Das, Kamala

Davis, Angela Yvonne

Day, Dorothy

Delaney, Lucy Ann

Derricotte, Toi

Dillard, Annie

Dinesen, Isak (Karen Blixen)

Dunbar-Nelson, Alice Moore

Duras, Marguerite

Elaw, Zilpha

Ernaux, Annie

Fisher, M.F.K. (Mary Frances Kennedy)

Foote, Julia A. J.

Frame, Janet Paterson

Frank, Annelies (Anne)

Fuller, (Sarah) Margaret

Gagnier, Regenia

Giovanni, Nikki (Yolande Cornelia Jr.)

Goldman, Emma

Gordon, Mary

Halkett, Anne, Lady

Heilbrun, Carolyn

Hildegard von Bingen

Hoffman, Eva

hooks, bell

Hurston, Zora Neale

Hutchinson, Lucy (née Apsley)

Jacobs, Harriet Ann

Jong, Erica

Jordan, June

Julian of Norwich

Karr, Mary

Kartini, Raden Adjeng

Kaysen, Susanna

Keckley, Elizabeth Hobbs

Kemble, Frances Anne

Kempe, Margery

Kincaid, Jamaica

Kingston, Maxine Hong

Koller, Alice

Kollontai, Alexandra Mikhailovna

Kollwitz, Käthe

Lamott, Anne

Lazarre, Jane

Lim, Shirley Geok-lin

Lionnet, Françoise

Lorde, Audre

Mairs, Nancy

Markham, Beryl

Martineau, Harriet

Mason, Mary Grimley

McKay, Nellie Y.

Menchú Tum, Rigoberta

Miller, Nancy K. (Kipnis)

Modjeska, Drusilla

Moody, Anne

Moraga, Cherríe

Morgan, Sally

Mukherjee, Bharati

Murray, Pauli

Nestle, Joan

Neuman, Shirley C.

Nin, Anaïs

Njeri, Itabari

Norris, Kathleen

Nussbaum, Felicity A.

Olds, Sharon

Olsen, Tillie

Plath, Sylvia

Prince, Mary

Pruitt, Ida

Rich, Adrienne

Ringgold, Faith

Santiago, Esmeralda

Sarton, May

Schenck, Celeste

Sexton, Anne

Shulman, Alix Kates

Silko, Leslie Marmon

Smith, Sidonie

Sone, Monica

Spacks, Patricia Meyer

Staël, Germaine Necker, Madame de

Stanton, Domna C.

Steedman, Carolyn Kay

Stein, Gertrude

Sui Sin Far (Edith Maude Eaton)

Suleri, Sara

Tompkins, Jane Perry

Truth, Sojourner

Walker, Alice

Watson, Julia

Wells, Ida B.

Welty, Eudora Alice

Williams, Donna

Wolf, Christa

Wong, Jade Snow

Woolf, Virginia

Titles

Autobiography of Alice B. Toklas, The

Book of Margery Kempe, The

Diary of a Young Girl, The

Harriet Martineau's Autobiography

I Know Why the Caged Bird Sings

Incidents in the Life of a Slave Girl

Journal of a Solitude

Moments of Being

Of Woman Born: Motherhood as Experience and Institution

Out of Africa

Woman Warrior, The

Zami: A New Spelling of My Name

Nationalities or Ethnicities

African American Women's Autobiography

African Women's Autobiography

American Women's Autobiography: Early Women Diarists and Memoirists

American Women's Autobiography: Nineteenth Century

American Women's Autobiography: Twentieth and Twenty-first Centuries

Asian American Women's Autobiography

Australian Women's Autobiography

British Women's Autobiography to 1900

British Women's Autobiography Since 1900

Canadian Women's Autobiography

Caribbean Women's Autobiography

Chinese Women's Autobiography

Eastern European Women's Autobiography

French Women's Autobiography

German Women's Autobiography

Irish Women's Autobiography

Italian Women's Autobiography

Japanese Women's Autobiography

Latin American Women's Autobiography

Latina Women's Autobiography

Middle Eastern Women's Autobiography

Native American Women's Autobiography

Philippine Women's Autobiography

Russian Women's Autobiography

Scandinavian Women's Autobiography

South Asian Women's Autobiography

Spanish Women's Autobiography

Genres and/or Styles

Autobiographical Fiction

Autoethnography

Biography

Captivity/Prison Narrative

Collaborative Life Narrative

Confession

Diary

Lesbian Autobiography

Letters

Memoir

Performative Autobiography

Personal Criticism

Personal Essay

Postcolonial Women's Autobiography

Relational Autobiography

Self-Help Narrative

Survivor Narrative

Travel Narrative

Key Words/Terms

Alterity

Autobiographics

Class

Embodiment

Feminism

Gender

Identity

Memoir

Memory

Mother/Daughter Relationship

Motherhood and Reproduction

Patriarchy

Postcolonial Women's Autobiography

Race

Rape and Sexual Abuse

Scriptotherapy

Sexuality

Space/Place

Voice

Preface

In 1987, Sidonie Smith began her seminal text on women's autobiography: "Suddenly everyone in the universe of literary critics and theorists seems to be talking about autobiography" (Smith 3). She built her own feminist analysis of the genre, in *A Poetics of Women's Autobiography: Marginality and the Fictions of Self-Representation*, on the previous thirty years and especially the preceding decade of scholarship in autobiography, a decade in which an ever increasing number of books, articles, and conference papers about autobiography appeared. In her introduction she attempted to explain some of the fascination with the genre: "This genre apparently so simple, so self-evident, so readily accessible . . . is ultimately as complex as the subject it seeks to capture in its representation and as various as the rhetorical expressions through which . . . that subjectivity reads itself into the world" (Smith 3).

When Smith began her own work of looking at autobiography through the lens of gender and recovering women's life writing texts nearly twenty years ago, she began what would be a parallel, yet perhaps even more explosive process. There has been, from 1987 through today in 2005, such a ferment of activity around women's life writing that one may safely say that suddenly everyone—but it appears to be a more inclusive "everyone"—is talking about women's auto-biography and probably will continue to talk about it for years into the future.

This activity, born of Smith's work and then followed by the works of a multitude of diverse and brilliantly vibrant scholars of women's autobiography and feminist theory is where we "went to school." In fact, we had the great good luck to have been students together in a feminist theory classroom with Sidonie Smith at the State University of New York at Binghamton and indeed owe her a tremendous debt for helping us to begin our lives as scholars and our partnership as editors. We acknowledge her for this beginning and gratefully dedicate these volumes to her.

SCOPE

The work and the writing of the 190 entries in the *Encyclopedia of Women's Autobiography* were done by a global electronic community of writers and scholars. This is the way information travels in the twenty-first century and we became very conscious of how quickly and efficiently such a writing community is formed and begins its work as we edited this encyclopedia. Initially, we were overwhelmed by the response and we presume that this is a further indication that women's autobiography is a topic of great interest to readers and scholars at many levels throughout the world, who will find this volume useful as they do research. We posted a "Call for Contributors" on two electronic Listserves used for this purpose and received more than 500 responses within a few days. The 138 contributors who were chosen are from 37 of the 50 United States and 15 other countries. All of our communications have been electronic, and we have not met most of the members of this community.

Our intention in producing the *Encyclopedia of Women's Autobiography* is to provide a compendium of information and a starting point for research for scholars, teachers, and students who study and write about women's life writing. Space limitations forced us to make choices. We hope readers will find that the helpful suggestions for further reading at the end of each entry will enrich understanding and fill any void found as a result of our choices.

The entries on individual women autobiographers and individual autobiographies are complemented by longer essays that are geographical (e.g., African Women's Autobiography) or historical (e.g., Nineteenth-Century American Women's Autobiography). In addition, there are entries on key terms in the study of women's autobiography, such as "Diary," "Identity," and "Personal Criticism." The focus throughout is on the writer's or the text's or the concept's relevance to the field of women's autobiography. For individual author entries, brief biographical details are included, but the emphasis is on the author's major autobiographical works.

The alphabetical organization is for the convenience of the student or the scholar and avoids the imposition of a value system in listing the entries. However, women's names often present problems since a writer may use a maiden or birth name, a married name, a pseudonym, even a slave owner's name. We have used the most common form whenever possible. Pseudonyms are used when a writer is known primarily by that name. All of the entries are cross-referenced within the entry text in boldface and can be used somewhat like an Internet site: the user may flip back and forth and enter increasing levels of complexity and interconnectivity among and between the entries. A "Guide to Related Topics" in the front matter arranges the entry terms by broad topic so that readers may, for example, see at a glance which writers have entry-length profiles, or what concepts or issues have entries. Two appendixes that list entry names by ethnicity or nationality and chronologically provide added access to the information in this book, and a general bibliography provides a selected list of good sources for the subject of women and autobiography. The index also offers deeper access to topics, names, and titles.

We are both very grateful to our many contributors from all over the United States and many countries who committed their time and talents to our project. We also want to acknowledge our very supportive and wise editors, Emmanuel Nelson, Anne Thompson, and George Butler. Vicki would like to thank her family, her SUNY Cortland colleagues, and her coeditor and friend, Jo Malin. Jo thanks the School of Education and Human Development at Binghamton University, especially Ted Rector and Scott Pionteck, for supporting her scholarship, Ted Brewster for his programming assistance, the Research Foundation of SUNY at Binghamton, her family, and Vicki for her superb and tireless editing and friendship. Amy Burtner, in particular, provided assistance in the final stages of the manuscript.

WORK CITED

Smith, Sidonie. *A Poetics of Women's Autobiography: Marginality and the Fictions of Self-Representation* (Bloomington: Indiana University Press, 1987).

ADDAMS, JANE (1860–1935) A widely respected American social reformer and public intellectual in her own time, Jane Addams is perhaps most famous today as the author of her classic **memoir**, *Twenty Years at Hull-House with Autobiographical Notes*. First published in 1910, the book has remained in print ever since. For generations, students and scholars have read it to learn about American nineteenth-century social history, urban and immigrant history, labor history, social work history, and settlement house history. Students and scholars of philosophy, English literature, and women's studies turn to it to understand Jane Addams' moral thought and her skills as a storyteller and as an autobiographer.

In the preface, Addams explains that she intends to provide a "faithful" record of the lessons that settlement life taught in the first twenty years. Her goal of self-effacement is well executed in the fourteen of the book's eighteen chapters that relate to Hull House. These chapters are essentially essays organized around topical themes relating to myriad issues, from poverty to labor legislation, to arts, to investigations that Hull House and its "residents"—volunteers who lived at the house—were involved with daily. The four chapters of "autobiographical notes" that open the book are more personal. There Addams tells touching stories

about her childhood adoration of her father, her fears and her dreams. Across the whole text, she creates a feeling of intimacy with the reader through her warm, at times self-probing, at times self-mocking, narrative voice. The result is a unique creation—not quite a true autobiography centered on the author.

The key event in Jane Addams' life and the pivot point, chronologically, that divides the autobiographical notes from the Hull House chapters is her decision to found a settlement house with her friend Ellen Gates Starr in Chicago. She arrived at this decision when she was twenty-seven years old and it would be two more years before she and Starr actually moved into their new home in Chicago in 1889. Dreamy and ambitious growing up, Addams had earned a B.A. when very few women did so and expected at first to work among the poor as a medical doctor. But her father's death the year after she graduated from Rockford Seminary, her own subsequent ill health, and her strong sense of duty to her family undermined her self-confidence for most of her twenties. Starr's friendship, along with a deepening of her own religious faith, strengthened her courage. Wide reading helped her justify leaving her family to take up social responsibilities, and a magazine article about a new kind of institution called a settlement house helped her formulate a new plan. Family wealth gave her the funds to finance the project.

The first settlement house in the world, Toynbee Hall, opened in London in 1884. Addams visited it in 1888 and was delighted with what she found. She and Starr opened their settlement house, Hull House, in Chicago in 1889 in a working-class, industrial section of the city. The house served as part educational institution, part clubhouse, part cultural institution, and part community center, with essential services for working-class people who lived in the neighborhood and for people of all classes. Staffed mostly by volunteers, some of whom lived at the settlement house and were called "residents," the institution offered college-educated young people a way to bring "culture" and "friendship" to working-class people while also educating themselves about the realities of urban industrial life. For Jane Addams, as well as for many of the residents, life at Hull House revealed the resourcefulness and compassion of her working-class neighbors, whom she had first misjudged because of their few economic resources and lack of formal education, and they in turn opened her eyes to the realities of poverty, power, **class**, and politics in the late-nineteenth-century United States.

Her awareness transformed, Addams was gradually drawn into various arenas of social reform—municipal government and education reform, legislative labor reform, woman suffrage, and so forth, where her skills in public speaking and the depth of her human understanding made her voice among the most influential in local, state, national, and eventually international circles. By 1910, her activism on behalf of workers, immigrants, women, children, world peace, and her steady public presence—conveyed through her many lectures, magazine articles, and books—had earned her the respect and affection of a wide portion of the American public. Though her pacifist stance during World War I and her continued progressivism in the conservative years of the early 1920s undercut that reputation for a time, it was restored in the 1930s, particularly after she received the Nobel Peace Prize in 1931. When Addams died in 1935, she was once more one of America's most admired women.

Jane Addams' cultural influence during her lifetime was primarily due to the ideals for which she stood. Many important social reformers and public intellectuals lived at or visited Hull House when they were young: the progressive historian Charles Beard, Frances Perkins, the first woman cabinet member in the federal government, Charlotte Perkins Gilman, the author and lecturer. Those who were friends and/or admirers of Addams included President Theodore Roosevelt, philosophers William James and John Dewey, British Labor Party leader John Burns, and India's Mahatma Gandhi.

Addams continues to wield influence through her thirteen books, which mostly deal with social issues, such as democracy, social ethics, urban youth, women's place in the culture, world peace, labor reform, and urban reform. In addition to *Twenty Years at Hull-House*, her two most important works are *Democracy and Social Ethics* (1902) and *Spirit of Youth and City Streets* (1909). In all her books Addams combines analysis and story to engage the reader in a freshly compassionate understanding of controversial social questions.

Further Reading: Addams, Jane. *Democracy and Social Ethics*. 1902. Reprint (Urbana: University of Illinois Press, 2002); Addams, Jane. *Spirit of Youth and City Streets*. 1909. Reprint (Urbana: University of Illinois Press, 2001); Addams, Jane. *Twenty Years at Hull-House*. 1910. Reprint (Urbana: University of Illinois Press, 1990).

Louise W. Knight

AFGHANI WOMEN'S AUTOBIOGRAPHY. *SEE* **SOUTH ASIAN WOMEN'S AUTOBIOGRAPHY.**

AFRICAN AMERICAN WOMEN'S AU-TOBIOGRAPHY Autobiographical writing seeks to reveal a person's life not only to him- or herself but also to his or her readers. Although the male tradition of self life writing (auto-bio-graphy) might have its antecedents in Plato's *Seventh Epistle*, by the middle of the eighteenth century, African American women and men used this genre both to interpret their experiences and to politicize their lives for their (mainly) white readers. Initially, it was African American males who gave voice to their lives in the form of slave narratives and spiritual conversion accounts, but it was not long before African American women would appropriate the form for their own purposes, not only to assert their identities and claim a public **voice** long denied them, but also to detail their secular and spiritual journeys as a way of transcending the proscriptions imposed on them because of their **race** and **gender**. During the eighteenth and nineteenth centuries, women used autobiography as the primary vehicle for raising readers' consciousness about the dehumanizing institution of slavery and as a way to assert their humanity and their intimate relationship with God. Even though slavery had been made illegal with the passing of the Thirteenth Amendment in 1865, twentieth-century black women continued to use autobiography to politicize the effects of racism and sexism and to communicate to the white world the heretofore effaced black self. While the content of African American women's autobiographies might have changed over time, their purpose remained the same: to expose the world to the material conditions facing all black women, regardless of **class**. In short, black women's autobiographies are stories of freedom, assertions of **identity**, and narrative exposés of white supremacist racist **patriarchy**.

The autobiographical form may be generally understood as a personal account of the writer's life written as historical **memoir** with the goal of rendering experience meaningful within the contexts of self and culture. Slave narratives and spiritual autobiographies, which arose at about the same time in the latter half of the eighteenth century, served the more specific purpose of chronicling the African American's life in the context of a racist society. Functioning as authentic representations of experience, both slave narratives and spiritual autobiographies wrote the (ex)slave or free black person into being. One might say such narratives were both ontological and rhetorical acts in that the author was able to write herself and her experience into history, into a collective historical consciousness. The act of writing, however, was not simply a gesture toward selfhood; rather, it was ultimately a political gesture toward freedom, for as early as 1740 it was illegal in many states to teach slaves to read or write. For blacks ostensibly silenced by such statutes, their texts became their voices, of deliverance and redemption.

Despite this, texts produced by former slaves and religious black women were not accepted at face value. Since most blacks could neither read nor write, those who could had to counter the assumptions that they were incapable of learning to read and write and were therefore less than human. African American writers faced the difficult task of needing to convince their primarily white audiences not only that they were bound together by virtue of their humanity but also that they would tell a truthful story. Both women's and men's slave narratives, as well as women's spiritual autobiographies, responded to this imperative in a number of ways. For example, male slave narratives and female spiritual autobiographies began with accounts of the writers' instruction in literacy (usually biblical), and ended with an "apology" for the writers' "inability" to use language with the same facility as their white readers, which often functioned as a veiled indictment against the system that prevented their intellectual development. Many texts, moreover, promised authenticity in the form of a validating statement made by a white editor. In **Harriet Jacobs'** (1813–1897) case, the prominent white abolitionist Lydia Maria Child refined Jacobs' manuscript and promoted it among her abolitionist friends and other antislavery sympathizers before and after the Civil War. Child wrote the introduction to *Incidents in the Life of a Slave Girl* (1861), promising readers that except for minor editorial changes, the work was entirely Jacobs' own. In the very act of relating her experience discursively, the female former slave, like many who wrote before and after her, intervened in the dominant culture by telling her story in her own words. That is, the black female autobiographer performed the double task of calling into question white constructions of black identity and of staking a claim for the right to be heard and acknowledged as a human being. African American women wrote their lives in the hope of enacting social change.

Dominant, white culture sanctioned African American autobiographies, but could not diminish the power of their messages. The very use of written language as an interpretive medium enabled slave narratives and spiritual autobiographers to serve as the discursive **memory** of an oppressed group, an essential element in understanding history as well as in understanding one's place in history. William Andrews explains, for example, that "autobiography became a very public way of declaring oneself free, of redefining freedom and then assigning it to oneself in defiance of one's bonds to the past or to the social, political, and sometimes even the moral exigencies of the present" (*Free Story* xi). For the first male African American autobiographers, writing was an act of establishing one's identity as "a man and a brother" (to a white audience), as a 1787 emblem engraved on the seal of the English Committee for Affecting the Abolishment of the Slave Trade declared. For women, it went beyond establishing one's claim to woman- and sisterhood and extended to the assertion of the right to be free from sexual exploitation.

Early Slave Narratives and Spiritual Autobiographies

Scholars of the black autobiographical tradition, including Andrews, locate the first black autobiography as early as 1760, a slave narrative dictated by Britton Hammon (*Free Story* 1986, 18). The first female slave narrative was published in 1787. "Belinda, or the Cruelty of Men Whose Faces Were Like the Moon," is noteworthy not only in that it is the first female slave narrative but also because it speaks directly of the violence of capture and eventual bondage of a young African girl who sought reparations from the New York legislature for her experience (Braxton 1989, 2). In the space of just forty-four years, from 1787 to 1831 when the next female slave narrative was published, women transformed this genre into a sharp indictment of slavery, specifically as it affected women. The themes of racism and sexual exploitation dominated African American women's autobiography in the nineteenth century both in slave narratives and in spiritual autobiographies, the two primary forms women used to express their morality, their identity, and their self-worth, as well as to negotiate the double bind of being black and female. Further, for women and men, autobiography served to "rend the veil of white definitions that misrepresent [them] to [themselves] and the world" in the words of Stephen Butterfield (1974, 136). Both the slave narrative and the spiritual autobiography were intended to do just this. Male and female autobiographers situated their narratives as metaphoric journeys that culminated in an awakening—both secular and spiritual. In other words, these narratives were expressed as journeys to consciousness of self in society and of self in relation to God. Either way, the writers used language as a vehicle for liberation, for declaring themselves free to define their place in the world.

Black women's autobiography entered the African American literary tradition at a crucial moment. Relegated to the shadows, these women were to be seen but not heard. They countered this cultural imperative by writing texts that asserted a black self capable of agency, worthy of inclusion in the category of "true womanhood." Whereas white, middle-class women in New England could automatically lay claim to such an appellation, black women had to prove that they, too, could uphold religious principles and maintain a stable household—the characteristics of a true (white) Northern woman. Whereas the early, antebellum male-authored slave narratives were straightforward documentaries that indicted the institution of slavery, the narratives recounted or written by women contained a more personal political edge. This is clearly evident in the next female slave narrative to appear, dictated to British social reformer Thomas Pringle by the illiterate West Indian slave **Mary Prince**. *The History of Mary Prince* (1831) is the first to allude specifically to the difficulties of satisfying the cultural expectations of "true womanhood," for women's sexual exploitation under slavery and their unique struggles to provide a secure and safe haven for their (illegitimate) children made such a goal nearly impossible. In order for women like Prince, and later, **Sojourner Truth** ([Isabella Baumfree] 1797–1883), and Harriet Jacobs to communicate to their readers how black women were challenged by these ideals, they needed to do more than chronicle their lives under slavery; thus, the slave narrative for women evolved into a political broadside against both the institution of slavery itself and the inhumane treatment black women faced at the hands of their white masters and mistresses. Prince's narrative, published by a British antislavery society, reflects the efforts of a woman intent on maintaining her selfhood and integrity, despite the brutality she experienced at the hands of her West Indian masters. Like Prince, Truth communicated her experiences as an exploited black woman not only through her speeches but also through her ethnobiography, an ac-

count of her life chronicled by two white abolitionists, Olive Gilbert and Frances Titus. Truth explicitly questioned the belief that white women alone could claim the status of (true) womanhood, reminding audiences that she had borne thirteen children, most of whom were sold into slavery. In her famous rhetorical refrain, Truth asks, "ain't I a woman," as she presents her challenging testimony, setting an important precedent in the slave narrative genre, prefiguring Jacobs' novel. Written in the form of the immensely popular sentimental fiction, Jacobs' *Incidents in the Life of a Slave Girl* exemplifies the brutality of slavery.

Narrated by Jacobs' alter ego, Linda Brent, *Incidents* is perhaps the most important female-authored slave narrative published in the nineteenth century. More a collection of incidents (hence the title) than a narrative proper, the novel features a young woman (Linda Brent) who must negotiate the reality of her sexual exploitation with the white, middle-class cultural imperative that at once disapproves of women's sexual promiscuity while it allows this exploitation to occur. The novel represents a critique of racism in the nineteenth century where a system of moral values paradoxically elevates women to the highest position while simultaneously supporting conditions that undermine them. Jacobs deftly discovered a way to articulate this dilemma in her story: The protagonist rejects the sexual advances of her white master and demonstrates her agency in choosing her own (white) sexual partner. Although she must struggle with a new set of issues (bearing two illegitimate children and then providing for them once she is able to gain her freedom), Brent nevertheless reconciles her choices because she made them in the cause of freedom. *Incidents* reflects not only her struggle for personal freedom but also freedom from the oppressive cultural conditions that imprison her. In a telling apostrophic address, the narrator asks readers not to judge her by the same standards as they would white women, for such standards are impossible for black women to uphold.

Antebellum slave narratives focused more on women's lives as slaves and the dilemmas they faced under a system that condoned their sexual exploitation; postbellum narratives also indicted the institution of slavery, but their authors directed readers' attention more explicitly toward their ability to exercise control over their freedom. These narratives feature a strong narrator who is able to resist oppression rather than succumb to it. Although antebellum narratives were closer to the antislavery polemics promulgated by leading abolitionists, after 1865 these accounts served as chronicles of African Americans' power to overcome the debilitating and dehumanizing aspects of slavery. Suffering as a way to salvation became the dominant trope, a theme whose presence was also ubiquitous in women's spiritual autobiographies.

Two prominent postbellum narratives reflect the themes of freedom and responsibility. **Elizabeth Keckley**'s (1824/5–1907) account, *Behind the Scenes* (1868) is a testament to former slaves' ability to survive and in fact flourish as freed persons. Keckley saw herself as a vehicle to promote the "reality" behind slavery and to reveal the radical inconsistencies of the cultural dictates of true womanhood. As the mother of an illegitimate mulatto boy, Keckley, like Jacobs, was forced to contend with the gendered norms constructed by a white society. Interestingly, Keckley does not apologize for her situation but instead blames it on the racist patriarchal system that enveloped nineteenth-century culture. As with all slave narratives, Keckley promises the reader a true story of enslavement and eventual freedom, where she becomes Mary Todd Lincoln's personal servant. Just as Keckley uses her narrative to reflect on her life as a former slave who succeeds as a freed person, so does Susie King Taylor (1848–1912) employ her literacy to reminisce on her life as the wife of a man em-ployed in the first colored Union army. In *Reminiscences of My Life in Camp with the U.S. 33rd Colored Troops* (1902), Taylor recalls her life as a young slave girl who, at age seven, was given the opportunity to live with her free grandmother in Savannah, Georgia. The author describes how as a slave she learned to read and write by participating in a "secret school," an incident evocative of one of the central themes in all slave narratives (qtd. in Braxton 1989, 44). Taylor proceeds to give an account of her life as the wife of a man who joined the First South Carolina Volunteers, the first black regiment of the Union army. Working with the regiment as nurse, teacher, and laundress, Taylor demonstrates the central role of women that went far beyond domestic servitude. Like Keckley, Taylor uses autobiography to indict the system that contributed in no small measure to the start of a war but moved beyond to develop the idea of herself as a responsible, able woman.

Spiritual Autobiographies

Slave narratives, whether ante- or postbellum, served the important purpose of representing slavery "as it is" to white audiences hungry to learn more about the inner workings of a system they either helped create or enabled to perpetuate. Presumably, these "first-person" accounts offered, as Andrews points out, compelling accounts of slavery that "promise[d] . . . intimate glimpses into the heart and mind of a . . . slave" and appealed more to skeptical audiences tired of (and perhaps immune to) the polemical accounts written by white abolitionists (*Free Story* 1986, 5). Such narratives gained respectability not simply by offering intimate glimpses of this institution, however, for it was the common belief that blacks possessed no soul and were therefore deemed not fully human. More important, these narratives artfully implied the presence of a people heretofore denied both voice and agency. Slave narratives authenticated blacks' identities and their experience and proved, despite the dominant culture's will to acknowledge them solely as chattel, that African Americans not only possessed souls but also shared a unique relationship with God. It is in this relationship, in fact, that black women ultimately found authorization to write their lives and to share their world. As more and more slaves converted to Christianity, the presence of the Spirit permeated their writing. Before they could even conceive of relating their experience, however, slaves had to demonstrate their personhood. Since whites perceived them as uncivilized savages, African Americans were forced to demonstrate evidence of their selfhood elsewhere—specifically, through Scripture. Although slave narratives generally reflected the dual themes of freedom and conversion, their rhetorical aim remained, nevertheless, to expose the effects of slavery on the individual. Spiritual autobiographies aimed more directly at authenticating one's humanity, to detail one's conversion from sin, and to bring this message to as many readers as possible. To be sure, all of the women who wrote about their relationship with God worked directly with people by speaking publicly, leading prayers, exhorting, and traveling countless miles as itinerant preachers spreading the Gospel. The written accounts of their experience were extensions of such efforts; they were, in effect, ministries in writing.

Spiritual autobiographical accounts countered the assumption that blacks were depraved brutes by declaring the enslaved (or free) self as free from both literal and figurative bondage once granted the gift of salvation. Like the slave narrative, whose dominant theme is freedom, the spiritual autobiography is both a linguistic and spiritual quest for freedom. In other words, freedom for African American women autobiographers meant being able to express themselves in writing and to live lives free from worldly constraints through their special relationship with God. The spiritual autobiographer's purpose was to "chronicl[e]

the soul's journey not only from damnation to salvation but also to a realization of one's place in the divine scheme of things" (Andrews, *Sisters* 1986, 10). Seeing their mission not only as spokespersons for their race but for all people, this genre of autobiography marked a significant turning point in women's life writing. The radical nature of these texts cannot be emphasized enough. Sue Houchins, editor of *Spiritual Narratives* (1988), underscores this radicalism by labeling spiritual autobiographers' works as feminist. Houchins argues that these women "read the Christ-story into and as their own personal story," claiming a personal relationship with God through their discourse (xxxviii–xxxix).

Protofeminist sentiments are clearly evident in the first autobiography written and published by an American-born black woman, a hybrid text featuring a spiritual **memoir** and a polemic detailing the racism and sexism experienced by the black community. Maria W. Stewart combined her 1831 pamphlet, *Religion and the Pure Principles of Morality, A Sure Foundation on Which We Must Build*; her spiritual autobiography, *Meditations* (1832); and her Boston speeches, delivered in 1832 and 1833, in *Productions from the Pen of Mrs. Maria W. Stewart* (1835). Published by the Friends of Freedom and Virtue in Boston, Stewart's text inaugurated a tradition of black women's autobiographical writing, whose aims included both racial uplift and an assertion of one's identity and voice. Beginning in 1835, when Stewart's *Productions* emerged, until the publication of Jacobs' *Incidents* in 1861, a number of women published their spiritual autobiographies. These texts sought, if not directly then at least obliquely, to justify African American women's rights to claim the same status as their white sisters. During the years following Emancipation, many more autobiographical writings were published, seeking the similar rhetorical purposes as their progenitors yet also focusing on their lives as missionaries. In addition to Stewart's *Prod-*

uctions (1835) other notable antebellum accounts include Jarena Lee's (1783–?) *Life and Religious Experience of Jarena Lee* (1836); **Zilpha Elaw**'s (c. 1790–?), *Memoirs of the Life, Religious Experience, Ministerial Travels and Labours, of Mrs. Zilpha Elaw, an American Female of Colour; Together with Some Account of the Great Religious Revivals in America* (1846); Nancy Prince's (1799–?), *A Narrative of the Life and Travels of Mrs. Nancy Prince: Written By Herself* (1850); and Rebecca Cox Jackson's (1795–1871), *Gifts of Power*, written between the years 1830 and 1864 (collected and edited by Jean Humez in 1981). Postbellum accounts include **Julia Foote**'s (1823–1900) *A Brand Plucked from the Fire: An Autobiographical Sketch by Mrs. Julia A. J. Foote* (1879); Amanda Smith's (1837–1915), *The Story of the Lord's Dealings with Mrs. Amanda Smith* (1893); and Virginia Broughton's *Twenty Year's* [sic] *Experience of a Missionary* (1907). All were created out of different contexts by women of different social classes, yet their presence suggest some uniformity, a connection to some larger mission of a self gaining authorization through the Bible. These authors had experienced a religious conversion and felt their work was sanctified by God. They used their writing to inform the public of the special role of women in a society where men's and women's work was divided according to their gendered spheres of influence.

The publication and proliferation of spiritual autobiographies were made possible by a number of forces. First, antebellum nineteenth-century American culture was experiencing a resurgence of religious devotion in the form of a series of revivals commonly known as the Second Great Awakening. Existing and newly converted Christians flocked to churches in unprecedented numbers seeking salvation by the grace of God. Women constituted the largest increase in church membership during this period, in which female churchgoers outnumbered men sixty to forty, particularly in the Southern states. Although they were not allowed to preach, women led

prayers, exhorted, and testified, which they did whenever possible. They took their roles seriously as Christian soldiers, marching to the beat of God's word. Using their newly acquired "authority" to encourage everyone, regardless of race, class, or gender, to live according to Christian principles that promoted the idea of faith as a way to salvation, women were a regular feature at camp meeting revivals in rural America, where they effectively led thousands of established and newly converted Christians toward this end.

An integral part of the Second Great Awakening was the rapid spread of Wesleyan Methodism and its offshoot, the Holiness movement. Wesleyan Methodism fed people's hunger for God. British theologian John Wesley promoted the idea that salvation was possible by renouncing willful sin against both God and man. Further, and more important, Wesley advocated these principles for all people, which signified to African Americans that not only was salvation possible, but that it could be earned in the same way by all members of the human race. Thus, Wesleyan Methodism was the second important element that made African American women's spiritual autobiographies possible. The Holiness movement promulgated the idea that two crises precipitate salvation. The sinner first undergoes a conversion experience by which she is freed from sin; next, she achieves full salvation, or sanctification, whereby she is liberated from the desire to commit moral transgressions. Although Wesley and the followers of the Holiness movement did not necessarily believe that conversion and sanctification would completely free a believer from sin, they promoted the idea that she should actively pursue a life that adhered to both moral and secular laws.

Having had conversion experiences and felt they were called to be messengers of the Word, women such as Lee, Elaw, Jackson, Foote, and Broughton thus capitalized on the power religion accorded them. Presumed to be "naturally" pious, they used their spiritual authority to promote a moral way of life for anyone, regardless of race, class, or gender. Their texts are remarkable in their resonance with each other. Following Methodist and Holiness principles, these African American spiritual autobiographers' accounts detail their three-phase spiritual development. First, the author narrates her experience of a sudden, traumatic conviction of sin in which she strives for redemption but struggles with guilt; second, she describes her journey toward salvation and eventual sanctification; and third, she relates her experiences of living a sanctified life parallel to that of an evangelist who, despite suffering, succeeds in faith in the same way that Christ and his disciples did. Inspired by the Puritan imperative to examine and reform one's life according to strict principles that would determine final salvation, followers of Methodism and of the Holiness movement committed themselves to obeying secular and moral law; they consciously eschewed sin; and they relied on the grace of God for the atonement of their sins. Further, believers in this theology promised to dedicate their lives entirely to God and to model this behavior for anyone seeking salvation.

After Stewart, spiritual autobiographies reflected their authors' experiences and metonymically acted as manifestations of bearing witness. Using their texts as discursive ministries, spiritual autobiographers recorded their evangelical lives in the hope that their texts would continue to work in their stead long after they had departed the material world. Generally speaking, these narratives spend less time on the author's conversion experience; the bulk of the texts are dedicated to evangelism, complete with the dominant metaphor of a journey. The authors undergo a number of dangers as they move from imperfection to perfection, from bondage in sin to spiritual freedom. The narratives often parallel Saul of Tarsus' conversion to Paul, the archetypal Christian. Although largely shaped by Puritan and New Testament sources,

these spiritual narratives also reflect distinctly African traditions, whose predominant features included praise songs and accounts from ancestral lives and times. Such elements refer to the oral tradition that defines African history. Further, these autobiographies are hybrids: They are conversion narratives, adventure stories, secular and spiritual journeys, and sermons featuring a call and response format. Indeed, the authors of these texts called out to their readers and demanded a response—a willingness to convert.

Paradoxically, a culture that celebrated women's natural piety was the same culture that expected them to remain in their proper sphere. Thus, women spiritual leaders encountered no small amount of resistance for doing what presumably came naturally to them. Recall that African American women were accorded almost no cultural caché except insofar as they could contribute their domestic skills to a culture that profited from women's unpaid labor. When they attempted to move beyond these boundaries, they were met with staunch resistance if not outright hostility. Stewart, for example, encountered such enmity from her own community that she eventually left Boston and the public stage, pursuing the culturally sanctioned work of teaching. Both Jackson and Broughton were pressured to cease their religious activities. Lee also encountered resistance to her persistent attempts to preach, a vocation reserved for the masculine domain. Traveling thousands of miles to conduct prayer services and lead camp meetings for women and men, free and enslaved, black and white, Lee believed she was both divinely inspired and divinely empowered to deliver God's message. Her convictions would serve her in the end, for although the African Methodist Episcopal (AME) Church refused to support Lee's efforts in 1849 to publish a revised and expanded version of her 1836 autobiography (it refused to endorse the publication of pamphlets or other materials written by traveling preachers), Lee financed the revised edition on her own. Despite the racism and gender bias women experienced during the nineteenth century, when most of these texts were published, black women proved that such obstacles would not deter them from their quest for voice. If they were not welcomed by their own communities, women simply went elsewhere. Lee, Elaw, Foote, Broughton, and Smith, for example, chose to spread their messages across thousands of miles in the East, New England, the Midwest, and even in some slave states, where they put themselves at risk of being captured and brought into slavery.

Cultural Critique and Identity in African American Autobiographies

As the twentieth century drew closer, African American women turned their attention even more acutely to cultural critique. From the antilynching campaign of **Ida B. Wells** (1862–1931) to the work of **Audre Lorde**'s (1934–1992), *Zami: A New Spelling of My Name* (1982), African American women used writing to express how the personal is political. After Broughton's narrative of her missionary activities, black women's life writing turned toward secular politics in an effort to call attention to the public black self. One of the first to do this was Wells in *Crusade for Justice* (1970), written during the late 1920s and early 1930s. An investigative journalist and newspaper publisher, Wells used autobiographical memoir to document the horrors of lynching during the latter nineteenth century and into the twentieth century as well as to chronicled her domestic life as a wife and a mother. The text serves as an important bridge between the freedom and conversion motifs of the previous centuries' slave narratives and the identity politics in the texts to follow. In *Crusade*, Wells accentuates the tension women faced when trying to negotiate a public persona with a private persona. Her work is a testament to the tenacity and self-assuredness of black women who recognized a cause worth

fighting for and knew how to accomplish their rhetorical purpose through writing. Notwithstanding, the posthumous publication of the text in 1970 when her daughter, Alfreda Duster, succeeded in publishing it, much of what is contained in *Crusade* found its way into editorials during the 1890s in the Memphis newspaper *Free Speech* and in Wells' own paper, the *Free Press*. Using the medium most accessible to a growing population of literate African Americans, Wells was able to effect social change, urging her black community on one particular occasion to leave Memphis as a result of a lynching, virtually paralyzing its economy. Wells is a key figure not only because her work reinforces the critiques of racism and sexism expressed in slave narratives such as Jacobs' but also because she was instrumental in helping to establish the black women's club movement, which galvanized women to work against racial oppression.

At the heart of the early- to mid-twentieth-century autobiographical writing by black women was identity. Although for Wells forming a positive black identity meant exposing draconian miscegenation laws and lynching practices, for Harlem Renaissance writer **Zora Neale Hurston** (1891/1901–1960), being black and female was a source of pride. During the 1920s and 1930s, black musicians, poets, and writers surged to the forefront of American consciousness as major contributors to this cultural renaissance. If blacks' artistic talents were buried beneath the relative obscurity of their days as slaves or itinerant preachers during the eighteenth and nineteenth centuries, this was far from the case in the twentieth century. The era of the "New Negro" witnessed the creative work of musicians such as Louis Armstrong and Duke Ellington; poets such as Jean Toomer, Langston Hughes, and Countee Cullen; and writers including Nella Larson and W.E.B. Du Bois. This era heralded a change in the demographic makeup and creative talent of major northern cities including

Chicago, Detroit, and New York as a result of the "Great Migration" in which African Americans, seeking both economic freedom and a respite from the enduring legacy of slavery in the south, headed north to secure what they hoped would be a better future. Never before had African Americans been able to take advantage of coming together to produce distinctive art, music, and literature that celebrated the black voice and black life. Although a controversial figure of the renaissance, Hurston was instrumental in shaping a new view of black culture. Along with several novels, plays, and anthropological studies, her 1942 autobiography *Dust Tracks on a Road* caused critics to regard her as a traitor to her culture for her honest portrayal of relationships within the black culture. Hurston celebrated black culture but she also portrayed it realistically, remarking for instance on the sexism evidenced by black men toward black women. Central to Hurston's work, however it is regarded, is the move to shape a more positive black (and female) self. Instead of seeing blackness as an impediment to true selfhood, she saw it as a source of pride and an ontological reality that warranted no pejorative connotation. **Alice Walker** (1944–), in her essay, "Zora Neale Hurston: A Cautionary Tale and a Partisan View," maintains that Hurston's work reflects "racial health; a sense of Black people as complete, complex, undiminished human beings" (1983, 85). *Dust Tracks* is emblematic of this attitude in its positive reflection of black consciousness. No longer did black women or men have to be judged according to patriarchal rules and white standards. Moreover, Hurston demonstrated that black women need be neither victims nor sexual objects: they were women in control of their destinies and could withstand the dust from the tracks, even if sometimes it seemed about to overwhelm them.

Just as the Harlem Renaissance signaled a turn toward African Americans shaping American culture through art, music, and letters, so too did women autobiographers seize this moment as a way to map new pathways that self-consciously laid bare their experience. Hurston's bold move to portray sexism within the black community may have met with severe criticism, but this critique did not deter later writers who were determined to offer insight into the impact of not only racial but also ethnic, and gender identity on their lives. **Gwendolyn Brooks** (1917–2000), the first African American to win the Pulitzer Prize (1950), used her poetry and fiction to portray the debilitating effects of racism and poverty on the lives of ordinary black people. Although social critique dominated her earlier work, she was influenced by emerging black nationalist leaders including LeRoi Jones, whose ideas infused Brooks' work with a political edge that characterized her writing up to her death in 2000.

Although considered a chauvinistic movement with its emphasis on the black man, black nationalism's politics attracted women as far back as the early nineteenth century, namely, Maria Stewart. At the core of black nationalism is knowledge of one's racialized identity, commitment to group cohesion as a way to maintain this, and achievement of a radical separation from the dominant white culture. Black nationalism, in a word, is a form of identity politics (in the most positive sense of this concept) that asserts the black person's right to define him- or herself in accordance with African American values and standards rather than Anglo American ones. Identity politics became the sine qua non of black women's autobiographical writing during and especially following the decades of the Civil Rights movement and manifested itself in black women's writing, autobiographical and otherwise, in a number of ways. During the 1960s and 1970s, the militancy of black nationalism permeated many women's writing as it never had before. Both **Nikki Giovanni** (1943–) and **Angela Davis** (1944–), for example, produced not only poetry and prose but also revolutionary autobiographies that interpreted their experience specifically through black consciousness and radical thinking that urged readers to struggle for blacks' rights and equality. For Giovanni, the personal is inextricably intertwined with the political. She expresses the centrality of her racialized and gendered position when, toward the end of *Gemini* (1971), she writes: "We Black women are the single group in the West intact. . . . We are the only group that derives its identity from itself" (143–144). The subject of black politics and power suffuses Davis' work even more than Giovanni's. Whereas Giovanni's work concerns the black female self as an instance of political identity, Davis' work deals more overtly with the political scene of which she is a part. *Angela Davis: An Autobiography* (1974) is less about the self and more about the oppression of black people, especially in the context of the criminal justice system. As the central focus of her autobiography, imprisonment reflects the dominant experience of African Americans, from slavery to the present. Indeed, as previously indicated, both slave narratives and spiritual autobiographies are structured on the metaphors of imprisonment and freedom, themes that exist either implicitly or explicitly in all African American autobiography.

If African American women were not writing about political freedom and racial equality, two themes that dominated the Civil Rights and black nationalist movements, they were speaking from their experience as black (and lesbian) women in the midst of the second wave of the **women's movement** that gained momentum during this same time period. Laudably, second-wave women activists organized a coherent coalition that advocated for women's rights to equal pay, equal opportunity, and equal access. But this movement represented a specific segment of this population: white, middle-class women. Key spokespersons such as Gloria Steinem could speak for some women from this limited perspective, but they ultimately

eclipsed the experience of women of color whose oppression stemmed from more than just economic inequality. Throughout history, African American women have suffered from the multiple and interlocking tyranny of race, class, and gender; **Maya Angelou** (1928–) exemplifies these injustices in her highly personal account, *I Know Why the Caged Bird Sings* (1969). Although not a political manifesto, *Caged Bird* may be understood as a text in which a woman shares her experience of the world through a racialized and gendered lens. Angelou struggles not only with her blackness and the shame this evoked, but also with her experience of being raped and the eventual acceptance of her black identity.

To assert their identity, black women needed to expose the racist and classist attitudes that blinded white, middle-class women to the unique experiences of their black sisters; most, if not all, African American women writers sharply criticized these white women for failing to take into account black women's struggles and their material realities. A number of black feminist scholars published books and essays that address these issues, including Patricia Hill Collins. In *Black Feminist Thought* (1991), Collins explains how black women's ideas have been historically suppressed as the result of a number of factors, including the exploitation of their labor, first as slaves and still today in many cases as low wage earners in the domestic labor market. Further, black women have historically been denied the same political and literacy opportunities and rights automatically granted to white males. And finally, black women have suffered from and continue to suffer from the "controlling images of black women that originated during the slave era" that portray images of women "from the mammies, Jezebels, and breeder women of slavery to the smiling Aunt Jemimas on pancake mix boxes, ubiquitous Black prostitutes, and ever-present welfare mothers of contemporary popular culture"

(6–7). These images contribute to the negative stereotypes that ultimately reinforce African American women's oppression. The women's movement in the 1960s and 1970s might have helped mitigate some of the effects of these negative images, but as Collins argues,

> Ironically, feminist theory has also suppressed Black women's ideas. Even though Black women intellectuals have long expressed a unique feminist consciousness about the intersection of race and class in structuring gender, historically we have not been full participants in white feminist organizations. (7)

Like Collins, other black, feminist heterosexual and lesbian writers have used their artistic talents to expose the aporias in mainstream feminist thought. A case in point is Audre Lorde. One of the most representative figures to give voice to the complexity of African American women's lives, this radical feminist was among the first to articulate **feminism**, lesbianism, and African American female selfhood in her poetry, prose, and in her autobiography, *Zami*. Lorde used writing to empower women who were either unable or afraid to speak for themselves. She is emblematic of all African American women who wrote their lives from multiple perspectives, proving once and again that although they share the common bonds of racial and sexual oppression, theirs is not a monolithic experience. Like the former slave narrators and spiritual autobiographers before her, Lorde used her poetry and her autobiography to name oppressions specific to women of color, thereby demonstrating the power of words to shape readers' consciousness and to affirm their valuable artistic contributions to American culture. Black women autobiographers may not have invented the genre, but they have made it their own. As Toni Morrison put it in her novel, *Beloved*, "definitions belon[g] to the definers" (1987, 190). To be sure, ours is a culture that has been defined by

white male standards of being and knowing, but marginalized groups have made significant inroads by questioning these standards and asserting the value of their own paradigms. African American women have, for example, redefined autobiography, using it to affirm their humanity; to assert their freedom; and to reinvent themselves in images that correct and expand the constructs of the dominant culture. Over the centuries, they have learned to "use the master's tools," in Lorde's words, to build their house of symbolic memory in order to shape a story of their past as they saw and experienced it. As **bell hooks** (1952–) explains, autobiography "is the act of writing . . . to find again that aspect of self and experience that may no longer be a part of one's life but is a living memory shaping and informing the present" (1998, 431). Black women's self life writing is, after all, an act of coming to consciousness and of declaring themselves free to tell their stories, in their own words.

Further Reading: Andrews, William. *Sisters of the Spirit: Three Black Women's Autobiographies of the Nineteenth Century* (Bloomington: Indiana University Press, 1986); Andrews, William. *To Tell a Free Story: The First Century of Afro-American Autobiography, 1760–1865* (Urbana: University of Illinois Press, 1986); Braxton, Joanne. *Black Women Writing Autobiography: A Tradition Within a Tradition* (Philadelphia: Temple University Press, 1989); Butterfield, Stephen. *Black Autobiography* (Amherst: University of Massachusetts Press, 1974); Giovanni, Nikki. *Gemini: An Extended Autobiographical Statement on My Twenty-Five Years of Being a Black Poet* (New York: Penguin, 1971); hooks, bell. "Writing Autobiography." In *Women, Autobiography, Theory: A Reader*, edited by Sidonie Smith and Julia Watson, 429–432 (Madison: University of Wisconsin Press, 1998); Houchins, Sue E., ed. *Spiritual Narratives*. Schomburg Library of Nineteenth Century Black Women Writers (New York: Oxford University Press, 1988); Morrison, Toni. *Beloved* (New York: Penguin, 1987); Walker, Alice. "Zora Neale Hurston: A Cautionary Tale and a Partisan View." In *In Search of Our Mothers' Gardens*, 83–92 (San Diego: Harcourt Brace, 1983); Smith, Sidonie, and Julia Watson, eds. *Women, Autobiography, Theory: A Reader* (Madison: University of Wisconsin Press, 1998).

Jami Carlacio

AFRICAN WOMEN'S AUTOBIOGRA-PHY   There are two categories of African women's autobiography that fit the Western definition of the personal history of an individual. One consists of life histories, published as early as the 1930s and as recently as 1998, which were transcribed and translated from various African languages by Western anthropologists, Christian missionaries, writers, and scholars. Many of these are either ethnographic portraits of one representative woman from a particular ethnic group or Christian conversion narratives in which one woman explains when and why she joined the mission community in her local area. The second category of African women's autobiography consists of those written between 1936 and 2002 in Arabic or one of the European languages by Western-educated African women from the various regions of the continent. Those written by women who live in Africa often emphasize their political development and resistance to colonial and postcolonial government policies designed to curtail their full participation in society. In many of these narratives, African women balance their roles as daughters, wives, and mothers, against their responsibilities as educators, factory workers, political activists, and social workers. Other African women autobiographers who live in Europe, Canada, or the United States locate their **subjectivity** at an intersection of traditional African and Western cultures. This cultural hybridity, for some, gives rise to the desire to pursue careers and lifestyles that conflict with traditional African practices, such as group interdependence, arranged marriages, and female circumcision.

African Women's Lives "As-Told-To"

Life histories "as-told-to" or "edited by" or "with the assistance of" an anthropologist, historian, missionary, or professional writer are a collaboration between two individuals. The African woman functions, in this case, as an insider whose particular life history provides an opportunity for non-African readers to observe an African society. Sarah Mirza and Margaret Strobel explain in their introduction to *Three Swahili Women: Life Histories from Mombasa, Kenya* (1989), that life histories from the start embody more than one person's agenda, purpose, and interests. In terms of form, a life history naturalizes the cultural insider's story by using the language and narrative techniques (such as linear chronology) of the non-African reading audience. Nevertheless, as the critic Judith Lutge Coulie argues "The Space Between Frames" (1996), life histories "provide textual space for articulation of experiences of black women" (132). As long as the person and the events she presents are not entirely invented, the narrative can provide significant cultural and historical information.

Women in Peril: Life Stories of Four Captives, edited by the historian Marcia Wright in 1984, is composed of four narratives that were previously published as early as 1930 by missionaries based in East Africa. Marcia Wright reissued the four women's narratives because of the historical information they provide about that particular region of East Africa. These Christian-conversion narratives were originally intended to show the trials, tribulations, and successes of doing "the Lord's work," on the part of both the missionaries and the East African women converts. Each of the four women was born in the late nineteenth century, lived in the region between Lake Nyasa and Lake Tanganyika (currently Zambia and Tanzania), and was caught up in the wars among rivaling tribes. Each also witnessed her village raided by Arabs and looted by

Germans. Each was captured as a slave by other Africans or Arabs, some as young girls, others as adults. In any case each had to learn the language of their various captors. These narratives recount the narrator's early life among her people, her capture, her escape or rescue, her return to her respective people, and her eventual conversion to Christianity when she enrolled in a mission school. In one case, the woman becomes a teacher at the mission school and begins translating the Bible into her indigenous language.

Another early example of an African woman's life history is "The Story of Nosente, the Mother of Compassion of the Xhosa Tribe, South Africa" recorded by Monica Hunter and included in the collection *Ten Africans*, edited by Margery Perham (1936). The Xhosa live in the eastern part of the Cape Province of South Africa. Nosente recalls her life in that region before and after the arrival of the British settlers. She compares her life as a traditional Xhosa woman with that of her daughter-in-law, whom she refers to as a "school person," to show the effect of the British presence on their cultural practices.

In 1978, the South African novelist and journalist Elsa Joubert published in Afrikaans, the language of the white South African descendants of the nineteenth-century Dutch settlers, *Die Swerfjare van Poppie Nongena*, the life history of a Xhosa woman with limited education. Joubert published the English version as *Poppie Nongena: One Woman's Struggle Against Apartheid* in 1981. This combination of autobiography, **biography**, and fiction was written at the request of a Xhosa woman who wanted to have her story told, but who insisted that her **identity** not be revealed for fear of possible reprisals from the South African government. Joubert assures the reader in her preface that the story is based on the actual life of a black woman living in South Africa. The literary critic Judith Coulie suggests that *Poppie Nongena* is important as an act of resistance, on Joubert's

part, to apartheid's designed displacement, and effacement, of millions of black South Africans.

In 1954, Mary F. Smith published *Baba of Karo: A Woman of the Muslim Hausa*. Smith, who accompanied her anthropologist husband, M. G. Smith to Zaria Provence, Northern Nigeria, where they were studying Hausa culture, conducted a series of interviews with the woman Baba because Muslim religious practices prohibited a male anthropologist from interviewing any of the local Hausa women. M. G. Smith did write the introductory essay to this life history in which he explains how Baba's story was collected and written and provides ethnographic information about the Hausa people. Of particular interest is his description of Baba's reluctance to let the Hausa community know that she was cooperating with the Smiths when they requested her life story. Baba understood her life as representative of the Hausa culture, and in the context of the British colonial setting in which she lived at the time, narrating her story to the Smiths was tantamount to betraying the cultural cohesion of her Hausa community. Baba was born in 1877 and died in 1951 before the narrative was published. The Smiths arrange Baba's life history according to the universal pattern of the life cycle: child, adult, elder. They include photographs of Baba, her family, and the compound in which she lives to document the narrative. Baba's memories include the arrival of the British settlers, which in turn affects the traditional patterns of her life.

The anthropologist Marjorie Shostak published *Nisa: The Life and Words of a !Kung Woman* in 1981. The !Kung people are hunter-gatherers living in southern Africa's Kalahari desert. Their traditional nomadic lifestyle shifted dramatically in the twentieth century due to the changing ecological and political environment of the region. In addition to revealing much about the life of Nisa and the !Kung through ethnographic discussions documented by a series of photographs of various !Kung girls and women, Nisa offers the reader important information about Shostak's values and her relationship with Nisa as she worked on this project. The reader can thus better evaluate the narrative presentation as an autobiographical duet about the lives of a young white woman anthropologist and an older black !Kung woman as they worked together.

The Calling of Katie Makanya, published in 1995 by Margaret McCord and awarded the *Johannesburg Sunday Times* Alan Paton Award, is similar to Elsa Joubert's *Poppie Nongena* in that it is a combination of autobiography, biography, and fiction. McCord, daughter of white South African doctor James McCord, grew up knowing Katie Makanya, who worked as her father's interpreter and assistant in the rural area of Amanzimtoti. Katie Makanya was born in 1873, when South Africa was a British colony, and died at age eighty-three in 1956, when apartheid was a firmly established policy (first established in 1948). In addition to Zulu, she was fluent in English, Dutch, Xhosa, and Sotho. As a young adult she was a member of the African Native Choir that toured England for two years from 1891 to 1893. She returned to South Africa to marry and raise a family. Katie Makanya asked Margaret McCord to write her life story. In the preface, McCord explains how she worked with Katie in South Africa during the early 1950s to record her story on tape. She then transcribed the tapes to more than eleven hundred pages of typescript. In the process of verifying Katie's story, McCord interviewed family and friends in the Northwestern Transvaal who knew her. She includes photographs of Katie as a young woman in the African Native Choir, places Katie lived, including Adams' mission station, and photographs of her own father, Dr. James McCord, for whom Katie worked. There is even a photograph of McCord and Makanya together in 1954 that verifies their acquaintance. This life history/novel about Katie Makanya, like that of Poppie Nongena, provides a picture of life in South Africa of a black woman who lived during a colonial rule designed to silence the black **voice**.

As editor of *Singing Away the Hunger: The Autobiography of an African Woman* (1996), the American actor, writer, and academic K. Limakatso Kendall, preserved much of Mpho 'M'atsepo Nthunha's form of English that is spoken only in Lesotho, a region of southern Africa. Mpho's English uses idioms resulting from literal translations of Sesotho expressions, and a smattering of Sesotho words. One clearly "hears" this life history as Kendall might have heard it while taping and transcribing it on weekends in 1992 and 1993. Mpho states in the first chapter that as a young child she did learn to read and write English, but has little time to read or write because of the demands of her family and job. She reveals a self-consciousness about producing a book about her life and wonders if anyone will want to read it. Hence, she is very aware of the contrast between her oral Basotho culture and the world of writing, books, and computers, a markedly different perspective than that of other African women's life histories published to date. The text is introduced by Ellen Kuzwayo, a prominent South African woman and member of Parliament, whose own self-scribed autobiography *Call Me Woman* (1985) received critical acclaim in South Africa and abroad. Kuzwayo's prefatory statement provides a sociological context for Mpho's story of her difficult life as a black woman who had to work at menial jobs to support her six children after her husband died. Photographs of Mpho, her family, and Mpho standing next to Limakatso Kendall are placed at the center of the text. In an afterword to *Singing Away the Hunger*, Kendall discusses her White American working-class background, her training in folklore and performance, and how she first met Mpho when she emigrated to South Africa in 1995. She carefully explains how she and Mpho worked: Mpho would read the pages and comment on the changes and arrangements of the stories after Kendall printed them out. Kendall's afterword reads as her own autobiographical statement of her identity as a White woman living in South Africa and her determination to minimize her own influence on *Singing Away the Hunger*.

Two other noteworthy works are by Miriam Makeba and Waris Dirie, that include numerous photographs of the authors at various stages in their lives in Africa and at different points in their international careers. *Makeba: My Story*, by the South African singer and antiapartheid activist, was published in 1987 with the editorial assistance of an American writer, James Hall. Waris Dirie, a Somalian who is now recognized as an international super model and a United Nations special ambassador for Human Rights, published her personal narrative, *Desert Flower*, with the assistance of Cathleen Miller in 1998.

African Women's Self-Scribed Autobiographies

The early history of African women's self-scribed autobiography begins with "The Story of Kofoworola Aina Moore, of the Yoruba Tribe, Nigeria, *written by herself*," published in 1936 as part of *Ten Africans*, a collection of African personal narratives edited by Margery Perham. After living in England for eleven years, Kofoworola Moore wrote her personal narrative a few months before she was due to return to Nigeria. Two sentences from the opening paragraph are typical of the personal identity conflict found in many African women's autobiographies published in subsequent decades: "The difference between these two places seems rather to coincide with the conflicting thoughts in my mind. My departure from Europe fills me at the same time with joy and with regret, with eager expectation and with anxiety." Women who remained in Africa also felt the personal anxiety between traditional African and Western cultures as well. In Charity Waciuma's, *Daughter of Mumbi*

(1969), the conflict is concentrated in the Kenyan emergency of the late 1950s, during the clash over land ownership between the British settlers and the Gikuyu peasants known as squatters. In a bold move for a Western-educated, Christian woman, Waciuma uses her personal narrative to celebrate and reclaim for herself the traditional Gikuyu culture of her grandparents, especially the practice of female circumcision.

In contrast, two Western-educated Egyptian feminists, Nawal El Saadawi and Laila Said, devote much of their adult lives to campaigning against traditional rituals, such as female circumcision, that are injurious to women. In her autobiographies, Nawal El Saadawi, a socialist, medical doctor, and novelist, angrily protests her own circumcision at age six in 1937, and the overall political and social oppression of women in North Africa and the Middle East in the current postcolonial era. First written and published in Arabic, the English translations of *Memoirs from the Women's Prison* (1986), and *Daughter of Isis: The Autobiography of Nawal El Saadawi* (1999) show the development of a defiant North African feminist crusader for women's rights. Laila Said, in *A Bridge through Time: A Memoir*, published in English in 1985, recounts her daring escape from an arranged marriage, her pursuit of an education in the United States, and her eventual return to Egypt where she founded her own theater company. She is viewed as "tainted" by some Egyptians because of her extended contact with Western culture, but this only strengthens her convictions as a feminist advocate for women's rights in postcolonial Egypt.

The Nigerian writer Buchi Emecheta, best known for her many novels depicting the plight of the African woman living in impoverished, postcolonial Nigeria, published two autobiographical narratives. *In the Ditch* (1972) is an autobiographical novel that details her experience as a poor, single parent in London. By using the fictitious African name Adah, meaning daughter, Buchi achieves the narrative distance of an observer of her own social reality. In 1986, Emecheta published *Head Above Water*, which depicts her many years of struggle to establish a career as a writer. Her failed marriage to a Nigerian who resented her efforts to write and publish novels and the demands of raising her children alone after her divorce were the first obstacles she faced to writing and publishing. Her eventual success as a writer who is acclaimed in Africa, Europe, and the United States, affords her the freedom to discover her own happiness without a husband. This constitutes a major break with all that she had been taught as a young girl growing up in Lagos, Nigeria, in the 1940s. But secure in her identity as an African woman living in London who can still appreciate life from "my own exotic African background," Emecheta concludes *Head Above Water* with an appreciation for the fullness of life.

Several autobiographies by women from Francophone Africa have received critical attention for the extent to which they correspond to the structures and ideologies of feminist autobiography. For instance, *Femme d'Afrique*, published by Aoua Keita in 1975, *Le baobab fou* by Ken Bogul [Marietou M'Baye] in 1984, *De Tilene au Plateau* by Nafissatou Diallo in 1975, and *My Country, Africa: Autobiography of the Black Pasionaria* in 1983, by Andree Blouin from Francophone Congo. Andree Blouin was born to an African woman and a French father. As a *metisse* she was sent to live in an orphanage administered by the Catholic Church for children of mixed racial backgrounds. This isolation from her African mother actually increased her passion for Africa, which led to her eventual involvement with the independence movement in Guinea in the 1960s. She ends her autobiography with a statement that solidifies her identity as an African woman: "[S]peaking of my life has been my way of speaking of Africa . . . I want Africa to be loved" (1983, 286).

As a loving gift to her European/African daughter, Sandra, Kesso Barry's *Kesso,*

Princesse Peuhle (1988) presents her life as a child born into a royal Fulani family in the Fouta-Djalon region of Guinea. Kesso Barry eventually met and married a French industrialist with whom she settled in Paris, where she became one of the city's most well-known fashion models. It is from this financially secure social position in Paris that Barry writes her autobiography as a means of mourning the loss of her traditional African culture, while at the same time critiquing many traditional African practices that prove injurious to women still living in Africa. Using memories of her own mother, a Fulani queen, as an example, Kesso Barry attacks female circumcision and polygamy as part of the traditional African patriarchal system that imposes restrictions on a woman's body. Yet, as the autobiography ends, Barry clings to her identity as an African woman living in Paris, fully accepting of the resulting personal ambiguities and vacillations of African cultural systems.

In 1986, Jane Tapsubei Creider, a Nandi woman from East Africa who resides in Canada, published *Two Lives: My Spirit and I*. The intersection of traditional African and modern Western cultures is interestingly portrayed in the combined autobiographies of the author and the first Tapsubei, of whom the author is the reincarnation. Inspired by the story she hears from her paternal grandmother about the first Tapsubei, who resorted to cattle raiding to win a better life for herself, Jane vows to use this example of feminine agency from her earlier incarnation to survive the many personal and social difficulties she confronts while living in colonial and postcolonial Kenya. Most difficult to resolve is the separation of her parents and the competing desires to live with both her westernized mother, who often wore business suits with trousers, and her father who, though Western educated, insisted on running his household according to traditional Nandi customs. Jane eventually migrates to Europe and Canada where she marries, raises a family, and develops as an artist and writer.

Three African women who currently live in the United States have also published autobiographies. In Dympna Ugwu-Oju's, *What Will My Mother Say: A Tribal African Girl Comes of Age in America* (1995), she portrays her Ibo-Catholic upbringing in eastern Nigeria, her coming to America to earn degrees from Briarcliff College and Syracuse University, her return to Nigeria for an arranged marriage, and her eventual return to the United States with her husband. This **autoethnography** closely examines the differences between Ibo and American women. It skillfully weaves portraits of American women who taught her how to be more assertive and to think independently with portrayals of Dympna's Ibo grandmother and mother from whom she learned a woman's role in traditional society. Her mother's frequent visits to the United States, and Dympna's to Nigeria means that she has a foot in each culture. This dual subjectivity in turn explains Dympna's view of herself as "Not quite American, not quite Ibo."

The poet and playwright Meri Nana-Ama Danquah's *Willow Weep for Me: A Black Woman's Journey through Depression, A Memoir* (1998) is a unique story of "a black woman's journey through depression." Danquah was born in Ghana and lived there with her maternal grandmother while her mother attended Howard University in Washington, DC. At age six she immigrated to the United States to live with her parents, but when they divorced two years later, Danquah experienced the first of many personal losses and accompanying melancholy that escalated over the years into a deep depression that would incapacitate her for days and weeks at a time. Unlike Dympna Ugwu-Oju, who insists that she drew personal strength from the example of stoicism set by her Ibo mother, Danquah maintains throughout her autobiography that the mythic strength of black women (both in Africa and in the United States) really

means hiding one's humanity and fallibility. Her own Ghanaian-American mother retreated behind a locked bedroom door with a "mournful resignation" that infected her two daughters. As successive personal crises occur in Danquah's life—her parents' divorce, her rape as a teenager by her mother's boyfriend, her witnessing the violent deaths of high school friends, her physically abusive relationship with her child's father, also a Ghanaian immigrant—she is overcome by a severe depression that she never tells anyone about because she had been taught that "suffering, for a black woman, was part of the package." *Willow Weep for Me* is Danquah's **confession** of need and the search for a therapist who helps her understand how **race**, **gender**, and her ancestral Ghanaian culture, interwoven with the modern American one in which she lives, all underlie her depression. Armed with this new understanding, and with strategies for managing her illness, including medication, Danquah's autobiography closes on a hopeful note.

Fauziya Kassindja was born in 1977 in Kpalime Togo, West Africa. She currently resides in the United States where she sought asylum from the cultural practice in Togo of female circumcision. Her autobiography *Do They Hear You When You Cry* (1998), written with the assistance of Layli Miller Bashir, is the story of her early, sheltered life in Togo, her protective father's sudden death, and her uncle's subsequent demand that she undergo the circumcision ritual prior to an arranged marriage. Kassindja's escape from this cultural prison (via Europe) does not at first lead to freedom in the United States. Ironically, she is imprisoned in a series of different INS detention centers for sixteen months. Hence, this narrative resembles the African women's prison memoirs of Winnie Mandela and Caesarina Makhoere in that it traces the emotional and physical toll of detention on her subjectivity. Fauziya Kassindja garners the unwavering support of a young law student, Layli Miller Bashir, who in turn enlists the assistance of the American University International Human Rights Clinic to plead her case for asylum on the grounds of gender-based persecution. Fauziya Kassindja was granted asylum on June 13, 1996.

The Devil That Danced on the Water: A Daughter's Quest (2002) by Aminatta Forna recounts the narrative of a daughter's quest to find the truth about her father's arrest, trial, and execution in Sierra Leone in 1975. The youngest of three children born to the bicultural/racial marriage of the Scottish Mildred Christison and Mohamed Forna, Aminatta was driven by memories of the day she last saw her father alive, when she was ten years old, being escorted away from their home in Koidu, Sierra Leone. He was a physician, trained in Aberdeen, Scotland, who returned to his home to set up clinics in the rural areas of the country. Eventually, his dissident stand against the tryannic postcolonial rulers of Sierra Leone cost him his life and Aminatta and her two older siblings their father. *The Devil That Danced on the Water* is Aminatta Forna's attempt to "piece together scraps of truth and make sense of fragmented images" of her past, especially the last ten years of her father's life. She defines her life as one of parallel realities: "There were the official truths versus my private memories, the propaganda of history books against untold stories; there were judgements and then there were facts, adult stances, and the clarity of the child's vision; their version, my version" (18).

Drawing on her training and work as a journalist in London, Aminatta Forna carefully gathered as much written and oral information as she could about the culture and politics of Sierra Leone to incorporate into her autobiography. She includes her memories of the period of time she and her siblings went into exile in Scotland the first time her father was arrested. For the first time she saw snow, wore thick wool clothing, and discovered another aspect of her mother's personality not noticed in Africa.

As the wife of the only doctor, and the only white woman in Koidu, Sierra Leone, her mother was revered but culturally isolated. In Scotland, among her own family and friends, Aminatta's mother was rejuvenated. As an adult discussing the eventual dissolution of her parents' marriage, Forna sees it as irreconcilable differences between their personalities and views on Africa. Although both parents focused on running the clinic, caring for patients, and raising their three children, "Nothing in her upbringing had prepared my mother for the reality of the Africa with which she was now faced; these were not her people and she did not share our father's passion or the political conviction that might otherwise have carried her through" (96). Aminatta Forna's determination to learn what happened to her father after he left home that night in 1975 motivates her to return to Sierra Leone, with her own husband. The resulting autobiography, *The Devil That Danced on the Water: A Daughter's Quest*, is the monument to her father's life and vision for post-independence Sierra Leone, but it is also Aminatta's milestone in her own personal journey.

By far the largest number of self-scribed autobiographies by African women are from South Africa. Noni Jabavu's two autobiographies, *Drawn in Colour: African Contrasts* (1960) and *The Ochre People* (1963), were the first published by a black South African woman and are examples of autoethnographies. These are personal narratives written by individuals indigenous to the culture under scrutiny, who are as concerned with examining their identities as members of that culture as they are with explaining, interpreting, and translating that culture to an audience of readers who are unfamiliar with it. As the granddaughter of John Tengo Jabavu, the first black African to own and edit a Xhosa-English newspaper, and daughter of Professor D.D.T. Jabavu, a linguist who published one of the first grammars of the Xhosa language, Noni Jabavu and her family belonged to the elite **class** of Christian, Western-educated Africans at that time. She left South Africa in 1933 to attend school in England. She eventually married an Englishman and had one daughter. In the course of writing these two autobiographies, Jabavu drew on her personal memories of her childhood in South Africa, which included close personal contacts with people of a variety of racial and ethnic backgrounds. As the adult narrator, she dismisses the apartheid regime as having had any repressive effects on her life as a child. She traveled back to South Africa in 1955 to attend the funeral of her only brother Tengo, who had been murdered in Johannesburg. His death marked the end of the Jabavu family line, hence it gives rise in her autobiographies to a deep sense of personal loss of her own Jabavu identity. She counterbalances this by proclaiming a broader identity as at once South African and British. *Drawn in Colour* opens with a note declaring this bicultural identity: "I belong to two worlds with two loyalties; South Africa where I was born and England where I was educated."

In most of the South African autobiographies published after those by Noni Jabavu, the women respond to the radical social changes in their lives brought about by the apartheid system of racial segregation legalized during the first decade of the twentieth century. A distinguishing structural feature of most of these texts is the inclusion of photographs taken at various times that depict the narrators, their families, and various personal and professional acquaintances. These photographs serve as documentation of the existence of the autobiographer, but also relate an important narrative of black life in South Africa, as we see the autobiographer age across time.

Joyce Sikakane was born in 1943 and raised in Soweto, the large, infamous black township just outside Johannesburg. She became a journalist at the *World* and *Rand Daily Mail* newspapers in South Africa before being arrested and jailed for seventeen months under the Terrorism Act. She was later prohibited from returning to journalism, and in 1973 she left South Africa to live in England. She eventually married a Scottish medical doctor with whom she raised a family of three children. In 1977, Joyce Sikakane published *A Window on Soweto*, a combined autobiography and sociological narrative of black life in Soweto under the apartheid regime. She carefully interweaves her sociological discussions of life in Soweto with her own personal experiences and reactions to life there as a child, young adult, and journalist. This autobiography, like those by Noni Jabavu published more than a decade earlier, serves to inform a white readership both inside and outside of South Africa about the life of South African blacks.

Ellen Kuzwayo, born in South Africa in 1914 into a Christian, Western-educated family, graduated from Adams College in Durban, South Africa, as a primary school teacher in 1933. In 1946, following the breakup of her six-year marriage, during which she had two sons, Kuzwayo joined the Youth League of the African National Congress and met a young Nelson Mandela and Walter Sisulu. After working as a teacher, Kuzwayo decided to train as a social worker at the Jan Hofmeyr School of Social Work from 1953 to 1955. One of her classmates there was the future activist Winnie Mandela. Kuzwayo assumed her first post as a social worker on the Johannesburg City Council in 1956. Then, from 1957 to 1962 she worked for the Southern African Association of Youth Clubs; was General Secretary of the YWCA from 1964 to 1976 and served as the only woman on the Soweto Committee of Ten in 1976. This synopsis of Kuzwayo's life shows that she had access to formal education and the limited power structures that existed for the indigenous Africans during the apartheid era. By the time she published her autobiography, *Call Me Woman* in London in 1985, Ellen Kuzwayo was a seventy-year-old grandmother. The narrative is, then, historical in its focus on the development of her own career and that of many other black South African women activists, doctors, and lawyers. Moreover, the fact that it narrates all of the public accomplishments of these women in the context of a political regime designed to economically and politically suppress the black South African community renders it an interesting narrative of black women's political resistance.

"How does a liberal white South African oppose apartheid?" This query launches Janet Levine's autobiography, *Inside Apartheid: One Woman's Struggle in South Africa* (1989). Labeled a "sickly pink humanist" and a danger to the state by the apartheid regime on the one hand, and summarily dismissed as irrelevant by black activists who said, "You have to be black to be oppressed, to be a part of the struggle," Levine remained steadfast in her anti-apartheid stance. As a student activist, then as a journalist, and later as an elected member of the Johannesburg City Council, Levine openly protested the government policies in numerous speeches and articles. She led the campaign of Helen Suzman, the Progressive Federal Party's member of Parliament. Levine speaks poignantly of Steve Biko, the black South African activist who died while in South African police custody on September 11, 1977. Though they worked on "disparate parameters" of the anti-apartheid campaign, Levine says that she respected Biko's intellect and rational leadership; and associated herself with Steve Biko because they were the same age, and "working for what we believed possible—a free, democratic South Africa" (163). Janet Levine's story of how she grew from her birth into a relatively sheltered, upper-middle class white family to become an anti-apartheid activist is documented with photographs. We can also understand from reading this narrative, how much she regretted having to abandon her political activities in the interest of her own and her family's safety to move with her husband

and two sons into exile in the United States in August, 1984.

The best-known South African woman novelist, Bessie Head, died in 1986 from hepatitis before she was able to publish her autobiography. In 1990, four years after her death, South African scholar Craig Mac-Kenzie edited a collection of essays by Bessie Head, *A Woman Alone: Autobiographical Writings*, a work that incorporates a number of overlapping genres, such as autobiography, fictional sketches, essays, **letters**, journalism, and explanatory notes about some of her novels. In 1991, Randolph Vigne, a political and literary friend whom Head had known when she lived in Cape Town, South Africa, published a selection of letters he had received from her between 1965 and 1979, when he lived in London. Titled *A Gesture of Belonging: Letters from Bessie Head, 1965–1979*, the letters cover topics that range from her own alienation as a mixed-race, "coloured" South African, to artistic concerns about her novels, to anger over the appalling political system that oppressed blacks in South Africa. In both collections of autobiographical writings, Bessie Head continually broods about her birth in a mental hospital in South Africa to a white South African woman from a prominent family. Rejected by her white mother's family, and without any precise information about the name of her black father, Head was haunted by a sense of alienation and aloneness for her entire life. She finally moved from South Africa to Botswana, where she wrote many novels and ethnographic and historical studies of Serowe, the village where she lived until her death.

Caesarina Kona Makhoere was a student in high school when she was arrested as an agitator following the 1976 student uprising against "Bantu education." She was detained without trial, convicted under the notorious Terrorism Act, and served six years in various South African jails. She was in solitary confinement and held incommunicado throughout her jail term.

Makhoere's narrative of her imprisonment, *No Child's Play: In Prison under Apartheid*, (1988), reveals her continued resistance even in an apartheid jail. Makhoere narrates her coming of age in political captivity and how she forgave her own father, who was a policeman, for turning her in to the authorities. She understands his act as the result of the apartheid regime that terrorized many black people into betraying their own families.

Sindiwe Magona published her two-part autobiography *To My Children's Children* (1990), which earned honorable mention in the 1991 Noma Award for Publishing in Africa, and *Forced to Grow* (1992). Both are written in the form of letters to her future grandchildren and great grandchildren to teach them about the era of South African history in which she was born. Magona assures them that in spite of the politically oppressive apartheid regime that denied black Africans the right to vote and to decent wages, her life as a child and young adult centered around her large extended family. She defines place less as a geographic location than as "a group of people with whom I am connected and to whom I belong. This is a given, a constant in my life." Magona expresses none of the personal alienation exhibited by Bessie Head because of the intricate web of family relationships to which she belongs.

Strikes Have Followed Me All My Life: A South African Autobiography by Emma Mashinini (1991), focuses on her work as secretary of the Commercial, Catering, and Allied Workers Union of South Africa. Her work with one of South Africa's largest trade unions ended when she was arrested without charge and held incommunicado for six months, much of that time in solitary confinement. A large section of the autobiography tells the story of her time in prison. In this it resembles a part of Ellen Kuzwayo's *Call Me Woman* (1985) and much of Winnie Mandela's *Part of My Soul Went with Him* (1984) that details her mistreatment while being detained in prison. Equally important is Mashinini's discussion of the "stokvel," women's collectives in the black townships that pooled their financial resources to help each other. This, too, is comparable to sections of Kuzwayo's *Call Me Woman* that describe the black collectives of social workers with whom she worked. *Strikes Have Followed Me All My Life* is an important record of the history of the black South African labor movement and the story of one woman's contribution to it.

Phyllis Ntantala, born in the 1920s in the Transkei to a family of black landed gentry, published her autobiography *A Life's Mosaic: The Autobiography of Phyllis Ntantala* in 1992 while living with her children in the United States. Her life was not one of poverty and brutal confrontations with the South African government. Of interest in this autobiography is the story of her own gradual politicization as an elite African wife of a college professor. When asked to write an essay in 1957 for the journal *Africa South*, Ntantala chose to write on the thousands of working class black South African women who struggled everyday to raise children while their husbands were away working in mining camps near Johannesburg. She continued to write essays during the late 1950s exposing the poor living conditions that resulted from apartheid regulations. Several of them were translated into different European languages, and one was reprinted in *An African Treasury*, an anthology edited by the Black American poet Langston Hughes. As the South African government increased its restrictions on the black population in 1961 and 1962, political demonstrations were on the rise at the University of Cape Town, where Phyllis Ntantala's two children attended school. The African National Congress also increased its protests against the apartheid regime when Nelson Mandela was arrested in 1962 and sentenced to life in prison. When Ntantala's husband was invited to lecture at a university in the United States, the entire family began to make plans to leave South Africa to avoid being arrested. They succeeded in doing this in the early 1960s, arriving in the United States at the height of numerous political demonstrations such as the Civil Rights and Black Power movements and demonstrations against the Vietnam War. Phyllis Ntantala's story, however, does not end happily with their arrival in the United States. Chapters in *A Life's Mosaic* detail the racial discrimination that they experienced as a black family in Milwaukee, Wisconsin. Two molotov cocktails were thrown at their house one night as protesters marched in the street outside their home. A few weeks later a swastika was burnt on their front lawn. Ntantala attributes these incidents to White extremists not affiliated with the university where her husband taught. Nonetheless, she credits her ability to cope to her experiences as a black from South Africa.

Mamphela Ramphele, *Across Boundaries: The Journey of a South African Woman Leader* (1995), was published in the postapartheid era. It relates a story similar to that of other black South African women: an early childhood and young adult years from 1947 through the early 1960s spent under the many laws restricting black life, yet it differs in depicting Ramphele's determination from a young age to become a doctor. Her motives were political—to provide health care to the black populations that the South African government neglected. To this end, she aligned herself with a group of political activists associated with Steve Biko, who formed the Black Consciousness movement. This caused the local police to maintain a constant surveillance of her activities; hence, when she established and ran one of South Africa's first community health centers in 1977, Ramphele was detained without trial and banned from the Transvaal. Once the order was lifted in 1983, she returned to school to pursue a doctorate in anthropology. Then, in 1996, she was appointed to an administrative position at the University of Cape Town that had always been held by a white man. Ramphele's autobiography gives us a glimpse into the pressures facing postapartheid South Africa as it adopts a new constitution, extends voting rights to all its citizens, and repeals its segregationist laws. Western women will find that Ramphele's life as a single, working mother parallels many of their own struggles to confront sexism in an industrial society.

This survey makes clear that whether "as-told-to" or self-scribed, there is more than a seventy-year history of African women's autobiography. The intended audience for these texts has shifted over the years from primarily non-African readers in Western countries to include Western-educated Africans living on the African continent or abroad in Europe and North America. To reach these expansive audiences, both the life histories and self-scribed autobiographies are written in (or translated into) Western languages. These narratives are evidence of the various types of African women and offer glimpses into their differing cultures and historical experiences from across the vast continent. The autobiographies of African women who reside in Europe, Canada, and the United States reveal a hybrid identity that most of them understand as the consequence of modernization.

Further Reading: Barry, Kesso. *Kesso, Princesse Peuhle* (Paris: Seghers, 1988); Blouin, Andree. *My Country, Africa: Autobiography of the Black Pasionaria*. Edited by Jean MacKellar (New York: Praeger, 1983); Boyce-Davies, Carole. "Private Selves and Public Spaces: Autobiography and the African Woman Writer." *CLA Journal* 24, no. 3 (1991): 267–289; Bugul, Ken [Marietou M'Baye]. *The Abandoned Baobab: The Autobiography of a Senegalese Woman*. Translated by Marjolijn de Jager (Brooklyn, NY: Lawrence Hill Books, 1991); Clayton, Cherry. "Ellen Kuzwayo." In *Between the Lines: Interviews with Bessie Head, Sheila Roberts, Ellen Kuzwayo, Miriam Tlali*, edited by Craig MacKenzie and Cherry Clayton, 57–68 (Grahamstown, South Africa: National English Literary Museum, 1989); Coulie, Judith Lutge. "(In) Continent I-Lands: Blurring the Boundaries between Self and Other in South African Women's Autobiographies." *Ariel* 27, no. 1

(1996): 133–148; Coulie, Judith Lutge. "The Space between Frames: A New Discursive Practice in Ellen Kuzwayo's *Call Me Woman*." In *South African Feminisms: Writing, Theory, and Criticism, 1990–1994*. Edited by M. J. Daymond, 131–153 (New York: Garland, 1996; Creider, Jane Tapsubei. *Two Lives: My Spirit and I* (London: The Women's Press, 1986); D'Almeida, Irene Assiba. *Francophone African Women Writers: Destroying the Emptiness of Silence* (Gainesville: University Press of Florida, 1994); D'Almeida, Irene Assiba. "Kesso Barry's *Kesso*, or Autobiography as a Subverted Tale." *Research in African Literatures* 28, no. 2 (1997): 66–82; Danquah, Meri Nana-Ama. *Willow Weep for Me: A Black Woman's Journey through Depression, A Memoir* (New York: W. W. Norton, 1998); Deck, Alice A. "Autoethnography: Zora Neale Hurston, Noni Jabavu, and Cross-Disciplinary Discourse." *Black American Literature Forum* 24, no. 2 (Summer, 1990): 237–256; Diallo, Nafissatou. *A Dakar Childhood*. Translated by Dorothy Blair (London: Longman Drumbeat, 1982); Dietche, Julie Phelps. "Voyaging toward New Freedom: New Voices from South Africa." *Research in African Literatures* 26, no. 1 (1995): 61; Djbar, Assia. *Fantasia, an Algerian Cavalcade*. Translated by Dorothy Blair (London: Quartet, 1987); Djbar, Assia. *A Sister to Sheherazade*. Translated by Dorothy Blair (London: Quartet, 1987); Djbar, Assia. *Vaste est la prison W* (Paris: Albin Michel, 1995); Eko, Ebele O. "The Undaunted Spirit of South African Womanhood: Ellen Kuzwayo's *Call Me Woman*." In *Literature and National Consciousness*. Edited by Ebele Eko, Julius Ogu, and Azubuiko Iboeje, 233–244 (Ibadan, Nigeria: Heinemann, 1989); Emecheta, Buchi. *Head Above Water: An Autobiography*, 1986. Reprint (Oxford: Heinemann Educational Publishers, 1994); Forna, Aminatta. *The Devil That Danced on the Water: A Daughter's Quest* (New York: Atlantic Monthly Press, 2002); Garritano, Carmela. "At an Intersection of Humanism and Postmodernism: A Feminist Reading of Ellen Kuzwayo's *Call Me Woman*." *Research in African Literatures* 28, no. 2 (1997): 57–65; Head, Bessie. *A Woman Alone: Autobiographical Writings*. Selected and edited by Craig MacKenzie (London: Heinemann, 1990); Head, Bessie. *A Gesture of Belonging: Letters from Bessie Head, 1965–1979*. Edited by Randolph Vigne (London: SA Writers, 1991); Hogan, Joseph, and Rebecca Hogan. "Autobiography in the Contact Zone: Cross-Cultural Identity in Jane Tapsubei Creider's *Two Lives*." In *True Relations: Essays on Autobiography and the Postmodern*, edited by G. Thomas Couser and Joseph Fichtelberg, 83–96 (Westport, CT: Greenwood Press, 1998); Hunter, Monica, recorder. "The Story of Nosente, the Mother of Compassion of the Xhosa Tribe, South Africa." In *Ten Africans*, edited by Margery Perham, 121–137 (London: Faber and Faber, 1936); Ibrahim, Huma. "The Autobiographical Content in the Works of South African Women Writers." In *Biography: East and West*, edited by Carol Ramelb, 122–126 (Honolulu: University of Hawaii Press, 1989); Jabavu, Noni. *Drawn in Color: African Contrasts* (New York: St. Martin's Press, 1962); Jabavu, Noni. *The Ochre People* (London: John Murray, 1963); Joubert, Elsa, trans. *Poppie Nongena: One Woman's Struggle Against Apartheid* (New York: Holt, 1987); Kassindja, Fauziya, and Layli Miller Bashir. *Do They Hear You When You Cry* (New York: Delacorte Press, 1998); Keita, Aoua. *Femme d'Afrique: La vie d'Aoua Keita racontée par elle-meme* (Paris: Presence Africaine, 1975); Kuzwayo, Ellen. *Call Me Woman* (San Francisco: Spinsters Ink, 1985); Levine, Janet. *Inside Apartheid: One Woman's Struggle in South Africa* (Chicago: Contemporary Books, 1989); Lionnet, Françoise. *Autobiographical Voices: Race, Gender, Self-Portraiture* (Ithaca, NY: Cornell University Press, 1989); Magona, Sindiwe. *Forced to Grow* (Claremont South Africa: David Philip Publishers, 1992); Magona, Sindiwe. *To My Children's Children*. 1990. Reprint (New York: Interlink Books, 1994); McCord, Margaret, trans. *The Calling of Katie Makanya: A Memoir of South Africa* (New York: John Wiley and Sons, 1995); Makeba, Miriam, and James Hall. *Makeba: My Story* (New York: New American Library, 1987); Makhoere, Caesarina Kona. *No Child's Play: In Prison under Apartheid* (London: The Women's Press, 1988); Mandela, Winnie. *Part of My Soul Went with Him*. Edited by Anne Benjamin and adapted by Mary Benson (New York: W. W. Norton and Co., 1984); Mashinini, Emma. *Strikes Have Followed Me All My Life: A South African Autobiography* (New

York: Routledge, 1991); Miller, Mary-Kay. "My Mothers/My Selves: (Re) Reading a Tradition of West African Women's Autobiography." *Research in African Literatures* 28, no. 2 (1997): 5–15; Mirza, Sarah, and Margaret Strobel, eds. *Three Swahili Women: Life Histories from Mombasa, Kenya* (Bloomington: Indiana University Press, 1989); Moore, Kofoworola Aina. "The Story of Kofoworola Aina Moore, of the Yoruba Tribe, Nigeria, *written by herself.*" In *Ten Africans*, edited by Margery Perham, 323–343 (London: Faber and Faber, 1936); Mortimer, Mildred. "Assia Djebar's Algerian Quartet: A Study in Fragmented Autobiography." *Research in African Literatures* 28, no. 2 (1997): 102–117; Ntantala, Phyllis. *A Life's Mosaic: The Autobiography of Phyllis Ntantala* (Berkeley: University of California Press, 1993); Nthunya, Mpho 'M'atsepo. *Singing Away the Hunger: The Autobiography of an African Woman.* Edited by K. Limakatso Kendall (Bloomington: Indiana University Press, 1997); Olney, James. *Tell Me Africa: An Approach to African Literature* (Princeton, NJ: Princeton University Press, 1973); Ramphele, Mamphela. *Across Boundaries: The Journey of a South African Woman Leader* (New York: The Feminist Press, 1995); Saadawi, Nawal El. *Daughter of Isis: The Autobiography of Nawal El Saadawi.* Translated from the Arabic by Sherif Hetata (London: Zed Books, 1999); Saadawi, Nawal El. *Memoirs from the Women's Prison.* Translated from the Arabic by Marilyn Booth (Berkeley: University of California Press, 1986); Said, Laila. *A Bridge through Time: A Memoir* (New York: Summit Books, 1985); Shostak, Marjorie. *Nisa: The Life and Words of a !Kung Woman.* 1981. Reprint (New York: Random House, 1983); Sikakane, Joyce. *A Window on Soweto* (London: International Defence and Aid Fund, 1977); Smith, Mary F. *Baba of Karo: A Woman of the Muslim Hausa* (New Haven, CT: Yale University Press, 1981); Ugwu-Oju, Dympna. *What Will My Mother Say: A Tribal African Girl Comes of Age in America* (Chicago: Bonus Books, 1995); Waciuma, Charity. *Daughter of Mumbi* (Nairobi: East Africa Publishing House, 1969); Watson, Julia. "Unruly Bodies: Autoethnography and Authorization in Nfissatou Diallo's *De Tilene au Plateau* [A Dakar Childhood]." *Research in African Literatures* 28, no. 2 (1997): 34–56; Wright, Marcia. *Women in Peril: Life Stories of Four Captives* (Lusuka: National Educational Co., 1984).

Alice A. Deck

ALEXANDER, MEENA (1951–) A prominent writer of the South Asian diaspora, Meena Alexander explores her self-construction and **identity** formation in the context of multiple migrations in her **memoir**, *Fault Lines* (1993). Resisting easy classification into generic category, her memoir focuses on various issues: the recuperation of childhood memories and her ancestral home in Kerala, India; her coming-of-age in Khartoum, Sudan; her Ph.D. years in Nottingham, England; and her experiences in Minneapolis and New York City. She articulates passionately the numerous concerns that evoke international allegiances and multifarious loyalties: racial and ethnic alienation in the United States; the state's attempt to control women's bodies in Khartoum; Hindu-Muslim riots in India; and the kinds of coalitions that can be built with other women of color in the United States. Identifying herself as a woman "cracked by mutiple migrations" (3), Alexander demonstrates a transnational identity and perspective through her meditations on home, nationality, **race**, ethnicity, and **gender**, making her work indispensable to courses in **postcolonial women's autobiography**, multiethnic, and women's studies.

Born into a highly respected Kerala family, Mary Elizabeth Alexander changed her Anglicized name to "Meena" when she turned fifteen. When her father, a meteorologist in the Indian government, was transferred, the family moved to Sudan, North Africa. She finished her education in Khartoum and entered the University of Nottingham to pursue a Ph.D. in British Romanticism, after which she moved back to India in 1974 and taught English at various universities. Before migrating to the United States she married David Lelyveld, an American historian of South Asia. Undoubtedly, her many migrations had a significant impact on Alexander's writing, and all her work, whether poetry, fiction, or autobiography, registers a profound sense of displacement and dislocation familiar to the migrant's restless (or restive) search for wholeness, home, and belonging. For example, she describes herself as "a woman with no fixed place, a creature struggling to make herself up in the new world" (*Fault Lines* 15). Thus, the memoir format allows Alexander to invent and establish a self and to create a persona in a newly adopted "home," one that also announces her "arrival" in America and initiates the process of her Americanization.

Fault Lines is a record of her childhood memories and experiences as she moved between four continents and various cities— Allahabad, Tiruvella, Khartoum, Pune, Hyderabad, Manhattan, Nottingham. Adopting a nonlinear, nonchronological narrative style, an apt model to describe the complex trajectory of her life, Alexander focuses nostalgically on her privileged childhood in Kerala, illustrating a keen awareness of the politics of **class**, gender and color in an evocative landscape. Alexander recalls her paternal grandmother's injunction about her being "so dark," which reveals the emphasis South Asians place on fair skin, their convoluted color consciousness having been shaped by thousands of years of Aryan and Muslim history and two hundred years of British colonialism.

In addition, Alexander elaborates on what it means to be a female child and woman in India by narrating her own childhood, her mother's life, and her grandmother Kunju's life, while also giving **voice** to the narratives of other women. Thus, the memoir, too, is about learning "how to grow up as a woman" (50). Thus, she articulates the contrast between her mother's acceptance of tradition, and her grandmother Kunju's resistance to patriarchal mores through her participation in the Indian nationalist movement, a movement that created a space for women to enter the public arena. In addition to being a coming-of-age story both in the country of her birth and in her current "home," *Fault Lines* also narrates the story of the birth of the Indian nation, from independence in 1947, to the Emergency of the mid-1970s, to its present-day flirtation with globalization. Alexander extends her examination of the Indian nation-state to include language, a concern she shares with other postcolonial writers. She agonizes over her use of English, the colonizer's tongue, which has "robbed" her of literacy in her mother tongue, while at the same time she demonstrates mastery of the English language and makes it her own. By the end of *Fault Lines*, English has been decolonized and made to bend and serve Alexander's purpose.

She not only shares the same concerns as other postcolonial writers, but also consciously aligns herself with other ethnic women writers in the United States, revealing an equal investment in the general concerns of immigrant women and describing how they negotiate their place in cultural patriarchies that exoticize and racialize them. Alexander narrates an incident where her own vulnerability as a racial minority— as a South Asian American woman—is exposed when a white male biker in Minneapolis calls her a "black bitch!" Shaken by the incident and afraid to tell her white husband, she tells an Indian friend who understands "what it mean[s] to be Unwhite in America" (169). Not even her privileged class position can provide complete shelter from a race-obsessed America.

In addition to *Fault Lines*, Alexander has published many volumes of poetry and prose, including *Stone Roots* (1980), *The Shock of Arrival: Reflections on the Postcolonial Experience* (1996) and *House of a Thousand Doors* (1988). *Shock* is a "mosaic" text that cannot be classified as a memoir proper, as it questions the construction of rigid genre distinctions and contains personal reflections interspersed with academic language, critical essays, and poetry. Standing tall and strong at the cusp of the postcolonial becoming ethnic American, Alexander's work resonates with a global and transnational awareness in which all political action is local. *See also* **South Asian Women's Autobiography**.

Further Reading: Alexander, Meena. *Fault Lines: A Memoir* (New York: The Feminist Press at CUNY, 1993); Alexander, Meena. *House of a Thousand Doors* (Washington, DC: Three Continents, 1988); Alexander, Meena. *The Shock of Arrival: Reflections on the Postcolonial Experience* (Boston: South End Press, 1996); Alexander, Meena. *Stone Roots* (New Delhi: Arnold-Heinemann, 1980); Shankar, Lavina Dhingra. "Postcolonial Diasporics: Writing in Search of a Homeland: Meena Alexander's *Manhattan Music, Fault Lines, and The Shock of Arrival*" *LIT: Literature Interpretation Theory* 12, no. 3 (September 2001): 285–312.

Anupama Arora

ALLISON, DOROTHY (1949–) Although Dorothy Allison has only written one relatively short **memoir**, *Two or Three Things I Know for Sure* (1995), which began its life as a performance piece, readers have come to understand much of her life through all of her works, which makes her a significant source for studying autobiographical writing. Her most obviously autobiographical work is her first novel, *Bastard out of Carolina* (1993). This type of fiction is generally labeled **autobiographical fiction**, but what makes Allison interesting for the purpose of studying autobiography is that she does not only limit her autobiographical impulses to her fiction. Her poetry and creative nonfiction essays also reveal facets of her autobiography.

Allison was born April 11, 1949, to a poor, unmarried fifteen-year-old mother. Her stepfather began abusing her when she was five years old, and this abuse continued for many years. Although she suffered because of the abuse and the effects of poverty, she remembers fondly the women in her family because of their strength and their abilities as storytellers. Allison gradu-

ated from Florida Presbyterian College in 1971 and took graduate courses at Florida State University. She completed her M.A. in 1987 at the New School for Social Research in New York City in urban anthropology. Before Allison began to write full time, she worked as a social worker, creative writing instructor, journalist, and editor for various gay/lesbian and feminist periodicals. She currently lives near San Francisco with her partner and their son, Wolf.

Allison's works portray a segment of Southern society that many people, including Allison, label as poor "white trash," and she counts herself a member of that society. Allison's objective in writing about this lower **class** of poverty-stricken whites includes providing them with an **identity** that had previously been denied to them or misrepresented. Before Allison, many depictions of this class were either the Slattery and Snopes version or the Waltons. She also wanted to present them with a **voice** in which to tell their stories. Her works reveal Allison's strong belief that class plays as large a role in identity formation as **gender**, **race**, and sexual orientation—a belief that she feels is not largely recognized by many people within the lesbian and feminist community.

In addition to portraying poverty and class as primary elements in creating identity, Allison also depicts male violence and child abuse as abhorrent but significant factors in the formation of one's identity. At the same time, she places herself at odds with her lesbian/feminist community by setting forth the possibility that women can express themselves creatively and sexually through violence. In her works and in interviews Allison examines the idea of promiscuity and butch-femme role-playing as viable prospects for exploration by mutually consenting adults.

As she reveals in numerous ways, the strong women in her family are her greatest influence and provide much of the source material for her writing. In 1975, Allison took a writing seminar where writers such as Rita Mae Brown and Mary Daly were present, but much of her admiration was reserved for Bertha Harris, who "took her breath away" (*Skin* 201). She later wrote "Bertha Harris, a Memoir" that first appeared in the *Village Voice* and was later included in her full-length work, *Skin*. In interviews she readily acknowledges Harris's influence on her own work. It remains to be seen about Allison's influence on writers, Southern and otherwise, but, judging by the popular and critical reception that her works, particularly *Bastard out of Carolina*, have received, one would expect her to influence another generation of writers.

As previously mentioned, all of Allison's works have autobiographical impulses. Her collection of poetry, *The Women Who Hate Me: Poetry 1980–1990* (1983), uses food as a prominent metaphor to explore the issues of poverty, class, and family dysfunction. *Skin*, a collection of essays, clarifies her views on many of these same issues along with other topics that are prevalent in feminist or lesbian debates, including her stance about the role of poverty and class in identity formation and her liberal position on sexual politics and a woman's private sexual life. *Two or Three Things I Know for Sure* is a loving look at the women who shaped her identity and influenced her writing. Her short story collection *Trash* (1988) is the basis of her novel *Bastard out of Carolina*. Allison acknowledges that the stories in *Trash* are an angrier version and that she had to write it first in order to get this anger out of her system. While critics acknowledge the intensity and grittiness of *Bastard out of Carolina*, most also recognize the loving portrayal of these poor "white trash" characters. Allison readily acknowledges the autobiographical elements but points out that unlike her, the protagonist, Bone, was able to escape child abuse at a relatively early age. Her novel also reveals Allison's ambivalent feelings toward a mother, like her own, who is aware of the ongoing violence against her children but does nothing to stop it. Allison's latest novel, *Cavedweller* (1998), is her

least autobiographical, but once again she explores the issue of a mother's failure and admits that it is based on the society and family from which she hails.

Allison has won numerous local and regional awards: Her novel *Bastard out of Carolina* was a finalist for the National Book Award, and the actress Angelica Huston made it into a controversial movie that several television networks refused to show because of its depiction of child sexual abuse. It did not win the Lambda award for lesbian fiction because the people who make this decision felt that it was not lesbian enough. Her most recent novel, *Cavedweller*, was not as well received by a popular or critical readership, but it won a Lambda award for lesbian fiction. Regardless, Allison's works exert significant influence on the way in which we look at autobiographical writing. Her works reveal that autobiography takes on many forms and can be depicted in various genres.

Further Reading: Allison, Dorothy. *Bastard Out of Carolina* (New York: Plume, 1993); Allison, Dorothy. *Skin* (Ithaca, NY: Firebrand Books, 1994); Allison, Dorothy. *Two or Three Things I Know for Sure* (New York: Dutton, 1995); Boyd, Blanche McCrary. "Dorothy Allison, Crossover Blues." *The Nation* 257, no. 1 (1993): 20–21; Moore, Lisa. "Dorothy Allison (1949–)." In *Contemporary Lesbian Writers of the United States: A Bio-Bibliographical Critical Sourcebook*, edited by Sandra Pollack and Denise D. Knight, 13–18 (Westport, CT: Greenwood Press, 1993).

Susie Scifres Kuilan

ALTERITY Derived from the Latin *alteritas* (meaning difference), alterity in its modern sense is normally used in opposition to **identity**. The word generally designates figures of otherness in relation to one's identity or ego. Using alterity in its etymological sense of "difference" broadens its range of meaning. In this case, it can refer to the *self* as well as to the Other, attesting, for instance, to one's own lack of self-transparency, or changeability over time, as in the case of the sixteenth-century humanist and autobiographical essayist, Michel de Montaigne, who made the startling claim that the more he studied himself, the more he appeared as Other to himself: "I have seen no more evident monstrosity in the world than myself. We become habituated to anything strange by use and time; but the more I frequent myself and know myself, the more my deformity astonishes me, and the less I understand myself" (*The Complete Works of Montaigne* 1967, 787). Self-study, or autobiographical writing, led Montaigne to a process of defamiliarization and to a lack of self-understanding based on alterity.

In the second half of the twentieth century, the word alterity has been closely associated with the Continental philosophy of Emmanuel Lévinas (1906–1995). According to Lévinas, alterity refers to "the radical heterogeneity of the other" (*Totality and Infinity* 1969, 36). Here alterity means the aspect of the Other that resists absolute comprehension or full understanding. The "face-to-face" encounter represents for Lévinas a seemingly immediate ethical moment or instance when the encountered Other unsettles his "world" by calling into question his (illusory) status as a self-sufficient subject. In this respect, the alterity of the Other needs to be seen as fundamentally traumatizing, for it effectively disrupts his ego and his familiarity with his surroundings. Lévinas is also known for his declaration that "ethics is first philosophy," meaning that his relation to the *human* Other cannot (should not) be a relation of knowledge, that is, an epistemological relation between a knower (the individual) and an object of knowledge (the other person).

In postcolonial criticism, alterity takes on primarily a political dimension, as otherness is linked to the subaltern Other (to any subordinated or colonized groups lacking power). Postcolonial critics, such as Gayatri Chakravorty Spivak (1941–) and Homi Bhabha (1949–), have called attention to the ways in which acts of dehumanization (the refusal to recognize the humanity of the Other) or the "process of othering" (inter-preting a person or group as fundamentally different from oneself) functions to disempower colonized people. Bhabba emphasizes *hybridity* and *mimicry*, subversive practices by which altered subjects can resist the ideal of colonial purity, overcome binary oppositions such as Self and Other, West and East, and effectively speak as political agents (e.g., as autonomous—free, self-determining—subjects). Bhabha argues for a position "which overcomes the given grounds of opposition and opens a space of translation: a place of hybridity, figuratively speaking, where the construction of a political object that is new, neither the one nor the other, properly alienates our political expectations, and changes, as it must, the very forms of our recognition of the moment of politics" (*The Location of Culture* 1994, 25).

In feminist criticism, alterity has been deeply interconnected with the question of sexual difference. Drawing on Lévinas' philosophy of the Other, feminists thinkers have argued that discourses dominated by men have failed to account for feminine alterity on its own terms. That is, such discourses merely see the concept of "woman" as the negation of the concept of "man"—"woman" is what "man" is not. Feminists argue that the place of women within Western philosophy has invariably been that of exclusion and marginalization. Within the binary opposition masculine/feminine, the feminine is seen as essentially inferior to the masculine. Luce Irigaray has even argued against Lévinas for his apparent failure to fully recognize women's **subjectivity**, the alterity of sexual difference, or the otherness of the feminine: "[T]he feminine, as it is characterized by Lévinas, is not other than himself. . . . The feminine is apprehended not in a relation to itself, but from the point of view of man" (Irigaray 1991, 109). In short, the feminine, even when perceived as an otherness, is usually considered a lesser Other, a derivative of, if not a subordinate to, the masculine Other.

Discussions surrounding sexual alterity have also opened up a larger debate between "essentialists" and "construction-ists," especially in relation to the question of **gender**. Is female alterity a metaphysical matter, as essentialists would argue (meta-physics is traditionally the branch of phi-losophy that deals with defining reality or existence), or in this case defining what a woman is? Or is it, as the constructionists feel, primarily a social question, concerning the ways in which gender (as opposed to one's biological sex) has been constructed by society throughout the centuries? For the essentialists, there is a perceived danger in neutralizing sexual difference and in as-suming that we are all first human beings and that our designated status as masculine and feminine is secondary. This would be unproblematic if the word "Man," which is intended to be inclusive of both sexes, did not in reality function to privilege the mas-culine over the feminine. Thus, alterity for the essentialist feminists denotes the pres-ence of sexual specificity. For the construc-tionists, however, sexual identity should not be understood in terms of a substance, an ahistorical entity representing woman-hood. On the contrary, the feminine or fe-male gender needs to be analyzed cultur-ally and socially and conceived as a social category. Indeed, feminists, for the con-structionists, should expose how empirical women, under patriarchal societies, have been formed as inferior alterities without positing or having recourse to a fixed fem-inine nature.

In the light of the diverse meanings of al-terity, the relevance of this key concept for an appreciation of women's autobiography becomes clear. Alterity can refer to one's own (alienating) past, when the autobiog-rapher, at the moment of writing, fails to co-incide or identify with his or her prior self. Figures of alterity (understood here as the Other) have also had a structuring role in women's autobiography, playing a crucial role in the practice of writing about oneself; indeed, there is an overall tendency to "defin[e] oneself in relation to significant others" (Marrone 2000, 8), especially in re-lation to the mother (Chodorow 1978 and Miller 1994). As a decentering textual prac-tice—moving away from a narcissistic *me* (of the type found in the autobiographies of Rousseau and Chateaubriand)—the female autobiographer offers her readers an alto-gether different kind of narrative, where re-lationality rather than an obsession with autonomy (ego, freedom, and textual self-mastery) governs the autobiographical project.

It is, of course, also the case that women autobiographers are alterities themselves, often writing from a socially marginal po-sition with respect to that of men; this is doubly the case for women whose **race** and/or **class** status makes it difficult for them to make their voices heard. This is es-pecially visible in women writing in a lan-guage that is not their own (Caribbean women autobiographers, for example). For this reason, women's autobiography invites feminist interpretations, since speaking for oneself is at the most basic level an em-powering practice—writing about one's lived experience in one's own **voice**. Yet, readers of women's autobiography should always keep in mind that female authors have been programmed to *imitate* male dis-course and that female experience is never pure or uncontaminated by social and ide-ological forces (Fuss 1994 and Scott 1994). The problem of female experience is, of course, tied to the more general debate over the status of sexual difference: can writing translate sexual alterity? Does *écriture femi-nine* (feminine writing) exist? Nevertheless, not all imitations are slavish and normaliz-ing; indeed, postcolonial and feminist criti-cism have especially taught us of the possi-bility for authors to subvert or manipulate preexisting models strategically—through the practice of mimicry and hybridity—for their own political, ethical, and aesthetic ends.

Further Reading: Bhabha, Homi. *The Location of Culture* (New York: Routledge, 1994); Chodorow, Nancy. *The Reproduction of Mothering: Psychoanalysis and the Sociology of Gender* (Berkeley: University of California Press, 1978); Fuss, Diana. "Reading Like a Feminist." In *The Essential Difference*, edited by Naomi Schor and Elizabeth Weed (Bloomington: Indiana University Press, 1994), 98–115; Irigaray, Luce. "Questions to Emmanuel Lévinas: On the Divinity of Love." Translated by Margaret Whitford. In *Re-Reading Lévinas*, edited by Robert Bernasconi and Simon Critchley, 109–118 (Indianapolis: Indiana University Press, 1991); Lévinas, Emmanuel. *Totality and Infinity: An Essay on Exteriority*. Translated by Alphonso Lingis (Pittsburgh, PA: Duquesne University Press, 1969); Marrone, Claire. *Female Journeys: Autobiographical Expressions by French and Italian Women* (Westport, CT: Greenwood Press, 2000); Miller, Nancy K. "Representing Others: Gender and the Subject of Autobiography." *Differences* 6, no. 1 (1994): 1–27; Montaigne, Michel. *The Complete Works of Montaigne*. Translated by Donald Frame (Stanford, CA: Stanford University Press, 1967); Scott, Joan W. "The Evidence of Experience." In *Questions of Evidence: Proof, Practice, and Persuasion across the Disciplines*, edited by James Chandler, Arnold I. Davidson, and Harry Harootunian, 363–387 (Chicago: University of Chicago Press, 1994); Spivak, Gayatri Chakravorty. "Can the Subaltern Speak?" In *Marxism and the Interpretation of Culture*, edited by Cary Nelson and Lawrence Grossberg, 271–313 (Urbana: University of Illinois Press, 1988).

Zahi Zalloua

AMERICAN WOMEN'S AUTOBIOGRAPHY: EARLY WOMEN DIARISTS AND MEMOIRISTS (TO 1800)

Early American women's diaries and memoirs are best understood in the context of women's diverse lived experiences. American women's lives varied widely according to geographical region, ethnicity, class, and religion as well as the broad historical contexts in which they were written, which literary scholars have generally defined as the colonial era (including seventeenth-century English settlement) and the Enlightenment eighteenth century (including the American Revolutionary and early Republican eras). With the emergence of women's and feminist studies in the academy, American literary studies have been energized by a broadening canon of American literature that includes a diverse range of writers and experiences. The recovery of early American women's writings has invigorated the field, particularly in the predominant genre of that time, autobiography, which includes diaries, journals, spiritual autobiographies, and conversion and **captivity** narratives. In addition to the critical reexamination of published texts in this genre, scholars over the past thirty years have focused on unpublished works as well. Because of the expense involved in printing and buying books in early America, many readers and writers participated in a thriving manuscript culture, exchanging **letters**, diaries, journals, poems, and commonplace books. The process of recovering the lost words of early American women involves not only a renewed attention to women's works but an examination of how our new knowledge about these works impacts what we already know about the literature, history, and culture of the period. Many scholars have discussed how women's writing has upheld, complicated, or resisted dominant cultural ideas about women. During the seventeenth and eighteenth centuries, the autobiographical works of American women reflected and sometimes challenged dominant cultural ideas about women's "place" in society and print culture.

Diaries, Spiritual Memoirs, and Captivity Narratives

Most seventeenth-century American women's diaries and memoirs emerged from New England, which was settled by English Puritans (Separatists and Congregationalists) in the early part of the century. Historian Laurel Thatcher Ulrich explains Puritan women's roles in terms of discrete duties: obedient wife and helpmeet, loving mother, community-minded neighbor, wise governor of servants and children, and faithful servant of God (*Good Wives* 1980). Women's roles derived from Calvinism's fixed and hierarchical worldview. According to this view, God's design was present and apparent in all things, including whether an individual was a member of the "elect," rich or poor, or high or low in stature. The family was an earthly microcosm for how God's will operated, and the husband was placed over the wife in authority and understanding, although he certainly took his wife's opinions into account. Through their work and conduct, women operated as supporting actors in their families, comporting themselves in their speech, manner, and dress with suitable industry and modesty. According to English Common Law, married women existed in a state of *coverture*, which meant that a wife's legal rights were subsumed under those of her husband. Upon their husbands' deaths, widows inherited at least a third of the household goods and were entitled to a third of the proceeds of the estate until they died or remarried.

The secondary yet crucial role of women in early New England impacted ideas about women's public and private writing and speech. From the notorious trials of the dissenter Anne Hutchinson to the scandal surrounding Mary Rowlandson's captivity and subsequent narrative, women's public words provoked public comment and, sometimes, criticism. Hutchinson was censured and banished for defying hierarchical authority that belonged to men after she expressed her religious views in mixed-**gender** gatherings. Her trial, known as the Antinomian Controversy, is a good lens through which to view cultural attitudes about women and their words. One of the judges stated that she had stepped out of her place and become a husband rather than a wife. John Winthrop dubbed Hutchinson an American "Jezabel," who "seduced" souls from the path of righteousness. In 1643, Winthrop linked women's reading and writing with infirmity and even madness, remarking that if Anne Hutchinson had busied herself with household and women's affairs, she would have kept her wits. Such commentary reveals that, in seventeenth-century New England culture, intellectual and scholarly pursuits were less important for women than domestic duties.

One notable exception is the publication of America's first poet, Anne Bradstreet's collection, *The Tenth Muse Lately Sprung Up in America* (1650). Anne Bradstreet, however, was a member of the Puritan elite and received her education in her father's library in England, where her work was first published by her brother-in-law, Thomas Parker. The publication of poetry by a woman author was so unusual that it merited twelve pages of prefatory explanation, including letters of recommendation attesting to Bradstreet's modesty and propriety as well as verification that she was, indeed, a woman.

Seventeenth-century American women's memoirs and diaries reflect their writers' awareness of woman's cultural position. Even ostensibly private documents might be understood as walking a tricky line between a woman's private life and her public roles. As Margo Culley (1985) asserts, the **diary** form has only recently become the purview of a "secret" or "private" life. Consistent with their roles of wise family instructors, dutiful wives, and faithful Christians, women's diaries recorded lives of good conduct for their children and descendants after their deaths. These texts were frequently circulated in manuscript and sometimes published by the families themselves subsequent to the authors' deaths. Such circulation and publication provided the community with moral barometers, examples of moral rectitude and Christian living. In this sense, early American women's diaries and memoirs operated as both public and private documents.

One important form of such writing was the spiritual autobiography, which traced an individual's spiritual growth and journey toward God and salvation. Since white women were taught to read but were not afforded the same formal training in writing as men, and since women's public speech was often a matter of concern, their spiritual autobiographies often appeared as conversion narratives, transcribed from the spoken word by ministers and elders into written church documents.

One variation of early American women's spiritual autobiography was the captivity narrative. Like conversion narratives, captivity narratives were frequently transcribed by male editors, booksellers, and ministers and sold in collections or as inexpensive pamphlets. Mary Rowlandson's *The Sovereignty and Goodness of God* (1682), the first prose narrative published in America by an English woman residing in America, and also a smash bestseller, exemplifies the use of spiritual autobiography to recount a woman's private life in a public forum. The text serves several intersecting purposes, both public and private. These include warning a backsliding New England community of its original Puritan errand into the wilderness to build "a City upon a Hill," recording and offering the English perspective on King Philip's war, helping its author make sense of her own survival when so many of her friends and family died, and providing a platform from which she can address accusations of lack of chastity and sinfulness raised by her captivity. Rowlandson's captivity and restoration tale represents her own spiritual journey from doubt to faith as a metaphor for the struggle with sin and the possibility of redemption faced by her entire community of readers.

According to the title page, Rowlandson's memoir of her two-month captivity among the Narragansetts, Nipmucks, and Wampanoags during King Philip's war in 1676 was written for the benefit of her children and family and made public only at the request of friends. The title page of the American edition suggests that this modest gentlewoman came forward only because others convinced her of the value of her narrative to benefit others afflicted by sin and despair. Should readers have any

doubt, the preface, perhaps written by Increase Mather, affirms Rowlandson's role as "dear Consort" of her husband, the Reverend Joseph Rowlandson, and alludes to the suspicions some readers may have had about the degree to which she herself was responsible for her own troubles. Instead, the preface insists that the narrator is one of God's elect, a modest and chaste gentlewoman in a company of barbarous heathens whose escape serves to illustrate God's love and mercy.

The narrative itself at once upholds and complicates the prefator's interpretation. At the outset, Rowlandson complies with images of her captors as bloodthirsty savages who prey upon innocent people. She describes in lurid detail the attack on Lancaster, the deaths of her family members and friends, and the arduous journey into the Massachusetts wilderness with her injured young child (who soon dies of a gunshot wound inflicted during the initial siege) in her arms. As the memoir progresses, however, Rowlandson demonstrates a remarkable conversance in her captors' language and habits, including a willingness to eat "Indian food" and serve an "Indian master." Through these developments, Rowlandson, whether intentionally or not, acknowledges the systematic practices of a coherent Native American culture. She records her resourcefulness in trade, knitting, and sewing for her captors in return for food and other niceties during wartime. Moreover, her narrative questions the competence of the English army and leaves the reader to wonder about the significance of her insomnia, despite her restoration to her friends and family at the narrative's end.

One important aspect of Rowlandson's authorship is her organization of the text into "removes," which break her text into episodic narratives of geographical displacements during her journey. In addition to her physical dislocation, these removes also suggest the social and emotional displacements that Rowlandson experienced as a result of her sudden immersion in an alien culture. At one point she laments, "All was gone, my husband gone . . . my children gone, my relations and friends gone, our house and home and all our comforts—within door and without—all was gone (except my life), and I knew not but the next moment that might go too" (144). This passage, as has been argued elsewhere, demonstrates the ways that Rowlandson's writing ties her **identity** to the duties and roles of a Puritan woman. Her life becomes merely parenthetical in this hierarchy of family and community obligations, for if she exists without the paradigm of her home, who is she?

Many scholars have noted the frequency with which Rowlandson cites scripture to accommodate the strange and tragic events she endures, and some critics have speculated that she collaborated with or that the text was ghostwritten by Increase Mather. This familiarity with scripture, however, should be expected from the wife of a minister, who may have read, listened to, or even assisted her husband as he wrote his sermons. Furthermore, early New Englanders operated in an oral culture; their reading and writing lessons came from the Bible. A woman such as Rowlandson, the most prominent woman in the frontier outpost of Lancaster, Massachusetts, would of course possess fluency with scripture and the genre of the sermon. Rowlandson's narrative was and remains today one of the most influential examples of autobiographical writing in early America.

Political Causes and Confessions in Women's Autobiographies

As some elements of Rowlandson's work suggest, American women diarists and memoirists during this time began to use the spiritual autobiography and captivity forms for complex spiritual and secular purposes. As these narratives gained popularity and influence, they garnered attention from prominent male figures in the community who wished to shape them to

their own agendas. Throughout the next century, captivity narratives not only presented the sensational experiences but also argued for the religious or political causes of their authors' communities. For example, Mary Lewis Kinnan's narrative, *A True Narrative of the Sufferings of Mary Kinnan* (1795), dictated by her to printer, Shepard Kollock, directs intense animosity at the British, whose military efforts in Ohio and Michigan lengthened her captivity. Elizabeth Hanson's captivity narrative, *God's Mercy Surmounting Man's Cruelty, Exemplified in the Captivity and Redemption of Elizabeth Hanson* (1728), written or dictated by Hanson, resembles many other early Quaker journals in its direct style and evenhanded portrayal of her captors despite the fact that they murdered her children.

Similar in their movement from sin to conversion were early criminal confessions and conversions that women ostensibly dictated to ministers before they went to the gallows. These narratives provide information about the lives of economically disadvantaged women who were perhaps illiterate and, but for their criminal conviction, would have disappeared from history and print culture. For example, *The Declaration and Confession of Esther Rodgers* (1701) includes the subject's **confession** of her "running out a Night" and falling into the "horrible Pit . . . of Carnal Pollution with the *Negro* man belonging to that House." After Rodgers' sexual adventures lead to pregnancy, she gives birth in a field, where she abandons the child to the cold, only to have the murder discovered by neighbors. The confession, according to her publisher, is "[T]aken word for word from her own Mouth" and is accompanied by prefaces and a sermon that explain its moral significance. *A Faithful Narrative of the Wicked Life and Remarkable Conversion of Patience Boston* (1738) relates the first-person conversion of a Native American servant woman who resisted the confines of servitude and eventually killed her master's grandson in revenge. These narratives, which seem to have been composed in collaboration with ministers and printers as their writers awaited execution, are vital documents that reveal the lives of otherwise obscure women in early America.

Many Quaker women's spiritual autobiographies, published by the Society of Friends, survive. Quaker theology not only supported women's speech and public preaching but encouraged the writing of such texts as a strategy for converting more followers to the faith. According to Quaker theology, all individuals, men and women of all classes and ethnicities, had access to a divine inner light, which was God's truth. Quaker meetings were conducted in silence unless someone felt the inspiration of God's light within and was moved to speak.

The best-known early American Quaker woman's autobiography is by Elizabeth Ashbridge, *Some Account of the Fore Part of the Life of Elizabeth Ashbridge* (1774). According to Carol Edkins, Quaker autobiographies observed the following general outline: early intimations of religious questioning, attempts to find religious life in prevailing doctrines, records of first knowledge of Quakers, struggle against surrender to God and the Quaker community, and submission to the divine and acceptance into the Society of Friends. Ashbridge's narrative follows this path yet also traces the life of a rebellious and passionate early American woman. Ashbridge eloped as a young teenager, but her marriage lasted only five months before she was widowed. Estranged from her father, she went to live with relatives in Ireland before deciding to immigrate to America, which resulted in indentured servitude with unscrupulous masters, one of whom seems to have sexually harassed her. In the meantime, she befriended a troop of actors and was well liked for her singing and dancing, through which she earned money toward her freedom. Finally paying off her indenture, she inexplicably married Sullivan, who becomes the antagonist whom she must overcome in order to convert to Quakerism.

While Ashbridge praises her mother's love and virtue, she frequently represents the important men in her life, including her father, a priest with whom she has a dialogue, her master, and her emotionally and physically abusive husband Sullivan, as her oppressors. Throughout the bulk of the narrative, her husband tries to "cure" his wife of her Quaker leanings through physical domination and punishment, public humiliation, and repeated relocations from friends who shared her religious tendencies. Ultimately, however, he concedes and even attends meetings with his wife, and the two apparently shared a brief but peaceful and stable life as schoolteachers until his death. Ashbridge's account is important not only as an example of Quaker women's autobiography but as a compelling record of an immigrant and nonelite woman's life. The Society of Friends' egalitarian views of women enable her to compose a spiritual autobiography that also examines the possibilities and pitfalls of women's cultural and social place in early America.

The *Memoirs of Mrs. Abigail Bailey* record its subject's efforts to make spiritual sense of her husband's domestic violence and incest. Published in 1815 with the memoirs of two other Congregationalist women, Bailey's narrative interweaves devotional diaries kept over the years of her marriage to justify to the public her private and domestic trauma, especially during the years 1788–1792, when her husband Asa sexually abused their teenage daughter Phebe. The *Memoirs* recount Bailey's emotionally painful relationship with a husband who was often cruel and who was accused of both adultery with and rape of household servants in the early years of their marriage. The devout Abigail describes her emotional and religious responses to her husband's behavior and her fear for his salvation, which, as a dutiful wife, she assiduously seeks to remedy. Once she becomes aware of the incest, however, she resolves to reach a property settlement with him so that they can separate. The narrative relies on both biblical and Indian captivity sources, as it presents Abigail's afflictions in Job-like terms and her acceptance of them as an example of God's love and grace. The captivity plot intensifies when her husband tricks his wife, also the mother of his seventeen children, into a forced march along the New York frontier, where property and divorce laws are less friendly to women. Asa's intent is to abandon his wife, penniless and friendless, to forever separate her from home and children, since she has no money or resources with which to return, and to recover all of their joint property for himself. Along the journey, Abigail is forbidden to read or write, but this ever resourceful wife convinces him to write down all the towns they have passed through, which she uses as a reverse map to find her way home, claim her property, and at last take him to court.

The *Memoirs* convey both spiritual and secular assertions of authority. Using excerpts from her devotional diaries, Bailey details her years of prayer and wifely obedience to a sinful man who cares nothing of God. Bailey's memoirs reveal her increasing dependence on God as she resists and defies her husband and insists on the value of that spirituality which he forbids. Her text conveys the deepest spiritual struggles of an eighteenth-century New England Congregationalist woman and justifies her distinctive behavior to her community from both religious and secular standpoints. As with Rowlandson, Ashbridge, and others, the spiritual autobiography of a religious convert serves clear personal and public purposes. These works provide us with a truer picture of the ways that early American women thought and behaved.

American Women's Accounts of Daily Lives up to the Nineteenth Century

In addition to recording the spiritual progress of their subjects, early American women's memoirs and autobiographies, in their various forms, served a range of purposes for their writers and for historians and literary scholars today. They recorded family and community events, thoughts on friendship, literature, and public issues and also preserved for loved ones the business of women's daily lives for those separated by relocation, travel, and death. While some diaries used brief entries crisply stating the facts, others used the form of extended letters that captured their daily concerns, struggles, and thoughts for distant friends and family.

Unpublished until 1825, Sarah Kemble Knight's 1704–1705 journal of her five-month trip from Boston to New Haven and New York City and back probably circulated in manuscript form to friends. Knight's narrative of her voluntary journey undertaken to help settle a will for her cousin's widow reveals a very different kind of Puritan woman from Rowlandson. The highly secularized Knight leaves her husband and daughter to embark on a difficult journey by horse through a great deal of rural territory. Her determination takes her away from the middle-class comforts she enjoyed in Boston to face with humor and whatever hapless guide she finds along the muddy and impassable roads, raging river crossings, and less than cosmopolitan accommodations and company. Knight's journey is secular rather than spiritual and reveals the shifting sensibilities of New England at the turn of the eighteenth century. Knight evinces a broad knowledge of business and trade, British and classical literature, and the ways of people. Episodic and often lighthearted, Knight's journal repeats the stories she witnesses or overhears along the way and directs jokes at those less privileged by urban living, class, ethnicity, and education. Yet her self-deprecating sense of humor almost redeems her, as when she mentions quarters too tight for her broad expanse or shares bits of highly stylized poetry apparently meant as doggerel for her audience. Critics often see her work as an example of America in transition, and her journal is also significant for recording an early American, white middle-class woman's business acumen and comic voice.

Elizabeth House Trist's 1783–1784 travel diary, rediscovered in 1976 by Annette Kolodny, traces her journey from Philadelphia, along the Mississippi River, to Natchez, where she intends to reunite with her husband, who has purchased property there. Kolodny suggests that Trist was probably influenced by the interests of her new friend, Thomas Jefferson, who became Trist's lifelong supporter once she returned north as a widow. Like Knight, Trist describes the hardships and dangers of eighteenth-century travel, including her fear of Native Americans and the difficulties of rural living. While Trist confides her illnesses and fears in her diary, she also describes, in the vein of eighteenth-century nature writers, such as Jefferson or Hector St. Jean de Crèvecoeur, the magnificent vistas and vast resources of the western territories. Her diary reveals that already the buffalo are depleted and the streams polluted, yet it also describes unique cultural exchanges that take place as English, French, and Native Americans come in contact along the Mississippi-Ohio border. Her diary is an unusual and intimate glimpse of a young woman's response to the frontier, to her unidentified female companion, Polly, and to separation from her beloved husband, whom we know has died months before she reaches him. As Trist's diary breaks off, she writes poignantly that she can "hardly keep [her]self alive," yet she knows that Mr. Trist will be "glad to see" her. Although only fragments of her travel diary survive, Trist's work offers a rare view of eighteenth-century frontier life from the perspective of an educated, white, mid-Atlantic middle-class woman.

Between 1754 and 1757, Esther Edwards Burr, daughter of renowned Congregational minister Jonathan Edwards and Sarah Pierpont Edwards, exchanged with her dear friend Sarah Prince a letter-journal, a series of letter "paquets" to be shared with friends that detailed their religious and intellectual lives. Although only Burr's half of the correspondence survives, it records the theological and political concerns of a minister's young wife, who ran a household of children, servants, frequent guests, and parishioners. The friends shared literary interests, spiritual goals, struggles, advice, and the events of their daily lives and conducted intellectual discussions about the role of women in literature, politics, and culture. Burr's letter-journal attests to the rich intellectual lives and thriving manuscript culture of economically privileged eighteenth-century women.

The journal and letters of South Carolina plantation mistress Eliza Lucas Pinckney provides an interesting contrast to her genteel northeastern counterparts. Pinckney's letterbook, which she kept from 1739 to 1762, recounts her many duties as a planter, wife, and mother. Responsible for her absent father's plantation from the age of seventeen, Pinckney documents her agricultural experiments with different crops, most notably indigo, and she is credited with pioneering its cultivation in the American south. Perhaps an effort to replicate her fine education in England, Pinckney's letterbook records an energetic daily routine that included two hours of reading, more hours of French, shorthand, and music practice, tutoring her sister and household slaves, and doing needlework in addition to plantation business and personal correspondence. Like Burr, Pinckney valued education and intellectual pursuits and kept a careful record of all that she read, from philosophical and scientific treatises to novels. After she married, she used her writing to contemplate her duties as a wife, mother, and educator of her children. She evinced discipline and energy in her domestic devotions and used her book to strive toward the goal of exemplary wife. Once widowed, she wrote from a woman's perspective about the political concerns of her country before, during, and after the Revolution. Her letterbook exhibits an unusual woman's life of the mind and spirit in the rural South. Further, like Burr and others, Pinckney offers an example of how women's roles were changing with the Revolution and the founding of the new republic. As Mary Beth Norton and Linda Kerber have argued, this period in history bestowed a sense of political awareness and activism in women, who saw firsthand how the affairs of men affected their personal and domestic concerns.

The diaries of ordinary women raise significant questions about how we might best approach them as literature. Even when manuscripts are edited by scholars and printed in textbooks and anthologies, early American women's diary literature proves challenging for a twenty-first-century literary readership trained to look for formal ambiguity and aesthetic complexity. For this reason, Margo Culley's "blueprint" for reading early American women's diaries is an essential tool. Culley suggests that readers notice how the text is shaped by its assumed contemporary audience, whether private and/or public. As well, readers should consider what textual elements are repeated, whether of plot, theme, image, or character. We might think about the ideas and values that shape the narrator's self-presentation and how those ideas and values are conveyed through imagery and symbolism. Culley notes that the repetition of elements can amount to a pattern of meaning. Most important, Culley asks us to look for "silences" in the text, places where the text does *not* say something. This blueprint can help to explicate these texts more effectively in the historical contexts in which they were produced and to work from a literary and cultural perspective on writing that may seem at first, like grocery lists and doodles on class notes, to render interpretation unnecessary.

Augusta, Maine, midwife Martha Moore Ballard kept her diary for twenty-seven years, from 1785 to 1812, a perfect example of the kind of ordinary writing that Culley discusses. Writing on ruled paper in almanac style, Ballard describes the weather and the major events of each day, which might include gardening, knitting, sewing, weaving, and other household tasks, births, deaths, people encountered, travel for social or medical reasons, and/or economic transactions. As she ages, the diary includes details of her illnesses, her family's financial struggles, which resulted in her husband spending a year in debtor's prison, her desire to remain independent despite her waning physical and monetary resources, and her bouts with mild depression. Occasionally, Ballard's daily life meshes with memorable town scandals, as when she delivers a child to a woman raped by a prominent selectman, and when she and her son discover the bodies of a neighbor, who has murdered his wife and eight children and then sliced his own throat with a razor. Ballard's diary, which some critics have dismissed as trivia or too ordinary, functions not only as a medical and economic history of the town but also as a window into the daily lives and concerns of a middle-class working woman in the late eighteenth century.

In contrast to Ballard, Philadelphia Quaker Elizabeth Drinker's financial means gave her the leisure to write thousands of diary pages, contained in thirty-three handwritten volumes, for nearly fifty years, from 1759 to 1807. In addition to keeping daily records of her family and community, she also recorded her thoughts on her wide reading in history, politics, the classics, literature, theology, natural history, and medicine. Her diary includes short book reviews of her reading, which enlighten about contemporaneous responses to important eighteenth-century works, including Samuel Richardson's *Pamela* (1740) and Mary Wollstonecraft's *Vindication of the Rights of Women* (1792). Since she remained in Philadelphia throughout the Revolutionary War, her diaries note historical, military, and political events next to social gatherings and daily family details. Pattie Cowell notes that Drinker's writings, like most diaries and letters of the period, were intended for an audience of family and friends, who would read selections aloud while visiting. As Cowell observes, Drinker herself spends time reading diaries and journals of close friends, a common practice in a culture where friends may be far away or visits not as frequent due to the obligations of marriage and family. In plain Quaker style, Drinker's diary reveals a life of literary pursuits and leisure strikingly removed from Ballard's rigorous endeavors.

Readers must keep in mind that any record is necessarily a partial reconstruction of the writer's life shared from her perspective alone. Like anyone keeping a diary or writing a memoir, early American women imagined audiences and specific purposes for their texts, and, based on their own determination, decided which details to include and how to organize them in the **space** of their books. How women wish to represent themselves and, in some cases, how friends, early American printers, ministers, booksellers, and editors wished to represent them, plays a big part in the persona we come to know through the pages of life writing. Margo Culley observes that the sense of an audience is the most important shaper of the diarist's details and self-presentation (12). To whom we are speaking has a great effect on what we say and how we say it. Neither the diary nor the memoir form allows full access to the real person behind the text because this writing is only a partial representation of the person who wrote it and who made literary and emotional choices about her work. For these reasons, autobiographical texts are best approached from a literary perspective that considers the diarist or memoirist as a narrator, persona, protagonist, central character, or subject of the book. By focusing on the literary patterns of language, image, character, and plot that make up the text, readers can determine how these elements shape its subject. Such textual analysis can give us a sense of some of the issues, ideas, and material details of the writer's life that inform the subject

whom we can only know through reading her diary or memoir.

Brief or extended, intended for public or private audiences, women's diaries and memoirs share a sense that, for whatever reason, their experiences and lives were worth recording. Perhaps the writer wanted to preserve her life, works, and thoughts for the edification of future readers or to clarify for herself and others the meaning of unusual events, such as travel, marriage, births, and deaths. The 1777–1778 diaries of Grace Growden Galloway, who lived in Philadelphia and defended her property rights as her Loyalist husband fled the Revolutionary army, and Sarah Wister, who lived in Germantown during the British occupation, document the ordinary lives of women experiencing extraordinary times. Because they preserve what has for many years been lost to us— the histories and voices that reside in the everyday—women's diaries and memoirs are vital to readers and scholars. If we wish to understand the legacy of women's voices in literature, the ways that women have represented themselves in writing, and the changing roles of women in American history and culture, we must read their words. Since the late 1970s, feminist scholars of American literature have been engaged in the work of recovering women writers whose works have been "lost" through the shifting aesthetic values of male-dominated publishing practices and the processes of canonization, or because their writings were never intended for publication. The recovery of women's autobiographies, diaries, and memoirs forces us to reconsider the role of women in history, literature, and culture. Moreover, this recovery insists that we rethink the ways in which we talk about historical periods, literary genres, and our assumptions about what counts as literature and how we should read, interpret, and value it.

Further Reading: Andrews, William L. *Journeys in New Worlds: Early American Women's Narratives* (Madison: University of Wisconsin

Press, 1990); Ashbridge, Elizabeth. *Some Account of the Fore Part of the Life of Elizabeth Ashbridge* (1774). Edited by Daniel Shea. In *Journeys in New Worlds: Early American Women's Narratives*, edited by William Andrews, et al., 117–180 (Madison: University of Wisconsin Press, 1990); Bailey, Abigail Abbot. *The Memoirs of Abigail Abbot Bailey* (1815). In *Religion and Domestic Violence in Early New England: The Memoirs of Abigail Abbot Bailey*, edited by Ann Taves, 51–198 (Bloomington: Indiana University Press, 1989); Ballard, Martha Moore. *The Diary of Martha Ballard, 1785–1812*. Edited by Robert R. McCausland and Cynthia MacAlman (Camden, ME: Picton Press, 1992); Burr, Esther Edwards. *The Journal of Esther Edwards Burr 1754–1757*. Edited by Carol F. Karlsen and Laurie Crumpacker (New Haven: Yale University Press, 1984); Culley, Margo. *A Day at a Time: The Diary Literature of American Women from 1764 to the Present* (New York: Feminist Press, 1985); Derounian-Stodola, Kathryn Zabelle, ed. *Women's Indian Captivity Narratives* (New York: Penguin, 1998); Drinker, Elizabeth. *The Diary of Elizabeth Drinker*. 3 vols. Edited by Elaine Forman Crane (Boston: Northeastern University Press, 1991); Drinker, Elizabeth. *The Diary of Elizabeth Drinker: The Life Cycle of an Eighteenth-Century Woman*. Vol. 1. Edited by Elaine Forman Crane (Boston: Northeastern University Press, 1994); Edkins, Carol. "Quest for Community: Spiritual Autobiographies of Eighteenth-Century Quaker and Puritan Women in America." In *Women's Autobiography: Essays in Criticism*, edited by Estelle C. Jelinek (Bloomington: Indiana University Press, 1980); Galloway, Grace Growden. "Diary of Grace Growden Galloway." Edited by Raymond C. Werner. *Pennsylvania Magazine of History and Biography* 55 (1931): 35–94; 58 (1934): 152–189. Reprint. *Diary of Grace Growden Galloway, Eyewitness Accounts of the American Revolution*, Series 3 (New York: New York Times and Arno Press, 1971); Hanson, Elizabeth. *God's Mercy Surmounting Man's Cruelty, Exemplified in the Captivity and Redemption of Elizabeth Hanson* (1728). In *Women's Indian Captivity Narratives*, edited by Kathryn Zabelle Derounian-Stodola, 61–80 (New York: Penguin, 1998); Kerber, Linda K. *Women of the Republic: Intellect and Ideology in Revolutionary America* (Chapel Hill: University of North Carolina Press, 1980); Knight, Sarah Kemble. *The Journal of Madam Knight*. Edited by Sargent Bush. In *Journeys in New Worlds: Early American Women's Narratives*, edited by William Andrews, et al, 67–116 (Madison: University of Wisconsin Press, 1990); Kollock, Sheperd. *A True Narrative of the Sufferings of Mary Kinnan* (1795). In *Women's Indian Captivity Narratives*, edited by Kathryn Zabelle Derounian-Stodola, 105–116 (New York: Penguin, 1998); Kolodny, Annette. Introduction to *The Travel Diary of Elizabeth House Trist: From Philadelphia to Natchez, 1783–84*. In *Journeys in New Worlds*, 183–200; Logan, Lisa. "Mary Rowlandson's Captivity and the 'Place' of the Woman Subject." *Early American Literature* 28, no. 3 (1993): 256–277; Mulford, Carla, with Angela Vietto, and Amy E. Winans. Introduction to *American Women Prose Writers to 1820*, edited by Carla Mulford, et al. *Dictionary of Literary Biography* 200 (Detroit: Gale Research, 1999), xvii–xxx; Norton, Mary Beth. *Liberty's Daughters: The Revolutionary Experience of American Women, 1750–1800* (Boston: Little, Brown, 1980); Pinckney, Eliza Lucas. *The Letterbook of Eliza Lucas Pinckney, 1739–1762*. Edited by Elise Pinckney (Chapel Hill: University of North Carolina Press, 1972); Rowlandson, Mary. *A True History of the Captivity and Restoration of Mrs. Mary Rowlandson* (1682). Edited by Amy Shrager Lang. In *Journeys in New Worlds: Early American Women's Narratives*, edited by William Andrews, et al., 11–66 (Madison: University of Wisconsin Press, 1990); Rowlandson, Mary. *A True History of the Captivity and Restoration of Mrs. Mary Rowlandson* (1682). In *Women's Indian Captivity Narratives*, edited by Kathryn Zabelle Derounian-Stodola, 1–52 (New York: Penguin, 1998); Shea, Daniel B. Introduction to *Some Account of the Fore Part of the Life of Elizabeth Ashbridge*. In *Journeys in New Worlds: Early American Women's Narratives*, edited by William L. Andrews, et al., 117–146 (Madison: University of Wisconsin Press, 1990); Sinor, Jennifer. *The Extraordinary Work of Ordinary Writing: Annie Ray's Diary* (Iowa City: University of Iowa Press, 2002); Taves, Ann, ed. *Religion and Domestic Violence in Early New England: The Memoirs of Abigail Abbot Bailey* (Bloomington: Indiana University Press, 1989); Trist,

Elizabeth House. *The Travel Diary of Elizabeth House Trist: Philadelphia to Natchez, 1783–84.* Edited by Annette Kolodny. In *Journeys in New Worlds: Early American Women's Narratives,* edited by William Andrews, et al., 181–232 (Madison: University of Wisconsin Press, 1990); Ulrich, Laurel Thatcher. *Good Wives: Image and Reality in the Lives of Women in Northern New England, 1650–1750* (New York: Vintage, 1980); Ulrich, Laurel Thatcher. *A Midwife's Tale: The Life of Martha Ballard, Based on Her Diary, 1785–1812* (New York: Vintage, 1990); Williams, Daniel E., ed. *A Faithful Narrative of the Wicked Life and Remarkable Conversion of Patience Boston* (1738). In *Pillars of Salt: An Anthology of Early American Criminal Narratives* (Madison, WI: Madison House, 1993), 119–141; Williams, Daniel E., ed. *The Declaration and Confession of Esther Rodgers* (1701). In *Pillars of Salt: An Anthology of Early American Criminal Narratives,* 94–109 (Madison, WI: Madison House, 1993); Williams, Daniel E. *Pillars of Salt: An Anthology of Early American Criminal Narratives* (Madison, WI: Madison House, 1993); Wister, Sarah. *The Journal and Occasional Writings of Sarah Wister.* Edited and introduction by Kathryn Zabelle Derounian (Rutherford, NJ: Fairleigh Dickinson University Press, 1987).

Lisa M. Logan

AMERICAN WOMEN'S AUTOBIOGRAPHY: NINETEENTH CENTURY Within the context of the newly formed United States of America and the burgeoning need among many of its citizens to identify and understand those qualities that would define them as Americans, autobiographical writings served as an important record of the many ways Americans engaged in acts of self-fashioning that differentiated them from their European ancestors. Autobiography also helped many Americans to identify and understand their roles and opportunities in the new American culture. In particular, the autobiographies of American women of this period contribute to the understanding of the young country by relating the stories of women marginalized by their sex, **race**, **class**, and ethnicity as well.

Women wrote their autobiographical narratives in a wide range of forms and experiences, from accounts of abusive marriages, to tales of slave life and escape, to narratives of their spiritual coming-of-age. Growing out of the literary and religious traditions of the seventeenth and eighteenth centuries, women wrote about their lives with a conscious desire to instruct their readers and to record their lives. In addition to the diaries, journals, and **letters** that had long been inscribed as components of the woman's sphere, women of the nineteenth century also wrote nonfiction, fictionalized narratives, and even political tracts, sermons, and other spiritual essays. By their acts of self-definition, they wrote themselves into the historical record, reserved until this time for men of the dominant culture engaged in the traditionally masculine sphere of public life.

Many of these autobiographies were written and published between 1800 and 1899, but some remained in manuscript form until the twentieth century. While the women themselves wrote the majority of these autobiographical texts, a number of them were narrated to an amanuensis, written collaboratively, or heavily shaped by an editor. Many appeared with authenticating papers—letters and statements from well-known figures that attested to the good character of the writer and the validity of the accounts contained in the published text. This was especially evident in the case of African American writers, as the strictures against literacy among slaves often prompted readers to question if in fact an educated white person had not written the narrative.

One of the traditions from which nineteenth-century women's autobiographies emerged is the Puritan conversion narrative. In her introduction to *American Women's Autobiography: Fea(s)ts of Memory* (1992), Margo Culley describes the dual nature of Puritan conversion narratives as similar in nature to women's autobiographies. Puritans sought their congregation's favorable judgment of the conversion testimonies they delivered publicly, and at the same time they hoped their experiences would be instructive to others. Women autobiographers also sought their readers' favor when, in prefatory material to their books, they expressed the desire to benefit their readers by publishing their works.

Such rhetorical engagement with female readers took on an apologetic tone, as well, indicating that the autobiographers' goals were not to glorify their own lives but to serve as instructive examples to others. The "cult of true womanhood" ideology that dominated many women's understandings of themselves and their relationships necessitated that women remain both literally and metaphorically within the private sphere. Publishing the story of one's life shifted a woman into the public eye, a move unbecoming to "true" women. This ideology, however, served to shape white women's experiences more than it did those of slave and immigrant women. Some autobiographies by women of color (and even those of some white women) during the century suggest an acceptance of this ideology, others demonstrate active resistance, while still others reveal themselves as operating under completely different sets of ideas about the nature and calling of women.

Sidonie Smith offers a means of understanding the significance of nineteenth-century women's autobiographies in relation to the history of autobiography and to the ideas of distinct **gender** differences as they developed in the nineteenth century. Theorizing that Western discourse has inscribed only white male **identity** as capable of existing separate from the physical body, all others—women, people of color—are thus designated Other. The concept of public and private—masculine and feminine—spheres that came to dominate nineteenth-

century theories of gender reinforced the notion that women's identities were tied to their bodies. Thus, autobiographies—narratives of self-imagining—conceived of their female subjects as both connected to the body as life-giving and nurturing, and resistant to that role in favor of a metaphysical self that transcends the material.

Literary women frequently turned their pens toward their own lives and wrote autobiographies. Critics note that a number of these women wrote about their lives without actually writing about themselves as writers. That is, they tended to focus on their childhood and youth, periods of time prior to their decisions to publish their works, instead of offering a significant look at the professional role and choices of the literary woman. Debate continues whether this is because of an interest in examining how their early lives led to their choice of métier, because focus on the childhood, domestic, and familial features of women's lives helped secure their position in a society that understood women's roles in narrow terms, or because this form replicated the realities of women's lives as interrelational.

Margaret Fuller's unfinished *Memoirs* (1852) provides a brief sketch of her childhood. The precocious daughter of a politician, Fuller received much of her education from her father. As a busy politician, however, he was gone for much of the day and saved his work with his daughter until the late hours of the evening when he returned home. Fuller's critical observations about her education and rather isolated upbringing are a central theme of her memoirs, which remained unfinished at Fuller's death at the age of thirty.

Catherine Maria Sedgwick's "Recollections of Childhood" (1871) was published as part of a collection of the writer's letters and papers. Written for her grandniece, Alice, as a record of the family's history, the work describes Sedgwick's young life among family and friends in Massachusetts.

Similarly, poet Lucy Larcom's *A New England Girlhood* (1889) also focuses on her childhood and relationships with her family and community. Other writers' autobiographies include *Recollections of My Childhood* (1854) by poet and essayist Grace Greenwood (pseud. Sara Jane Clarke Lippincott), "Looking Back on Girlhood" (1892), by fiction writer Sarah Orne Jewett, and *Chapters from a Life* (1896) by Elizabeth Stuart Phelps, best known for her religious fiction.

Journalist Edith Maud Eaton (**Sui Sin Far**) wrote her autobiographical essay "Leaves from the Mental Portfolio of an Eurasian" (1909) as a record of her life as a woman of British and Chinese descent living in England, Canada, and the United States. Her work is one of the first published accounts in the United States to speak about the racist treatment of Chinese immigrants.

Although many women authors of note did not leave autobiographical writings, many did, including such works as Lydia Howard Sigourney's *Letters of Life* (1866), Julia Ward Howe's *Reminiscences* (1899), Rebecca Blaine Harding Davis' *Bits of Gossip* (1904), and Ella Wheeler Wilcox's *The Story of a Literary Career* (1905).

In a culture that valued women's silence and domesticity, writers who asserted themselves both professionally and economically may have focused on childhood experiences in their autobiographies as a means to justify their professional choices. Childhood experiences often proved important in the autobiographies of religious women, as well. As in the Puritan tradition, spiritual autobiographies of the nineteenth century illustrated the author's Christian conversion experience and offered readers an opportunity to witness the workings of the divine in an individual's life. Generally, these narratives follow a pattern in which the subject of the work initially resists conversion (often in childhood) by rebelling against God and religious ideas. She then relates a moment or series of events that ul-

timately cause her to commit her life to Christianity and Christian service.

African American Women's Autobiographies in the Nineteenth Century

The autobiographies of three African American women, Jarena Lee, **Zilpha Elaw**, and Julia A. Foote, illustrate the complexity of the experiences of women marginalized both by their gender and their race. In addition to their marginalization as black women, as the writer of the preface to Foote's narrative points out, these women suffered further marginalization by their call to evangelism, seen by many as an attempt to usurp the existing power structure in Christian church organizations. Foote's autobiography begins in her youth and describes her "sinful" behavior, and her family, who were not strongly religious although apparently not hostile to Christianity. Following the description of her conversion to Christianity, the remainder of the book describes her experiences as a visionary and evangelical preacher. She suffered racial and gender discrimination at the hands of people of all faiths, but throughout her life, she held firm in her conviction that she was called by God to preach.

Jarena Lee describes the spiritual state and conversion experience of a black woman who ultimately adopted the African Methodist Episcopal Church as her spiritual home. A self-described liar, her text demonstrates her struggle toward telling the truth as one sign of her gradual conversion. As Richard Douglass-Chinn (2001) demonstrates in his essay on the works of Jarena Lee and Zilpha Elaw, Lee also demonstrates an acute understanding of the flexibility of language and its use by a black woman in a predominantly white society to construct the truth as she understands it, a truth that takes on different shapes for black and white communities.

Among the autobiographies of black female preachers, Lee's addresses race and gender politics most explicitly. In the 1849 expanded edition of her autobiography, her attention to racism and abolitionism becomes significantly more developed as a theme. In addition (in her early version of the narrative), she rejects the white ideal of womanly behavior by, at one point, leaving her sick son in the care of someone else while she travels on her preaching circuit.

Zilpha Elaw's *Memoirs of the Life, Religious Experience, Ministerial Travels and Labours of Mrs. Zilpha Elaw, an American Female of Colour* (1846), also describes her conversion and her life as an itinerant preacher. Like Lee, Elaw also left a child at home in order to respond to what she saw as a call to preach. Unlike Lee, Elaw's narrative is characterized by a highly elaborate literary style that seems intended to appeal to a white audience. Her concern with this audience is reiterated by her direct exhortation to her readers to renounce wealth and the dubious respectability it provides as well as the "pride of a white skin [that] is a bauble of great value with money."

More difficult to categorize as an autobiography, but which nevertheless demonstrates features of the genre, is *The Narrative of Sojourner Truth,* who published the details of her life in two forms, both of which were collaborations between herself and one or more white amanuenses. The 1850 version, transcribed by Olive Gilbert, tells the story of **Sojourner Truth**'s early life and career as a traveling preacher. The 1878 version, prepared by Truth, Olive Gilbert, and Frances Titus, includes a variety of works about Truth by other white writers along with her own narrative, which provides a broader set of perspectives on her life and work, but also removes the text further from the strict definitions of autobiography. The 1850 narrative, while written in the third person, takes on a tone and form similar to that of other black evangelists' spiritual autobiographies. The book begins with an account of Truth's childhood as Isabella, the enslaved daughter of parents who are freed when she is small. Young Isabella moves among a variety of slave-holding families, ending up in the home of the Dumont family, where she plots her escape. Dumont had reneged on his promise to free her on July 4, 1827, claiming she had not finished her work for him, so she dutifully completed the work, then ran off with her infant son and was taken in by the Van Wagener family. The narrative also details Truth's religious life and conversion. Although raised as a Christian, she did not fully embrace the faith, making repeated promises to God to "be good" if he would only improve her quality of life. When she had a visionary experience in which she claimed she saw Jesus, she dedicated her life to evangelism, changed her name to Sojourner Truth, and began her work as a traveling preacher. The majority of the book is dedicated to this portion of her life.

Among middle-class white women of the nineteenth century, conversion narratives followed similar patterns to those of black women. The authors narrate a prelude to their conversions in which the women typically resisted the change and clashed with family and friends over their spiritual convictions. Following the actual conversion experience or period, however, the women describe their move out into the world through publication of their works or public speaking, and deny any interest in the celebrity that publication might bring. They simply hope to provide instructive tales for their readers. Among these are the autobiographies of Harriet Livermore (1826) and Harriet Cooke (1861), whose narrative illustrates the effect one woman's conversion can have on others. As the head of a girl's school in Middlebury, Vermont, she provided guidance to students undergoing conversion and narrates their experiences alongside her own.

Spiritual autobiographies also help provide some shape for slave narratives of the nineteenth century. Tracing a slave's journey through slavery and toward freedom, slave narratives appealed to their white readers in part through a shared (with the reader) sense of morality grounded in the

Christian tradition. One of the earliest known slave narratives is Nancy Prince's *A Narrative of the Life and Travels of Nancy Prince, Written by Herself* (1850), the story of one woman's sexual and physical abuse at the hands of a cruel master. **Harriet Jacobs'** well-known autobiography *Incidents in the Life of a Slave Girl* (1861), also traces her life from her childhood through her escape and freedom in the North. An attractive and light-skinned woman, Jacobs had a pleasant childhood, claiming not to have known she was a slave until age six. Following the death of her mother, however, and her subsequent sale to a master who attempted to rape her and constantly harassed her, Jacobs became painfully aware of the particular atrocities of slavery experienced by women. She escaped her master's domination by hiding for seven years in the attic crawl space of her freed grandmother's house, not far from her master's property. She narrates the extensive psychological abuse that she suffered at the hands of her lustful master and decries the fact that as a slave woman she cannot rise to the same standard of womanhood set for white women. As a black woman, she is considered inherently sexual and thus unable to be pure; she is denied property, and thus cannot be domestic; she is not allowed to attend church or read her Bible, and thus cannot be pious (Yellin 1987). Her book consciously appeals to northern white women readers, encouraging them to identify with black women on the basis of gender.

A more ambiguously categorized narrative is that of the recently discovered manuscript by Hannah Crofts, which also narrates the experience of a black woman and her escape from slavery. Purportedly a fictionalized account, *The Bondwoman's Narrative* was probably written between 1853 and 1861. Treated well by her master's wife, who turns out to be passing for white, the two escape together and are haunted by a malicious lawyer who makes it his business to return the two women to their status as property. The narrator and her mistress successfully elude the lawyer, only to be captured by another slave trader. Eventually, the narrator is sold to a careless woman who pays so little attention to her that she escapes, disguised as a man.

Similar in form to Crofts' novel is Harriet Wilson's *Our Nigor, Sketches from the Life of a Free Black, in a Two-Story House, North Showing that Slavery's Shadows Fall Even There* (1859). The novel is not technically a slave narrative because the central figure is born free in the north, but as the title implies, it chronicles the hardships of a mulatto woman living in the antebellum context of racist society. In the novel, the father of the central character, Frado, dies and her mother abandons her, forcing her into indentured servitude. She is mistreated by the family for whom she works, marries an escaped slave who abandons her after she gets pregnant, and ends up homeless with an infant to care for.

Other accounts of black women's lives as slaves and free women are available in numerous autobiographies of African American women, including **Elizabeth Keckley's** *Behind the Scenes, or Thirty Years a Slave and Four Years in the White House*; Annie L. Burton's *Memories of Childhood's Slavery Days* (1909); Octavia V. Roger's *The House of Bondage*; Bethany Veney's *The Narrative of Bethany Veney, A Slave Woman* (1889); Amanda Smith's *An Autobiography: The Story of the Lord's Dealings with Mrs. Amanda Smith, the Colored Evangelist Containing an Account of Her Life Work of Faith, and Her Travels in America, England, Ireland, Scotland, India, and Africa, as an Independent Missionary* (1893); Susie King Taylor's *Reminisces of My Life in Camp*; Maria Stewart's *Productions*; and Elizabeth (last name unknown), *A Coloured Woman Author*.

Quaker women's autobiographies were generally published posthumously, several examples of which are Chloe Willey's *A Short Account of the Life and Remarkable Views of Mrs. Chloe Willey, of Goshen N.H., Written by Herself* (1807); Rachel Hinman Lucas's *Remarkable Account* (1806); Mary Mitchell's

A Short Account of the Early Part of the Life of Mary Mitchell, Late of Nantucket, Deceased, Written by Herself (1812); Harriet Livermore's *Narrative of Religious Experience* (1826), Elizabeth Collins' *Memoirs* (1833) and *A Narrative of Some of the Exercises and Christian Experiences in the Early Part of Her Life* (1838); and Margaret Cummin's *Leaves from My Port Folio, Original and Selected Together with a Religious Narrative* (1860).

Women Social Reformers and Autobiographical Writing

In the category of reform autobiographies, many women social reformers chronicled their lives as crusaders for causes such as women's rights and health, prison, and educational reform.

Reformer Mary Gove Nichols published her fictionalized autobiography, *Mary Lyndon, or Revelations of a Life, an Autobiography* (1855) in response to negative portrayals of her in other publications. Beginning with her childhood, Nichols relates her early interest in medicine and health to the death of her sister, who died as the result of wearing a corset and too few clothes in cold weather. The narrative follows her through her disastrous first marriage to and divorce from Hiram Gove, the kidnapping of her daughter by her ex-husband, the establishment of her own schools for girls, and her administration of Grahamite boardinghouses. She also relates her happy second marriage to Thomas Lowe Nichols. As a reform text, the narrative speaks about health and diet reform as well as the legal status of women in and after marriage.

Elizabeth Cady Stanton's *Eighty Years and More: Reminiscences, 1815–1897* (1898) lays out her lifelong interest in the status of women in the United States. As numerous critics point out, Stanton's work is curiously shaped around the idea of her domesticity although actually saying little about her husband and children. *Eighty Years and More* traces the personal elements of Stanton's life, beginning with her childhood and her early distrust of religion and

law, both of which she precociously recognized as human constructs. She continues with the discussion of her courtship and marriage to Henry Stanton, an abolitionist. The two spent their honeymoon in London at the World's Anti-Slavery Convention of 1840. Here, Stanton, a lifelong abolitionist, recognized the unfair treatment of women who were not allowed to vote even as delegates, a result of the claims by clerics in attendance that women must not vote according to biblical principal. Stanton's autobiography describes in some detail her political efforts and career following the 1848 Seneca Falls women's rights convention, which she organized with Lucretia Mott. What is striking about her autobiography, however, is the extent to which she features her private life over her public one. The book ends with her as a grandmother, enjoying and appreciating the quotidian domestic life.

Sidonie Smith argues that Stanton's autobiography, like that of Harriet Jacobs', both resists and embraces the idea that a woman's identity must be associated with her body and its biological and social functions. It ostensibly describes Stanton's domestic life and concerns of a very public woman, but the overt attention to domesticity in fact serves to move this otherwise extraordinary woman (because of her highly public role) into the ordinary (Sidonie Smith 1992). Estelle Jelinek asserts that Stanton's autobiography was written for two purposes: to establish herself as "both an ordinary and exceptional woman" and to further the cause of woman suffrage (1986, xiv).

Although published in the early twentieth century, another pioneering suffragist's autobiography, *Pathbreaking* (1914), by Abigail Scott Duniway, recounts the turn-of-the-century work of a woman who devoted her energies to gaining the right to vote for women in the Pacific Northwest. Concentrating on her adult activism, Duniway also includes a number of speeches she delivered in her work for woman suffrage. Her tenure as a leader in the Northwest was not without its controversies, and Duniway's book serves in part as a defense of her position as well as an argument against moving in the direction of activism against prohibition, which the regional organization did following their success in gaining the vote for Oregon women in 1912.

Other women who wrote about their work toward improving the political, legal, and social lives of women included Frances Willard's *Glimpses of Fifty Years: The Autobiography of an American Woman* (1889) and Mary Rice Livermore's *The Story of My Life; or the Sunshine and Shadow of Seventy Years* (1897). Willard served as president of the Women's Christian Temperance Union for a decade, and Livermore lectured on women's political and legal issues on the lyceum stage. Late in the century, Elizabeth Blackwell published her autobiographical work, *Pioneer Work in Opening the Medical Profession to Women* (1896). The book details her experience as the first woman graduate of an American medical school and her struggles to establish a medical practice in a professional world dominated by men. **Jane Addams'** work on behalf of the working poor of Chicago serves as the background for her autobiography, *Twenty Years at Hull-House* (1910). A prominent reformer of the late nineteenth and early twentieth centuries, Addams established Hull House as a center of grassroots political activity, and her autobiography tells the story of the political and educational efforts that took place there at the turn of the century.

Reformers of the nineteenth century also included writers such as Elizabeth Packard, whose *The Prisoner's Hidden Life; or, Insane Asylums Unveiled* (1868) argued for changes in the way mental patients were understood and treated in nineteenth-century asylums. Packard's text employs the forms of narrative, letters, and political treatises to illustrate the abuse of patients and in defense of herself as sane. Writing about fellow patient Sophie Olsen as well as herself, Packard frames her story as the struggle between good and evil, a move identified by scholar Mary Elene Wood (1994) as an appeal to her readers to see the instructive value in her personal story. Additional autobiographies of women held in insane asylums include Ada Metcalf's *Lunatic Asylums: And How I Became an Inmate of One: Doctors, Incidents, Humbugging* (1876), Anna Agnew's *From Under the Cloud; or, Personal Reminiscences of Insanity* (1886), Lydia Smith's *Behind the Scenes* (1879), and Clarissa Caldwell Lathrop's *A Secret Institution* (1890). Each of these works exposes the inhumane and oftentimes cruel treatment of women in institutions through the use of medical and social practices that infantilized them.

Works by women who were tried or incarcerated for crimes also served in some senses as reform texts, laying bare the injustices accorded to women in a society that did not afford them legal or political standing and restricted their activities to the private and religious spheres. Hannah Hanson Kinney's *A Review of the Principal Events of the Last Ten Years in the Life of Mrs. Hannah Kinney: Together with Some Comments upon the Late Trial, Written by Herself* (1841) relates her experience of having been accused of the murder of her third husband. A combination of epistolary and narrative forms, Packard's autobiography demonstrates her will to prove her innocence, and in fact, she was ultimately acquitted. Abigail Abbot Bailey's *Memoirs* (1815) recounts her experience as the wife of an abusive husband, and while it does not make direct calls for the reform of marriage laws, it inherently speaks to the need for protections for women and children from abusive husbands and fathers.

Native American Women, Adventure Narratives, and Civil War Autobiographies

The nineteenth century witnessed some of the earliest Native American writings published in English, few of which are formal autobiographies in the European and

American tradition. Writing stories that featured Native American myths and history, Sarah Winnemucca's *Life Among the Paiutes* (1883) stands out among both Native American writings and women's autobiographies of the nineteenth century in its resistance to the conversion narrative forms of earlier Native American writers and the sentimental heroines of much of nineteenth-century women's fiction and nonfiction narratives, according to A. LaVonne Brown Ruoff (1990). Winnemucca's book outlines some of her childhood, her tribe's history and ethnography, and an account of her adult experiences as an activist against injustices perpetrated on Native Americans by whites. She relates a number of significant events for the Paiutes, including their removal to Yakima lands and the invasion of the reservation by cattle ranchers grazing their herds as a result of an unscrupulous white, land agent.

The popularity of captivity narratives of the seventeenth and eighteenth centuries had abated slightly by the nineteenth century when several new ones were published. Mary Jemison's life among the Seneca people presents a challenge to the genre of captivity narratives. Traditionally written to illuminate God's protection or to portray the "savagery" of the Native American people, Jemison's account does neither. Because she narrated her story to James E. Seaver, who published *A Narrative of the Life of Mrs. Mary Jemison* (1824) we don't know the extent to which her story has been reshaped. Filtered through her own **memory** and Seaver's editorial hand, the story is still told as a first-person narrative that details her life from her initial capture as a teenager and adoption by her Seneca captors through her marriages, children, and adulthood among her tribal family. Choosing to remain with her adoptive tribe rather than return to her white culture, Jemison provides a more sympathetic account of life among Native Americans than was the case for many captivity narratives of the era.

Despite the ideology of separate spheres that dominated the nineteenth century, many women nevertheless had to support their families when their husbands could not do so. Writing was an option for many such as Harriet Beecher Stowe and Louisa May Alcott, but many women pursued alternate routes of employment. Writing about her professional life as an entertainer, Anna Cora Mowatt's *Autobiography of an Actress, or Eight Years on Stage* (1853) recounts the story of a woman who endured the scorn of her community in order to earn an income for her family by working on the stage.

Unlike Mowatt, who worked under her own name, many women went to work disguised as men. Some of these women, such as Lucy Brewer, took jobs in order to avoid work in brothels. Brewer took a job as a sailor for three years and detailed her experiences in *The Adventures of Lucy Brewer* (1815), retitled *Female Marine* in later editions. Ellen Stephens also took a job at sea, in her case to find her child who had been kidnapped by her husband. *The Cabin Boy's Wife* (1840) relates her tale and her advice to young women readers to marry for character rather than money.

Autobiographical works by women written during and about the Civil War are more plentiful among Southern women. Many Southern women wrote about domestic life under the conditions of war rather than explicitly writing about the politics or military aspects of the Civil War period, and few were critical of slavery. Among the more recognizable of these is Mary Boykin Chesnutt, the wife of one Southern politician and the daughter of another. Her writing is based partly on the **diary** she kept during the war and partly on her reflections about the Civil War period written in the 1880s. The earliest publication of her work in 1905 excludes much of her personal commentary on the implications of slavery for white women, though later editors have included some of this information in an edition titled *Mary Chesnutt's Civil War* (1981). Mary Ann Webster Loughborough's *My Cave Life in Vicksburg*

(1864) focuses on the three-month period of the war in which the Northern armies attacked Vicksburg, Mississippi. Other works by confederate women include Fannie A. Beers' *Memories: A Record of Personal Experience and Adventure during Four Years of War* (1888), Eliza Frances Andrew's *The War Time Journal of a Georgia Girl, 1864–1865* (1908), and Sarah Morgan Dawson's *A Confederate Girl's Diary* (1913).

Extant autobiographies by Northern women include that of the wife of Ulysses S. Grant, titled *The Personal Memorial of Julia Dent Grant* (1975), a work that was not published until well after Grant's death. Louisa May Alcott's *Hospital Sketches* (1863) is based on the author's letters to family and friends written while she worked briefly as a nurse during the war at the Union Hotel Hospital in Georgetown, Washington, DC. Two additional works by women married to Northern men involved in the war are Setima Maria Levy Collis' *A Woman's War Record, 1861–1865* (1889) and Mary Ames' *From a New England Woman's Diary in Dixie in 1865* (1906).

Autobiographies of Pioneer Women

During the increased westward expansion of white people in the nineteenth century, many women wrote accounts of their travels and trials as pioneers. They wrote generally of domestic life on the pioneer trails, and their work provides a much-needed balance to the more publicly focused writings of their husbands, fathers, brothers, and sons. Christiana Homes Tillson's *A Woman's Story of Pioneer Illinois* (1873) tells the story of her honeymoon trip with her husband and settlement in Illinois. Anna Howard Shaw's *The Story of a Pioneer* (1915) features an account of her family's life as they established a home in Michigan.

Although not published until 1938, Mary Ann Hafen's *Recollections of a Handcart Pioneer of 1860: A Woman's Life on the Mormon Frontier*, nevertheless describes her frontier experience in the mid-nineteenth century. Born in Sweden to a family that converted to Mormonism, she emigrated with them as a child to the United States. The autobiography describes the family's trek as they pulled a handcart filled with their belongings from New York to southern Utah and follows Mary Ann's life through two polygamous marriages.

Spanning the transition of the nineteenth and twentieth centuries, *Plain Anne Ellis* (1931) narrates the life of Anne Ellis, whose ambition helped her move from the role of caretaker and oldest sibling to county treasurer in Colorado. Having spent much of her childhood raising her six siblings, Ellis had little formal education, but educated herself and earned enough experience to win the local election. Even though she described herself as an ordinary woman, scholars have argued that in fact, she was anything but ordinary.

The autobiography of Josephine Sarah Marcus Earp remains in manuscript form but has been the basis for the stories printed in Glenn Boyer's *I Married Wyatt Earp* (1976), a book that chronicles the life of the wife of the now infamous Tombstone, Arizona, lawman, Wyatt Earp. Their lives together were spent traveling throughout the western United States and Alaska, and the book reveals Josephine's hunger for adventure.

The story of "Mountain Charley" in E. J. Guerin's *Mountain Charley, or the Adventures of Mrs. E. J. Guerin, Who Was Thirteen Years in Male Attire* (1861) illustrates the measures taken by some women to protect and raise their children. Married at age twelve and a widow with two children three years later, Guerin gave her children over to the Sisters of Charity and disguised herself as a man so that she could get work. Working as a cabin boy on a steamer, a brakeman on the railroad, a gold prospector, a saloon owner, and finally a rancher, she occasionally returned to her women's clothing and visited her children.

This history of autobiography among nineteenth-century women illustrates well the variety of women's experiences that existed beyond the traditional dichotomy of the public and private spheres. Although many women's lives were proscribed by this separation of duties, many who wrote autobiographies did so knowing that the autobiographical act of inserting one's life into the public record was itself resistant against the dominant ideology of the time. Still other women—including African Americans, Native Americans, and immigrant women—may have been well aware of the ideology but clearly did not see themselves as operating within this tradition. Women's autobiographies of the nineteenth century demonstrate a breadth of experience, talent, education, drive, energy, and interest that resists easy categorization.

Further Reading: Boyer, Glenn. *I Married Wyatt Earp: The Recollections of Josephine Sarah Marcus Earp.* (Tucson: University of Arizona Press, 1976); Braxton, Joanne. *Black Women Writing: Autobiography: A Tradition within a Tradition* (Philadelphia: Temple, 1989); Brereton, Virginia Lieson. *From Sin to Salvation: Stories of Women's Conversions, 1800 to the Present* (Bloomington: Indiana University Press, 1991); Culley, Margo, ed. *American Women's Autobiography: Fea(s)ts of Memory* (Madison: University of Wisconsin Press, 1992); Douglass-Chinn, Richard J. *Preacher Woman Sings the Blues: The Autobiographies of Nineteenth-Century African American Evangelists* (Columbia: Columbia University of Missouri Press, 2001), 75–110; Jelinek, Estelle, ed. *The Traditions of Women's Autobiography: From Antiquity to the Present* (Boston: Twayne, 1986); Jacobs, Harriet. *Incidents in the Life of a Slave Girl* (Cambridge, MA: Harvard University Press, 1987); Jewett, Sarah Orne. *Selected Letters of Sarah Orne Jewett: A Critical Edition with Commentary.* Edited by S. F. Stoddart (University of Illinois at Urbana-Champaign, 1988); Keckley, Elizabeth. *Behind the Scenes: Or, Thirty Years a Slave, and Four Years in the White House* (New York: Oxford University Press, 1988); Larcom, Lucy. *A New England Girlhood* (Boston: Houghton Mifflin, 1889); Rogers, Octavia. *House of Bondage, Or, Charlotte Brooks and Other Slaves* (Oxford, 1988); Sigourney, Lydia Howard. *Letters of Life* (New York: D. Appleton and Co., 1866); Smith, Sidonie. "Resisting the Gaze of Embodiment: Women's Autobiography in the Nineteenth Century." In *American Women's Autobiography: Fea(s)ts of Memory*, edited by Margo Culley (Madison: University of Wisconsin Press, 1992); Stanton, Elizabeth Cady. *Eighty Years and More (1815–1897): Reminiscences of Elizabeth Cady Stanton* (Boston: Northeastern University Press, 1992); Truth, Sojourner. *The Narrative of Sojourner Truth* (New York: Vintage Books, 1993); Wilson, Harriet. *Our Nig, or, Sketches from the Life of a Free Black, in a Two-Story House, North Showing That Slavery's Shadows Fall Even There.* 1859. Reprint (New York: Vintage Books, 1983); Wood, Mary Elene. *The Writing on the Wall: Women's Autobiography and the Asylum* (Chicago: University of Illinois Press, 1994).

Annemarie Hamlin

AMERICAN WOMEN'S AUTOBIOGRAPHY: TWENTIETH AND TWENTY-FIRST CENTURIES

In the decades since 1900, American women's autobiography has proven to be an ever more vibrant compositional form than it had been in the past. To read the self-told stories from this span in history is to discover the shared triumphs and tragedies, writing traditions and revolutions, social movements and counter-movements that shape the American woman's contemporary cultural situation. As historical and social shifts made it easier for women to write and publish their life stories, the resulting volume and variety of work has had the effect of recasting autobiography as an enterprise in substantive ways: changing the definitional considerations in autobiography, reexamining the generic requirements or tendencies of the writing form, revisiting the rhetorical perils and possibilities of gendered autobiography, reseeing the nature and limits of language used to testify to life experience, and shifting notions of why personal narratives prove so compelling to writers and readers alike.

Debate and Critical Theory about Women's Autobiographies

Equally remarkable during this period is the extent to which women's autobiography has emerged as the site for a tremendous amount of critical debate and literary/cultural theory. In the process of reckoning women's accounts within discussions of autobiography, old questions about the genre's nature and meaning take on more and different meanings, and new questions emerge. Does each of us have a single, stable, unified, and coherent **identity**? Do we each possess a self, or do we invent one? Does an autobiography reveal a self, or does it construct one? Do we define ourselves, as individuals or through our relationships socially or culturally? What are the politics of women's identity, particularly on the page? How are theories of human development demonstrated or contested through the autobiographical act? How do women autobiographers negotiate the public rhetoric of the genre to address private experiences and insights? How do autobiographers resist the forces of both literary and cultural scripts, with their false self-images, constraining narrative structures, and the residue of a language that has itself been one of the instruments of women's oppression? How is autobiography simultaneously an illustration of the power and the limits of human memory? What does all the above mean for autobiographers, particularly for women of color, working-class women, disabled women, and lesbians? Responses to these questions hold the potential to redefine autobiography as a field of writing and scholarship. Movement toward this reevaluation of autobiography has been nothing short of a crisis of self-representation.

In the twentieth century, the United States marked an explosion in the publication of women's writings and, in particular, women's life stories, typically offered by their male antecedents or counterparts as book-length autobiographies. A traditional definition of autobiography might limit such a discussion to only those texts that correspond to the canonical and male-identified criteria associated with the form, with its male-coded hubris, individualism, and claims to a life's singularity. A more expansive definition of the term "autobiography," here interpreted as autobiographical writings, however, seems most helpful and inclusive when attending to women's texts. Such a definitional framework allows consideration of a wide range of texts in which language becomes the medium through which women offer accounts of their lived world experiences and their lasting implications. In addition to book-length works offering versions of the traditional autobiography, this more inclusive and eclectic approach admits into evidence other important, albeit more humble, forms of autobiographical writing such as **memoir**, journals, diaries, correspondence, **personal essay**s, and even cookbooks. In other words, it may be most accurate to describe American women's autobiography of the twentieth and twenty-first centuries as a body of writings rather than as entirely self-contained and rigidly rule bound. To address autobiography through these more expansive criteria is to cast the form as dynamic rather than static, a dynamism that would appear to be the sustaining interest both writers and readers find today in autobiographical texts.

The problematics of women's autobiography are embedded in issues and theories of sexual difference. That is, if the term "autobiography" has customarily been applied to, and implied accounts of, the lives of men by men, what happens when women write their own testimony? If lives are journeys guided by desire, so are autobiographies accounts of yearning. Why assume that this phenomenon is the same, or, for that matter, essentially different for men and women as autobiographers? A more satisfactory notion of sexual difference in autobiography requires greater nuance than to equate, essentialize, or reduce to binaries the complex dynamic between **gender** and autobiography.

Still, it is undeniable that some social and literary constructions of gender do surround the role of the autobiographer. Two of the most poignant accounts of the embattled history of women's literature, and with it American women's autobiography, are **Tillie Olsen**'s *Silences* (1978) and Joanna Russ' ironically titled, *How to Suppress Women's Writing* (1983). Both books identify and comment on the social and cultural impediments to women's production and publication of literature. Olsen notes how infrequently women's literary work has been recognized, and, observes further, how few women writers who published during their lifetimes also married or had children. Russ, with her parody of women's sexual and textual oppression, chronicles the strategies of prohibition, constraint, disparagement, inattention, double standards, false categorization, and denial that threaten women's expression, particularly as it attests to and affirms women's experiences. Taken together with books such as poet/critic **Adrienne Rich**'s *On Lies, Secrets and Silence: Selected Prose, 1966–1978* (1979), Olsen's and Russ' texts chronicle and contribute to what women's literature we have, but at the same time evoke the loss of women's literature. That haunting absence pervades, where it does not preempt entirely, the study of women's writing, and American women's autobiography represents no exception to that rule. Therefore, students of women's life writings engage in both recovery and analysis of texts.

As the term "author" suggests, an autobiographer proceeds by claiming for him/herself the authority to speak. The writer must devise a strategy by which to assert the text's importance and the writer's entitlement to render it on the page. Since the convention of autobiography is to claim the weight of a single life and its telling, women autobiographers must accept, con-

test, or modify this convention as they authorize their acts of self-representation through writing. This is no simple feat in a patriarchal society, in which women must arrive at a sense of their own centrality despite the ways in which society marginalizes women's experiences and voices.

In so doing, women autobiographers must engage this centrality within the genre of autobiography itself. If the life featured is truly singular, of what relevance is its recounting to the reader? With what can the reader identify? At the same time, if the life featured appears wholly ordinary, of what special benefit is its retelling to the reader? What can it reveal to the person who already recognizes the tale?

As autobiographers, American women have had to inhabit a middle space, poised between self-congratulation and self-effacement. They must value their own insights enough to reflect at length on the lives lived. They must discern and convey the consequence of that testimony in order to produce it in print. They must discover points of convergence between the life of the writer and the life of the reader if they are to engage an audience through publication. Simply put, in offering an autobiography, women must find a **voice** dignified enough to honor their perspectives and yet approachable enough to welcome their readers. Women autobiographers need to find in the written word a bridge between identity and community, humility and agency, tradition and innovation.

As many scholars of autobiography have noted, women's life stories tend to operate outside many of the content and style criteria that characterize the androcentric traditions of autobiography. Women's autobiographies frequently shift the emphasis, if not the typical content, of traditionally male defined and dominated autobiography. Where, for instance, men's narratives tend to dwell on the individual's impersonal deeds and public profile, women's texts more often address private acts and everyday moments in a lifetime. While the autobiographical canon favors a heroic model of individualism, women tend to understand and articulate their lives through relation rather than isolation. Where men in a patriarchal society may presume an authoritative stance, women autobiographers must seek and/or challenge such authority to ensure that their stories will be heard.

Women autobiographers tend to deliver their distinct content with an even more distinctive style. Rather than building their autobiographies around the scaffolding of a linear, cohesive, and polished whole, women are more likely to write autobiographies characterized by more oblique, open-ended, subdued, and ruminative approaches. Introverted rather than self-aggrandizing, collective rather than solitary, fragmented rather than totalizing, reflective rather than progressive, women's autobiographies pose a challenge to any definition of the genre formulated before the twentieth century or on the basis of male autobiography alone. Just as literature more generally has shifted from the representational to the abstract, autobiography's conventions have taken a turn toward experimental, unorthodox, and diverse expression.

Prior to the twentieth century in America, autobiography had not been recognized as a legitimate writing form or a reliable historical source. Traditionally speaking, autobiography has never enjoyed the status of other literary forms. Perhaps it is because everyone has a life story. Its democratic access as a frame of reference—the very thing that makes autobiography both popular and profound—may have kept autobiography from recognition as part of the canon of writings in English. Of course, while literary properties of an autobiographical writing contribute considerably to the reader's pleasure and understanding, their very artfulness may simultaneously place into question the truthfulness of its account. A seemingly guileless text may be supposed more accurate or reliable in its lack of obvious craft. In this regard, the

woman autobiographer faces a double bind. If her work is too skillful, it will become suspect. If it lacks skill, however, it will be dismissed altogether.

Autobiography in Interdisciplinary Study

The middle decades of the twentieth century witnessed a dramatic increase in the interest in interdisciplinary study, along with added recognition for its institutional homes, such as in American Studies programs at colleges and universities. Autobiographies have proven a crucial genre for studying both the literary and the historical past in American studies and remain standard texts featured in introductory courses on the subject. From William Bradford's *Of Plymouth Plantation* (1647) and Benjamin Franklin's *Autobiography* (1811), to Frederick Douglass' *Narrative of the Life of Frederick Douglass* (1853) and Henry David Thoreau's *Walden* (1884), Henry Adams' *Education of Henry Adams* (1918) and Richard Wright's *Black Boy* (1945), to Malcolm X's *Autobiography* (1965) and Norman Mailer's *Armies of the Night* (1968), life stories have functioned as staples in the study of American experience and its representations. On the premise that the American past might be understood best by scrutiny of first-person narratives and the immediate messages they convey, secondary school and college educators have engaged their students with autobiographies relevant to the study of an era, a movement, a population, or a theme. Still, these efforts to personalize America's past typically omitted or under attended the experiences and accounts of women's lives.

While surveys of the American past typically have focused on the perspectives and experiences of men, the advent of women's studies, multicultural studies, and gay/lesbian/bisexual/transgender studies has helped to right this balance. For instance, it is now fairly commonplace to study American women's history by reading autobiographies. To make a study of the antilynching campaign and other efforts toward racial equality, one might read the testimony of a movement leader, *Crusade for Justice: The Autobiography of Ida B. Wells* (1970). To understand the utopian zeal of the Progressive age, one reads **Jane Addams'** account of the settlement house movement, *Twenty Years at Hull-House* (1910), or Ida Tarbell's memoir of muckraking and corporate greed in the oil industry, *All in the Day's Work: An Autobiography* (1939). To gain insight into the bohemian radicalism of Greenwich Village in the 1920s, one picks up **Emma Goldman's** *Living My Life* (1931). For a life story from a critic of male-centered systems of economics, medicine, or architecture, one might examine *The Living of Charlotte Perkins Gilman* (1935). If curious about the battle to make birth control available and affordable to American women, one might consider Margaret Sanger's *Margaret Sanger: An Autobiography* (1938). To read first-hand accounts of Japanese Americans internment during World War II, one might consult Jeanne Wakatsuki Houston's *Farewell to Manzanar* (1973) or Yoshiko Uchida's *Desert Exile: The Uprooting of a Japanese American Family* (1982). To uncover the experience of the segregation era of the Civil Rights movement, one turns to **Anne Moody's** account of the segregation-era south, *Coming of Age in Mississippi* (1968) or Jo Ann Gibson Robinson's memoir of the sit-in era, *The Montgomery Bus Boycott and the Women Who Started It* (1987). To probe the convictions and actions of the struggle for racial equality, one looks to countercultural icon **Angela Davis'** *Angela Davis: An Autobiography* (1974), Assata Shakur's *Assata* (1987), Elaine Brown's *A Taste of Power: A Black Woman's Story* (1992), or Gloria Wade-Gayles' *Pushed Back to Strength: A Black Woman's Journey Home* (1993). For virtually every era or event in twentieth- and twenty-first-century American history, there are women's autobiographies to provide a human dimension to its study.

The Issues of Identity and Inviting the Reader In

With the advent of women's studies, multicultural studies, and gender studies as fields of inquiry came a dramatic rise in published autobiographies by women of color during the 1980s. Examples of this wave in late-twentieth-century American women's autobiography include **Cherríe Moraga's** *Loving in the War Years* (1983), **Gloria Anzaldúa's** *Borderlands/The New Mestiza* (1987), Michelle Cliff's *Claiming an Identity They Taught Me to Despise* (1980), and **Nikki Giovanni's** *Gemini: An Extended Autobiographical Statement on My First Twenty-Five Years of Being a Black Poet* (1971). During this era, some key anthologies also addressed the relative silence in autobiography from radicals, lesbians, and women of color. These works include Barbara Smith's edited collection, *Home Girls: A Black Feminist Anthology* (1983) and *This Bridge Called My Back: Radical Writings by Women of Color* (1983), edited by Cherríe Moraga and Gloria Anzaldúa.

Similarly, as sexual pluralism became more accepted within American society, writings by lesbians became more numerous and more readily available in bookstores and libraries. Adrienne Rich's *What Is Found There* (1993), **Audre Lorde's** *Zami: A New Spelling of My Name* (1982), and **May Sarton's** *Journal of a Solitude* (1973) are three examples of **lesbian autobiography**. Along with these works of well-known authors are a great many more lesbian autobiographies, such as **Joan Nestle's** *A Restricted Country* (1987), Toni McNaron's *I Dwell in Possibility: A Memoir* (1992), **Dorothy Allison's** *Bastard out of Carolina* (1992) and Kim Chernin's *My Life as a Boy* (1997). Together, these autobiographies break a longstanding silence, even within American women's autobiography, until nearly 1950.

As women become more comfortable as autobiographers with their audiences, they sometimes find ways to renegotiate the form's generic value of uniqueness by inviting readers into a dialogical relationship. For instance, an autobiographer might frame her story around a distinct life but use a common experience that has shaped it in lasting ways, ranging anywhere from **sexuality** and the body to love and its loss. By centering the narrative around a familiar or shared experience, the autobiographer joins with the reader in a mutual effort to make sense of it. The result is a cycle of remembering, composing their lives, engaging their readers, and reflecting together with other women about the underlying meanings of universal or widely shared experiences.

Often, American women's autobiographies take their greatest connection from a particular stage or aspect of a life's journey, such as childhood, relationships to parents, coming-of-age, parenthood, and aging. Many of the reflections on childhood years are simultaneously meditations on the nature of human memory as the vehicle for autobiographical memory. Such is the case with Mary McCarthy's *Memories of a Catholic Girlhood* (1957), but it is also to a degree true of other recollections of youth, such as **Annie Dillard**'s *An American Childhood* (1987). Of course, truth telling is more of a proposition than an exhibited property within a given life story, but it persists as an expectation of autobiography as a mode. Anthologies such as *Fathers: Reflections by Daughters* (1983) and single-authored texts such as **Alix Kates Shulman**'s *A Good Enough Daughter: A Memoir* (1999) portray the child's complicated connection to a parent. Adrienne Rich's *Of Woman Born* (1976) speaks to her perceptions of motherhood. For every chapter in a woman's life, there are autobiographies to read as a point of reference, connection, or contrast.

Other markers of mutuality—professional lives, adversities, and traumas—may also assume center stage within women's autobiography. For example, numerous American women's autobiographies take their shape from the author's history with an illness, such as cancer. Two works that exemplify this are **Audre Lorde**'s *The Cancer Journals* (1980) and Marilyn French's *A Season in Hell: A Memoir* (1998). Both are tales of survival and a renewed savoring of life.

Life Stories in American Women's Autobiography

Predictably perhaps, the most extensive subcategory of American women's autobiography during the twentieth century consists of life stories by those who make writing their profession. Literary autobiographies, then, are a plentiful subcategory and offer rich insight into the lives of the century's American women of letters. Zelda Fitzgerald's *Save Me the Waltz* (1953), Edith Wharton's *A Backward Glance* (1934), Ellen Glasgow's *The Woman Within* (1954), Lorraine Hansberry's *To Be Young, Gifted, and Black* (1969), Doris Lessing's *The Memoirs of a Survivor* (1974), **Sylvia Plath**'s *The Journals* (1982) and *Letters Home: Correspondence, 1950–1963* (1975), **Anne Sexton**'s, *Anne Sexton: A Self-Portrait in Letters* (1977), **Leslie Marmon Silko**'s *Storyteller* (1981), and Adrienne Kennedy's *People Who Led to My Plays* (1986) all represent examples of the rich tapestry women writers weave with their lives and language.

Memoirs proved an important means of expression for American women during this period, as suggested by the works of such scholars as Helen M. Buss, Janet Mason Ellerby, **Carolyn Heilbrun**, and **Jill Ker Conway**. As usual, literary women produce the most memoirs, perhaps because of their sustained and nuanced relationship to the written word. Examples of multiple memoirs by individual women writers include Lillian Hellman's *An Unfinished Woman: A Memoir* (1969), *Pentimento* (1973) and *Scoundrel Time* (1976). Hellman, like bohemian Mabel Dodge Luhan before her, as well as other women who came after her, realized that the work of an autobiographer is recursive and so is never complete until the life itself is concluded.

The 1990s marked the publication of many new memoirs by America's contemporary women writers, including **Meena Alexander**'s *Faultlines: A Memoir* (1993), Alice Kaplan's *French Lessons: A Memoir* (1993), **Shirley Geok-lin Lim**'s *Among the White Moon Faces: An Asian-American Memoir of Homelands* (1996), Rita Mae Brown's *Rita Will: Memoir of a Literary Rabble-Rouser* (1997), and Bobbie Ann Mason's *Clear Springs: A Memoir* (1999). This trend toward memoirs among women of letters continues into the twenty-first century in America, with such works as Linda Hogan's *The Woman Who Watches Over the World: A Native Memoir* (2001) and Marge Piercy's *Sleeping with Cats: A Memoir* (2002).

Even those women who did not think of themselves chiefly as writers and who declined or hesitated to reveal their entire life stories, found in memoir a way to share an aspect or phase of their lives with an audience. Distinguished women outside the literary world have sometimes ventured into autobiographical writing: First Lady Eleanor Roosevelt published her story in 1961; groundbreaking African American singer Marion Anderson recorded her experiences in *My Lord, What a Morning!* (1956); documentary photographer Margaret Bourke-White penned her autobiography, *Portrait of Myself* (1963); and Congresswoman **Shirley Chisholm** related her development in *Unbought, Unbossed* (1970). Anthropologist Margaret Mead wrote her story in *Blackberry Winter: My Earlier Years* (1972); iconoclast and reformer Mother Jones framed her own legacy with *The Autobiography of Mother Jones* (1972); and field researcher on animal behavior Dian Fossey wrote an 1983 autobiography that was subsequently made into a film bearing the same name, *Gorillas in the Mist*. **Pauli Murray**, a leader in the **women's movement** and Civil Rights struggle committed her story to print in *Pauli Murray: The Autobiography of a Black Activist, Feminist, Lawyer, Priest and Poet* (1989), and Marian Wright Edelman's account of her life of advocacy

for children and families appeared as *Lanterns: A Memoir of Mentors* in 1999. With their autobiographies, these American women leave behind a legacy of accomplishment, treasured by both readers and fellow autobiographers.

Late-twentieth-century American readers had a seemingly endless appetite for the life stories of the celebrated or notorious, so no depiction of women's autobiography of the period could overlook these works. Katharine Hepburn's *Me* (1991), for example, affords the screen star an opportunity to provide her perspective on an already much-reported life. **Susanna Kaysen**'s account of life in a psychological ward, *Girl, Interrupted* (1993) was popular enough to warrant a film adaptation of the same name. Whether portraying the lives of the glamorous or the vulnerable, such autobiographies extend the view of women's experiences available elsewhere in print.

Added to the ranks of fully self-authored life stories are oral histories and assisted autobiographies. Oral history anthologies, gathered by interviewers from Studs Terkel to John Langston Gwaltney, offer transcriptions of the spoken language of women's lives, autobiographies from a wider spectrum of women than would be likely to commit their testimony to more traditional book-length autobiographies. To the extent that interviewers render such accounts intact, oral histories stand as a body of autobiographical texts. Similarly, even some women who agree to impart their life stories as books do so with the partnership of editors and collaborators. This is especially the case where a woman does not yet enjoy a reputation as a writer, or may lack the confidence or literacy skills that would facilitate writing on her own. Joining the ranks of "as-told-to" male autobiographies such as Theodore Rosengarten's *All God's Dangers* (1974), Nell Irvin Painter's *Narrative of Hosea Hudson* (1979), and Alex Haley's *Autobiography of Malcolm X*, then, are books about their female counterparts, such as Thordis Simonsen's and Sara Brooks' document of a woman sharecropper, *You May Plow Here: The Narrative of Sara Brooks* (1986) and William Dufty's collaborative narrative of the life of blues singer Billie Holiday, *Lady Sings the Blues* (1956).

Writing with a Voice

With the arrival of the twenty-first century and its postmodern and post-structuralist moves to challenge claims to textual neutrality or authorial objectivity, recent scholarly writing about autobiography has tended to acknowledge and even proclaim its **subjectivity** of voice. Rather than a flaw of the text, such writers assert personal perspective as the feature, indeed perhaps the signature feature, of their work. Setting aside the pretense of a third-person pose, such authors explore in direct ways what it means to write in an era so acutely conscious of the sociocultural positions that writers and readers occupy. In this important sense, the genre of autobiography loses its edge as a writing category, as writers from journalists to academics inscribe their own voices, and thus their own experiences and reflections in the texts they write.

As the volume of criticism generated on the topic of interplay between fact and fiction attests, women's autobiography has shaped women's fiction in profound ways. Contributors to this volume cite such works as Isabel Allende's *The House of the Spirits* (1985) and Clarice Lispector's *The Stream of Life* (1989) as works bearing such an influence. In terms of American women's fiction, examples such as **Gertrude Stein**'s *The Making of Americans* (1934), Doris Lessing's *The Diaries of Jane Somers* (1984), and Paule Marshall's *Brown Girl, Brownstones* (1959) suggest some of the ways autobiography as a form of reflection and address, finds its way into fiction writing.

Even many scholarly forms of writing, customarily the province of detached, third-person prose, increasingly embody the voices, perspectives, and lived world memories of their writers in ways that recall autobiography. This **personal criticism**, or confessional criticism, as it is sometimes called, finds champions among such writers as literary critic **Jane Tompkins**, women's historian Elizabeth Fox-Genovese, cultural theorist Gayatri Chakravorty Spivak, and visual culture scholar Marianne Hirsch. These works take many forms, from **autoethnography** to autobiographically informed literary criticism. Diane P. Freedman's work on the "New Belletrism" explores the resulting hybrids of writing forms that emerge in literary works as divergent as Gloria Anzaldúa's *Borderlands/The New Mestiza* (1987), **Alice Walker**'s *In Search of Our Mothers' Gardens: Womanist Prose* (1983), **Nancy Mairs**'s *Remembering the Bone House: An Erotics of Space and Place* (1989), Susan Griffin's *Made from this Earth* (1982), Marge Piercy's *Parti-Colored Blocks for a Quilt* (1982), Tess Gallagher's *A Concert of Tenses* (1986), **Maxine Hong Kingston**'s *The Woman Warrior* (1976) and *China Men* (1980), Jane Gallop's *Thinking through the Body* (1988), and Cherríe Moraga's *Loving in the War Years* (1983). Freedman further identifies books by academic writers outside literature who join this unabashed turn toward positioned prose: Ruth Behar's *Translated Woman: Crossing the Border with Esperanza's Story* (1993), Norma Field's *In the Realm of a Dying Emperor* (1991), Eunice Lipton's *Alias Olympia: A Woman's Search for Manet's Notorious Model and Her Own Desire* (1992), Sara Ruddick's *Maternal Thinking: Toward a Politics of Peace* (1989), Patricia Williams's *The Alchemy of Race and Rights* (1991), and **Carolyn Kay Steedman**'s *Landscape for a Good Woman* (1987). All find a new place of possibility where autobiography joins other rhetorical forms in writing. As they advance their projects, autobiography becomes less distinct and discreet as a genre, but more pervasive in its impact on the written words and imaginative lives of American women.

Further Reading: Addams, Jane. *Twenty Years at Hull-House*. Reprint (New York: Signet Classics, 1999); Allison, Dorothy. *Bastard Out of Carolina* (New York: Plume Books, 1992); Anderson, Linda. *Women and Autobiography in the Twentieth Century: Remembered Futures* (New York: Prentice Hall, 1996); Anderson, Marion. *My Lord, What a Morning!* Reprint (Urbana: University of Illinois Press, 2002); Anzaldúa, Gloria. *Borderlands/The New Mestiza* (San Francisco: Aunt Lute Books, 1999); Ashley, Kathleen, Leigh Gilmore, and Girald Peters, eds. *Autobiography and Postmodernism* (Amherst: University of Massachusetts Press, 1994); Behar, Ruth. *Translated Woman: Crossing the Border with Esperanza's Story* (Boston: Beacon Press, 1993); Bell, Susan Groag, and Marilyn Yalom. *Revealing Lives: Autobiography, Biography, and Gender* (Albany: State University of New York Press, 1990); Bloom, Harold, ed. *Women Memoirists* (Philadelphia: Chelsea House Publishers, 1998); Bourke-White, Margaret. *Portrait of Myself* (New York: Simon and Schuster, 1963); Braham, Jeanne. *Crucial Conversations: Interpreting Contemporary American Literary Autobiographies by Women* (New York: Teachers College, Columbia University, 1995); Braxton, Joanne M. *Black Women Writing Autobiography: A Tradition within a Tradition* (Philadelphia: Temple University Press, 1989); Brodzki, Bella, and Celeste Schenck. *Life/Lines: Theorizing Women's Autobiography* (Ithaca, NY: Cornell University Press, 1988); Broughton, Trev Lynn, and Linda Anderson, eds. *Women's Lives/Women's Times: New Essays on Auto/Biography* (Albany: State University of New York Press, 1997); Brown, Elaine. *A Taste of Power: A Black Woman's Story* (New York: Anchor, 1992); Brown, Rita Mae. *Rita Will: Memoir of a Literary Rabble-Rouser* (New York: Bantam, 1997); Brownley, Martine Watson, and Allison B. Kimmich, eds. *Women and Autobiography* (Wilmington, DE: SR Books, 1999); Buss, Helen. *Repossessing the World: Reading Memoirs by Contemporary Women* (Waterloo, Ontario: Wilfrid Laurier University Press, 2002); Cahill, Susan, ed. *Writing Women's Lives: An Anthology of Autobiographical Narratives by Twentieth-Century American Women Writers* (New York: HarperPerennial, 1994); Chernin, Kim. *My Life as a Boy* (Chapel Hill, NC:

Algonquin, 1997); Chisholm, Shirley. *Unbought and Unbossed* (Boston: Houghton Mifflin, 1970); Cliff, Michelle. *Claiming an Identity They Taught Me to Despise* (Watertown, MA: Persephone Press, 1980); Coleman, Linda S., ed. *Women's Life-Writing: Finding Voice, Building Community* (Bowling Green, OH: Bowling Green State University Popular Press, 1997); Conway, Jill Ker. *When Memory Speaks: Reflections on Autobiography* (New York: Knopf, 1998); Conway, Jill Ker. *Written by Herself: An Anthology* (New York: Vintage Books, 1992–1996); Cosslett, Tess, Celia Lury, and Penny Summerfield, eds. *Feminism and Autobiography: Texts, Theories, Methods* (New York: Routledge, 2000); Culley, Margo, ed. *American Women's Autobiography: Fea(s)ts of Memory* (Madison: University of Wisconsin Press, 1992); Culley, Margo, and Leonore Hoffman, eds. *Women's Personal Narratives: Essays in Criticism and Pedagogy* (New York: Modern Language Association, 1985); Davis, Angela. *Angela Davis: An Autobiography*. Reprint (New York: International Publishers, 1989); Dillard, Annie. *An American Childhood* (New York: Harper and Row, 1987); Dufty, William, and Billie Holliday. *Lady Sings the Blues*. Reprint (New York: Penguin, 1984); Edelman, Marian Wright. *Lanterns: A Memoir of Mentors* (Boston: Beacon, 1999); Ellerby, Janet Mason. *Intimate Reading: The Contemporary Women's Memoir* (Syracuse, NY: Syracuse University Press, 2001); Field, Norma. *In the Realm of a Dying Emperor* (New York: Pantheon, 1991); Fitzgerald, Zelda. *Save Me the Waltz* (London: Grey Walls Press, 1953); Fossey, Dian. *Gorillas in the Mist* (Boston: Houghton Mifflin, 1983); Fowler, Lois J., and David H. Fowler, eds. *Revelations of Self: American Women in Autobiography* (Albany: State University of New York Press, 1990); French, Marilyn. *A Season in Hell: A Memoir* (New York: Knopf, 1998); Gallagher, Tess. *A Concert of Tenses* (Ann Arbor: University of Michigan Press, 1986); Gallop, Jane. *Thinking through the Body* (New York: Columbia University Press, 1988); Gilman, Charlotte Perkins. *The Living of Charlotte Perkins Gilman: An Autobiography*. Reprint (Madison: University of Wisconsin Press, 1991); Gilmore, Leigh. *Autobiographics: A Feminist Theory of Women's Self-Representation* (Ithaca, NY: Cornell

University Press, 1994); Gilmore, Leigh. *The Limits of Autobiography: Trauma and Testimony* (Ithaca, NY: Cornell University Press, 2001); Giovanni, Nikki. *Gemini: An Extended Autobiographical Statement on My First Twenty-Five Years of Being a Black Poet* (New York: Macmillan, 1971); Glasgow, Ellen. *The Woman Within* (New York: Harcourt, Brace, 1954); Goldman, Anne E. *Take My Word: Autobiographical Innovations of Ethnic American Working Women* (Berkeley: University of California Press, 1996); Goldman, Emma. *Living My Life* (New York: Dover, 1930); Griffin, Susan. *Made from This Earth* (New York: Harper and Row, 1982); Hallett, Nicky. *Lesbian Lives: Identity and Auto/biography in the Twentieth Century* (London and Sterling, VA: Pluto Press, 1999); Hansberry, Lorraine. *To Be Young, Gifted, and Black* (New York: S. French, 1969); Hepburn, Katharine. *Me: Stories of My Life* (New York: Ballantine, 1991); Heilbrun, Carolyn. *Women's Lives: The View from the Threshold* (Toronto: University of Toronto Press, 1999); Hellman, Lillian. *Pentimento* (New York: Signet, 1973); Hellman, Lillian. *Scoundrel Time*. Reprint (Boston: Little, Brown, 2000); Hellman, Lillian. *An Unfinished Woman: A Memoir*. Reprint. (Boston: Little, Brown, 1999); Hogan, Linda. *The Woman Who Watches Over the World: A Native Memoir* (New York: W. W. Norton, 2001); Houston, Jeanne Wakatsuki. *Farewell to Manzanar* (New York: Bantam, 1973); Jelinek, Estelle C. *The Tradition of Women's Autobiography from Antiquity to the Present* (Boston: Twayne Publishers, 1986); Jelinek, Estelle C., ed. *Women's Autobiography: Essays in Criticism* (Bloomington: Indiana University Press, 1980); Jones, Mother. *The Autobiography of Mother Jones* (Chicago: C. H. Kerr, 1972); Kaplan, Alice. *French Lessons: A Memoir* (Chicago: University of Chicago Press, 1993); Kaysen, Susanna. *Girl, Interrupted* (New York: Vintage, 1993); Kennedy, Adrienne. *People Who Led to My Plays* (New York: Knopf, 1986); Kingston, Maxine Hong. *China Men*. Reprint (New York: Vintage, 1989); Kingston, Maxine Hong. *The Woman Warrior* (New York: Knopf, 1976); Lessing, Doris. *The Memoirs of a Survivor* (New York: Knopf, 1974); Lifshin, Lyn, ed. *Lips Unsealed: Confidences from Contemporary Women Writers* (Santa Barbara, CA: Capra Press, 1990); Lim, Shirley Geok-Lin. *Among the White Moon Faces: An Asian-American Memoir of Homelands* (New York: Feminist Press at CUNY, 1996); Lipton, Eunice. *Alias Olympia: A Woman's Search for Manet's Notorious Model and Her Own Desire* (New York: Pantheon, 1991); Lorde, Audre. *The Cancer Journals* (San Francisco, CA: Spinsters Ink, 1980); Lorde, Audre. *Zami: A New Spelling of My Name* (New York: Crossing Press, 1982); McCarthy, Mary. *Memories of a Catholic Girlhood* (New York: Harcourt, Brace, 1957); McNaron, Toni. *I Dwell in Possibility: A Memoir* (New York: Feminist Press, 1992); Mairs, Nancy. *Remembering the Bone House: An Erotics of Space and Place* (Cambridge: Harper and Row, 1989); Mason, Bobbie Ann. *Clear Springs: A Memoir* (New York: Random, 1999); Mead, Margaret. *Blackberry Winter: My Earlier Years* (New York: Washington Square Press, 1972); Moody, Anne. *Coming of Age in Mississippi* (New York: Dell, 1968); Moraga, Cherríe. *Loving in the War Years* (Cambridge, MA: South End Press, 2000); Moraga, Cherríe, and Gloria Anzaldúa, eds. *This Bridge Called My Back: Radical Writings by Women of Color*. Reprint (Berkeley, CA: Third Woman Press, 2002); Morgan, Janice, and Colette T. Hall. *Gender and Genre in Literature: Redefining Autobiography in Twentieth-Century Women's Fiction* (New York: Garland, 1991); Murray, Pauli. *Pauli Murray: The Autobiography of a Black Activist, Feminist, Lawyer, Priest and Poet* (Knoxville: University of Tennessee Press, 1989); Nestle, Joan. *A Restricted Country* (San Francisco: Cleis Press, 2003); Neuman, Shirley, ed. *Autobiography and Questions of Gender* (London and Portland, OR: F. Cass, 1991); Olney, James, ed. *Autobiography: Essays Theoretical and Critical* (Princeton, NJ: Princeton University Press, 1980); Olsen, Tillie. *Silences*. Reprint (New York: Feminist Press at CUNY, 2003); Owen, Ursula, ed. *Fathers: Reflections by Daughters* (London: Virago, 1983); Personal Narratives Group. *Interpreting Women's Lives: Feminist Theory and Personal Narratives* (Bloomington: Indiana University Press, 1989); Piercy, Marge. *Parti-Colored Blocks for a Quilt* (Ann Arbor: University of Michigan Press, 1982); Piercy, Marge. *Sleeping with Cats: A Memoir* (New York: William Morrow, 2002); Plath, Sylvia. *The Journals* (New York: Dial, 1982); Plath, Sylvia. *Letters Home: Correspondence, 1950–1963* (New York: Harper and Row, 1975); Polkey, Pauline, ed. *Women's Lives into Print: The Theory, Practice and Writing of Feminist Auto/Biography* (New York: St. Martin's Press, 1999); Rich, Adrienne. *Of Woman Born: Motherhood as Experience and Institution* (New York: Bantam, 1976); Rich, Adrienne. *On Lies, Secrets and Silence: Selected Prose, 1966–1978*. Reprint (New York: W. W. Norton and Co., 1995); Rich, Adrienne. *What Is Found There* (New York: W. W. Norton and Co., 2003); Rodriguez, Barbara. *Autobiographical Inscriptions: Form, Personhood, and the American Woman Writer of Color* (New York: Oxford University Press, 1999); Robinson, Jo Ann Gibson. *The Montgomery Bus Boycott and the Women Who Started It* (Knoxville: University of Tennessee Press, 1987); Ruddick, Sara. *Maternal Thinking: Toward a Politics of Peace* (Boston: Beacon, 1991); Russ, Joanna. *How to Suppress Women's Writing* (Austin: University of Texas Press, 1983); Sanger, Margaret. *Margaret Sanger: An Autobiography*. Reprint (New York: Cooper Square Press, 1999); Sarton, May. *Journal of a Solitude* (New York: W. W. Norton and Co., 1992); Sexton, Anne. *Anne Sexton: A Self-Portrait in Letters* (Boston: Houghton Mifflin, 1977); Shakur, Assata. *Assata* (Chicago: Lawrence Hill Books, 1987); Shulman, Alix Kates. *A Good Enough Daughter: A Memoir* (New York: Schocken, 1999); Silko, Leslie Marmon. *Storyteller* (New York: Seaver Books, 1981); Simonsen, Thordis, and Sara Brooks. *You May Plow Here: The Narrative of Sara Brooks* (New York: Norton, 1986); Smith, Barbara. *Home Girls: A Black Feminist Anthology*. Reprint (New Brunswick, NJ: Rutgers University Press, 2000); Smith, Sidonie. *A Poetics of Women's Autobiography: Marginality and the Fictions of Self-Representation* (Bloomington: Indiana University Press, 1987); Smith, Sidonie. *Subjectivity, Identity, and the Body: Women's Autobiographical Practices in the Twentieth Century* (Bloomington: Indiana University Press, 1993); Smith, Sidonie, and Julia Watson, eds. *De/colonizing the Subject: The Politics of Gender in Women's Autobiography* (Minneapolis: University of Minnesota Press, 1992); Smith, Sidonie, and Julia Watson, eds. *Getting a Life: Everyday Uses of Autobiography* (Minneapolis: University of Minnesota Press, 1996); Smith, Sidonie and Julia Watson, eds. *Reading Autobiography: A Guide for Interpreting Life Narratives* (Minneapolis: University of Minnesota Press, 2002); Smith, Sidonie, and Julia Watson, eds. *Women, Autobiography, Theory: A Reader* (Madison: University of Wisconsin Press, 1998); Stanley, Liz. *The Auto/biographical I: The Theory and Practice of Feminist Auto/biography* (Manchester and New York: St. Martin's Press, c. 1992); Steedman, Carolyn. *Landscape for a Good Woman* (New Brunswick, NJ: Rutgers University Press, 1987); Stone, Albert E., ed. *The American Autobiography: A Collection of Critical Essays* (Englewood Cliffs, NJ: Prentice-Hall, 1981); Tarbell, Ida. *All in the Day's Work: An Autobiography* (Urbana: University of Illinois Press, 2003); Uchida, Yoshiko. *Desert Exile: The Uprooting of a Japanese American Family* (Seattle: University of Washington Press, 1982); Veeser, H. Aram, ed. *Confessions of the Critics* (New York: Routledge, 1996); Wade-Gayles, Gloria. *Pushed Back to Strength: A Black Woman's Journey Home*. Reprint (New York: Avon, 1995); Walker, Alice. *In Search of Our Mothers' Gardens: Womanist Prose* (San Diego, CA: Harcourt Brace Jovanovich, 1983); Wells, Ida B. *Crusade for Justice: The Autobiography of Ida B. Wells*. Reprint (Chicago: University of Chicago Press, 1991); Wharton, Edith. *A Backward Glance*. Reprint (New York: Scribner, 1964); Williams, Patricia. *The Alchemy of Race and Rights* (Cambridge: Harvard University Press, 1991).

Linda S. Watts

ANGELOU, MAYA (1928–) Maya Angelou is the author of six autobiographical volumes written over a period of more than thirty years. These volumes reveal a woman in process—someone who continues to gain understanding through her travels, from the lives and wisdom of family members, and from the metaphorical peaks and valleys of her own life. Rather than being intensely self-focused, Angelou departs from autobiographical tradition by defining herself largely in relation to key moments in history as well as in relation to others. Consequently, Angelou serves as an exemplar, according to *Voices from the Gaps*, "a point of consciousness for African-American people and especially for black women seeking to survive masculine prejudice, white illogical hate and Black lack of power." Yet Angelou strives not simply to survive, but to endure with her courage and wit in tact. Moreover, she wants to speak not only about the black experience, but about everyone's sorrows and joys. It is precisely this unique combination of visionary idealism and realism that creates the dynamic tension in Angelou's works.

Born Marguerite Johnson on April 4, 1928, Angelou grew up in St. Louis, Missouri, and then, after her parents divorced when she was age three, in rural, segregated Stamps, Arkansas. There, she and her brother were raised by her paternal grandmother, who ran the town's only black general store. After graduating from the eighth grade with honors from the segregated Lafayette Training School, she moved to San Francisco to live with her mother and won a scholarship in drama and dance to the California Labor School. Angelou has been married three times: to a Greek-born former sailor, Tosh Angelos, in 1951 or 1952; unofficially, to a South African dissident lawyer, Vusumzi Make, in 1961; and to an English builder and writer, Paul Du Feu, in 1973.

Angelou's list of achievements is extensive. She was the northern coordinator for the Southern Christian Leadership Conference (1959–1960); associate editor of *The Arab Observer* in Cairo (1961–1962); and was feature editor of the *African Review* in Accra, Ghana (1964–1966). For her documentary, *Afro-Americans in the Arts*, a PBS special, she received the Golden Eagle Award. *Georgia, Georgia* (1972), a film about the response of white society to two black women traveling in Switzerland, was the first screenplay by a black woman to be filmed. She was nominated for a Tony Award for her Broadway debut in *Look Away* (1973) and an Emmy Award for her performance as Kunta Kinte's grandmother in *Roots* (1977). She was appointed by President Gerald Ford to the Bicentennial Commission (1974) and later by President Jimmy Carter to the Commission for International Woman of the Year. In 1981, she accepted a lifetime position as the first Reynolds Professor of American Studies at Wake Forest University in Winston-Salem, North Carolina.

Hailed as a renaissance woman, Angelou speaks five languages fluently, has received more than thirty honorary degrees from different institutions, and lectures extensively on topics such as creativity, spirituality, and politics. She has worked diligently to improve conditions for women in the Third World, particularly in Africa. Angelou's novels are widely read and taught in schools and universities across the nation. Her first volume of poetry, *Just Give Me a Cool Drink of Water 'Fore I Diiie* (1971), was nominated for a Pulitzer Prize. For Bill Clinton's first presidential inauguration in January 1993, Angelou wrote and recited her poem, "On the Pulse of Morning," an honor she shared with only one person before her, Robert Frost, who read one of his poems at John F. Kennedy's inaugural ceremony in 1961. Angelou also read her poem, "A Brave and Startling Truth," for the fiftieth anniversary of the United Nations in 1995. *Writer's Digest* named her one of the top 100 writers of the twentieth century, and in 2000, she received a National Medal of Arts. Her poetry, especially favorites such as "Phenomenal Woman" and "Still I Rise," is widely acclaimed by the public.

Among those people who pay tribute to Angelou's influence in their lives are television host Oprah Winfrey; rhythm and blues songwriters and performers Nickolas Ashford and Valerie Simpson; and spiritual leaders Andrew Young, the Reverend Barbara King, and Coretta Scott King. Meanwhile, Angelou has been influenced by several writers and acknowledges her indebtedness to the sonnets and plays of William Shakespeare; the novels of Charles Dickens; and the poems of Edgar Allan Poe, James Weldon Johnson, and Langston Hughes. Throughout her life, Angelou has been an avid reader—so much so that she refers to the Bible and *Roget's Thesaurus* as her two greatest friends. From these two sources she has gleaned much of her vocabulary and style.

While Frederick Douglass, Malcolm X, and Richard Wright are other black autobiographers to whom Angelou might be compared, several of Angelou's writing techniques are different from theirs. First, Angelou often flashes forward and backward in time, chronology being less important to her than thematic connection making. Second, she frequently amplifies the autobiographical tone by using dialogue, for example, when her grandmother prays before spending a long day picking cotton; when the sheriff tells her grandmother that Angelou's crippled Uncle Willie should hide from the Ku Klux Klan as they come through town; and when members of different black churches join together for their spirited, annual revival meetings. Third, Angelou even imagines some scenes, blending fact with welcomed fiction. In one memorable scene, Angelou's grandmother stands up to a white dentist who refuses to treat the young Maya, the result being that the dentist not only relents, but also profusely thanks Angelou's grandmother for sparing his life even as she turns the doctor's nurse into a sack of chicken feed. For these reasons, some critics classify Angelou's narratives as **autobiographical fiction** rather than autobiographies. Yet simultaneously, Angelou's keen sensitivity to historical events during her coming-of-age story (cf., George Eliot's *The Mill on the Floss*) strongly locate her personal narratives in reality. For example, in her first autobiography, *I Know Why the Caged Bird Sings* (1970)—from which the previous examples are taken—Angelou incorporates some of the effects of the Great Depression, Prohibition, President Roosevelt's declaration of war against Japan, and internment of the Japanese on the West Coast on her neighborhood and family.

I Know Why the Caged Bird Sings, which was the basis of a two-hour television special on CBS (1979), was also on the *New York Times* bestseller list for more than two years. The title comes from Paul Lawrence Dunbar's poem "Sympathy," in which a bird beats its wings against its cage's bars in a desperate bid for freedom. Angelou is symbolically that bird, and consequently, Angelou's first autobiography, like slave and prison narratives, contains the themes of captivity, mistreatment, a desire to escape, and self-education. When, at age seven, Angelou is raped by her mother's boyfriend and is then forced to testify at her rapist's trial and finds out that her rapist has been found beaten to death in an alley, she becomes mute for the next five years, fearful that speaking will lead to someone else's death. During this time a teacher befriends her and introduces her to the world of literature, an experience that helps her find her **voice** again. As an oppressed outsider, though, Angelou cannot escape the injustices of the world around her. Consequently, she reflectively questions her God-fearing grandmother's passive resistance to white girls' taunting; painfully relates a graduation speaker's racist remarks about the future of black boys as basketball players; and explains how, in an act of righteous indignation, she breaks the dishes of a white employer who repeatedly chose to call her by another name. She also worries about her sexual orientation, a crisis that leads her to a single sexual encounter with a neighborhood boy when she is sixteen. The birth of her son, Guy, as a result of this encounter, marks another turning point in Angelou's life.

Angelou's second autobiography, *Gather Together in My Name* (1974), explores Angelou's multiple conflicts among motherhood, work, and men. More often than not, these conflicts leave Angelou guilt ridden. In this work, Angelou specifically departs from traditional expectations of autobiography by telling her readers much more of the truth than some of them may want or expect to hear, and telling it in a way that produces an effect of fragmentation rather than wholeness. As a madam, prostitute, and chanteuse, Angelou wrestles with demons that threaten to keep her imprisoned in a world of fear and hopelessness, unable to trust herself and others. Also worthy of note is Angelou's focus on clothes, symbolic of the "costuming" of one's self. Angelou learns that drugs and easy money do not bring success, but carefully made decisions, hard work, and perseverance can change one's life. Like self-acceptance, it is an ongoing process, fraught with danger and full of rewards.

Singin' and Swingin' and Gettin' Merry Like Christmas (1976) details Angelou's many adventures as she marries a white man, enters show business, and tours twenty-two countries in Europe and Africa as a dancer in George Gershwin's *Porgy and Bess*. Yet, Angelou still struggles with tremendous guilt, having left her son behind, but to whom she ultimately returns and with whom she goes to Hawaii to restore their relationship. In *The Heart of a Woman* (1981), their relationship remains tender even as her son becomes a rebellious teenager. Other relationships are delineated, from her friendship with Billie Holiday and Malcolm X to her camaraderie with numerous people working alongside her in the fight for civil rights, reveal Angelou as both strong and vulnerable. Here Angelou also emerges as a budding writer in the Harlem Writers Guild.

The journey motif continues in *All God's Children Need Traveling Shoes* (1986). Going to Africa on a quest for **identity** and self-enlightenment, Angelou fails to achieve those goals, and, as a result, her romanticized views of Ghana are shaken. Her extensive adventures finally conclude in West Africa. Only after she has moved toward autonomy can she, paradoxically, accept her dual heritage and truly define herself in relation to others, as a mother and as a woman. She does so with an unusual combination of humility and pride.

In her sixth autobiographical volume, *A Song Flung Up to Heaven* (2002), Angelou records her devastation by the assassinations of Malcolm X and Martin Luther King Jr. She subsequently withdraws from the world and is then reintegrated into it when James Baldwin takes her to a dinner party, where the idea for writing about her childhood is born. Coming full circle, *A Song Flown Up to Heaven* ends as Angelou writes the first sentences of *I Know Why the Caged Bird Sings*: "What are you looking at me for? I didn't come here to stay" (3). Ironically, these lines, which reflect Angelou's intense self-awareness and her sense of alienation and displacement, are the ones that best help Angelou's readers to reflect on the growth of her critical self-awareness throughout her six autobiographical volumes. They also help readers fully appreciate Angelou's new understanding of "home" as places where the heart resides. Angelou seeks to share her understanding with others, whatever their **race**, **class**, or **gender**. So, too, is her message that while all human beings will face many trials, they must not give in to despair. Indeed, the indefatigability of the human spirit is what Angelou repeatedly celebrates with her call to replace ignorance with caring, an ethic that testifies to the redemptive powers of honesty, forgiveness, and love.

Further Reading: Angelou, Maya. *All God's Children Need Traveling Shoes* (New York: Random House, 1986); Angelou, Maya. *The Complete Collected Poems of Maya Angelou* (New York: Random House, 1994); Angelou, Maya. *Gather Together in My Name* (New York: Random House, 1974); Angelou, Maya. *I Know Why the Caged Bird Sings* (New York: Random House, 1970); Angelou, Maya. *A Song Flung Up to Heaven* (New York: Random House, 2002); Angelou, Maya. *The Heart of a Woman* (New York: Random House, 1981); Angelou, Maya. *Singin' and Swingin' and Gettin' Merry Like Christmas* (New York: Random House, 1976); Angelou, Maya. "Voices from the Gaps: Maya Angelou." *Voices from the Gaps: Women Writers of Color.* http://www.voices.cla.umn.edu/authors/MayaAngelou.html; Angelou, Maya. *Wouldn't Take Nothing for My Journey Now* (New York: Random House, 1993); Braxton, Joanne M. *Black Women Writing Autobiography: A Tradition within a Tradi-*

tion (Philadelphia: Temple University Press, 1989); Eliot, George. *The Mill on the Floss.* Harvard Classics Shelf of Fiction. Vol. 9 (New York: Collier, 1917); Lupton, Mary Jane. *Maya Angelou: A Critical Companion* (Westport, CT: Greenwood Press, 1988); McPherson, Dolly A. *Order Out of Chaos: The Autobiographical Works of Maya Angelou* (New York: Peter Lang, 1990).

Laurie A. Dashnau

ANZALDÚA, GLORIA (1942–2004) Gloria Anzaldúa represents the growing presence of women of color in women's autobiography. One of the few autobiographies by a Chicana author in the late twentieth century, *Borderlands/La Frontera: The New Mestiza* (1987), examines the condition of women in Hispanic culture, Chicanos in white American society, lesbians in "straight" culture, and activists in academe. The larger context for her own life is the colonial legacy of the conquest of the Americas. In *Borderlands*, American and Mexican history and culture are equally contested terms that shape her life. As a Chicana she rejects the traditional roles of daughter, sister, wife, and mother, yet she identifies with the language, folklore, mythology, and country that continues to influence her and other Mexican Americans. These issues, rarely addressed in women's autobiography, constitute the center of Anzaldúa's writings.

Anzaldúa's autobiography seizes on the feminist practice of making the personal political and also critiques the difficulties that women of color face in attempting to tell their own stories. She addresses what she saw as the reluctance in many white women's autobiographies to examine their tendencies to universalize their life experiences. Instead, Anzaldúa's narrative illustrates that the **subjectivity** of women of color is expressed in its nonuniversalizing difference from others. In this way, Anzal-dúa's autobiography identifies a different political strategy for women's autobiography.

Gloria Anzaldúa, a self-described "chicana dyke-feminist, *tejana patlache* poet, writer, and cultural theorist," was born to Mexican parents on September 26, 1942, in Jesus Maria of the Valley, Texas. After relocating at age eleven to the city of Hargill, Texas, she began to work in the fields. The family worked on ranches and farms along the U.S./Mexican border, and for one year they worked in Arkansas. The family eventually moved back to Hargill in order to provide the children with schooling and a more stable life. The stability was short-lived when Anzaldúa's father died when she was fourteen years of age. His death meant that Anzaldúa needed to help the family financially by working in the fields throughout high school and college.

In spite of these obstacles, Anzaldúa finished high school and earned two college degrees. After earning a B.A. in English, Art, and Secondary Education from Pan American University in 1969, she earned an M.A. in English and Education, at the University of Texas, Austin. Her academic advisers in Texas discouraged her from pursuing Chicana topics, and eventually she left for the University of California-Santa Cruz to work on feminist theory and cultural studies.

Anzaldúa has taught **feminism**, Chicano studies, and creative writing at a number of universities including the University of Texas, Austin; Vermont College of Norwich University; and San Francisco State University. It was during a two-year teaching stint in Vermont where, feeling isolated and alienated, she began to write segments of *Borderlands*.

Anzaldúa has won numerous awards for her works, including the Lambda Lesbian Small Book Press Award (1990) and an NEA Fiction Award (1991). *Borderlands*, which combines the genres of autobiography, poetry, and political, cultural, and historical analysis, was chosen as one of the thirty-eight best books of 1987. The work grapples with the issues of narrative representation, reality, and truth. Gloria Anzaldúa died in May 2004 of complications from diabetes.

Borderlands is divided into two parts. The

first section is a personal narrative in which Anzaldúa questions received ideas about her **gender** and culture. The second primarily consists of poetry. In both sections, the recurring focus of the work is language. Anzaldúa uses a variety of Spanish dialects and two variations of English. The multilingual nature of her work, and the bilingual title, express her ideas about Chicana **identity**, which requires women to constantly switch between "codes" never settling on one language (or identity) exclusively.

Anzaldúa poses a postmodern critique of the American autobiography. Her individuality, while as inconsistent and performative as the canonical autobiographies of, say, Benjamin Franklin and Henry Adams, does not transcend the irregularities of time and space. In other words, she does not record the achievement of a fully integrated self, but the struggle to remain intelligible as a subject, to herself and others, without resorting to the fiction of a naturally, inevitably coherent self. In many ways, the subject of her autobiography is as much about the political work of deconstructing herself (parsing links among words and ideas and endlessly revising their meaning in the process) as it is about her own life. In *This Bridge We Call Home*, she addresses the need for people to think of themselves as transnational subjects: "Living in multicultural communities and the complexities of our age demand that we develop a perspective that takes into account the whole planet" (2002, 3).

Further Reading: Anzaldúa, Gloria. *Borderlands/La Frontera: The New Mestiza* (San Francisco: Spinsters/Aunt Lute, 1987); Anzaldúa, Gloria, and Cherríe Moraga, eds. *Lloronas, Women Who Howl: Autohistorias-Torias and the Production of Writing, Knowledge, and Identity* (San Francisco: Aunt Lute, 1996); Anzaldúa, Gloria, ed. *Making Face, Making Soul/Haciendo Caras: Creative and Critical Perspectives by Feminists of Color* (San Francisco: Aunt Lute Foundation Books, 1990); Anzaldúa, Gloria, and Analouise Keating, eds. *This Bridge We Call Home: Radical Visions for Transformation* (New York and London: Routledge, 2002); Brady, Mary Pat. *Extinct Lands, Temporal Geographies: Chicana Literature and the Urgency of Space* (Durham, NC: Duke University Press, 2002); *Cassell's Encyclopedia of Queer Myth, Symbol and Spirit: Gay, Lesbian, Bisexual and Transgender Lore* (London and Herndon, VA: Cassell Academic, 1998); Keating, AnaLouise, and Gloria Anzaldúa, eds. *Interviews/Entrevistas* (New York: Routledge, 2000); Keating, AnaLouise. *Women Reading Women Writing: Self-Invention in Paula Gunn Allen, Gloria Anzaldúa, and Audre Lorde* (Philadelpia, PA: Temple University Press, 1996); Moraga, Cherríe, and Gloria Anzaldúa, eds. *This Bridge Called My Back: Writings by Radical Women of Color* (Watertown, MA: Persephone Press, 1981); Martin, Biddy. "Lesbian Identity and Autobiographical Difference[s]." In *Life/Lines: Theorizing Women's Autobiography*, edited by Bella Brodzki and Celeste Schenck, 77–103 (Ithaca, NY: Cornell University Press, 1988); Raiskin, Judith. "Inverts and Hybrids: Lesbian Rewritings of Sexual and Radical Identities." In *The Lesbian Postmodern*, edited by Laura Doan, 156–172 (New York: Columbia University Press, 1994).

Rekha Rosha

ASIAN AMERICAN WOMEN'S AUTOBIOGRAPHY Asian American women's autobiography refers here to autobiographical writings by women of Asian descent who were either born in North America or have lived or migrated here. The writers so defined come from a range of countries including China, India, Japan, Korea, Pakistan, and Vietnam.

Definition of Asian Americans

The term "Asian American" emerged in the 1960s as a result of the Asian American movement, which sought to unify Americans of Asian ancestry to resist racism and seek cultural inclusion. When the term was originally conceived, the major Asian-origin immigrant groups in the United States were Japanese, Chinese, Filipino, Korean, and Asian Indian. As a result of changes brought about by the Immigration and Nationality Act of 1965, however, the Asian American community has grown more diverse and now includes people from all the countries in South, Southeast, and East Asia. The Immigration and Nationality Act of 1965 was a watershed event in Asian American history because it put an end to several decades of legislative restrictions on Asian immigration and led to the influx of large numbers of immigrants. Thus, the rubric Asian American has come to encompass an increasingly heterogeneous formation defined by differences of **race**, **class**, national origin, **gender**, **sexuality**, religion, and culture. This heterogeneity, framed by a shared structural position as a liminal racial group neither black nor white and a fraught and shifting political history between Asian nations and the United States, is crucial to understanding the writings of Asian American autobiographers.

It is important at the outset to specify the limits of the way the term Asian American will be used here. Asians who have their origins in West Asian countries like Saudi Arabia, Iraq, and Afghanistan are not classified as Asian Americans by the census and other government entities. There has been some discussion within Asian American studies about the need to include West Asians within the label Asian American because of experiences of racism, marginalization, and an image as perennial aliens that they share with other Asian-origin groups in the United States. West Asian American community groups have also petitioned government bodies for a change in their classification but have been unsuccessful thus far. The prevailing practice in Asian American Studies has been to include as Asian American those groups that are officially categorized as such, while remaining cognizant of the artificiality and historical contingency of the category: the term could be expanded further to include new subgroups in the future, as it has been in the past. Yet another demarcation that scholars have argued for is the need to retain a separate critical framework in treating the local literary production of Hawai'i because of the distinc-

tive colonial history of the Pacific Islands (Sumida, "Postcolonialism, Nationalism"). Thus, this essay defines as Asian Americans writers from Bangladesh, Bhutan, Burma (present-day Myanmar), Cambodia, China, Philippines, Japan, Korea, India, Indonesia, Laos, Nepal, Pakistan, Sri Lanka, Thailand, and Vietnam.

The term Asian American as used here includes writings by Asian Canadian women because of the historical similarities in the experiences of Asian groups in the United States and Canada (exclusion, discrimination, and internment). Moreover, several of the women whose autobiographies are included here (**Bharati Mukherjee** and the Eaton sisters) lived and wrote in the United States and Canada and hence their work cannot be restricted to a singular location. Finally, in an attempt to keep this a bibliography of manageable size, only autobiographical writings in English have been included. Autobiographies by Asian American women have been written in several Asian languages and English translations of some of these writings do exist but more extensive archival and critical work on Asian American literature in Asian languages remains to be undertaken.

The definition of autobiography is deliberately kept flexible and incorporates a range of texts including oral histories, autobiographical novels, and more conventional autobiographies. Since the field of Asian American literature is in the early stages of development, it is preferable to be inclusive so as not to prematurely exclude texts by criteria that need themselves to be retheorized in the light of historically changing and culturally specific autobiographical practice. The archival work of constituting a canon of Asian American women's autobiography provides a means of challenging dominant models of self and life story through an analysis of the range of minority autobiographical writing.

Although literary studies have historically privileged the autobiographies of writers with a strongly literary bent (Eakin

1991, 5), current critical theory offers a broader definition of autobiography because the use of the traditional aesthetic criteria would exclude a number of Asian American women's autobiographies. Instead, this essay situates autobiographical writing within the larger field of public discourse in order to highlight the social and political conditions that determine literary production. As Susan Schweik notes in exploring the way in which the internment shaped Japanese American women's poetry, it is necessary to read the literature "pre-poetically, by necessity." She cites Ann Rosalind Jones' statement about the importance of studying "the conditions necessary for writing at all, and the way those conditions shape the lyrics of . . . women writers" (1989, 89). For instance, some of the Asian American women whose writings are included here, like **Monica Sone**, Nien Cheng, and Cynthia Chou, were not creative writers and their autobiographies signify their solitary excursion into literature. For still other Asian American women, the long struggle with mastering English as a second language curtailed their productivity, made evident in the production of one autobiography in English written late in the author's life and often at the behest of sponsors or publishers.

Finally, the growing importance of oral history has emphasized giving **voice** to ordinary, marginalized, or nonliterate people and this trend has, in turn, enabled the reexamination of established ideas of autobiography. Oral history projects that document the lives of old-timers and newer immigrants have been very influential in Asian American Studies. The Asian American movement and the literary projects that emerged from it were shaped by the effort to overcome the historical silencing of Asian Americans within American culture, and the project of recovery at the heart of oral history coincides with this political impetus. Oral histories represent the convergence of the disciplines of history, anthropology, and literature, and the discursive

position of the subaltern female subject in collaborative works, like Mary Paik Lee's *Quiet Odyssey: A Pioneer Korean Woman in America* (1990), edited by Sucheng Chan) and *Through Harsh Winters: The Life of a Japanese Immigrant Woman* (Kikumura 1981) (produced by "Michiko Tanaka" [pseudonym] and her daughter Akemi Kikumura). Such texts open up a rich field of investigation for autobiography as the site of multiple discourses of **subjectivity** and legitimation. For instance, when we open *Through Harsh Winters*, we realize that the Akemi Kikumura to whom authorship of the text is attributed on the cover page is a trained anthropologist who has written the introduction, epilogue, and appendices of a life history, which is narrated by "Michiko Tanaka," her Issei (first generation Japanese American) mother, in Japanese. Kikumura serves as editor and translator of her mother's text. But although the cover page attributes authorship to Kikumura, she prefaces her mother's account with the following comments: "The following history is my mother's, the memories she chose to tell me about her past life. The interviews were tape recorded in Japanese; I have translated it and made a few rearrangements to bring disconnected anecdotes together. But the story is my mother's" (15). Kikumura's comments signal the multiple mediations through which her mother is given voice in a text that breaks down the boundaries between **biography** and autobiography. Her insistence, "but the story is my mother's," signals a political and filial urgency to attributing authorship to her mother and points to the limitations of the available language of authorship to represent their collaborative project. Kikumura also attempts, through the singular life history of her mother, to represent the collective subject of Issei womanhood. Of this generation of women she writes, "[E]fforts at orienting themselves to their new environment were hindered by the inability to speak English, by confinement to home and children, by lack of relatives or any network of social organizations and friends, and by the barriers of racism and discrimination." She adds, "This book was written out of respect and admiration for these courageous women who had managed to transform hardship, suffering, and despair into determination, understanding, and hope" (ix). This statement not only highlights the gendered and racialized exclusion of women like her mother from the public sphere but also foregrounds the role of autobiography in retroactively inserting a collective female subject within this domain, thus claiming a historical **space** for marginalized subjects.

In the production of oral histories and collaborative autobiographies, which represent a significant proportion of Asian American women's autobiographical production, Asian American and white historians, anthropologists, sponsors, editors, translators, and coauthors have played a pivotal role. The cultural politics shaping these forms of collaborative authorship have parallels with the production of African American slave narratives, native American autobiographies, and Latina/o American *testimonios* in that the self that emerges in these narratives is shaped by dominant constructions of minority groups, the historical limits of the available discourses, and the conventions of the genre. But these collaborative works also demonstrate the ability of Asian American women and other minority subjects to shape rhetorical strategies that subvert or elude such discursive constraints. As William L. Andrews notes of early African American slave narratives, these autobiographical texts require of the reader "an exercise in creative hearing" (qtd. in Eakin 1991, 9).

Asian American Autobiography within American Culture

Any account of Asian American autobiography must acknowledge the privileged position of autobiography within Asian American literary production where, in contrast to mainstream literature, autobiography has served until the 1980s as the most

marketable genre for Asian American writing. The common perception of Asians as exotic outsiders and racial aliens created an audience for Asian American autobiographical texts that provided ethnographic representations of their homelands or their ethnic communities in the United States. As critics have noted, Asian American autobiographers often served as cultural ambassadors, initiating outsiders to the mores, customs, or practices of their cultures in an effort to close the gap between themselves and most of their readers and to combat dominant stereotypes of Asian cultures (Kim, "Asian American Literature," 1988, 812). In contrast to the scholars and diplomats who produced the earliest autobiographies, the vast majority of Asian immigrants to the United States from the mid-nineteenth century through 1924 (by which time legislative exclusion had been enacted against most Asian immigrant groups) were non-English-speaking laborers whose lives and struggles go unrecorded in the autobiographies of that time. Most of the earliest Asian American autobiographies like Yan Phou Lee's *When I Was a Boy in China* (1887) and New Il-Han's *When I Was a Boy in Korea* (1928) focus on the upper-class childhoods of the protagonists in their homelands and offer portraits of privileged Asian groups. A few Asian American women did publish their life stories in the early twentieth century, but the low numbers of these publications indicate not only how few women there were among the early immigrant groups (which were largely "bachelor societies") but also that for most working-class Asian women, domestic responsibilities, economic struggles, and a lack of knowledge of English excluded them from literary production in English. But the few early autobiographies by Asian American women that did appear reveal a greater diversity of perspective than that of their male counterparts and can be less easily assimilated to the stance of the cultural ambassador.

The earliest known autobiographical

pieces by an Asian American woman are two essays by the biracial Chinese and English journalist and short story writer Edith Maud Eaton who wrote under the Chinese pen name of **Sui Sin Far**. The essays, "Leaves from the Mental Portfolio of an Eurasian" (1909) and "Sui Sin Far, the Half Chinese Writer, Tells of Her Career" (1912), describe the anguish of her predicament as a biracial and single woman, assert the dignity and worth of the Chinese people, and challenge the prejudices of Chinese and white alike against those of mixed-race **identity**. Another important early autobiographical writer was Edith Eaton's sister, Winnifred Eaton, who disavowed the Chinese heritage her sister publicly proclaimed, opting instead to pass as a woman of part-Japanese ancestry. Winnifred Eaton published her work under the Japanese pseudonym of Onoto Watanna. Her choice of a Japanese pseudonym was driven by the need to deflect the racism directed against the Chinese in North America and to capitalize on the current vogue for *Japonisme*. Onoto Watanna's romantic novels, many of them set in Japan, proved very popular and she was a successful Hollywood screenplay writer by the time she set about writing an autobiographical novel, *Me, A Book of Remembrance* (1915). *Me*, which has a Eurasian protagonist called Nora Ascough, was published anonymously and reveals the paradoxical desire for revelation and concealment that characterized Winnifred Eaton's public persona. While some earlier Eaton scholars tended to polarize the writings of the two sisters on political grounds, Annette White-Parks invoked the trope of "tricksterism" to highlight the performative aspects of race and gender in Winnifred Eaton's self-representations, thus paving the way for recent revisionist accounts of their writings. In her book-length study of the Eatons, Dominika Ferens observes, "[W]hen criticism indulges in the 'good sister-bad sister' paradigm, both Winnifred's subtle antiracist interventions and

the muted Orientalism of Edith's work go unnoticed" (2).

In contrast to the autobiographies of the Eaton sisters, which sought in different ways to address issues of racial passing, poverty, and gender stereotypes, another autobiography written in the early decades of the twentieth century, Etsu Inagaki Sugimoto's *A Daughter of the Samurai* (1925) conforms more closely to the ethnographic mode seen in Asian American men's autobiographies of the time. Sugimoto's narrative, which covers her life in Japan as the daughter of a samurai and her subsequent marriage to a Japanese merchant in the United States, restricts itself largely to describing Japanese culture and customs to an American audience and contains little description of personal feelings, social conflicts, or painful experiences. Well received by contemporary reviewers, *A Daughter of the Samurai* reveals less about Etsu Sugimoto's life than about the limits of the available discursive positions for upperclass Asian American women in their exchanges with the West.

Although the number of Asian American women who produced autobiographies during the early decades of the twentieth century was low, with the emergence of an American-born generation, and the political changes produced by World War II, the number of women writing autobiographies grew significantly so that by the later decades of the twentieth century women's voices came to dominate the production of Asian American life writing.

Asian American Autobiographies in the 1940s and 1950s

The women who wrote autobiographies during the 1940s were nearly all Westernized, foreign-born, and from upper-class or diplomatic backgrounds (Han Suyin, Maimai Sze, Helena Kuo, and Adet and Anor Lin) and most were from Christian families where sons and daughters were likely to receive a Western education (Ling, *Between Worlds* 1990, 58). But English-language proficiency, even for those who were Westernized, was a hard-won accomplishment and thus the struggle for a public voice often appears as a central thematic in their life narratives. But in addition to these barriers to finding a public voice, Asian American women also had to overcome the social constraints associated with publishing or becoming a writer. In her foreword to *Destination Chungking*, Han Suyin writes, "Ladies of the diplomatic corps do not write books. The set in which I lived considered writing an unwomanly occupation, destructive of one's moral character, like acting" (qtd. in Ling, *Between Worlds* 1990, 67).

The political context of the 1940s is crucial to understanding the nature of the autobiographies produced by Asian American women and their reception. Pearl Harbor marked a turning point in popular perceptions of Japanese and other Asian Americans in the United States. World War II positioned most Asian nations as allies of the United States, except Japan, and created a sympathetic public for stories of the political oppression and hardships of Asian nations invaded or threatened by Japan. The political sympathy for Asian allies extended toward stories about these immigrant groups in the United States as evident in the wide acclaim achieved by the American-born writer **Jade Snow Wong**'s depiction of Chinatown family life in *Fifth Chinese Daughter* (1950). The two frameworks that emerge in these autobiographies would reappear in later autobiographical writings by Asian American women. The first identified the female autobiographical subject with the cause of a suffering people and constructs her position as a witness and an intercessionary figure making known this political oppression in the West. The second produces a narrative of feminist emergence within the context of an ethnic community and combines criticism of the

racism of the dominant community (albeit often muted) with criticism of patriarchal constraints in the ethnic community. The first type of autobiography can be seen in the pro-Chinese narratives of the 1940s by the Lin sisters and Han Suyin, but would be followed in later decades with anti-Communist life narratives like Bette Bao Lord and Sansan's *Eighth Moon* (1964) and Nien Cheng's *Life and Death in Shanghai* (1987). Jade Snow Wong's autobiography provided the model for the second type of autobiography and is an important antecedent for **Maxine Hong Kingston**'s *The Woman Warrior* (1976).

The politicization of Japanese American identity after Pearl Harbor and the internment of Japanese Americans in the United States and Canada had a profound impact on the emergence of Japanese American women's autobiography during this period. The historical silence surrounding the internment in the dominant culture and within the Japanese American and Japanese Canadian communities made it difficult to address the issue directly. Yet the internment so profoundly transformed the Japanese American community that autobiographical narrative was deeply marked by these changes. Monica Sone's *Nisei Daughter* (1953), Jeanne Wakatsuki Houston's *Farewell to Manzanar* (1973), and Yoshiko Uchida's *Desert Exile* (1982), all written by second-generation Japanese American (Nisei) women, were praised by reviewers for their neutral, cheerful, or conciliatory tones. However, critics like **Shirley Geoklin Lim**, Sau-ling Wong, and Traise Yamamoto have pointed out the importance of not taking the superficial tone of these texts too literally. Yamamoto uses the trope of "masking" to characterize the autobiographical subjects of these narratives: "[T]he tropical deployment of masking constructs encoded narratives that resist and criticize the dominant ideology that erases Nisei women as subjects. These autobiographies attest to a crisis of raced subjectivity wherein the impulses of disavowal and abjection compete with the equally strong necessity of identifying with the raced self associated with the Japanese mother" (6). The time lag in the appearance of these autobiographies, published many years after the end of the internment, and the contrast between the strong political critique in Sone's 1979 preface to *Nisei Daughter* and her 1953 text reveal the fraught terrain of self-disclosure negotiated by these texts and their role in transforming the discursive boundaries that shaped their own production. These writings can be seen as part of a long process of breaking silence culminating in the redress movement of the 1980s that called for an official apology and financial compensation for the losses suffered by Japanese Americans. A striking feature of these Nisei women's autobiographies is the way in which they use the singular "I" of autobiography to give utterance to the collective subject of an oppressed community. The focus on identity in relational terms highlights the intersubjectivity of Japanese American meanings of family and community. The incorporation of **letters**, diaries, journals, and historical documents into Nisei autobiographical novels like Joy Kogawa's *Obasan* (1981) emphasize the inextricability of self-representation and historical reconstruction in Nisei autobiographies dealing with the internment.

Civil Rights and the Women's Movement in the United States

In the 1960s and 1970s, civil rights struggles, the **women's movement**, the antiwar movement, and the Asian American movement dramatically transformed the meanings of Asian American subjectivities, creating an environment in which autobiography offered a powerful vehicle for exploring and constructing new forms of self and community. Maxine Hong Kingston's *The Woman Warrior: Memoirs of a Girlhood among Ghosts*

(1976), often described as one of the most widely read books by an American writer, won the National Book Critics Circle Award for nonfiction in 1976, thus achieving unprecedented national success and recognition for an Asian American text. The powerful feminist narrative with its critique of Chinese American sexism and its lyrical and extravagant mythmaking that invented new models of womanhood from fictional and real Chinese women's lives won a wide audience and generated a critical firestorm. While some mainstream reviewers praised the book in Orientalist terms or appropriated its feminist critique to confirm stereotypes of Asian culture, several prominent Asian American male critics condemned the text as pseudoautobiographical, assimilationist, and self-Orientalizing (Chin, Chan). However, for several Asian American feminist scholars, this very reception served as a critical parable for the difficulties of articulating an Asian American feminist critique (Cheung 1990; S.C. Wong). The fluid and conflicted subjectivity at the center of the text and Kingston's transgression of generic boundaries set an important precedent for Asian American women's autobiographies that followed and shaped discussions of Asian American sexual politics and cultural nationalism.

The next three decades witnessed a proliferation of autobiographical writings by Asian American women. The growing numbers of foreign-born writers in this group (**Sara Suleri**, Le Ly Hayslip, **Meena Alexander**) and their use of diverse constructions of self have created a rich and heterogeneous field of writing that draws on multiple literary traditions and concepts of selfhood. The institutionalization of women's studies, ethnic studies, and postcolonial studies courses at universities, the growing theoretical interest in women's autobiographies, the establishment of feminist presses and journals for women of color, and the influence of multiculturalism in all cultural spheres has created a growing audience for life writing by Asian American women. The university has played a crucial role in creating a cultural space for this literature. Thus, it is not surprising that many contemporary autobiographies have been written by women who are academics or creative writers (Bharati Mukherjee, Sara Suleri, Meena Alexander, and Shirley Geok-lin Lim), and in many cases their autobiographies have appeared in university or feminist presses.

The incredible heterogeneity of these texts and the multiplicity of the subject positions they examine make it difficult to offer generalizations that encompass the range of contemporary Asian American women's autobiographies. But several themes recur in Asian American women's life writings from the 1980s to the present. One of the most prominent is the use of personal narrative to interrogate official histories of colonialism, nationalism, globalization, and ethnic identity (Theresa Hak Kyung Cha, Sara Suleri, Meena Alexander). Several of these autobiographies have focused on the racially marked and gendered body as the site for the production of new forms of knowledge and consciousness (Nunez, Suleri, Cha). Other autobiographies, particularly those by immigrant women writers, explore the possibility of making homes in language (Suleri, Alexander, Lim). Rather than emphasizing a unitary concept of self, some recent autobiographies have highlighted the fault lines underlying ideas of selfhood and have highlighted the fictiveness of reconstructions of the self. Thus, while recent autobiographies reveal a greater self-reflexiveness in the construction of the autobiographical subject, it is as much a product of the conjunction of diverse literary traditions, languages, and histories as it is influenced by developments in postmodern fiction or poststructuralist theory. Asian American women's autobiographical writing represents a rich, complex field of literary production that draws from and transforms contemporary debates about identity and history.

Further Reading: Primary Texts: Alexander, Meena. *Fault Lines* (New York: Feminist Press, 1993); Cha, Theresa Hak Kyung. *Dictee* (1982; Berkeley: Third Woman, 1992); Cheng, Nien. *Life and Death in Shanghai* (New York: Grove, 1986); Chennault, Anna Chan. *The Education of Anna* (New York: Times Books, 1980); Chou, Cynthia L. *My Life in the United States* (North Quincy, MA: Christopher, 1970); Chuang Hua [pseud.]. *Crossings* 1968. Reprint (Boston: Northeastern University Press, 1986); Han, Suyin. *Destination Chungking* (London: Jonathan Cape, 1942); Hayslip, Phung Thi Le Ly, and Jay Wurts. *When Heaven and Earth Changed Places: A Vietnamese Woman's Journey from War to Peace* (New York: Doubleday, 1989); Hayslip, Phung Thi Le Ly, and James Hayslip. *Child of War, Woman of Peace* (New York: Doubleday, 1993); Houston, Jeanne Wakatsuki, and James D. Houston. *Farewell to Manzanar*. 1973. Reprint (New York: Bantam, 1995); Kikumura, Akemi. *Through Harsh Winters: The Life of a Japanese Immigrant Woman* (Novato, CA: Chandler and Sharp, 1981); Kingston, Maxine Hong. *The Woman Warrior: Memoirs of a Girlhood among Ghosts* (New York: Knopf, 1976); Kogawa, Joy. *Obasan* (Toronto: Lester, Orpen, 1981); Kuo, Helena [Ching-Ch'iu]. *I've Come a Long Way* (New York: Appleton-Century, 1942); Lau, Evelyn. *Runaway: Diary of a Street Kid* (Toronto: HarperCollins, 1989); Lee, Mary Paik. *Quiet Odyssey: A Pioneer Korean Woman in America*. Edited by Sucheng Chan (Seattle: University of Washington Press, 1990); Liang Yen [Margaret Yang Briggs]. *Daughter of the Khans* (New York: Norton, 1955); Lim, Shirley Geok-lin. *Among the White Moon Faces: An Asian-American Memoir of Homelands* (New York: Feminist Press, 1996); Mukherjee, Bharati, and Clark Blaise. *Days and Nights in Calcutta* (1977; Rev. and enl. ed. (Markham, Ontario: Viking-Penguin, 1986); Sone, Monica. *Nisei Daughter*. Reprint with an introduction and preface to the 1979 edition, original 1953 (Seattle: University of Washington Press, 1991); Sugimoto, Etsu Inagaki. *A Daughter of the Samurai* (1925; Rutland, VT: Tuttle, 1966); Sui Sin Far [Edith Maud Eaton]. "Leaves from the Mental Portfolio of a

Eurasian." *Independent* 7 (January 1909): 125–132; Suleri, Sara. *Meatless Days* (Chicago: University of Chicago Press, 1989); Sze, Mai-mai. *Echo of a Cry: A Story Which Began in China* (New York: Harcourt, Brace, 1945); Tan Yun [Adet Lin], and Anor Lin. *Our Family* (New York: Day, 1939); Uchida, Yoshiko. *Desert Exile: The Uprooting of a Japanese-American Family* (1982; Seattle: University of Washington Press, 1989); Uchida, Yoshiko. *The Invisible Thread: An Autobiography* (New York: Simon and Schuster, 1991); Watanna, Onoto [Winnifred Eaton]. *Me, A Book of Remembrance* (New York: Century, 1915); Wong, Jade Snow. *Fifth Chinese Daughter*. Reprint with an introduction to the 1989 edition (1945; Seattle: University of Washington Press, 1989); Wade, Jade Snow. *No Chinese Stranger* (New York: Harper and Row, 1975); Wong, Su-ling [pseud.], and Earl Herbert Cressy. *Daughter of Confucius* (New York: Farrar, Straus, 1952). **Secondary Texts**: Ammons, Elizabeth, and Annette White-Parks, eds. *Tricksterism in Turn-of-the-Century American Literature: A Multicultural Perspective* (Hanover, NH: University Press of New England, 1994); Boelhower, William. "The Making of Ethnic Autobiography in the United States." In *American Autobiography: Retrospect and Prospect*, edited by Paul John Eakin, 123–141 (Madison: University of Wisconsin Press, 1991); Cheung, King-Kok. "The Woman Warrior versus the Chinaman Pacific: Must a Chinese American Critic Choose between Feminism and Heroism?" In *Conflicts in Feminism*, edited by Marianne Hirsch and Evelyn Fox Keller, 234–251 (New York: Routledge, 1990); Chin, Frank. "This Is Not an Autobiography." *Genre* 18, no. 2 (1985): 109–130; Eakin, Paul John, ed. *American Autobiography: Retrospect and Prospect* (Madison: University of Wisconsin Press, 1991); Ferens, Dominika. *Edith and Winnifred Eaton: Chinatown Missions and Japanese Romances* (Urbana: University of Illinois Press, 2002); Huang, Guiyou, ed. *Asian American Autobiographers: A Bio-Bibliographical Critical Sourcebook* (Westport, CT: Greenwood Press, 2001); Kim, Elaine H. *Asian American Literature: An Introduction to the Writings and Their Social Context* (Philadelphia: Temple University Press, 1982); Kim, Elaine H. "Asian American Literature." In *Columbia Literary History of the United States*, edited by Emory Elliott, 811–821 (New York: Columbia University Press, 1988); Koshy, Susan. "Mother-Country and Fatherland: Re-Membering the Nation in Sara Suleri's *Meatless Days*." In *Interventions: Feminist Dialogues on Third World Women's Literature and Film*, edited by Bishnupriya Ghosh and Brinda Bose, 45–61 (New York: Garland, 1997); Ling, Amy. *Between Worlds: Women Writers of Chinese Ancestry* (New York: Pergamon Press, 1990); Ling, Amy. "Revelation and Mask: Autobiographies of the Eaton Sisters." *Auto/Biography Studies* 3, no. 2 (1987): 46–52; Ling, Amy. "Creating One's Self: The Eaton Sisters." In *Reading the Literatures of Asian America*, edited by Shirley Geok-lin Lim and Amy Ling, 305–318 (Philadelphia: Temple University Press, 1992); Schweik, Susan. "The 'Pre-Poetics' of Internment: The Example of Toyo Suyemoto." *American Literary History* 1, no. 1 (1989): 89–108; Sue, Karen. "Jade Snow Wong's Badge of Distinction in the 1990s." *Hitting Critical Mass: A Journal of Asian American Cultural Criticism* 2 (1994): 3–52; Sumida, Stephen H. "Protest and Accommodation, Self-Satire and Self-Effacement, and Monica Sone's *Nisei Daughter*." In Multicultural Autobiography: American Lives, edited by James Robert Payne, 207–243 (Knoxville: University of Tennessee Press, 1992); Sumida, Stephen H. "Postcolonialism, Nationalism, and the Emergence of Asian/Pacific American Literatures." In *Interethnic Companion*, 274–288; Wong, Sau-ling Cynthia. "Immigrant Autobiography: Some Questions of Definition and Approach." Eakin, 142–170; Wong, Sau-ling Cynthia. "Autobiography as Guided Chinatown Tour?" In Maxine Hong Kingston's *The Woman Warrior* and the Chinese-American Autobiographical Controversy. Payne, 248–279; Yamamoto, Traise. *Masking Selves, Making Subjects: Japanese American Women, Identity and the Body* (Berkeley: University of California Press, 1999).

Susan Koshy

AUSTRALIAN WOMEN'S AUTOBIOGRAPHY Any consideration of Australian women's life writing should take into account the British Empire's incursion (from 1788) into lands already occupied by indigenous peoples and the effect that the dynamic of colonization has on the self-representation of both the settlers and those who have been displaced by imperial imperatives. Women's sense of self and their place in the world is influenced by social constructions of **gender** within their society, the demands of family, community and employment, and the constant negotiations their individual situations require for survival.

Nonindigenous Australians have long been concerned with national **identity** and how to establish a sense of identity that is separate from and yet connected to its European beginnings. Also of importance is what it means to be part of a country that is home to a diverse population of Aboriginal peoples who have occupied the land for thousands of years as well as immigrants of substantial cultural diversity. People have come to Australia in varying circumstances for the past two centuries, initially as convicts and free settlers of the British Empire, and more recently as refugees from war-torn homelands, or migrants seeking a new life for their families in a place frequently advertised in utopian terms. The greatest influx of immigrants occurred following World War II, when new arrivals came predominantly from Italy, Greece, and Central Europe. More recently new immigrants are from Asia, primarily China, Korea, and Vietnam. Australia is now perceived as a multicultural nation, with communities representative of many different cultures.

Autobiography in the Early Letters Home and Memoirs

The earliest evidence of Australian women's autobiographical writing is in **letters** sent from the newly established British colonies in the eighteenth and early nineteenth centuries. Many letters were written in serial form due to the vagaries of an unreliable postal system in the early years of settlement. Women relied on passengers or sailors to transport their letters back home by ship and there was no guarantee of safe arrival or a speedy answer by return mail. Letters, diaries, journals and memoirs penned by women who were estranged from family and friends in distant England demonstrate their sense of alienation in a strange and often hostile land. They reveal hardships endured, descriptions of new flora and fauna, activities of both immigrant and indigenous peoples, and details of lives being lived in a wide range of circumstances.

The autobiographical writing of Australian settler women reflects the complexities inherent in the experience of migration and life in a new **space**—partings, crossings, nostalgia for what was lost and adjustment to extreme difference. For the early Australian settler women there was rarely any prospect of return to the homelands they left behind. They came from diverse backgrounds and cultural bases, bringing with them the entrenched attitudes and behaviors of their particular location, **class**, ethnicity, and gender. The experiences they write vary, depending on their circumstances and the ways in which each woman responded to the challenges of unfamiliar landscapes and situations and the way in which each chose to represent herself in narrative form.

Dale Spender (1988) points out that many of the letters written by settler women were in serial form and that a distinctive Australian women's literary tradition can be traced back to this early letter writing, one that demonstrates common concerns such as exile and transformation. These characteristics continue to be evident in a range of women's writing across the past two centuries of European occupation in Australia.

Some significant works from early Australian settlement include a rare self-representation (through her letter writing) of a convict woman's experience from penal servitude to colonial citizenship: Margaret Catchpole (1762–1819) was a convict woman who was transported to the penal colony of New South Wales for stealing a horse. Elizabeth Macarthur (1769–1850), the educated wife of John Macarthur, the prosperous owner of Elizabeth Farm at Paramatta in New South Wales, documented her twelve years of farm and domestic management in her husband's absence; Louisa Anne Meredith (1812–1895), a writer and artist, chronicled the flora, fauna, and society of the colony in New South Wales and Tasmania; Rachel Henning (1826–1914), a Victorian gentlewoman wrote of life in the new country in letters to her family in England, cataloguing pioneer life in a lively, daily anecdotal account of the adventures that befell her, as well as her brother, Biddulph, and sisters, Amy and Annie. Her narrative ended with Rachel's marriage to a Mr. Taylor. Others were Georgiana McCrae (1804–1890), daughter of an aristocrat, an artist whose exquisitely illustrated diaries listed the activities of her family and acquaintances and served to allay some of her frustration with being unable to realize her artistic creativity amidst the demands of family life; Ellen Clacy (1830–?), who wrote a descriptive and colorful account of her experience traveling to Australia with her brother in 1852, led an adventurous life walking unaccompanied in the streets of Melbourne, and living with her husband amidst the Victorian goldfields; and Catherine Helen Spence (1825–1910), esteemed South Australian social reformer, teacher, writer, and lay Unitarian preacher, who wrote of her migration to Adelaide at age fourteen, when the South Australian colony was only three years old and detailed her enormous contribution to the new society during those years of early settlement.

Joy Hooton (1990) suggests that though these kinds of autobiographical texts are frequently utilized to reflect on Australian social history, many critics remain ignorant of other significant narratives such as Jane Watt's *Memories of Early Days in South Australia* (1882), a fine memoir of early pioneering penned in response to personal grief; Agnes Gosse Hay's *After-Glow Memories* (1905), a memoir of family; and Sarah Conigrave's *My Reminiscences of Early Days* (1914), which outlines her childhood during early settlement on Hindmarsh Island in South Australia in the mid-nineteenth century. Hooton's text is a tremendous contribution to scholarship in the area of Australian women's autobiography at a time when research continues to be compromised by lack of bibliographic guides and finding aids in Australian libraries and archives. Exclusion of women from serious consideration in historical narratives and from the literary canon in Australia has resulted in substantial gaps in knowledge of women's activities and contributions to the nation, as well as the opportunity to assess their self-representation through autobiographical writing. Since the 1970s much work has been done to retrieve evidence of Australian women's stories, revealing a wealth of material that is gradually being made more accessible to the public.

The Purposes of Documentation of Women's Lives in Australia

It is necessary to read women's writing in relation to the means of expression available to them and the cultural frameworks of their particular times. Social, religious, and class conventions have contributed to prescribed standards of feminine behaviors, which often prevented women from articulating their experiences directly. Much of the published autobiographical writing of women in the first centuries of Australian settlement follows Western conventions of self-representation that were prevalent at the time of writing. Such conventions favored documentation of men's activities—administration, scientific endeavor, exploration, adventure, politics, commerce, and contribution to the processes of British imperial expansion. The privileging of masculine endeavors, to the exclusion of serious consideration of women's endeavors throughout Australia's history, has impacted considerably on the ways in which women have been able to represent their lives in narrative form.

Gillian Whitlock (2001) asserts that "it is in autobiographic writing that [the] discourses which structured domestic subjects are taken up, rehearsed and reformulated in terms of the individual life; it is a location where gendered, racial identities are embodied, resisted, articulated" (*The Intimate Empire* 57).

Sanitizing the content of women's writing according to the conventions of social acceptability (as well as a certain sentimentality that infused all of nineteenth- and early-twentieth-century writing) is evident in a great deal of the content of diaries, journals, memoirs and letters. Women have always written within specific societal constraints, operating within a gendered division of labor and usually within the institutionalized subordination of women to men. Female roles have been strongly dictated and in many cases rigidly enforced. Women's lives have been fragmented, conflicting demands have been made on their time and energies, and their creative endeavors have been trivialized. Women were (and still are) complicit in the imposition of social constraints on the activities and efforts of their gender in Western societies. Women stood in judgment of other women's behaviors and were instrumental in quelling aberrant conduct within their networks of family and community. Such tensions are evident in women's writing, whether their works were intended for private or public consumption.

For many women, self-representation through autobiographical writing provided a literary outlet that allowed them freedom to be writers, readers, and subjects, while appearing to comply with acceptable forms of gendered behavior. In the hypermasculine culture of Australia, autobiographical writing, within the socially acceptable forms of letters, diaries, journals, and travel memoirs, provided an outlet for women to express their individual life experiences in a manner that usually conformed to perceived ideals of appropriate female behavior.

In many of these representations, particularly those earlier works that were published at the time of their creation, un-pleasant experiences, graphic details of hardships endured, or descriptions of negative responses by the subject to perceived or real horrors rarely receive direct attention. Such writing, for the most part, has been constructed by middle-class women who had the advantage of an education. There is little published representation from working-class or uneducated women, except through secondary consideration by others who were literate and had time and resources available to them to put pen to paper. Personal accounts of the grinding realities of domestic life, birthing, incivility, barbarity, and all the harshness that was frequently experienced by many women living in often primitive conditions are for the most part absent from such writing, or glossed over with minimal information provided. This self-censorship may have been in part a strategy to protect relatives and friends from undue anxiety, but it was also the result of general compliance with notions of propriety prevalent at the time.

Across the range of available autobiography, however, individual **voice** and style are evident in the material. The treatment of a diversity of women's experiences and responses to their environments reveals the personalities of the authors and a wide variety of representation of their circumstances. More recently, retrieved autobiographical works that have been made available through publication of excerpts from letters and **diary** entries at times demonstrate a less self-censored representation of settler women's life experiences. Lucy Frost's text, *No Place for a Nervous Lady* (1984), for example, contains personal accounts of several mid-to-late-nineteenth-century women such as Anna Cook, who reveals her delight in emigration to Queensland with her large family on the *Scottish Hero* in 1883, detailing life aboard ship and its similarity to English village life. Sarah Davenport, in contrast, documents the series of mishaps, tragedies, and hardships that were her experience of emigration to New South Wales and Victoria, providing a more graphic description of her vulnerability in the face of the violence of colonial life in 1843, as well as the toughness and resourcefulness required of her to survive. Penelope Selby details the disappointments she endured in Victoria following her great expectation that her family would make their fortune in the colony. Hard work did not enable the Selby family to succeed in Australia and only her strong Protestant faith kept her resilient in the face of incessant personal defeats that included the birth of seven stillborn infants.

The writing of women in early Australian settlement times was received with interest by those in the "Mother" country, both for its presumed exoticism and as a connection with loved ones and community members who had disappeared to an unknown and little understood **space**. Autobiographical writing served differing purposes for the authors. Such life writing was often utilized as a way of managing loneliness, homesickness, and extreme isolation from all that was known and familiar; as a form of conversation and connection with loved ones; as a means of placing the self as central to the new environment being experienced; as a methodical means of ordering one's life; as a way of preventing mental unraveling; as an educative narrative for those who did not directly share the experience; or as a way of bringing oneself into being, a literary construction of self that could be viewed from the vantage point of observer as well as participant.

Some of the many examples of life writing—letters, diaries, journals, and memoirs—evident in early Australian colonial history were published, more were not, and are still to be found buried in attics and archives. Retrieval and publication of the documentation of women's experiences since settlement of Australia by the British in 1788 continues into the twenty-first century, evidenced by texts such as Lucy Frost's *A Face in the Glass: The Journal of Annie Baxter Dawbin, 1858–1868* (1992), a publication drawn from thirty-two notebooks of the subject's life in Tasmania, New

England, and Victoria. In *Wildweeds and Windflowers: The Life and Letters of Katharine Susannah Prichard* (1975) Ric Throssell attempts to flesh out the character of the subject further than did Prichard's autobiography, *Child of the Hurricane* (1963), in which she writes of her childhood in Tasmania, presenting her experience indirectly in relational form. Prichard was an intensely private woman who burned most of her personal papers before her death and did not wish to have her life, as a celebrated author, playwright, and a foundation member of the Communist Party of Australia, open to public scrutiny. Issues of privacy continue to be of concern to scholars of women's autobiographical works. Publication of previously unpublished manuscripts requires editors to take into account the nature of private diaries, journals, and memoirs that were often not intended for an audience by their authors, to be sensitive to the wishes of the author.

Many female autobiographers write with a strong sense of **place**, but most focus on family and community life. It is particularly evident in colonial writing that women's lives and self-representation are relational. That is, they write themselves in relation to significant others: parents, partners, offspring, community members, or their God. Great historical or public events, the focus of masculine autobiography and men's relation to nation building, appears to be in the background in much of Australian women's writing. The vast majority of women do not seem to view their lives in a direct connection to large-scale world or national histories. Their focus is more frequently on the ways that people interact with one another and the land itself, so the subject matter is more concerned with the ways in which lives are lived, rather than with the depiction of the self as an individual who is representative of the process of nation building, politics, or history making. There are, of course, exceptions. Women with a strong social conscience who were politically active, such as Catherine Helen

Spence, wrote of her contribution to reform that was directly related to the political, economic, and social conditions of South Australian colonization. Several other writers were also politically active, writing about their experiences of association with various political organizations and social reform endeavors. As **Drusilla Modjeska** points out in her text, *Exiles at Home: Australian Women Writers 1925–1945* (1981), the impact on international politics of the rise of Fascism, the world wars and the Great Depression, as well as an emerging consciousness of an Australian literary cultural heritage, are reflected in the writing of several literary women of this period, some examples of which are the personal and public works of Katherine Susanna Prichard (1883–1969), Kylie Tennant (1912–1988), Eleanor Dark (1901–1985), Dymphna Cusack (1902–1981), Christina Stead (1902–1983), Henry Handel Richardson (1870–1946), Marjorie Barnard (1897–1987), Flora Eldershaw (1897–1956), and Dorothy Hewett (1923–2002). Evidence of the sense of community and shared ideals of some of these renowned authors may be read in the letters of support they wrote to one another, samples of which are found in Marilla North's work, *Yarn Spinners: A Story in Letters: Dymphna Cusack, Florence James, Miles Franklin* (2001). Franklin, Richardson, and Stead became expatriates, appearing to need to leave Australia in order to realize their identities as writers. In much of the literature that these writers produced, themes of departure and the journey, home, origin, and exile are a strong feature.

Susan Sheridan, in *Along the Faultlines* (1995), examines women's writing in Australia "from the end of the nineteenth century into the 1930s" and insists that, "Since at least the 1840s, women have been a significant presence in the white Australian cultural scene; they were never the silenced outsiders that later historians and critics rendered them" (viii). She asserts that women worked within and against conventions and patriarchal constraints, negotiating their lives, creativity, and self-representations as their circumstances dictated, making the most of the materials available to them and contributing a great deal to the social, historical, and literary realms of their nation.

Many of the published autobiographies of Australian women from the nineteenth century onward are of subjects who were prominent people deemed interesting to a general reading public: successful writers, actors, musicians, and artists, women associated with social or political reform, wives or daughters of esteemed men and those rare women who excelled in sports or activities dominated by men. Significant among such autobiographies are texts such as *My Australian Girlhood* (1902) by Rosa Praed (1851–1935), a successful writer and spiritualist who wrote of her childhood in rural Queensland, where her father was a squatter in the contact zone of the mid-nineteenth century, at the headwaters of the Logan River. Her family was actively involved in the conflict between the European settlers and the local indigenous people, in particular the Yiman tribe. Rosa Praed's interaction with the Aboriginal people provided material for her writing and was to have a significant impact on her emerging interest in spirituality, a strong focus during her adult expatriate years in England.

Judith Wright, reared by her wealthy pastoral family on a substantial property near Armidale in New South Wales, is one of Australia's most highly regarded poets. Wright is noted for her awareness of the plight of indigenous peoples and their culture and the imperative of taking responsibility for care of the living world and the land. Her autobiography, *Half a Lifetime* (1999), reveals her as a woman with a strong social conscience and a committed environmentalist who took a great interest in the historical constructions and politics of her country.

Dame Mary Gilmore (1864–1962), another esteemed poet, penned *Old Days, Old Ways:*

A Book of Recollections (1934), which outlines her life in rural New South Wales as a schoolteacher and her participation in the Labor Movement of the 1890s. *Childhood at Brindabella* (1963), a memoir by Miles Franklin (1879–1954), likens the author's formative years on the family farm to living in a mythical Eden, mirroring the treatment of her central character's (Sybella Melvyn) life experience in the controversial novel, *My Brilliant Career* (1901). Franklin was bewildered by the response of family and friends to her first novel. They saw the work as autobiographical with unflattering parallels to known personalities, so Franklin withdrew it from sale in 1910. Stella Bowen's (1895–1947) autobiography, *Drawn from Life* (1941), details life with her partner, the novelist Ford Madox Ford, and her attempt to negotiate her artistic endeavors alongside Ford's needs and a demanding domestic life. Lady Joan Lindsay (1896–1984), author of *Picnic at Hanging Rock*, was married to Daryl Lindsay (brother of the revered artist, Norman Lindsay) and recounted her connection with the entertaining Lindsay clan in *Time without Clocks* (1962).

Ada Cambridge's *Thirty Years in Australia* (1903), Jessie Couvreur's (Tasma) *Not Counting the Cost* (1895), Dymphna Cusack's *A Window in the Dark* (1991), Dulcie Deamer's *Queen of Bohemia: The Autobiography of Dulcie Deamer* (1998), and Jean Devanny's *Point of Departure* (1986), demonstrate in various ways the life experiences of creative women grappling with the demands made on their time by family and community as they forged careers for themselves in the arts. Most of these women were politically active, and their writing reflects ideological concerns and a desire for substantial social change. For example, Kylie Tennant published *The Missing Heir* in 1986, in which she is highly critical of her dominating father, "the Parent," and declares her strong objection to the valorization of war.

Oriel Gray's (1920–) memoir, *Exit Left: Memoirs of a Scarlet Woman* (1985), was con-

structed in four acts, and details the author's progression toward life as a "free spirit." Dorothy Hewett, a highly acclaimed poet and playwright (and once an active member of the Communist Party), wrote *Wild Card: An Autobiography 1923–1958* (1990), in which she outlines the physical and emotional hardships she endured with a difficult partner and three children she reared virtually single-handedly. At her death in 2002, the second volume of her autobiography remained incomplete. Barbara Hanrahan (1939–1991), writer and artist, wrote *The Scent of Eucalyptus* (1989), an exquisitely lyrical memoir of her childhood in Adelaide, while the author was living with her mother, grandmother, and a great-aunt who had Down Syndrome. **Jill Ker Conway**'s (1934–) autobiography, *The Road from Coorain* (1989), outlines the author's harsh life as a child obliged to take on a taxing workload on the family farm in far western New South Wales, during many years of drought and extreme hardship. Conway also documents her education in Sydney and eventual decision to pursue an academic life in the United States. She is critical of the situation she finds in Australia, where intelligence in a woman is generally viewed as a social handicap. As an intellectual woman, Conway writes a compelling historical overview of Australian rural life in her memoir. Beverley Farmer's *Body of Water: A Writer's Journal* (1990) is composed of fragments of literary efforts, poetry, personal experiences, observations, and thoughts across a year of her life. Farmer reveals her inner life through exposure of her literary concerns, demonstrating some of the different options available to contemporary women through autobiographical writing.

Modern Literary Construction and Understanding and Autobiographical Writing

The latter part of the twentieth century and early twenty-first century have been marked by changes in the way that literature is constructed, received, and perceived. Due to the influence of contemporary literary theory (in particular, postmodern, poststructural, postcolonial, and feminist criticism), there has been an increase in deconstruction of literary texts to expose the cultural practices and underlying ideologies that affect their creation and production. Such changes in reading and critical practice challenge the veracity of both historical and literary texts by revealing them to be written constructions from a specific cultural location, profoundly influenced by the authorial position, time, and place of their writing.

In response to changes in reader reception, literary works are emerging more frequently in which authors self-consciously draw attention to their writing practice, further encouraging readers to question those stories that appear seamless and truthful. This is particularly evident in autobiographical writing that conventionally relies on a pact (between author and reader) that the content will be a true accounting of a life lived. The supposition that autobiography is based on truth allows that much of what is written may not be the truth. As there are many different perspectives available on any given event, it may be virtually impossible to uncover a single truth. Some facts may be verifiable, many are merely speculative, and some are certainly fabricated or distorted. Choices made by the author regarding inclusion or exclusion of information and the unreliability of **memory** ensure that certain aspects of a life may be misrepresented.

Traditionally, autobiographical writing has been presumed to be the written account of an individual life, a testimonial of remembered experience by an author claiming the authorial "I" and constructing a text containing the facts of his/her own life. Therefore, the gender of the writer and the subject of the text are of substantial importance in the writing and reception of autobiographical and biographical works. As **Bella Brodzki** and **Celeste Schenck** sug-

gest, "The very authority of masculine autobiography derives from the assumption held by both the author and reader that the life being written and read is an exemplary one" (*Lifelines* 1998, 2–3). If a judgment is made about whether a subject is worthy of public scrutiny, it appears that such judgment favors male subjects. Men are more likely to have been involved in public activities than women, who, in the past, have more frequently been required to function in domestic spaces and have been actively excluded from the public domain. Therefore, women who have written autobiographical works for public consumption have been required to presume a sense of self-importance that may have run counter to their indoctrination as female subjects in a patriarchal society. The tension between what women wish to express through literary self-representation and societal expectations of public female representation is reflected in many of their autobiographical works.

Questions about the veracity of autobiographical and biographical narratives have prompted several contemporary writers to adopt strategies that expose their writing practices in a self-conscious manner in order to demonstrate the difficulties inherent in constructing true life stories and to privilege the different types of responses that are utilized in the critical literary environment of our times.

Drusilla Modjeska's three texts, *Poppy* (1990), *The Orchard* (1994) and *Stravinsky's Lunch* (1999) are concerned with the production of truth about people's lived experience. In different ways, all three interrogate the way life stories are constructed. In particular, Modjeska is concerned with women's lives and the ways in which they have negotiated their creativity within the constraints imposed on women within patriarchal societies. *Poppy*, arguably her most celebrated work, demonstrates Modjeska's attempt to write her mother's life story, an ambition complicated by the author's discovery that she cannot comprehend her mother's life without first considering her own life in relation to her mother. The text that begins as a biographical work thus becomes autobiographical. Further, when it is clearly impossible to establish the truth of her mother's life story, Modjeska fictionalizes the text. Throughout *Poppy*, the author draws attention to her narrative construction, to the choices she makes in her writing and her reasons for making them. The book becomes a generic blending of fiction, autobiography, **biography**, and a consideration of contemporary literary theory. Modjeska maintains a certain discomfort about *Poppy*, stating that, "Too much of it came from my life to call it fiction, and too much of it was invented to call it biography. As neither term seemed right, I opted for both. . . . But if I'm honest, it was a compromise I'm still not easy with. . . . And I don't mean I'm uneasy with the blend, the bend, between fiction and not. What I don't like is the polarity of true or untrue as if there were just one register of truth" (*Timepieces* 2002, 67–68).

Modjeska's concern with the difficulties of truthful representation of women's life experience is echoed by Joy Hooton, who draws attention to a subversive trend by Australian women writers to write their experience indirectly through fictional works rather than directly in autobiography. Her investigation of a wide range of women's published texts reveals a variety of strategies of self-representation, with fictionalized treatment of autobiography particularly evident in texts such as *My Brilliant Career* (Miles Franklin 1901), *The Getting of Wisdom* (Henry Handel Richardson 1910), *The Man Who Loved Children* (Christina Stead 1940), *We of the Never Never* (Aeneas Gunn 1987), or more recently, *Puberty Blues* (Gabrielle Carey and Kathy Lette 1979). There are many other examples of fictional works that appear to be strongly autobiographical in Australian women's literature.

Such interrogation of literature reveals a current ambivalence toward traditional literary conventions that appear to favor

Western men's writing endeavors and have in the past disadvantaged the reception of women's works or those of indigenous and marginalized peoples. However, autobiographical writing continues to gain popularity in contemporary Australia where there is a broad range of women's stories covering diverse topics that include testimony of illness or hardship, migration and relocation, exile, experience of war and natural disasters, success stories of public and private achievement, exposure of dark personal secrets, religious experience, and sporting or artistic prowess. As women's lives have moved into the public domain over the past fifty years, their autobiographies reflect a range of experience that is not limited to the domestic sphere but embraces all aspects of women's lives.

Indigenous Writers in Australia

The effects of colonialism are evident in all representations of self in colonized spaces. Since European settlement of Australia began in 1788, Aboriginal peoples have been dispossessed and oppressed. Their historical representations have been limited to Western interpretation and documented in relation to Western constructions of events. It should be noted that there were many Aboriginal nations and language groups present in Australia prior to European colonizations and it is therefore important to stress the multiplicity of their experiences, histories, and forms of self-expression.

Indigenous histories are remembered within Aboriginal communities and passed on through a tradition of oral storytelling, but literary articulation through the writing of their own versions of history has been a fairly recent occurrence. The transmission of stories is a social act. Oral transmission of narratives evokes a familiarity and intimacy between speaker and audience that allows the transfer of knowledge and experience to the audience in a very direct manner. Written storytelling by Aboriginal writers frequently maintains this sense of direct speech and is an important aspect of such writing. Indigenous writers may intend to address a mixed audience, inclusive of the indigenous community and the broader western community, or their intention may be to primarily address the indigenous community. Anne Brewster posits that indigenous narratives "frequently invoke the presence of a listener and reader. As performative acts, drawing upon a repertoire to meet the social requirements and conditions of the occasion, these texts are above all contingent and local" (*Literary Formations* 1995, 54). Further, Brewster suggests that "in the transition from orality to literature, story becomes history, at least in the sense that Aboriginal historians construct it; namely, a discourse that establishes continuities between past and present" (*Literary Formations* 54). For many indigenous writers, it is important to stress their resourcefulness and survival in the face of oppression and disadvantage, to preserve their cultural heritage for future generations, and to focus on central concerns of family, parenting, kinship, the land, politics, and movement toward autonomy and self-governance. Kateri Akiwenzie-Damm and Josie Douglas, editors of the indigenous anthology *Skins* (2000) point out that though early indigenous writing came from the necessity of activism and contemporary works evolved from this, many of the stories articulated in *Skins* "don't necessarily have a blatant message. What they do is open the reader up to an emotion, a feeling, an insight into Aboriginal culture, the subtleties of Aboriginal humour, irony and expression and our adaptation and usage of English alongside our own languages" (*Skins* ix).

There was a proliferation of indigenous writing from the 1980s, much of it autobiographical, most of it intensely political, emphasizing contentious topical issues of displacement and alienation, the stolen generation(s) (a process during which many children were removed from their families and placed in service or orphanages in an institutionalized attempt to "white out" their origins and assimilate indigenous peoples into the dominant culture, an official Australian government policy from the late nineteenth century until the 1970s), incarceration in prisons and deaths in custody, domestic violence, substance abuse, and past and ongoing oppression. There are stories, too, of personal achievement and public success. Many of the writers of these works are Aboriginal activists who attempt to draw attention to the plight of their peoples, to past wrongs perpetrated by their European usurpers, and to ongoing negative effects of the colonial process.

Indigenous women's autobiographical writing forms a substantial part of those emerging texts that serve to illuminate previously silenced perspectives on Aboriginal history in Australia and to provide counternarratives to those of the dominant Western culture. Texts such as Mum Shirl and Roberta Syke's *Mum Shirl* (1981), Elsie Roughsey's *An Aboriginal Mother Tells of the Old and the New* (1984), **Sally Morgan**'s *My Place* (1987), Ruby Langford Ginibi's *Don't Take Your Love to Town* (1988), Alice Nannup's *When the Pelican Laughed* (1992), Jackie and Rita Huggins *Auntie Rita* (1994), and Roberta Syke's three volume autobiography, *Snake Dreaming* (1997) give voice to Aboriginal women's experience and move some way toward establishing an empathy in their readers that may help facilitate reconciliation between the indigenous communities and immigrant cultural groups. These autobiographies and the many stories contained in anthologies of short fiction and poetry by indigenous women outline remarkable experiences of endurance and survival. *The Stolen Children: Excerpts from Their Stories* (1998), edited by Carmel Bird, is an important text that contains excerpts of autobiographical narratives taken from the Australian government's stolen generation(s) report. Prepared by the Human Rights Commission, "Bringing Them Home" (1997) deals with material gathered during the national inquiry into the separation of Aboriginal and Torres Strait Islander children from their families, documenting "the terrible grief and loss" (*The Stolen Children* 2) incurred by the indigenous peoples who lost their parents, culture, and connection to home and relationships, as well as the opportunity to learn parenting skills with which to rear their own children. Texts such as Carmel Bird's bring to broader public attention actions that in the past have been hidden, and it is hoped that the acknowledgment of past wrongs may allow indigenous peoples to begin the long process of healing.

Drawing on an oral tradition of storytelling, Aboriginal autobiographical writing varies in style and tone from conventional Western autobiography, as writers utilize a range of narrative strategies, such as multiple authors and voices, a strong sense of immediacy when dealing with the past, the importance of kinship ties, and a focus on journeying toward traditional lands and activities. Much of this writing is marked by compassion and humor. Many indigenous women's texts blur the boundary between autobiography and biography in that they frequently include outlines of the lives of extended family members as well as that of the author. The treatment of family and community within a consideration of self reflects indigenous women's cultural practices and focus.

There are ongoing concerns with indigenous autobiography in regard to issues of authenticity and collaborative processes. Involvement of Western writers, researchers, and editors in the publication process continues to be questioned. In her text, *The Intimate Empire* (2001), Gillian Whitlock states that black women's autobiographical writing is emergent (146). "Publication has frequently required the services of the white amanuensis, editor, patron or collaborator. These autobiographies are hostages to publishers, the tastes of the reading public, and shifts in the political,

cultural and social life of the nation" (9). Such writing must be viewed within its specific local context in order that the reader may comprehend the complexity of its production and reception. Issues of the individual author's **subjectivity**, identity formation, and agency, as well as public reaction to indigenous women's attempts at self-representation, both within the indigenous communities and the broader reading public, continue to impact on the ways in which autobiographical writing from oppressed peoples is constructed and received.

It is important to note that the issue of collaboration remains sensitive, given that self-representation of Aboriginal peoples may be adversely influenced by attempts to sanitize material in a palatable form for Western audiences and to appropriate indigenous stories for commercial gain or to feed a current western appetite for spiritual and mythical cultural material. Care must be taken not to continue to make indigenous authors into the Other by exerting western control over representation by nonindigenous collaborators and recognizing the extreme differences between dominant western and indigenous consciousnesses and perspectives. Aileen Moreton-Robinson, an esteemed academic and indigenous woman of the Koenpul people of Quandamooka in Queensland, states:

> An Indigenous woman's standpoint is informed by social worlds imbued with meaning grounded in knowledges of different realities from those of white women.... All Indigenous women share the common experience of living in a society that deprecates us. An Indigenous woman's standpoint is shaped by the following themes. They include sharing an inalienable connection to land; a legacy of dispossession, racism and sexism; resisting and replacing disparaging images of ourselves with self-defined images; continuing our activism as mothers, sisters,

aunts, daughters, grandmothers and community leaders, as well as negotiating sexual politics across and within cultures (Collins 1991). Such standpoint does not deny the diversity of Indigenous women's experiences. Indigenous women will have different concrete experiences that shape our relations to core themes. (*Talkin' Up to the White Woman* 2000, xvi)

Moreton-Robinson draws attention to the inadvertent racialization of indigenous peoples by those who, with the best of intentions, attempt to assist Aboriginal writers to articulate their experience through publication of autobiographical works. She stresses that some differences are incommensurate. Thus, there is a need to examine individual positions and motivations during the process of collaboration between indigenous writers and white editors and publishers so that inequitable power relations are made transparent and addressed, in order to resist further colonization of indigenous people's cultures and creative endeavors.

Autobiographical Work by Women from Nonpredominant Cultures

Inclusion of writings by women from different cultural, ethnic, and racial groups is also essential to any consideration of Australian literature. Initially, the colonizing settler groups in Australia were predominantly from England and Ireland, and the dominant culture of Australia remains Anglo-Celtic, with English the dominant language. Literature produced by writers from non-Anglo-Celtic backgrounds has been termed migrant, ethnic minority, or multicultural writing. None of these terms adequately represent the diversity of the writing that is emerging from authors whose backgrounds and cultural affiliations place them outside mainstream Anglo-Celtic literature in Australia. It is essential to situate each work within the cultural, social, historical, and gendered site of

its creation and production in order to accept their differences and the significance of such works to an Australian literary heritage.

In her work, *Framing Marginality* (1994), Sneja Gunew draws attention to the difficulties inherent in qualifying literatures from non-Anglo-Celtic Australian writers. She states that "the term migrant . . . conjures up subjects whose presence in the dominant culture is merely temporary, and whose orientation is towards a past nostalgically conceived of as a lost motherland and lost mother tongue" (7). This does not allow for situation of the writing of a range of women who may be second, third, or fourth generation offspring of migrant settlers or for the differences that exist between those who speak English as their first language and those whose primary language is not English, or for any writer who does not share the presumed common history, language, and culture of the dominant Anglo-Celtic population. Many writers who are categorized as "migrant" have stated that they wish their work to be considered Australian, not merely an example of marginalized migrant writing. Gunew's project is to insert the writings of non-Anglo-Celtic women "into the mushrooming domain of women's writing" where it may be "considered as part of literature rather than sociology" (9). Toward this end Gunew has been involved in a process of compiling anthologies of the writing of ethnic minority women and a bibliography of multicultural writers in Australia, fostering ongoing debate regarding dissemination of such works and their place in the national literature and equitable recognition, through the application of awards and funding grants, while drawing attention to the necessity for their inclusion on reading lists in educational institutions.

Because of Australia's cultural diversity, various governments have attempted to assimilate migrant or refugee populations into the dominant Anglo-Celtic Australian cultural base. This process has involved various strategies, depending on the incoming migrant groups, at specific points in history. The White Australia Policy, which was aimed at limiting immigration to Western peoples, was dropped in 1965. The Racial Discrimination Act was introduced in 1975, and since 1978, there have been a range of multicultural policy statements. Anne Brewster argues that multicultural policy has been instituted in order to "manage a racially segmented workforce, and to sustain social order and productivity" (Brewster 1995, 42). Government policy has had a profound impact on public opinion and on who is able to speak, write, and be published, and who is included and who is not. Sneja Gunew (1994) provides an overview of many different theoretical positions on the production and reception of literatures from a range of ethnic minority writers in Australia and points out that, "Minority discourse is . . . not simply an oppositional or counter-discourse: it also undoes the power of dominant discourses to represent themselves as universal" (Gunew, *Framing Marginality*, 42).

Much of the writing of women of ethnic and cultural diversity in Australia is autobiographical. As with consideration of indigenous literatures, it is important to place each work within the context of its author's situation and location, in order to encourage a greater understanding of different subjectivities, experiences, and perceptions. For many writers from marginalized groups, their stories remain unspeakable until they have overcome barriers of language, literacy, and trauma and until a site becomes available that enables them to voice their stories. Many of the autobiographical works produced by ethnic minority groups are infused with a sense of dislocation, alienation, and loss. Frequently they deal with the memory of homeland, melancholy, and mourning for what has been lost, and revisit traumatic experiences

of migration and relocation to an unfamiliar and often hostile space. There is often, too, a sense of hope for a better future in new spaces.

Significant among such works are Rosa Cappiello's *Paese Fortunato* (published in Italian in 1981) (*Oh Lucky Country* 1984), a rollicking parodic account of the impressions of this Italian/Australian migrant woman to her adopted country; Lolo Houbein's *Wrong Face in the Mirror: An Autobiography of Race and Identity* (1990), the personal account of a Dutch immigrant in Asia, Papua, and Australia, where she settled in 1958 at age twenty-four; Malaysian/Australian Beth Yahp's *Family Pictures* (1994), an anthology of eleven stories about family and relationships; Gillian Bouras' *Aphrodite and the Others* (1994), which reveals the relationship between the author and her Greek mother-in-law when she visits her Peloponnese village, and *Starting Again: In Search of a Home* (1999), which details the author's experience of family life and her sense of alienation in England, Greece, and Australia, where she was born and reared; Italian/Australian Anna Maria Dell'Oso's *Songs of the Suitcase* (1998), a blend of autobiography and fiction consisting of six stories and a novella, a first-person account of family anecdotes, generational conflict, and life experience; Chinese/Australian Adeline Yen Mah's *Falling Leaves* (1997), an autobiography of a childhood of emotional abuse, and, in spite of extreme disadvantage, her achievement as an anaesthesiologist, and *Watching the Tree* (2000), a combination of personal disclosure and Chinese wisdom and belief systems.

Autobiography is extremely popular in contemporary Australia, and women's writing forms a large portion of works currently published. The self-representations of Australian women, in all their diversity, reflect an ongoing concern with issues of identity (individual, national, ethnic, racial), family and community, relationships, agency, histories that continue to inspire debate, the impact of national and global politics on personal lives, and hopes for a future of unity, peace, and security.

Further Reading: Akiwenzie-Damm, Kateri, and Josie Douglas, eds. *Skins: Contemporary Indigenous Writing* (Alice Springs, NT: Jukurrpa Books, 2000); Bird, Carmel, ed. *The Stolen Children: Excerpts from Their Stories* (Milsons Point, New South Wales: Random House, 1998); Bowen, Stella. *Drawn from Life* (London: Collins, 1941; Virago, 1984); Brewster, Anne, Angeline O'Neill, and Rosemary Van Den Berg, eds. *Those Who Remain Will Always Remember: An Anthology of Aboriginal Writing* (Fremantle, WA: Fremantle Arts Centre Press, 2000); Brewster, Anne. *Reading Aboriginal Women's Autobiography* (Sydney: Sydney University Press, 1996); Brodzki, Bella, and Celeste Schenck. *Lifelines: Theorizing Women's Autobiography* (Ithaca, NY, and London: Cornell University Press, 1988); Clarke, Patricia, and Dale Spender, eds. *Life Lines: Australian Women's Letters and Diaries 1788–1840* (Sydney: Allen and Unwin, 1992); Collins, Patricia Hill. *Black Feminist Thought: Knowledge, Consciousness, and the Politics of Empowerment* (New York: Routledge, 1991); Colmer, John, and Dorothy Colmer, eds. *The Penguin Book of Australian Autobiography* (Victoria: Penguin, 1987); Conway, Jill Ker. *The Road from Coorain* (London: William Heinemann Ltd., 1989); Conway, Jill Ker. *When Memory Speaks* (New York: Knopf, 1998); Ferrier, Carole, ed. *As Good as a Yarn with You: Letters between Miles Franklin, Katherine Susannah Prichard, Jean Devanny, Marjorie Barnard, Flora Eldershaw, Eleanor Dark* (New York: Cambridge University Press, 1992); Franklin, Miles. *My Brilliant Career* (Edinburgh and London: William Blackwood and Sons, 1901); Franklin, Miles. *My Career Goes Bung* (Melbourne: Georgian House, 1946); Franklin, Miles. *Childhood at Brindabella* (Sydney: Angus and Robertson, 1963); Frost, Lucy. *No Place for a Nervous Lady* (Victoria: McPhee Gribble, 1984); Frost, Lucy. *A Face in the Glass: The Journal and life of Annie Baxter Dawbin, 1858–1868* (Melbourne: William Heinemann, 1992); Gilmore, Mary. *Old Days, Old Ways: A Book of Recollections* (Sydney: Angus and Robertson, 1934); Grossman, Michele, ed. *Blacklines: Contemporary Critical Writing by Indigenous Australians* (Melbourne: Melbourne University Press, 2003); Gunew, Sneja, and Jan Mahyuddin. *Beyond the Echo: Multicultural Women's Writing* (St. Lucia, Queensland: University of Queensland Press, 1988); Gunew, Sneja. *Framing Marginality: Multicultural Literary Studies* (Melbourne: Melbourne University Press, 1994); Hewett, Dorothy. *Wild Card: An Autobiography 1923–1958* (Victoria: Penguin, 1990); Houbein, Lolo. *Wrong Face in the Mirror: An Autobiography of Race and Identity* (St. Lucia, Queensland: University of Queensland Press, 1990); Houbein, Lolo. *Ethnic Writings in English from Australia: A Bibliography by Lolo Houbein* (Adelaide: University of Adelaide, 1984); Holmes, Katie. *Spaces in Her Day: Australian Women's Diaries of the 1920s and 1930s* (St. Leonards, NSW, Australia: Allen and Unwin, 1995); Hooton, Joy. *Stories of Herself When Young: Autobiographies of Childhood by Australian Women* (Melbourne: Oxford University Press, 1990); Modjeska, Drusilla. *Exiles at Home: Australian Women Writers 1925–1945* (Sidney, NSW, Australia: Angus and Robertson, 1981); Modjeska, Drusilla. *The Orchard* (Sydney, NSW, Pan MacMillan, 1994); Modjeska, Drusilla. *Poppy* 1991. Reprint (Victoria, Australia: Penguin, 1996); Modjeska, Drusilla. *Stravinsky's Lunch* (Sidney, NSW, Australia: Picador Pan MacMillan, 1999); Moreton-Robinson, Aileen. *Talkin' Up to the White Woman: Indigenous Women and Feminism* (St. Lucia, Queensland: University of Queensland Press, 2000); Praed, Rosa. *My Australian Girlhood* (London: T. Fisher Unwin, 1902); Richardson, Henry Handel. *The End of Childhood and Other Stories* (London: Heinemann Ltd., 1934); Richardson, Henry Handel. *The Getting of Wisdom* (Melbourne: William Heinemann Ltd., 1910); Richardson, Henry Handel. *Myself When Young* (New York: W. W. Norton, 1948); Robinson, Portia. *The Hatch and Brood of Time: A Study of the First Generation of Native-Born White Australians 1788–1828.* Vol. 1 (Melbourne: Oxford University Press, 1985); Sheridan, Susan. *Along the Faultlines* (St. Leonards, NSW: Allen and Unwin, 1995); Smith, Sidonie, and Julia Watson, eds. *Women, Autobiography, Theory: A Reader* (Madison: University of Wisconsin Press, 1998); Spence, Catherine Helen. *Catherine Helen Spence:*

An Autobiography (Adelaide: W.K. Thomas, 1910); Spender, Dale, ed. *The Penguin Anthology of Australian Women's Writing* (Rihgwood, Vic. Australia: Penguin, 1988); Webby, Elizabeth, ed. *The Cambridge Companion to Australian Literature* (Cambridge: Cambridge University Press, 2000); Whitlock, Gillian, ed. *Autographs: Contemporary Australian Autobiography* (St Lucia, Queensland: University Queensland Press, 1996); Whitlock, Gillian, ed. *The Intimate Empire: Reading Women's Autobiography* (London: Cassell, 2001).

Brenda Glover

AUTOBIOGRAPHICAL FICTION Autobiographical fiction is a genre (or subgenre) in which an author fictionalizes portions of her life and presents it as a novel. In this type of writing, the life of the writer and narrator are so closely intertwined that, often, very little distinction can be made between the two. Although autobiographical fiction is not new, modern critical reception of this genre, especially by women authors, has created a new emphasis and area for academic study. Autobiographical fiction is often classified as a bildungsroman or coming-of-age novel—a classification that has contributed to its interest as an area for study. Another reason for the increase in autobiographical fiction writing and analysis of such is the acknowledgment by most critics of the fluid nature of **identity** and **subjectivity**. Recent practitioners of women's autobiographical fiction include **Dorothy Allison**, **Margaret Cavendish**, **Dorothy Day**, **Audre Lorde**, **Tillie Olsen**, **May Sarton**, and **Christa Wolf**, who are all included in these volumes.

Some autobiographical fiction is only thinly disguised, a very transparent reworking of the author's real life, such as *Bastard out of Carolina* by Dorothy Allison (1992), while other authors, such as Rebecca Wells who wrote *The Divine Secrets of the Ya-Ya Sisterhood* (1996) and *Little Altars Everywhere* (1992) deny any strong connection to their own lives, regardless of evidence to the contrary. Autobiographical fiction is often written as a means for a writer to create a **space** for her **voice** that has generally been marginalized and rendered powerless. The relationship between marginalized writers and autobiographical fiction is fairly clear when one considers the number of disempowered writers from non-Western cultures who write autobiographical fiction.

Researchers who attempt to determine a genealogy of autobiographical fiction can generally trace early examples to the time when the novel was emerging. Daniel Defoe's *Moll Flanders* (1722) is an often-cited example. Critics claim the subgenre began during this time as a way of making the novel more acceptable to skeptical readers. Autobiographical fiction reveals the problematic nature of autobiography, with some critics arguing that all autobiography is fiction in some respects. Since autobiography is a look back at a person's life, the writer inevitably interprets her life, but inherent in this is some recasting. Another contention is that faulty **memory** and biased interpretation will render problematic the facts on which an autobiography is based: settings must be remembered, dialogue must be re-created—hence, the fine line between autobiography and autobiographical fiction. What separates autobiographical fiction from autobiography is the author's more liberal and acknowledged use of fiction. For example, Dorothy Allison's protagonist, Bone, in *Bastard out of Carolina*, lives in the same area where Allison grewup, with many similar family members, and experiences some of the same events that Allison did; however, Bone escapes her abuser at a relatively early age, a fact that Allison is quick to point out did not happen to her until she left for college. In casting her life in fiction, Allison creates a fantasy world in which she escapes her abuses and creates power over her life and life story. Creating new directions is one of the primary appeals for writing autobiographical fiction.

A closely related type of writing is fictional autobiography. In fictional autobiography, the author adopts a persona in order to create an autobiography of someone who never existed or to reinterpret historical events. As previously mentioned, many critics cite Daniel Defoe's *Moll Flanders* as an example of fictional autobiography. Using fictional autobiography to portray alternative versions of history would include recent fictional portrayals of the Rosenbergs, who were executed for treason by the United States government. Fictional autobiography differs from autobiographical fiction in that it does not purport to be real at all, it just uses many of the characteristics of the genre. Because fictional autobiography shares these characteristics with autobiography and autobiographical fiction, researchers can analyze them for the function and effect of the autobiographical "I."

Researching autobiographical fiction as a separate and specialized genre is difficult because few critics focus on it as a specialized genre in and of itself. Most critics fix their attention on a particular author and then proceed to label the author's writing as autobiographical fiction, but the focus remains on the author, not the specialized genre. Much of this type of analysis has been on male authors, such as Daniel Defoe and Charles Dickens. Only recently, with the renewed interest in female *bildungsroman*, have scholars focused their critical energy on women authors who employ this type of writing. Other critics concentrate on autobiography and discuss the fictional impulses that are inherent in writing autobiography, or the reverse phenomenon, of autobiographical tendencies being intrinsic in much fiction. One cannot help but notice the autobiographical impulses in much of the fiction written by women today, and researchers can generally find sources discussing these elements within individual works or by certain authors, but additional, secondary sources about autobiographical fiction as a genre distinct from autobiography have yet to be published.

Further Reading: Eakin, Paul John. *Fictions in Autobiography: Studies in the Art of Self-Invention* (Princeton, NJ: Princeton University Press, 1985); Felber, Lynette. *Literary Liaisons: Auto/biographical Appropriations: Modernist Women's Fiction* (Dekalb: Northern Illinois University Press, 2002); Smith, Sidonie. *A Poetics of Women's Autobiography: Marginality and the Fictions of Self-Representation* (Bloomington: Indiana University Press, 1987).

Susie Scifres Kuilan

AUTOBIOGRAPHICS   Drawing on Michel Foucault's ideas about the conjunction of discourse and power, Leigh Gilmore, in *Autobiographics: A Feminist Theory of Women's Self-Representation* (1994), examines the ways in which women autobiographers negotiate the constraints of a genre that traditionally has failed to authorize women's speaking. Gilmore generates a feminist theory of reading that draws attention to autobiographers' multiple and experimental constructions of **identity**. Committed to nonessentialist analysis, Gilmore addresses an assumption of early (1980s) feminist autobiography criticism, which regarded women's narratives as marked by greater thematic and/or stylistic discontinuity than men's. Although Gilmore focuses exclusively on texts by women, drawing out the contradictory elements of these works, she indicates that autobiographies by men as well as women can be read using her theory (11).

Gilmore describes autobiographics as both a method of self-representation and a reading practice (42). Her examples are of Western women autobiographers through the ages, from medieval mystics through European and U.S. autobiographers of the twentieth century. In Gilmore's definition, autobiographics consists of "those changing elements of the contradictory discourses and practices of truth and identity which represent the subject of autobiography" (13). Refusing definitions of autobiography that limit it to a mode of "telling the truth," Gilmore presents her theory instead as a means of exploring how autobiographers use self-representation as a way to claim agency as self-representational subjects (12). Choosing noncanonical autobiographies (including those not traditionally viewed as autobiographies, and those whose authors choose new names for their narratives, such as **Audre Lorde**'s *biomythography*), Gilmore shows how women who are marginalized in mainstream Western societies—women who are lesbians, women of color, women without **class** privilege, mystical and religious women, women less famous than their husbands—shape subject positions by resisting and refiguring the strictures society has placed on them. Interruptions and contradictions are key elements of autobiographics—rhetorical practices Gilmore refers to as "technologies of autobiography." Though these methods of resistance and destabilization do not always result in a "liberated" female subject (63), they nonetheless highlight the methods of experimentation in which many autobiographers engage.

Autobiographics is a strategy of reading that complicates the assumptions of traditional autobiography criticism, developed by theorists such as Georges Gusdorf and Paul de Man. Rather than regarding autobiography as a "genre" per se, for example, autobiographics enables readers to unsettle the idea of a predefined genre and to ask, instead, what constitutes the autobiographical and its representation (42). For many women autobiographers, especially those with socially marginalized positions such as lesbians and women of color, writing (of) one's life and experiences may involve "a profound renegotiation of the terms and forms of self-representation" (2). The act of writing, itself, then, is a central focus of autobiographics (13).

A key tenet of Gilmore's theory is that the "I" of autobiography is an unstable entity, and that, as a result, the author's name becomes a site of experimentation rather than a confident contract of identity (42). Departing from Philippe Lejeune's idea of an "autobiographical pact," in which the author's name on the title page is assumed to reflect the narrative presence in the text, Gilmore posits a resistant, ambivalent "I." She demonstrates how many narratives can be read as autobiographical although the narrators are not named within the text as representations of the living author. In her exploration of Sandra Cisneros' *The House on Mango Street* (1983) and **Jamaica Kincaid**'s *Annie John* (1985), for example, Gilmore examines the ways acts of (re-)naming break familiar codes for women's autobiography.

Gilmore also questions the ideal of truth in autobiography. Conventionally viewed as a more "real" means of representation than fiction, autobiography, as Gilmore reminds us, is no more essentially "truthful" than other forms of writing. Referring to the ways one well-known autobiographer (Mary McCarthy) continually destabilizes the apparent distinctions between truth and fiction, Gilmore notes that confessing is never a simple act (121), especially when the narrator announces herself as a confessional subject.

Along with its emphasis on multiple discourses of truth telling and identity, autobiographics is, for Gilmore, a theory in which women's bodies matter. A body's presence in a self-representational text is less an announcement about **gender** than "evidence of certain preoccupations about gendered identity" (132). Gilmore suggests that, like the category "women" (effectively disrupted by feminist theorists of the postmodern, such as Judith Butler), "the female body" is no such generic and essential thing, but rather a shifting and unpredictable entity. Gilmore also shows that autobiographics' emphasis on discourses of physicality—eroticism, pleasure, pain—necessarily includes exploration of representations of violence (often against female bodies) in women's autobiographies.

Gilmore's theory of autobiographics shapes a **space** for further readings of autobiography that examine the constraints faced by speakers unauthorized within traditional conceptions of autobiography and in mainstream popular culture(s)—including women of color, lesbians, women living outside the United States, and women whose lives seem shrouded in mists of history. Discussed in seminal volumes on reading autobiography (see Further Reading), autobiographics invites ways of reading that explore writers' resistances to and within traditional autobiographical forms.

Further Reading: Gilmore, Leigh. *Autobiographics: A Feminist Theory of Women's Self-Representation* (Ithaca, NY: Cornell University Press, 1994); Gilmore, Leigh. *The Limits of Autobiography: Trauma and Testimony* (Ithaca, NY: Cornell University Press, 2001); Smith, Sidonie, and Julia Watson. *Reading Autobiography: A Guide for Interpreting Life Narratives* (Minneapolis: University of Minnesota Press, 2001); Smith, Sidonie, and Julia Watson, eds. *Women, Autobiography, Theory: A Reader* (Madison: University of Wisconsin Press, 1998).

Jennifer Love

AUTOBIOGRAPHY OF ALICE B. TOKLAS, THE Modernist writer and art collector **Gertrude Stein** wrote *The Autobiography of Alice B. Toklas* in 1933. It is unique in that it is actually a mixture of **memoir** and **biography** (written by Stein, about her life partner Toklas), nonfiction and fiction (Stein pretends to be Toklas, writing in a style that approximates Stein's dry, understated personality). Ironically titled an "autobiography," this imaginative memoir recounts the lives of the two American women living in a house at 27 rue de Fleurus in Paris. The autobiography describes the women's social life among the many, great painters and writers of the late nineteenth and early twentieth centuries, and also reveals Stein as a powerful proponent of artists and a vital life force of her own. Stein is seen through the eyes of her lover, whose acerbic **voice** is revealed through the diction and decisive judgments of the narrator. Although Stein wrote as Toklas, she knew that people reading the autobiography would learn more about her than they would learn about her partner; in fact, the double voice of the narrator captures the love and lives of the two women, whose twenty-five years together as a couple had to be couched in coded terms and deflected in print. The book reveals Stein's great need for Toklas' approval and her own enjoyment of barely convincing disguises.

During the period recounted in the book, the two women met, entertained, and championed many of the most prominent early-twentieth-century painters, including Pablo Picasso, Henri Matisee, Georges Braque, and Amedeo Modigliani. They also traveled in Europe, began to work together writing and promoting Stein's writing, and drove a reconditioned Ford called "Aunty" to do war work in France. In this original pseudoautobiography, readers get a strong sense of the relationship between Toklas and Stein, and also of the changing character of Paris before and after World War II, seen through the life of art collectors and artists. Current events of their daily lives are chronicled in a free-associative, gossipy style, from the cook refusing to make soufflé for Matisse to Toklas learning French from Picasso's first wife, Fernande; it casts its net near and far, describing their lives in rough chronological order and then what happened later to the same artists, art works, and their relationships with each other. This tale of self, seen through the eyes of the loved one, opens with the fictional "Toklas" describing her life before she met Stein, where she lived, comfortable but unstimulated, in San Francisco, among friends and family. When she met the visiting Stein, through Stein's brother Leo, Toklas says, "[My] new full life began" (*The Autobiography of Alice B. Toklas* 5).

First struck by Stein's coral broach and voice, Stein as writer opens their love story by explaining, through Toklas's voice, that she instantly recognized Stein to be a genius. The narrator says that each time she has met a genius, a "bell within me rang" (5), and that she knew, upon meeting her, she had met such a person. Told through her eyes (but created through Stein's own pen), Stein is shown to be a bold, decisive genius with early insight into the promise of the new, unknown painters. The meandering storyline is laced with intimate, affectionate, offhand details that underscore the seemingly unsophisticated and dry voice of Toklas. In her circular, unfiltered style, she gives equal time to cooks and art exhibitions, revealing herself as an wide-eyed witness to some of the greatest changes in European art and history. Her narrative reveals intimacy through the art of living—especially poignant in the scenes where Stein protects her (as when she urges her not to turn on the light, but to come sleep downstairs during a Zeppelin attack) or when Toklas's superiority is described (they each were awarded medals for bravery during the war; Toklas' bravery without pause, but Stein's was for only bravery).

From their showings at Stein's salon, which had a key only for show since "these pictures had no value" (13), to Toklas's French lessons with Pablo Picasso's estranged wife, who "had two subjects, hats and perfumes. This first day we talked hats" (14), the human, unstructured style of the novel heralds Stein's future style and points to her influence not only in the world of literature but also in the world of art. Early in the book, Toklas mentions—in one of her most "Steinian" styled passages, full of constant repetitions, that as Stein's companion, she dined with many geniuses' wives. Stein here seems to present Toklas as one of those wives—and conversely, herself as one of those geniuses.

The second half of the book reveals the women's lives during the German invasion of France, from their difficulties returning to Paris from England at the beginning of World War II to their American Fund for the French War Wounded. During the war, Stein is even more vocal and proud of her American heritage and of what she understands of American character. From a policeman who brought them coal when none was to be found to their postwar salons that included writers Sherwood Anderson, Djuna Barnes, Ezra Pound, Ernest Hemingway, and F. Scott Fitzgerald, it is a portrait of a time, a place, a relationship, and of self-imposed American exiles in France, feeling connected to their country even in their distance from it.

The book's chapter titles refer to people, locations, and dates, deceptively suggesting a chronological description of Toklas's life. Some chapters, however, are solely about Stein, and even take place before Toklas knew her, for example, Chapter 3, "Gertrude Stein Before She Came to Paris." There is little doubt about the main character and focus of this "autobiography." The narrative, like Stein's sentences themselves, is blatantly circular rather than linear, with stories interrupted with later events, as the events and the later revisions of time, and relationships are all visible at once. For instance, sections involving Pablo Picasso frequently are "dated" by the woman currently at his side; on one page, the time and wives change three times in two paragraphs, only to return, after the time-traveling detours, to the present time of that chapter. Events, later events, relationships, the change of some relationships all play fancifully, almost dizzyingly, across the steady certainty of the underlying voice and relationship between Stein and Toklas. All other things change, but this relationship, it seems, remains.

Prior to the publication of this book, Stein's writing often had been considered obscure and abstract, with a repetitive style and simplicity similar to the paintings she loved. Simple forms and small sentences, restated numerous times for emphasis, marked much of her writing; plot frequently did not exist, or was secondary to word-play or character sketches. The elements of language (words, sentences, grammar) were pulled apart and used in a style more like modernist painting than the nineteenth century writers whose thorough narratives and well-explained characters her work rebels against. Like many modernist texts, her writing also used irony and reused traditional phrases and material in distinct new ways. This experimental and eccentric style seemed unfocused or unreadable to many early-twentieth-century readers, who had little other modernist writing to train them in this way of writing and reading. In contrast, *The Autobiography of Alice B. Toklas* was much more conversational and understandable, with little punctuation and a childlike simplicity, and was the most publicly acclaimed—and also criticized—of her writings.

Written after a "dead" period in which Stein had written little, *The Autobiography of Alice B. Toklas* struck a chord with readers both in the United States and in France; she received scores of **letters** as soon as the first installment of the book appeared in *The Atlantic Monthly* magazine, and even earned the first real money she had ever received for her writing. After a period of obscurity, Stein was invited to speak, read, and dine with many well-known publishers, writers, and an appreciative popular audience in the United States and Europe. The serialization in *The Atlantic Monthly* (1933) brought Stein's work to many readers previously unfamiliar with her, and its gossipy look at the "behind the scenes" world of many famous painters' early years appealed to fans of art and writing both. However, this insider **memoir** also alienated many of the artists and intellectuals described in the book.

Six painters mentioned in the book published their "Testimony Against Gertrude Stein" in the journal *transition* (1934–1935 supplemental copy). They argued against many factual details, criticizing Stein's **memory** (much of the work was written from her own remembrances, often thirty years after the events occurred). However, they were more offended by her judgments and assumptions that she could weigh their importance and narrate the meaning of their works and the history of their careers in relation to modern art. Even after Stein's brother Leo, who is barely mentioned, had read the book, he complained to a friend that his sister was a liar.

At first the authorship was questioned, as some readers assumed that it was too artful for Toklas to have written, and others argued that it revealed Toklas as the author or an influence on Stein' other works. Richard Bridgman (1970) even argues that the book was written by Toklas, although Timothy Dow Adams (1990) and others concur that there is no evidence for that claim; the two women instead, perhaps, deeply influenced one another's writing style and drew synergy from each other's speaking style and thinking. The borrowed voice of Toklas reveals a common life and a shared **identity**.

The work's influence on other writers has rarely been written about. Its blunt, multifocused style can be seen in writing and theory in France, England, and the United States, however, and this, as well as other Stein works, may have influenced the French feminists of the 1970s, whose *L'ecriture feminine* theorizes and enacts the circular language earlier used by Stein, James Joyce, and other modernists as "feminine writing." Later, the introductions to the revised versions of many of Stein's papers suggest her influence on writer and art critic John Ashbery and other American L-A-N-G-U-A-G-E and experimental poets, writers, and postmodernists of the late twentieth century. Whether directly or indirectly influencing other writing, *The Autobiography of Alice B. Toklas* gives an intuitive, natural sense of the central female characters' time and relationships, and heralds contemporary theories of autobiography as a fiction of its own.

Further Reading: Adams, Timothy Dow. *Telling Lies in Modern American Autobiography* (Chapel Hill: University of North Carolina Press, 1990); Bridgman, Richard. *Gertrude Stein in Pieces* (New York: Oxford University Press, 1970); Brinnin, John Malcolm. *The Third Rose: Gertrude Stein and Her World*. 1959. Reprint (Reading, MA: Addison-Wesley, 1987); DeKoven, Marianne. *A Different Language: Gertrude Stein's Experimental Writing* (Madison: University of Wisconsin Press, 1983); Hobhouse, Janet. *Everybody Who Was Anybody* (New York: G. P. Putnam's Sons, 1975);

Stein, Gertrude. *The Autobiography of Alice B. Toklas* (New York: Harcourt Brace, 1933).

Jan VanStavern

AUTOETHNOGRAPHY An analytical/objective personal account about the self/writer as part of a group or culture, autoethnography usually includes a description of a conflict of cultures and an analysis of the experience of an outsider. Because an autoethnography is written for an audience that does not have membership in the writer's group or culture, the genre provides an opportunity to explain differences from an insider's perspective and to explain how one becomes Other. The autoethnographer attempts to see herself as others might see her. Autoethnography is both a method—something one does—and a text—something one writes: it is a way of including one's awareness of and emotions toward the subject through some personal accounting of oneself.

Autoethnography combines autobiography, an account of oneself through personal narratives, with ethnography, an account of a particular social group through such activities as participant observations of events, interviews, transcribed conversations, audio and video recordings, and written field notes. In 1991, Mary Louise Pratt, in her essay "Arts of the Contact Zone," first used the 350-year-old text of an insider, Guaman Poma, a native Andean Incan, written to King Philip III of Spain, as an example of autoethnography. She provides a well-known definition of autoethnography as "representations that the so-defined others construct *in response to* or in dialogue with" readers (35). Poma uses his native language and the language of his Spanish conquerors to describe the conflict of cultures and to critique what the Spaniards were doing to the Incas. Writers of autoethnographies—whether in their actual accounts, narrative constructs, or literature—appropriate the dominant language by bringing it into their service, reproducing it, and inserting themselves into it through a variety

of means. In other words, these writers incorporate the narrative style of the oppressor into their counterhegemonic discourse. Their writing is rich with the emotions of those who experienced them, emotions barely suppressed by the cultures in which they find their source.

More recently, scholars of autoethnography incorporate current theory as they describe the genre. Deborah E. Reed-Danahay, editor of *Auto/Ethnography: Rewriting the Self and the Social* (1997), argues that autoethnography "is a useful term with which to question the binary conventions of a self/society split, as well as the boundary between the objective and the subjective." Thus, the autoethnographic "postmodern/postcolonial conception of self and society is one of a multiplicity of identities, of cultural displacement, and of shifting axes of power" (2). As "something one does," autoethnography includes making sense of what happens, sorting out meanings, arriving at interpretations about the significance of actions and events, providing analysis with description and writing fiction—a product of negotiation between one's culture and one's self. In autoethnography, writers refuse to deny both their experiences of the physicality of their bodies and the experiences of being from a particular culture. These women appropriate language in order to tell and recover their relationship to their language. Their lives have been informed and defined by their communities, which in turn carry collective memories of oppression and suffering, including death or exile.

Because the autoethnographer is writing from a perspective of displacement, her act of writing "involves a rewriting of the self and the social" (Reed-Danahay 4). She must provide a middle **voice** to negotiate the two communities so that she can retain membership in both. An autoethnographer researches a social group as participant and then writes the results, thereby negotiating between individual and collective identities and among a variety of textual styles and genres. For example, Lorraine Kenny, in *Daughters of Suburbia: Growing Up White, Middle Class, and Female* (2000), writes from within a group of white, middle-class suburban teenage American girls, locating herself in the center of her research. By recognizing and making official the multiplicity of historical voices, women who write autoethnography strategically discuss and negotiate alternate ways to inform and define their contemporary communities. Carolyn Ellis and Arthur P. Bochner (*Composing Ethnography* 1996) argue that "instead of masking our presence, leaving it at the margins, we should make ourselves more personally accountable for our perspective" (15). They continue by arguing for an "involved, situated" scholar who is an "integral part of the research and writing process" (18). Autoethnographers are often careful to write from the "I" position in order to maintain a reliable account not only from their own perspectives as both insider and outsider (and so, perhaps, neither), but from the perspectives of the participants in the project. The temptation is strong to give up the difficult position of "I"—in its specificity and humility—in favor of a general and communally sanctioned "we." The latter position silences the object of the written work and gives power to the subject. However, autoethnography conserves stories rather than erasing them, stories rich with events exposing the emotions of a people. When a woman begins to let herself experience emotion about being from a particular group, she begins to remember. She begins to see the story. More important, she begins to see herself as a character in the story. And she begins to see other women around her as characters in the story.

Further Reading: Brodkey, Linda. "Writing Permitted in Designated Places Only." In *Higher Education Under Fire: Politics, Economics, and the Crisis of the Humanities*, edited by Michael Bérubé and Cary Nelson, 214–237 (New York: Routledge, 1995); Denzin, Norman K. *Interpretive Ethnography: Ethnographic Practices for the 21st Century* (Thousand Oaks, CA: Sage, 1997); Ellis, Carolyn. "Evocative Autoethnography: Writing Emotionally about Our Lives." In *Representation and the Text: Re-framing the Narrative Voice*, edited by W. Tierney and Y. Lincoln, 116–139 (Albany: State University of New York Press, 1997); Ellis, Carolyn. "Heartfelt Autoethnography." *Qualitative Health Research* 9, no. 5 (1999): 669–683. Ellis, Carolyn, and Arthur P. Bochner. "Autoethnography, Personal Narrative, Reflexivity: Researcher as Subject." In *Handbook of Qualitative Research*, edited by Norman K. Denzin and Yvonna S. Lincoln, 733–768 (Thousand Oaks, CA: Sage, 2000); Ellis, Carolyn, and Arthur P. Bochner, eds. *Composing Ethnography: Alternative Forms of Qualitative Writing* (Walnut Creek, CA: AltaMira, 1996); Kenny, Lorraine Delia. *Daughters of Suburbia: Growing Up White, Middle Class, and Female* (New Brunswick, NJ: Rutgers University Press, 2000); Pratt, Mary Louise. "Arts of the Contact Zone." *Profession* (1991): 33–40; Reed-Danahay, Deborah E., ed. *Auto/Ethnography: Rewriting the Self and the Social* (Oxford: Berg, 1997), 1–17; Smith, Sidonie, and Julia Watson, eds. *De/colonizing the Subject: The Politics of Gender in Women's Autobiography* (Minneapolis: University of Minnesota Press, 1992).

Violet A. Dutcher

B

BEAUVOIR, SIMONE DE (1908–1986)
Best known as the author of the founding
text of second-wave **feminism**, *Le Deuxième
Sexe* (1949, [*The Second Sex*]), Simone de
Beauvoir (her full name is Simone Lucie
Ernestine Marie Bertrande de Beauvoir) has
been called the "emblematic intellectual
woman of the twentieth century" (Moi
1994, 1). A prolific writer, she authored novels, short stories, a play, philosophical
works, and a sizeable corpus of autobiographical writing. The latter includes a
memoir in four volumes correspondence,
diaries, **travel narrative**s, and accounts of
both the death of her mother and that of
Jean-Paul Sartre, her lifelong companion.
Her oeuvre continues to spark interest
among literary critics, historians, philosophers, and feminists.

Born January 4, 1908, into a well-to-do
Parisian family, Beauvoir was the eldest of
two daughters. Despite the fact that she became a world traveler, her permanent residence was never very far from the home in
the 14th arrondissement in Paris where she
was born. Educated in private schools
through high school, her family's financial
troubles caused her and her sister to be destined to work rather than be married, because there would be no dowry for either
of them, a situation she welcomed. Against
her father's wishes, she decided to become

a teacher and attended the Sorbonne, earning degrees in literature, math, and philosophy. At age twenty-one, she passed the
agrégation de philosophie, a rigorous compet-
itive examination leading to the highest
ranked teaching posts in the French secondary education system. She was the
youngest person in France ever to have
done so. The year that she prepared for the
exam, she first met and became linked both
intimately and intellectually with Jean-Paul
Sartre. In rejection of the bourgeois values
of her social background and in affirmation
of the existentialist values to which they adhered, Beauvoir chose not to marry Sartre
or cohabitate with him, and to live a free existence, sexually and otherwise. She earned
her living as a high school teacher, first in
Marseille, then in Rouen, and later in Paris,
until the successes of her books allowed her
to live as an independent writer. Her first
published work was *L'Invitée* (1943 [She
Came to Stay]), a fictionalized account of
the triangular relationship she and Sartre
had with Olga Kosakievicz. She founded
the journal *Les Temps Modernes* with Sartre
and Maurice Merleau-Ponty in 1945. In
1954, she was awarded the prestigious
Goncourt Prize for her novel *Les Mandarins*
(1954 [The Mandarins]). Though early on
Beauvoir was not engaged politically, she
went on to become a political activist, es-

pecially known for her opposition to the Algerian war of independence and her promotion of abortion rights in France. In the last years of her life, she adopted Sylvie le Bon, a young philosophy teacher, to ensure that her intellectual legacy be passed on to subsequent generations. She died in Paris on April 14, 1986, and was buried in the same plot as Sartre at Montparnasse cemetery with thousands in attendance.

Beauvoir stated that she always envisioned her life as a "lovely story that became true as I told it to myself" (*Mémoires* 1958). The self-written and the self-writing thus entwined to support the self-in-construction model she uses as part of the basis for her understanding of **subjectivity**. While many of Beauvoir's works are autobiographical, critics generally consider her autobiography to consist of the four volumes of memoirs. The first, *Mémoires d'une jeune fille rangée* (1958 [Memoirs of a Dutiful Daughter]), is a bildungsroman recounting her birth, early childhood, and adolescence. In this work, the greatest distance between the authorial self and the narrated self is evident as is the attempt on the part of the author to connect the development of her early self to the later adult she would be. Recognizing the fragmentation of the subject in relation to the Other as well as to past selves, is a constant theme throughout her autobiography. The next two books, *La force de l'âge* (1960 [The Prime of Life]) and *La force des choses* (1963 [The Force of Circumstance]), chronologically recount her adult years during the time of German occupation of France and the postwar era. The last volume, *Tout compte fait* (1972 [All Said and Done]), is approached thematically rather than chronologically, as the author chooses to review a life she views as no longer progressing, but near its end. Beauvoir published two other works critics often place in the category of her autobiography or auto/**biography**, *Une mort très douce* (1964 [A Very Easy Death]), her representation of her mother's illness and

death and her reactions to it, and *La Cérémonie des adieux* (1981 [A Farewell to Sartre]), which narrates Sartre's decline in the last few years of his life and his death in 1980. Both works place the self in conjunction with the Other and demonstrate Beauvoir's continued commitment to exploring and inscribing self-Other relations as well as her interest later in life in the processes of aging and dying, and the situation of the elderly in (mostly Western) society, which she also analyzed in her philosophical work, *La Vieillesse* (1970 [Old Age]), an attempt to do for the elderly what *Le Deuxième Sexe* did for women.

Early critics of Beauvoir's autobiography condemned her for not being truthful enough and for sometimes contradicting herself, or by feminist critics for not sufficiently asserting herself or her **sexuality** in her autobiography. More recent analyses understand her project as fundamentally testimonial rather than confessional and underscore the fact that Beauvoir not only justifies her choice not to include sensitive material in her autobiography, but also recognizes that her sociohistorical circumstances may have censored her. Indeed, what Beauvoir called the situation of the subject—not only what we now often call **identity** (**race**, **class**, **gender**, sexuality, and so forth), but the identity of the subject in relation to others and society in general—undoubtedly influenced both the scope and focus of her autobiographical enterprise. Examples of omissions that fall under this rubric are changing certain names and details to respect others, choosing not to write about her lesbian relationships, and not providing details of her intimate relationship with Sartre, not only the sexual part of their relationship, but also the tensions and philosophical differences. Beauvoir has also been called a "witness to [the twentieth] century" (Wenzel 1986), and her autobiography is used by historians and literary critics for the first-hand information one can find there about the important historical events and intellectual figures in France of her time. The publication in recent years of Beauvoir's correspondence and diaries has raised issues and venues for new critical perspectives. For some, these works present the opportunity to verify that the facts add up, while for others the recent publication represents new evidence of Beauvoir's important, though often overlooked, contributions to existentialist philosophy and to the French literary traditions of life writing.

Critics and biographers of Beauvoir and Sartre compare their accomplishments, asking who influenced whom. Throughout her life, Beauvoir portrayed herself as second fiddle to Sartre's genius and has often been criticized for it. While she always denied having played an important role in Sartre's intellectual development and thinking, her influence, especially in the field of existential morality has become apparent. A great difference between them that is relevant to the context of autobiography is that while Sartre wrote a great deal more abstract philosophy, Beauvoir's works intertwine philosophical thinking with detailed illustrations of the facts of material existence, using herself as a case study in her autobiographical writing and others, most often women (real or imagined), elsewhere. While Sartre never felt as compelled as Beauvoir to write explicitly about himself, it is in her self-representation that one can find some of her most sophisticated philosophical ideas along with their application. Rather than attempting to pull the philosophy out of the autobiography or vice versa, it is more fruitful to envision the autobiographical and philosophical as means to the same existentialist end, an understanding of the human condition, and in the case of Beauvoir, also of the feminine condition.

Indeed, upon examination of the circumstances of her initial desire to produce an autobiography, the conflation of the two is justified. Her primary reason for wanting to be a writer was to share her self with her readership. Furthermore, when she first set out to write her autobiography in the 1940s, Simone de Beauvoir states, she realized she first needed to analyze the degree to which having been born female had been an influence on her life. The result was *Le Deuxième Sexe*. Her famous formulation from this work, "One is not born, but becomes a woman," offers a social constructionist understanding of the subject that is apparent in all of her writing, perhaps best of all in her self-representations. Kate Millet, in comparing *Le Deuxième Sexe* with her autobiography, stated that while the former taught women how to think, the latter taught them how to live (cited in Tidd 1990, 61). An important author of her time, Simone de Beauvoir's influence on the international women's movement is still felt today, and her autobiographical work is among the most significant of the twentieth century.

Further Reading: Bair, Deirdre. *Simone de Beauvoir* (New York: Summit, 1990); Beauvoir, Simone de. *Adieux: A Farewell to Sartre*. Translated by P. O'Brian (Harmondsworth: Penguin, 1986); Beauvoir, Simone de. *All Said and Done*. Translated by P. O'Brian (Harmondsworth: Penguin, 1987); Beauvoir, Simone de. *America Day by Day*. Translated by Patrick Dudley (New York: Grove Press, 1953); Beauvoir, Simone de. *The Force of Circumstance*. Translated by R. Howard (Harmondsworth: Penguin, 1985); Beauvoir, Simone de. *Journal de guerre: septembre 1939–janvier 1941*. Edited by Sylvie le Bon de Beauvoir (Paris: Gallimard, 1990); Beauvoir, Simone de. *Letters to Sartre*. Translated by Q. Hoare (New York: Arcade, 1991); Beauvoir, Simone de. *The Long March*. Translated by Austryn Wainhouse (New York: World, 1958); Beauvoir, Simone de. *Memoirs of a Dutiful Daughter*. Translated by James Kirkup (Harmondsworth: Penguin, 1987); Beauvoir, Simone de. *The Prime of Life*. Translated by P. Greene (Harmondsworth: Penguin, 1986); Beauvoir, Simone de. *A Very Easy Death*. Translated by P. O'Brian (Harmondworth: Penguin, 1985); Beauvoir, Simone de. *The Second Sex*. Trans. of *Le Deuxieme Sexe*. Translated and edited by H.M. Parshley (New York: Vintage Books, 1974); Beauvoir, Simone de. *A Transatlantic Love Affair: Letters to Nelson Algren. 1947–1964*. Edited by Sylvie le Bon de Beauvoir, et al. (New York:

The New Press, 1998); Fallaize, Elisabeth, ed. *Simone de Beauvoir: A Critical Reader* (London and New York: Routledge, 1998); Hewitt, Leah. *Autobiographical Tightropes: Simone de Beauvoir, Nathalie Saurraute, Marguerite Duras, Monique Wittig, Maryse Condé* (Lincoln: University of Nebraska Press, 1990); Moi, Toril. *Feminist Theory and Simone de Beauvoir* (Oxford: Blackwell, 1990); Moi, Toril. *Simone de Beauvoir: The Making of an Intellectual Woman* (Oxford: Blackwell, 1994); Pilardi, Jo-Ann. *Simone de Beauvoir Writing the Self: Philosophy Becomes Autobiography* (Westport, CT: Greenwood Press, 1999); Tidd, Ursula. *Simone de Beauvoir: Gender and Testimony* (Cambridge and New York: Cambridge University Press, 1990); Wenzel, Hélène Vivienne, ed. "Simone de Beauvoir: Witness to a Century." *Yale French Studies* 72 (1986).

Mary C. Ekman

BENSTOCK, SHARI (1944–) Author and editor of more than a dozen books that explore the complex interrelations between **gender**, history (particularly modernism) and **biography**, Benstock distinguishes herself in the field of women's studies for pioneering critical and literary methodologies by which to theorize women's autobiographical writings. Beginning with her early work on James Joyce, *Who's He When He's at Home: A James Joyce Directory* (1980), to her study of expatriate women artists, writers, and booksellers, *Women of the Left Bank: Paris, 1900–1940* (1986), to her most comprehensive compiling of essays on women's autobiographical writings in *The Private Self: Theory and Practice of Women's Autobiographical Writings* (1988), Benstock has focused on the cultural importance of delegitimized processes of autobiographical self-creation.

The historical and cultural contexts within which the "feminine" has been conventionally defined calls attention, Benstock shows, to the psychosexual determinants by which female autobiography has been categorized and often misread. Organized around key concepts of "privacy," "self," and "theory," *The Private Self* is divided into two parts:

"Theories of Autobiography" and "Autobiographical Practices." The six essays in Part I interrogate how the autobiographical self has traditionally been legitimized and defined as a (usually male) totality of unified selfhood. These essays range from "Writings of Afro-American Women," to an analysis of **Simone de Beauvoir**'s fears of aging, to an examination of eighteenth-century women's writings. Part I foregrounds **race**, **class**, culture, and religion as determining dispersed and dislocated subjects who negotiate vulnerable ego boundaries in their writings.

Part II of *The Private Self* analyzes autobiographical discourse as a practice that underwrites or subverts dominant conventions of self-representation. From Mary Wollstonecraft's "pedagogy of self-expression," to Jane Austen's **letters**, or Dorothy Wordsworth's journals, and Charlotte Forten Grimke's "search for a public voice," the struggle these essays articulate is one that dramatizes the fluid, interrelational terms by which these women have achieved self-expression. It is a model of selfhood Benstock tells us in her essay, "Authorizing the Autobiographical" in Part I, which deconstructs a Western model of the individualistic, monolithic self. The cumulative point these essays make clear is what Benstock proposes in her introduction: that given women's disenfranchised positions in dominant, mainstream social orders, the autobiographical form provides an opportunity for articulating a self left fragmented by conventions that have marginalized her; autobiography as a genre allows women to "express that which cannot be expressed in other forms" (6).

The Private Self makes fundamental connections between language and **subjectivity** and highlights how women's autobiographical writings are located in **spaces** restricted, undermined, or erased by patriarchal systems of meaning. Benstock chooses a range of **voices** and autobiographical styles (journals, letters, **memoir**s) to underline the varied ways by which women (for all their differences) have managed to subvert or rewrite predetermined social structures that have subordinated or silenced them. The fragility and permeability of the boundaries of what constitutes selfhood in these autobiographical writings is what has made the genre so particular, and so important to female self-expression.

In *Textualizing the Feminine, On the Limits of Genre* (1991), Benstock gives even broader theoretical attention to the idea of the feminine as a symbol of absence in dominant systems of language that impose and structure themselves to achieve a "fiction of self-consistency" (xxx). Using the theoretical contributions of Freud, Lacan, and Derrida as well as that of the feminist theorists, Irigaray, Cixous, and Kristeva, Benstock delineates how the feminine, as a principal of otherness, has come to express itself through the unsettled and uneasy divisions of conscious/unconscious, genre/gender. As in *The Private Self*, Benstock's arguments in *Textualizing the Feminine* mine cultural investments in maintaining consistent, and therefore socially legible, terms of self-representation, which, Benstock has consistently argued, robs women of articulating selves "illegible" (or marginal) in the social contexts that have complicated and limited them.

Textualizing the Feminine investigates theoretical and linguistic determinants in the construction of the subject through key modernist texts. If *The Private Self* explores the sociohistorical world of the female autobiographical self, *Textualizing the Feminine* focuses on the linguistic fissures within the text itself, or how the speaking subject tries, through "textual body parts" (the title of Part II), to make connections of meaning: the "ellipses" in **Virginia Woolf**'s *Three Guineas* (1938, Chapter 5) are used to unveil truths kept covered by Western thinking and patriarchal law, and **Gertrude Stein**'s linguistic experiments of "non-sense" are in fact efforts to speak the language of the female body (Part I).

Throughout Benstock's writing, editing, and teaching career, as professor of English and associate dean for faculty affairs at the College of Arts and Sciences at the University of Miami, and former director of the Center for Study of Women's Literature at the University of Tulsa, as well as former editor of *Tulsa Studies in Women's Literature*, Benstock's work, as a *body* of work, encompasses the multifaceted and interrelated strands of the autobiographical subject she has spent her life articulating.

Further Reading: Benstock, Shari, ed. *The Private Self: Theory and Practice of Women's Autobiographical Writings* (Chapel Hill: University of North Carolina Press, 1988); Benstock, Shari. *Textualizing the Feminine: On the Limits of Genre* (Norman: University of Oklahoma Press, 1991); Benstock, Shari. *Women of the Left Bank: Paris, 1900–1940* (Austin: University of Texas Press, 1986); Broe, Mary Lynn, and Angela Ingram, eds. *Women's Writing in Exile* (Chapel Hill: University of North Carolina Press, 1989); Jacobus, Mary, ed. *Women Writing and Writing about Women* (New York: Barnes and Noble, 1979).

Adrianne Kalfopoulou

BIOGRAPHY   Biography, especially modern Western biography, is still frequently seen as a patriarchal genre, dominated by eminent male writers writing about famous male subjects. It is often regarded as opposed to (or even instrumental in suppressing) other forms of life writing, such as women's autobiography. It is not yet widely recognized how much the field of biography has been altered by **feminism** or how biographers are now grappling with issues (such as relational conceptions of the self) that are also central to women's autobiography.

The perception of biography as patriarchal sometimes obscures the existence of early biographies of women. Women's biography is today a junior partner in the life writing field: books using the postmodern term "auto/biography" normally concentrate most of their attention on autobiography. Historically, however, biographies of women have had equal or greater importance than autobiographies of women. The first-known biography of women comes from China: it is *Lienü zhuan* [A Biography of Famous Women] by Liu Xiang. This is a collective biography, which historically has been one of the most common forms that women's biographies have taken. Arabic literature (which is especially rich in biography), includes many biographies of women, dating back as far as the seventh century. Ibn Sa'd (writing in the ninth century) gave considerable attention to Muhammed's wives, as did many other Arab biographers. This strong tradition of women's biography, which included biographies of women written by women, had consequences that can seem surprising to the Western reader. It meant that collective biographies of women by women were extremely common in Egypt in the nineteenth and early twentieth centuries, with the tradition arguably being disturbed by Western influences. In other areas of the world, biographies of women frequently focused on the lives of religious martyrs and saints (this was particularly common in medieval Europe), as well as on the lives of aristocratic and royal women. In Europe, Giovanni Boccaccio wrote the lives of more than one hundred famous women; Jacopo Filippo Foresti published *On Certain Famous Women* in 1497; Ann Thicknesse's collective biography, *Sketches of the Lives and Writings of the Ladies of France*, was published in 1780.

Elizabeth Gaskell's full-length biography of Charlotte Brontë (1887) ushered in a new tradition in Europe, and numerous nineteenth-century women wrote biographies of other women. Full-length biographies of women increased rapidly in the twentieth century, partly as a result of female historians wishing to reclaim lives that had become obscure. This tendency has been most marked in Western countries. In China, some twentieth-century authors used biography to single out a "patriotic heroine" for praise (*Zhongguo aiguo nüjie Wang Zhaojun zhuan* [Biography of Wang Zhaojun: A Patriotic Heroine of China] and *Kangri yingxiong*

Zhao Yiman [Zhao Yiman: A Heroine in the War of Resistance against Japan]).

It is nonetheless true that the majority of biographical subjects have been eminent males. Consequently, a frequent charge against modern Western biography is that its focus on public achievement and its linear form have made it an uncongenial vehicle for relaying the experiences of women. In order to see what opportunities are available in this field for both feminist biographers and feminist critics, it is vital to see how greatly this genre has been changed by the advent of feminism. Feminism has altered the genre of modern Western biography in three ways: it has massively increased the range of biographical subjects now considered; it has radically altered the ways in which lives are written; and it has made tools of feminist analysis available to literary critics, opening up the ways in which works are evaluated and analyzed.

The range of biographical subjects is today much wider than it has ever been. There is now keen interest, for example, in the life of Dorothy Wordsworth (rather than an exclusive focus on her famous brother, William Wordsworth). There is an interest in the experiences of women who were oppressed and silenced by their historical conditions, such as poverty or slavery. There is a growing realization that any life can potentially provide interesting biographical information, not merely the lives of men renowned for their public achievements.

Moreover, even today when the lives of acclaimed men are written, the depiction of their lives is often radically different from those written in the past. Ray Monk's biography of Bertrand Russell (2000), for example, differs greatly from an earlier biography of Russell by Ronald Clark (1978). Clark focuses on Russell's public achievements. Monk takes a different approach, contrasting Dora Russell's willingness to care for their mentally ill son with Bertrand Russell's exclusive concentration on public achievement. The role of the male self (seen and lived as single, autonomous, and focused on public achievement) is, Monk suggests, far easier to maintain than the role of the relational care-giving self traditionally both assumed by and imposed on women. Seemingly "canonical" texts (biographies of famous male figures) thus can reveal a substantial engagement with feminist thought.

Feminism has opened up new ways of analyzing both the cultural role of biography and the particular forms it has taken. **Virginia Woolf** was keenly aware of biography's potentially oppressive cultural role, its capacity to celebrate the public achievements of men and overlook the lives of women. In *A Room of One's Own* (1929) she wrote an imagined biography of Shakespeare's sister, pointing to the ways in which a woman of Shakespeare's talent would have been condemned to failure by the constraints of her era. However, she was also alert to the ways in which biographical constraints could be altered: she wrote two mock biographies, *Orlando* (1928) and *Flush* (1933), the latter of which sees the world from the viewpoint of a dog's eye. Woolf's biographical experiments point to **space**s that are open in the genre today, the possibilities of radically altering biographical forms. Both *Orlando* and *Flush* can be seen as forerunners to postmodernism in their blending of fact and fiction and their self-referential playfulness. They can also be seen as forerunners to the currently popular genre of fictionalized biographies, which offer a way of representing partially documented lives, for instance Fay Weldon's *Rebecca West* (1985) uses fictional dialogue between Weldon and West. There is now an awareness that the lack of documentation of many women's lives can present an opportunity for experimenting with the form of biography; thus, Brian Matthews turns the lack of evidence about Louisa Lawson's life into an investigation of the uncertainties and gaps within any biographical narrative (*Louisa* 1987).

In addition to the possibility of experi-menting with form, feminist approaches allow the reanalysis of the assumptions of earlier eras. Margaret Forster, for instance, notes that earlier biographers found Elizabeth Barrett Browning's "antisocial attitude" and her negative opinion of marriage incomprehensible (Iles 1992), whereas for Forster, Elizabeth's opinion reflects the way marriage operated as an institution in nineteenth-century England. Feminist critics and biographers are also able to reanalyze the evidence on which assumptions of influence were made: initial assumptions, for example, that **Simone de Beauvoir** simply followed Sartre's ideas have now been overturned.

Feminist approaches have combined with queer theory in highlighting the relationships between women, rather than assuming women's primary relationships are with male partners. Thus biographies such as Kathleen Jones' *A Passionate Sisterhood: The Sisters, Wives and Daughters of the Lake Poets* (1997) highlight the bonds between a group of women.

Despite the potential for new approaches, questions about the role of biography in relation to feminism are likely to persist. Biographies of women continue to have a controversial relationship with feminism partly because of questions about the ethics of biography. Some earlier traditions of life writing (the medieval tradition of writing about saint's lives, in particular) were wholly celebratory. However, since the publication of Lytton Strachey's *Eminent Victorians* in 1918, the pendulum has swung away from hagiographic presentations. In *Eminent Victorians*, Strachey used a debunking style, often presenting his subjects as ridiculous, rather than emphazing their dignity or their achievements. He also argued strongly for the biographer acting as an artist, shaping the life he presented. Since the publication of *Eminent Victorians*, biography has split into many strands. While celebratory biographies are still published, many biographers have followed Strachey's lead, portraying their subjects as less than admirable, or as monsters. As a result, biographers are now often accused of being intrusive, trespassing into the privacy of people's lives, exposing every detail to the world's critical gaze. Where living subjects are involved, biographies are also potentially destructive. There are conflicting views over the role of feminist biographers and the stance they should take toward their subjects. Janet Malcolm, in her biography, *The Silent Woman: Sylvia Plath and Ted Hughes* (1994), has severely criticized the way in which biography can become a blood sport, with **Sylvia Plath**'s husband being hounded by generations of biographers.

Collections of essays on biography (often by practicing biographers) highlight the many problems and controversies of the genre (see Homberger and Charmley 1988 and Salwak 1996). Diane Wood Middlebrook's decision to include material from the tapes of **Anne Sexton**'s sessions with her psychiatrist is one of many that could be considered controversial, because of the way it invades Sexton's private life. Joyce Antler raises a more subtle problem in her essay "Having It All, Almost: Confronting the Legacy of Lucy Sprague Mitchell" (1984). As Antler notes, most feminist biographers have a strong commitment to considering both the private and public lives of their subjects (see Ascher, DeSalvo, and Ruddick; Alpern et al., and Iles). Antler asks, Does considering the private life of a biographical subject hold them to impossible standards, asking them to be perfect in every area of their lives?

In the context of women's autobiography, the ethics of biography can be especially fraught. As Alice Wexler has written (1992), for the biographer, the subject's own autobiography can be "a major ally, obstacle, and rival" ("Emma Goldman and the Anxiety of Feminist Biography" 38). How is a biographer (particularly a feminist biographer) to square the subject's account with her own interpretation of the subject's life, one that may be wildly different? For many feminist biographers, questions of empathy, of critical distance from their subject, of identification with their subject, are part of the challenge of life writing, with no final answers.

Further Reading: Alpern, Sara, Joyce Antler, Elizabeth Israels Perry, and Ingrid Winther Scobie, eds. *The Challenge of Feminist Biography: Writing the Lives of Modern American Women* (Urbana: University of Illinois Press, 1992); Ascher, Carol, Louise DeSalvo, and Sara Ruddick, eds. *Between Women: Biographers, Novelists, Critics, Teachers, and Artists Write about Their Work on Women* (Boston: Beacon Press, 1984); Booth, Marilyn. *May Her Likes Be Multiplied: Biography and Gender Politics in Egypt* (Berkeley: University of California Press, 2001); Clark, Ronald. *The Life of Bertrand Russell* (Harmondsworth: Penguin, 1978); Forster, Margaret. *Elizabeth Barrett Browning: A Biography.* 1990 (London: Flamingo, 1993); Gaskell, Elizabeth. *The Life of Charlotte Brontë.* 1857. Edited by Alan Shelston (London: Penguin, 1975); Homberger, Eric, and John Charmley, eds. *The Troubled Face of Biography* (New York: St. Martin's Press, 1988); Iles, Teresa, ed. *All Sides of the Subject: Women and Biography* (New York: Teacher's College Press, 1992); Jones, Kathleen. *A Passionate Sisterhood: The Sisters, Wives and Daughters of the Lake Poets* (London: Constable, 1997); Malcolm, Janet. *The Silent Woman: Sylvia Plath and Ted Hughes* (London: Picador, 1994); Monk, Ray. *Bertrand Russell 1921–70: The Ghost of Madness* (London: Jonathan Cape, 2000); Oldfield, Sybil. "Women's Biographies." Vol. 2 of *Encyclopedia of Life Writing: Autobiographical and Biographical Forms.* Edited by Margaretta Jolly, 948–950 (London: Fitzroy Dearborn, 2001); Salwak, Dale, ed. *The Literary Biography: Problems and Solutions* (Iowa City: Iowa University Press, 1996); Strachey, Lytton. *Eminent Victorians.* 1918. Reprint (London: Chatto and Windus, 1928); Weldon, Fay. *Rebecca West* (New York: Viking, 1985); Woolf, Virginia. *Flush: A Biography.* 1933. 2nd ed. (London: Hogarth Press, 1947); Woolf, Virginia. *Orlando: A Biography.* 1928. Reprint. Edited by Rachel Bowley (Oxford: Oxford University Press, 1992); Woolf, Virginia. *A Room of One's Own.* 1929. Reprint (London: Grafton Books, 1977).

Susan Tridgell

BOOK OF MARGERY KEMPE, THE (c. 1436–1438)

Almost six hundred years ago, an illiterate, devout, opinionated, and tireless English matron decided, after many years and many miles, to tell the story of her life—from pregnancies to pilgrimages, housewifery to heresy, human love to divine love—in order to praise, explain, and illustrate the love and mercy of Jesus Christ and God for all, as she knew it from direct experience. This decision, like most decisions **Margery Kempe** made, was not usual. Devotional writings of varying quality and value were plentiful in the fifteenth century, but Kempe's creation was not devotional writing as it was then known, although that is probably what she thought she was doing. Rather, what became *The Book of Margery Kempe* in turn, became not only the first autobiography by an English woman, but also the first-ever English autobiography, breaking literary as well as **gender** and religious barriers.

Even if it was not considered the first autobiography in English, *The Book of Margery Kempe* would still be a phenomenon. In 1936, the medievalist Hope Emily Allen experienced a true "eureka" moment. Dr. Allen had been asked by Colonel Butler-Bowdon of Lancashire, England, to examine an aged manuscript that had been in the family since the 1538 dissolution of the monasteries under Henry VIII. When she started reading the manuscript—which a notation indicated had once been in the possession of Mount Grace, a Carthusian monastery in Yorkshire—she could not believe what she held in her hands. The content of the manuscript was the life story, spiritual and physical, of a dimly known, fairly well-to-do, and extremely well-traveled, middle-class English woman named Margery Burnham Kempe of Lynn, told in her own words.

Margery Kempe was known in scholarly circles as a minor medieval mystic, whose few examples of her ecstatic visions were sometimes included in collections of mystical writings by the English mystics Walter Hilton, Richard Rolle, and **Julian of Norwich**. But this manuscript was a complete book. Such a document was not merely rare; it was unprecedented. While seeming to be in the tradition of Julian of Norwich (*A Book of Showings*) and Bridget of Sweden (*Revelations*), the full, found text transcended its assumed confessional and revelatory purpose and was as much a character and cultural study as a religious testament. Judging from her book, Margery Kempe took everything very personally and her "book" is, perforce, uniquely personal.

The Book of Margery Kempe is written in Middle English, not Latin, as would be the more common practice for religious treatises; it is written in prose, not verse, which was the more usual mode for "popular" writing at the time; its author is a laywoman—a wife, mother, and businesswoman—not a churchwoman or a member of the nobility, who were the more likely to be writers in this period. And *The Book of Margery Kempe* is a dictation. Kempe herself says in the *Book* that she could neither read nor write, which is somewhat odd since women of her social standing in England in the late fourteenth and early fifteenth centuries generally had access to schooling. This could be a disingenuous or rhetorical gesture (comparable to Chaucer's saying that he had "little Latin"), either for propriety's sake or because her skill was limited or because she wished to emulate women religious who, though literate, traditionally dictated their revelations to their confessors. If she was truly illiterate, this still did not keep her from understanding (and promoting) the importance and influence of the written and spoken word. She had a sharp **memory** (not unusual for a culture that still had a strong oral tradition of both secular storytelling and of religious sermonizing) and always asked to be read to. This can also explain her exceptional knowledge of both biblical text and commentary as well as English and Continental devotional treatises by such female visionaries as Julian of Norwich, Bridget of Sweden, and Elizabeth of Hungary. Indeed, Kempe identified particularly with Bridget, who died shortly before Kempe's birth, and the Bridgettine Syon Abbey was not far from the city of Lynn. Bridget is frequently referenced in the *Book*, often with Christ telling Margery how she resembles Bridget. Kempe's pilgrimages deliberately followed those of Bridget's, and Kempe was in Rome when Bridget was canonized.

In any case, and for whichever reason, Kempe dictated her book but needed urging to do so. Her confessor wanted her to record her visions and confessions, but she demurred for twenty years until God told her directly that she should do it. The dictation thus began sometime around 1430, when Kempe was about sixty-years-old and had already made pilgrimages to Santiago de Campostela and to the Holy Land. *The Book of Margery Kempe* was written down by at least two scribes—someone who had impossibly illegible handwriting and who may also have been Kempe's son, and a local priest (possibly Kempe's confessor) who rewrote the first, badly written attempt and continued on for the whole book. The proem to the *Book* is telling. Written by her second scribe in 1436, after completion of the long first part of the *Book*, it is his heaved sigh, his expostulation—of frustration, guilt, weariness, pride, admiration, bemusement and awe. Yet another brief preface from 1438 to the second, shorter part of the *Book* expresses similar feelings in light of the scribe actually having accompanied Kempe on her German pilgrimage.

Although the author of her own life, Margery Kempe was not its writer and so—inversely, perversely, and appropriately—she was her book's editor, and a demanding one at that (as her scribe records). God may have told her to write, but she would tell her scribe what to write and then read it back to her, and he had better get it right. *The Book of Margery Kempe* is not a strict, chronological, linear narrative (although it does start with Kempe's marriage at age twenty and her temporary madness following the first of her fourteen pregnancies, a mania that brought on her first vision of Christ). Rather, it is almost stream of consciousness, unusually employing dialogue from remembered conversations along with regular descriptive narration, with an internal and idiosyncratic logic that employs richly detailed descriptions of divine visions and worldly domesticities. Its minimal organization seems to follow progressions based on visitations by Christ and saints, on tribulations and their resolutions, meetings and their outcomes—all demonstrating Kempe's call to a spiritual life in the world, rather than removed from it. Kempe tells her story in the third person, referring to herself as "this creature," the name "Margery" appearing infrequently and only then as part of a quoted statement addressed to her. This third-person narration is a type of "conceit" meant to underscore the narrator's humility, not to imply that the scribe is the actual author. Nor does this narrative technique discount consideration of *The Book of Margery Kempe* as an autobiography, but it does make it more than simply an autobiography.

During her lifetime, Margery Kempe disquieted people with her loud and endless ecstatic weeping, her visions of Christ, and her challenges to authority—essentially, she refused to be quiet, literally and figuratively—and it is not difficult to sympathize with some of the folk who had to put up with her. True to her self, Kempe's book did not shy from depicting the trouble she made for others and for herself (including accusations of pre-Protestant heresy), all for the greater glory of God. After 1439, Margery Kempe disappears from the record books, but her own book was expertly and cleanly copied in its entirety at least once, c. 1440, by a skilled copyist who identified himself as Salthows at the end of the document. And it was this lone and unique manuscript copy that the Butler-Bowdon family had preserved unawares and that Dr. Allen recognized nearly five centuries later.

Before its full resurrection in 1934, Margery Kempe's book did have a life after her death, but in a deliberately truncated form. The reasons for the full text being left to oblivion can be debated. Books get lost, people copy out and save what they like and discard the rest, sensibilities are offended by too frank language and so sections are censored. That Kempe was considered a difficult personality at best during her life is well attested to—she herself includes the (sometimes funny) comments people would hurl at her during her "ravings." That she was not quite a proper mystic was the predominant assessment, and so she was trimmed and edited to acceptable portions and proportions. Her book is indeed frank, in that it is unrestrained; Kempe gives full **voice** to her feelings and thoughts, submerging herself fully into the perhaps unsettling but wholly orthodox vision of Christ as bridegroom. She also gives full voice to her feelings and thoughts about those who helped her and hurt her and, in her opinion, hurt the Church. The monks of Mount Grace, where the 1440 full-text edition ended up, were of a similar ecstatic mind to Kempe's. As their thoughtful marginal comments and annotations to the manuscript show, they were not averse to her demonstrative receptions of the Godhead (many of which display significant familiarity with *The Song of Songs*). But the larger world was more sensitive. So, rather than the full text, short, deliberative, devotional (and unrepresentative) excerpts of Kempe's book were published in 1501 by Wynken de Worde (and again in 1521 by Henry Pepwell) and were widely read, the sixteenth century having a particular appetite for mystical treatises. By this time Kempe was being referred to as "Anchoress Margery Kempe," that is, a cloistered recluse similar to Julian of Norwich. There is no evidence for this, although one priest did say to Kempe in exasperation that he wished she would wall herself up. In one way "anchoress" is an honorific that Kempe may have welcomed; in another

way, it completely misrepresents who she was and what she did. This residency among the traditions of medieval mystics in general, and medieval women mystics in particular, was all the world knew of the lady from Lynn until Dr. Allen dusted her off and exposed her full textual self to the light. Then, though silent for centuries, she managed to unsettle folks all over again.

When Margery Kempe burst onto the scholarly world in her entirety in a facsimile edition in 1940, the old criticisms of her contemporaries were also resurrected—she was possessed, she was not a true mystic, she was a heretic and blasphemer, she was mad (as in both angry and insane). Added to these were new, modern criticisms of exhibitionism, hysteria, neurosis, pathology, and indiscretion, if not actual obscenity. The reaction is not wholly surprising, Kempe was a stranger from a strange time and her voice was an unfamiliar one on first hearing, even for medievalists. As counterpoint to the psychological approach to *The Book of Margery Kempe* and its author, a literary assessment started to develop, suggesting Kempe as a real-life version of Chaucer's Wife of Bath or Moll Flanders, as the progenitor of autobiographical writing, as a patriarchal victim, or a feminist icon. Neither theology nor literature was sure who should claim her, if either. An illustration of the confusion is seen in the modernized English version of the book by Colonel Butler-Bowdon that came out in the 1940s—the British edition used smaller print for the revelatory and visionary passages while the American edition relegated those passages to an appendix, presumably to create a more normal narrative but in both cases diminishing the importance of Kempe's religious visions. All the critiques, until recently, seemed to balk at taking Kempe seriously and on her own terms. What was forgotten, or ignored, was that ultimately Kempe was convincing, even though she did not garner a contemporary following—she overcame the heresy charge, she was granted audiences with leaders of the Church, she won over her scribe. For Kempe was serious about her religion, and she was serious about telling the truth, as she saw it, about her life—her vanities, her indiscretions, her confrontations, her successes, her piety. Her goal was redemption but also a full-throated declaration of the love of God. The complexity of her presented self and her accomplishment can be as irritating as the real woman probably was, but it can also be rewarding and revelatory, if not in the way she may have intended.

Margery Kempe was an extraordinary woman, and it was her ordinariness that made her so. The formalities, protocols, and training of the religious orders were not hers; she was not a traditional mystic or ascetic; she was a townswoman whose manifestations of faith were as real to her as the ale she brewed; she was proof that God could touch the plain. In her book Kempe recounts "felyngs," "trewth," and "experiens," and these terms refer both to her encounters with Christ and with earthly folk. A truly individual and personal text—especially in that Kempe's self is integral rather than suppressed as in the cases of those women mystics she so admired—*The Book of Margery Kempe* wavers between the genres of religious treatise and hagiography and of autobiography, being all and none. It is pious and picaresque equally, with neither attribute undermining the other. Kempe is not an easy character—she was no saint—but however one responds to her, Margery of Lynn is undeniably an exceptional and singular witness, of her time and for her God and her own restless, vocal soul.

Further Reading: Atkinson, Clarissa W. *Mystic and Pilgrim: The "Book" and the World of Margery Kempe* (Ithaca, NY: Cornell University Press, 1983); Kempe, Margery. *The Book of Margery Kempe: A Modern Version*. Translated by W. Butler-Bowdon (London: Jonathan Cape, 1940); Kempe, Margery. *The Book of Margery Kempe*. Translated by W. Butler-Bowdon. Introduction by R. W. Chambers (New York: Devin-Adair, 1944); Kempe, Margery. *The Book of Margery Kempe*. Facsimile edition. Edited by Sanford Brown Meech. Preface by Hope Emily Allen. Original Series 212 (London: Early English Text Society/Oxford University Press, 1997); Kempe, Margery. *The Book of Margery Kempe*. Translated and edited by B. A. Windeatt (London: Penguin, 1985); McEntire, Sandra J., ed. *Margery Kempe: A Book of Essays* (New York: Garland, 1992); Staley, Lynn. *Margery Kempe's Dissenting Fictions* (University Park: Pennsylvania State University Press, 1994); Stone, Robert Karl. *Middle English Prose Style: Margery Kempe and Julian of Norwich* (The Hague: Mouton, 1970).

Elizabeth Dominíque Lloyd-Kimbrel

BOYCE, NEITH (1872–1951) This founding member of the Provincetown Players wrote an autobiography that saw print in 2003, exactly 100 years after the events appended in her travel **diary**. Well known in the first two decades of the twentieth century for modernist novels, plays, and short stories, Neith Boyce was "recovered" in the 1970s. Her innovative writing and role as the wife of radical journalist Hutchins Hapgood (1869–1944) seemed to prefigure the politics of personal life that were important to the New Left and feminist ideology. Her autobiography, however, reveals her reluctance to marry.

Although crafted in 1939–1940, her autobiography ends with her marriage in 1899 and avoids reporting on the bulk of her life, an existence shaped by a forty-five-year alliance with a major experimenter in sexual relations. Rather, we witness Boyce's development as a writer: publication as a teenager of "short pieces" in California newspapers and magazines; the change to a more "realistic" style after the Boyce family moves east; and, in her mid-twenties, success in Greenwich Village. She disregards her later novels, dozens of short stories, and plays that explore the nuances of male-female relationships as well as marital problems.

Born in Indiana in 1872, Neith Boyce was

named for the chthonic Egyptian goddess by her schoolteacher mother. Her father, Henry H. Boyce, was a decorated Civil War hero and an intermittently successful businessman, often connected to the printing trade but also involved in other speculations. Writing in the third person, Boyce used pseudonyms for nearly everyone, including herself. Her mother, Mary, is among the few characters with a real first name. Her father is called the "Captain." Young Iras [Neith] loves him very much, even as she feels somewhat rejected by her intellectual mother.

An omnipotent narrator looks down on their extended family group and charts, rather naturalistically, the efforts and failures of their "Great American Saga": the move west by the Carolans [Boyces] and Smiths. They struggle for middle-class respectability, economic security, and love and experience tragedy along with the transcendent joy that comes from art. Fate, a character in the book, intervenes in their lives. Boyce ignores her father's scandalous divorce in order to marry Mary.

The autobiography opens in 1880 in Milwaukee, where "Captain Carolan" works as a "book agent" and Mary is raising five small children. Iras/Neith's blissful childhood comes to a crashing end when all four of her siblings die of diphtheria within a week. Crushed, the diminished family moves to Southern California, where Henry Boyce cofounds the *Los Angeles Times* in 1884 and Mary establishes an art club and charity organization. Two more daughters are born. The Carolans/Boyces are leading citizens and wealthy—for a time. Iras begins publishing "small pieces" in her father's newspapers and short stories in small California magazines and belongs to the city's Bohemian circle. She falls in love with a man whose life is ruined after he accidentally kills his best friend.

In the early 1890s the family pattern of boom and bust—with touches of scandal—sends them to Boston. There, Iras and Mary work on B.O. Flower's progressive *Arena*

magazine, of which the Captain is part owner for a time. Iras is skeptical of the reformers she meets on the magazine, but enjoys its freedom of thought.

The family abandons Boston for Manhattan, then Mount Vernon, New York. Iras begins selling short stories and "pieces" (genre-bending writing now called creative nonfiction) to major magazines in New York. The editor of *Vogue* introduces her to Norman Hapgood (1868–1937), who helps her get work on New York's *Commercial Advertiser*. Its city editor [muckraker Lincoln Steffens (1855–1936)] hires recent Ivy League graduates interested in writing—and Iras. She moves into the Judson Hotel on Washington Square. Soon she is on the copy desk, where she edits the work of those bright young men.

One of them is Hutchins Hapgood, Norman's younger brother. Simply called H. in the autobiography, Hapgood pursues Iras romantically. Iras confides that something bad happens to every person that she likes; therefore, she eschews romance in favor of writing. However, "Iras at times felt herself melting in this warmth and had a panicky feeling. It was true what she told him, that she didn't want to love or marry. She was afraid of it" (DeBoer-Langworthy 2003, 177). Along with this romance, readers experience the allurements of New York in the late nineteenth century. Recognizable characters flit anonymously through the pages. Iras sells her short stories to magazines and newspapers, including the *Commercial Advertiser*. The city editor asks her, "Why don't you have some happy endings?" (155).

Boyce's great reserve and enormous autonomy are discussed. One of Iras's friends warns her that, "You don't trust anyone, you have walled yourself up—you will never be a good sweetheart, but if you marry you will be a good mother" (148). When this friend, a Danish immigrant struggling in the New World, commits suicide, Iras recognizes that implacable figure of Fate. Happiness is not a realistic expectation for the human **race**, she concludes.

Hapgood, with his great capacity for love and friendship, continues pursuing Iras ardently. Frightened, she quits the newspaper and retreats to an aunt's house in Mount Vernon. Debating the pros and cons of marriage, she publishes a nine-part humorous manifesto against traditional marriage in *Vogue*. But finally Iras determines that they can have it all: love, family, and mutual lives dedicated to art and intellectual pursuits along the tenets of the "New Marriage." The autobiography ends with a traditional marriage ceremony and their wedding night in the Carolan family home in Mount Vernon. Contemporary readers know that the remainder of Boyce's life was dedicated to working out the small print in that contract. Hapgood's consistent infidelity was a source of distress that interfered with Boyce's literary production.

When Boyce typed up her autobiography, she added her "Diary—1903," an account of her first trip to Italy with Hapgood and their first son. Bernard and Mary Berenson, Gertrude and Leo Stein, and other later-famous Florentines surface in this document. Boyce's first novel, *The Forerunner* (1903), appears while they tarry in Italy. All seems well. But happiness in Italy and the publication of her first novel exact a price. Fate interrupts the daily entries to announce the death of the Captain. Neith becomes Iras again and the diary reiterates the theme of the autobiography: Life is hard, happiness is fleeting, and even love cannot placate Fate. The young family returns to the United States.

These linked narratives ponder the ties that bind. Iras, their main character, reflects that the family "was something different from individual relationships. You didn't choose the family, it happened, and it was more than the sum of its parts" (171). This may have been Boyce's stoic rationale for staying in her marriage. She died in Provincetown on December 2, 1951.

Further Reading: DeBoer-Langworthy, Carol, ed. *The Modern World of Neith Boyce: Autobiography and Diaries* (Albuquerque: University of New Mexico Press, 2003). http://www.neithboyce. net; Trimberger, Ellen Kay, ed. *Intimate Warriors: Portrait of a Modern Marriage, 1899–1944. Selected Works of Neith Boyce and Hutchins Hapgood* (New York: The Feminist Press, 1990); France, Rachel, ed. *A Century of Plays by American Women* (New York: Richard Rosen Press, 1979).

Carol DeBoer-Langworthy

BRITISH WOMEN'S AUTOBIOGRAPHY TO 1900 Thanks in large part to feminist efforts at recovering forgotten texts, access to women's autobiographies has greatly expanded in the last thirty years. At the same time, autobiographic studies have extended the range of works that fall under this heading in order to gain a wider range of information about women's literary and social history. According to Carolyn Barros and Johanna Smith in *Life-Writings by British Women, 1660–1815* (1999), the standard definition of autobiography as a "full record of a life or a linear narrative of development" texts excludes many of the valuable nonfiction by women that have been uncovered (3). Thus, critics have increasingly focused on women's life writing as textual sources, including a broad spectrum of autobiographic forms: life stories, **letters**, **memoir**s, journals, prefaces, **travel narrative**s, *mémoires scandaleuses*, and so forth. As Estelle Jelinek points out in *Women's Autobiography* (1980), in addition to traditional autobiographies, women's letters, and diaries are valuable resources because they contain historically significant information otherwise unavailable.

The feminist critics, such as Jelinek, who drew our attention to women's life writing sought to uncover and identify a unique female literary tradition. Other theorists involved in this project include **Carolyn Heilbrun** (*Writing a Woman's Life* 1988), **Sidonie Smith** (*Poetics of Women's Autobiography* 1987), Sheila Rowbotham (*Woman's Consciousness, Man's World* 1974), and **Shari Benstock** (*The Private Self: Theory and Practice of Women's Autobiographical Writings* 1988). While Jelinek is widely viewed as originating this line of inquiry, Heilbrun introduced the study of women's writing and recovery work to a more general audience beyond the academy and feminist movement. In her writing, Heilbrun notes that traditional women's autobiographies disguise women's anger and desire for autonomy and power, instead striving to find "beauty even in pain and to transform rage into spiritual acceptance" (12). Shari Benstock outlines a new way to read autobiographies that accounts for the differences between men's and women's autobiographies. Men's are generally written to present an idealized version of themselves and celebrate their accomplishments, and women's tend to be critical and self-effacing. These theorists established that it is no longer adequate to read autobiographies as accounts of personal achievements. Smith posits that women turned more often to autobiographical writing because of the social stigma attached to public speech: Historically, rather than extolling their public successes, women have employed autobiography to work through and explain private dilemmas. When they did write about themselves, women showed reluctance to assume narrative authority, often elaborately explaining their reasons for writing.

These early feminist accounts of women's autobiographical practices, along with other tenets of the feminist movement, proved too narrow because the assumption that the main, identifiable quality of women's autobiography was **gender** ignored **class**, ethnic, racial, religious, regional, and political differences. Attempts to identify a uniquely female tradition were based on theories of women's development in relation to others and the dominant social and cultural values of the time, privileging an essential female self that did not account for the diversity of women and their writing. Theorists have since complicated earlier critical constructs of women's life writing, seeking to de-essentialize our understanding of women's life writing by emphasizing the differences across women's autobiographies. In *Traditions of Victorian Women's Autobiography: The Poetics and Poli-*

tics of Life Writing (1999), Linda Peterson recently asserts that using gender as a "hermeneutic key" proved inadequate because women's writing may be influenced by a spectrum of factors, including a desire to write against a female tradition (2). Critics Sidonie Smith and **Julia Watson** in *Women, Autobiography, Theory* (1998) examine how women have employed autobiographical forms to build **identity** and agency, allowing them to "write themselves into history" (5). In this light, life writing becomes an invaluable tool for studying alternative historical narratives across social, racial, and ethnic divides.

Early Autobiographies in Britain

The earliest autobiographies in Britain emerged from the religious tradition of self-examination and spiritual witness. **Julian of Norwich**, considered the first British woman of letters, wrote an influential series of *Revelations of Divine Love* (1998) based on a mystical vision of God that she experienced on May 8, 1373. After her vision, she moved to St. Julian's in Norwich where she remained as an anchoress (recluse) at the small church for the rest of her life. From her cell, she prayed, wrote out her revelations, and gave spiritual advice to those who consulted her. To this day, her work continues to be respected as a profound statement of faith. Another female autobiographer from the late medieval period, **Margery Kempe** (c. 1373–after 1439), outlined her religious experiences and pilgrimages to Jerusalem, Rome, Germany, and Spain in *The Book of Margery Kempe*. She claims to have first seen Christ when she was pregnant with her first child and to have continued to be visited by him throughout her life. In many ways her memoir conforms to our expectations of a conversion narrative: She gives a detailed account of her path from sin to salvation. Like Julian of Norwich, Kempe focuses on spiritual and religious matters without revealing any personal details other than those of her spiritual life. Kempe was a highly problematic figure during her lifetime because many doubted her claims to speak to Christ and were unimpressed by her "trances" during which she would cry and scream. *The Book of Margery Kempe* also troubles critics who question whether, and to what extent, one of the scribes who wrote it out for her may have revised and rewritten it (Kempe herself was illiterate).

Throughout the fifteenth and sixteenth centuries, as handwriting became a more widely shared skill, a greater number of women kept a **diary** and chronicled their lives than in earlier periods. Women, for the most part, continued to focus on spiritual matters, although, as a sense of the self as individual developed throughout the Renaissance, they increasingly examined their world in order to understand their relation to it. The most common biographical and autobiographical form in this period was the *exemplum*, an anecdote intended to present a moral example for the reader or listener. For example, Anne Askew (1521–1546), an outspoken Protestant who was imprisoned by Henry VIII and in 1546 tortured and burned at the stake, wrote about her life in order to show others the strength of her faith. In *The Examinations of Anne Askew*, she details how she was questioned repeatedly on theological issues and refused to renounce her beliefs. Her experiences demonstrate, she writes, that faith can triumph over adversity.

Religious narratives were not the only forms of life writing that women produced in this period. Both the structure and content of Martha Moulsworth's (1577–16??) 1632 poem entitled "Memorandum of Martha Moulsworth, Widow" reflect the Enlightenment impulse to catalogue and define the world. Her "Memorandum," written in her fifty-fifth year, is composed in verse, exactly fifty-five couplets. In this poem, she takes stock of her life, expressing both satisfaction and loss, and relays a sense of the circumscribed life she, and most other women in the period, endured.

In the seventeenth century, women's re-lationship to the Church continued to shape identity, and thus much autobiographical writing in early modern England relates directly to religious experience. These writings usually take the form of conversion narratives or accounts of a life lived through faith. In these spiritual autobiographies, women explore their identity through their discovery of and relationship to God. In *The Life and Christian Testimony of That Faithful Servant of the Lord*, Elizabeth Stirredge (1634–1706), for example, relates a fairly typical religious "awakening," including her temptation to sin, fear of God, and her conversion.

Anna Trapnel (1620?–1660?), a member of a radical Puritan sect that believed that Jesus was soon to return to earth, describes her ecstatic visions and prophecies, as well as the religious persecution that she suffered, in her *Report and Plea* (1654). An itinerant preacher, she attracted large crowds to her spiritual "performances." In her trances, she criticized Cromwell's authority and called on him to resign. The Cromwell government arrested her for witchcraft, and her account describes how her faith helped her to triumph. During her trial, she was accused of unwomanliness, witchcraft, and lunacy, and it was to refute these claims that she wrote her *Report*. While, in the main, she relates an episode of religious persecution, hers is not purely a spiritual account: Her text presents both a political argument and personal narrative, concluding with her claim to have convinced her audience that she is not a witch.

Alice Thornton (1627–1707) also wrote an account of how her faith helped her to withstand physical and emotional adversity. Like many women of the period, Thornton spent a significant portion of her adult life bearing children and, in her *Autobiography* (1875), she describes how she suffered during pregnancy, labor, and motherhood. She explains that each physical hardship helped to continually renew her faith in God each time she recovered.

The Enlightenment sense of a stable

self, as well as the move to gain scientific information through firsthand observation, contributed to the impulse to write autobiographies. The autobiographies of the sixteenth and seventeenth centuries, in their adherence to first-person observation, differed from the accounts of conversion and faith that flourished in the previous century. Women, who had no separate identity under the law, found it difficult to define themselves as subjects of their own stories, and the autobiographies from this period frequently begin with the author justifying why she is writing about herself.

Secular Approaches to Autobiographies

In *Memoirs of Lady Fanshawe*, Ann, Lady Fanshawe (1625–1679), addresses her son in her autobiography, describing the travels and adventures that she and Sir Richard Fanshawe, to whom she was devoted, had experienced together. She frames the text as an account of her husband for her son's benefit, as well as a lesson in avoiding his parents' mistakes. She and her husband were Royalists and spent the greater portion of their married life running from Cromwell's government until the monarchy was restored in 1660, and they were finally able to return to England. She details her adventures, including her travels, a shipwreck, and an occasion when she dressed as a cabin boy to visit her husband on the deck of a ship. The memoirs end abruptly after her husband's death.

Another seventeenth-century author, Aphra Behn (1640–1689), was the first English woman to earn a living through writing. Little is known about her, and the autobiographical elements in her fiction do not always match historical detail. Her most autobiographical work was *Oroonoko, the Royal Slave* (1688), part memoir, part **travel narrative**, part novel. She based this work on her experiences visiting the Dutch colony of Surinam in 1663–1664. At the outset, she asserts that her narrative is a true story, without embellishment, of an event that she witnessed, and, for the most part, the details appear to match the loose chronology of her life that critics have reconstructed. The title character is a noble African prince who is enslaved and tortured by "civilized" white Christians. Many believe that her account of his treatment played a role in igniting the antislavery movement. Whether Behn portrays events factually, *Oroonoko* succeeds both as a memoir and as a novel and is considered one of the first philosophical novels in English.

As *Oroonoko* contains both fictional and nonfictional elements, it points to a central generic issue in the field of autobiography studies. If *Oroonoko* is both novel and memoir, should we include other loosely autobiographical novels, such as Charlotte Brönte's *Jane Eyre: An Autobiography* (1847) and Charles Dickens' *The Personal History of David Copperfield* (1850), in the spectrum of life writing? The distinction between a loosely autobiographical novel and life writing can be thin at times, especially as critics have called into question whether some of the elements of particular autobiographies that were written for publication were fictional.

Questions about "truth" and "authenticity" surround the critical tradition of autobiography. These distinctions were called even further into question by *mémoirs scandaleuses*, which employed many of the same narrative strategies as novels. These sensationalist memoirs most obviously call into question the blurred relationship between fact and fiction. They most often describe intrigue in high society, generally the royal court, or the life story of a transgressor, especially a prostitute or courtesan. Authors of *mémoires scandaleuses* included Ann Sheldon and Elizabeth Gooch. This subgenre points to a major theoretical issue in autobiography studies: the question of truth and authenticity versus fiction. Many autobiographies contain fictional elements, including novelistic narrative techniques, and at times, especially with scandalous memoirs, the distinction becomes blurred.

Delarivière Manley's (1672–1724) thinly veiled autobiographical novel, *The History of Rivella* (1714) is one of the most famous "scandal chronicles." As a *roman à clef*, the real life people who are represented as involved in political and sexual intrigue in her work were easily recognizable to contemporary audiences. She wrote this "novel" during a period in which women were not supposed to be involved in politics, and in many ways it is a piece of political propaganda. The last ten pages of the book deal almost exclusively with the Tory versus Whig controversy of the period. She employed novelistic narrative techniques, and this work was extremely popular with contemporary audiences. Her contemporary, Lady Grace Elliot, mixes politics with an account of her experiences as royal courtesan and prisoner. These accounts were scandalous because they recount the lives of courtesans—flaunting the expectation that "fallen women" hide their shame—and expose the activities of politically and socially prominent men.

Autobiographies by both male and female authors proliferated during the eighteenth and nineteenth centuries for various reasons, not the least of which is to resist the loss of individuality resulting from rapid industrialization. Critics have identified the negotiation between the private and public self—how one's consciousness is expressed in daily life—as a central concern in autobiographies. Another reason for the popularity of the autobiographic form at this time was the commercial success of two memoir-styled novels, Daniel Defoe's *Moll Flanders* (1722) and Samuel Richardson's *Pamela* (1740).

During this period, many women's autobiographies bear witness to the author's spirituality while also providing a space for self-analysis. Margaret Fell Fox (1614–1702) wrote *A Relation of Margaret Fell* (1710) after she was imprisoned under one of the Quaker Acts of 1662–1664, which declared that anyone who refused to swear an oath of allegiance to the king would be imprisoned. Quakers were targeted because their principles of equality stopped them from swearing oaths of allegiance.

Justification for Writing Autobiographies: Women Who Wrote to Clear the Record and to Survive Economically

In the eighteenth century, the ascendancy of empirical research methods and self-analysis gave rise to many autobiographies. This is also the period when people began keeping diaries in a serious way. The eighteenth century witnessed a shift in women's autobiographical writings with an increasing number of memoirs written with the aim of clearing their author's name and enlisting sympathy by presenting her as a victim. A memoir could be an effective means of recourse for women who had no other socially respectable public options for presenting her side of the story. **Charlotte Charke**'s (1713–1760) autobiography describes her struggles to survive during the long periods of economic hardship after her husband abandoned her. This document is also witness to her resourcefulness: In one episode she reveals that she once dressed as a man to get a job as a waiter to a lord. Charke, actress and daughter of playwright and actor Colley Cibber, originally wrote *A Narrative of the Life of Mrs. Charlotte Charke* (1755) as a full **confession** and as an appeal for financial help from her estranged father. However, when he rejected her appeal, sending a blank sheet of paper as his reply, she published the memoir, hoping that her connection to her father, as well as her own notoriety, would help make it a financial success (and an embarrassment to her father). Another actress, George Anne Bellamy (1731?–1788), wrote *An Apology for the Life of George Anne* (1785), both for money to pay her debts and to salvage her reputation. In her *Apology*, she describes the men who had misused her, her debts, and the hardships that actresses faced, especially those caused by the common perception of actresses and women playwrights as equivalent to prostitutes. By the time she published her memoir, she was completely impoverished, and the royalties all went to her creditors.

Keeping an epistolary journal removes the necessity of justifying why the author is writing about herself and thus was a popular format for women autobiographers. While writing in a journal was seen as unladylike, especially in the eighteenth century, letters were acceptable because they involved valuable social skills. Lady Elizabeth Craven (1750–1828) wrote *Letters from the Right Honorable Lady Craven, to His Serene Highness the Margrave of Anspach* (1789) to disprove the stories that were being told about her. She was notorious in England and often written up in the press, especially after she was separated from her husband and children and denied her jointure—a legal ruling suggesting that she was responsible for the separation. People believed that she was the margrave's mistress, and she did eventually marry him after both of their spouses died.

Anne, Lady Halkett (1623–1699) wrote *The Memoirs of Anne, Lady Halkett* (1979), in which she describes her personal thoughts and feelings, but rarely refers to current events. She also discusses two men that she loved in vain, as well as her husband. As a gentlewoman with no dowry, she had few options as to marriage. Her love affair with Colonel Joseph Bampfield ended in misery when she learned that he had deceived her into believing that he would marry her when, instead, he married an earl's daughter. She focuses at length in her memoir on his treachery.

Within this tradition, Margaret Lucas Cavendish, duchess of Newcastle (1623–1673), author of *A True Relation of My Birth Breeding and Life* (1656), is considered the first Englishwoman to have published a straightforward autobiography, albeit as an appendix to a **biography** that she wrote about her husband, *The Life of William Cavendish* (189?). Cavendish, who was maid of honor to Queen Henrietta Maria, was also a prolific writer and wrote a biography of her husband, Lord Cavendish, that Martine Brownley and Allison Kimmich (1999) point out was extremely influential in the development of the genre. One goal of her autobiography, as well as her biography was to undermine the gossip that was circulating about them both, and that she was a social climber. Her autobiography emphasizes her relationships, having a loving childhood, and her family's "natural" aristocracy (in order to bolster her claim to a higher class status), as well as her love for her husband and her determination to stay with him despite their impoverishment and opposition from Queen Henrietta Maria.

In some cases, these "apologies" were not aimed simply at countering gossip or as a temporary economic stopgap. Mary Blandy (1720–1752) wrote *Miss Mary Blandy's Own Account of the Affair between her and Mr. Cranstoun* (1752) after she was convicted of poisoning her father. Her case had the questionable distinction of being the first to use circumstantial evidence, which involves inventing a narrative based on appearances, thus blurring the distinction between fact and fiction in legal proceedings. Her *Account* tells her side of the story, and right before she was executed, she asked that it be published. Blandy's version further blurred the distinction between fact and fiction because she created yet another plausible narrative through which to interpret the events that led to her execution. Blandy's memoir was subversive because she dared to correct the official record.

Travel Narratives

Imperial expansion and colonialism inspired another category of autobiography the travel narrative, generally written by the wife of a royal officer or administrator. These narratives are often an apology for colonialism, describing the exoticism and lack of "civilization" in British territories.

These accounts provide different images of the territories than those by men because the women often described intimate details and firsthand experiences of daily life rather than political or economic negotiations. The *Letters of the Right Honourable Lady M___y W___y M___e* (1763) is an example of this type of travel narrative. In her letters, Lady Mary (1689–1762) describes her travels to Turkey with her husband, detailing the customs and culture of Turkish society and drawing comparisons with England. She directly challenges the prevailing travel narratives written by men, asserting that as a woman and as an intellectual she had an advantage in understanding the culture. Her description of a Turkish bathhouse, or bagnio, deliberately subverts male authors' accounts of sensual exoticism. She defuses the mystique of the bathhouse tradition by comparing it to an English coffeehouse where people congregate to relax and socialize. Another famous travel narrative was Anna Maria Falconbridge's, *Narrative of Two Voyages to the River Sierra Leone* (1793) that describes a trip she made with her husband, in which she expresses her horror at the "uncivilized" conditions in which the free blacks of Sierra Leone lived.

Unsurprisingly, literary figures also wrote epistolary memoirs that reveal a less public side of their character. During an extended trip to Scandinavia, Mary Wollstonecraft (1759–1797) wrote a series of letters to her lover, Gilbert Imlay. She insightfully comments on the society that she visited and her letters reflect an aesthetics of class and gender in her descriptions of its picturesqueness. On her return, she arranged to have this epistolary journal published as *Letters Written During a Short Residence in Sweden, Norway, and Denmark* (1796), but withheld the identity of the "you" to which the letters are addressed.

First Autobiographies of Working-Class Women and Women of Color

In the process of recovering literary and historical documents by women, scholars have had less access to life writings by working class women, in part because a high proportion of these women were illiterate. Locating these texts takes on particular urgency as, in many cases, they represent the only record of women's lives that are available. Jane Rendall (1997) is one of many critics who have focused on finding and cataloguing working women's life writing. Rendall emphasizes that these women had less time to write about themselves, and many of the documents that have been uncovered are appeals for support from potential middle-class patrons (31–50). For example, Ann Candler wrote *Poetical Attempts . . . with a short narrative of her life* (1803) while in the workhouse in hopes of middle-class patronage. Eliza Macauley, author of the *Autobiographical Memoir of Miss Macauley* (1835), and Mary Ann Ashford, author of *Life of a Licensed Victualler's Daughter* (1844), who were both from the working class, explicitly distinguish their work from romantic fiction to emphasize the "truth" of their narratives. Elizabeth Kenning, a former prostitute and alcoholic, wrote a repentance tract, *Some account of the life of Elizabeth Kenning* (1829), another common genre in which "fallen" women would tell their life stories for a benevolent society that offered them shelter in exchange. In appeals for support, women did not only lay out the often tragic story of their lives; in many cases, they wrote poems or other short literary pieces in hopes of attracting the reader's interest and attention. Although she was a barrister's daughter, in Jane Jowitt's autobiography, *The Poor Poetess* (1844), defines herself primarily in relation to her poverty. Jowitt supported herself in her later years by writing poetry for the gentry, and hers was one of the few working-class women's autobiographies to be published during her lifetime.

Very few autobiographies by British women of color survive to this day, but most famously, **Mary Prince's** (1788–?) autobiography, *The History of Mary Prince, A*

West Indian Slave, Related by Herself (1831) is significant for a number of reasons. Prince was the first British woman to escape from slavery and her narrative relates the details of the vicious beatings and sexual abuses that she suffered at the hands of her owners. When Prince escaped in London, she received help from members of an anti-slavery society who eventually helped her to attain full emancipation. The society was publishing a series of slave narratives that emphasized the virtuous female slave's victimization by her master, and they were interested in publishing her story to use as propaganda. Realizing that they were not interested in publishing accounts of subversion, instead preferring to focus on victimization, Prince did not explicitly describe the sexual abuse that she received. Like many other slave narratives published in the nineteenth century, including **Harriet Jacobs**'s *Incidents in the Life of a Slave Girl* (1861), Prince's memoir was framed by detailed testimonials as to its truth and her reliability, as well as her virtue, from her white advocates.

Writing as a Career for Women

As more women entered the literary profession in the late eighteenth and nineteenth centuries, their autobiographies revealed their ambivalence and guilt about pursuing careers as writers. The novelist **Frances (Fanny) Burney** (1752–1830) felt guilty enough about writing that at age fifteen she burned all the poems, letters, stories, and other fragments that she had written up to that point. However, Burney's desire to write soon overcame her scruples, and she began her diary nine months later, addressing herself to "nobody" because "To Nobody can I be wholly unreserved—to Nobody can I reveal every thought, every wish of my heart" (*Journals and Letters* 1). Another author, Anna Brownwell Jameson (1794–1860) produced three autobiographical works: *Diary of an Ennuyé* (1826), a fictionalized travel journal based on elements from her own life; *Winter Stud-*

ies and Summer Rambles in Canada (1838), another travel book, although this one was not fictional; and "A Revelation of Childhood" (1854) detailing her personal reminiscences (*Studies, Stories and Memoirs* 1866). In Jameson's *Winter Studies,* she does not simply recount her experiences, but analyzes the thoughts and actions of other people, especially the Canadian Indians with whom she traveled. Jameson used fragments from her letters and travel journal to piece together her autobiographical work, which, in a similar rhetorical gesture to Fanny Burney's "nobody," she addresses to "a friend."

Women's literary autobiographies also describe how they came to think of themselves as a writers. In Elizabeth Barrett Browning's (1806–1861) record of her life from age three to age fourteen, "Glimpses into My Own Life and Literary Character" (*Hitherto Unpublished Poems and Stories* 1914), she recounts her development from precocious child to writer and how her family encouraged her to think of herself this way. In many ways, these authors use their autobiographies to justify choosing a literary career.

Dorothy Wordsworth, William Wordsworth's sister, wrote several journals, most famously *The Alfoxden Journal* (1798) and *The Grasmere Journal* (1800–1803), which were "family journals," meaning that they were written with the intention of sharing them with her family. Her journals demonstrate an intuitive sense of detail and understanding of nature and poetry, and her writing has been closely associated with the development of nature writing. She did not write, however, with her own literary career in mind, but rather to assist her brother, and by extension their good friend, Samuel Taylor Coleridge, with their work. Both poets incorporate images, especially of nature, directly from her journal.

The term "autobiography" per se did not come into use until the nineteenth century. According to Linda Peterson, one of the earliest attempts to identify and collect autobiographies, including those by women, was undertaken by the Quakers (1999, 7). Between 1837 and 1850, historians William and Thomas Evans published a collection of Quaker autobiographies, entitled *The Friends Library*, with the intention of recording a history of Quakerism. The collection contains more than twenty accounts by women. Other women whose autobiographies appear in *The Friends Library* include Elizabeth Ashbridge (1715–1733), Jane Pearson (died c. 1775), and Sarah Morris (1704–1775). Another early-nineteenth-century recovery project was undertaken by the publishing firm of Hunt and Clarke, which, according to Peterson, gathered autobiographies for the first collection of autobiographies as a literary form.

The nineteenth century was the era of the domestic memoir, popularized from 1830 onward and reflecting the institutionalization of separate spheres. Sara Coleridge (1802–1852), the daughter of the poet Samuel Taylor Coleridge, began a diary in 1830 to record the events of the early years of her infant son, Hartley. Increasingly, however, her entries became more introspective, describing in detail her weak health and severe depression, which relieved her loneliness and gave her an intellectual outlet. Weakened by pregnancy, and nervous and sensitive, she explains her difficulty with motherhood and her reluctance to have more children. Her physical illnesses likely stemmed from depression and frustration, but at the time she was unable to discover why her health was so poor. She wrote her brief autobiography for her daughter, Edith, addressing her at the beginning. She had meant for the memoir to be more complete, but she died before she could finish it. It was published as *Memoirs and Letters of Sara Coleridge* in 1870.

Victorian Autobiographies

Valerie Sanders explains that Victorian women's life writing predominantly dealt with childhood, family life, lack of access to education, and efforts involved in striving for success (*Encyclopedia* 2001, 947). **Harriet Martineau**'s *Autobiography* (1877) depicts her unhappy, illness-ridden childhood and how it impacted her later philosophy of reform. The novelist Margaret Oliphant's *Autobiography* (1899) recounts her writing life and the economic hardships that she endured, especially after becoming the sole support of her family. She also records her sadness at her children's sicknesses and deaths. The sense of missed opportunity and regret, especially of a more successful literary career, emerges clearly from this work.

Although nineteenth-century memoirs were generally silent on the subject of sex, Anne Lister's (1791–1840) four-million-word diary, *I Know My Own Heart* (1988), reveals her emotional and sexual development throughout her lifetime. Lister's diary is a sensitive account of her relationships with her family and the women she loved, especially a woman named Marian. She examines her attraction to other women, and historians point to Lister's diary as evidence that lesbian identity existed long before Havelock Ellis and other sexologists formulated it as a pathology at the end of the nineteenth century. Although about one-sixth of it is written in a cryptic code that Lister invented, she gave the key to the code to several of her lovers to use in their letters and diaries, perhaps envisioning them as potential readers of her journal.

Charlotte Tonna's (1790–1856) *Personal Recollections* (1841) are addressed to an anonymous reader/listener in response to a request for her life story. Unlike many women's autobiographies that begin by elaborately justifying the author's reasons for writing, Tonna explains her reluctance (another common rhetorical move) to relinquish her privacy that she has closely guarded, even to the extent of not keeping a journal or any other written document that could give information about her personal life. Tonna had become famous for the social-problem novels that she wrote under the pseudonym Charlotte Elizabeth to frustrate her estranged husband's attempts to claim her earnings. In her memoir, however, her tone is direct and matter-of-fact: She explains that she has decided to write her story before someone else has an opportunity to misrepresent her. At the outset, she announces her intention of stating her opinions on every possible subject, including politics and public affairs, so that no one has to guess or look through her other writings searching for her point of view. Her autobiography focuses on her intellectual and moral development as a writer through her relationship to God and continues the tradition of religious introspection.

Toward the end of the nineteenth century, in reaction to the dramatic social changes in women's status and rights, women's autobiographies took on a more confident tone as they recounted their political, social, and literary experiences. **Frances** (Fanny) **Anne Kemble** (1809–1893), an actress who came from a theatrical family, wrote *Records of a Girlhood* (1879), in which she recounts her early experiences in the theater and her success in the 1830s, as well as her friendship with Lord Byron and Sir Walter Scott. Kemble is perhaps best known for her work as an abolitionist in the United States. After a theatrical tour to New York with her father, Kemble stayed in America to join the abolitionist movement. Deeply committed to the antislavery movement, she was horrified to discover, after marrying Pierce Butler in 1834, that her new husband owned a plantation in the South on which he kept slaves. Kemble's *Journal of a Residence on a Georgian Plantation* (1863) records her years with her husband and her perception of American's attitude toward **race**.

Mary Kingsley (1862–1900) published several memoirs, including an addendum to her father's *Notes on Sport and Travel* (1892) and "In the Days of My Youth: Chapters of an Autobiography" (1899), both of which are primarily concerned with her lonely childhood and troubled relationship with her parents whom she characterizes as selfish and cruel. Kingsley's most famous autobiography is her narrative, *Travels in West Africa* (1897), an account of her excursions into Sierra Leone and West Africa. Kingsley's *Travels* was immensely popular, in no small part because she was the first white woman to explore these regions without an accompanying European. In contrast to Lady Mary Montagu, who traveled as a helpmeet for her husband and recorded the exotic from the "woman's" point of view, Kingsley's travels and autobiography reflect the rapid changes both in women's status and in life writing in the last several hundred years.

Further Reading: Barros, Carolyn A., and Johanna M. Smith, eds. *Life-Writings by British Women, 1660–1815: An Anthology* (Boston: Northeastern University Press, 1999); Benstock, Shari, ed. *Authorizing the Self: Theory and Practice of Women's Autobiographical Writings* (Chapel Hill: University of North Carolina Press, 1988); Broughton, Trev Lynn, and Linda R. Anderson. *Women's Lives/Women's Times: New Essays on Auto/Biography* (Albany: State University of New York Press, 1997); Brownley, Martine, and Allison Kimmich, eds. *Women and Autobiography*. Worlds of Women 5 (Wilmington, DE: Scholarly Resources, Inc., 1999); Heilbrun, Carolyn. *Writing a Woman's Life* (New York: W. W. Norton and Co., 1988); Jolly, Margaretta, ed. *Encyclopedia of Life Writing: Autobiographical and Biographical Forms*. 2 vols. (London: Fitzroy Dearborn Publishers, 2001); Kanner, Barbara Penny. *Women in Context: Two Hundred Years of British Women Autobiographers* (New York: G. K. Hall and Co., 1997); Peterson, Linda. *Traditions of Victorian Women's Autobiography: The Poetics and Politics of Life Writing* (Charlottesville: University of Virginia Press, 1999); Sanders, Valerie. *The Private Lives of Victorian Women: Autobiography in Nineteenth-Century England* (New York: St. Martin's Press, 1989); Smith, Sidonie, and Julia Watson. *Women, Autobiography, Theory* (Madison: University of Wisconsin Press, 1998).

Sigrid Anderson Cordell

BRITISH WOMEN'S AUTOBIOGRA-PHY SINCE 1900 The twentieth century has witnessed significant growth in British women's autobiographical writing. As a consequence of sociopolitical developments affecting women, particularly education and employment opportunities, women have increasingly utilized autobiographical modes to document their experiences and their artistry. In **letters** and diaries, published and unpublished, through literature, and in visual, theatrical, and online **spaces**, women have disclosed and declared their personal lives and their politics. These writings, through their similarities and differences, have actively shaped women's autobiographical writing more generally, whether by restricting or enabling certain modes of autobiographical expression at particular historical moments. In the twenty-first-century Britain, autobiography has become the most significant space from which self-awareness and **identity** are articulated.

It would be impossible to effectively summarize developments in British women's autobiography across the range of media outlined above. Thus, the discussion here is mostly limited to readily accessible, published autobiographical monographs, rather than, for instance, **biography**, diaries, letters, or online publishing. It is important to recognize the limits that this imposes on this discussion and to acknowledge the diverse forms of British women's autobiographical writing in the twentieth century that cannot be covered here comprehensively.

Scholars of early-twentieth-century British women's writing have found **Virginia Woolf**'s infamous statement to Ethel Smyth a useful starting point. In 1940, Woolf wrote, "[T]here's never been a woman's autobiography." Contrary to Woolf's suggestion, women did utilize autobiography to represent themselves in this period. This writing, however, did not often occur within the traditional, masculine, literary forms against which Woolf and others evaluated them. Women's autobiographical writing of the early twentieth century var-

ied in format and was burdened by external and internal conflicts relating to self-representation, **subjectivity**, and the cultural expectations of women's writing.

During the late nineteenth century, British women writers had embraced particular modes of autobiography. These modes were distinct from conventional autobiographies that concerned themselves with narrating "great lives." For example, British women wrote **autobiographical fiction** and **memoirs** to avoid criticism that they were focusing too closely on their own experiences and intimacies. And yet this period was also characterized by a shift toward more "controversial" issues being represented in women's autobiography: unhappy marriages and social inequalities, for example.

The Early Twentieth Century

British women's autobiography ebbed and flowed during the early part of the twentieth century. In comparison to its progress in the late nineteenth century, women's autobiographical writing languished prior to, and during, World War I. Though educational and occupational opportunities were rising at this time, and women were engaged in substantial war work, as nurses, doctors, teachers, and rights campaigners, a new conservatism regarding sex and **gender** roles was affecting Britain (Sanders 137). These conditions generated a particular mode of political autobiography. According to Philip Dodd, there are roughly forty women's autobiographies about World War I (Sanders 160). The most notable autobiographies from this period were concerned with the early twentieth-century suffrage movement, some of which are Millicent Garrett Fawcett's *What I Remember* (1924), Mary Gawthorpe's *Up Hill to Holloway* (1962), Cicely Hamilton's *Knight Errant* (1935), Annie Kenney's *Memories of a Militant* (1924), Hannah Mitchell's *The Hard Way Up* (1968), Christabel Pankhurst's *Unshackled: The Story of How We Won the Vote* (1959), Emmeline Pankhurst's *My Own Story*—based on an interview and eventually published as an autobiography (1914), Sylvia Pankhurst's *The Suffragette Movement: An Intimate Account of Persons and Ideals* (1931), Emmeline Pethick-Lawrence's *My Part in a Changing World* (1938), Mary Richardson's *Laugh a Defiance* (1953), Lady Rhodda's *This Was My World* (1933), and Evelyn Sharp's *Unfinished Adventure: Selected Reminiscences from an Englishwoman's Life* (1933), the diaries of Ruth Slate and Eva Slawson, Helena Swanwick's *I Have Been Young* (1935), and Mrs. Humphry Ward's (Mary Augusta Ward) *Writer's Recollections* (1917).

These autobiographies document the experiences of the National Union of Women's Suffrage Societies (NUWSS) and the Women's Social and Political Union (WSPU). They relate these women's experiences of winning particular women's rights campaigns against the backdrop of war. They were produced at a time when the suffragette campaign was losing public support and experiencing a significant amount of internal wrangling. These autobiographies are largely performances of selflessness, reflecting the self-consciousness of women writers occupying autobiographical forms. Whether these writings sustained or challenged bourgeois femininity, the suffragettes immersed autobiography within an explicitly feminine context (Corbett 1992, 150). Suffragette writers embrace the autobiographical mode to serve their politics, choosing memoir as their form, yet using a more self-consciously impersonal style to demonstrate the scope of their experiences. A consequence of this was that for many reviewers at the time, suffragette autobiographies were not autobiographical enough (Sanders 1989, 141). Thus, these autobiographies not only reflect the overt political struggles of the suffragettes, but also their conflicts as women writers.

Other significant autobiographical writings of the early twentieth century came from artists and scholars. Writer, composer, and suffragist campaigner Ethel Smyth (the recipient of Woolf's aforementioned letter) was a prolific autobiographer most noted for her work *Impressions That Remained* (1919). Critics celebrated its apparent openness in revealing her personal ambitions (Sanders 1989, 142). Actress Ellen Terry's *The Story of My Life* (1908) was important to the suffragette movement as Terry "mirrored the projections of spectating consumers" (Corbett 1992, 150). Sociologist Beatrice Webb wrote *My Apprenticeship* (1926), a narrative of personal and professional development as a "scientific worker . . . a child, unmarried woman, wife and citizen" (1). She later wrote another autobiography *Our Partnership* (1948).

Dorothy Richardson's thirteen-volume *Pilgrimage* (1915–1938), an auto/biographical fiction, or documentary novel of an independent woman's life in the early twentieth century, is considered by many to be one of the great works of modernism. *Pilgrimage* is styled via contemporary cultural theories such as modernism, sexology, and psychoanalysis, resulting in an exploration of women's **sexuality**. Margaret Llewelyn Davies' *Life as We Have Known It* (1931), an anthology of working-class women's autobiographies, documents working women's descriptions of their jobs and families in the early twentieth century. The recurrent narratives in this book are of women in domestic service or working in factories. In particular, Davies' anthology is concerned with accounting for the political awakenings of working-class women of this period through their involvement in the Women's Co-operative Guild movement.

Vera Brittain's *Testament of Youth*, a feminist, pacifist autobiography was published in 1933. Brittain's retrospective account was inspired by the events of World War I and adapted from **diary** entries she had made at the time. Brittain considered writing her story as a novel or as a diary before recognizing that autobiography offered the perspective she required. She believed that autobiography would allow her to present "a complete picture" (12). Yet, throughout her autobiography she acknowledges the complexities of writing in this mode, for example, the impossibility of reconstructing feelings and perspectives from the past. *Testament of Youth* provides a woman's response to war alongside prevalent male commentators such as Siegfried Sassoon. In so doing, Brittain asserts the significance of her experiences and claims an authoritative space for women's autobiographies of war. She served in Britain and abroad as a nurse and suffered the deaths of her brother, fiancé, and several friends. Like the suffragette autobiographies, Brittain's text juxtaposes personal life with historical events. *Testament of Youth* recounts her own political development toward becoming a committed pacifist, but the autobiography also functions as a collective biography of the people she lost. This consciousness of the "representativeness" of her writing is a significant feature of Brittain's autobiography. For example, it is one of the ways in which Brittain justifies writing in this mode, amid criticisms of the solipsism of autobiographical writing or the inappropriateness of women engaging in this mode of expression. Brittain went on to write three additional autobiographies: *Testament of Friendship* (1940), *Testament of Experience* (1957), and *Testament of Faith* (unpublished). Though it is her first autobiography that is widely recognized, in her later writings, particularly *Testament of Experience*, Brittain demonstrates an increasing awareness of the role that gender has played in her writing. For example, in *Testament of Experience*, Brittain discusses masculine responses to her writing as a means to explore the difficulties she experienced with autobiography.

Bloomsbury writers generated memoirs and were also responsible for important early-twentieth-century literary criticism of autobiography. Throughout her fictional and nonfictional work, Virginia Woolf's interest in how women can write their lives. Woolf considered autobiographical writing to be a "crucial part of women's move from the private to the public sphere," an important step in "redressing patriarchal dominance"

(Snaith 2000, 96). She was concerned that so many women's lives remained marginalized or unrecorded. Reflecting on ideas of fact and fiction, self and consciousness, and the relationship between identity and writing, Woolf's experiments in autobiography reflect the promises and limitations of women's autobiography of the period.

Though Woolf did not write an autobiography, she did write autobiographically via diaries and letters, which have subsequently been published. Woolf also wrote autobiographically in her essays, particularly in *A Room of One's Own* (1929) and *Three Guineas* (1938). In these two pieces, Woolf writes at length about the constraints of Victorian manners and of the inequalities suffered by women, which, in turn, affected their ability to write. As **Shari Benstock** suggests, Woolf extended and reconstructed the boundaries of autobiographical genres: "[s]he used the diary to pose theoretical and practical questions of *writing*" (1988, 17). For instance, in these writings Woolf replaced linear time with fragmented moments; her writing proposed that experiences are indefinite—multiple, diverse, unconnected, and contradictory. Woolf experimented with fictional biography in *Orlando* (1928) and *Flush* (1933). She regarded autobiography as a masculine mode of writing, but as Linda Anderson suggests, "Woolf's extremely subtle and provocative thinking about women's autobiographical writing seems to prefigure many of the contemporary debates about writing and sexual difference: she saw the importance of autobiography for women as well as how it was inseparable from the process of its own self-questioning, from a discursive leap into the unknown" (1997, 46).

After her death, five autobiographical sketches were pieced together in ***Moments of Being*** (1976). When read chronologically these sketches resemble a memoir. Three of these autobiographical sketches: "22 Hyde Park Gate," "Old Bloomsbury," and "Am I a Snob?" were read to her contemporaries at a Bloomsbury Memoir Club. The remaining two sketches are the well-known pieces "Reminiscences" (1907), which describes the birth of her first nephew, Julian Bell, and "A Sketch of the Past" (1938–1940), a deeply moving piece that relates a diversity of experiences, from the sensations of childhood to the death of her mother and sister. Woolf was a great reader of memoirs and in "A Sketch of the Past" she explores the complexities of **memory**, the possibilities and impossibilities of remembering and the compulsion to remember and record the past via writing. Carefully crafted experimental writing and suggestive visual imagery characterize this sketch.

Mid-Twentieth Century

The mid-twentieth century saw the publication of British women's experiences of World War II. Accounts can be found in autobiographies such as Frances Partridge's *A Pacifist's War* (1978) and Christabel Bielenberg's *The Past Is Myself* (1962), which describes her experiences of being an Irish woman in Germany during the war. Naomi Mitchison kept a diary during World War II at the request of the social research organization, Mass Observation. The result was *Among You Taking Notes* (1939–1945, published in 1985). It contained sharp descriptions of this social period and Mitchison's place within it. Mitchison wrote many other autobiographical texts including *Small Talk* (1973), *All Change Here* (1975), *You May as Well Ask* (1979), and *Mucking Around* (1981), which summarized, among other things, her socialist politics and extensive travels.

The boom period for women's autobiography in the twentieth century occurred from the 1960s to 2000s. This period witnessed the publication of countless autobiographies by British women. The developments in British women's autobiography during this period are difficult to summa-

rize, a consequence of their volume and variety. The growing recognition that women's literary voices had been silenced has resulted in a recovery and celebration of the particular modes of writing that women had traditionally occupied: autobiography, diaries, and letters. Increasingly, second-wave feminists and women in academia are recognizing and utilizing autobiography, particularly in public forms of writing: sociological tracts, and literary and popular autobiography.

The 1960s to 1980s were predominantly characterized by literary autobiographies as well as autobiographies by artists and entertainers. Controversial writer Edith Sitwell's *Taken Care Of* (1965) was published shortly after her death. Poet and critic Kathleen Raine wrote a series of autobiographies: *Farewell Happy Fields* (1973), *The Land Unknown* (1975), and *The Lion's Mouth* (1977), while biographer Anita Leslie wrote *The Gilt and the Gingerbread: An Autobiography* (1981). Storm Jameson, who is recognized as one of the most important British literary figures of the 1918–1945 period, authored *Journey from the North* (1969). Bloomsbury autobiographies published during this period include Angelica Garnett's *Deceived with Kindness* (1984), Juliette Huxley's *Leaves of the Tulip Tree: Autobiography* (1986), and Frances Partridge's *Memoirs* (1981). In addition, actress Anna Neagle's *Anna Neagle Says "There's Always Tomorrow"* (1974), television personality Katie Boyle's *What This Katie Did* (1980) and quiz show contestant/entertainer Irene Thomas' *A Bandsman's Daughter* (1979), represent some of the autobiographies written by women entertainers of this period. The autobiographies of philanthropists, such as Baroness Sue Ryder and Baroness Muriel Dowding, were also published in the 1970s and 1980s. Ryder wrote two volumes of autobiography, *And the Morrow Is Theirs* (1975) and *Child of My Love* (1986). Dowding, an animal rights campaigner, wrote *Beauty—Not the Beast: An Autobiography* (1980).

The End of the Twentieth Century and the Beginning of the Twenty-First

In the latter part of the twentieth century and the early part of the twenty-first century, British women from all walks of life have written various styles of autobiographies. Political autobiographies such as Margaret Thatcher's *The Downing Street Years* (1993) and Barbara Castle's *Fighting All The Way* (1993) highlight the mixed paths of British women in politics. Actor Vanessa Redgrave explores her career in *Vanessa Redgrave: An Autobiography* (1991) and Sarah, duchess of York exposes her experiences as a royal in *My Story* (1996). Jackie Kay writes her autobiography in poetry in *The Adoption Papers* (1991) and journalist Yasmin Alibhai-Brown considers the complexities of multicultural Britain in *No Place Like Home* (1995). There has also been a move toward autobiographies by so-called "ordinary" women, for example, women who were not well known before writing their autobiographies. One such example is Ruth Picardie, author of *Before I Say Goodbye* (1998). Like Woolf before them, these writers are fascinated by the implications of writing in the autobiographical mode—and test the possibilities, meanings, and limitations of such writing.

Recent British women's writing has significantly extended the boundaries of autobiographical representation, particularly in relation to issues such as social inequality, sexuality, illness, violence, and abuse. Autobiographies published during this period have become a site for the close examination of particular moments in twentieth-century history, for example, cultural memory of the 1950s–1970s. Historian and sociologist **Carolyn Kay Steedman** is part of a generation of feminist scholars in Britain, which includes Lorna Sage and Annette Kuhn. Steedman, like Sage and Kuhn, entered university in the 1960s as a result of educational reforms aimed at increasing the numbers of working- and lower-middle-class children

in grammar schools and universities. Her part auto/biography, part sociology *Landscape for a Good Woman* (1986) traces the childhoods of Steedman and her mother. It locates their stories within socio political developments of the 1920s and 1950s, particularly **feminism** and psychology. Steedman's work is an example of "academic memoir," an autobiographical mode that has developed in recent times. Various literary critics, gender theorists, sociologists, philosophers, anthropologists, and cultural studies theorists have worked within this mode in recent years. These autobiographies commonly work as an explanation or justification of the particular vocation of the writer. For example, in identifying themselves as working class, academics are better able to explain their ideologies, politics, and conflicts. Other examples of academic memoirs are Annette Kuhn's *Family Secrets: Acts of Memory and Imagination* (1995), Ann Oakley's *Taking It Like a Woman* (1984), Gillian Rose's *Love's Work* (1995), and Lorna Sage's *Bad Blood* (2000). Kuhn's is not a life story organized as a linear narrative, but, rather, an autobiographical meditation on personal and collective memory, using autobiography as a cultural critique. Sage's *Bad Blood* is an autobiography of childhood set in the 1950s, which is predominantly concerned with Sage's literary development via her rural, working-class family. Sage's childhood memories are shaped in terms of the feminist literary critic that she becomes. Sage implicates her own story within broader social changes that enabled the social mobility of herself and others. This allows *Bad Blood* to employ a sociological stance in explaining the inequality suffered by working-class, rural children in 1940s and 1950s England.

A number of other recent British women's autobiographies attempt to redress inequalities suffered by women such as Leila Berg's *Flickerbook* (1997) and Meg Henderson's *Finding Peggy* (1994). Like Sage's *Bad Blood*, Berg's *Flickerbook* is a feminist autobiography of childhood. Berg's autobiography is set in

Salford, Lancashire, in the 1920s and 1930s. Far from being a "golden age," this was a time when girls were isolated from knowledge, social activities, and careers. For Berg, autobiography becomes a means for writing her experiences into history in a way that was impossible before the 1990s. Berg's narrative reinstates a knowing child into her past who, via first-person, present-tense narration, critiques the ignorance of adults and asserts the intelligence of children. *Flickerbook* progresses through eighteen years of Berg's childhood to adulthood and is told using vignettes or "flickers" of stories. This creates the impression of a narrator with a fast-developing intellect, and of childhood as a phase of rapid and disorientating development. Like Sage's narrative, *Flickerbook* reflects a need to "write back" as an accomplished, educated adult and acknowledge one's origins to offer pointed criticisms of the education system in which she succeeded in spite of its discrimination toward girls.

Girls' sexuality is an important feature in the autobiographies of Berg and Sage. Sage writes of finding herself pregnant at sixteen, without knowing she had actually had sex. And just as autobiography allows Sage to identify herself publicly as an adolescent mother, the autobiographical form permits Berg to reveal that she had an abortion during her adolescence. Through these acknowledgements of youthful sexuality, Berg and Sage are able to assert a space for themselves as radical pacesetters, concerned about the rights of women and children. Sage ends her autobiography by looking to the future via her daughter: "[S]he's the real future, she tells the world that we broke the rules and got away with it, for better and for worse, we're part of the shape of things to come" (2000, 278). This statement is a call to action whereby the reader is encouraged to see and respond positively to women's social change.

Another "autobiography" dealing with girlhood sexuality is Jeanette Winterson's *Oranges Are Not the Only Fruit* (1985). This text is significant on a number of fronts.

Thematically, Winterson's text explores the protagonist's "coming-out" as a lesbian amid the religious conservatism of 1950s, working-class Britain. The most commonly asked question about *Oranges Are Not the Only Fruit* is, "to what extent is it autobiographical?" The generic ambiguity of this text is one of its primary appeals. *Oranges Are Not the Only Fruit* is most often referred to as "autobiographical fiction," or "semi-autobiographical," rather than autobiography. It interweaves allegorical fairy tales within its narrative to disrupt an autobiographical reading.

Like the autobiographies of Winterson and Kuhn, Jenny Diski's *Skating to Antarctica* (1997) is a transgeneric text. It weaves together previous "fictions," travel writing, and autobiography. Novelist Diski merges the story of her 1950s–1960s childhood with a travelogue of a 1990s trip to Antarctica. Traveling to Antarctica represents Diski's desire for peace, quiet, and emptiness, which she believes she will find in the "whiteness" of Antarctica. What the experience does provoke, however, is memories of her youth and childhood, of the whiteness of the psychiatric institutions she found herself in as a child.

Throughout *Skating to Antarctica* the narrator refers to herself as "Jenny Diski," author of previous novels, who is preoccupied with questions of consciousness and **memory**. Such gestures imply that this will not be a conventional autobiography; *Skating to Antarctica* exudes ambiguity and even contradiction. There is very little reassurance of its "truth"; it is not chronological and the narrator presents the story of her childhood—from birth to mid-adolescence—in two pages. The narrator approaches her childhood memories with a great deal of postmodern skepticism (perhaps appropriate for a writer of literary fiction). She refers to her childhood self in the third person, and slips between first and third person throughout the narrative as she painstakingly establishes herself as an unreliable narrator. The narrator muses over the possibilities of self-representation.

Diski's autobiography is also a narrative of child abuse. Diski's narrative, Andrea Ashworth's *Once in a House on Fire* (1998) and Carolyn Slaughter's *Before the Knife: Memories of an African Childhood* (2002) represent very different journeys from childhood abuse to becoming writers and intellectuals. Ashworth's autobiography represents her journey from working-class Manchester to Oxford University. In *Before the Knife*, Slaughter's narrator is unable to narrate her abuse without first discussing and contextualizing her childhood as a colonial childhood spent in Africa. Slaughter's narrative is framed as a forgiving narrative that seeks to explore beneath the surface of her "ordinary English family living in a very remote part of southern Africa during the lingering last years of British colonial rule" (1).

Illness narratives also emerged in the 1990s; examples include Gillian Rose's *Love's Work* (1995) and Ruth Picardie's *Before I Say Goodbye*. Picardie's is an edited collection of her columns from the *Observer* newspaper, letters from readers, e-mail correspondence with friends, and final accounts written by her sister and husband after the author's death. Picardie's autobiography records the development of her terminal breast cancer and explores her feelings about her illness. Linda Grant's auto/biography *Remind Me Who I Am, Again* (1999) recounts the author's experiences coping with her mother's dementia and the questions about identity, memory, and independence that it raises. The rise of lifestyle autobiographies, such as television presenter Sally Magnusson's *Family Life* (1999), perhaps functions as a balance for illness narratives. Lifestyle narratives—which commonly confer advice on rearing families, gaining fitness, or renovating houses or gardens—work to reassure readers that they are part of a community of like-minded people.

Illness and lifestyle narratives work to blur the boundaries between private and public life, challenging preconceptions of what can be spoken about, particularly by women, in public forums. Another type of autobiography that has raised the issue of private and public lives, but in a very different way, is the tell-all autobiography. This is a recent publishing phenomenon in Britain and in the United States in particular. For example, Margaret Cook's *A Slight and Delicate Creature: The Memoirs of Margaret Cook* (1999), written by the ex-wife of former British Foreign Secretary Robin Cook, made headlines in Britain when it was published because of its intimate revelations about a leading political figure.

Celebrity autobiographies are endemic of the more general rise of celebrity. Such narratives are often controversial and are commonly best sellers in the United Kingdom. For example, ex-Spice Girl Geri Halliwell has penned two autobiographies *If Only* (1999) and *Geri: Just for the Record* (2002). Television presenter Ulrika Jonsson wrote *Honest* (2002); her disclosure of being raped by a television personality caused a sensation and resulted in the media clamoring for further details.

Where many early theorists of women's autobiography were concerned with confirming the existence of these autobiographies, recent theorists of British women's autobiography have focused on particular movements and key figures of these writings. Major theorists of twentieth-century British women's autobiography include Linda Anderson, Shari Benstock, Mary Jean Corbett, Margaretta Jolly, Valerie Sanders, Liz Stanley, and Carolyn Steedman. Anderson's *Women and Autobiography in the Twentieth Century* (1997) uses feminist, psychoanalytic, and poststructuralist theory to (re)read the works of six women autobiographers of the modern era including Woolf and Brittain. Other theorists of Woolf's autobiographical writing include Shari Benstock and Anna Snaith; each proposes that Woolf is a key figure in both British women's autobiographical writing and its theory. Marie Jean Corbett, Maroula Joannou, Valerie Sanders, and Elaine Showalter have written on suffragette autobiography in a duel project to unveil these writings as autobiography and to explore the complexities, characteristics, difficulties, and contradictions of these diverse texts.

Carolyn Steedman's work, which looks at women's writing from the eighteenth to the twentieth centuries, is concerned with the myriad ways in which people construct self-identity, while Margaretta Jolly has completed extensive scholarship in the field of British women's letters. Julia Swindells has focused on the political and educational contexts of autobiography in literature and theater from the eighteenth to the twentieth century. Her work has considered the writings and oral testimonies of working-class women and others speaking from the margins. Many articles on British women's autobiography have appeared recently in the popular press; articles by Kathryn Hughes and Ann Treneman explore the contemporary phenomena of autobiography within a British context, engaging in particular with sensationalism and accusations of solipsism in contemporary British autobiography.

What each of these critics share is a recognition of the occurrence and consequence of British women's autobiography in the twentieth century. Throughout this period, British women writers have written their disparate experiences into limited cultural spaces. In doing so, these writers have used the contested space of autobiography to write themselves into history.

Further Reading: Alibhai-Brown, Yasmin. *No Place Like Home* (London: Virago, 1995); Anderson, Linda. *Women and Autobiography in the Twentieth Century* (London: Prentice Hall, 1997); Ashworth, Andrea. *Once in a House on Fire* (London: Picador, 1998); Benstock, Shari. *The Private Self: Theory and Practice of Women's Autobiographical Writings* (London: Routledge, 1988); Berg, Leila. *Flickerbook* (London: Granta, 1997); Bielenberg, Christabel. *The Past Is Myself* (London: Corgi, 1984); Boyle, Katie. *What This Katie Did* (London: Weidenfeld and Nicolson, 1980); Brittain, Vera. *Testament of Friendship* (London: Virago, 1992); Brittain, Vera. *Testament of Youth* (London: Victor Gollancz, 1933); Castle, Barbara. *Fighting All The Way* (London: Macmillan, 1993); Cook, Margaret. *A Slight and Delicate Creature: The Memoirs of Margaret Cook* (London: Weidenfeld and Nicolson, 1999); Corbett, Mary Jean. *Representing Femininity: Middle-Class Subjectivity in Victorian Women's Autobiographies* (New York: Oxford University Press, 1992); Davies, Margaret Llewelyn. *Life as We Have Known It* (London: Virago, 1977); Diski, Jenny. *Skating to Antarctica* (London: Granta Books, 1997); Donnell, Alison, and Pauline Polkey. *Representing Lives: Women and Auto/biography* (London: Macmillan, 2000); Dowding, Baroness Muriel. *Beauty—Not the Beast: An Autobiography* (London: C. W. Daniel, 1980); Ferguson, Sarah. *My Story* (London: Pocket, 1997); Garnett, Angelica. *Deceived with Kindness* (London: Pimlico, 1995); Garret Fawcett, Millicent. *What I Remember* (Honolulu: University Press of the Pacific, 2004); Gawthorpe, Mary. *Up Hill to Holloway* (Penobscot, ME: Traversity Press, 1962); Grant, Linda. *Remind Me Who I Am, Again* (London: Granta, 1999); Halliwell, Geri. *If Only* (London: Bantam, 1999); Halliwell, Geri. *Geri: Just for the Record* (London: Ebury Press, 2002); Henderson, Meg. *Finding Peggy* (London: Corgi Books, 1994); Hughes, Kathryn. "I Have Seen the Past and It Works." *Guardian Unlimited.* July 11, 1999; November 8, 1999. http://www.guardianunlimited.c . . . Article/0,4273,3882243,00.html; Hughes, Kathryn. "Remembering Imagination: Have We Had Enough of Memoir?" *The Observer.* November 17, 2001. http://www.observer.co.uk/review/story/0,6903,538944,00.html; Huxley, Juliette. *Leaves of the Tulip Tree: An Autobiography* (Oxford: Oxford Paperbacks, 1987); Jameson, Storm. *Journey from the North* (London: Virago, 1984); Jelinek, Estelle. *The Tradition of Women's Autobiography: From Antiquity to the Present* (Boston: Twayne, 1986); Joannou, Maroula. "Gender, Militancy and Wartime." In *The Uses of Autobiography*, edited by Julia Swindells, 31–44 (London: Taylor and Francis, 1995); Jolly, Margaretta, ed. *Dear Laughing Motorbyke: Letters from Women Welders in the Second World War* (London: Scarlet Press, 1997); Jonsson, Ulrika. *Honest* (London: Pan, 2002); Kay, Jackie. *The Adoption Papers* (Gwynedd, UK: Bloodaxe Books, 1991); Kenney, Annie. *Memories* *of a Militant* (London: Arnold, 1924); Kuhn, Annette. *Family Secrets: Acts of Memory and Imagination* (London: Verso, 1995); Leslie, Anita. *The Gilt and the Gingerbread: An Autobiography* (London: Hutchinson, 1981); Magnusson, Sally. *Family Life* (London: HarperCollins, 1999); Mitchell, Hannah. *The Hard Way Up* (London: Virago, 1977); Mitchison, Naomi. *Mucking Around* (London: Victor Gollancz 1981); Mitchison, Naomi. *Among You Taking Notes* (London: Gollancz, 1985); Mitchison, Naomi. *Small Talk* (Sydney: Macmillan, 1988); Mitchison, Naomi. *You May as Well Ask* (London: Victor Gollancz, 1979); Neagle, Anna. *Anna Neagle Says "There's Always Tomorrow."* (London: W. H. Allen, 1974); Pankhurst, Christabel. *Unshackled: The Story of How We Won the Vote* (London: Ebury, 1987); Pankhurst, Sylvia. *The Suffragette Movement: An Intimate Account of Persons and Ideals* (London: Virago, 1997); Partridge, Frances. *Memoirs* (London: Gollancz, 1981); Partridge, Frances. *A Pacificist's War* (London: Phoenix, 1999); Pethick-Lawrence, Emmeline. *My Part in a Changing World* (London: Hyperion, 1976); Picardie, Ruth. *Before I Say Goodbye* (Harmondsworth, UK: Penguin, 1998); Raine, Kathleen. *Farewell Happy Fields* (London: Braziller, 1977); Raine, Kathleen. *The Land Unknown* (London: Hamish Hamilton, 1975); Raine, Kathleen. *The Lion's Mouth* (London: Hamish Hamilton, 1977); Redgrave, Vanessa. *Vanessa Redgrave: An Autobiography* (London: Random House, 1994); Richardson, Dorothy. *Pilgramage* (London: Virago, 1979); Richardson, Mary. *Laugh a Defiance* (London: Weidenfeld and Nicolson, 1953); Rhondda, Lady. *This Was My World* (London: Macmillan, 1933); Rose, Gillian. *Love's Work* (London: Chatto and Windus, 1995); Ryder, Sue. *And the Morrow Is Theirs* (London: S. Ryder Foundation, 1975); Ryder, Sue. *Child of My Love* (London: The Harvill Press, 1998); Sage, Lorna. *Bad Blood: A Memoir* (London: Fourth Estate, 2000); Sanders, Valerie. *The Private Lives of Victorian Women: Autobiography in Nineteenth-Century England* (New York: Harvester Wheatsheaf, 1989); Sharpe, Evelyn. *Unfinished Adventure: Selected Reminiscences from An Englishwoman's Life* (London: John Lane/The Bodley Head, 1933); Showalter, Elaine. *The Female Malady: Women,* *Madness and English Culture, 1830–1980* (London: Virago, 1987); Sitwell, Edith. *Taken Care Of* (London: Hutchinson, 1965); Slaughter, Carolyn. *Before the Knife: Memories of an African Childhood* (London: Black Swan, 2002); Smith, Sidonie, and Julia Watson. "Introduction: Situating Subjectivity in Women's Autobiographical Practices." In *Women, Autobiography, Theory: A Reader*, edited by Sidonie Smith and Julia Watson, 3–52 (Madison: University of Wisconsin Press, 1998); Smyth, Dame Ethel Mary. *Impressions That Remained.* 2 vols. (London: Longman's, Green, 1919, 1920); Snaith, Anna. " 'My Poor Private Voice': Virginia Woolf and Auto/biography." In *Representing Lives: Women and Auto/biography*, edited by Alison Donnell and Pauline Polkey (London: Macmillan, 2000); Stanley, Liz. *The Auto/biographical I: The Theory and Practice of Feminist Auto/biography* (Manchester: Manchester University Press, 1992); Stanton, Domna C. *The Female Autograph: Theory and Practice of Autobiography from the Tenth to the Twentieth Century* (Chicago: University of Chicago Press, 1984); Steedman, Carolyn. *Landscape for a Good Woman: A Story of Two Lives* (London: Virago Press, 1986); Steedman, Carolyn. "Stories." In *Women, Autobiography, Theory: A Reader*, edited by Sidonie Smith and Julia Watson, 243–254 (Madison: University of Wisconsin Press, 1998); Swanwick, Helena. *I Have Been Young* (London: Victor Gollancz, 1935); Swindells, Julia. "First Person Suspect, or, the Enemy Within." In *Representing Lives: Women and Auto/biography*, edited by Alison Donnell and Pauline Polkey, 34–42 (London: Macmillan, 2000); Terry, Ellen. *The Story of My Life* (London: Schocken Books, 1998); Thatcher, Margaret. *The Downing Street Years* (London: HarperCollins, 1995); Thomas, Irene. *A Bandsman's Daughter* (London: Macmillan, 1979); Thompson, Tierl, ed. *Dear Girl: The Diaries and Letters of Two Working Women, 1897–1917* (London: The Women's Press, 1987); Treneman, Ann. "When Did You Last See Your Panda?" *Independent.* November 8, 1999; Ward, Mary Augusta. *Writer's Recollections.* 2004. Indypublish.com; Webb, Beatrice. *My Apprenticeship* (London: Longman's, 1926); Webb, Beatrice. *Our Partnership* (Cambridge: Cambridge University Press, 1975); Winterson, Jeanette. *Oranges Are Not the Only Fruit* (London: Vintage,

1996); Woolf, Virginia. *Collected Essays*. 4 vols. (London: The Hogarth Press, 1929); Woolf, Virginia. *The Diary of Virginia Woolf*. Edited by Anne Oliver Bell. 5 vols. (London: The Hogarth Press, 1982); Woolf, Virginia. *The Letters*. Edited by Nigel Nicholson. 6 vols. (London: Granada, 1978); Woolf, Virginia. *Moments of Being: Unpublished Autobiographical Writings*. Edited by Jeanne Schulkind (New York: Harcourt Brace Jovanovich, 1976); Woolf, Virginia. *A Room of One's Own* (London: The Hogarth Press, 1929).

Kate Douglas

BRODZKI, BELLA (1951–) A leading critic in women's autobiography studies, Brodzki has written on Holocaust testimonies, Francophone literature, Jorge Luis Borges, slavery, translation studies, and feminist theory. Born in Munich, Germany, the daughter of Polish Holocaust survivors, she studied at Sarah Lawrence College and Hebrew University before earning her Ph.D. at Brown University. She taught at Smith College and Lewis and Clark College before joining the faculty at Sarah Lawrence College in 1984.

Brodzki coedited, with **Celeste Schenck**, a highly influential collection of essays, *Life/Lines: Theorizing Women's Autobiography* (1988). This collection addresses the conflicting concepts of selfhood in contemporary criticism. On the one hand, the essentialist self is prevalent in much of American and French feminist theory and considers factors as diverse as **race**, maternity, labor issues, and sexual politics. On the other hand, the post-structuralist self is purely textual; selfhood is a textual effect stripped of individualizing characteristics and therefore fails to represent the real lives lived by real women. In their introduction, the authors formulate a theory of female autobiography that acknowledges the problematic, or mediated, status of the female autobiographical self, even while reclaiming it from the masculine autobiographical tradition, a tradition in which texts mirror unified, undistorted, transcendent selves.

Furthermore, the authors propose "a feminist reappropriation of the mirror" (7) modeled on French psychoanalyst and theorist Luce Irigaray's image of the speculum. *Life/Lines* complements and extends criticism begun in the 1970s, when interest in women's autobiography surged. The collection specifically responds to Estelle Jelinek's *Women's Autobiography* (1980) and **Domna C. Stanton**'s *The Female Autograph* (1984). Brodzki and Schenck's revisionist aim is to enlarge the canon of Jelinek's female autobiographical tradition and to restore to feminist autobiographical theory the bio, or life, deleted by Stanton. Brodzki and Schenck assert that reducing female **identity** to only a textual representation potentially disallows the relevance of crucial personal issues in female identity. Reaffirming the relevance of these aspects of identity grounds feminist theory in the real lives of women. The book is ambitious— even revolutionary—in its attempt to preserve rather than reconcile "the tension between life and literature, between politics and theory, between selfhood and textuality" (14). The work's inclusive theoretical premise anticipates the next decade's debates over identity politics, debates about which position (or positions) to privilege in understanding the complexity of identity formation: **gender**, sexual orientation, nationality, culture, race, **class**, victim status, geographical location, age, disability, and others.

Brodzki's earlier critical writing on female identity in Borges' fiction introduces an important theoretical motif: the limitations of both deconstruction and feminist theory and, thus, the need for new critical approaches to bridge critical impasses. Later, she and coauthor Schenck delineate such a critical move in "Criticus Interruptus: Uncoupling Feminism and Deconstruction," (1989) in which their readings of female identity in three **Jamaica Kincaid** stories exuberantly escape the limitations imposed by a solitary contemporary critical method. Here, the authors wield a hybrid, flexible, and responsive critical approach that accommodates the reading of women's autobiography rather than formulaically applying established critical methods such as deconstruction, with its ultimate focus on undoing binary opposites.

Brodzki has also written extensively about postcolonial Caribbean and African texts, foregrounding the connection between the autobiographer's impulse to write and the desire to restore or create collective and individual memories. Her work repeatedly examines the identity problems involved in the particular versus the universal. For example, in her essay, "Nomadism and the Textualization of Memory in André Schwarz-Bart's *La Mulâtresse Solitude*," (1993) she provocatively questions the privileged status of the terms Holocaust and exile; explores "the role of memory and resistance in Guadeloupean and Holocaust history and literature" (214); and notes the frequency with which French Caribbean texts equate Africa, the unknown continent, to the lost mother (1993). "Reading/Writing Women" in Myriam Warner-Vieyra's *Juletane* (1982) points out Western feminist criticism's inadequacy in readings of Francophone African women's literature. Such readings, Brodzki argues, require an intercultural context prohibited by Western **feminism**'s reductive assumptions about literacy and political power.

Drawing on Walter Benjamin's work about translation, Brodzki investigates the relationships among trauma, narration, personal identity, historical **memory**, and translation, particularly in the transmission of memory from mother to daughter. As she explains in her analysis of the autobiographies of Nathalie Sarraute and **Christa Wolf**, the mother is the "pre-text" for the daughter's literary project, whose purpose is to establish a discourse with the lost or absent mother and re-create the maternal legacy. In "Trauma Inherited, Trauma Reclaimed: Chamberet: Recollections from an Ordinary Childhood" (2001), she relies on Benjamin's analogy of the shattered vessel, which likens language translation to the assembling of unlike pieces in order to reconstruct an original. Brodzki parallels the translator's desire to re-create a written or oral text's original language and meaning to the autobiographer/daughter's attempt to recover the mother-daughter bond ruptured by the trauma of the Holocaust.

Brodzki incorporates Jacques Derrida's translation theory as well, in her analysis of Nigerian T. Obinkaram Echewa's novel (written in English). She emphasizes the cultural burden of postcolonial writers who, in translating their cultural legacy, must ensure the survival of the preceding generation's culture and history, as well as embody both pre- and postcolonial identities. Thus, the translator's task exceeds mere preservation and approaches ethnography; the hybrid text not only survives but creates its own terms of existence, separate from origin or translator (1999).

Bella Brodzki's groundbreaking work articulates the tensions and challenges at the intersection of feminism criticism, poststructuralism, postcolonial theory, and cultural studies. It is a significant contribution to the scholarship of women's autobiography. *See also* **Autoethnography**; **Mother/Daughter Relationship**; **Schenck, Celeste**; **Stanton, Domna**; **Subjectivity**; **Survivor Narrative**.

Further Reading: Benjamin, Walter. "The Task of the Translator." In *Illuminations*, translated by Harry Zohn, 69–82 (New York: Schocken, 1968); Brodzki, Bella. "Nomadism and the Textualization of Memory in André Schwarz-Bart's *La Mulâtresse of Solitude*." *Yale French Studies* (1993): 213–230; Brodzki, Bella. "Trauma Inherited, Trauma Reclaimed: Chamberet: Recollections from an Ordinary Childhood" *Yale Journal of Criticism* (2001): 155–167; Brodzki, Bella and Celeste Schenk. "Criticus Interruptus: Uncoupling Feminism and Deconstruction." In *Feminism and Institutions: Dialogues on Feminist Theory*, edited by Linda S. Kauffman (Oxford, New York: Basil Blackwell, 1989); Brodzki, Bella and Celeste Schenk, eds. *Life/Lines: Theorizing Women's Autobiography* (Ithaca: Cornell University Press,

1988); Fuss, Diana. *Essentially Speaking* (New York and London: Routledge, 1989); Roof, Judith, and Robyn Wiegman, eds. *Who Can Speak? Authority and Critical Identity* (Urbana and Chicago: University of Illinois Press, 1995).

Gerri Reaves

BROOKS, GWENDOLYN ELIZABETH

(1917–2000) The first African American to win a Pulitzer Prize in any field, Gwendolyn Brooks was one of the most influential American poets of the twentieth century. Celebrated internationally for her poetry, Brooks was also a grassroots educator. She combined formal resourcefulness with a quintessentially urban idiom in order to speak to the African American who was not the usual audience for poetry during the earlier part of her lifetime.

Author of many books of poetry and fiction—including the Pulitzer Prize–winning *Annie Allen* (1949), a novel entitled *Maud Martha* (1953), and several children's books—Brooks also composed an autobiography in two volumes: *Report from Part I* (1972) and *Report from Part II* (1996). Here Brooks narrated her development as a poet and as an African American as the historical and cultural events in the latter part of the twentieth century unfolded, most notably the Civil Rights era and the Black Power movement of the 1960s. Rather than put forward a chronological autobiography, these volumes offer a collage of Brooks's multifaceted concerns, including interviews with herself and her own introductions of other writers during her year as poetry consultant to the Library of Congress in 1985–1986. The volumes read almost as oral transcripts: conversational, casual, at times confrontational—but always written with an exacting humanity and warmth that so many people associated with Brooks, who was a beloved figure in the African American community and beyond.

Born in Topeka, Kansas, in 1917, Gwendolyn Brooks spent the majority of her life living in the South Side of Chicago. Perhaps the most celebrated Chicago poet since Carl Sandburg, Brooks held the position of Illinois poet laureate from 1968 until her death in 2000. From the beginning, her work focused on African American urban culture; and her first book, *A Street in Bronzeville* (1945), described characters and domestic situations in a poor Chicago neighborhood. Brooks herself, along with some of her critics, was to critique this early work for its failure to express an acute enough understanding of the racist society that created the subculture, and the economic hardships, that constitute the book's subject. Indisputably, however, *A Street in Bronzeville* put Brooks on the map and established her as a poet who excelled in portraying character, especially in the genre of the persona poem.

Brooks's poetry always combined strong formal work with vernacular music. Her language's startling marriage of clarity and syntactic complexity revealed her schooling in the classics and her grounding in the spoken **voice** of African American communities. Brooks's formal versatility was akin to that of Langston Hughes, the foremost poet of the Harlem Renaissance and a figure to whom she was devoted.

Annie Allen (1949), Brooks's second book of poetry and recipient of the Pulitzer Prize in 1950, created the character of a romantically minded young African American woman during wartime. The centerpiece, *Annie Allen*, is a mock epic in tetrameter entitled "The Anniad" (with the obvious play on Homer's epic) that tells a young girl's story, including her trials and tribulations with a philandering husband. Though Brooks clearly looked on the Annie Allen character with a somewhat jaundiced eye, the poem employs high and lyrical diction to describe the character's foibles and dramas. The volume also contains Brooks's famous sonnet sequence, "The Children of the Poor," as well as ballads and other poems in the spirit of *A Street in Bronzeville*.

In *The Bean-Eaters* (1960), written in the heady days of the Civil Rights movement, Brooks turned to a less self-consciously literary mode that led some of her critics to accuse her of abandoning poetry for politics. The volume includes two poems on Emmett Till, "The Ballad of Rudolph Reed" (which treats hate crimes against an African American that prompt him to kill whites, and then to be killed himself), and the often-anthologized, "We Real Cool," spoken in the voice of a disaffected street gang. These and many other poems in *The Bean-Eaters* seemed to indicate that Brooks was testing the literary and racial equilibrium she had established in her first two books. Brooks herself, however, felt that she did not fully integrate her poetry with racial consciousness until quite a few years later, in 1967, to be exact.

"Until 1967 my own blackness did not confront me with a shrill spelling of itself," Brooks wrote in *Report from Part I* (83). Indeed, Brooks consistently hailed "The Black Writer and Human Rights" Conference at Fisk University in 1967 as the turning point in her development as a poet and as an African American. Here she was first introduced to some of the writers who were the movers and shakers of the Black Power movement, including Amiri Baraka (still known at the time as LeRoi Jones). Some have questioned the near reverence with which Brooks treated the younger writers associated with this movement; one could indeed argue that Brooks had, in her own manner, developed a powerful racial consciousness long before this unquestionably important conference occurred. Nevertheless, from this moment, Brooks made racial awareness the centerpiece of her writing, striving to speak in a language that would be accessible to the African American whose experience was not addressed by the literary elite of the time. In *Report from Part I*, Brooks also represents a trip to Kenya as seminal for her self-definition as an African American.

Her later works—including *In the Mecca* (1968), inspired by an apartment building in Chicago—made good on these concerns, embracing the political and social power of blackness and daringly indicting American racism. Though her poetry never lost the complex lyricism that was its trademark, Brooks had clearly revolutionized her notion of audience and her goals for what her poetry should accomplish in the world. It was also after the publication of *In the Mecca* that Brooks decided to publish with African American publishing houses rather than mainstream literary presses; both Broadside Press and Third World Press brought out her subsequent works, which included poetry collections (including *Riot* in 1969, *Family Pictures* in 1970, and *To Disembark* in 1981) and books for children. In the 1980s, Brooks established her own publishing company called The David Company, named after her father, David Brooks.

Brooks was also steadfastly committed to the education of inner-city youth in Chicago and elsewhere, asserting that children in the primary grades should be exposed to poetry writing and to the creative arts in general. Brooks visited classrooms and sponsored writing contests for young children as well as for college students, often using her own money to support such endeavors. Though she consistently asserted that her poems were not polemical, she also maintained an impassioned belief that poetry could change urban social life in America, even before the "slam" poetry scene of the 1990s. When she served as consultant in poetry to the Library of Congress, Brooks tirelessly promoted poetry in schools, prisons, and churches, often inviting students to her office.

Though *Report from Part I* and *Report from Part II* are spoken in a largely public voice, Brooks was personally committed to family life and motherhood, and sometimes nearly legislated the latter as the superior life choice for women. A daughter of supportive and well-read parents, David and Keziah Brooks, wife to Henry Blakely, and mother to son, Henry Jr., and daughter, Nora, Brooks felt that what she termed "the black family" needed to be emphasized culturally in order to counteract media images of African American dissipation. Moreover, she remained dedicated to the **memory** of her loving parents, devoting a large section of *Report from Part II* to her mother's memory and commonsense words of wisdom, spoken in Keziah's own voice.

It is also clear, however, that Brooks juggled the demands of family and career before this dilemma was a commonplace for American women. In *Report from Part I*, Brooks comes across as a woman for whom family life is essential, but who also struggles within these confines to maintain her productive **identity** as a writer. Separated from Blakely in 1969 (and reunited with him in 1973), Brooks describes the particular challenges of a successful and creative wife and mother prior to the advent of second-wave **feminism**.

Gwendolyn Brooks died in her home in Chicago on December 3, 2000. She was eighty-three years old. It would be almost impossible to overestimate Brooks' influence on African American and white poets, but perhaps it is African American women poets, from **Nikki Giovanni** to Elizabeth Alexander, who have expressed most eloquently the importance of Brooks' poetry and person for their particular development as writers. From all indications, Brooks's literary and cultural legacy will endure.

Further Reading: Brooks, Gwendolyn. *Report from Part I* (Detroit: Broadside Press, 1972); Brooks, Gwendolyn. *Report from Part II* (Chicago: Third World Press, 1996); Brooks, Gwendolyn. *Selected Poems* (New York: Harper and Row, 1963); Brooks, Gwendolyn. *The World of Gwendolyn Brooks* (New York: Harper and Row, 1971); Kent, George E. *A Life of Gwendolyn Brooks* (Lexington: University Press of Kentucky, 1990).

Christina Pugh

BURNEY, FRANCES (FANNY) (1752–1840)

Celebrated in her own time for her innovative novels and dubbed by **Virginia Woolf** as the "Mother of English Fiction," Burney kept a seventy-year journal whose publication in 1842 gained her recognition as the preeminent diarist of her time. Her journal remains a vivid record of the life and times of a woman on the cusp of modernity, struggling to shape a writing life and a life in writing.

A daughter of respected musicologist Charles Burney and his first wife, Esther Sleepe, who died when Fanny was ten, Burney grew up in a large family of musical and linguistically talented siblings. Given a great deal of freedom as a girl, she read voraciously and interacted with her father's wide circle of literary and artistic friends, among them the famed actor-producer David Garrick. Burney wrote prolifically from an early age; at fifteen she began the journal—initially addressed to the alter-ego "Nobody"—that she would continue until her death. In 1778, she secretly published her anonymous epistolary novel, *Evelina, or The History of a Young Lady's Entrance into the World*, widely admired for its pointed social satire and dramatic flair. When her authorship became known, she was adopted into the social circle of wealthy and cultivated writer Hester Thrale (later Piozzi), under whose mentorship she became the darling of literary celebrities like Richard Brinsley Sheridan and Samuel Johnson. Encouraged to write for the theater, Burney completed a comedy, *The Witlings*, in 1779, but was persuaded to suppress it to avoid scandalizing the Bluestocking circle of literary women it satirized. (Only one of Burney's eight plays—the tragedy *Edwy and Elgiva*—was produced in her lifetime.)

In 1782, Burney's novel *Cecilia, or Memoirs of an Heiress* appeared, and in 1786 she was appointed second Keeper of the Robes to Queen Charlotte, wife of King George III. Strained physically and emotionally by restrictive court etiquette, she resigned this prestigious position after five years and was awarded a pension. In 1793, Burney married French émigré Alexandre D'Arblay, a former aristocrat whom the Revolution had deprived of property and title. The couple built a cottage in Surrey from the proceeds of her 1796 novel, *Camilla, or A Picture of Youth*, where they lived with their son in happy semiretirement. A trip to France in 1802 to recover D'Arblay's confiscated property would become a decade-long sojourn when the renewal of the Napoleonic wars stranded the family in Europe. In 1814, Burney published her last novel, *The Wanderer, or Female Difficulties*, and after a final trip to France settled with her family in Bath. Following her husband's death in 1818, Burney moved to London where, entrusted with the management of her family's voluminous papers, she labored to ensure her father's reputation, publishing his **biography**, the *Memoirs of Doctor Burney*, in 1832.

The journal that cemented Burney's literary fame consists of a combination of **diary** entries, **letters** to her sisters and other family and friends, and novelistic incidents reconstructed from memos, correspondence, and an extraordinary **memory**. When *The Journals and Letters* first appeared in 1842, edited by her niece Charlotte Barrett from a selection Burney herself had made, reviewers accused the author of vanity and self-absorption, criticizing her revelation of the unvarnished conversations of famous figures and the mundane details of her life. These same minute details, however, conveyed in lively vernacular and sparkling dialogue in an effort to inform and entertain family and friends, have prompted more recent critics to acknowledge Burney's autobiographical innovations; J. N. Waddell, for example, describes her as a "transcriber of the ordinary, as well as a pioneer in the unusual" (qtd. in Harman 2000, 57).

On subjects ranging from court life to courtship, from the harrowing account of a mastectomy she underwent without anesthesia, to a meeting with Napoleon, Burney writes with deep feeling, with a knack for creating character through dialogue, and a verbal richness and flexibility that have contributed scores of memorable words and phrases to the English language. (To Burney's journal we owe such coinages as "social-cheerful," "tranquilizer," "break-up," "enrage," and—appropriately—"diarize").

Her writing reveals influences ranging from the sentimental fiction of Samuel Richardson to dramatists like Thomas Otway, Susanna Centlivre, and Hannah Cowley. Especially important was Burney's family friend and correspondent Samuel "Daddy" Crisp, who urged her to surprise him with spontaneous, conversational prose.

Burney's lively side, however, was less apparent in public. Shy and self-conscious by nature, her self-expression was further hampered by society's demand for female respectability and self-effacement: the resulting tension, a recurrent thread in her fiction, found release in Burney's private writing. Her half sister Sarah Harriet Burney observed that Fanny, under pressure to appear modest and polite, "bottled it all up.... But what was kept back, and scarcely suspected in society, wanting a safety valve, found its way to her private journal" (qtd. in Harman 2000, 367). What else found its way into her journal was a fictionalized version of the truth.

Scholars have observed that at times Burney's journal plays fast and loose with the facts. Burney herself, betraying a highly modern awareness of the complexity of personality, the constructedness of **identity**, and the permeability of life and art, believed her private diaries complemented her published work, composing a body of writing that served to actualize her life. Perhaps this conviction helps explain readers' perplexity at the inconsistent personality that emerges from Burney's life writing: at times apologetic, anxious, even prudish, and at other times bold, racy, and self-promoting. What her journal ultimately reveals are the progress and pitfalls of a gifted, observant woman's efforts to legitimize herself, her family, and her fiction in the face of personal and cultural ambivalence about women's place in the public sphere.

This enterprise, and the works that resulted, influenced the fiction of contemporaries Maria Edgeworth, Charlotte Smith, and Jane Austen (all of whom, like Burney, would address the difficult position of women in a male-dominated culture), as well as Dickens, Thackeray, and Woolf. Further attesting to her importance, Burney's novels, letters, and journals remain in print after 200 years, and her once-neglected plays are now being published and performed. As more of her papers emerge, scholars under the aegis of the Burney Project at McGill University in Canada are engaged in an ongoing project to restore, edit, and publish the life writing of this "Nobody" whose literary quest to become "Somebody" we read with delight today.

Further Reading: Burney, Fanny. *Frances Burney: Journals and Letters*. Edited by Peter Sabor and Lars E. Troide (New York: Penguin, 2001); Burney, Fanny. *The Journals and Letters of Fanny Burney (Madame D'Arblay) 1791–1840*. Edited by Joyce Hemlow, et al. 12 vols. (Oxford: Clarendon, 1972–1984); Doody, Margaret. *Frances Burney: The Life in the Works* (New Brunswick, NJ: Rutgers University Press, 1988); Harman, Claire. *Fanny Burney: A Biography* (New York: Knopf, 2000); Lang-Peralta, Linda. "'Clandestine Delight': Frances Burney's Life-Writing." In *Women's Life-Writing: Finding Voice/Building Community*, edited by Linda S. Coleman (Bowling Green, OH: Popular, 1998).

Jan Wellington

**CANADIAN WOMEN'S AUTOBIOGRA-
PHY** Just over two decades ago, Susan
Jackel (1987) referred to Canadian women's
autobiography as "an insoluble riddle" (97)
and a "problem for literary criticism" (101).
Pointing to the marginal status of Canadian
literature, women's writing, and autobiography as a literary genre, Jackel argues that
"Canadian women's autobiography," em-
bodying all three of these often-overlooked
categories, has been particularly undervalued and discredited. However, the reception
of women's writing, autobiography, and
Canadian literature has improved significantly since Jackel wrote this essay in 1981.
Many exciting developments have occurred
both in the production of autobiographical
texts and in their reception. Feminist theorizing has challenged the marginalization of
women's autobiographical writing, and
Canadian literature has received international recognition. "Canadian women's autobiography" no longer bears the triple-
stigma attributed to it in the past.

Canadian women's autobiographies stem
from diverse influences, both national and
international, and assume a variety of literary forms. Most feminist criticism on Canadian women's autobiography has highlighted the fact that many of these texts blur
the boundaries between autobiography and
other literary genres. Canadian women

writers, particularly since the mid-1960s,
have challenged the boundaries of autobiography by incorporating elements of fiction, poetry, and literary theory.

In the opening essay of her edited collection, *Essays on Life Writing* (1992), Marlene
Kadar reappropriates the eighteenth-
century label "life writing" because it is
more inclusive than **biography** or autobiography and allows for the consideration of
letters and diaries, as well as more experimental forms of personal writing that challenge the boundary between fiction and autobiography and allow us to transcend
dualistic frameworks that draw sharp distinctions between these genres. Kadar argues for life writing as a "critical practice"
to be used for "looking at more or less autobiographical literature," but reminds us
that " 'autobiographical' is a loaded word,
the 'real' accuracy of which cannot be
proved and does not equate with either 'objective' or subjective truth" (10). Kadar argues that life writing as a critical practice
enables the reader to develop new strategies for identifying the "self-in-the-writ-
ing" (12). In addition to genres that are conventionally assumed to reflect aspects of
the author's own **identity** such as autobiography, journals, letters, and anthropological life narratives, Kadar considers their
"fictionalized equivalents, including self-

reflexive metafiction" where life writing serves the double function of representing the self in writing while simultaneously challenging the overdetermination of the autobiographical subject. Kadar's definition of life writing is broad enough to include a diversity of genres, thus allowing a consideration of texts that have usually been devalued and labeled "non-literary," such as letters and diaries alongside texts that have been deemed "literary," such as poetry and metafiction. Life writing as critical practice helps us move away from judging autobiographical texts on the basis of how closely they adhere to autobiographical "truth" and enables us to question the hierarchies we have internalized that grant more status to public genres and devalue private genres.

In her contribution to the *Literary History of Canada: Canadian Literature in English* (1990), **Shirley Neuman** also opts for the label "life writing" over "autobiography," arguing that the most sophisticated, innovative, and interesting literary attempts to inscribe the self in writing transgress "the borders between auto/biography and fiction in order to question static and holistic conceptions of the writing subject" (333). Neuman edited a special issue of the journal *Essays on Canadian Writing* (*ECW*) in 1995 that focused specifically on autobiography. In the introduction to this issue of *ECW*, she makes reference to the "unwieldiness" of the term "life writing" as deployed in her chapter of the *Literary History of Canada*, but attributes this to the constraints of having to discuss such a wide range of material, including autobiographies, **memoirs**, letters, diaries, travel writing, and biography within a single chapter (5). Neuman notes the relative lack of engagement among scholars of Canadian autobiography with the scholarly debates about the poetics and aesthetics of autobiography that occurred in the United States and Britain in the 1970s and 1980s. She identifies this as a split between a nationalist and a generic approach, a "chasm between the rapidly emerging and various poetics of the genre and a highly localized discussion of Canadian autobiography" (2). A possible reason for this, she suggests, is the difficulty of applying the generic conventions of autobiography to a settler culture such as Canada "where the poetics of genre might be seen as largely irrelevant to, or inaccurate about, the experiences being recollected" (3). Neuman argues that Anglophone critics in particular tend to see autobiographies as historical and sociological rather than as literary texts, but that Francophone writers and theorists have been more open to reading autobiographical texts as creative and aesthetic works.

In their editorial in a special issue of *Canadian Literature* devoted to "Auto/biography," Susanna Egan and Gabriele Helms note the proliferation of theorizing on autobiography that has occurred in Canadian literary studies since Shirley Neuman made this observation. They suggest that the recent popularity of personal narratives in Canada may be linked to their illumination of personal and communal history, insofar as they give **voice** to personal and national experiences (9). Egan and Helms insert a slash between "auto" and "biography" to draw attention to the continuum of life writing texts that purport to be about the self and the Other, and to illustrate the blending of genres and the theoretical questions brought to bear on the field in recent years.

In *Mapping Our Selves: Canadian Women's Autobiography in English* (1993) Helen Buss decides to use the word autobiography as opposed to life writing to describe texts written by women about their lives. While acknowledging the appeal of Marlene Kadar's conception of life writing as a critical practice, Buss opts for "autobiography" out of a desire to refresh and reclaim old terminologies rather than inventing new ones (14). In actual fact, both "life writing" and "autobiography" are older terms, redeployed by Kadar and Buss for the consideration of women's personal writings that have traditionally been left out of discussions of autobiography as a literary genre. Under the heading of autobiography, Buss considers a range of texts by women, some of which adhere to standard autobiographical conventions, and others that blur the boundary between autobiography and other genres. Buss and Kadar both argue persuasively that a consideration of autobiographical writings by Canadian women will inevitably lead to texts that may not adhere to the standard definition of autobiography. Despite their differences in terminology, Helen Buss and Marlene Kadar bring similar questions to the discussion of Canadian women's autobiography. They recently coedited a book entitled *Working in Women's Archives* (2001) that explores some of the complex issues feminist scholars must consider when turning to the archives to research women's lives and life writing.

Buss identifies what she sees as the two main branches of autobiography: the humanist strain that treats the subject as a stable entity whose life can and should be accurately recorded by language, and the postmodernist strain that calls into question the subject's control over her linguistic self-representation. Both versions, she argues, exclude female experience because they assume a male cultural and historical experience. Women are prohibited from laying claim to the position of the humanist subject, and thus they are denied a stable identity to deconstruct. Buss suggests that a different model is required for a study of autobiographical writings by Canadian women. She employs the metaphor of mapmaking as a way of conceptualizing her investigation, arguing that mapmaking can represent both the subject's psychic development in language and the activity of a specifically female oriented writing of the self. As a historian of women's autobiography, Buss sees herself as performing archeological mapmaking, unearthing texts that have been devalued, forgotten, and ignored.

Surveying Autobiography in Canadian Women's Writing

Autobiography has been an important element of Canadian women's writing as far back as the eighteenth century, when accounts of travel and settlement were first written and published by female pioneers and adventurers in Canada. One of the most persistent themes in Canadian autobiographies is immigration. Canada was a settler colony, and thus many of its early texts were accounts of travel, emigration, and settlement. This has remained a strong component of Canadian women's autobiography, although more recent texts frequently address a more racially and ethnically diverse range of immigrant experiences, and focus more explicitly on the urban experience of the newly-arrived immigrant rather than the rural experience of clearing the land and establishing settlements in the rugged wilderness.

Many early Canadian women's autobiographical works were not actually written as autobiographies, but rather as books of advice for women in Britain who were contemplating immigrating to Canada. Because these books draw heavily on personal experience, however, they are autobiographical in theme and content. Susanna Moodie's work, *Roughing It in the Bush* (1852), and her sister Catharine Parr Traill's *The Backwoods of Canada* (1836) recount leaving the middle-class comforts of England to set up a homestead in the wilderness near Peterborough, Ontario, in the 1830s. Moodie and Traill are arguably the most famous early Canadian female autobiographers, but many others also wrote about their experiences of homesteading in the Canadian wilderness. The letters that make up *Our Forest Home* (1889) by Frances Stewart record fifty years of settlement in Peterborough from 1822 to 1872. Other accounts of pioneer settlement in the area include *A Gentlewoman of Upper Canada* (1967), by Anne Langton, and *The Journals of Mary O'Brien (1828–1838)* (1968).

Although the vast majority of published pioneer women's settler accounts originate from the region once known as Upper Canada and now known as Ontario, accounts from other regions of the country do exist. *A Pioneer Gentlewoman of British Columbia, The Recollections of Susan Allison* is an account of early settlement in an isolated area of British Columbia in the 1860s. Allison gave birth to the first white child in the Similkameen Valley and went on to have thirteen more children. Facing challenging living conditions with courage, Allison countered her loneliness by turning to writing. Ellenor Ranghild Merriken's *Looking for Country: A Norwegian Immigrant's Alberta Memoir* (1960) is another retrospective examination of pioneer life, documenting a young woman's experience of immigration to the Alberta prairie in 1910 and the challenges posed by farming and homesteading in this harsh environment. Many of these autobiographical accounts were based on diaries or letters written to friends and family overseas and later edited and published as book-length narratives.

In the nineteenth century, the wives of some Canadian politicians published accounts of their lives. Lady Dufferin, whose husband was the governor-general of Canada from 1872 to 1878, published *My Canadian Journal* in 1891 based on a series of letters written to her mother in England. This account of Canadian political life and her travels across Canada was popular with both Canadian and British readers. Elizabeth Simcoe, the wife of the first lieutenant governor of Upper Canada, kept an account of her life in Canada which she addressed to her friend Mary Anne Burgess, in whose charge she left four of her children before accompanying her husband to Canada. Helen Buss reads Lady Simcoe's **diary** as a rich account of female **subjectivity** that reveals, especially through its absences, the linguistic limitations placed on women in the late eighteenth and nineteenth centuries. The birth and death of Simcoe's daughter in Canada are signified through the absence of entries. There was no language available with which to adequately express the experiences of childbirth, maternal affection, and the grief associated with the loss of a child. Since topics such as **sexuality**, pregnancy, and childbirth could not be written about directly, one often has to read these texts for their absences as well as their narrative content.

The **travel narrative** was another popular form of early Canadian autobiographical writing. Anna Bronwell Jameson's *Winter Studies and Summer Rambles in Canada* (1836) is arguably the most popular piece of nineteenth-century Canadian travel literature. Although Jameson is not actually Canadian, her book has been claimed by Canadian scholars and publishers as an early work of Canadian literature. *Winter Studies and Summer Rambles* has been republished as part of the New Canadian Library Series, a set of inexpensive paperbacks published by McClelland and Stewart with the mandate to provide affordable paperback editions of Canadian classic works. The vast majority of travel accounts by women in Canada were written after the Canadian Pacific Railway was completed in 1885, when women were finally able to travel across the country with relative speed and comfort. Narratives such as Mrs. Arthur Spragge's *From Ontario to the Pacific by the C.P.R.* (1887) and Isabel Gordon's *Through Canada with a Kodak* (1893) recount the experience of traversing Canada by rail when such rapid and comfortable travel was still a novelty. The publication of many of these narratives was funded by the emerging Canadian tourist industry and by land developers in western Canada who were actively encouraging settlement in the areas recently made accessible by the railway. Although a great many of these travel narratives are written by British women visiting Canada and thus are arguably not "Canadian," they do provide insights into women's experiences in Canada in the late nineteenth century. They are also directly linked to settlement and immigration and are part of the body of Canadian women's life writing and autobiography.

Accounts of settlement, travel, and politics by women are of particular importance to feminist literary scholars and historians because they reveal important details about the daily lives of Canadian women in the nineteenth century. Specifically, they illuminate details that have been left largely unrecorded by historiographers who have traditionally focused on public events such as politics, economics, and war. Some of these writings remained unpublished and forgotten in archives, only to be "rediscovered" and published decades later to satisfy a growing feminist demand for firsthand accounts by female pioneers. During the 1980s, the Canadian Institute for Historical Mircroreproduction (CIHM) made many relatively obscure accounts of travel, immigration, and settlement available on microtext in university libraries and government archives. More recently, CIHM has made thousands of early Canadian texts available on the Internet, including many autobiographical publications by female missionaries, settlers, and travelers.

Narratives of travel and settlement continued well into the twentieth century. Georgina Binnie-Clark's *A Summer on the Canadian Prairie* (1910) is in many ways typical of a late-nineteenth- or early-twentieth-century settler account. It is a humorous text, largely written to inform the British reader of the conditions of travel and life in Canada. Binnie-Clark travels to Canada to investigate the progress of her somewhat inept brother, who is unsuccessfully farming a piece of land in the prairies. When she arrives, she finds that homesteading has proven to be too much for him. The book ends with Binnie-Clark purchasing a plot of land that she plans to farm herself. Her second book, *Wheat and Woman* (1914), is a much more descriptive account of the three years Binnie-Clark spends farming wheat on the Saskatchewan prairies. One of the most interesting elements of this book is its illustration of how Canadian homesteading

laws discriminated against female farmers by denying women the right to claim ownership of land.

The Twentieth Century and Beyond

The emergence of **feminism** in the early twentieth century signified a new interest in women's identities and experiences. Susan Jackel argues that debates about Canadian national identity occur at roughly the same time as the emergence of Anglo-American feminist activism, resulting in a close association between a feminist and national consciousness in Canada (99). This connection is evident in several early-twentieth-century autobiographical texts, including Laura Goodman Salverson's *Confessions of an Immigrant's Daughter* (1939). Salverson recounts her life from her birth in 1890 to the publication of her first novel in 1923, writing of her family's emigration from Iceland to Canada and their struggles with poverty and hardship as they attempt to establish themselves in a new country. In addition to retracing Salverson's early life, this book is primarily concerned with the rights of women, immigrants, and the poor, and as such can be read as social commentary. The book makes reference to the emergence of feminism, temperance, and suffrage on the prairies in the early twentieth century, and it can also be read as a defense of immigrants, who have not always been welcomed to Canada.

Salverson was friends with another prominent Canadian writer and feminist, Nellie McClung. The two women mention each other by name in their works and offer each other constructive criticism on their writing. Like Salverson, McClung's autobiographical writing reveals as much about social issues in Canada during the early twentieth century as it does about its author. *Clearing in the West* (1935) recounts McClung's life from her birth to her marriage, but does not mention her political involvement in feminist causes. Salverson told McClung that *Clearing in the West* was too concerned with events and that autobiography should reveal "the mind and soul of the writer" (145). Taking this criticism into account, McClung shaped her second book, *The Stream Runs Fast* (1945), as a more introspective social commentary, exploring her emerging political and social consciousness and her activism on behalf of the suffrage movement and other feminist causes.

The connection between a feminist and a geographic consciousness is also evident in Emily Carr's writings, although Carr's identification is with region rather than nation. Best known for her paintings depicting west coast scenery, Emily Carr also wrote four books based on her life. She arranged to have *Growing Pains* (1946) published posthumously as an autobiography, although she wrote it a number years prior to her death. Essentially a "portrait of the artist as a young woman," *Growing Pains* traces Carr's development as an artist from her childhood in Victoria to her training in San Francisco and England, and her eventual return to Canada. Carr writes at length about the isolation and marginalization she experienced as a female artist and the solace she sought in the wild landscape of Canada's west coast among the native people of British Columbia. Looked down upon in England as a "colonial" and ridiculed by fellow western Canadians who found her art too experimental, Carr was greatly underappreciated. This reception changed when she came into contact with a group of artists from eastern Canada known as the Group of Seven. Carr writes about the profound impact these artists had on her, especially Lawren Harris who became her mentor. Although *Growing Pains* is the only one of Carr's books to be officially classified as an autobiography, her other three books are also based on her experiences and thus can easily be classified as autobiographies. *Klee Wyck* (1941) describes the time Carr spent painting in isolated native communities on Canada's west coast. "Klee Wyck," which means "laughing one," was the name given to Carr by the

Nuu-Chah-Nulth people. *The Book of Small* (1942) describes her childhood rebellion against her parents' loyalty to the church, the Queen, and Victorian values. In addition to painting a vivid portrait of herself as a vibrant, intelligent, and precocious child, Carr's text also offers a great deal of insight into the cultural life of Victoria in the late nineteenth century. *The House of All Sorts* (1944), written shortly before Carr's death, is a humorous account of her time spent as a landlady and a breeder of sheepdogs.

Carr's biographer, Maria Tippett, was inspired to write *Becoming Myself: A Memoir* (1996) after the success of her award-winning biography of Emily Carr and her election into the Royal Society of Canada in 1992. Tippett struggled through school, barely graduating from high school. Resuming her education later in life, she excelled at university and at the time of writing her memoir was a senior research fellow at Cambridge. Tippett begins with a reference to the death of the author and foregrounds her suspicion of autobiographies that claim to be "true life stories." She invokes **Simone de Beauvoir**, **Gertrude Stein**, Margaret Mead, **Janet Frame**, **Maya Angelou**, and Mary Miegs, situating herself in a tradition of female authorship and experimental autobiographical writing, firmly rejecting the traditional male autobiographical subject. The book concludes with an account of the process by which she wrote her biography of Emily Carr. Remarkably, her life seems to fuse with Carr's, and the final chapter is as much about her own biographical subject as it is about herself, enacting the fluidity of autobiographical subjectivity she makes reference to at the outset of her memoir. Tippett's memoir implicitly raises the issue of the biographer's identification with her subject, and suggests that the line between biography and autobiography is not always straightforward.

Elspeth Cameron, another well-known Canadian biographer, also turns the biographer's gaze on herself in her 1997 memoir, *No Previous Experience*, an intimate account of the author's gradual awareness of her romantic feelings for a female friend and her subsequent decision to leave her husband and pursue a lesbian relationship. Although not explicitly addressed by Cameron, her account raises the issue of what it means to go from "biographer" to "autobiographer." When one has made her mark by telling the life stories of others, what does it mean to then tell her own story? How do these processes differ? In a similar vein, Helen Buss, theorist of Canadian women's autobiography, recently published an account of her own childhood, *Memoirs from Away: A New Found Land Girlhood* (1999). Buss uses the occasion of the writing of her own memoir to directly address some of the theoretical issues raised by herself and other literary critics who study autobiography. Through frequent, self-reflexive authorial intrusions, Buss draws our attention to her anxiety about her audience, the impossibility of constructing an accurate and complete textual representation of one's life, and the ever unstable boundary between truth and fiction. Buss's relation to self-representation through language is complicated even further by the fact that she has written a novel under a pen name. In her exploration of the impossibility of writing a memoir without recourse to literary devices such as symbols that inevitably alter the text by adding a layer of artifice, Buss confesses that she made up an image in a previous passage and admits that these are the "confessions of a sometimes fiction writer trying to walk the constantly moving line between what happened and what is made from what happened" (18).

Many Canadian writers who are primarily known as poets and novelists have written autobiographies. Their autobiographical accounts shed light on their writing in other genres by tracing their various influences and outlining the steps that led them to become writers. Canadian poet Dorothy Livesay has written three autobiographical works. *Right Hand Left Hand* (1977) is a collection of letters, photos, personal recollections, poems, and other miscellaneous fragments that detail the development of Livesay's political convictions as well as her emergence as a prominent Canadian poet in the 1930s. In *Beginnings: A Winnipeg Childhood* (1975) Livesay distances herself from her autobiographical subject by adopting what Shirley Neuman calls a fictionalized veneer that allows her to record "diverse epiphanic and disjunctive moments without self-reference and without tracing a pattern of development" (Neuman 1990, 369). Livesay's *Journey with My Selves, A Memoir 1909–1963* (1991) is written in a more conventional fashion, although Livesay warns us in her introduction that "Autobiography, or memoirs, are not written to satisfy a secret, personal urge. They are written as an actor who performs behind a mask" (15). She claims to be the sum of the series of selves she puts forward in this text. Livesay's warning resonates with current theories of autobiography and life writing that treat truth claims in autobiographical narratives with suspicion.

Gabrielle Roy, a well-known Francophone novelist, wrote an autobiography tracing the key developments that led her to become a writer. Roy's *La détresse et l'enchantement* (1984) retraces the first twenty years of Roy's life. The autobiography was initially planned to consist of four parts, but Roy only managed to complete the first two before she became too ill to continue; it was her last book. One of the central themes of Roy's autobiography is her persistent search for belonging. As a Francophone in a predominantly Anglophone province, Roy always felt out of place. As a young woman, Roy travels to Paris and London in search of a sense of community but finds herself lonely and isolated. She eventually returns to Canada and settles in Montreal where she begins her writing career. Roy's close relationship with her mother dominates the first half of the book, while the second half focuses on Roy's desire to define herself in a world far removed from her mother and the small town of St. Boniface. The narrative concludes in 1939, when Roy returns to Canada to settle in Montreal on the eve of World War II and just a few years before she gained international recognition for *Bonheur d'occasion* (1945) (translated by Alan Brown under the title *The Tin Flute*, 1980).

Margaret Laurence wrote *Dance on the Earth* (1989) shortly before her death in 1987. In some respects, Laurence's book resembles a traditional autobiography. She discusses her family background, her childhood years, the time she spent living in Africa, her political involvement in the environmental, peace, and pro-choice movements, and her career as a writer. The narrative trajectory, however, is not strictly linear, as each chapter is structured around themes that do not necessarily unfold chronologically. Laurence pays homage to her "three mothers" (her birth mother, her stepmother, and her mother-in-law), women who had powerful, positive influences over her own development as a writer and mother. Laurence honors these women by writing in detail about their lives. This is as much a biography about her three mothers as it is an autobiography of Laurence, and she consciously and carefully displaces the primacy of the autobiographical "I." Laurence titles the second, third, and fourth chapters after these women, and reserves Chapter five, "Margaret," for an extended discussion of her own career as a novelist. Ironically, Laurence died before completing *Dance on the Earth*, and her own daughter Jocelyn completed the manuscript, adding an additional layer of complexity to the mother-daughter relationships so important to this book.

Many autobiographies by Canadian women feature women who grow up in rural areas and leave for big cities when they come of age. The symbolic split between rural and urban Canada becomes configured as the split between childhood and adulthood. Fredelle Bruser Maynard

wrote two autobiographical texts; the first, *Raisins and Almonds* (1972) is composed of recollections of her experiences of isolation and discrimination as a Jewish child growing up in a series of predominantly Christian prairie towns. Although she writes in detail about her family's marginalization and the anti-Semitism prevalent in small towns in Canada in the 1930s, she also nostalgically recollects the excitement of local church bazaars and Christmas pageants, and the much-anticipated arrival of the Eaton's catalogue with its depictions of the latest fashions. *Raisins and Almonds* strikes an interesting balance between nostalgia and critique. It focuses on her early years and ends with her entrance into the University of Manitoba and the beginning of her career as writer and scholar. *The Tree of Life* (1988) picks up where the first book ends. Darker than the earlier volume, Fredelle Bruser Maynard explains in the introduction that this book is "tougher" than the first one because it is an attempt to make sense of her adult life, rather than a random collection of childhood memories. She states that she now feels freer to write truthfully about details she omitted from the earlier text. She recounts her tumultuous marriage, her fraught relationships with her sister (who is barely mentioned in the first book), and her ambivalent relationship with her mother. The second book illuminates the many gaps and oversights of the first, thus underscoring the extent to which autobiography is carefully selected and constructed by the author, and as such is always partial, subjective, and situated in relation to the details that the author chooses not to record. *The Tree of Life* tells the story of a woman suffering through an extremely difficult marriage, searching for outlets for her intellect in a world where maternity is seen in direct opposition to intellectual ambition.

Maynard's family came to Canada before World War II, along with many Jewish people who immigrated to Canada during and after the war. A number of Jewish Canadian Holocaust survivors have written memoirs describing their horrific experiences in the concentration camps of Nazi Germany. These memoirs are not exclusively or even primarily "Canadian," and perhaps are more accurately classified as part of Jewish diasporic writing. What makes these autobiographies significant as examples of Jewish diasporic writing and Canadian immigrant narratives, is the fact that many Jewish people immigrated to Canada and wrote about their experiences. Eva Brewster's *Vanished in Darkness* (1984) is an account of her involvement in the resistance movement and her imprisonment at Auschwitz where her husband and young daughter were killed. After the war she remarried and settled in Alberta where she had an active career in writing and in television. Faye Schulman's *A Partisan's Memoir: Woman of the Holocaust* (1995) and Ibolya Szalai Grossman's *An Ordinary Woman in Extraordinary Times* (1990) are also written by Jewish women who survived the Holocaust and immigrated to Canada.

Accounts of survival and immigration by Jewish writers represent one strand of an increasingly diverse field of autobiographical writing. Nineteenth-century published immigrant narratives were predominantly written by immigrants of British descent. During this time, however, immigrants were also arriving from a variety of other countries, including China, Japan, India, Norway, Iceland, and Germany. In addition, Canada provided refuge to many African Americans who fled from the southern United States to escape slavery after the Fugitive Slave Act was passed in 1850. The life stories of many of these people were not written or simply were not published, and these groups were largely omitted from the official narrative of nation building. In recent years, interest in the lives and stories of these "forgotten" pioneer voices has increased, and historians and biographers have attempted to recover some of these narratives.

The increased diversity of Canada's pop-

ulation in the latter half of the twentieth century was reflected in the scope of autobiographical voices. While some immigrant writers recount the traumatic situations they left behind, many write about the alienation and racism they experience on arrival in Canada. For women who are socially and economically disempowered, acquiring the literacy skills needed to write an autobiography and gaining access to publishers are difficult tasks. Consequently, most autobiographies in Canada are written by relatively privileged women. The accounts included in Makeda Silvera's *Silenced* (1983) give **voice** to those women whose personal stories are most often left unrecorded and expand the kinds of autobiographical immigrant narratives included in the Canadian national psyche. Silvera, herself an immigrant from the Caribbean, interviews ten women who have moved to Canada from the West Indies to work as domestics. The women speak of the racism they experience in Canada and the exploitation they endure as domestic workers with few rights and low pay. Although these women's autobiographical narratives are mediated by the interview process, Silvera's editorial decisions, and the existence of the book itself, she avoids dictating the direction and content of their stories by allowing the women to talk about the issues that they feel are most urgent. The book is situated somewhere between biography, autobiography, and ethnography, framed by Silvera, but including the firsthand accounts of the ten women she interviews.

Although Dionne Brand has not written an autobiography, many of her essays, novels, and poems contain strong autobiographical elements. Much of Brand's writing focuses on the sense of exile and displacement she felt on moving to Toronto from Trinidad and on her direct experiences of racism in Canada. These themes are dealt with directly in her long poem *No Language Is Neutral* (1990) and in much of her other writing. Brand is uncomfortable with the term nation-state and resists defining herself as either Canadian or Trinidadian. Although her rejection of these categories make it somewhat problematic to include her in a discussion of Canadian women's writing, her work sheds insight into her own experience as an immigrant in Toronto.

In contrast to the many autobiographies written by those who arrive in Canada from elsewhere, Jan Wong, a Canadian-born journalist for the *Globe & Mail*, wrote an account of leaving Canada. Wong's *Red China Blues* (1996) details the years she spent in China as a university student in the 1970s and as a journalist in the 1980s and 1990s. It is as much an account of China's movement from the Maoism of the 1970s to a fledgling capitalist state in the early 1990s as it is an account of Wong's own experiences there. In fact, national politics and Wong's personal experiences are closely linked, since she went to China as a self-identified Maoist in the 1970s and maintained an interest in Chinese politics when she covered the 1989 student uprisings as a journalist. Wong writes of her initial impassioned Maoism, her growing skepticism with the restrictions it placed on Chinese citizens, and her mixed feelings regarding China's emerging capitalism.

Vancouver writer Evelyn Lau's *Runaway: Diary of a Streetkid* (2001), is an autobiographical narrative about life as a teenage drug addict and prostitute. This arguably sensationalistic work is an account of the three years Lau spent living on the streets of Vancouver. *Runaway* was based on a **diary** Lau kept between age fourteen and age seventeen and was published when she was only eighteen. The book is a survival narrative of sorts, written with the goal of publication in mind. Lau makes several references to her potential audience and her plans for publication. The popularity of *Runaway* set Lau's literary career in motion. Now in her early thirties, she is the author of several books of poetry, short stories, essays, and a novel. Unlike most autobiographical texts, which are typically written

close to the end of their author's life, or at least when the author is well into middle age, the events of *Runaway* were experienced and transformed into a text while the author was still a teenager.

Native Women Autobiographers in Canada

Accounts of residential school abuse represent another type of autobiographical **survivor narrative** in Canada. Until the late 1960s, many native children in Canada were taken from their homes and placed in church-run residential schools, where a great number of them suffered physical, sexual, and psychological abuse. In recent years, a number of First Nations people have spoken up about their mistreatment at these schools. *Out of the Depths*, by Isabelle Knockwood (1992), is one such account. Knockwood writes a detailed account of her own experience at the Indian Residential School in Shubenacadie, Nova Scotia and supplements her firsthand testimony with the inclusion of interviews she conducted with others who attended the school.

In addition to the body of writing devoted to exposing their mistreatment, native writers in Canada have produced several autobiographical texts. Maria Campbell's *Halfbreed* (1973) is widely acknowledged as the first published autobiography by a Native writer in Canada. Campbell's moving account of her family's struggle against poverty and discrimination in Saskatchewan and her subsequent battles with drug and alcohol addiction and prostitution paint a vivid picture of the difficulties many Native people continue to face in Canada. Campbell grounds her narrative in the history and tradition of Métis culture, highlighting the history of oppression, and presenting her grandmother (Cheechum) as a figure of great wisdom and strength.

Lee Maracle's *Bobbi Lee: Indian Rebel* (1975) is an autobiographical account of her childhood in Vancouver and her turbulent young adulthood in California, Toronto, and Vancouver. Maracle writes of her struggles with racial oppression, poverty, and drug abuse and her later involvement in the Native Alliance for Red Power, where she first encountered antiracist and left-wing activism. The book was revised and republished in 1990 with an added preface and epilogue that serve to frame the book and to "fill in the missing pieces" (201) which, on reflection, she felt were needed in order to tell her life story. Maracle's epilogue suggests that an author's perception of the events that constitute her life story shifts over time as certain events become more significant and others wane in importance.

Francophone Autobiographies

While Anglophone Canadian writing has a rich autobiographical tradition, particularly in the form of immigrant and settler narratives, autobiography has been a less prevalent genre in Quebec. In *Distinctly Narcissistic: Diary Fiction in Quebec* (1993) Valerie Raoul argues that although it was fashionable for upper-class young women to keep diaries in nineteenth-century Quebec, most were destroyed by the diarists themselves or by nuns at the convent schools (47). One of the only surviving examples of personal writing by a Quebecoise woman from this time is the diary of Henriette Dessaulles, but this remained unpublished until 1971. In *Women and Narrative Identity: Rewriting the Quebec National Text* (2001), Mary Jean Green suggests that the significance of the individual autobiographical subject in Quebec has historically been eclipsed by a focus on the collective culture. Quebec has struggled to preserve its French language and its distinct society in the face of the cultural and linguistic encroachment of English Canada; hence, its literature has been largely interested in the preservation and definition of a collective Quebecois identity.

While the autobiographical tradition may not be as strong in Quebec, Quebecoise female writers have been among the most inventive and creative in their explorations of autobiographical writing. In conjunction with the development of the feminist movement in Quebec, the past thirty-five years have been marked by an increase in women's autobiographical writings. New forms of "collective identity" have emerged to address other forms of inequality in Quebec.

Influenced by feminist theory from France and America, female writers in Quebec sought ways to articulate their subjectivity and experiences. France Théoret's *Nous parlerons comme on écrit* (1982) utilizes the interplay of multiple voices, genres, and narratives to construct a plural female subject. Combining autobiography, theoretical essay, fiction, and travelogue, the text mediates between the personal life story and the collective autobiography of Quebecoise women. Similarly, Madeline Gagnon combines fiction, autobiography, and theory to reflect on everyday experience in *Autographie* (1982).

Jovette Marchessault's autobiographical trilogy is an exploration of the ability of women to nurture and sustain one another through a rejection of patriarchal religious systems in favor of a maternal, goddess-oriented religion. Marchessault explicitly resists the Catholicism that dominated Quebec for so many years and that she sees as contributing to the oppression of Quebecoise women. The first book in the trilogy, *Comme une enfant de la terre/ 1. Le crachat solaire* (1975) (translated by Yvonne M. Klein under the title *Like a Child of the Earth*, 1988) won the prix France-Quebec in 1976. Marchessault uses native mythology to trace her own native origins and her search for a mother goddess. *La mère des herbes* (1980) (translated by Yvonne M. Klein under the title *Mother of the Grass*, 1989) and *Des cailloux blancs pour les flôrets obscures* (1987) (translated by Yvonne M. Klein under the title *White Pebbles in the Dark Forests*, 1990) continue Marchessault's search for identity and her exploration of the creative and nurturing potential of lesbianism, native spirituality, and feminism.

Manuscrits de Pauline Archange (1969) by Marie Claire Blais roughly follows the life of its author. Mary Jean Green notes that the book was met with criticism on publication, particularly by male reviewers who found it lacking in logic, order, and plot, but argues that it is an important work because it undertakes an exploration of women's experience that anticipates the feminist writing produced in Quebec in the 1970s and 1980s.

Valerie Raoul's *Distinctly Narcissistic* uses the psychoanalytic theory of narcissism to draw our attention to diaries and diary fiction as a form of autobiography in Quebecoise literature. One of the texts Raoul discusses is Nicole Brossard's *Journal intime* (1984). Originally written for radio as part of a program that examined various writers' lives, Brossard adopts the diary form only to deconstruct it, illustrating the impossibility of narrating the self. The diary becomes a comment on diary writing and by extension, the construction of the self through language. Brossard poses an implicit challenge to the traditional stable subject of autobiographical writing and examines how the story of one's "life" is produced through various literary and social conventions.

Brossard also utilizes autobiography to explore how fiction structures women's lived experiences in *La Lettre aérienne* (1985 [The Aerial Letter]). Brossard's essays explore the utopian possibilities opened up when women, whose stories she believes have long been told by intermediaries, begin to write about themselves. As she explains, "Only through literally creating ourselves in the world do we declare our existence and from there make our presence known in the order of the real and the symbolic" (134). While *The Aerial Letter* is written in the first person, its "I" often appears to be a collective one. By contrast, the second-person narrative presented in *She Would Be the First Sentence of My Next Novel/Elle Serait La Première Phrase De Mon Prochain Roman* (1998), which features a side-by-side French and English narrative, finds Brossard referring to herself as "the author," reflecting on her development as a female writer in Quebec and as a French writer in English Canada and on her commitment to exploring the possibilities of "writing in the feminine." Here, she explicitly links this practice to autobiography and its deconstruction, explaining that "writing in the feminine" encourages narratives that retrace censored stories while simultaneously disrupting those worlds known as "novelistic" that are ultimately "steeped in autobiographical matter" (93).

While traditionally there has been limited crossover between Anglophone and Francophone writing in Canada, the *Tessera* collective, formed in 1984 by Barbara Godard, Daphne Marlatt, Kathy Mezei, and Gail Scott, has done much to bridge this gap. The collective has a mandate to create dialogue between feminist writers, artists, and theorists working in both official languages and publishes the bilingual journal *Tessera*. In a special issue devoted to the theme of "Auto-graph(e)," Louise Cotnoir summarizes the questions raised by asking: "[W]hat is written when the hand that writes is a woman's hand? How is it that the feminine writes (itself)? How does the body, tracing, overflowing and displaying itself, inscribe its marks in words?" (12). In other words, the articles collected in this issue of *Tessera* each examine the connection between female identity and writing.

Daphne Marlatt, one of the founding members of *Tessera*, published an essay in the Auto-graph(e) issue in which she coined the term "fictionalysis" to describe her writing. Fictionalysis is, in Marlatt's words, "a self-analysis that plays fictively with the primary images of one's life, a fiction that uncovers analytically that territory where fact and fiction coincide" (*Readings from the Labyrinth* 1998, 124). Fictionalysis also suggests an alternative to psychoanalysis because it offers a mode of self-examination that is not predicated on notions of lack or phallocentrism. In her poetry, novels, and essays, Marlatt challenges the boundaries between genres, employing autobiographical elements while raising questions about inscribing a feminine subjectivity in language. In the introduction to *Ghost Works* (1993), a collection of three of her previously published works, Marlatt writes about the difficulty of women's autobiography in cultures where women's stories are systematically erased and their lives are reduced to ghostlike shadows. Marlatt suggests that because of the lack of historical accounts of our foremothers' lives, we must reimagine our pasts through fiction. In *How Hug a Stone* (1983), she combines the forms of journal, travelogue, and long poem to write about a journey to England with her son to visit her mother's family. Marlatt records her literal and metaphorical reconnection with the maternal. She has also written several collaborative pieces with her former lover, Betsy Warland. *Double Negative* (1988), coauthored with Warland, also combines the journal with the long poem to record a voyage by train across Australia.

Self, Language, and Culture in Canadian Autobiographies

Susana Egan and Gabriele Helms identify a subgenre of autobiography in Canada that combines autobiography and essay as a way of exploring the relationship between self, language, and culture. As examples they name Daphne Marlatt's *Readings from the Labyrinth* (1998), Di Brandt's *Dancing Naked* (1996), and Dionne Brand's two collections of essays, *Bread Out of Stone* (1994) and *A Map to the Door of No Return* (2001). Also, Gail Scott's *Spaces Like Stairs* (1989), Nicole Brossard's *La Lettre aérienne* (1985), and Aritha van Herk's *In Visible Ink* (1991) could be added to this list as examples of writing that combine fiction, poetry, literary criticism, and autobiography.

Van Herk's *Places far from Ellesmere* (1990) combines elements of autobiography, travel narrative, and revisionist literary criticism to write what she calls a "feminist geografictione." Through the exploration of **memory** maps, van Herk writes about the intimate relationship between self and **place**. The longest and final section of the book outlines a trip she took to Ellesmere Island in the Canadian Artic. Van Herk brings along Tolstoy's *Anna Karenina*, and the autobiography becomes a feminist rereading of Tolstoy's novel. Ellesmere Island, with its twenty-four hour summer sunlight, becomes a metaphorical place of escape for Anna, van Herk, and, by extension, all women. Through the extensive use of wordplay, van Herk presents landscapes, lives, and literary characters as texts to be read and reread, "a fiction of geography/geography of fiction: coming together in people and landscape and the harboured designations of fickle memory. Invented; textual: un/read; the hieroglyphic secrets of the past" (40).

As Tolstoy's character Anna Karenina functions as a literary muse for van Herk, so too does **Virginia Woolf**'s Lily Briscoe in Mary Meigs' *Lily Briscoe: A Self Portrait* (1981). Meigs, originally from the United States, moved to Canada with her lover, the Quebecoise writer Marie Claire Blais. Through repeated references to Lily Briscoe, the artist from Virginia Woolf's *To the Lighthouse* (1927), Meigs establishes an identification with the androgynous, lone figure of the female artist. Rather than recounting a chronological sequence of events, Meigs' autobiography is selective in what it recounts. Near the end of her narrative she explains, "[I]t is not a book about my life's events, of which I hardly speak, but an attempt, rather, to define myself through its inscape (254). She writes at length about growing up in a repressed household where sex was rarely discussed, coming out as a lesbian, and her relationships with Barbara Deming and Marie Claire Blais. Primarily, however, Meigs writes about her own emotional insecurities and her struggles as an artist.

Autobiographical writing by women in Canada is extraordinarily diverse. Perhaps one of its most striking features is the persistent use of hybrid genres. Although this is most notably a characteristic of more recent writings, it is also present in many autobiographical texts dating back to the nineteenth century. Susanna Moodie's *Roughing It in the Bush* contains poems, songs, and sketches, while Anna Jameson's *Winter Studies and Summer Rambles* (1836) devotes long passages to and an extended analysis of German Romanticism. Perhaps the only absolute claim to make about autobiographical writing in Canada is that it provides a **space** for the inscription of the self into being through language, and in doing so allows the autobiographical subject to construct and deconstruct notions of identity and belonging in national, literary, and gendered contexts.

Further Reading: Blais, Marie Claire. *Manuscrit de Pauline Archange* (Montreal: Editions du Jour, 1968). Translated by Derek Coltman under the title *The Manuscripts of Pauline Archange* (Toronto: McClelland and Stewart, 1982); Brand, Dionne. *A Map to the Door of No Return* (Toronto: Doubleday, 2001); Brossard, Nicole. *Journal intime: Ou voilà donc un manuscrit* (Montreal: Les Herbes Rouges). Translated by Barbara Godard under the title *Intimate Journal or Here's a Manuscript* (Toronto: Mercury, 2004); Buss, Helen M. *Mapping Our Selves: Canadian Women's Autobiography in English* (Montreal: McGill-Queen's University Press, 1993); Cameron, Elspeth. *No Previous Experience* (Toronto: Penguin, 1997); Campbell, Maria. *Halfbreed* (Halifax: Formac, 1973); Carr, Emily. *Growing Pains.* 1946. Reprint (Toronto: Irwin, 1986); Egan, Susanna, and Gabriele Helms. "Auto/biography? Yes. But Canadian?" *Canadian Literature* 172 (Spring 2002): 5–16; Gagnon, Madeleine. *Autographie* (Montreal: VLB, 1982); Jackel, Susan. "Canadian Women's Autobiography: A Problem of Criticism." In *Gynocritics: Feminist Approaches to Canadian and Quebec Women's Writing*, edited by Barbara Godard, 97–110 (Toronto: ECW Press, 1987); Kadar, Marlene, ed. *Essays on Life Writing: From Genre to Critical Practice* (Toronto: University of Toronto Press, 1992); Lau, Evelyn. *Runaway: Diary of a Street Kid* (Toronto: HarperPerennial Canada, 2001); Laurence, Margaret. *Dance on the Earth: A Memoir*

(Toronto: McClelland and Stewart, 1989); Livesay, Dorothy. *Journeys with My Selves: A Memoir, 1909–1963* (Vancouver: Douglas and McIntyre, 1991); Marlatt, Daphne. *Readings from the Labyrinth* (Edmonton: NeWest, 1998); McClung, Nellie. *Nellie McClung, the Complete Autobiography: Clearing in the West and the Stream Runs Fast.* Edited by Veronica Strong-Boag and Michelle Lynn Rosa (Peterborough: Broadview, 2003); Moodie, Susanna. *Roughing It in the Bush.* 1852. Reprint (Ottawa: Tecumseh, 1997); Neuman, Shirley. "Life Writing." Vol. 4 of *Literary History of Canada: Canadian Literature in English.* 2nd ed. Edited by W. H. New (Toronto: University of Toronto Press, 1990), 333–370; Neuman, Shirley. "Reading Canadian Autobiography." *Essays on Canadian Writing* 60 (Winter 1995); Raoul, Valerie. *Distinctly Narcissistic: Diary Fiction in Quebec* (Toronto: University of Toronto Press, 1993); Roy, Gabrielle. *La détrisse et l'enchantement* (Montreal: Boréal Express, 1984). Translated by Patricial Claxton under the title *Enchantment and Sorrow* (Toronto: Lester and Orpen Dennys, 1987); Salverson, Laura Goodman. *Confessions of an Immigrant's Daughter.* 1939. Reprint (Toronto: University of Toronto Press, 1981); Scott, Gail. *Spaces Like Stairs* (Toronto: The Women's Press, 1989); Traill, Catharine Parr. *The Backwoods of Canada.* 1836. Reprint (Ottawa: Carlton University Press, 1997); Van Herk, Aritha. *Places Far from Ellesmere* (Red Deer: Red Deer College Press, 1990); Warland, Betsy. *The Bat Had Blue Eyes* (Toronto: The Women's Press, 1993).

Heather Milne

CAPTIVITY/PRISON NARRATIVE Women autobiographers too often have encountered restrictions based on **gender**, **race**, and **class**. In some special situations, writers may add to these restrictions the limitations of literal confinement, which have led to a variety of types of life writings: testimonials, wartime internment memoirs, Holocaust **survivor narrative**s, prison literature, and captivity narratives. The last two literary modes are discussed here.

The richly diverse literature written by imprisoned women is both international and historical, beginning as early as the

Passion of Saint Perpetua, an account of imprisonment preceding martyrdom in Carthage in 203 C.E. Many of the international works are available in English translation. Forms of life writing, encompassing **letters**, diaries, **memoir**s, and autobiography, have traditionally been the genres chosen by women prison writers, but post–World War II prison literature increasingly includes fiction, poetry, and essay forms.

Most incarcerated women have not written about their experiences; until the twentieth century, only educated, political, and religious prisoners left written records. Some, like Madame Roland, executed in 1793 during the French Revolution, have written letters and prison memoirs to vindicate themselves before history; others, such as Quaker Katharine Evans, who describes her imprisonment in Malta by the Inquisition in 1661, have written to support a cause or belief. Letters and memoirs of imprisonment by politically active women are truly global, including those by Caesarina Makhoere, imprisoned in 1976 in South Africa under apartheid, and Krystyna Wituska, executed by the Nazis in 1944. Prison narratives typically begin by describing the trauma of the prison intake process, and continue with details about conditions and deprivations, stories of companions, and accounts of the writer's strategies for psychological survival. A major difference from men's prison literature has been women's emphasis on relationships and family concerns and the special torment experienced by imprisoned mothers.

In the United States of the 1970s, political prisoners like **Angela Davis** continued the narrative tradition of educated women prisoners, but went beyond accounts of personal experience to speak out on behalf of their incarcerated sisters. The emergence of writing workshops, often sponsored by universities, helped give a new character to women's prison literature of this period. Increasing numbers of women from the general prison population began to speak in their own **voice**s for the first time through

their writings. Today, a new political consciousness and sense of solidarity inform the writings of imprisoned women, crossing lines of race and class and uniting imprisoned women of all backgrounds in their concern for issues affecting all women prisoners. In keeping with this atmosphere of collectivity, some recent writing is collaborative, such as *Breaking the Walls of Silence* (1998), compiled by the Women of the AIDS Counseling and Education (ACE) Program of the Bedford Hills Correctional Facility in New York State.

A major difference between prison and captivity narratives is that writing from prison is both historical and current. Unlike captivity narratives, which were generally promoted and published with the support of the establishment, prison narratives, especially those written by women, have sometimes been suppressed and generally have been unknown or ignored by the mainstream reading public.

Although the genre of captivity narrative, when viewed broadly, includes diverse personal histories, such as those of slaves and Native Americans, the term generally denotes the captivity by Native Americans of European women living in the American colonies. These accounts are more consistent in form and more concentrated in historical time periods, centering on the late seventeenth through early nineteenth centuries, than the more varied time periods of prison narratives. A fundamental question about captivity narratives is that of authorship, since many accounts were composed by others, often male clergy, with religious or political agendas.

The most widely cited captivity narrative by a woman is Mary Rowlandson's *A True History of the Captivity and Restoration of Mrs. Mary Rowlandson*, published in 1682. The wife of a Puritan clergyman, Rowlandson was captured in 1676 from Lancaster, Massachusetts, during Metacom's or King Philip's War. During the twelve weeks she spent traveling with her captors, Rowlandson suffered the death of her young daughter. After her ransom and release, Rowlandson wrote her account, whose publication, scholars assume, was supported by Increase Mather.

The account of Hannah Dustan's captivity, on the other hand, was published by Cotton Mather in 1697, and was not written by Dustan. Her capture in 1697 by the Abenaki Indians resulted in her escape and subsequent vengeance, when she and her companions scalped ten of their captors. Dustan's heroics were praised by the community and cited by the clergy as a spiritual example. Quite different in tone is the 1728 narrative of Elizabeth Hanson, a Quaker wife and mother captured by the Abenakis in New Hampshire and taken to Canada, where she was ransomed and released to her husband. She dictated her narrative, which is characterized by its quality of submissiveness to adversity and its attempts to understand her captors' actions.

Captivity narratives were well-received publications that provided moral instruction for the community; the former captive served as a cultural model, simultaneously demonstrating the trials of Christians in a new, uncivilized world and the necessity of trusting in God's mercy. Recent critical interpretation of women's captivity narratives, however, describes a complex interplay of this surface conservative message with an underlying, subversive theme. Undermining the power of racial and gender stereotypes is the voice and character of a woman whose captivity ironically frees her to question established institutions and see herself and others in radically new ways.

Further Reading: Burnham, Michelle. *Captivity and Sentiment: Cultural Exchange in American Literature, 1682–1861* (Hanover: University Press of New England, 1997); Castiglia, Christopher. *Bound and Determined: Captivity, Culture-Crossing, and White Womanhood from Mary Rowlandson to Patty Hearst* (Chicago: University of Chicago Press, 1996); Chevigny, Bell Gale, ed. *Doing Time: 25 Years of Prison Writing—A PEN American Center Prize Anthology* (New York: Ar-

cade, 1999); Derounian-Stodola, Kathryn Zabelle, ed. *Women's Indian Captivity Narratives* (New York: Penguin, 1998); Franklin, H. Bruce, ed. *Prison Writing in 20th-Century America* (New York: Penguin, 1998); Gelfand, Elissa. *Imagination in Confinement: Women's Writings from French Prisons* (Ithaca, NY: Cornell University Press, 1983); Harlow, Barbara. *Barred: Women, Writing, and Political Detention* (Hanover, NH: University Press of New England, 1992); Namias, June. *White Captives: Gender and Ethnicity on the American Frontier* (Chapel Hill: University of North Carolina Press, 1993); Scheffler, Judith, ed. *Wall Tappings: An International Anthology of Women's Prison Writings, 200 to the Present* (New York: Feminist Press, 2002); Strong, Pauline Turner. *Captive Selves, Captivating Others: The Politics and Poetics of Colonial American Captivity Narratives* (Boulder, CO: Westview Press, 1999).

Judith A. Scheffler

CARIBBEAN WOMEN'S AUTOBIOGRAPHY   To talk about Caribbean women's autobiography is to talk about an expansive genre, one that resists rigid definitions and raises many complex questions. The history of Caribbean women's autobiography is perhaps best described as the history of the struggle to define what it means to be, and to write about being, Caribbean and a woman. The very terms "Caribbean," "women," and "autobiography," are not unproblematic, for they represent loose categories that constantly need to be reexamined. Although the geographic borders of the Caribbean are debated (the Caribbean generally refers to the West Indies islands, yet many writers and critics argue that as a concept or culture, the Caribbean extends to the countries bordering the Caribbean Sea, who share a similar history), diasporas and migrations have also led to the establishment of Caribbean communities throughout the world. Thus, writers like **Audre Lorde** or Paule Marshall, both born in the United States but steeped in the culture of their West Indian parents, might to some extent be considered "Caribbean."

Diverse Cultures in the Caribbean Region

These considerations aside, it is even more important to recognize that because of its specific history, the Caribbean is a place where multiple cultures and languages overlap, blend, and collide. With Europe's "discovery" of the New World in the fifteenth century began a long period of brutal conquest, resettlement, and slavery for the peoples of the Caribbean. European invaders—the Spanish, English, French, and Dutch—exterminated virtually all of the indigenous Arawak and Carib populations, then began transporting slaves from western Africa to work as laborers in the new Caribbean colonies. After the abolition of slavery in the nineteenth century, European colonizers sought out laborers from other locations, and the Caribbean witnessed an influx of East Asians (mainly from India). In the nineteenth and twentieth centuries, many West Indian islands (like Haiti, Cuba, and a number of British possessions) gained their independence, while others (Guadeloupe and Martinique) were assimilated into the political structure of their colonizers. These movements and contacts between various populations have produced in the Caribbean, as Allison Blakely describes it, "a mixture of peoples, languages, religions, and all other aspects of human culture, creating new colors and new sounds that are reflected in enrichment of the respective European and African languages involved, as well as in creation of new hybrid languages."

Although the Caribbean's history makes it today a site of creativity and rich cultural forms, the traumas of slavery, violence, and racism have also left scars. Autobiography has been one way for Caribbean authors to interrogate and work through this difficult past. Some critics maintain that autobiography is valuable to the process of decolonization, or the deconstruction not only of the political structures in place under colonization, but, and perhaps more important, of the mental structures and dispositions imposed on colonized peoples. In writing autobiography, in analyzing one's self and one's past, and questioning how to put one's life experience into words, authors often confront two of the main tools of colonization: education and language. Many Caribbean authors have examined the contradictions involved in belonging to a West Indian culture while speaking the language of the colonizer and conforming to certain European educational models. While writing about the self is a source of renewal for some, for others, written literature itself is problematic, or viewed as a Western import to be de-emphasized in favor of oral traditions.

> While noting a recent increase in literary production on Dutch St. Martin, Fabian Badejo has described St. Martiners' relation to writing as problematic. If St. Martiners are generally multi-lingual, and move between English, Dutch, Spanish, and Papiamentu according to the social situations in which they find themselves, "their command of these languages is, however, often suspect, while the fact that their mother-tongue is not the language of instruction at school often undermines their self-assurance and self-esteem. Consequently," Badejo continues, "they do not really speak and write any of these languages confidently enough to express themselves creatively." ("Introduction to Literature in English in the Dutch Winward Islands" *Callaloo* 21, no. 3 [1998]: 676–679)

For Caribbean women, the problems of language, racial discrimination, and political or economic marginalization felt by Caribbean societies as a whole are often doubled by the difficulties they encounter as women in traditionally patriarchal cultures. Finding a **voice** as a Caribbean and as a woman can be an arduous and complex task. Making one's individual or private life public—traditionally a defining characteristic of autobiography—has long been an obstacle for women in particular, who have generally been confined to private, domestic **space**s and are seen as transgressing social norms. If autobiography as a genre has been dominated through much of history in the West by men and male conceptions of the self, as critics such as **Sidonie Smith** and Leah Hewitt have argued, the genre's loss of status among twentieth-century literary critics poses additional problems for women writers seeking to articulate their views of **subjectivity**. Autobiography traditionally relies on the notion that the author is a self-conscious, autonomous individual who faithfully represents him or herself through the tool of language, a notion that twentieth-century philosophers and literary critics (such as Jacques Derrida, Roland Barthes, Michel Foucault, and Jacques Lacan) have discredited. With the "death of the author" also comes, for certain critics, the death of autobiography. Rather than renouncing autobiography altogether, however, recent Caribbean women writers have attempted to navigate between a desire to find and assert their voices, and the recognition that coherent identities are often constructed through words by turning to **autobiographical fiction** and exploring generic innovations in order to articulate their views. Still, the critic must ask to what degree Caribbean women's voices remain silenced due to the perceived inferiority of autobiographical modes of writing. If women in general have been vulnerable to charges of narcissism and self-indulgence when they write about their lives, Caribbean women's autobiography in particular is subject to charges of political apathy or indifference in an environment where literature is often looked on as a means to promote political change. Françoise Lionnet is a staunch critic of such claims, arguing in *Autobiographical Voices: Race, Gender, Self-Portraiture* (1989) that it is because women's writing tends to interrogate subtle issues and to refuse "all rigid, essentializing approaches to questions of race, class, or gen-

der" that female authors have been unfairly dismissed.

Autobiography as a Genre: Caribbean Modes

Recent years have seen much formal innovation in autobiographical writing. Yet autobiography has always been a difficult genre to define, one that overlaps with many others. While some traditional autobiographies exist in the Caribbean (in the sense of a life story, organized chronologically), Caribbean women's autobiographical writing spans various forms: histories, travel writing, spiritual autobiography, memoirs, testimonials, lyric poetry, autobiographical novels, diaries, **letters**, and criticism. Their works can be written, oral, or dictated. They write for varying publics, sometimes for a limited readership (an academic audience or a relatively small language community), sometimes for a broad public. The goals of each of these forms are of course diverse; each can also take on several functions. Whatever the primary motivation of the text, most Caribbean women's autobiography engages in social criticism, which will be examined further. The following discussion is not an exhaustive survey, but a sample of the multiple forms Caribbean women's autobiography has taken since the nineteenth century and the many uses to which it has been deployed. It must be recalled, of course, that these generic divisions often overlap, and must be regarded as useful, rather than essential, distinctions.

Autobiographical History

Some of the earliest known Caribbean women's autobiographies take the form of histories. The individual life stories of the authors who chose to write in this vein are related in respect to the history of a larger social group or movement. The personal becomes exemplary of the social, and often made public ostensibly for the common good. Such is the case of sisters Anne Hart

Gilbert and Elizabeth Hart Thwaites (Antigua), who each published a "History of Methodism" in 1804, as well as **Mary Prince** (Bermuda), whose antislavery tract, *The History of Mary Prince, a West Indian Slave, Related by Herself* appeared in 1831. Composed at a time when women had no right to vote and were generally consigned to the domestic sphere, these historical autobiographies are oriented toward social and political goals, and rely on existing institutions and figures of authority in order to promote their cause. As women of color in the early-nineteenth-century English colonies, these three women authors faced additional obstacles. Although privately educated and born into a family of free blacks and plantation owners, the Hart sisters were the targets of racism and insults after their marriages to white men, while Mary Prince, born a slave, suffered abuse and harsh working conditions for years.

The Hart sisters' histories were both written at the request of Reverend Richard Pattison, who asked the two to write on the state of Methodism in Antigua. As Sandra Pouchet Paquet (2002) points out in her study of their texts, the sisters' close relationship perhaps led them to collaborate, for their narratives relate varying but complementary aspects of their involvement with the Methodist Church: Anne's text relates the ups and downs of the Methodist Church in Antigua, only touching on her own activism as it relates to a general history, while Elizabeth's is a more personal account of her own spiritual life and is organized around the chronology of her life rather than the church. Articulating their life stories as a part of church history lends legitimacy, in the eyes of their readers, to their antislavery project by drawing on an established, influential institution (the Methodist Church), while allowing the women to "reinscribe black womanhood so as to project both their own sense of innate value and their social mission in ideal terms" (26).

Mary Prince similarly relied on the Methodist Church, and on two of its members, Thomas Pringle and Susanna Strickland, in her struggle with her owners for freedom. *The History of Mary Prince* is a transcription of Prince's life story, published along with a supplement by Pringle summarizing the antislavery debate and additional documentation given as evidence of conditions under slavery. As a slave, Mary Prince was aware of her weak position of authority, and multiplies details and corroborating facts in order to persuade the reader of the merits of her account. In addition to an autobiographical account of her personal life and trials in Bermuda and England, Mary Prince and her editors create a document of legal history, intended to serve as evidence for the argument against slavery. Since the account is transcribed and edited, the extent to which Prince's own voice is conveyed can be questioned. Yet Paquet argues that the text retains a specifically West Indian quality and language, and articulates the self-consciousness of West Indian slaves through the techniques of oral literature. Prince defines herself as a West Indian, as a member of a coherent, oppressed community. She identifies with both male and female slaves, and speaks as the proponent of their common cause.

While history in these cases is both a strategy and a constraint for Caribbean women attempting to convey their life stories and make their voices heard, in recent years, it is autobiography that has been used as a way of telling history differently. In *Havana Dreams: A Story of Cuba* (1998), Wendy Gimbel merges her own experience of Cuba with the story of Doña Natica, her daughter Naty Revuelta (Fidel Castro's former mistress), their family, and the Cuban revolution. Unlike historical accounts that strive for an impersonal objectivity and a vast picture of the causes leading to events, Gimbel's book focuses on one family, and specifically on the women in that family, and the ways in which different generations interact and clash in a changing social and political environment. Something of a history, and something of a **memoir**, the book has received mixed reviews, some critics favor her innovative and appealing personal account, others oppose her mixing of genres and her focus on sentimental life.

Travel Writing and the Immigrant Experience

Much of Caribbean women's autobiography stems from the experience of travel or exile. Whether travel is voluntary or obligatory, it entails an encounter with different cultures that often leads to a reflection of one's own **identity**. Caribbeans have often left their countries for political and economic reasons, and a large body of literature exists that details the experience of immigration and the difficulties of acculturation in foreign lands. Children of immigrants also write about their own immersion in two cultures, that of their parents, and that of their birthplace, cultures that sometimes enrich and sometimes conflict with each other. Among such autobiographical works are those of **Esmeralda Santiago**, a woman born in Puerto Rico who moved to New York City at age thirteen. Her two memoirs, *When I Was Puerto Rican* (1994) and *Almost a Woman* (1998) relate her experiences of childhood and adolescence in the 1950s and 1960s, the happiness and hardship of life in Puerto Rico, and her struggle to find her identity growing up in American society. Her books evoke larger social issues as well, including immigration laws, education, and **sexuality**.

Julia Alvarez's works also draw from her own experiences, her flight from political turmoil in the Dominican Republic at age ten and arrival in New York City, but her choice to write fiction allows her to explore varying points of view. *How the Garcia Girls Lost Their Accents* (1991) and its sequel, *¡Yo!* (1997), explore similar themes, found in Santiago's works, yet give a fictive account of the lives of four sisters from the Dominican Republic. Similarly, Paule Mar-

shall, the daughter of Barbadian immigrants, creates a semiautobiographical account of a young girl's life in New York and her return to her parents' homeland as an adult in *Brown Girl, Brownstones* (1959). Marshall's groundbreaking first novel explores **gender** dynamics and the relation between knowing one's heritage and forging an identity. The novel was also noted for its attention to West Indian dialect.

Caribbean women have also written about the experience of travel, as opposed to settling in a place. In travel writing, a physical journey is often paralleled by an emotional or intellectual journey, though the goals in publishing a travel account vary. Dulce María Loynaz's *Un verano en Tenerife* (1958 [A Summer in Tenerife]) has been described as a lyric interpretation of the Canary Islands and the author's memories of her time there. The Canary Islands (located in the Atlantic Ocean, off the northwestern coast of Africa) have long had a place in myth and literature. The islands were subject to European invasion in the fifteenth century and were finally conquered by Spain in 1404. Christopher Columbus made his last stop there before voyaging west. Historical connections between the Canary Islands and the Caribbean are increased twofold for Loynaz by personal ones; her second husband was born there. Among other things, traveling to Tenerife is also an occasion for Loynaz to reflect on geographic insularity and its effects on the mentality of island inhabitants. Loynaz was also a poet and novelist whose works were neglected for decades after the Cuban revolution because they were deemed apolitical.

For one earlier writer, Mary Seacole, travel is a way to assert freedom and redefine her identity. Her work, *Wonderful Adventures of Mrs. Seacole in Many Lands* (1857), details her career as a doctor in Kingston, Jamaica, her travels in the Caribbean and to London, and her decision (after being rejected by the army) to travel to the Crimea on her own to serve as a nurse during the Crimean War (1853–1856). Seacole fashions herself as a mother (she was known as Mother Seacole among the soldiers), yet goes against expectations by stepping outside the private space of the home. Although Seacole contests, or redefines, the role of women in society (a widow, she does not remarry, but chooses to work and move freely around the world), she does so from the standpoint of a British imperial subject. That is, she accepts colonialism and British values and sets out to aid the British army in its civilizing mission. As Paquet puts it, "Seacole's self-constitution as emblematic of colonial progress . . . carries with it an assertion of black women's power in the vacuum created by the cult of domesticity; however, it also speaks to an adoption of British colonial culture as a model of authentic being" (2002, 54). As a "mulatto" (she is the daughter of a free black Jamaican woman and a Scottish man), she encounters racism, but focuses on her ability to achieve her goals through practice and determination. Autobiography, for Seacole, is a way to celebrate these achievements. A businesswoman throughout her life, Seacole also publishes her work with the pragmatic intention of earning profits. Writing for her is not so much a means to discover an inner self as a way to preserve the memory of her public acts (70).

Exile and Testimony

Although travel can be a productive encounter with difference, it often entails great pain, especially when leaving is an urgent necessity. The topic of exile has been widely discussed among literary critics, who have often focused on writing as a strategy for dealing with the trauma of displacement. For people living in exile, writing can serve several purposes. It can be a highly personal form of therapy, or a way of drawing public attention to political problems and crimes in hopes of change. It can be a way to record events for posterity; it can also be a way to connect with others,

or to forge communities. To some extent, a great deal of Caribbean literature, including fiction, can be described as testimonial, in that it is in part driven by a desire to testify to certain realities and events, namely to social, political, and personal turmoil, and to the strategies adopted in response to these realities.

How to speak about exile or trauma (or whether to speak at all) has often been hotly contested among literary critics. Yet, testimonial works can often generate great sympathy among a wide audience or mobilize public opinion. For writers, testifying about their experience of oppression, brutality, and displacement is often felt to be a duty or a pressing need. The four examples that follow are all recent works that deal with two countries, Haiti and Cuba, whose major political upheavals resulted in large migrations and internal conflict. In *The Butterfly's Way: Voices from the Haitian Dyaspora* [sic] *in the United States* (2001), Edwidge Danticat, a Haitian writer who has lived in the United States since age twelve, has collected diverse reflections from a number of Haitians living abroad. It includes essays and poetry and is organized by multiple themes: such as childhood, migration, first-generation experience, and return, from both male and female perspectives. *The Butterfly's Way* represents one way of testifying to an experience—that of *diaspora*, or dispersion—that has many sides and affects various members of society differently. Danticat, who includes some reflections on her own migration in the introduction to the volume, has also attempted to portray the Haitian immigrant experience through her novels, notably, *Breath, Eyes, Memory* (1994).

Like Danticat's collection, which focuses on the question of what it means to be Haitian, María de los Angeles Torres' anthology, *By Heart/De Memoria: Cuban Women's Journeys In and Out of Exile*, focuses on the problem of exile, yet brings gender to the center of debate. The book includes testimony from women across generations, and from those who left Cuba during and after Castro's revolution in the late 1950s, and from those who stayed. Ana Rodriguez's chronicle, written with Glenn Garvin, of her imprisonment, *Diary of a Survivor: Nineteen Years in a Cuban Women's Prison* (1995) attempts to testify to the brutality of political repression under the Castro regime. Once in favor of the revolution, Rodriguez became critical of Castro's methods and was imprisoned after being denounced. Although Cuban prison conditions and torture have long been the subject of international debate and criticism, Rodriguez also focuses on attitudes toward women in Cuban society and the treatment of women deemed political criminals. **Diary** is used here in a figurative sense and evokes the vividness with which Rodriguez and Garvin seek to portray her recollections; the story is related as a narrative, using the past tense.

Anthropologist, writer, and Cuban native, Ruth Behar turned to film in 2002 as a medium for tracing her own heritage as a Cuban Sephardic Jew, attesting to the resilience and multifaceted character of this community. *Adio Kerida* [Goodbye Dear Love] explores themes of expulsion, exile, and cultural transformation. Behar herself appears onscreen, and her encounters with her father and brother, who disagree with aspects of her project, are also given a place in the film. Autobiography in this form is a means of reconciliation for Behar. Through *Adio Kerida*, Behar sets out to recover a heritage that she has forgotten after leaving Cuba as a child, yet she also acknowledges the voices of those who approach the memory of Cuba differently.

Memoirs and Autobiographical Fiction

Françoise Lionnet has convincingly argued that defining autobiography as a first-person, nonfiction narrative ignores many of the ways women have attempted to make their personal voices heard and to convey their thoughts on female identity and female worldviews. Sensitive to the way the genre of autobiography has been shaped by men, women often choose literature as a means of expressing "those elements of the female self which have been buried under the cultural and patriarchal myths of selfhood" (1989, 91). Literature, Lionnet contends, "can show us new means of constructing the world, for it is by changing the images and structures through which we encode meaning that we can begin to develop new scripts and assign new roles to the heroines of the stories we recount in order to explain and understand our lives" (91).

Caribbean women writers have often staged the problem of writing about the self and have stretched the traditional borders of the genre of autobiography in many ways. Some have adopted, and adapted, the practice of writing memoirs (a subgenre of autobiography often focusing on memory) to call attention to the writing situation, the fragmented nature of memory, and the changes to identity and to interpretation of events over time. Guadeloupean novelist Maryse Condé published a set of memoirs, *Le coeur à rire et à pleurer* (1999 [Tales from the Heart]), whose title is taken from a popular French folksong, and whose subtitle, *Contes vrais de mon enfance* [True Tales from My Childhood], points out that to speak of oneself is to tell a story, and to create a sort of fiction. Condé's book does not give a chronological account of her life, but selectively recounts certain scenes, events, and family stories passed down to her regarding her birth, childhood, and adolescence. The memoirs are dedicated to Condé's mother, who is also a central figure throughout the text.

Jamaica Kincaid, an Antiguan, combines the memoir and essay forms in *My Garden (Book)* (1999), a collection of meditations ranging from personal recollections to thoughts on colonialism, gardening, and gardens throughout the former British Empire, and to reflections on the process of creativity. While much of Kincaid's work has been described as semiautobiographical, two particular texts, in addition to *My Garden (Book)*, center on the problem of female identity and autobiography: *The Autobiography of My Mother* (1996) and *My Brother* (1997). Narrated by a character named Xuela, a Dominican woman whose mother (an indigenous Carib woman) died during her birth, *The Autobiography of My Mother* deals with the (impossible) recuperation of female ancestry and history in the Caribbean, reflecting on the relation between language, absence, and remembrance (cf., Guadeloupean novelist Simone Schwartz-Bart's *Pluie et Vent sur Telumée Miracle* (1972 [The Bridge of Beyond]) which similarly explores female lineage). *My Brother*, a personal memoir, also revolves around the question of remembrance and identity, but tells the story of the death, from AIDS, of Kincaid's brother Devon Drew. The contrasts and intersections between Kincaid's life as a successful writer and married woman living in Vermont and Devon's physical decline in Antigua point to the contingency of identity. Kincaid alternately identifies with and distinguishes herself from her brother, and reflects that her life could have ended prematurely as well, but for causes that remain unknown. Autobiography functions here as a means of grieving and a project of preservation, both of which are fraught with ambivalence. In particular, Kincaid explores the relation between writing or creativity and her conflicted relationship with her brother, and the ways both of these are mediated by her mother. The role of the social in the construction of identity is examined here through the question of sexuality, as Kincaid learns of her brother's hidden homosexual life, the revelation of which again provokes a crisis of identification and a movement of self-interrogation.

American writer Audre Lorde and Puerto Rican novelist Rosario Ferré have also interrogated the line between fiction and autobiography. Lorde created a form she calls "biomythography" in **Zami: A New Spelling of My Name**, while Ferré fictionalizes history in *The House on the Lagoon*

(1995) and *Eccentric Neighborhoods* (1998). In *House on the Lagoon*, Ferré's first novel recounts Isabel Monfort's attempts to write an autobiographical chronicle of her family's past and her husband's conflicting view of this history, which he expresses by writing his own, alternative chapters to her book. *Eccentric Neighborhoods* is based on characters in the author's own family and various political figures and recounts the story of two branches of the narrator's wealthy Puerto Rican family. Both novels, written in English rather than Spanish (the language of her earlier work), provoked strong responses, both favorable and disapproving. Ferré's own political views (first as an advocate for Puerto Rican independence, then later a proponent of American statehood) have much to do with the critical response, as well as her choice to write directly in English. In *Eccentric Neighborhoods*, her focus on upper-class landed families and industrialists was also lauded for its unusual portraiture and criticized as a narrow vision of Puerto Rican society.

A large number of Caribbean women authors have chosen the novel as their means to express a female view of **race** relations, education, neurosis and madness, the political and economic position of women in society, mothering, and other topics concerning the feminine condition. Only a limited number of authors can be mentioned here, but their work provides a point of entry into a large body of literature in which women's voices are increasingly present. Mayotte Capécia's *Je suis martiniquaise* (1948) and Michèle Lacrosil's *Sapotille et le Serin d'Argile* (1960) give insights into French education and alienation (both women have been the subject of much criticism, although their work has recently received renewed interest). Merle Hodge, a Trinidadian, in *Crick Crack, Monkey* (1981) explores **class** and racial discrimination from a child's point of view, while Martinican writer Françoise Ega's *Le temps des madras* (1966) focuses on childhood with an emphasis on mother-daughter relationships. Haitian writer Marie Chauvet explores racial prejudice in *Fille d'Haïti* (1954), the story of a mulatto daughter of a prostitute, while her well-known trilogy, *Amour, colère et folie* (1968), explores, among other themes, women's frustrating confrontations with society, and writing as a means of forging and affirming female identity. (*Amour, colère et folie* was banned in Haiti because it condemned the corruption of the Duvalier regime. Chauvet went into exile, where she died in 1973.) Maryse Condé created a narrator she has described as an "anti-me" in *Heremakhonon* (1976) in order to creatively explore the traumatic events she witnessed in Guinea in 1962. Another Guadeloupean writer, Gisèle Pineau, has also drawn on her own life and relationship with her grandmother in many of her novels.

When considering literature as autobiographical texts, readers must remain wary of reading fiction as a mere transposition of the authors' lives. Although writers generally draw on their own experiences, fiction provides a way of altering these experiences to achieve various goals. In interviews, Surinamese writer Astrid Roemer has remarked that she writes fiction in order to discuss sensitive social issues without inflicting pain on specific community members (Rowell, Charles H. "An Interview with Astrid Roemer." *Callaloo* 21, no. 3 [1998]: 508–510). In most cases, Caribbean women writers view literature as a way to get beyond the confines of one's own life, to explore new themes and places, and to set out new visions of language and society for the future.

Poetry

Like novels, poetry provides a means for writers to express personal views creatively. Lyric poetry (poetry written in the first person) has a long tradition in literature, but takes on particular significance for Caribbean women writers, who have sometimes favored poetry for its closeness to oral traditions, and its generic flexibility,

which allows for the creation of new forms. Surinamese novelist and poet Astrid Roemer disrupts formal conventions in her works, and developed what Wim Rutgers describes as "a feminist form of 'song verse'" in *En wat dan nog* (1984 [And Now What]) and *Noordzee Blues* (1985 [North Sea Blues]) ("Dutch Caribbean Literature" *Callaloo* 21, no. 3 1998, 542–555). Johanna Schouten-Elsenhout, a self-taught woman, also from Suriname, draws heavily on oral traditions in her poems, which are composed in Sranantongo (also called Sranan for short), the primarily oral language spoken by descendents of African slaves in Suriname. Grace Nichols, born in Guyana, is the author of the famous, *I Is a Long-Memoried Woman* (1983), a collection of highly expressive poems dealing with history and memory. Cuban anthropologist Ruth Behar has published two bilingual collections of poetry, *Everything I Kept/Todo lo que guardé* (2001) and *Poemas que vuelven a Cuba/Poems Returned to Cuba* (1995) (both are presently available only in rare, handmade and illustrated editions from the Cuban publishing company Ediciones Vigía). For Caribbean women writers, poetry is a particularly fluid form that allows for innovation and acute attention to problems of language and female voice. Poetry is a space in which personal, collective, or lost voices can be reimagined and asserted. *See also* **African American Women's Autobiography**, **Autobiographical Fiction**, **Postcolonial Women's Autobiography**, **Race**.

Further Reading: Criticism: Araújo, Nara. *El alfiler y la mariposa: Género, voz y escritura en Cuba y el Caribe* (Havana: Editorial Letras Cubanas, 1997); *Callaloo* 15, no. 1 (Winter 1992). "The Literature of Guadeloupe and Martinique." Edited by Carroll F. Coates, Yanick Lahens, Maximillien Laroche, and Charles H. Rowell; *Callaloo* 15, no. 2–3 (Spring–Summer 1992). "Haitian Literature and Culture."; *Callaloo* 17, no. 3 (Summer 1994). "Puerto Rican Women Writers." Edited by Consuelo López (Springfield); *Callaloo* 21, no. 3 (Summer 1998). "Caribbean Literature from Suriname, the Netherlands Antilles, Aruba, and the Netherlands." Introduction by Hilda van Neck-Yoder; Condé, Maryse. *La parole des femmes* (Paris: L'Harmattan, 1979); Cudjoe, Selwyn, ed. *Caribbean Women Writers: Essays from the First International Conference* (Wellesley, MA: Calaloux Publications; Amherst: Distributed by the University of Massachusetts Press, 1990); Davies, Carole Boyce. *Black Women, Writing, and Identity. Migrations of the Subject* (London: Routledge, 1994); Davies, Carole Boyce, and Elaine Savory Fido. *Out of the Kumbla: Caribbean Women and Literature* (Trenton, NJ: Africa World Press, 1990); Davies, Catherine. *A Place in the Sun? Women Writers in Twentieth-Century Cuba* (London: Zed Books, 1997); Ferguson, Moira. *Colonialism and Gender Relations from Mary Wollstonecraft to Jamaica Kincaid: East Caribbean Connections* (New York: Columbia University Press, 1993); Hewitt, Leah D. *Autobiographical Tightropes* (Lincoln: University of Nebraska Press, 1990); Lionnet, Françoise. *Autobiographical Voices: Race, Gender, Self-Portraiture* (Ithaca, NY: Cornell University Press, 1989), xii; Luis, William, ed. *Voices from Under: The Black Narrative in Latin America and the Caribbean* (Westport, CT: Greenwood Press, 1984); Paquet, Sandra Pouchet. *Caribbean Autobiography: Cultural Identity and Self-Representation* (Madison: University of Wisconsin Press, 2002); Pineau, Gisèle, and Marie Abraham. *Femmes des Antilles; Traces et voix cent cinquante ans après l'abolition de l'esclavage* (Paris: Stock, 1998); Shepherd, Verene, Bridget Brereton, and Barbara Bailey, eds. *Engendering History: Caribbean Women in Historical Perspective* (London: James Currey, 1995). **Primary Works**: *Adio Kerida* [Goodbye Dear Love]. Directed by Ruth Behar. Video documentary. Women Make Movies, 2002. 82 min.; Alvarez, Julia. *How the Garcia Girls Lost Their Accents* (Chapel Hill, NC: Algonquin Books of Chapel Hill, 1991); Alvarez, Julia. *¡Yo!* (Chapel Hill, NC: Algonquin Books of Chapel Hill, 1997); Badejo, Fabian. "Introduction to Literature in English in the Dutch Winward Islands." *Callaloo* 21, no. 3 (1998): 676–679; Behar, Ruth, and Rolando Estévez Jordán. *Everything I Kept/Todo lo que guardé* (Matanzas, Cuba: Ediciones Vigía, 2001); Behar, Ruth, and Rolando Estévenz. Jordán. *Poemas que vuelven a Cuba/Poems Returned to Cuba* (Matanzas, Cuba: Ediciones Vigía, 1995); Blakely,

Allison. "Historical Ties Among Suriname, the Netherlands, Antilles, Aruba, and the Netherlands." *Callaloo* 21, no. 3: 472–478; Bridges, Yseult. *Child of the Tropics: Victorian Memoirs*. Edited by Nicholas Guppy. 1980. Reprint (Trinidad: Aquarela Galleries, 1988); Capécia, Mayotte. *Je suis martiniquaise* (Paris: Corréa, 1948); Chauvet, Marie. *Amour, colère et folie* (Paris: Gallimard, 1968); Chauvet, Marie. *Fille d'Haïti* (Paris: Fasquelle, 1954); Condé, Maryse. *Le coeur à rire et à pleurer* (Paris: Robert Laffont, 1999); Condé, Maryse. *Heremakhonon*. 1976. Reprint (Paris: Robert Laffont, 1997); Danticat, Edwidge. *Breath, Eyes, Memory* (New York: Vintage Books, 1994); Danticat, Edwidge, ed. *The Butterfly's Way: Voices from the Haitian Dyaspora in the United States* (New York: The Soho Press, 2001); Dominique, Jan J. *Mémorie d'une amnésiaque* (Port-au-Prince, Haïti: Imprimerie H. Deschamps, 1984); Ega, Françoise. *Le temps des madras* (Paris: Editions Maritimes et d'Outre-Mer, 1966); Ega, Françoise. *Lettres à une Noire* (Paris: L'Harmattan, 1978); Ferguson, Moira, ed. *The Hart Sisters: Early African Caribbean Writers, Evangelicals and Radicals* (Lincoln: University of Nebraska Press, 1993); Ferré, Rosario. *Eccentric Neighborhoods* (New York: Farrar, Straus and Giroux, 1998); Ferré, Rosario. *The House on the Lagoon* (New York: Farrar, Straus and Giroux, 1995); Gimbel, Wendy. *Havana Dreams: A Story of Cuba* (New York: Knopf, 1998); Hodge, Merle. *Crick Crack, Monkey* (London: Heinemann, 1981); Kincaid, Jamaica. *The Autobiography of My Mother* (New York: Farrar, Straus and Giroux, 1996); Kincaid, Jamaica. *My Brother* (New York: Farrar, Straus and Giroux, 1997); Kincaid, Jamaica. *My Garden (Book)* (New York: Farrar, Straus and Giroux, 1999); Lacrosil, Michèle. *Sapotille et le Serin d'Argile* (Paris: Gallimard, 1960); Lionnet, Françoise. *Autobiographical Voices: Race, Gender, Self-Portraiture* (Ithaca, NY: Cornell University Press, 1989); Loynaz, Dulce María. *Poesía completa* (Havana, Cuba: Editorial Letras Cubanas, 1993); Loynaz, Dulce Mavia. *Un verano en Tenerife* [A Summer in Tenerife] 1958. Reprint (Havana, Cuba: Editorial Letras Cubanas, 1994); Mahase, Anna, Sr. *My Mother's Daughter: The Autobiography of Anna Mahase Snr., 1899–1978* (Trinidad: Roynards, 1992); Marshall, Paule. *Brown Girl, Brownstones* 1959. Reprint

(New York: Feminist Press at The City University of New York, 1981); Nichols, Grace. *I Is a Long-Memoried Woman* (London: Caribbean Cultural International; Karnak House, 1983); Prince, Mary. *The History of Mary Prince, a West Indian Slave, Related by Herself.* 1831. Reprint (Ann Arbor: University of Michigan Press, 1993); Rhys, Jean. *Smile Please: An Unfinished Autobiography* (Berkeley, CA: Creative Arts, 1979); Rodriguez, Ana, and Glenn Garvin. *Diary of a Survivor: Nineteen Years in a Cuban Women's Prison* (New York: St. Martin's Press, 1995); Roemer, Astrid H. *En wat dan nog* (Alkmaar: Furie, 1985); Roemer, Astrid H. *Levenslang gedicht* (Haarlem: In de Knipscheer, 1987); Roemer, Astrid H. *Nergens ergens* (Amsterdam: In de Knipscheer, 1983); Roemer, Astrid H. *Noordzee Blues* (Breda: De Geus, 1985); Roemer, Astrid H. *Sasa: Mijn actuele zijn* (Paramaribo: n.p., 1970); Santiago, Esmeralda. *Almost a Woman* (Reading, MA: Perseus Books, 1998); Santiago, Esmeralda. *When I Was Puerto Rican* (New York: Vintage Books, 1994); Seacole, Mary. *Wonderful Adventures of Mrs. Seacole in Many Lands.* 1857. Reprint (New York: Oxford University Press, 1988); Schouten-Elsenhout, Johanna. *Sranan pangi* (Paramaribo: Bureau Volkslektuur, 1974); Schouten-Elsenhout, Johanna. *Awese.* 1965. Reprinted in *Spiegel van de Surinaamse Poëzie*, edited by Michiel van Kempen (Amsterdam: Meulenhoff, 1995); Schwartz-Bart, Simone. *Pluie et Vent sur Telumée Miracle* (Paris: Editions du Seuil, 1972); Torres, María de los Angeles, ed. *By Heart/De Memoria: Cuban Women's Journeys In and Out of Exile* (Philadelphia: Temple University Press, 2003); Vianen, Bea. *Ik eet, ik eet, tot ik niet meer kan* (Amsterdam: Querido, 1972).

Nicole Simek

CAVENDISH, MARGARET (LUCAS), DUCHESS OF NEWCASTLE (1623–1673)

Margaret Cavendish was the first Englishwoman to write an autobiographical excursus for print. Her apparent purpose in composing the forty-page "A True Relation" (1656, see Cavendish *Paper Bodies*, 2000) was to defend her kin in the face of suggestions that they were socially inferior to her husband's family. Thus, she begins by pointing out that her father, who was wealthy, was pressed to purchase a title but refused because he believed that titles should be earned rather than bought. Before long, however, she shifts her focus from defense and instead describes her family in terms that are often intimate and homey. Along the way, she writes a good deal about her own character, in particular that she was painfully shy while a maid of honor at the court of Queen Henrietta Maria during the 1640s. Later biographical sketches, including that in George Ballard's influential *Memoirs of Several Ladies* (1752), have suggested on this basis that she was shy throughout her life, but there is reason to believe that Cavendish was quite bold during the 1660s. Much current understanding of her poetry, fiction, plays, and scientific writing is based on a long, sometimes mistaken tradition of reading "A True Relation."

Cavendish chronicles her childhood education in "singing, dancing, playing on music, reading, and writing." She says that she was poor at the study as well as the practice of foreign language. Although she grew up in Colchester, she made visits in the winters to London, where she and her siblings attended the theater and strolled in Hyde Park. She was the youngest in the family, and often she stayed in London with a favorite married sister, Catherine Lucas Pye, about whom she also writes in *Sociable Letters* (1664). Cavendish describes in some detail the indignities that her family endured during the English Civil Wars and praises her mother for having fortitude in these difficult times as well as for having skill in farm management. Independent evidence suggests that Elizabeth Lucas was a tough-minded woman, who deftly navigated the dangers of the Court of Wards at the time of the death of her husband. After the wars were over, families on the losing side, which included the Lucases and the Cavendishes, tried to reach accommodation with the government of Oliver Cromwell. Cavendish, who had fled to the Continent with the court of Queen Henrietta Maria, married William, marquis of Newcastle, and returned to England as her husband's agent in an attempt to regain his sequestered estates by payment of a fine. Cavendish explains how she worked through her brother, Lord Lucas, to gain the cooperation of Cromwell's Committee for Compounding and was unsuccessful. Her narrative of the events of her life ends shortly thereafter with the death of her much-loved brother-in-law, Sir Charles Cavendish.

She continues, however, by first describing her husband's character and then her own, concluding with a discussion of the process by which she composed her books. She is, she says, solitary and melancholic, "of a lazy nature and not of an active disposition." Many biographers have concluded that she was too lazy to revise what she wrote, though what she probably meant by "lazy" was she did not care to travel and was not inclined to take exercise. **Letters** from the physician Theodore Mayerne show that she did not exercise as he thought she should. She also explains that she composed what she later wrote down by first speaking out loud in a disorganized fashion. She then found that she could commit to paper what had, through this process, become orderly, though she confesses that her handwriting is such that her manuscripts cannot be taken to the press. She does not say so, but she probably used a family secretary, as her husband did, to create clean copy. She often claimed in the prefaces to her books that she did not borrow plots from classical authors, as did Shakespeare, Jonson, and others. Instead, she writes in "A True Relation" that she developed what she composed out of her own fancies and contemplations, like "silk worms that" spin "out of their own bowels." In point of fact, she openly relied on Plutarch for portions of *Sociable Letters* and transformed story lines found in Shakespeare for such plays as *The Convent of Pleasure* (1668) and *The Unnatural Tragedy* (1662).

"A True Relation" was not printed separately but rather was added as an afterthought to a collection of stories in verse and prose, *Nature's Pictures* (1656). It was dropped from the second edition of that book (1672) probably because Cavendish no longer felt the need to defend her family. "A True Relation" was privately reprinted by Sir Egerton Bridges at the beginning of the eighteenth century but did not become widely available until the last portion of the nineteenth century, when it appeared in a dozen or more printings together with the **biography** that she had written of her husband. **Virginia Woolf**'s review of the biography/autobiography combination for *TLS* was harsh (see Woolf, *The Common Reader* 1925). The introduction to the most recent edition of "A True Relation," edited by Sylvia Bowerbank and Sara Mendelson (2000), is more sympathetic. It notes that "in a period when spiritual and political autobiographies predominate, Margaret Cavendish's 'A True Relation' offers an unusually vivid example of a personal and secular autobiography."

If her project was to defend her family against suggestions that it did not compare to her husband's, Cavendish succeeded not by listing her family's many accomplishments but by allowing her readers to identify with the Lucases as human beings who enjoyed ordinary pleasures like strolling in Hyde Park and who suffered during the Civil Wars in the manner of so many other families.

Further Reading: Battigelli, Anna. *Margaret Cavendish and the Exiles of the Mind* (Lexington: University Press of Kentucky, 1998); Cavendish, Margaret. *Paper Bodies: A Margaret Cavendish Reader*. Edited by Sylvia Bowerbank and Sara Mendelson (Peterborough, Ontario: Broadview Press, 2000); Cavendish, Margaret. *Sociable Letters*. Edited by James Fitzmaurice (New York: Garland, 1997); Fitzmaurice, James. "The Life and the Literary Reputation of Margaret Cavendish." *Quidditas: The Journal of the Rocky Mountain Medieval and Renaissance Association* 20 (1999): 55–74; Whitaker, Katie. *Mad Madge: The*

Extraordinary Life of Margaret Cavendish, Duchess of Newcastle, the First Woman to Live by Her Pen (New York: Basic Books, 2002).

James Fitzmaurice

CHARKE, CHARLOTTE (1713–1760)

Actor, playwright, novelist, and most notably the author of her autobiography, *A Narrative of the Life of Mrs. Charlotte Charke* (1755), Charke's work is an entertaining account of her life, in which she presents herself at times as a penitent daughter seeking reconciliation with her famous father and at times as a resourceful female rogue well known for cross-dressing as a man both on and off the stage.

The *Narrative* begins with an account of Charlotte Cibber's childhood as the youngest child of Colly Cibber, playwright, actor, and poet laureate of England. Born when her mother was forty-five years old, Charlotte writes, "I came as an unexpected and unwelcome guest into the family." The account of her childhood and youth reveals her talent for acting and impersonation. At age four she dressed up in her father's clothes and wig and walked into town. Later, when still living at home, she set up an apothecary, and fooled adults who believed that she was trained in medicine. This flair for dramatic posturing and energetic pursuit of theatrical entertainment characterized much of her life.

After attending boarding school, Charlotte Cibber quickly married Richard Charke, a musician, who exploited her connection to the Cibber family. The marriage failed within twelve months, leaving Charlotte Cibber, now Charke, with an infant daughter to support. She took to the stage. The *Narrative* vividly describes the life of a London actress in the eighteenth century. When Charke began her acting career in 1730 her father was one of the patent holders for Drury Lane Theater. Her family name helped her begin her career by playing and working as an understudy for female parts. She then moved to playing "breeches roles" (women characters who spend part of the

time disguised as men) when acting with her brother's (Theodophilus Cibber) company at the New Haymarket Theater. Relations between Charke and her brother became strained, however, when she found herself competing with other actresses for roles she thought were exclusively hers. She finally broke with her brother's company and briefly set up a company of her own at the Haymarket to perform her own satirical play, *The Art of Management, or Tragedy Expell'd* (1735). She then returned to Drury Lane with the help of her father in a rare instance of paternal concern. But in 1735, when she was again out of work, Charke joined the Great Mogul's company, where Henry Fielding was manager. Fielding first hired Charke to play a parody of Colly Cibber, her father. Using her talent for male impersonation, Fielding cast Charke to play male parts in his productions: as Lord Place in *Pasquin*; Mr. Hen in *The Historical Register*; Mr. Spatter in *Eurydice Hissed*; and short parts in other plays.

Charlotte Charke had the most success while working for Fielding, but it came at a cost. Apparently because of the antagonism between Colly Cibber and Fielding, Cibber publicly disowned his daughter once she joined Fielding's theater. When the Stage Licensing Act of 1737 made it impossible for her to act on a London stage, Charke was out of work and without recourse as she was estranged from her family. She would live the rest of her life on the margins of society, pursuing a variety of ways to make a living, as a puppeteer, sausage maker, innkeeper, and waiter.

From 1737 to 1745, Charlotte Charke continued to cross-dress in order to hold jobs usually reserved for men; in London she worked as a street peddler, a gentleman's valet, and a tavern bouncer. She became notorious for wearing men's clothes in public. Barely eking out a hand-to-mouth existence for her and her daughter, Charke landed in debtor's prison several times, was bailed out, and finally decided to leave London in order to avoid her creditors.

After 1745, Charke joined different traveling acting troupes, and played male roles. During much of this time she went in public as Mr. Charles Brown and traveled with a "wife." Whereas she had previously dressed as a man to gain attention, she now cross-dressed to hide her **identity** from creditors. Her male impersonation was successful enough to have gained the attention of a young heiress who supposedly fell in love with Charke posing as Mr. Brown, until Charke convinced her that she was "the youngest daughter of Colly Cibber."

When Charlotte Charke returned to London in 1754 she had given up cross-dressing. At this time, she began writing novels, and her autobiography, but with little financial success. She wrote the first part of the *Narrative* in one more attempt to raise some cash, but also used the book as a way to bring public pressure on her father to take in his penitent daughter. In return, she would suppress the rest of her story. Receiving no response from her family, Charke continued to publish her *Narrative* in several parts. Later, she brought out the completed version as a book, printed in 1755.

Following the *Narrative*, Charke wrote a novel, *The History of Henry Dumon, Esq.; and Miss Charlotte Evelyn . . . With Some Critical Remarks on Comic Actors*, which she sold to her publishers for ten guineas. The novel was printed in 1756, although the *Critical Remarks* were never included. Charke's other publications appeared during the last few years of her life, including *The Mercer; or, Fatal Extravagance* (1755) and *The Lover's Treat; or, Unatural Hatred* (1758). When writing failed to provide her with enough income, she attempted unsuccessfully to return to the stage. Charlotte Charke then disappeared from sight in 1759 and died a year later at age forty-seven, alone and destitute.

Further Reading: Baruth, Philip, ed. *Introducing Charlotte Charke: Actress, Author, Enigma* (Urbana: University of Illinois Press, 1999); Charke, Charlotte. *A Narrative of the Life of Mrs. Charlotte Charke*. 1755. Reprint. Edited by Leonard Ashley. Facsimile (Gainesville, FL: Scholars' Facsimiles and Reprints, 1969); Mackie, Erin. "Desperate Measures: The Narratives of the Life of Mrs. Charlotte Charke." *ELH* 58, no. 4 (Winter 1991): 841–865.

Rebecca C. Potter

CHERNIN, KIM (1940–) Psychoanalyst, writing consultant, and author of fourteen books and multiple essays and articles, Kim Chernin is best known for her works *The Obsession* (1981), *In My Mother's House* (1983), *The Hungry Self* (1985), and *The Woman Who Gave Birth to Her Mother* (1998). Other works by Chernin include, *A Different Kind of Listening: My Psychoanalysis and Its Shadow* (1994); *My Life as a Boy* (1997); *Reinventing Eve: Modern Woman in Search of Herself* (1987); and *Sex and Other Sacred Games: Love, Desire, Power and Possession* (1989) with coauthor Renate Stendhal.

Chernin's work is multidisciplinary and difficult to classify. Her works have been characterized as "memoir, fiction, poetry, psychological study, and a psycho-sociological/religious study of women's search for self" (Fisher 2003). She is renowned for her storytelling, and her writing is at once poetic, theoretical, lyrical, autobiographical, analytical, psychoanalytic, and introspective. Her work is used by writers who discuss and theorize about the body, **embodiment**, Jewish American women's literature, autobiographical theory, psychoanalysis, **sexuality**, **gender** studies, eating disorders, **identity**, body image, and issues of self-representation. While her works are deeply personal, they strike a cord in diverse readers. Her works, *The Hungry Self* and *The Obsession* have contributed significantly to the canon on eating disorders and body-image issues in women. Chernin's work on themes such as sexuality, a daughter's relationship to her parents, the hunger for spirituality as well as for physical nourishment, read and appreciated by theorists, academicians, and mainstream readers. In addition to book-length works and articles, discussions of Chernin's work also appear in texts that address **race**, **class**, and gender, as well as Jewish American women and twentieth-century American women writers.

Chernin not only has worked as a writer and psychoanalyst, but also cofounded Edgework Books in 2001, for which she serves as CEO (Creative Executive Officer) and member of its editorial board. Edgework Books is a grassroots publishing collective founded by Chernin and other writers, therapists, and women over the age of fifty, who wanted to create an alternative to the mainstream, commercial book publishers. Edgework Books was born to put power in women's hands, giving them the freedom to write about topics that larger publishers would reject. Chernin's publishing company has been a vehicle for women to share their own (unfiltered) messages. Related to her work with Edgework Books is her work as an online writing consultant. To Chernin, her goal as a writing consultant is to help "people embark on, conceptualize, work with and through the problems that arise in the course of a writing project" (Fisher 2003). In her capacity as a psychotherapist, Chernin counsels those who suffer from eating and identity disorders and who are "in profound spiritual distress" (Fisher 2003).

Chernin was born in the Bronx, New York. Her parents, Rose Chernin and Paul Kusnitz, were both Marxists who encouraged their daughters' involvement in and knowledge of leftist writings and politics. The storytelling of her parents and her grandmother influenced Chernin's own use of storytelling and writing as an outlet, and her encouragement of other women in this way. She was also heavily influenced by the death of her only sister, Nina, from Hodgkin's disease when Chernin was four-years-old, and by what she felt was a lack of fully mourning her sister's loss by her family. After Nina's death, the family moved to central Los Angeles where her mother dealt with depression and being ar-

rested because of her involvement with the Communist Party. Chernin began to feel uncertain about the status of her family life and caused her to be teased at school. At age eighteen, after informing her mother that she was no longer a Marxist, Chernin moved to Berkeley, California, identifying herself as a mystic and a poet, rather than the way in which her mother had identified herself. She married in 1958, moved to Oxford (England) in 1963 with her husband, soon after giving birth to her daughter, Larissa. After divorcing and rethinking her feelings for her mother, Chernin changed her name back to Chernin, her mother's last name. While her feelings for her mother have been complicated and emotionally charged, this relationship has "fueled not only Kim's writing about her own life, but also her studies of contemporary women's ambivalent responses to their mothers" (Fisher 2003). In her autobiographical texts, she often works through these feelings and issues, particularly in both *In My Mother's House* and *Crossing the Border* (1994). In 1971, after her father's death, Chernin traveled to Israel, married again in 1972, and divorced in 1978. She then lived with Susan Griffen and their daughters. Chernin traveled to Paris in 1985, renewing a friendship and developing a relationship with Renate Stendhal, with whom she lives and writes in Berkeley, California.

Further Reading: Barker-Nunn, Jeanne. "Telling the Mother's Story: History and Connection in the Autobiographies of Maxine Hong Kingston and Kim Chernin." *Women's Studies* 14, no. 1 (1987): 55–63; Burstein, Janet Handler. *Writing Mothers, Writing Daughters: Tracing the Maternal in Stories by American Jewish Women* (Urbana: University of Illinois Press, 1996); Chernin, Kim. *The Hunger Song* (St. Paul, MN: Small Press Distribution, 1983); Chernin, Kim. *Crossing the Border: An Erotic Journey* (London: The Women's Press, 1994); Chernin, Kim. *In My Father's Garden: A Daughter's Search for a Spiritual Life* (Chapel Hill, NC: Algonquin Books, 1996); Chernin, Kim. *The Girl Who Went and Saw and Came Back: A Novel* (Berkeley, CA: Edgework

Books, 2002); Fisher, Jerilyn. "Kim Chernin."
July 11, 2003. http://www.kimchernin.com.

Emily C. Martin-Hondros

CHINESE WOMEN'S AUTOBIOGRA-PHY Autobiography as a literary genre is not common within the Chinese literary tradition. The sense of an independently thinking individual with critical abilities, values, and feelings has not been a prominent concept guiding the development of the Chinese mentality until the beginning of the twentieth century, when mass importation of Western learning and knowledge created a Chinese version of the Italian Renaissance in the May Fourth Movement. Ancient Chinese scholars do sometimes express their political aspirations and philosophical ponderings about life and death in their writing, but these ideas and thoughts are usually subtly embedded in layers of metaphors for self protection from political prosecution.

Women's autobiography in China is an even more recent genre. While there were a number of famous Chinese women poets in ancient China, a distinct female **voice** talking about her own experience in particular or even in general has not been a mainstream development. In its five-thousand-year history, China has always been a male-dominated society. For the most part, the female community has been relegated to domestic **space**s that do not provide equal opportunities for receiving education or even participating in public discussions about the issues in their lives. This hierarchical dominance of the male as well as rigid **class** distinctions have not favored the growth of female voices. Not until the beginning of the twentieth century did women have a public voice. This shift was the result of new opportunities for education, and the importation of liberal Western ideas created a more cordial environment for women to be heard publically.

Chinese women's autobiography as a specific literary genre within the modern period, however, is a complex anomaly within Chinese literary development. The dramatic events documenting modern Chinese history create a network of historical, literary, and cultural environments that makes even defining such a genre a complicated discussion. The very essence of Chinese **identity** is a problematic issue today, the result of a series of events: the civil war between the Communists and the Nationalists resulted in the political separation between Mainland China and Taiwan; the mass emigration of Chinese people to overseas countries created diasporic Chinese communities; and the return of colonies, such as Hong Kong and Macau, to Mainland sovereignty, resulted in Special Administrative Regions. This cultural context strongly affects the production of women's autobiography.

Apart from external forces acting directly on China, internal, social, and cultural values shift in response to international contexts and change people's day-to-day lives. After the establishment of the People's Republic of China, uniting China under Communist rule, political instability struck China once again in the late 1950s and early 1960s, when a series of bad harvests put the mainly agricultural population at the mercy of famine. In an attempt to stabilize the situation, and to divert people's attention from what might be considered mismanagement by the government, the Cultural Revolution, which lasted for ten years, was begun in 1967. This political event engaged the entire population in a series of time- and energy-consuming actions that ended in confusion and loss for many people. Into the 1980s, after the country had recovered from the political turmoil, a one-child policy was issued to control population growth. Nationwide movements such as these leave an indelible mark in the collective **memory** of the Chinese people.

It is with this background that Chinese women's autobiography should be read and understood. When referring to the works of Chinese women, one may be talking about women from any of the Chinese lands and diasporic communities. In this way, the concept of being Chinese embodies a full range of different material experiences as well as psychological and emotional responses. While one Chinese woman's story talks about the hardship of rural life, another woman's narrative may be about a sense of emptiness in the face of extreme material wealth in a fast-moving society. While a second-generation Chinese American mourns the loss of her Chinese roots, another woman living in one of the metropolitan cities in Mainland China may be eager to demonstrate the highly Westernized life she is living.

Chinese Women's Autobiography in the Twentieth Century

One of the earliest autobiographies published in China ostensibly as one woman's own real life story is Xie Bingying's *Autobiography of a Chinese Girl* (1936). Xie was a figure in a transitional period in China's history, as she was born at the beginning of the twentieth century into a landowning feudal family but received an education based on Western, democratic ideas. Her self-narrated autobiography talks about her early antagonism with her mother, who was a powerful enforcer of traditional patriarchal principles governing women's behavior. This early antagonism changed into open confrontation with the system her mother represented when she refused to marry the man her family chose for her, and instead ran away from them to become a soldier for her country. The time was the Sino-Japanese war and manpower was critical for the defense of the country. Due to the exceptional situation, Xie became one among a group of similarly minded young women who managed to escape their domestic destiny and participate in actions defending their country.

The appearance of Chinese autobiography in the twentieth century bears the generic marks of historical and cultural crises. Chinese autobiography is always a narrative of crises, and it is always the narrative of a specific personal crisis in relation to the larger crises in the country. Zhang Rong's *Wild Swans: Three Daughters of China* (1991) is one of the more widely known narratives, which have come to be known as Scar Literature, a type of literature that recalls individuals' lives during the Cultural Revolution. Written a decade after the Cultural Revolution, the story is a cross-generational documentation of the lives of three women in China: Zhang's grandma who belonged to feudal China, her mother who was an important official during the Cultural Revolution, and Zhang as a teenager at the start of this political movement, but who later managed to leave China and settle in Britain. At the end of the book is a personal reflection on the history of modern China and its impact on her own family.

Wild Swans was internationally acclaimed, partly because it is an insider's view of such an extended period of history that has been a secret to outsiders. Its success raises not only awareness but also interest in the history of modern China, as reflected in a surge of publications at the time. More "hidden" events were disclosed when Steven Mosher's *A Mother's Ordeal: One Woman's Fight Against China's One-Child Policy* was published in 1993. It was a narrative written from extensive interviews with Chi An, a Chinese woman who was trained to be a nurse to carry out the one-child policy, but who unfortunately became a victim a few years later when she wanted to have a second baby against the rules of the policy. Apart from her firsthand experience of carrying out the various population control measures, Chi An also speaks as a woman who sees her life's completion in motherhood. These two contradictory experiences substantiate the narrative and give it a depth of feeling.

An important subgenre of Chinese women's autobiography is the Chinese diaspora. Looking for a better life by immigrating to foreign countries has been a significant reality since the beginning of the twentieth century, resulting in an ever growing population of overseas Chinese in different parts of the world. The difficulty of immigrants mixing with the mainstream culture on the other hand, and the importance of recognizing one's "Chinese-ness" on the other hand, have been the dual focus of these narratives. An early example is found in **Jade Snow Wong**'s *Fifth Chinese Daughter* (1950). Wong is the first generation of her family to be born in America. Like other kids born in America, she received a regular American education; but at the same time her family enforced traditional Chinese rules concerning morality, social behavior, and hierarchies of identity. Wong's growth is a process of personal struggle to understand and hopefully compromise between these two very different cultural imperatives.

While Jade Snow Wong's narrative focuses more on the practical issues of day-to-day life, such as customs to follow, festivals to celebrate, or even ways to address different people, **Maxine Hong Kingston**'s *The Woman Warrior* (1977) opens up more deeprooted issues of cultural mixing, and questions of the location of Chinese-ness in these Chinese American identities. Kingston's use and transformation of traditional legends and icons in Chinese culture, such as Fa Mu Lan and Yue Fei, gives the narrative a playful dimension of cultural interaction. Another significant feature of the text is the employment of the mother-daughter framework, similar to Western self-narratives of women. Mother and daughter represent not just two generations, but two different origins of identity, two views on life and the importance of culture, and two people who can finally come to a full understanding of each other.

Back in Mainland China, where most Chinese live, women's self-narratives have also undergone a change. In 1928, when young female writer Ding Ling published her second story "Miss Sophie's Diary," the reading public was shocked by the narrator's admission of female desires and yearnings. It brought immediate fame to the writer because her frankness in such personal matters was very unusual in preRepublican China. Although the narrative is a series of fictional **diary** entries, the parallel between the young writer and the narrator of the story, who is also a young woman, arouses interest and comparisons, drawing attention to the emotional and psychological world of single women as a space of literary exploration.

Zhang Jie's collection, *Fang Zhou* (1983 [The Ark]) captured attention when it was first published. The title story tells the experience of three single women who are struggling to survive at a time of transition after the Cultural Revolution. On the one hand, the post-Revolution era possessed a liberal feeling of independence and openness, but, on the other hand, the protagonists, single women from different backgrounds, still experience oppression from class discrimination, sexist views, and narrow-minded bureaucracy. This autobiographical narrative once again reminds Chinese readers that women, who constitute half of the population, are still being mistreated as a result of age-old biases in Chinese society. This breakthrough in the subject matter in contemporary Chinese literature was followed by an even more personal narrative ten years later, when Zhang Jie wrote *Shi jie shang zui teng wo de na ge ren qu le* (1994 [Gone Is the One Who Held Me Dearest]), a record of her mother's last days in the form of diary entries. Mother, daughter, and granddaughter once again become an unbreakable chain within which love circulates.

At the beginning of the twenty-first century, Mainland China is still torn between basic problems of sustenance and the psychic emptiness of cities that have developed too fast, and too much in touch with international, ultramodern, metropolitan cities. These problems are at the root of current autobiographical trends. *Shanghai Baby* (2001) by Wei Hui is an unashamedly, self-professed autobiography, written for the sole purpose of making the writer famous. Firmly positioning herself in Shanghai, a glamorous city with the mixed charm of contemporary materialism and the old aura of colonialism, the narrator, Coco, indulges in all sorts of sensual and material pleasures, but finds it difficult to come to terms with herself. Moving among her two lovers, her extremely clever but dysfunctional friends, and broken relationships all around her, Coco gives a picture of contemporary China as materially saturated but spiritually empty. While some critics applaud the reality of the sentiment and the daring subject matter, others see it as nothing more than a non-self using consumer brand names and catchy ideas to patch herself up.

Chinese women's autobiography has blossomed during the twentieth century. External influences and internal developments have given rise to new forces of stimulation, urging women to write about their own lives in a time of transition and change.

Further Reading: Becker, Jasper. *Hungry Ghosts: China's Secret Famine* (London: J. Murray, 1996); Kingston, Maxine Hong. *The Woman Warrior: Memoirs of a Girlhood Among Ghosts* (London: Pan Books, 1977); Lee, Robert. *Multicultural American Literature: Comparative Black, Native, Latino/a and Asian American Fiction* (Edinburgh: Edinburgh University Press, 2003); Mosher, Steven. *A Mother's Ordeal: One Woman's Fight Against China's One-Child Policy* (New York: Harcourt Brace, 1993); Ng, Janet. *The Experience of Modernity: Chinese Autobiography of the Early Twentieth Century* (Ann Arbor: University of Michigan Press, 2003); Wei, Hui. *Shanghai Baby*. Translated by Bruce Humes (London: Robinson, 2001); Wong, Jade Snow. *Fifth Chinese Daughter* (New York: Harper, 1950); Xie, Bingying [Hsieh, Ping-ying]. *Autobiography of a Chinese Girl*. 1936. Reprint. Translated by Chi Tsui (London: Pandora, 1986); Zhang, Jie. *Fang Zhou* [The Ark] (Beijing: Xinhua shudian, 1983); Zhang, Jie. *Shi jie shang zui teng wo de na ge ren qu le* [Gone Is the One Who Held Me Dearest] (Hong Kong:

Tian di tu shu you xian gong si, 1994); Zhang, Rong [Chang Jung]. *Wild Swans: Three Daughters of China* (London: HarperCollins, 1991).

Amy Wai-sum Lee

CHISHOLM, SHIRLEY ANITA ST. HILL (1924–2005)

A controversial politician and one of the leading female orators in the United States, Shirley Chisholm is the author of two autobiographies. The first, *Unbought and Unbossed* (1970), was published in 1970, and records her family history, birth, early life, and career until 1970. *The Good Fight* (1973) is the story of her 1972 bid for the Democratic Party's presidential nomination. Together, these two autobiographies give us an insider's view of the turbulent political atmosphere of the 1960s and 1970s from the point of view of one of the most inspirational women of our times.

Chisholm writes in the introduction to *Unbought and Unbossed* that she hopes to be remembered for "what I have done, not for what I happen to be" (xii), but she will always be remembered as the first black woman to be elected to the United States Congress (1968–1982) and the first black person to seek the Democratic Presidential nomination (1972). Chisholm's narrative emphasizes her political rather than her private life. Although some personal details are included, she mainly chronicles her political career and what shaped it. She emphasizes that she speaks for herself, not for anyone else, nor does she suggest motives others may have had for their decisions. Chisholm's two political autobiographies chart the history of her career through the 1972 presidential election.

Shirley St. Hill Chisholm was the oldest of the four girls born to immigrants Charles and Ruby Seale St. Hill, in Brooklyn, New York. At age three, her parents sent her to be reared by her maternal grandmother in Barbados until she was ten-years-old. Chisholm recounts an idyllic island life and a strong academic background. She returned to New York, attended Girls' High School in Brooklyn, and later majored in sociology at Brooklyn College, graduating in 1946. While in college she joined the Harriet Tubman Society, the Political Science Society, and was active in campus politics, campaigning for women candidates for Student Council and serving as a volunteer for the National Urban League and the National Association for the Advancement of Colored People (NAACP).

Chisholm began what she believed would be her lifelong work with children at the Mt. Calvary Childcare Center in Harlem in 1946. After seven years she moved to the position of director of the Friends Day Nursery in Brooklyn. She attended Columbia University earning a master's degree in education in 1952 and later served as an educational consultant for New York City's day care division. In 1953, as a member of the 17th Assembly District Democratic Club she and her mentor, Wesley McD. Holder, helped elect Lewis S. Flagg, Jr., the first black judge in Brooklyn's history, to the municipal court. But it was not until 1964 that her own political career took off when she won her campaign for the New York State Assembly. Between 1965 and 1968 she authored legislation that provided college funding to underrepresented youth, secured unemployment insurance for domestics and day care providers, and voted to increase funding for schools.

In 1968, Shirley Chisholm won a seat in the House of Representatives when she defeated James Farmer. She became known as a liberal champion of human rights who opposed the Vietnam War and favored social reforms including full employment, higher minimum wage, federal funding for day care facilities, the Equal Rights Amendment, and legalized abortions. She served on the Education and Labor committee and secured federal grants for businesses in her district. She claims that college students started her thinking about running for president, and in 1972 she campaigned for the presidency, as "a candidate of the people" winning 152 delegates before withdrawing from the race.

After retiring from Congress in 1982, Shirley Chisholm was active as an educator both at Mount Holyoke College (1983–1987) where she held the Purington chair and as a visiting scholar at Spelman College in 1985. She was a spokesperson for women's rights and participated in Jesse Jackson's campaign for the presidency in 1980. She created and chaired the National Political Congress of Black Women, was a founder of the National Women's Political Caucus, and served on the Advisory Council of the National Organization for Women.

Shirley Chisholm credited Eleanor Roosevelt, Harriet Tubman, and her grandmother as having the greatest influences on her life. Chisholm said that she faced more discrimination as a woman than she did as a black person. She writes in *Unbought and Unbossed*, "I want the time to come when we can be as blind to sex as we are to color" (75).

In her autobiographies, Chisholm emerges as a courageous individual. Her intellect, constancy to her political goals, integrity, and challenges to the political system are legendary. In *The Good Fight*, she writes "The next time a woman runs, or a black, a Jew or anyone from a group that the country is 'not ready' to elect to its highest office, I believe he or she will be taken seriously from the start. The door is not open yet, but it is ajar" (3–4). Her political autobiographies allow us to see what one person can accomplish.

Further Reading: Brownmiller, Susan. *Shirley Chisholm: A Biography* (New York: Doubleday, 1970).

Dianna Laurent

CLASS   When writing about women's autobiography, literary critics have more often than not concerned themselves primarily with issues of **gender**. Early critics in the field of autobiography looked to women's autobiography to learn how women experienced their lives differently than men and what concerned women in all aspects of their lives. Typically, these theorists were dealing with the autobiographies of white, middle-class women. In response to critiques of such a narrow frame of reference, critics expanded their purview of women's autobiographies to include those of different ethnic and racial backgrounds. What has gone missing in much of the discussion of women's autobiography, however, is how a person's social class informs the formation of self, in particular, a gendered self.

Since the 1990s, some literary critics have made an attempt to interrogate women's autobiographies with an eye toward how class informs life histories. These critics have a number of concerns when investigating the issue of class and class formation in women's autobiographies: First, they are careful to locate their discussions of class within a specific historical time period because they acknowledge that different historical moments can translate into different interpretations of class and gender. Second, these critics are also aware that social class helps inform how women will construct their autobiographies and what issues women autobiographers will address. For example, social class can influence and determine what a woman can or cannot say in her autobiography. The nexus of class and gender is an important consideration when reading and analyzing women's autobiographies, since women experience and interpret their lives differently depending on their social class.

In order to understand how social class informs autobiography, an examination of women's autobiographies from different social strata will serve to highlight some of the differences among women. In her book, *Representing Femininity: Middle-Class Subjectivity in Victorian and Edwardian Women's Autobiographies* (1992), Mary Jean Corbett looks specifically at middle-class women's autobiographies that were written during the nineteenth and early twentieth centuries. At issue for women writers during this period was their relationship to the public sphere. Since middle-class women lived on the border between their domestic lives in the home and their emerging public lives as writers, they had to negotiate between this private/public **space** in order to write their autobiographies.

Among the options available for middle-class women during the nineteenth century were spiritual and secular autobiographies. When middle-class women wrote spiritual autobiographies, they were able to keep their private lives more or less intact. Writing an autobiography from the perspective of one's religious ideals meant a woman's autobiography was just an extension of her private life. The spiritual autobiography helped inculcate a domestic ideology for its intended audience: other women. Women, thus, wrote about their lives as models of exemplary behavior from which they expected others could learn.

However, when middle-class women wrote secular autobiographies, suddenly these writers had to confront the issue that their private lives would be made available for public consumption through publication of their works. Writing for them meant doing so at the expense of revealing their private lives. As a way to negotiate between their private lives and the public act of writing autobiography, many middle-class women autobiographers turned to writing memoirs instead. The **memoir** enabled them to downplay their own private lives while focusing their attention on other people's lives. Thus, women wrote about famous family members or literary people about whom the public might be interested in learning more. Their autobiographies, in effect, emphasized other people's lives and stories while limiting how much they told of their own lives. As a result, women writers could enter the public domain without publicizing their own private lives.

In her work, *Subjectivities: A History of Self-Representation in Britain, 1832–1920* (1991), **Regenia Gagnier** writes about women's working-class autobiographies. Her project is to locate these women and their autobiographies in the context of their economic, social, and historical circumstances. She explains that unlike most nineteenth-century, middle-class men's autobiographies, which concerned themselves with exploring the individual self, working-class autobiographers had other rhetorical concerns.

First, women's working-class autobiographies are more pragmatic in nature. They communicate specific ideas in expository prose. They were interested, for example, in giving information about their own labor history or in helping other workers. For the most part, regardless of their topic, these working-class autobiographers had little interest in discovering themselves through writing. They wrote because they had reasons to do so that had less to do with themselves as individuals than with informing their audience.

Because their lives were necessarily different from their middle-class counterparts, the narrative trajectory of working-class autobiographies takes a different shape. Thus, for example, working-class writers typically begin their narratives by apologizing for themselves. Moreover, their autobiographies seldom include a narrative of either their education or of their early childhood. Due to economic circumstances, these writers were forced to go to work at an early age, which precluded a childhood or education that conformed to middle-class norms. Instead, their autobiographies document their lives of constant work. As a result, working-class autobiographies typically end in the middle of a person's life since their narrative trajectories do not lead toward a "successful" resolution, in middle-class terms. By looking at nineteenth-century women's working-class autobiographies in the context of their social, historical, and economic circumstances, one comes to learn how such forces help define a person's life.

At the opposite end of the spectrum is Julia Bush's article "Ladylike Lives? Upper Class Women's Autobiographies and the Politics of Late Victorian and Edwardian Britain" (2001). Bush demonstrates that upper-class women had different issues to contend with in regard to their public selves. Her study of thirteen upper-class women's autobiographies reveals a number of commonalities that all of these women writers shared. Significantly, none of the women focus on their own achievements or their singularities as individuals. Instead, their autobiographies are other directed; thus, upper-class women typically chose "Great Men" as the subjects of their autobiographies. These men could include great men the writers had known as a result of family and political connections, or they could be the authors' fathers or husbands. By shaping their autobiographies around the theme of "Great Men" they had known, upper-class women autobiographers, like their middle-class counterparts, thus limited their own personal exposure to the public.

Writing their autobiographies about "Great Men," rather than focusing primarily on themselves as the subject, rendered these men a significant service by helping ensure that they would figure prominently in the future because of their past deeds. But at the same time, the reader cannot help but notice that these women themselves held a certain amount of social sway because of their personal familiarity with these great figures of history. In telling the "Great Men" story, upper-class women autobiographers also reveal their access to important people and places.

Increasingly, their autobiographies also demonstrate how these women were in a sense obliged to participate in a more public life since their husbands and family members were directly involved in politics. Women married to political figures began to play a more active role in their spouses' lives, helping them politically and participating in public appearances. Such a change in roles for upper-class women at the beginning of the twentieth century demonstrated their increasing participation in a more public sphere.

The historical accounts of how women autobiographers negotiated their private/

public lives reveal how class and gender function together to construct women's lives. But these historical accounts only render broad generalizations about the autobiographers studied. Herein lies the problem for **Carolyn Kay Steedman**. She argues that when cultural critics write about and analyze working-class people, critics typically depict them in terms of psychological simplicity. Steedman contends that critics need to spend more time considering the individual psychological makeup of the writer along with her working-class status in order to understand how social class informs everyday life.

Thus, in her autobiography *Landscape of a Good Woman* (1986), Steedman takes a different approach to discussing and analyzing her own working-class background and that of her mother. She tells their dual story because she believes that her mother's story has yet to be told in any of the books written about the British working class of the 1950s, since it did not conform to the working-class paradigm of the time. In many historical accounts, the theorist tends to see the lives of the working class as overdetermined by economics and material deprivation. What gets lost in such histories, according to Steedman, are issues of personal "pain, loss, love, anxiety, and desire" (12). Because they talk in broad generalities about the working class, with an emphasis on rendering the collective experience of the group, historians of the working class pay little attention to the personal nuances of an individual's life. Moreover, they lack understanding about interfamilial relations and the psychic pain that can take place in such families. Steedman remains opposed to any grand narrative about working-class people and their lives; instead, she contends that when looking at the working class, the theorist needs to consider the psychological development of the individual alongside the social context (18).

Steedman's own autobiography complicates the twin issues of gender and class by going beyond an economic understanding of class to look at the psychological consequences of social class and how they inform her life. It is this story that Steedman wants to tell about both herself and her mother. However, narrating her individual autobiography necessitates going back in history to tell the story of her mother's desire and longings, which helped to shape her life experiences. Steedman locates her mother's personal story in a particular time and place in order to historicize the social and economic situation that her mother has to traverse. Psychological loss and personal exclusion are the driving dynamic in her mother's life. These losses and exclusions associated with social class inevitably make up the person that she becomes, and from which her daughter will also learn the experience of social class. By linking the social with the psychological, Steedman fleshes out the experiences of both herself and her mother, which enables her to understand how another person's past (her mother's) informs her present (Steedman's).

Much of the work on class and gender in autobiography has been done by looking at the British experience. It is clear from these studies that class remains a fraught category of analysis because of the multiple ways one can attend to a discussion of class; however, it is also clear that such studies of necessity need to be undertaken in order to understand how social class and gender help construct a person's life and her daily lived experiences. Middle-class autobiographies only tell part of the story of social class, and future accounts of both the upper class and working class need to be pursued in order to render more fully how each social class functions. Finally, analyzing the American experience of social class in women's autobiography is a largely untapped field that awaits further study.

Further Reading: Smith, Sidonie, and Julia Watson, eds. *Women, Autobiography, Theory: A Reader* (Madison: The University of Wisconsin Press, 1998).

Phoebe S. Jackson

COLLABORATIVE LIFE NARRATIVE

The increasing visibility of collaboration in life narrative has highlighted the limitations of the traditional term "autobiography." Strictly speaking, "collaborative autobiography" is a contradiction in terms, for "self-life-writing" implies that one single person lives, narrates, and writes her or his own life. In practice, few people compose life narratives wholly by themselves: even the most traditional *self* life writers check their memories of events not only against historical documents but also against the memories of friends and family members. Some make this consultation process more or less transparent to their readers. Margaret Mead and Mary McCarthy, for example, juxtapose their own memories with family members' different recollections of the same events. Other single-authored narratives owe a good deal—perhaps even their very existence—to the work of editors. **Harriet Jacobs'** *Incidents in the Life of a Slave Girl* (1861) was published through the intervention of the editor, Lydia Maria Child. Mourning Dove (Christine Quintasket) wrote her narrative in her second language, English, and apparently intended to have it edited; fifty-four years after her death it was found, edited, and published as *Mourning Dove: A Salishan Autobiography* (1990).

The terms "collaborative life narrative" and "collaborative autobiography," however, are generally reserved for cases in which two (or occasionally more) people are directly involved in negotiating and producing a text. These two collaborators are the "subject"—that is, the person who lived and now tells the life—and the "writer." The writer's role varies: he or she may be an aggressive interviewer or passive dictation taker; the writer may determine the final shape of the text or have little influence on how the materials are organized. If a book results from a collaboration, the subject's name generally comes first, with the writer's name appearing, in smaller print, after one of these phrases: "as told to," or "with," or even "edited by."

"As-told-to" life narratives range from celebrity autobiographies to ethnographies. (In the latter, the subject is known as the "informant," the writer as the "ethnographer.") Some celebrity autobiographies are ghostwritten; that is, the writer's name does not appear at all; at the opposite extreme is the ethnographic case study, with the writer's name alone in the byline and the name (or pseudonym) of the informant appearing only in the narrative and perhaps the title, as with Marjorie Shostak's *Nisa: The Life and Words of a !Kung Woman* (1981). A collaborative case study in mainstream American culture is Susan Cheever's *A Woman's Life* (1994), where the subject remains anonymous—known only as "Linda." While Shostak presents Nisa's story in the first person (Nisa, the subject, is "I"), Cheever refers to Linda in the third person. Thus, Linda's story lies somewhere between **biography** and autobiography.

Occasionally, and especially in women's life writing, other patterns of collaboration emerge. For example, two people who have shared certain experiences—sisters, perhaps, or longtime friends—also share in communicating those experiences. Counter to the usual pattern of collaborative autobiography, they are both subjects and writers at once; but unlike the solo autobiographer, they must find ways to negotiate their separate and differing memories into a coherent text. In *Imaginary Parents* (1996) Sheila Ortiz Taylor and Sandra Ortiz Taylor collaborate to produce a family history; Sheila writes the account based on the sisters' memories, and Sandra creates art "as a separate but parallel narrative to the text" (xvi). *In the Land of the Grasshopper Song* (1957) is Mary Ellicott Arnold and Mabel Reed's **memoir** of two years (1908–1909) as matrons for the Bureau of Indian Affairs among the Yurok in California's Klamath River country. In this text, a single rather than a double strand of narrative, the voice is Arnold's, but she reports in the foreword that she and Reed wrote two separate accounts of each day's events and later compared what they had recalled, "in order to arrive, as nearly as possible, at a true statement of what our friends had said and done."

Collaborative life writing poses a number of important ethical questions, some of them so insistent that the writer-collaborator must discuss them in their introductions or epilogues. Broader ethical issues are taken up by scholars with background in such areas as anthropology and critical and narrative theory: a comprehensive and helpful example is G. Thomas Couser's "Making, Taking, and Faking Lives" (2001). Most pressing is the question of ownership: whose story is it, anyway? The life is the subject's, the writing is the writer's, and the text is the result of their dialogue and negotiation—but sometimes it is difficult to determine the boundaries of life, writing, and text. Further complicating the situation, translators, editors, publicists, or coresearchers may be involved in the project as well. Issues of ownership can be approached personally (through subject-writer discussions of their relationship), legally (with copyright and royalties), and professionally (subjects must have an opportunity to review the manuscript they have helped produce, even if this requires an ethnographer to have the text translated back into the informant's language).

Collaborative life narrative is potentially exploitive. Despite good intentions, subject and writer may not share equitably in both the rewards and drawbacks of the collaboration. Telling a life story can be a volatile act, and stories abound of broken, difficult, or unsatisfactory collaborations: a subject who became angry or fearful and stopped the project, a writer who willfully distorted the subject's story, a subject who became unhappy with the text after publication, a writer who knew that some of the subject's claims were untrue. Furthermore, as Couser points out, the balance of power between subject and writer is rarely even: a celebrity autobiographer has more power than her hired ghostwriter. And not all collaborations are voluntary: a written **confession**

obtained through interrogation or torture is a form of collaborative autobiography.

While subjects struggle to remember and to decide what to say, writers contend with the ethics of representation: how to portray the subject appropriately, accurately, and fairly. To add to the complexity, many collaborations are cross-cultural and bilingual. (Nearly all nineteenth- and early-twentieth-century Native American life narratives were the product of what critic Arnold Krupat (1985) calls "original bicultural composite composition.") In such collaborations, it is difficult for subject and writer to understand each other's motivations and cultural assumptions and for the subject to give "informed" consent. Even the ideas of what makes for a good life narrative, or a well-told story, vary from culture to culture, and most writers have shaped their subjects' stories to fit Western tastes and understandings.

Knowing the potential difficulties of collaborative life writing, many writers provide careful descriptions of the circumstances of the collaboration: the physical and cultural context, the difficulties encountered, and the roles played by writer and subject. Several decades after first publishing *Papago Woman* (1979) the life narrative of Maria Chona, anthropologist Ruth Underhill added a lengthy introduction, explaining how she had elicited Maria Chona's stories and later organized them. In the introduction to *I, Rigoberta Menchú: An Indian Woman in Guatemala* (1984), Elisabeth Burgos-Debray not only discusses the interview and translation process but also makes claims about the personal relationship between her and the subject. Although some readers object that detailed introductions call too much attention to the writers, others find it crucial to know something about the process by which the text was produced, so that they can be aware of how the subject's life narrative was mediated through this process.

Despite all the potential (and actual) pitfalls in the process, collaborative life narrative is an important practice, a potential force for diversity and even for justice. It provides a way for mainstream culture to hear from "underrepresented" people; it is a means for voices of resistance to mainstream values to be heard. The autobiography of those who do not write is inclusive not only of those who do not have skill or time to write their own stories, but also of those who are ill or disabled, or who would normally be denied the means to write. In her discussion of "out-law" genres of autobiographical narrative—genres that challenge and subvert traditional mainstream autobiography—Caren Kaplan mentions Third World women's prison narratives and *testimonios* (testimonial narratives by Latin American women resisting oppression). These narratives, too, are collaborative, and they allow marginalized voices to be heard.

Further Reading: Couser, G. Thomas. "Making, Taking, and Faking Lives: Ethical Problems in Collaborative Life Writing." In *Mapping the Ethical Turn: A Reader in Ethics, Culture, and Literary Theory*, edited by Todd F. Davis and Kenneth Womack, 209–227 (Charlottesville: University Press of Virginia, 2001); Kaplan, Caren. "Resisting Autobiography: Out-Law Genres and Transnational Feminist Objects." In *De/Colonizing the Subject: The Politics of Gender in Women's Autobiography*, edited by Sidonie Smith and Julia Watson, 115–138 (Minneapolis: University of Minnesota Press, 1992); Krupat, Arnold. *For Those Who Come After: A Study of Native American Autobiography* (Berkeley: University of California Press, 1985); Sands, Kathleen M. "Cooperation and Resistance: Native American Collaborative Personal Narrative." In *Native American Representations: First Encounters, Distorted Images, and Literary Appropriations*, edited by Gretchen M. Bataille, 134–149 (Lincoln: University of Nebraska Press, 2001).

Kathleen Boardman

CONFESSION Literary confessions are most often associated with the so-called confessional poets, a group of New Englanders writing in the 1960s–1970s that in-

cludes W.D. Snodgrass, Robert Lowell, **Anne Sexton**, **Sylvia Plath**, and John Berryman. These authors revolutionized poetry by writing with unprecedented frankness about previously taboo subjects. Before confession was a movement, however, it was a mode of writing with a long and illustrious literary history. A confession combines an autobiographical methodology with a subject matter focused primarily on sin, transgression, and redemption. Unlike autobiography, which is generally understood to present a self that is crafted and constructed, confession implies a much more transparent interrelation between author and subject; just as one speaks the truth in the Catholic ritual of confession, from which the genre takes its name, so is one assumed to speak the truth about oneself in a confessional narrative. Confessions take many and varied forms, from the novel passing as autobiography to the sensationalist and shockingly intimate **memoir**, from poetry to prose. Most confessions, however, follow a narrative framework that can be traced back to one of two prominent authors: Augustine or Rousseau. Each provides a distinctive model for confessional writing.

Augustine's *Confessions* (c. 397) centers on a conversion experience: sins are detailed, even celebrated, but are ultimately renounced. In the end, Augustine is transformed and redeemed through the act of confession. The standard prohibition against frank discussion of sin, especially of the sexual sin that typically lies at the heart of confessional narratives, is lifted by Augustine's narrative replication of the privileged locus of the Catholic confessional; in this sacrosanct space, the silence and repression that govern the topics of **sexuality** and sin give way to a mandate to detail one's transgressions. Just as the Catholic confessional was the place where a discussion of sex and other transgressions was not only permitted but in fact required, so too do confessional narratives touch on subjects that strict autobiographies could not. This explicit subject matter is enabled through the implicit renunciation of and atonement for sin—the regulation of desire—that is inextricably linked with contrition.

Jean-Jacques Rousseau's *Confessions* (1781) recounts the secular experiences that contributed to the author's maturation; where Augustine's narrator moves from sinner to saint, Rousseau's moves from boy to man. Rousseau presents sinning as a natural part of the coming-of-age process, and repentance seems a hasty afterthought, a doff of the hat to societal conventions. Rousseau's use of the confessional mode disguises the lack of repentance in his own narrating persona; the genre enables a frank explication of sexual exploits precisely because it presupposes the renunciation of sin and the transformation of sinner into a saint. That the transformation never really takes place marks a profound change in the conventions of the confessional literary genre: the deployment of the rhetoric and ritual surrounding the act of confession allows for the discussion of sexually explicit subject matter in the guise of piety while challenging prevailing notions concerning the nature of sin itself.

It is no coincidence that both of these founding texts are written by men. Until the second wave of **feminism** and the sexual revolution, transgression was a luxury that only men could afford; the double standard promised forgiveness to men for their sins while branding women social pariahs for equivalent offenses. Nevertheless, women who were in a position to write their autobiographies were to a large extent already transgressors, both in the act of writing and in the aspects of their lives that rendered their life stories noteworthy. For many of these women the confessional framework proved particularly useful, softening the blow of their transgressive acts by locating themselves within a literary tradition based on a structure of penitence, whether religious or purely rhetorical.

With the advent of the sexual revolution came an increased openness about previously taboo subjects. It was in this cultural moment that the mode of confessional writing became a movement within American literature, giving rise to the confessional poets. Marking a transition away from the prevailing aesthetic of the impersonality of poetry as outlined by T. S. Eliot in his influential essay, "Tradition and the Individual Talent" (1919), their work turned the spotlight on the individual, exploring issues concerning **identity** and **subjectivity**. Using the first-person **voice**, confessional poetry confronted intimate topics such as marital infidelity, childhood trauma, sexuality, alcoholism, mental breakdown, and suicidal depression. (Significantly, all the poets were analysands and most were suicides, facts that inevitably inform one's reading of their work.) While these topics were controversial, Sexton and Plath in particular created a stir by writing about aspects of women's experience previously not spoken of in polite society, much less written about in lyric poetry (for example, Sexton's "Menstruation at Forty" and "Woman with Girdle"). By linking their depression and anger to the dysfunctions of the family and **gender** roles, they launched incisive feminist critiques.

To some extent, all writers mine their personal experiences for use in their work, but the confessional poets appeared to do so with a lack of reserve, with no regard for the private or potentially embarrassing, and without speaking through personae. The intimate details provided combined with the seemingly direct and naked form of address imparted their work with a convincing facade of verisimilitude. It is important to note, however, that autobiographical accuracy, or "truth," is the desired effect of the poetry and not the mode of producing it; truth is as complicated and contested a category in confession as it is in autobiography. Making use of facts and situations from their lives, the poets challenged the applicability of a universal self; rendering transparent the veil between author and persona, they alternately dissected and reconstructed, analyzed and mythologized the self. The resulting poetics are thus uniquely positioned to interrogate the tensions between public and private, between self and society, and between life and art.

One of the most significant movements in postwar poetry, confessional poetry enjoyed an unprecedented popularity; highlighting the divide between academic and popular opinion, the poems were initially denigrated by critics for their lack of craft and for the sensational nature of their subject matter even as they were embraced by the reading public for the same reasons. The confessional poets inaugurated a new era in American literature and influenced many important writers. They enabled the personal explorations of new generations of writers, including the contemporary postconfessionals, who continue to explore childhood, **memory**, trauma, and identity. Given its emphasis on sexuality and its unflinching discussion of taboo topics, the confessional mode has proven particularly useful to lesbian writers such as **Adrienne Rich** and **Audre Lorde**, as well as to gay Beat writers such as Allen Ginsberg, who has himself sometimes been classified as a confessional. Moreover, confessional poetry undoubtedly paved the way for the memoir craze that began in the 1990s, in which authors competed to reveal shocking accounts of sexaholism, adult incest, and drug abuse. As an adjective, "confessional" has become associated with the sensationalist, the lurid, and the self-promoting. Viewed in its historical context, however, confessionalism has complicated notions concerning self, truth, and subjectivity, pushed the boundaries of acceptable narratives, and created **space** for alternative identities to find expression. As a contemporary phenomenon, confessional writing continues to enrich the body of autobiographical literature.

Miranda Sherwin

CONWAY, JILL KER (1934–) Jill Ker Conway is best known for her compelling

autobiographical trilogy that narrated her educational journey from a child in the Australian outback to first female president of Smith College in Hanover, Massachusetts. Her interest in women's educational narrative led her to study and anthologize autobiographical writings of women worldwide, as well as write about women's **memoirs** from a historical perspective. Trained as a historian at Harvard University, Conway brings her skills to bear on both historical and literary texts.

In penning her autobiography, Conway set out to fill a perceived void in literary representation: women's education narrative. Conway notes, "So far as women's life of the mind went, I could see that there weren't any female counterparts to the classic male stories of an education. . . . I'd try to write a lively picture of the way a woman's mind developed and how her intellectual vocation was formed" (*A Woman's Education* 2001, 122). Conway wrote this story in three volumes that explore the development of her ideas and career— through conversations with fellow students and faculty, research of historical women's **letters** and diaries, and study of the needs of individuals within educational institutions.

Her critically acclaimed volumes, *The Road from Coorain* (1990), *True North* (1994), and *A Woman's Education* (2001), have been praised for their lyricism, sense of **place**, and depiction of the rewards of intellectual work. In them, Conway credits her childhood on an isolated ranch in New South Wales for the self-reliance and intellectual curiosity that have sustained her academic career. *The Road from Coorain* poignantly describes Conway's troubled relationship with her mother, a woman with similar talents but fewer opportunities. Their relationship is central to the 2002 film version produced for public broadcasting's Masterpiece Theatre. Following a series of family tragedies and a move to Sydney with her mother and brother, Conway earned a degree in history at the University of Sydney.

Experiencing a lack of support for her interest in women's history and barriers to career advancement as a woman, she left Australia to pursue a Ph.D. at Harvard University.

The later memoirs depict Conway's education and career in North America, painting a vivid picture of her struggles for recognition and equal pay as a female academic, as well as her experience of the cultural differences between Australia, the United States, and Canada. *True North* chronicles Conway's doctoral research on the first generation of female American college graduates, her marriage to Harvard history professor John Conway, and her professorial appointment at the University of Toronto, where she also served as vice president in charge of internal affairs. *A Woman's Education* begins in 1975, when Conway became president of Smith College. The volume details Conway's tenure at Smith, including her efforts to not only document women's educational lives, but to improve them. At Smith, Conway sought to articulate the modern relevance of a women's college and to foster research on women's issues. She also helped make college education possible for mothers, welfare recipients, and older women by developing scholarship and child care programs. After a decade at Smith, Conway accepted a position as visiting scholar and professor at MIT and has continued her career in administration as chair of Lend Lease Corporation and member of several corporate boards.

Along with traditional Western philosophy, such as the Socratic method and Hegelian dialectic, Conway has been influenced by the ideas of feminist precursors and colleagues. As a scholar and administrator, Conway has contributed to the feminist goals of integrating women's works and research into the literary and historical canons. Yet Conway eschews what she calls "sentimental feminism" that depicts women's nature as fundamentally different from men's. She also rejects postmodern theory that she views as inaccessible for a majority of nonacademic readers. This differentiates Conway's works from much of the writing of contemporary ("third-wave") feminist theorists who draw on postmodernist philosophy and discuss women's **subjectivity** in theoretical language.

Conway's academic works are known for their accessibility and clarity, rather than their theoretical complexity, as critics have noted. The issues of **gender** and culture foregrounded in her memoirs are evident in works such as *When Memory Speaks* (1998), in which Conway explores how gender and culture have shaped the writing of Western autobiography. This text argues that, while male autobiographers have modeled their works on a Ulysses-like quest, female autobiographers have masked their ambition in the form of the romance, in order to make their messages more palatable to readers.

In her three edited anthologies of women's autobiography—*Written by Herself* (1992) volumes 1 and 2, and *In Her Own Words* (1999)—Conway presents diverse women's **voices** (including **Harriet Jacobs**, **Isak Dinesen**, **Sally Morgan**, and **Meena Alexander**) narrating their own life stories, some of which are out of print in their original versions. In editing the collections, Conway continues her valuable project of furthering representation of the intellectual lives of women around the globe. With the anthologies, along with her own well-read memoirs, she helps to ensure the availability and perseverance of a tradition of women's education narrative.

Further Reading: Conway, Jill Ker. *The Road from Coorain.* (New York: Vintage, 1990); Conway, Jill Ker. *True North: A Memoir* (New York: Knopf, 1994); Conway, Jill Ker. *When Memory Speaks: Reflections on Autobiography* (New York: Knopf, 1998); Conway, Jill Ker. *A Woman's Education* (New York: Knopf, 2001); Conway, Jill Ker, ed. *In Her Own Words: Women's Memoirs from Australia, New Zealand, Canada and the United States* (New York: Vintage, 1999); Conway, Jill Ker, ed. *Written by Herself: Autobiographies of American*

Women (New York: Vintage, 1992); Conway, Jill Ker, ed. *Written by Herself, Volume II: Women's Memoirs from Britain, Africa, Asia, and the United States* (New York: Vintage, 1996); Gudzowsky, Nicole. "Telling It Straight: How the Girl from Coorain Became a Scholar with a Social Conscience." *Horizon Magazine* (October 1998). April 2, 2003. http://www.horizonmag.com/1/conway.htm. Hoy, Pat C. "Jill Ker Conway: A Father's Daughter." *Sewanee Review* 108 (2000): 448–457; McCooey, David. "Parents, Crisis and Education: Jill Ker Conway's *The Road from Coorain.*" *Australian and New Zealand Studies in Canada* 11 (1994): 91–102; Newman, Joan. "The Heroic Type in Australian Nationalist Autobiography." In *Myths, Heroes and Anti-Heroes: Essays on the Literature and Culture of the Asia-Pacific Region*, edited by Bruce Bennett and Dennis Haskell, 175–184 (Perth: Centre for Studies in Australian Literature, 1992); White, Naomi Rush. "'The Best Years of Your Life': Remembering Childhood in Autobiographical Texts." *Children and Society* 12 (1998): 48–59.

Natalie Stillman-Webb

D

DAS, KAMALA (1934–) Although better known as one of India's most controversial poets, Kamala Das has also published a number of autobiographical works of which only one **memoir**, *My Story* (1976), has been translated into English. Her literary oeuvre includes, in addition to her many volumes of poetry, a novel, *The Alphabet of Lust* (1976). As the title of the novel indicates, Das' work is characterized by an intense sexual candor, thereby earning her more than a fair share of notoriety in India.

The contribution of her memoir to women's autobiography in general and to Indian women's autobiography more specifically is noteworthy. In narrating her life freely and frankly, she has broken the gendered boundaries of what is considered appropriate for a woman to discuss and write about. Moreover, the autobiography's preoccupation with the life of the artist also gives us remarkable insight into the creative development of one of India's leading, albeit contentious, women poets.

Das was born in 1934 in the south Indian state of Kerala. She was married at a young age and has three sons. After experiencing a peripatetic childhood involving sojourns all over India, including the metropolitan cities of Delhi and Calcutta, Das now lives in her home state of Kerala. In 1999, she converted to Islam, calling herself Kamala Suraiya, a decision—like almost everything else in Das' life—that provoked immense controversy in India, especially among the right-wing Hindu constituency.

My Story gives important insights into the mind of an artist—as well as the body of a woman—affronting the strictures of a deeply patriarchal society. In the preface, Das claims that writing the autobiography was a cathartic experience for her, one with which she "could depart when the time came with a scrubbed-out conscience" (*My Story* 1976, Preface). Her critics would say that the volume involves more scrubbing out than necessary, its contents revealing more information about Das' intimate life than required. Her supporters, however, would retort that Das is claiming for herself, and for women's writing in general, a new mode of narration: one that refuses to be confined by social standards of decorum.

A powerfully reflective tone characterizes *My Story*. While Das is painfully aware of her own ordinariness and writes often of her perceived lack of physical beauty, she is also aware of her extraordinary potential as an artist. She began writing poetry at the young age of six. Even then she is aware of the isolation of the artist, particularly of the female artist. Her memories of her literary progress are interwoven with reflections on her sexual development. The "shock value" associated with this narrative is reinforced by Das' description of certain homosexual encounters in her childhood and adolescence. For example, she describes at length her first kiss with a woman (71), a description bound to enrage more conservative Indian readers. The tone of the narrative is also somewhat digressive, however, repeatedly distracting us from Das's **confession** of her sexual encounters. At one point, Das writes about a love letter she received as a child from another female schoolmate when she suddenly switches to talking about a stern, albeit caring, uncle (19). This gives the narrative a certain stream of consciousness style, a postmodern attribute that takes the reader wherever Das' **memory** wants to go.

The narrative also moves from Das' own anxieties, sexual and literary, to the immediacy of her cultural background: the autobiography describes at length the worship of the goddess Kali in the month of Makaram (26) and her wealthy young widowed neighbor who was implicated in a marital scandal (48). This contradicts the title of the autobiography: *My Story* is not just the story of Kamala Das, but also the story of her cultural and social milieu.

Das is most iconoclastic in her uncensored discussion of sex; especially the lack of sexual fulfillment for Indian women trapped in hastily arranged marriages. She describes sex as "the principal phobia of Nair women" (22) and claims that women are constantly indoctrinated with the idea of sex as illicit, brutal, and above all physically unsatisfying. She describes her own wedding night as "rape" (79) and her married life as an extension of that brutalization. For Das, writing then becomes a catharsis, a way out of the trauma of a deeply unhappy marriage. She writes:

> Writing became my only hobby. I wrote almost two stories every week and mailed them, borrowing the money for stamps from my husband. . . . Each story took me one full night to finish, for it was not pos-

sible to write when the children were awake. (122)

Das articulates the misery of a woman writer who does not have the financial wherewithal to sustain her creative endeavors. Her writing is also constantly interrupted by her domestic responsibilities, a frustration she repeatedly expresses in this narrative. Das describes writing as a terrible, lonely profession fraught with bitterness and isolation for the writer: "As I wrote more and more, in the circles I was compelled to move in . . . I felt that my loneliness was a red brand on my face" (157).

It is in the country, when she returns to her childhood home of Nalapat, that Das finds spiritual and intellectual solace. Eventually, however, the villagers begin to resent her, especially the power of the pen that she wields. Later, while reviewing her life and her artistic career, Das defiantly asserts that despite all the scorn and hatred that has been poured upon her, she is satisfied with the way she has led her life and the books she has written. Kamala Das' lot seems to be that of a maligned, often even unacknowledged, writer—and as her autobiography attests—she has borne this burden with exemplary courage.

Further Reading: Das, Kamala. *The Alphabet of Lust* (New Delhi: Orient Paperback, 1976); Das, Kamala. *My Story* (New Delhi: Sterling Publishers, 1976); Jaidka, Manju. "Kamala Das." In *South Asian Novelists in English: An A to Z Guide*, 43–46, edited by Jaina Sanga, (Westport CT: Greenwood Press, 2003); Kumar, Uday. "Kamala Das." In *Encyclopedia of Life Writing*, edited by Margaretta Jolly, 261–263 (London: Fitzroy Dearborn Publishers, 2001).

Pallavi Rastogi

DAVIS, ANGELA YVONNE (1944–) A controversial political figure and fiercely committed activist, Angela Y. Davis is author of one of the most compelling autobiographies of the twentieth century in the United States. Titled *Angela Davis: An Auto-*

biography, it was published in 1974 when she was barely thirty. It remains one of very few book-length autobiographies published by women directly involved in the Black Power politics of the 1960s.

In the preface, Davis makes it clear that hers is not a conventional self-representational text. Her instinctive reserve, she concedes, would not allow her to create a thoroughly confessional narrative. Rather than focus on the details of her personal life, she opts to use the autobiographical format to assess the public significance of her life experiences. The result, therefore, is a political autobiography: the narrative focus is not on the private but on the political dimensions of her life. The book maps the formation of her revolutionary consciousness and the emergence of her radical **subjectivity**.

At the center of the autobiography is an alleged crime. In February 1970, Davis had become the leader of a campaign to free the Soledad (Prison) Brothers, three black inmates accused of murdering a notoriously racist prison guard. On August 7, 1970, there was an armed revolt at the Marin County (California) Courthouse initiated by Jonathan Jackson, a seventeen-year-old brother of one of the defendants. The shootout resulted in the deaths of the presiding judge, two defendants, and Jonathan himself; several others were injured. One of the guns used by the young assailant was registered in Angela Davis' name. Though she was nowhere near the scene of the crime, she was implicated in the revolt and charged with murder, kidnapping, and conspiracy. She had been, for quite some time, under surveillance by various law enforcement agencies because of her militant activism. Jackson's use of her gun therefore became a convenient way to justify criminal action against her and silence her politically. The Federal Bureau of Investigation (FBI) placed her on its list of the Ten Most Wanted. Davis' autobiography is a riveting account of the events that led to the shootout, her flight and subsequent capture, her

suspiciously long pretrial imprisonment, the trial itself in which she eloquently defended herself, and her acquittal on all charges by an all-white jury on June 4, 1972. Woven into this gripping legal drama are the less public, but largely sketchy details of her childhood in a violently racist Birmingham, Alabama; her adolescent years in New York City where she attended a Greenwich Village high school; her university education in Boston, Paris, and Frankfurt; and her discovery of Utopian Socialism, which became the basis for her insurgent political philosophy.

Ever since Davis emerged as a public figure in the late 1960s, she has provoked a range of responses. Her detractors demonize her; her public image, constructed and circulated by the mainstream media, has led uninformed people to view her as a misguided and thuggish character with an insane political agenda. But her supporters, both in the United States and internationally, see her as an iconic figure who is simultaneously a symbol of the institutionalized victimization of African Americans and a defiant emblem of black resistance. Her autobiography helps dismantle some of these myths and misconceptions. Because of her relentless foregrounding of the public events of her life, her narrative offers us only fragments of her personal life. Nevertheless, when fleeting glimpses emerge of her interior life, we find a highly complex individual vastly different from the mono-dimensional, mythical figure frozen in the public imagination. She is neither a demonic character nor a flawless heroine.

In the pages of her autobiography, Davis emerges as an immensely courageous yet deeply vulnerable individual. Her intellectual sophistication, instinctive identification with the most victimized members of society, and her articulate challenges to the various structures of oppression are amply evident in the book. However, what is somewhat troubling is her willingness, at least at the time she composed her autobiography, to see Marxism as a panacea for all social malaise. The narrative of her epiphanic discovery of Marxism and her conversion to its philosophy, for example, is startlingly similar to the descriptions of religious conversions so common in early African American autobiographies. Yet there is a poignancy to her unassailable faith in her newfound religion. It is apparent that a romantic streak drew her to a belief system that promises to create a heaven on earth. What frames her political philosophy and activism is her utopian vision of a just and genuinely emancipated global community of human beings. The clarity of that vision is the foundation for her action. Her political autobiography allows us to see, at least briefly, the woman behind the activist persona: a visionary, a dreamer.

Further Reading: Davis, Angela. *Angela Davis: An Autobiography.* 1974. Reprint (New York: International Publishers, 1988); Perkins, Margo V. *Autobiography as Activism: Three Black Women of the Sixties* (Jackson: University of Mississippi Press, 2000).

Emmanuel Nelson

DAY, DOROTHY (1897–1980) The founder, with Peter Maurin, of the Catholic Worker movement, Dorothy Day spent her life as an advocate for the disadvantaged, establishing a newspaper and a network of farms and houses where the poor could be fed, clothed, and housed. Her autobiography, *The Long Loneliness* (1952), traces, with grace and passion, her evolution from a socialist to a supporter of Catholic social action and borrows heavily from an earlier account of her conversion, *From Union Square to Rome* (1938).

Day was born in Bath Beach, a section of Brooklyn, New York, on November 8, 1897, to John and Grace Satterlee Day, the third of five children. A sportswriter, John Day moved his family to San Francisco in 1903, then, after the earthquake, to Chicago in 1906. "Haunted by God" from the beginning, Day recalls reading the Bible, attending a Methodist Church with neighbors,

learning about the saints from a Catholic friend, and seeing her Catholic neighbor, Mrs. Barrett, kneeling in prayer. In Chicago, she attended an Episcopal church, studying the catechism in order to be baptized and confirmed. At age thirteen she read some of John Wesley's sermons, and, later, Mary Baker Eddy's *Science and Health*. By age fifteen, she had developed a social conscience, and as a student at the University of Illinois, she began to swear, joined the Socialist Party, and rejected religion, which she saw in Marxist terms as an opiate.

After two years at the university, Day began working for the New York *Call*, a Socialist publication, and later wrote for *The Masses*. Arrested in Washington, DC after picketing with suffragists, she participated in a prison hunger strike, during which she decided that she would never again be free of responsibility to the oppressed. During the hunger strike she read the Bible and found her childhood faith partially restored. Nevertheless, Day again rejected religion and began writing for the *Liberator*, the successor to *The Masses*. In Manhattan, she associated with people connected to the Provincetown Playhouse, including Eugene O'Neill. At times, after spending the night in taverns, she would go to early mass at St. Joseph's Church. A pacifist, Day worked during World War I as a nurse at King's County Hospital, Brooklyn, where, convinced that worship was a necessary human activity, she began attending Sunday mass with another nurse, Miss Adams.

After the war she returned to writing, working for a time in Chicago where she was falsely arrested on a morals charge while staying at a hotel run by the International Workers of the World. After an unhappy love affair in Chicago, she returned to New York and entered into a common-law marriage with Forster Batterham, an English anarchist and biologist identified in her autobiography only by his first name. Their New York friends included Malcolm Cowley, Kenneth Burke, Allen Tate, Caroline Gordon, and Hart Crane. At home in lower Manhattan and on Staten Island, Day read Tolstoy, Dostoyevsky, Dickens, the Bible, and *The Imitation of Christ*.

In *The Long Loneliness*, Day writes engaging vignettes about famous and obscure people, though her lover, Forster, an "inarticulate" man who "became garrulous only in wrath" remains a shadowy figure in the book. At the beach house, she began to pray and attend mass regularly, and believes her relationship with Forster and its "natural happiness" brought her to God; ironically, her relationship with God ended her relationship with Forster.

Day feared she was unable to bear a child because of a previous abortion (not mentioned in her autobiography). When she became pregnant, she resolved to have the child baptized, and at the birth of Tamar Teresa Day recognized that she had to choose between the Church and Forster, who was hostile to religion. Still, though she wanted to become a Catholic, Day believed that in her conversion she would betray the poor. Unaware until later of Catholic social teachings, she saw the Church as a bastion of complacency and wealth. Following an illness diagnosed as "nervous," she determined to break with Forster and become a Catholic.

After a short stint as a writer in Hollywood and a period in Mexico, she returned to New York and wrote for *The Commonweal*, whose editor, George Shuster, was responsible for her introduction to Peter Maurin, a practitioner of voluntary poverty. Maurin taught Day Church history and together they began, in 1933, *The Catholic Worker*, still available for one cent per copy. They worked together until Maurin's death in 1949, establishing houses of hospitality and farms, aiding strikers, and spreading the social Gospel. Maurin and Day championed ownership by workers of the means of production, the abolition of the assembly line, decentralized factories, crafts, and ownership of private property. Critical of the welfare state, they preferred individual initiative. Commenting that some deem poverty or community the most significant element of the Catholic Worker movement, Day concludes that "the final word is love," the only solution to the long loneliness of human existence. Day continued working for the movement she and Maurin founded until her death on November 29, 1980.

Further Reading: Coles, Robert. *Dorothy Day: A Radical Devotion* (Reading, MA: Addison-Wesley, 1987); Day, Dorothy. *The Eleventh Virgin* (New York: Boni, 1924); Day, Dorothy. *From Union Square to Rome* (Silver Spring, MD: Preservation of the Faith Press, 1938); Day, Dorothy. *House of Hospitality* (New York: Sheed and Ward, 1939); Day, Dorothy. *I Remember Peter Maurin* (Cambridge, MA: American Friends Service Committee, 1958); Day, Dorothy. *Loaves and Fishes* (New York: Harper and Row, 1963); Day, Dorothy. *The Long Loneliness: The Autobiography of Dorothy Day* (New York: Harper, 1952); Day, Dorothy. *Meditations* (New York: Newman Press, 1970); Day, Dorothy. *On Pilgrimage: The Sixties* (New York: Curtis, 1972); Day, Dorothy. *Therese* (Notre Dame, IN: Fides Publishing Association, 1960); Ellsberg, Robert, ed. *By Little and By Little: The Selected Writings of Dorothy Day* (New York: Knopf, 1983); Miller, William D. *All Is Grace: The Spirituality of Dorothy Day* (Garden City, NY: Doubleday, 1987); Miller, William D. *Dorothy Day: A Biography* (San Francisco: Harper and Row, 1982).

Anita G. Gorman

DELANEY, LUCY ANN (c. 1824–c. 1900) Lucy Delaney is now best known for her slave narrative, *From the Darkness Cometh the Light; or, Struggles for Freedom*, which was published c. 1891, though she seems to have counted her civic involvement in St. Louis' black community as her major accomplishment. Her autobiography first came to widespread notice when it was included in the Schomburg Library of Nineteenth-Century Black Women Writers in 1988 and has begun to enter classrooms and scholarship as a transitional text in the trajectory of African American women's self-representation.

Delaney actually begins her narrative before she was born, with the kidnapping of her mother, Polly Crockett, a free African American sold into slavery. After briefly being owned by Missourian Thomas Botts, Crockett was bought by Major Taylor Berry, a prominent resident of St. Louis, for his wife Frances (Fanny) W. Christy Berry. Crockett married another Berry slave whose name remains unknown, and the couple had two children, Nancy and Lucy Ann. Most scholars date Delaney's birth to around 1830, but she was actually probably born closer to 1824, based on census data.

When Berry was killed in a duel with Abiel Leonard in 1824, his slaves went to his wife, with the stipulation that they be freed at her death. Two years later, Fanny Berry married jurist Robert Wash. Delaney spent much of her childhood in the Wash home; when Fanny died—in late 1836 or early 1837—though, the Crocketts were not freed. Nancy was taken by one of the Berry's daughters, Mary, who had just married Henry Sidney Coxe (Cox in the narrative), and Polly's husband was sold South. Nancy, at the urging of her mother, escaped to Canada while the Coxes took a long honeymoon trip around the North. When the Coxes returned, they took the young Lucy to care for their first child and, soon after, sold Polly. Polly escaped to Chicago, but eventually returned to St. Louis, where, with the aid of friends, she filed suit for her freedom and won.

In the meantime, Lucy had been moved to the home of the other Berry child, Martha, who had recently married David D. Mitchell, later the notorious superintendent of Indian Affairs. Martha Mitchell was a hard mistress, Lucy rebelled, and David eventually attempted to sell her. With the aid of her mother, Lucy began the long process of proving her claim to freedom through the courts. After an almost two-year ordeal, which Delaney claims included time in jail and arguments on Delaney's behalf by future attorney general Edward Bates, Delaney was finally granted her freedom in 1844.

After a short marriage to Frederick Turner, who was killed in a steamboat explosion, Delaney married Zachariah Delaney, a free black from Cincinnati who had settled in St. Louis, on November 16, 1849. The couple had four children, but all died before reaching age twenty-five. St. Louis city directories show that Zachariah Delaney worked at a succession of jobs, most often cook and porter; it is likely that Lucy Delaney supplemented their income by sewing, a skill she learned as a child. Delaney became active in St. Louis' black community. She joined the Methodist Episcopal Church in 1855, was the first treasurer of the Siloam Court (a part of the Heroines of Jericho, an organization for women related to masons), and was active in the women's auxiliary to the Colonel Shaw GAR post. She stayed in touch with her sister Nancy, who lived in Toronto, and, in about 1870, found her father living in Vicksburg, Mississippi. Her narrative relates with heart-rending simplicity the difficulty she had seeing her father return to St. Louis only to feel like "a stranger in a strange land" and finally return to Mississippi.

Lucy Delaney penned her sixty-four-page narrative around 1891. (Although her narrative is undated, in the text she notes that she has been married to Zachariah for forty-two years.) She dedicates the work to the GAR and notes that several friends have urged her to write it, in part so that those who never lived through slavery could find in reading it "interest and sympathy" for former slaves (viii). The volume was published by J. T. Smith, a small local St. Louis house that published primarily religious texts during the 1890s; the run was likely small, and the audience, localized. What happened after the publication of her narrative remains conjecture; most scholars place her death sometime in the 1890s, although there is limited evidence that suggests that she was alive as late as 1910.

Timing, content, distribution, and character have limited the attention paid to Delaney's narrative. William Andrews notes that writing long after the heyday of slave narratives, Delaney focuses much more on "the liberating feats of slave motherhood" than traditional themes of "escape, literacy, and the achievement of freedom" (*Oxford Companion* 1997, 205). Critics have paid much more attention to the roughly contemporary *Iola Leroy* (1892), by Frances Ellen Watkins Harper, ironic in that one of that novel's characters, as P. Gabrielle Foreman reminds us, is named Lucille Delany.

Still, Delaney's work is what Foreman rightly calls a "feisty autobiography" (341), one that offers an important, albeit later, counterpoint in terms of region and focus to better known autobiographical texts like those by **Harriet Jacobs**, Harriet Wilson, and William and Ellen Craft. Further, like its contemporaries, *Iola Leroy* as well as Anna Julia Cooper's *A Voice from the South* (1892), it struggles with how to treat the **memory** of slavery in the context of a generation of readers removed from slavery's horrors.

Further Reading: Andrews, William L. "Delaney." In *Oxford Companion to African American Literature* (New York: Oxford University Press, 1997); Delaney, Lucy Ann. *From the Darkness Cometh the Light; or, Struggles for Freedom*. In *Six Women's Slave Narratives*, edited by William L. Andrews (New York: Oxford University Press, 1988) (available online from the New York Public Library, Digital Schomburg at http://www. digilib.nypl.org:80/dynaweb/digs/wwm97254 /@Generic_BookView); Foreman, P. Gabrielle. " 'Reading Aright': White Slavery, Black Referents, and the Strategy of Histotextuality in *Iola Leroy*." *The Yale Journal of Criticism* 10, no. 2 (1997): 327–354.

Eric Gardner

DERRICOTTE, TOI (1941–) Fiercely honest and minutely self-critical, Toi Derricotte has written a **memoir**/autobiography that is an in-depth exploration of internalized oppression, of the privileges that come with a white skin tone, and of the ways in which people psychologically manipulate their thoughts to block out difficult ques-

tions of **race**, privilege, and entitlement. *The Black Notebooks: An Interior Journey* was published in 1997 and was a book that was twenty years in the making. In *The Black Notebooks*, Derricotte brings together **diary** entries from various times in her life, linking them by theme and topic. The entries detail her exploration of her feelings toward her light skin, her ambivalence over her ability to pass as white, and the multiple ways in which society's definitions of "race" intersect in her choices, actions, and attitudes.

Derricotte was born into a middle-class family, grew up in Detroit, and graduated with a B.A. in special education from Wayne State University in 1965. She is known mainly for her poetry, having published multiple volumes, including *The Empress of the Death House* (1978), *Natural Birth* (1983), *Captivity* (1989), and *Tender* (1997). Her middle-class values, well-educated sensibilities, and the ability of many of her family members to pass as white, gave her a unique perspective on white culture and its racial strictures. Her work explores these perspectives and also examines the ways in which her upbringing and her family dynamics contributed to her negative self-image as she probes her anxieties about her marriage, the usefulness of her ability to pass when she and her husband buy a home, the lessons she teaches her students, and the messages she gets from her colleagues at artists' colonies and poetry readings.

Derricotte's text deals with many of the same themes about passing as white that earlier literary predecessors do: loss of racial **identity**, fear of being caught, dislocation from family and friends, and exploration of society's definitions of racial categories. In this respect, *The Black Notebooks* follows in a long line of fiction, such as *Autobiography of an Ex-Colored Man* (1912) by James Weldon Johnson, *Plum Bun* (1929) by Jessie Fauset, *Iola Leroy* (1892) by Frances E. W. Harper, and *Passing* (1929) by Nella Larsen. In terms of present-day autobiography/memoir, Derricotte is a leader in exploring contemporary politics involved in racial identity as it develops among light-skinned African Americans.

In her introduction, Derricotte describes her purposes and objectives in publishing a text that probes so deeply into her psyche. She also outlines the methods by which she has constructed, deconstructed, and reconstructed her notions of self. She explains that the work looks at the structures of society that have been so deeply internalized that they hold in place each citizen's notion of self. She articulates that the same structures that have oppressed black people for centuries have also become an intrinsic part of their psychological framework. She further indicates that black people have struggled to "forget" racist attitudes in order to survive; however, in *The Black Notebooks* she is making the excruciating effort to "unforget" or to "remember" herself as a black person. This journey of remembering her racial past and remembering her mind and body comes at a price. Her quest is marked by clinical depression, inclinations toward suicide, estrangement from her husband, and bouts of writers' block during her most depressive stages.

In writing about her experiences where she forced herself to "remember" or "confront" her identity as a black person, she began publicly to take on an identity about which she was ambivalent. She hoped to resolve conflicting aims and voices in her record of "the language of self-hate" (20), causing readers to think more deeply about racism and its devastating effects on black Americans. She does so because "we carry the unfinished business of the past forward. We are compelled to resolve, not only our personal wounds, but the wounds of our ancestors" (21). Theorizing about the legacy of racism is woven around examples and vignettes from her own life. For example, in the chapter titled "The Club," Derricotte details her search for belonging in a neighborhood in New Jersey. Passing as white in order to be shown houses in the neighborhoods she and her husband would like to

live in, Derricotte sees and buys a house in Upper Montclair, New Jersey. When the couple moves in, they find that all the other families on the block are friendly to them, but the neighbors also belong to a social club that blacks are not allowed to join. At a dinner party that she has for some friends of color, Derricotte expresses her anger at this discrimination. Later in the evening, however, she is unsure whether she is really angry or whether she expressed anger "to fit in with the others" at the dinner party (49). She understood then that her entire life had been based on not knowing which group she should choose and about the fear that making that choice would hurt her. Further, she wonders whether she's a "real" black person, whether she can actually have an "authentic" black **voice**, and wonders about which side she's on (64–65).

In her memoir, Derricotte forces herself to "undo" the protective wall she has built around her self-concept, to "confront [her] own complicity" in disavowing her own emotions, ideas, and life force, and to "unforget" her past, her ancestors' past, and the past of the country (65). She comes to the conclusion that her remembering leads her to search for a "home," a safe place for her complexities and beauties, and that while she cannot find that physical home in the world, she has created it in language.

Further Reading: Davidson, Phebe. *Conversations with the World: American Women Poets and Their Work* (Pasedena, CA: Triology Books, 1998), 37–74; Derricotte, Toi. *The Black Notebooks: An Interior Journey* (New York: W. W. Norton, 1997); Rowell, Charles H. "Beyond Our Lives: An Interview with Toi Derricotte." *Callaloo* 14, no. 3 (Summer 1991): 654–664.

Samantha Manchester Earley

DIARY The diary is one of the earliest forms of women's autobiography. Historically, when women could write nothing else, they were allowed, even encouraged, to keep a record of their days. For a long time, diaries were one of the few examples of life writing that testified to a woman's presence and her experience.

The diary is not a static genre. Today, what we consider a diary—a personal record of daily life—has evolved over the centuries. Robert Fothergill traces the historical progression of the diary in its Western form, beginning with four protodiaries. These protodiary categories include seventeenth-century journals of conscience, diaries kept by the religious—mostly Puritans and Quakers—to record moments requiring repentance or marking spiritual progress; travel journals found throughout the sixteenth, seventeenth, and eighteenth centuries; public journals, like ships' logs and those documenting military campaigns; and, finally, journals of personal memoranda, containing lists of expenditures and visitors to the home.

These early forms are found in some combination in personal diaries written in the nineteenth century, the century that marked the apex of the diurnal form. The evolution of the diary is a movement from the occasional to the everyday. As Stuart Sherman suggests in his work, beginning in the seventeenth century with changes in the way clocks told time, diarists, Samuel Pepys in particular, began recording their passage through time, rather than recording moments in time. Diaries became, in other words, daily writings.

What makes a diary a distinct form of autobiography, different from a **memoir** or a letter, is found in its etymology. The term "diary" comes from the Latin, *dies*, meaning "day." That a diary is kept every day has important implications for the form. Writing within the day creates the immediacy associated with the diurnal form. There is no foreshadowing, no plot development, little sense of how this particular day will fit into the days making up the diarist's life. In addition, diaries lack closure, unfolding without a sense of beginning or end. Neither are they selective, but instead account for everything, so that the mundane and the significant share equally on the page.

Because the diary is less a "shaped" text, in the way autobiography proper is shaped, diaries were historically considered outside the limits of autobiography. Few diaries rose, in scholarly opinion, to the level of art.

More recently, attitudes toward the diary have changed. In fact, many scholars consider the diary, in its daily accounting of an individual's passage through the days, as the ultimate form of autobiography, rendering crafted, less exhaustive texts "the more lifeless form" (Lensink 1987, 43). In particular, recent interest in the diary as a genre has focused on the performance of the writer's **identity**. **Felicity Nussbaum** suggests that the diurnal form allows the contradictions of the self to exist on the page. By recording daily life, the diarist creates both a continuous sense of self, what Nussbaum calls "an enabling fiction of a coherent or continuous identity," and a discontinuous, changing self—I am not the same as I was yesterday (Nussbaum 1988, 134). Such a contestory **space** is arguably a much more accurate "metaphor of self" than traditional autobiography provides.

While men have historically kept (and continue to keep) diaries, beginning in the nineteenth century diaries became a form associated with women's writing. As diaries became a more personal experience of time, they also became more private, and, given nineteenth-century ideologies, more female. There is a strong correspondence between women's lives, at least historically, and the diurnal form; namely, both are fragmented, cyclical, inward, and inclusive. While diaries are not inherently female, the nature of writing in the day has allowed women to write against more patriarchal forms of expression, thereby empowering them.

The diary is democratic. It may be kept by the famous, the infamous, the ordinary, the literary, the artistic, the young, and the old. Throughout history women have had different reasons for keeping a diary. Women in the nineteenth century kept diaries as family histories, as documents to be passed down to their children. American homesteaders kept diaries to record the journey westward so that others might follow their path. Literary figures might keep diaries as "creative blueprints" for later work. And many contemporary diarists use them for therapeutic reasons, writing to heal from a trauma or to reflect on daily life. When **Virginia Woolf** referred to her diary as "a capacious hold-all," she was heralding the ability of the diurnal form to serve simultaneously as a confidant, a record of expenditures, an almanac, an heirloom, a healer, or a creative wellspring.

Given the purpose and backgrounds of diarists across the centuries, distinctions need to be drawn between ordinary or manuscript diaries and diary literature. Many diarists keep them with the intention (or the hope) of publishing them someday. They edit and craft their diaries as they write and then again upon revision. **Anne Frank**, **Anaïs Nin**, and **May Sarton**, among others, have kept diaries with a larger audience in mind. Such diaries form the canon of diary literature—diaries we might read as we would a novel, for entertainment or for information. The vast majority of diarists, though, write for themselves rather than for a greater public. Their diaries, some held in manuscript form in historical museums or libraries, others in attics, many lining the bookshelves of ordinary people, are not edited, crafted, or revised. They often tell ordinary stories, about ordinary events, in ordinary lives. While perhaps not as interesting to read or as readily accessible, these diaries, too, must be included in the study of women's autobiography.

Further Reading: Bunkers, Suzanne L., and Cynthia Huff, eds. *Inscribing the Daily: Critical Essays on Women's Diaries* (Amherst: University of Massachusetts Press, 1996); Fothergill, Robert A. *Private Chronicles: A Study of English Diaries* (Oxford: Oxford University Press, 1974); Hampsten, Elizabeth. *Read This Only to Yourself: The Private Writings of Midwestern Women, 1880–1910* (Bloomington: Indiana University Press, 1982);

Johnson, Alexandra. *The Hidden Writer: Diaries and the Creative Life* (New York: Anchor Books, 1997); Lensink, Judy Nolte. "Expanding the Boundaries of Criticism: The Diary as Female Autobiography." *Women's Studies* 14 (1987): 39–53; Moffat, Mary Jane, and Charlotte Painter, eds. *Revelations: Diaries of Women* (New York: Random House, 1974); Nussbaum, Felicity A. "Towards Conceptualizing Diary." In *Studies in Autobiography*, edited by James Olney, 128–140 (Oxford: Oxford University Press, 1988); Podneiks, Elizabeth. *Daily Modernism: The Literary Diaries of Virginia Woolf, Antonia White, Elizabeth Smart and Anais Nin* (Montreal, Quebec: McGill-Queen's University Press, 2000); Sherman, Stuart. *Telling Time: Clocks, Diaries, and English Diurnal Form, 1660–1785* (Chicago: University of Chicago Press, 1996).

Jennifer Sinor

DIARY OF A YOUNG GIRL, THE   Since it was first published posthumously in June 1947 as *Het Achterhuis*, Dutch for *The Secret Annex*, **Anne Frank**'s private journal, written between June 14, 1942 and August 1, 1944, has been translated into more than 50 languages and read by more than twenty-five million readers. Her **diary**, a candid self-portrait of a young girl in extraordinary times, has become perhaps the most important **voice** for all who were persecuted during the Holocaust. It has never been out of print since its first appearance, and has achieved international success as a Tony Award–winning and Pulitzer Prize–winning 1955 play adaptation, a 1959 motion picture, and a 1980 television movie. The name Anne Frank has been associated with schools and institutions, a ballet, cantatas, and even a species of rose, and her diary is required reading in schools worldwide. What began as the inner thoughts of a normal, Jewish thirteen-year-old girl has become a human document that examines what it is like to be persecuted. Her unique insights into the ordinary life of a young girl now speak moral truths for all of us.

Annelies Marie Frank was born in Frankfurt, Germany, in 1929, and with her family immigrated to Holland in 1933 when the Nazis came to power. She and her family were living in Amsterdam when, on her thirteenth birthday, she received, among other gifts, a red-and-white-checkered, clothbound book that she called "maybe one of my nicest presents" (Otto Frank 1995, 1). She began writing in her diary, entries addressed to "Kitty," that same day. In it she recorded her innermost thoughts about her family and her schoolmates. From the start, she wanted her diary to be her friend and confidante. When her older sister Margot received a call-up from the Nazi SS—The Netherlands had been under German occupation since 1940—the family clearly understood it to mean deportation to a concentration camp, and on July 6, the family went into hiding in the now famous secret annex on the third floor of her father's office building. Anne's carefree life was turned upside down, and one of the first things she packed was her diary because, as she says, "Memories mean more to me than dresses" (20).

Anne kept her diary for nearly twenty-six months, recording in both print and cursive writing the everyday life of those in hiding with her. In addition to the four members of her own family, three members of the van Pels family—Hermann, a business partner and friend of Otto Frank; his wife Auguste; and their teenage son Peter (renamed the Van Daans in her diary)—and Fritz Pfeffer (renamed Albert Dussel)—a dentist and acquaintance of Otto Frank—all shared the hiding place at 263 Prinsengracht. Anne would write in her bedroom or in the attic and put her diary in her father's leather briefcase for safekeeping; everyone knew she kept a diary, though no one else in the annex read it. Besides writing about the life she might see a small glimpse of on the streets of Amsterdam and what she heard over the radio about the progress of the war, Anne used her diary to express the natural fears and frustrations of a girl going through puberty. Since it was private, she could use her journal to air her

resentment of her parents' perceived favoritism toward Margot, her sixteen-year-old sister. She also records her contempt for her mother and their numerous quarrels, and her unflinching devotion to her father, whom she idolized. Because of the unique historical perspective of Anne's diary, we see not only what life was like for Jews in occupied Holland, but also problems common to all young people.

Throughout her 761 days in hiding, Anne's diary serves as a mirror in which she sees herself as an ugly duckling, yet also as someone determined to be happy in spite of the dangers around her. She admits to being a bundle of contradictions; she has longings, self-pity, and at night ponders her sins and shortcomings. Periodically, she rereads her diary and comments on the superficial Anne Frank of a year earlier. She could be both an optimist who knew God was watching over her and her family, and the others in the annex, and a realist who knew how lucky they were compared with those facing the daily terror of life on the outside. From her growing infatuation with Peter to her lack of privacy and frustration in coping with the personalities of seven other people in such an artificially contrived circumstance, the Anne Frank who emerges in the pages of her private journal is someone who refused to let life get her down. She knew her voice would be heard some day, and her determination to write is a daily driving force in her coming to terms with life in the annex.

It is misleading to think of one diary because there were, in fact, several diaries and several versions of the diary as published. In addition to the small red-and-white checkered book she received on her thirteenth birthday, Anne wrote down her thoughts in a number of school exercise books, notebooks, and account books. She also added photographs and wrote comments alongside them. One of the reasons there are several versions of her diary is that on March 29, 1944, after hearing Dutch Cabinet Minister Bolkestein ask that wartime diaries and **letters** be kept for publication after the war, Anne began editing and rewriting her diary on loose sheets of blue and pink onion-skin paper. With an eye to publication, she inserted comments made about earlier entries, changed the names of those living in the annex, and rearranged, expanded, and abbreviated previous material, which she had already planned to call *Het Achterhuis*. After two and a half years, she had 324 handwritten pages. As Anne was writing daily entries in her diary, she also started writing a book, *Stories and Events from the Secret Annex*, mixing real life and fiction. These short stories, fables, reminiscences, essays, and *Cady's Life*, an unfinished novella, were published in 1984 as *Tales from the Secret Annex* or *Tales from the House Behind*.

The last entry in Anne's diary is August 1, 1944, three days before German SS officer Karl Silberbauer and three Dutch security policemen discovered the eight occupants of the secret annex. In the course of the arrest and ransacking of the annex, the contents of Otto Frank's briefcase, containing the loose pages, notebooks, and journals that were Anne's diary, were emptied onto the floor. Of all those in hiding with Anne Frank, only her father, Otto, survived the war. He returned to Amsterdam on June 3, 1945. On the day he learned that Anne had died of typhus at Bergen-Belsen concentration camp in late February or early March 1945, Miep Gies, Otto's secretary, gave him all of Anne's personal writings, which she and fellow company secretary Bep Voskuijl had retrieved five days after the family's arrest and kept locked in a drawer, unread.

Otto Frank, surprised and delighted at his daughter's literary talents and insights, decided to have Anne's diary printed as a memorial to her. He began to type up copies of the diary and sent one to his mother who was living in Switzerland. Other copies were circulated among friends and close acquaintances. Jan Romein's article on Anne's diary, "A Child's Voice," in the newspaper *Het Parool* on April 3, 1946, received unanimously favorable reviews, and various publishers contacted Otto Frank about publishing it. A Dutch university professor, who saw a typed copy, urged him to have it published. In June 1947, 1,500 copies were published by the Dutch firm, Contact Publishers, as *Het Achterhuis* [The Secret Annex], and included excerpts from Romein's article and Anne's favorite photograph of herself, taken in May 1939. However, *Het Achterhuis* did not include approximately 30 percent of the original diary. Otto Frank, in effect, created a third version by choosing to omit graphic references to Anne's budding **sexuality** and her unflattering comments about her mother. In 1950, the diary was published in a French translation; the German translation that same year sold 900,000 copies. In 1952, the diary was published in England and in the United States. The American version, with an introduction by Eleanor Roosevelt praising the writer's nobility of spirit, was titled *Anne Frank: The Diary of a Young Girl*. The subsequent play and motion picture versions solidified the book's international reputation and success, and Anne's diary, once the innocent, naïve exuberance of a teenage girl, became for many the most powerful indictment of Nazi Germany.

The work has also had its detractors, and since its 1947 publication, there were those who claimed the diary was a fraud. Otto Frank, before he died on August 19, 1980, left the manuscripts to the Dutch state, which deposited them with the Netherlands Institute for War Documentation (RIOD). In 1986, the institute published the so-called Critical Edition. Included were the results of extensive forensic tests performed on the paper, ink, and handwriting to prove their authenticity and to answer the critics who argued against the diary's legitimacy. The critical edition includes almost all of the different versions of the diary, as well as information on the Frank family's background, their life in hiding, and the betrayal that led to their arrest. Otto Frank appointed the Anne Frank Foundation in Basel, Switzerland, as his legal heir and as the copyright owner of Anne's works.

In 1995, on the fiftieth anniversary of Anne's death, the Definitive Edition was published, edited by Otto Frank and Mirjam Pressler, and translated by Susan Massotty. It contained material omitted from Otto Frank's version and the 1947 Contact Publishing edition. Based on Anne's "b" version of her diary, the one she rewrote for possible postwar publication, the definitive edition contains Anne's later comments on earlier entries in a chronological format. In 1998, another controversy over the diaries arose when it was discovered that there were five missing pages. Cor Suijk, a former employee of the Anne Frank Foundation, said that shortly before his death, Otto Frank had given him the pages as a gift, which included an introduction written by Anne and three pages, dated February 8, 1944, concerning her parents' marriage. The Anchor Books paperback edition includes these missing pages.

In her entry for Tuesday, April 4, 1944, Anne Frank wrote, "I want to go on living even after my death!" (251). She succeeded in a way no one would have expected. *The Diary of Anne Frank* is a meaningful document that, despite the horror of the times, inspires millions to believe, as she did, in the ultimate goodness of humanity. A born writer, Anne Frank used her diary as her apprenticeship into the adult world. Alternately silly and serious, immature and insightful, the Anne Frank of the diary is a multitalented and multifaceted young woman who longed to be a writer and journalist. She is just as critical of herself as she is of her family and friends; she admits to being a chatterbox, and a lonesome, fearful person. Her diary becomes her friend, her confidante. Time and again, she says, she can tell her diary what she cannot tell anyone else. Because she also had access to good books and biographies in the years she was writing her diary and was dili-

gently doing schoolwork, her own style matured. The diary reveals a precocious teenager, however self-doubting and irresponsible, and her observations on human nature reveal all the qualities of the emerging novelist. The importance of her work, beyond its obvious and lasting identification with the Holocaust, is what it reveals about the diarist herself.

Further Reading: Barnouw, David, and Gerold van der Stroom, eds. *The Diary of Anne Frank: The Critical Edition*. Translated by Arnold J. Pomerans and B. M. Mooyart (New York: Doubleday, 1989); Frank, Otto H., and Mirjam Pressler, eds. *The Diary of a Young Girl: The Definitive Edition*. Translated by Susan Massotty (New York: Doubleday, 1995); Kopf, Hedda Rosner. *Understanding The Diary of a Young Girl: A Student Casebook to Issues, Sources, and Historical Documents* (Westport, CT: Greenwood Press, 1997); Rittner, Carol, ed. *Anne Frank in the World: Essays and Reflections* (Armonk, NY: M. E. Sharpe, 1998).

Gary Kerley

DILLARD, ANNIE (1945–) Annie Dillard was only twenty-nine years old when she completed the book that would win the 1975 Pulitzer Prize. *Pilgrim at Tinker Creek* (1974), Dillard's first book-length work of nonfiction, brought her literary celebrity and firmly established her as one of the most important American women writers working in autobiography. Though she has also published poems, short stories, literary criticism, and a novel, Dillard is best known for her nonfiction prose. Her personal narratives explore spiritual and philosophical themes such as the development of consciousness, the nature of suffering, and the mystery of God.

Dillard was born April 30, 1945, in Pittsburgh, Pennsylvania, as Meta Ann Doak, to Frank and Pam (Lambert) Doak. The eldest of three sisters, Dillard came of age in an affluent society that included an education at a prestigious private school for girls. In 1963, she left her hometown for Roanoke, Virginia, entering Hollins College to study literature and creative writing. Her experience at Hollins was deeply formative in that it introduced her to the landscape of Tinker Creek and also to her first husband, Richard Henry Wilde Dillard, a poet and professor. They married in 1965 and she remained in school, completing her B.A. in 1967 and an M.A. the following year. Between 1975 and 1989, Dillard would publish six books and marry two more times. She spent these years living in Bellingham, Washington, and Middletown, Connecticut, working as scholar-in-residence at Western Washington University (1975–1978, 1981–1982), and as a visiting professor at Wesleyan University (1979–1980), and later as writer-in-residence at Wesleyan from 1983 to the present.

Dillard's unique contribution to women's autobiography comes through her ability to evoke a sense of **place** and a sense of the self in place. Rather than explicit discussions of **gender** or the role of the woman writer, Dillard's books document her evolving interest in the individual life and how one can make it meaningful despite the knowledge of pain, suffering, and certain death. She challenges traditional conventions of autobiography, insisting that one need not be famous to have an important story to tell. Her work demonstrates how individual lives intersect: she writes from personal experience and often includes profiles of others whose lives have influenced her own.

Dillard's literary influences include the British Romantics and their American counterparts, though she is most often associated with the American tradition of transcendentalism and the works of Ralph Waldo Emerson and Henry David Thoreau. Her pursuit of understanding the nexus of nature, consciousness, and God echoes Emerson's philosophical concerns with perception and Thoreau's descriptions of natural phenomena. In her early work, Dillard so closely aligns herself with these two writers that she is most often classified as a nature writer.

Certainly *Pilgrim at Tinker Creek* (1974)

has done much to fuel Dillard's reception as a latter-day transcendentalist. The book is part natural history and part spiritual autobiography, and its structure is similar to Thoreau's *Walden* (1854). Both narratives offer a year-long account of each author's life in a local landscape: Thoreau at Walden Pond, on the outskirts of Concord, Massachusetts, and Dillard at Tinker Creek, near Roanoke, Virginia. She links her project to Thoreau's in her desire to explore the immediate environment. She contemplates the intricacy and extravagance of the natural world, from the careful arrangement of blood cells, scales, and gills of a goldfish, to the millions of insect eggs that are laid, hatched, and eaten in a single summer day. Her daily excursions force Dillard to examine humanity's place in this ongoing matrix of life and death. She uncovers the remarkable in the ordinary, reminding readers that mystery and adventure constantly surround them.

Three years later Dillard published *Holy the Firm* (1977), a book decidedly more theological than her first one. As in *Pilgrim at Tinker Creek*, Dillard meticulously describes her natural environment and the isolated cabin where she lives on an island in Puget Sound. Though she claims that nothing will happen in this narrative, *Holy the Firm* proves otherwise. This book records three days in Dillard's life and the parallel story of young Julie Norwich, who survives a plane crash but is left disfigured by the burns she sustains. This book depicts Dillard's struggle to find meaning in this accident and an understanding of God. It is an intense exploration of the fundamental question of human suffering and religious faith.

With *Teaching a Stone to Talk* (1982), Dillard returns to the humorous style of her earlier work in *Pilgrim at Tinker Creek*; through detailed observation, she exposes the idiosyncrasies that characterize the human condition. She examines the human desire for exploration, recounts her experiences traveling in Ecuador, and shares her terrifying vision of a solar eclipse. Other essays include memories from her childhood and from her years of living in the Pacific Northwest. Five years later, Dillard published *An American Childhood* (1987), her most traditional autobiographical work. This book covers thirteen years of her life, from age five to age eighteen. She portrays the loving family and small community that fostered her interest in science and nurtured her sense of self. While her depictions are personal, they are not confessional. This book provides another angle from which Dillard can explore the nature of consciousness, from childhood to adulthood.

In 1989 Dillard published *The Writing Life*, a book based on her philosophy and practice of being a writer. She advises would-be writers of the hard work and dedication required when one chooses writing as a profession. Her most recent work, *For the Time Being* (1999), recalls her travels in China and Israel but also includes a range of subjects from the natural history of sand and the formation of clouds, to the wisdom of Eastern European Hasidic Jews and the mystery of human birth defects. She weaves together these disparate elements to show that humans past and present struggle with the same questions of existence.

Dillard's writing reveals a pattern in which she constantly measures the individual life against universal human conditions. Through this act she finds meaning and demonstrates the importance of attending to both.

Further Reading: Dillard, Annie. *An American Childhood*. 1987. Reprint (Boston: G.K. Hall, 1988); Dillard, Annie. *For the Time Being*. 1999. Reprint (New York: Vintage Books, 2000); Dillard, Annie. *Pilgrim at Tinker Creek*. 1974. Reprint (New York: Harper and Row, 1985); Elliott, Sandra Stahlman. "Annie Dillard: Biography." http://www.well.com/user/elliotts/smse_dill ard.html; Smith, Linda L. *Annie Dillard* (New York: Twayne, 1991).

Susan M. Lucas

DINESEN, ISAK (KAREN BLIXEN) (1885–1962)

A well-known writer of the early twentieth century, Isak Dinesen was born into an aristocratic and wealthy Danish family in 1885. She studied painting and writing in Europe when she was in her late teens and early twenties, traveled to Africa and married her cousin Baron Bror von Blixen at the age of twenty-nine, officially separated from him at age thirty-six, divorced when she was forty, took control of their coffee farm in Africa from age thirty-six to forty-six. She lost the farm at age forty-six, and in 1937, at age forty-nine, began publishing her works to pay off debts and finance the building of a hospital in Kenya. When she died in 1962 at age seventy-seven, she had published twenty-three books, numerous essays and magazine articles, and many **letters** in Danish and English, but had abandoned the idea of a hospital. Most of her work was of such fine quality that her name was often mentioned in connection with the Nobel Prize for Literature. She was acknowledged in Hemingway's Nobel acceptance speech in 1954 and lost the Nobel Prize to Albert Camus in 1957. Her work was selected for five Book-of-the-Month Club offerings, and she was featured in *Life* magazine in 1959. Since her death, her works have been published in several languages. One book, ***Out of Africa*** (1937), and two short stories, "Babette's Feast" (1953) and "The Immortal Story" inspired films of the same name. In addition, her life inspired a one-woman play by William Luce entitled *Lucifer's Child*.

Dinesen's **memoir**, *Out of Africa* (1937), was the second of her published works to gain critical acclaim and the first to describe the soul of the **place** that haunted much of her writing. Sparse, yet exotic and evocative, the work barely touches upon the everyday aspects of her pioneering farm life twelve miles from Nairobi, Kenya, before, during, and after World War I. Opening with, "I had a farm in Africa, at the foot of the Ngong Hills," Dinesen eulogizes an

Africa that served as a refuge for noble natives and grand aristocrats, an Africa whose residents lived in a vanishing present tinted with folklore and myth. After sketching several aspects of life in the foothills, her work ends with a farewell glimpse of the mountain "whose hills had flattened out in the distance." "I know a song of Africa," she wrote. That song is a rhapsody filled with similes and metaphors that arouse the senses and invite readers to grasp the tragic, exquisite, humorous beauty of human existence.

The work is divided into five sections. The first three sections focus on the African natives whom Dinesen sees as a "bygone people, full of wit, gallantry and humanity." She begins by describing the landscape and then proceeds to narrate a tale of murder, custom, and legal proceedings, a tale filled with eccentric cooks, amusing houseboys, loyal assistants, enigmatic chiefs, and the occasional European immigrant aristocrat. In the middle section of the work, she forgoes all pretense to a coherent narrative to create brief sketches of the immigrants, natives, wildlife, and natural beauty that she grew to love during her stay in Africa. She also includes occasional metaphorical meditations on the meaning of life and homages to impressionistic ideas and feelings, as if they were afterthoughts. In the final section, she presents an encapsulated narrative of the loss of her farm. Sparse, respectful, stoic, written with no sentiment, no sense of pity, no bitterness, this part of her tale ends with the selling of her possessions and the formal petition for settlement land for her beloved Kikuyu. The few Europeans who appear in this section, including Denys Finch-Hatton, Berkeley Cole, Lord Delamere, and the Prince of Wales, are treated with respect and fondness. Whether casual acquaintances, lovers, or good friends, these men are important to Dinesen. They enrich her solitude and relieve her loneliness by showering her with the gifts she loves the most: wine, music, good conversation, romantic safaris in the bush, and exhilarating flights over the plains.

Perhaps one of the most interesting aspects of Dinesen's memoir is what she leaves out. Her book contains no references to her childhood, no references to her father—a writer and adventurer who committed suicide when she was ten—no references to the syphilis that plagued her as it had her father, no discussion of her miscarriage from the time she spent with Finch-Hatton, and no references to her husband, Baron Bror von Blixen or Blixen's twin brother Hans, her first love. She does not dwell on the boredom of the farm nor the nightmare of her finances. Rather, her intimacy with Finch-Hatton is summarized in brief references to shooting lions and casual mention of intense conversations long into the night. And her various letters begging for money and lengthy trips to Europe to cure her illnesses are treated as inconvenient interruptions to daily life.

In addition to her controlled, restrained presentation of characters and events, Dinesen also controls her presentation of the many eccentricities that intrigued her biographers. Fascinated with the image as well as the spirit of nobility, for example, Dinesen loved being addressed as Baroness and was hurt when Bror remarried and she had to forfeit her title. Yet, her autobiography barely refers to the title or the fact that she made her houseboys wear white gloves in the farmhouse and dressed her attendants in lavish costumes when she took them to Europe. In addition, when Dinesen entertained at the farm, she was the consummate hostess; her carefully prepared meals were served on elegant China and accompanied by exquisite music and fascinating stories. Although her autobiography barely touches on this aspect of her personality, a later tale, "Babette's Feast," offers an ironic variation of this theme.

Most of Dinesen's other stories also develop exquisitely ironic variations of the themes of nobility, loss, mystery, and adventure that appear in *Out of Africa*. *Seven Gothic Tales* (1935), her first Book-of-the-Month Club selection in America, features stories of gloomy and grotesque eighteenth-

and nineteenth-century artists and aristo-crats who fall prey to eerie natural and su-pernatural events. In "The Dreamers," the most interesting tale in the book, Dinesen tells the story of an opera singer, Pellegrina Leoni, who loses her voice and reinvents her **identity** several times in order to live a more adventurous life. *Angelic Avengers* (1944), a novel published under the pseudonym Pierre Andrezal, presents a story of heroic actions in Nazi-occupied Denmark. *Winter's Tales* (1943) and *Last Tales* (1957) contain references to Nordic and Mediterranean folk tales that emphasize the enigma of human existence. *Shadows on the Grass* (1960) features vignettes of many of the natives in *Out of Africa*. And *Anecdotes of Destiny* (1958) boasts two famous stories: "The Immortal Story," an adaptation of the old metaphorical tale of impotence, power, and mortality, was in turn adapted to the film of the same name by Orson Welles (1968) and "Babette's Feast," a tale of a cook's sacrifice and love, was transformed into a film by Gabriel Axel (1985). Dinesen's posthumous publications offer more straightforward versions of her familiar themes. *Carnivals, Entertainments, and Posthumous Tales* (1977), a collection of stories written before and after Dinesen's residence in Africa, also deals with nobility, innocence, and loss. And *Letters from Africa* (1981) sheds more light on many of the characters and events mentioned in *Out of Africa* and *Shadows on the Grass*.

Like the opera singer Pellegrina Leoni, Dinesen was a woman with many faces and many names, but whether her readers referred to her as Isak Dinesen (as she was known in America), Karen Blixen (as she was known in Europe), the Baroness Christence Karen von Blixen Feneche (as she was known in Africa), Tanne (as known by her family), or Isak, the Danish translation of Isaac, the Hebrew name for laughter, it is clear that Dinesen enjoys playing with image and identity. Yet, no matter how out-landish the role, Dinesen's narrative tone is always one of gentle restraint, quiet respect, and subtle wit. Whether this tone repre-sents the true Karen Blixen is difficult to say. "I know a song of Africa," she wrote in her memoir, "Does Africa know a song of me?"

Further Reading: Brantly, Susan C. *Understanding Isak Dinesen* (Columbia: University of South Carolina Press, 2002); Dinesen, Isak. *Out of Africa*. 1937. Reprint (New York: Modern Library, 1992); Hannah, Donald. *"Isak Dinesen" and Karen Blixen: The Mask and the Reality* (New York: Random House, 1971); Langbaum, Robert Woodrow. *Isak Dinesen's Art: The Gayety of Vision* (Chicago: University of Chicago Press, 1975); Mowatt, Donald. "A Profile of Karen Blixen." The Arts Tonight, Vancouver: The Canadian Broadcasting Corporation, December 1, 1995; Parmenia, Michael. *Titania: The Biography of Isak Dinesen* (New York: Random House, 1967); Thurman, Judith. *Isak Dinesen: The Life of the Storyteller* (New York: St Martin's Press, 1982).

Emily B. Golson

DUNBAR-NELSON, ALICE MOORE (1875–1935)

Perhaps now as remembered for her tumultuous marriage to the poet Paul Laurence Dunbar as for her own writings, Alice Dunbar-Nelson's life and works walked the color line omnipresent in nineteenth- and early-twentieth-century African American literature. The fair-skinned writer's works chronicle turn-of-the-century through early-Depression-era America, with particular attention paid to life in New Orleans and the vivacity of black literature, including essays entitled "Negro Literature for Negro Pupils" and "The Negro as a Modern Literary Subject." She began to collect her daily thoughts in a **diary** in 1921 and seems to have kept it more or less continuously for the following decade, though the entries for 1922–1925 are missing. Gloria T. Hull collected, edited, and extensively commented on what remains of Dunbar-Nelson's diary, publishing it as *Give Us This Day* in 1984. The text remains not only an important historical chronicle of African American arts and letters in post–World War I America, but also a testament to one woman's experiences in the traumatic **gender** and **race** struggles of the 1920s.

Alice Ruth Moore was born July 19, 1875, in New Orleans, Louisiana, took her degree at Straight College, and sought further education at such institutions as Cornell, Columbia, and the University of Pennsylvania. She was fair skinned enough to pass for white in order to subvert the Jim Crow laws; indeed, she recounts in her diary instances in which she was forced to move to the front of the bus because other passengers believed her to be white. Her position on race is an important and often troubling one. Though a diligent champion for black rights in America, which included a visit to President Harding alongside James Weldon Johnson regarding the protection of sixty-one black soldiers imprisoned in Houston, Texas, after a race "riot" during which no whites were arrested, Dunbar-Nelson reveals her own blatant color and **class** biases. She often dismisses darker-skinned blacks in her writings as inferior, especially those without an education comparable to her own. The problem appears to be as much a case of class bias as a reaction to darker-skinned blacks who ostracized her throughout her life. Her writings reflect an access to the high society she esteemed (operas, and so forth), which would have been denied her darker-skinned, fellow Americans; she tends not to recognize the differences in treatment—claiming to have developed no sense of color. Despite this, her life's work is consumed by the desire to bring equality between the races and the sexes. Clearly, her racial position offers interesting problems, as she moves within both worlds, though not ever completely of either black or white America. Indeed, her life exemplifies that of the **space** of the New Orleans' Creole.

The events recalled in her diary range from daily minutiae to extended accounts of political and social activities. What becomes clear above all else is her commitment to the advancement of black American arts and politics, as well as education. She recounts her life as a teacher, writer, critic, and keeper of her late ex-husband's literary **memory**. Despite being faced with nearly overwhelming debt through much of the 1920s, Dunbar-Nelson writes of seeking loans to found a black-owned newspaper and of helping to found a state school for black girls. Dunbar-Nelson married twice: first to American poet Paul Laurence Dunbar from 1898 until their separation in 1902, and to journalist and civil rights activist Robert Nelson from 1916 until her death in 1935.

As might be expected, the intended reader of her diary is the author herself; nothing indicates that Dunbar-Nelson planned to publish the diary's text, though her writing profoundly appeals to readers other than herself. She even remarks that she fully expects her husband Robert Nelson to read the diary with or without her consent. Thus, the **voice** of the text is caught in a double bind—a series of them, in fact. Her diary is seemingly torn between her private and public worlds. She is often highly euphemistic in her recordings, especially those regarding her intimate relationships with women, in order to disguise the truth from prying eyes. Thus, in a space in which she craves the ability to write her private thoughts as freely as she can think them, she is forced to hide them and remain as deceptive in her private world as she must be in the public one.

Dunbar-Nelson published her first fiction collection, *Violets* (1895), at just twenty years of age. Her second, *The Goodness of St. Rocque* (1899), followed four years later. These would prove to be the only collections of her fiction works to be published in her lifetime. They revolve around life for the Creole in New Orleans and are most remarkable for their intense focus on sensory details, especially "A Carnival Jangle." In this story she captures the chaotic movement of sight and sound during Mardi Gras, a setting that becomes the background and veil to a murder rendered inconsequential against the celebration. The stories tend to be short and, often, not thematically concerned with race, but consumed instead by gender, as in the title story in *Rocque*. Her fiction is often rushed and faulty and her poetry commonplace; nevertheless, the works she produced are important in their vision of the standards of color and class so apparent in the author's lifetime. Dunbar-Nelson can be credited not only for her lectures and essay works to increase the readership of black authors, but of adding to the vitality of African American literature.

Though her place in African American literature is as uncertain and complex as her racial position in the public sphere, her diary is an important document of racial, gender, and literary politics of the 1920s. Readers find a woman constantly caught between spaces, trying as best she can to survive, write, and change the racial and gender paradigms in America.

Further Reading: Dunbar-Nelson, Alice Moore. *Give Us This Day: The Diary of Alice Dunbar-Nelson.* Edited by Gloria T. Hull (New York: W. W. Norton, 1984); Dunbar-Nelson, Alice Moore. *The Works of Alice Dunbar-Nelson.* Edited by Gloria Hull. Vols. 1–3 (New York: Oxford University Press, 1988); Hull, Gloria T. *Color, Sex, and Poetry: Three Women Writers of the Harlem Renaissance* (Bloomington: Indiana University Press, 1987).

Kristen Simmons Roney

DURAS, MARGUERITE (1914–1995)

Marguerite Duras, a prolific writer of literature, theater, and film scenarios from 1950 to 1995, preferred a form of writing in which she deliberately blurred the boundaries of autobiography and fiction, putting herself into a story that stands somewhere between the two. She first achieved wide public recognition in 1950 for *The Sea Wall*, a fictionalized account of her early years. In this early work she invented a kaleidoscope of images and relationships that would shift several times over her life until as recently as 1991, with *L'Amant de la Chine du nord* [The Lover from the North of China]. *L'Amant* [The Lover], published in 1984, returns to the period covered in *The Sea Wall* and was understood to be her first real "autobiography," but, like her other works, it does not strictly follow the rules that ordinarily define the autobiographical genre. Duras is very clear about rejecting autobiography of the usual sort, which is presumed to be entirely nonfictional, because it seems to her totally inauthentic. She thus upsets any received notion of a distinction between autobiography and fiction, going even further than other French women writers (such as Colette and **Simone de Beauvoir**) of the twentieth century in redefining the autobiographical genre itself.

Marguerite Donnadieu (later changed to Duras) was born near Saigon in 1914. The daughter of French colonial schoolteachers, she lost her father at an early age and watched her mother struggle financially to raise her and her two brothers. She lived through the catastrophe of her mother's using her entire life savings to buy a parcel of land that turned out to be flooded each year by the Pacific and therefore useless for cultivation. This early experience of colossal injustice and her ruined mother's doomed attempts to build a dam to hold back the ocean are present in much of Duras' autobiographically based work. These repeated accounts allowed Duras to explore her concern with an unfair distribution of power in personal relationships and in society. After earning her baccalaureate, she left for France where she affiliated herself with an international community of intellectuals. Her personal experience of the occupation of France during World War II and the deportation of her husband, Robert Antelme, increased still further her sensitivity to suffering, and she played an active role in the French resistance. She lived a somewhat scandalous existence after the war with Antelme and Dionys Mascolo, the father of her son, following no established model for a wife and mother. She became an important intellectual figure in Paris and regularly received other intellectuals in her apartment in the rue St. Benoît, much as Sartre and Beauvoir were doing during this same period.

In 1958, she published *Moderato Cantabile* and was considered for a time to be a member of the *nouveau roman* school. Her cycle of books involving the character Lol V. Stein were written in an elliptical style that required the reader to puzzle out the plot, a characteristic of the *nouveau roman*. But in later life she returned to less elliptical autobiographical writing, reworking the material in *Un barrage contre le Pacifique* [The Sea Wall] and *L'Eden cinéma* (1987), and winning the prestigious Prix Goncourt for *L'Amant* [The Lover] in 1984. In this book that catapulted her to almost cult status in France, she describes her first love affair at age fifteen with an older Chinese man in Saigon. In subsequent works she continues to explore her early life with her mother and two brothers, and her Chinese lover (*L'Amant de la Chine du nord* [The Lover from the North of China] 1991), her experience of awaiting the return of her husband from a concentration camp in 1945 (*La Douleur* [The War] 1985), and then her love relationship with Yann Andrea, a gay man much younger than herself, with whom she lived her last years (*Les Yeux bleus cheveux noirs* [Blue Eyes, Black Hair] 1986), *Yann Andréa Steiner* (1992), *Emily L.* (1987). Many of her later texts are addressed to a particular reader, more or less precisely identified, and they are increasingly insistent on the will and the need to establish an intimate, loving connection through words with that person.

Duras experimented with many styles, usually preferring a simple, poetic form of prose. Because she was constantly exploring and innovating, Duras' writing became increasingly transgressive, disobedient, and difficult to classify over time. She had a heightened awareness not only of sorrow but also of anger, and her willingness to express her anger directly sets her work apart from her major compatriot women writers, including Simone de Beauvoir. She was increasingly sexually explicit, alluding to many sexual practices and situations that had previously been found only in pornographic books and movies. She also wrote openly about her addiction to alcohol.

While never officially a feminist, she proved in *Les Parleuses* [Women Speaking] and in her film *Nathalie Granger*, which portrays in detail the hour-by-hour experience of two women friends in their home, that she found the company of her women friends empowering, especially during her fifties. In a manner typical of French feminists, she was intent on discovering what she considered to be the specificity of woman's nature, but she differs from most French women writers in her awareness of women's exclusion from many arenas of social and political life and in her willingness to talk about it.

Duras' best known works include the script for *Hiroshima mon amour*, *Un barrage contre le Pacifique* [The Sea Wall], *Moderato Cantabile*, *Le Ravissement de Lol V. Stein* [The Ravishing of Lol V. Stein], *L'Amant* [The Lover], and *La Douleur* [The War].

Further Reading: Adler, Laure. *Duras* (Paris: Gallimard, 1998); Duras, Marguerite. *The Sea Wall*. 1950. Reprint (New York: Perennial Library, 1986); Duras, Marguerite. *The Lover* (New York: Pantheon Books, 1997); Evans, Martha Noel. *Masks of Tradition: Women and the Politics of Writing in Twentieth Century France* (Ithaca, NY: Cornell University Press, 1987); Lebellay, Frédérique. *Marguerite Duras ou le poids d'une plume* (Paris: Grasset, 1994); Vircondelet, Alain. *Marguerite Duras* (Paris: Editions François Bourin, 1991); Willis, Sharon. *Marguerite Duras: Writing on the Body* (Chicago: University of Illinois Press, 1987).

Bethany Ladimer

E

EASTERN EUROPEAN WOMEN'S AU-TOBIOGRAPHY In terms of current geopolitics, the Eastern European region includes Albania, Bulgaria, the former Czechoslovakia (the Czech Republic and Slovakia), Hungary, Poland, Romania, and the former Yugoslavia (Bosnia-Herzegovina, Croatia, Macedonia, Montenegro, Serbia, and Slovenia). In addition, since about 1991, countries of the former Soviet Union—Belarus, Estonia, Latvia, Lithuania, Ukraine—are now regarded as Eastern European although they are not discussed in this entry (see **Russian Women's Autobiography**). Because these countries all had Communist systems until the late 1980s, they were perceived as a single entity despite having quite different cultures, traditions, and histories. Yet a common past of foreign domination under either the Hapsburgs or the Ottoman Empire does loosely unite these countries as does a preoccupation with national survival. Predictably, both Ottoman and Hapsburg rule suppressed the development of a women's consciousness and the dearth of women in the literary canon unites the history of women's writing within this region (Hawkesworth 1991, 102).

Prior to the nineteenth century there were few women writers in Eastern Europe and, as might be expected, most of the early writers were aristocratic women known for autobiographical writing with religious overtones. For example, the Czech aristocrat Zuzana Černinová z Harasova (1601–1654) wrote letters about the travails of the Thirty Years' War; Countess Kata Bethlen (1700–1759), a Hungarian living in Transylvania, wrote the **memoir** *A Short Description of the Life of Countess Kata Bethlen Written by Herself*. Published posthumously in 1762, the book recounts the suffering and self-loathing of this Protestant woman who was forced at age seventeen to marry her Roman Catholic half brother.

Initially a form of expression used by women whose work was neglected and deemed nonliterary because it did not conform to male-dominated genres, women's life writing in Eastern Europe—considered here as autobiography, **memoir**, journal, **diary**—may be viewed as "an 'intermediate' medium, characteristic of the search for new forms among women writers today" (Hawkesworth 1991, 103). For example, the diary was the preferred genre of Croatia's first woman writer, Dragolja Jarnević (1812–1875). In her diaries she identifies familiar sources of societal tension for women: "the conflict between intellectual activity and household chores . . . and the conflict between her desire for independence and her sexual drive" (103). And in the 1930s, the works of the American suffragist movement, particularly those by Agnes Smedley with their themes of social injustice and political rights influenced the Serbian writer, Milka Žicina's autobiographical novel *Kajin put* (1934 [Kaja's Journey]).

It appears that the desire and need to write autobiographies and memoirs became preeminent in post–World War II Eastern European literature. In the twentieth century, Eastern Europe has been the location of several of humankind's great tragedies: World War II, the Holocaust, and the subsequent redrawing of national borders; dramatic social change under Communism and currently, post-Communism; and the war and "ethnic cleansing" in the former Yugoslavia. The most salient themes captured in countless personal written and oral narratives and interviews by women as well as in their autobiographies, deal with the death, suffering, and displacement of masses of people. More broadly, the relationship between **memory** and survival as well as the function of memory in creating meaning, for often chaotic, irrational events are central motifs in these works. As a representative text, *Escape through the Balkans: The Autobiography of Irene Grünbaum* (1996), discovered at the Institute of Austrian Resistance in Vienna, recounts the life of Grünbaum, a German Jewish woman living in Belgrade at the beginning of World War II who escapes to Brazil via the Balkans and Albania after her husband is killed. Grünbaum (1909–1983) portrays a complex part of wartime Europe about which little has been written, as well as her own travails of a female traveling alone in hunger and in poverty, encountering partisans, thieves, Fascists, and various ethnic groups, many of whom gave her kind assistance but who were also embroiled in ethnic hatreds.

Women's voices constitute a small portion of the millions of words written about World War II, yet numerous autobiographies and memoirs have been written by East European women, many of whom are Jewish. These recount the horrors and pathos of women's lives and experiences in the Polish resistance, the Warsaw uprising, Nazi concentration camps, the partisan insurgency, and in labor camps in Soviet Siberia. Two examples of such female life writing are *A Partisan's Memoir: Woman of the Holocaust*, and *The Horror Trains: A Polish Woman Veteran's Memoir of World War II*. *A Partisan's Memoir* (1995) is the story of Faye Schulman who at age nineteen escaped the Nazis who murdered her family and joined the partisans on the Polish-Soviet border. She trained herself as a nurse and as a photographer while surviving in the forest and fighting a guerilla war. In *The Horror Trains* (1999), Wanda E. Pomykalski recounts how in 1939 she set out to join the Polish army, was captured by the Soviets and deported first to Odessa and then to Siberia. Following the amnesty given to Poles held in Soviet prisons, Wanda reaches the Polish army and is assigned as a clerk-typist for the Polish forces and is stationed in many countries.

The phenomena of displacement and life in a new country is well represented in the autobiographies of three scholars: *Between Worlds: In Czechoslovakia, England, and America* (1991) by Susan Groag Bell, *Budapest Diary: In Search of the Motherbook* (1996) by Susan Rubin Suleiman, and **Eva Hoffman**'s *Lost in Translation: A Life in a New Language* (1989). All three emigrated as children from Czechoslovakia, Hungary, and Poland respectively, Bell during World War II, Suleiman in 1949, and Hoffman in 1959, and all established influential careers in North America. Each writes about the search for their childhood and national identity, made sharper by subsequent visits to their homelands; the sense of alienation and feelings of loss so connected with the immigrant experience is addressed by all authors. Hoffman pays particular attention to the relationship between language, culture, and self-identity; Bell describes the cultured world she lost when she became a refugee, her teen years in London, and her postwar return to a Czechoslovakia in which, she realizes, she no longer fits; and Suleiman's diary, written largely in 1990 when she returns to Budapest as an academic, recounts how she comes to feel an "at-homeness" there within the context of being a Hungarian American despite the unpalatable aspects of Hungarian and European nationalism that destroyed Hungary's Jewish community, including members of her own family.

The complex war in the former Yugoslavia that began in the early 1990s with the breakup of the federation into separate countries is the background for several pieces of life writing that give insight into women's experiences and perspectives in a region undergoing dramatic social transition. *Zlatin dnevnik* (1994 [Zlata's Diary: A Child's Life in Sarajevo]) by Zlata Filipović is a child's testimony about the war in Sarajevo, Bosnia. Begun in September 1991 when Zlata was age eleven and completed in October 1993, the diary follows this typical preteen as her interests in MTV, Madonna, school friends, and piano lessons evolve into real concerns about the horrors of war: water, food, and gas shortages, bombings, and snipers. It is a compelling description of the ravages of war and its effect on one adolescent. An adult view of the Bosnian conflict is Elma Softić's diary, *Sarajevski dani, sarajevske noci* (1995 [Sarajevo Days, Sarajevo Nights]). Written between April 1992 and June 1995, the book revolves not only around Softić's diary, but her correspondence with relatives in Zagreb, Croatia that recounts the effects of the siege of the city on herself, family, friends, and neighbors.

As well as life writing of memories—of writing in order not to forget or be forgotten—Eastern European women's self-writing encompasses such universal themes as illness, poverty, gender discrimination, and childbearing. Two widely translated contemporary Eastern European writers who have written autobiographical novels are the Croatian women Irena Vrkl-

jan and Slavenka Drakulić. *Hologrami straha* (1987 [Holograms of Fear]), an exceptional work by the journalist Drakulić, relates her experience with kidney dialysis and a subsequent transplant and is a reassessment of her life following a life-threatening illness. Similarly, the poet Vesna Krmpotić recounts in her autobiography, *Brdo iznad oblaka* (1988 [A Hill above the Clouds]) the story of her son's death from leukemia, her exploration of treatment alternatives for him, as well as her own arrival at a faith encompassing such philosophies as those of ancient Egypt and India.

Irena Vrkljan, an established poet, has written an autobiographical novel *Svila, škare* (1984 [Silk, Scissors]) that questions literary conventions through its use of letters that provide her own as well as her sisters' perceptions of a shared upbringing; traditional categories of "femininity" are defied through the expression of "the young woman's developing awareness of discrimination, [and] a real sense of anger" (Hawkesworth 1991, 124). Another of Vrkljan's works is about the Russian poet Marina Tsvetaeva, *Marina, ili o biografji* (1986 [Marina, or about Biography]); it is interesting for its mixture of autobiography and **biography** and "offers an honest appraisal of the extent to which a 'biography' may be separated from its author's own perceptions in a mixed genre ... [and] explores the way fragments of the lives of other people, known or unknown, live in us" (Hawkesworth 124). Perhaps this work represents that age-old search for forms, which best express Eastern European women's perceptions and experiences.

Further Reading: Bell, Susan Groag. *Between Worlds: In Czechoslovakia, England, and America* (New York: Dutton, 1991); Drakulić, Slavenka. *Holograms of Fear*. Translated by Ellen Elias-Bursać (New York: Norton, 1992); Drakulić, Slavenka. "'Six mortal sins' of Yugoslav feminism." In *Sisterhood Is Global*, edited by R. Morgan, 736–738 (New York: Anchor Books, 1984); Farris, June, Irina Livezeanu, Christine Worobec, and Mary Zirin, eds. *Bibliography on Women and*

Gender in Russia, the Successor States of the Former Soviet Union, and East Central Europe (Armonk, NY: M.E. Sharpe, in press); Filipović, Zlata. *Zlata's Diary: A Child's Life in Sarajevo.* Translated with notes by Christina Pribichevich Zoric (New York: Viking, 1994); Grünbaum, Irene. *Escape through the Balkans: The Autobiography of Irene Grünbaum.* Translated and edited by Katherine Morris (Lincoln: University of Nebraska Press, 1996); Hawkesworth, Celia. "Feminist Writing in Eastern Europe: The Problem Solved?" In *Textual Liberation: European Feminist Writing in the Twentieth Century*, edited by Helena Forsas-Scott, 100–129 (London: Routledge, 1991); Hoffman, Eva. *Lost in Translation: A Life in a New Language* (New York: Dutton, 1989); Krmpotić, Vesna. *Brdo iznad oblaka* (Zagreb: Globus, 1988); Lukić, Jasmina. "Women-Centered Narratives in Contemporary Serbian and Croatian Literatures." In *Engendering Slavic Literatures*, edited by Pamela Chester and Sibelan Forrester, 223–243 (Bloomington: Indiana University Press, 1996); Pomykalski, Wanda E. *The Horror Trains: A Polish Woman Veteran's Memoir of World War II* (Pasadena, MD: Minerva Center, 1999); Schulman, Faye, Sarah Silberstein Swartz. *A Partisan's Memoir: Woman of the Holocaust* (Toronto: Second Story Press, 1995); Softić, Elma. *Sarajevo Days, Sarajevo Nights* (Toronto: Key Porter Books, 1995); Suleiman, Susan Rubin. *Budapest Diary: In Search of the Motherbook* (Lincoln: University of Nebraska Press, 1996); Vrkljan, Irena. *Svila, škare* (Zagreb: Grafički zavod Hrvatske, 1984); Vrkljan, Irena. *Marina, or About Biography.* Translated by Celia Hawkesworth (Zagreb: The Bridge and Dirieux, 1991); Wolchik, S.L. and A.G. Meyer. *Women, State and Party in Eastern Europe* (Durham: Duke University Press, 1985); Žicina, Milka. *Kajin put* (Belgrade: Nolit, 1934).

Teresa L. Polowy

EATON, EDITH MAUDE. *SEE* SUI SIN FAR.

ELAW, ZILPHA (c. 1790–AFTER 1845)

Zilpha Elaw is important in both the history of black women evangelists and black women autobiographers—a nexus embodied in her 1846 narrative, *Memoirs of the Life, Religious Experience, Ministerial Travels, and Labours of Mrs. Zilpha Elaw: An American Female of Colour*, one of the earliest spiritual autobiographies by an African American woman—though her contemporary and occasional partner, Jarena Lee, has received more critical attention.

Most scholars believe that Elaw was born around 1790 near Philadelphia. Her narrative reports that she was one of only three of her parents' twenty-two children to survive childbirth. We do not know Elaw's parents' names, and our knowledge of her childhood is drawn solely from her narrative, which notes that, following her mother's death in childbirth, her father placed her with Pierson and Rebecca Mitchel, where she lived and worked until she turned eighteen. Her father died soon after he placed her with the family. The Mitchels were a large, devout Quaker family who seem to have regularly hired free blacks as live-in help (the 1810 census lists two free blacks living with the family of nine).

Some critics have simplistically suggested that Elaw rebelled against the quiet meetings of Quaker practice, choosing instead the volume and vigor of the evangelical Protestant camp meetings and revivals that surrounded her. Sometime around 1804, she began seeing visions and had a conversion experience soon after; sometime around 1808, she joined a Methodist Episcopal society. Still, Elaw's narrative is much friendlier to Quaker theology; she also notes that the Mitchels later aided her financially and recounts with some fondness a later meeting with two of the Mitchel sons.

Elaw married Joseph Elaw in 1810, and the young couple continued to live in the Philadelphia area before moving to Burlington, New Jersey. They had one daughter, Rebecca, in 1812, but Joseph did not share Elaw's faith and so the marriage was rocky from the outset. Elaw's narrative represents her sister Hannah's death—soon after her marriage—as a turning point in her life; with expected sentimental tropes, she shows Hannah's deathbed scene, at which Hannah has a vision of Elaw preaching. Elaw did not accept this call until much later—after a near-fatal illness and a set of visions of her own at a camp meeting in about 1817. Scholars guess that she began preaching in about 1819 with the support—rare for her time—of the others in her society. Her husband, however, objected strenuously, and the marriage grew worse.

Joseph Elaw died, though, in early 1823. Financial need forced Elaw and her daughter into domestic work; eventually she was able to open a small school for black children in Burlington, which was funded in part by area Quakers. By 1828, though, the call to preach was too strong, and Elaw closed the school, left her daughter, and traveled to Philadelphia, Maryland, and Virginia as she preached.

Elaw's sense of sanctification, in some ways like Jarenna Lee's, embraced a nondenominational focus, though she remained associated with Methodist Episcopals for much of her life. She was noted for her extemporaneous delivery and her fiery exhortations. She was also avowedly antislavery and antiracist, but, though she defended women's right to preach, at times she seems to have embraced dominant notions of women's subservience.

Until 1840, she traveled as an itinerant evangelist throughout the northeast and the mid-Atlantic regions, occasionally returning to Philadelphia and Burlington. In the summer of 1840, she felt called to do missionary work in England, where she arrived on July 24. She self-published her narrative in London in 1846.

We know little of Elaw's final years; most accounts assume she died in England. Her daughter Rebecca, who is not named in the narrative, married and had two sons before 1846. She seems to have stayed in the United States when her mother left for England, and there is some evidence that, later in life, she became the third wife of Nantucket African American minister, James E. Crawford.

Elaw's narrative is fairly dense and difficult to read; the combination of early sentimentalist and fervent evangelical rhetoric have limited its attention by contemporary readers. Still, Elaw directly confronts questions of slavery, racism, and **gender** discrimination, and she astutely comments on the complexities of itinerant evangelism—even noting bluntly that some people came to see her simply because she was a curiosity: a black woman preaching. The narrative is also important as an early text in the transatlantic dialogue on slavery and **race**—a book by "an American female of colour" directly addressed to the British. Elaw herself deserves note as one of the earliest black women evangelists and autobiographers, as a **voice** in the early-nineteenth-century debates over the place of women in public discourse, and as an important precursor to the mid-nineteenth-century African American presence in England.

Further Reading: Andrews, William. "Zilpha Elaw." In *The Oxford Companion to African American Literature* (New York: Oxford University Press, 1997), 249; Elaw, Zilpha. *Memoirs of the Life, Religious Experience, Ministerial Travels, and Labours of Mrs. Zilpha Elaw: An American Female of Colour*. Reprinted in *Sisters of the Spirit: Three Black Women's Autobiographies of the Nineteenth Century*, edited by William L. Andrews, 49–160 (Bloomington: Indiana University Press, 1986); Grammer, Elizabeth Elkin. *Some Wild Visions: Autobiographies by Female Itinerant Evangelists in Nineteenth-Century America* (Oxford University Press, 2003); Johnson, Robert. "Black-White Relations on Nantucket." http://www.nha.org/pdf/johnson%20article.pdf. LaPrade, Candis. "Zilpha Elaw." In *Notable Black American Women*, edited by Jessie Carney Smith, 317–319 (New York: Gale, 1996); Moody, Joycelyn. *Sentimental Confessions: Spiritual Narratives of Nineteenth-Century African American Women* (Athens: University of Georgia Press, 2001); Tate, Gayle. "Zilpha Elaw." In *Black Women in America*, edited by Darlene Clark Hine, 388–389 (Bloomington: Indiana University Press, 1993).

Eric Gardner

EMBODIMENT   A complex concept, embodiment, centers on the idea that to be a "self," that is, a human being in a world of other human beings, is to have a physical existence. The embodied self is material, but at the same time is socially situated.

Conceptualizations of embodiment can be historically traced through the works of philosophers such as Friedrich Nietzsche, Jean-Paul Sartre, and Gabriel Marcel. These early explorations of embodiment were a response to the traditional approach to human existence rooted in the system of Cartesian dualities: man/reason/spirit versus woman/emotion/body. These dualities were based on a Platonian ideal that saw the body as the irrational part of the soul that must be kept in check. If the body is allowed to overtake the rational soul, then it is an impediment to the acquisition of knowledge, goodness, reality, beauty, love, and statehood. For millennia, "woman has been portrayed as essentially a bodily being, and this image has been used to deny her full status as a human being wherever and whenever mental activity as over against bodily activity has been thought to be the most human activity of all" (Spelman 1982, 123). Embodiment theories allowed for the reunification of the formerly disembodied self, and, moreover, provided the platform for a growing feminist position.

One of the most influential figures in developing the theory of embodiment was the phenomenologist Maurice Merleau-Ponty (1908–1961). Merleau-Ponty reshaped the way theorists view the connection between self and world—and thus between subject and object. The basis of his claim is the significance of the existential body, which he believed that traditional philosophy undervalued, seeing it as a mere servant of the mind. Instead of merely performing actions, the body, and the extensions thereof, such as eyeglasses or technology, is actually the center of human interaction with the world. Building on these ideas, George Herbert Mead suggested that an individual self develops from bodily interaction with the world; thus, our sense of self is dependent on both the physical and social selves. These views form the nexus of the classical social constructivist approach, which sees the body as an entity that both derives meaning from and gives meaning to social and cultural processes.

Later work by Michel Foucault (1926–1984) also provided a platform for current studies about embodiment. Foucault presented the body as a site of power that is central to the formation of **subjectivity**. While this model allows for analysis of the repressive and productive nature of power, it also overlooks some sites of **identity** formation. Poststructuralist theory has allowed for further examination of embodiment and subjectivity, particularly in connection with performance theory. Within these frameworks, bodies both destabilize and institute discourses. Still, some scholars are critical of poststructuralist reliance on discourse over material relations.

Embodiment and **feminism** have had a long and turbulent relationship. Through feminism, the significance of theories of embodiment to all areas of investigation was revealed. In other words, the identity of the investigator and/or the producer is crucial to the production, distribution, and substantiation of knowledge within discourses and communities. Furthermore, the development of the self is closely linked to the collective entities to which one belongs.

Early feminists, in particular, **Simone de Beauvoir**, and, later, Shulamith Firestone, developed their own take on embodiment. Both Beauvoir and Firestone view women's experience with embodiment in a predominantly negative light. A major premise of this position is that women are enslaved by their biology, especially the reproductive aspects thereof. Beauvoir takes the stance that women's bodies are more immanent (meaning more difficult to surpass completely) because of menstruation, which is repetitive, and pregnancy; thus, female embodied experience is less desirable than male embodiment. Firestone maintains that reproduction creates a natural and inherent inequality between men and women. Recently, these views have been made problematic by gynocritics, primarily due to issues of authenticity. Gynocritics claim that Beauvoir and Firestone, as well as their followers, need to be deconstructed because they assume the male embodied experience is the norm for authentic human activity and go on to define women's embodied experience as different from this norm. In particular, gynocritics have sought to overturn these ideas by restoring value to procreation and motherhood. These scholars begin with the premise that women's reproductive biology has a natural value that has been denied and suppressed through **patriarchy**. Moreover, women are more clearly integrated into the natural pattern because of their biology, where men are separated from nature and must create artificial points of connection. This position however, is also problematic for a variety of reasons. In particular, this viewpoint reduces women to being defined by the womb and articulates the stance that women become authentic through their unity with nature (i.e., through childbirth). This theory defines women who actively choose to remain child-free as inauthentic.

The idea of embodiment is intrinsically linked to the concepts of subjectivity and agency, as well as **gender** performance and difference. In turn, all of these foreground the contribution of embodiment to autobiographical writing and life writing. Moving beyond purely physical embodiment, many feminist theorists argue that identity is a multidimensional concept that covers various levels of experience: the individual self, the social and political apparatuses in which individuals function, and levels of symbolic images and representations. Thus, the body is no longer simply a biological entity; rather, it is a complex intersection of given and acquired characteristics.

Theorists such as Judith Butler built on earlier interpretations of the acquisition and development of agency and identity as related to the body and its actions. Butler pioneered the concept of gender performance. In her framework, identity is established based on *"stylized repetition of acts.* Further, gender is instituted through the stylization of the body; and, hence, must be understood as the mundane way in which bodily gestures, movements, and enactments of various kinds constitute the illusion of an abiding gendered self"* ("Performative Acts" 1988, 402, original emphasis). In this way, performance—gender performance in particular—is a structure of embodiment.

New directions in studies of embodiment include explorations of virtual and constructed bodies. Donna Haraway published *A Cyborg Manifesto* in 1985. In this work, she illustrates the value of contemporary biological and technological research that can be used in deconstructing the traditional Cartesian dualities. By making problematic these dualities, Haraway further complicates the notion of gender. The cyborg is her vehicle for this exploration. As a fusion of biology and technology, the cyborg, which stands between the boundary of the natural and mechanical, helps illustrate how the body both constructs and is constructed by technology. Haraway's ideas about an ambiguously gendered technological body opens up multiple possibilities for researchers in many other areas, particularly those examining the virtual landscape(s) of the Internet and those involved with disability studies.

One of the clearest ways theories of embodiment are related to women's autobiography is through the concepts of subjectivity and agency. Women's self-representation has increasingly been examined in light of contesting notions of a universal/unified "I" and replacing it with multiple, fractured subject positions. The explosion of the Internet and other virtual landscapes has opened the field of autobiography and embodiment to a wide range of self-representational strategies. The virtual landscape allows disembodied expression and the creation of multiple alter-personae. In this environment, subjectivity is truly dependent on speaking the self. In turn, speaking the self is linked in important ways to speaking the experience of female embodiment. **Sidonie Smith** outlines the intersection of subjectivity and body that occurs in autobiography:

> When a specific woman approaches the scene of writing and the autobiographical "I," she not only engages the discourses of subjectivity through which the universal human subject has been culturally secured; she also engages the complexities of her cultural assignment to an absorbing embodiment. And so the autobiographical subject carries a history of the body with her as she negotiates the autobiographical "I," for autobiographical practice is one of those cultural occasions when the history of the body intersects the deployment of subjectivity. ("The Universal Subject" 1993, 22–23)

Smith's ideas can be linked back to the works of Merleau-Ponty, who held the position that the body is a historical idea, but is not limited by that history; instead, it gains meaning through historically mediated expression.

These are important concepts in feminist thought because they keep open the possibility of the variability of the body, as well as the autobiographical subject. Historical (re)presentation is important in reaffirming female agency. Moreover, some theorists suggest that the female body is a site of potential power, knowledge, and rebellion, all of which may threaten the status quo of male privilege and power. Surely, embodiment is a central concept in the field of women's autobiography.

Further Reading: Diprose, Rosalyn. *The Bodies of Women: Ethics, Embodiment, and Sexual Difference* (London: Routledge, 1994); Smith, Sidonie. "The Universal Subject, Female Embodiment, and the Consolidation of Autobiography." In *Subjectivity, Identity, and the Body:*

Women's Autobiographical Practices in the Twentieth Century (Bloomington, IN: Indiana University Press, 1993), 1–23; Spelman, Elizabeth V. "Woman as Body: Ancient and Contemporary Views." *Feminist Studies* 8, no. 1 (1982): 109–131.

Michelle M. Sauer

ERNAUX, ANNIE (1940–) In her first novel, *Cleaned Out* (1974), Annie Ernaux explored a theme that was to become central in her work: the painful social separation endured by a woman cut off from her working-class origins by education and marriage into a bourgeois family. Her fourth narrative, *A Man's Place* (1984), was a turning point in her work, bringing official recognition (Prix Renaudot) and public success, and above all, marking her departure from the novel. From then on, she resolutely adopted the autobiographical form and pledged to write about her life. Being a social-class defector led her to her subject. She considers social dimension a deciding factor in the acquisition of her **identity**: being a member of the voice-deprived sex mattered less than having been born into the working class. While she may not be a feminist standard-bearer or enjoy being listed under the heading "women's literature," she recognizes in her writing her sex-bound condition.

In her works, she recalls her childhood in a small Normandy town—her parents' café/grocery store and her Catholic school. Her unconventional parents did not adhere to traditional sex roles. Her mother, a born fighter, embodied the couple's social ambition. Annie Ernaux's narratives show her growing up torn between her home language and the school's norm, experiencing her "in-between" state early between two languages, two cultures, two social worlds. As a consequence, she felt like a social misfit. Her parents had wished for their only child to become a schoolteacher; she became a laureate of the Agrégation (1971). Very soon, writing became an essential part of her life; she kept a **diary** from age sixteen, and from 1962, attempted novel writing in the nouveau roman style. Her writing matured under the strain of such experiences as an illegal abortion in 1963, narrated in *Happening* (2001); her marriage in 1964, a conjugal trap depicted in *A Frozen Woman* (1981); her father's death (1967), which led her to analyze her own **class** betrayal in *A Man's Place* (1984); and finally, her mother's Alzheimer's disease and death in 1986, evoked in *A Woman's Story* (1968) and *I Remain in Darkness* (1997). Meanwhile, she remained a teacher, which gave her financial independence from her husband, whom she divorced in 1982. In the 1980s, Annie Ernaux became popular, but, especially after *Simple Passion* was published in 1993, some academics and critics expressed doubt. They cast her off to the edges of the literary world because she disturbed their ideas about literature. However, this situation proved to be temporary; today, Ernaux enjoys wide acclaim.

Her style has evolved substantially. The familiar, vindictive, fertile, and syncopated language of *Cleaned Out* was followed with *A Man's Place* and afterwards by a "flat" tone and an economical style. Annie Ernaux strives to write in the least circuitous way, favoring descriptions (comments on photographs, background settings, enumerations), and rejects the contrivance of passé simple. From 1984, she also breaks with the derisive tone of her first novels and strains to rid her writing of any signs of elitist cultural connivance. While she refuses to "elevate" her testimony, she succeeds with her exactitude and will to reveal. When she sounds disturbing, shocking, or moving, it is because she has managed to express the untold and to make the written word an instrument of social and sexual transgression.

Annie Ernaux wishes to make her works explicit and her method clear; hence, the presence of metadiscourse in her works and her willingness to grant interviews to critics and journalists. When asked about influential figures, she quotes in turn Sartre, Breton, Proust, Perec, Bourdieu, and **Simone de Beauvoir**. Her mother's model and Beauvoir's writings have combined to create her deeply rooted and spirited **feminism**. She pays tribute to Bourdieu for having made her bold enough to talk about what she found shameful. It may be said that, with her works, she has given a whole generation of class defectors, products of public education, the right to explore the self and the intimate in writings that disclose social and collective dimensions.

In her works, we can find the traces of autobiography and diary. Among her autobiographical narratives, *A Man's Place, A Woman's Story, Shame*, and part of *Happening* are more auto/sociobiographical than strictly autobiographical. *Simple Passion* and *Occupation* are analyses of intimate passions in an impersonal mode. Her diaries are multiform. In addition to her diary proper (only a fragment of which has been published, *Se Perdre* 2001), she keeps a writing diary in which she discusses difficulties in composing her writing as well as occasional published diaries: *I Remain in Darkness* is a diary Ernaux kept during her mother's illness, and two "ethnotexts" are records of everyday life in a Parisian suburb (*Exteriors* in 1993 and *La Vie Extérieure* in 2000). In her works, personal experience meets historical experience, with no hint of miserabilism or populism, and style is a scalpel that lays reality bare.

Further Reading: Ernaux, Annie. *Happening*. Translated by Tanya Leslie (New York: Seven Stories Press, 2001); Ernaux, Annie. *A Man's Place* 1984. Translated by Tanya Leslie (New York: Four Walls Eight Windows, 1992); Ernaux, Annie. *Shame*. Translated by Tanya Leslie (New York: Seven Stories Press, 1998); Ernaux, Annie. *Simple Passion*. Translated by Tanya Leslie (New York: Four Walls Eight Windows, 1993); Ernaux, Annie. *A Woman's Story*. 1968. Translated by Tanya Leslie (New York: Four Walls Eight Windows, 1991); Thomas, Lyn. *Annie Ernaux. An Introduction to the Writer and Her Audience* (Oxford: Berg, 1999); Tondeur, Claire-Lise. *Annie Ernaux ou l'exil intérieur* (Amsterdam and Atlanta: Rodopi, 1997).

Françoise Simonet-Tenant

FEMINISM Complex, diverse, and increasingly theory based, feminism in the early twenty-first century has become a household word. However, recent feminist theorists, seeking to recognize its complexities, have pluralized the word and speak not of "feminism" as if it were a single unified idea, but of "feminisms." Because we want to emphasize the multiplicity of feminist thinking and action, we adopt this plural usage. Though feminism, in all its many manifestations, has been centered and still centers on issues of women and power, it is surely not a unitary movement. Politically, feminists range from the far left to the moderate right. Academically, feminisms range from the highly philosophical and finely pointed to the broad based and accessible, with the most complex available only to those who can understand the specialized vocabulary that confronts difficult ideas in difficult prose. Though feminisms have become more powerful as a result of academic rigor and brilliant scholarship, many feminists, both women and men, argue that feminism should be inclusive, pragmatic, and accessible. On the other hand, broadly accessible forms of feminism fall prey to omitting, oversimplifying, or collapsing trains of feminist thought as if they were not fraught with difference. In fact, the most successful and useful feminisms have cultivated a critical awareness of the various strands and conflicts among schools of thought while acknowledging the unifying urge to alleviate **gender** inequity, oppression, and power imbalance. The following provides a broad description of feminism before discussing the academic feminisms that bear on the field of women's autobiography. This brief history of feminism and the political spectrum help characterize feminist political points of view.

Three Waves: A Brief History

There are several ways to distinguish among feminisms. One is historical and generational, by distinguishing among first-wave, second-wave, and third-wave feminism. In North America, the first wave falls between the Seneca Falls, New York, Women's Rights Convention of 1848 and women winning the right to vote in the 1920s. It was a movement for equal rights with men. One of its primary documents is *The Declaration of Women's Rights*, modeled on the United States' *Declaration of Independence*. In the mid-eighteenth century first-wave feminism was very much linked to the antislavery movement. African Americans such as Frederick Douglass and **Sojourner Truth** (who gave her famous "ain't I A Woman" speech at the 1851 Women's Rights Convention in Akron,

Ohio) were key figures in this campaign, as were Susan B. Anthony, Lucy Stone, Lucretia Mott, and Elizabeth Cady Stanton, all European Americans. After the Civil War, however, black men received the right to vote, and there was an unfortunate split in the **women's movement** due to the entrenched segregation and white privilege of U.S. society. In the late nineteenth century, feminists of color and white feminists fought for their rights on separate fronts, the former focusing on both racism and sexism, the latter more exclusively on sexism. The African American leader **Ida B. Wells-Barnett** not only fought against lynching but also against cultural stereotypes defining black women as immoral and white women as pure. Black women, such as Josephine St. Pierre Ruffin, Mary Church Terrell, and Anna Julia Cooper, organized the black women's club movement, and, though they did not see themselves as feminists, they focused on the rights of black women and girls. White feminists organized for equality in areas such as the right to own property, to divorce, for birth control, and to vote. Similar struggles around equal rights characterized feminism in Europe during the same time period, though socialist, anarchist, and communist movements were stronger there as the legacy of women like Eleanor Marx, Alexandra Kollentai, **Emma Goldman**, and Clara Zetkin attests.

After the World War II, power shifts were evident all over the world. Struggles against European colonialism in Asia and Africa, the Civil Rights movement in the United States, and resistance to the war in Vietnam inspired women to recognize their own unique forms of oppression. The Women's Liberation Movement or second-wave feminism ensued. This "rebirth" of feminism added a new dimension to theories about women: "the personal is political." In consciousness-raising groups, women supported each other and examined every aspect of their lives for patterns of oppressive relations with men. An ex-plosion of feminist theory and political activity created scores of new publications and legal reforms. Title IX of the Educational Amendments of the United States (1972) provides an example of the sorts of reforms instituted against sex discrimination during this period. Outlawing different treatment in both academics and athletics, it read: "No person in the U.S. shall, on the basis of sex be excluded from participation in, or denied the benefits of, or be subjected to discrimination under any educational program or activity receiving federal aid." By the 1980s, however, the unity that had marked much of the early movement had splintered. The 1980s saw tremendous disagreement over theoretical principles. A period of creative tension deepened as many debated whether the movement was marred by white privilege and heterosexual privilege. During this time black feminism became powerful and feminists became more attuned to the differences among women's experiences.

In the 1990s third-wave feminism emerged. Assuring doubters that feminism was not dead, this movement's leaders are primarily young women who resist what they see as rigid and limiting visions of liberation promulgated by their "mothers." Third wavers want equal rights, but they want to reclaim feminine **sexuality** and behavior in rebellious ways. These young women fight for self-empowerment, and they assert themselves as sexual beings, dressing and acting as they want to in an assertion of joyful energy and power. They often focus on cultural and personal issues and have been inspired by Madonna, movies like *Buffy the Vampire Slayer*, Kathleen Hanna (feminist "thrillseeker"), activist groups like Riot Grrrl, and books like Elizabeth Wurtzel's *Bitch*. Though not always defining themselves as feminists, their mottos are "Girls Rule!" and "Grrrl Power!" They champion diversity and also organize around issues in the workplace, especially sweatshops, violence against women, reproductive freedom, queer—gay, lesbian, bisexual, or transgendered—**identity**, welfare rights, and so forth.

A Political Spectrum of Feminisms

Feminist theories can also be differentiated politically by placing them along the spectrum of right (conservative), center (liberal), and left (anticapitalist). In the heady days of second-wave feminism, a successful feminist theory was expected to accomplish the following: accurately describe women's lives, explain the sources of women's oppression, and provide a concrete strategy for improving women's status. Currently, given the postmodern critique of grand "master" theories and the tendency to privilege one perspective over another, expectations are not so high.

Also, the influence of multiculturalism and postcolonial studies has been immense. Feminists now recognize the superficiality of claiming "all women are sisters, regardless of race or class." Intersectionality analysis is crucial; feminists try to illuminate the matrices of cultural, political, physical, and economic influences that construct women's experience. Feminist theory has become more descriptive and local. Nevertheless, many still pursue the agenda of theory building, and it is possible to use a standard account of abstract political theory to make distinctions among feminisms.

In the history of philosophy, classical liberalism (called conservatism by the eighteenth century) was the theory of social change in modern Europe. In the transition from feudalism to industrial society, the middle class took power from the landed aristocracy and the nobility, proclaiming that all "men" are created equal. Liberty could be achieved through a free market and the opportunity to own property. Government authority was acceptable only if ruled by laws guaranteeing the rights of the individual. By the nineteenth century, however, it became obvious that great disparities in wealth and opportunity could accompany a system built on private property. Contemporary liberalism (simply called liberalism today) and socialism emerged as alternative political perspectives. On the one hand, contemporary liberals are procapitalist but seek to humanize it through state intervention. Welfare programs, affirmative action, and policy changes in schools, the government, and corporations can make reforms deep enough to provide equality among classes, races, and sexes. Socialists, on the other hand, see those sorts of changes as superficial: the root cause of inequality is capitalism, which must be abolished through revolution. The current dominance of global neoliberalism (the push for a "free" market and cutbacks in government services) is a backlash against welfare state liberalism, socialism, and national liberation movements.

Transposing these standard distinctions onto feminism, one can identify several political forms of feminist theory. Straightforward conservatives, however, cannot be realistically considered feminists. Though they might provide lip service to the idea of equal rights for women, their tendency to see woman's place in society as conditioned by her biology limits their vision as to the possibility of significant changes in what women do. Therefore, in the following, we will distinguish among feminisms of the liberal, "radical," or socialist variety.

At the right side of the feminist spectrum, moderate liberal feminists can be described as those who seek minimal changes to society to enable women to become equal to men. In this view, sexism is seen at an individual level and is primarily due to outdated traditions and bad attitudes. Thus, someone may not hire a woman because of prejudice or ignorance. Discrimination is seen as primarily an individual phenomenon, and it is not that widespread. Society is gradually improving, which is all we can expect. It is interesting to note that even among moderate thinkers, prejudice and stereotypes against women are frowned on. The tremendous success of the women's movement has made many feminist assumptions mainstream, particularly in the mass media.

Feminists on the center and left sides of the spectrum have been more outspoken in their critiques of sexism. They agree on several things: discrimination against women goes beyond prejudice; it is ubiquitous and deep; it is found in both personal and public forms; and it is rooted in institutional policies. Liberal feminists, as their philosophical heritage suggests, believe women should be free to make their own choices in private life. The right to abortion, for example, is defended by the idea that laws should not prevent women from choosing whether to have a baby. Liberals argue for a distinction between sex and gender; the former refers to genetic, biological being and the latter to social norms of masculinity and femininity. They do not believe that biological difference should influence women's status, but they are divided as to whether laws should eliminate any differential treatment of men and women or provide special treatment and services for women because of their procreative and family roles.

Moreover, since liberal feminism seeks to correct classical modern philosophy, it seeks to eliminate the economic and social disparities of capitalism. *All* humans must be treated equally and protected by laws. Liberal feminists see discrimination against women as the result of cultural norms and routine institutional practices or policies. Women are socialized by their families and in schools to expect less of themselves; they are steered into sex-typed, less influential, and less well-paid careers than men; they are not given the same opportunities. Affirmative action is a paradigmatic example of a liberal feminist reform.

Radical feminism, emerging in the late 1960s, has been one of the most influential forms of feminism. Radicals see liberal orientations as entirely inadequate. They push for revolutionary change and want to get to the *roots* of women's oppression. **Patriarchy**, the most basic form of all oppression, is a system of male dominance that has existed from the beginning of human history. Rad-

ical feminists have been stereotyped as "man-haters" because of their emphasis on uprooting male power, but that characterization is unfair. They embody a no-nonsense approach to detecting sexism in all its forms and are more aptly seen as militantly *pro-woman*.

Radical feminists typically stress the importance of the body and sexuality, theorizing that "women are made, not born" (Monique Wittig). They refuse to accept the distinction between private and public spheres of life on which liberals rely. Oppression is personal; it exists even in the minute details of everyday chores (Marilyn Frye). And male privilege is all the more powerful because men control the female body, procreation, and sexuality. Some radical feminists became lesbian separatists and extended their theoretical analysis to forms of socially compulsory heterosexuality. Radical feminists' analysis of gender, sex, and the body has stimulated a great many debates and theoretical advances. Postmodern radical feminists have argued that there are a multiplicity of genders and that sex too may be socially constructed.

During the 1970s, socialist feminism became popular among those who felt that both liberal individualism and radical feminism were unsatisfactory. The former could not grasp the collective nature of gender oppression, and the latter lumped all men together as the enemy and failed to theorize how significantly **class** structured women's experience. Marxism, though revolutionary, seemed insufficient as well. This stance was due to an economic determinist interpretation of Marx, which led people to assume that his method made gender invisible due to its sole focus on public production and class. By the early twenty-first century, anti-Marxist forms of socialist feminism declined, and socialist feminists have typically adopted a more sympathetic reading of Marx for at least two reasons: first, because of his insights into how the accumulation of capital creeps into every interstice of our lives, even the most intimate ones; and second, because of his emphasis on how capitalist competition for profit draws all the world's people into its incessant drive for wealth. Socialist feminists are particularly concerned to produce clear accounts of how the multiple aspects of women's lives intersect. Though they do not agree on one form of theoretical explanation, "all socialist-feminists see class as central to women's lives, yet at the same time none would reduce sex or race oppression to economic exploitation. And all of us see these aspects of our lives as inseparably and systematically related; in other words, class is always gendered and raced" (Holmstrom 2).

Academic Feminisms and Women's Autobiography

In a complementary way, both feminist theory and scholarship in women's autobiography have posed rich and sometimes contentious readings of key concepts: the self, the subject, experience, agency, and truth. Conflicts have arisen around the question of what it means to be a woman. Feminists have argued about whether definitions of women according to particular gender traits and roles are useful and empowering or oppressive. Those who work in the field of women's autobiography are interested in these questions because most of women's life writing features a specifically gendered narrator, a character who speaks of herself, taking herself as her subject. Her self-definition, however she chooses to frame it, is central to her autobiographical project. Whether she embraces the gender conventions that have historically marked individuals as women or whether she subverts, resists, or refuses those social conventions is an important matter for the autobiographer. The woman autobiographer and the feminist theorist share the central concern about how to define and describe gender.

Some feminists argue that feminisms' strengths lie in the very attributes marked as feminine, including such traits as cooperation and caring, characteristics that are taken to be predetermined, biologically hardwired, or sociologically and psychologically inevitable for women. Others argue, however, that these conventional descriptors of the feminine are problematic because they essentialize women, describing them forever in the same ways, inscribing them as they have always been, leaving no room for difference, besides the conventional differences that mark women as diametrically opposed to men. In fact, one of the most important debates among feminist theorists centers around women's identities and essentialism. Those thinkers who critique essentialized versions of women argue that the female subject (also known in the humanist tradition as the *self*) is constructed through social forces that mold the individual. Postmodern feminisms have been particularly articulate in this critique, appropriating current theories of power and discourse to make their arguments.

On the other hand, some feminisms protest this antiessentialist view because it destabilizes identity and throws concepts of self and experience into question. Postcolonial feminisms, for example, concentrate on racialized identity and the shared struggles of women of color. Some of these feminists have argued that the unstable postmodern subject is a liability. Theorizing the *self* as a malleable *subject* that exists only as a product of discursive social forces undermines efforts to identify oppression based on the shared experience of oppressed individuals. Postmodern theories, which posit destabilized subjects—fluid, fragmented, and fictional—as the model of the individual, erase the possibility of naming the self as a material, historically consistent entity who can know and articulate herself and can claim "authenticity" and "speak her truth." In contrast, postcolonial feminisms have a stake in the connection of particular identities with particular traits and experiences—traits such as racialized skin color, experiences such as racial discrimination. Postcolonial feminisms emphasize the importance of speaking out about the common experiences of oppression in order to find common cause with others and to act. These feminists find antiessentialist theory suspect. Is identity discursive and determined by social forces as postmodern theorists argue? Or is it firmly anchored in essential attributes of gender, race, class, and other such impositions? For the feminist theorist and the scholar of women's autobiography, this conflict exemplifies important differences in thinking about women.

Conflicts among feminisms have both enriched and troubled those who work on issues of gender and power, including those who work in the field of women's autobiography. Especially as autobiography concentrates on the lived experience of a gendered subject, it is a genre that has testified to the many ways that women have understood what it means to be a woman and how the power of gender has shaped their lives. Various feminisms have provided powerful tools for thinking about gendered *selves*—the political, social, and cultural makeup of the woman subject—and for articulating these *selves* in ways that allow readers to see deeply into gendered identities. While feminisms interrogate gender and sex, autobiography interrogates the individual woman as a character of her own meditation on a *self*. However, feminisms differ and explain the self-narrative of autobiography differently. For instance, with the advent of postmodern feminist theory, women's life writing has been coupled with and illuminated by the social construction of the subject. This feminism raises questions about how aspects of the *self* are created by forces of social and cultural history and how the *self* is formed by the contexts that it occupies and the histories that occupy it. These recent theories offer a critique of the seamless life narrative built on a truth claim, a linear representation of life, and a unified version of *self*.

In terms of women's autobiography, academic feminisms offer diverse theories of the self or subject and of experience, concepts crucial to the study of autobiography. Recent feminist scholars, especially those in philosophy and literary studies, have consciously asked theoretically loaded questions about the nature of women's identities, questions that are critical to women's autobiography. Who are the subjects of feminism—the essentialized woman, the psychoanalytic feminine, the socially constructed, gendered subject? Can essentialized versions of women be useful politically? If so, how? How do identity, agency, experience, language, and culture weigh in as relative influences for feminisms and the narrative of women subjects? What influence have feminisms had on identifiable and increasingly powerful versions of the self/subject? And what influence has the rich and contentious thought and debate among feminists had on writers of women's autobiography? A short list of current, prominent feminist theories will illustrate the multiple perspectives among feminisms and will show the arguments that distinguish them. These distinctions bear on the way women think and write about themselves.

Liberal feminist theory is rooted in the tradition of liberal humanism, with its emphasis on the individual unified "self" and on universal human experience. Human agency is a distinct possibility within this frame, and political change is wrought through changes in individuals. A women's expression of her personal experience and the consciousness-raising that accompanies it are defining characteristics of this theory with its slogan "the personal is the political." This theory has had much influence and has inspired autobiographical writing. Women have come to value their experience and to write it. Since liberal feminism focuses on women's inclusion in areas dominated by men, the life writing of women succeeding in a man's world exemplify this view. Its democratic ideal is evident in autobiographies in which strong women assert themselves and gain the power and respect of their male contemporaries. Many women's autobiographies fall into this category, including **Isak Dinesen**'s *Out of Africa*, and **Beryl Markham**'s *Westward into the Night*.

The academic activities of liberal feminists include examining how women have been excluded and how to rectify that exclusion. For instance, in literary studies, liberal feminists unearth lost women's texts and work to incorporate them into mainstream publication, thereby affecting canon formation. They also strive to recuperate strong women figures and to trace images of women in texts by women and men, seeking to elucidate the roles of women and to interpret women as important characters and cultural actors. Collections of diaries, **letters**, and other nontraditional autobiographical texts have been unearthed and popularized through the efforts of these academic feminists.

Liberal feminist theory, with its emphasis on equity and inclusion, appeals to many women. It also has gained popularity because it focuses on the importance of the individual *self* coming to **voice**. Though it tends not to make problematic forces of culture and language, it does encourage the celebration of women's voices and the valuing of women's expressions. Perhaps the most accessible and nonconflictual forms of feminism, it posits that changes within the individual go hand in hand with political change; finding the genuine *self* results in coming to terms with a world in which men have more power than women and doing something about this state of affairs in one's own life. Women may become individual agents of social change, making the world a more hospitable place for all people.

In contrast to liberal feminism's desire to integrate, cultural feminism seeks to separate men from women on the levels of identity, language, and culture. This feminism defines an essential set of differences between man and woman, critiques the patriarchal history of devaluing the woman's side, and revalues her identity. A few of the binary elements often cited include: feminine/masculine, collaborative/competitive, connection/individuation, private/public, inclusive/exclusive, relational patterns/linear patterns, nurture/combat, body/mind. As cultural feminism valorizes the left side of the binaries and critiques the right, it offers utopian visions of a future culture based on woman's identity and capable of "revisioning" the patriarchy. **Adrienne Rich**'s work, particularly her autobiographical essays and her book, *Of Woman Born*, provide key examples of cultural feminism. This feminist orientation often relies on the ethical and critical perspectives of outsider women as theorists, those who are capable of re-visionary insights unavailable to insiders. This outsider status is evident in cultural feminism's experimental language practices, which link these theorists to French, postmodern, and postcolonial feminisms.

Cultural feminist theory asserts that the feminine should be the basis for activism because the values that women embody are superior to the manly values of the patriarchy. This feminism has tied the feminine to specific practices that seem to grow out of women's innate and/or culturally assigned characteristics. In this way, cultural feminism has imported the binary oppositions that are its hallmark.

Both liberal and cultural feminist theories have had a major influence on academic feminist thinking and action. These two theories share an ideology based on individualism, subordinating language and culture to the higher power of the *self*, who is largely free to choose and direct her actions and to access her "authenticity" through her personal experience and her unique self-expression. In terms of autobiography, this focus on the individual has had productive results: it has prompted women to value self-expression; it has encouraged feminists to reclaim devalued forms, such as letters and diaries, and to argue that these literary genres should be taken seriously; and it has inspired women to think of their experience as valuable and worthy of recording. These conceptions contrast to the next three categories of feminism, all of which share a tendency to regard language and culture as inextricable and as powerful determiners of identity and agency.

French feminist theory offers a radical alternative to liberal feminism, especially in the arena of discourse. This theory argues that the female body can interrupt, disrupt, and redirect conventional, patriarchal perspectives that dominate our thinking. Psychoanalytic thought provides the foundation for this brand of feminism. Stylistically, French feminism makes a case for experimental writing based on the female body as a means to disrupt patriarchal discourse.

French feminism rereads psychoanalytic theory in order to appropriate the body as a linguistic and stylistic locale for revolutionary practice. The female body has its own (non)language, outside of the phallogocentric system of language that shapes and controls identity. Woman can gain revolutionary agency by disrupting the phallic law encoded in language. The difference between the strategic stylistic practices of the cultural feminists and those of the French—called *ecriture feminine*—is the specifically psychoanalytic point of view of the French, who adopt and revise the Lacanian idea that language (the *symbolic*) shapes identity and culture at the psyche's foundation. Hélène Cixous' and Luce Irigaray's "writing the body" and Julia Kristeva's semiotic disruptions of language exemplify French feminism's practices: language experiments that place the speaking woman subject at the center of the writing. This writing opens up possibilities for a different kind of autobiography—one that tests the boundaries of self and that "steals" and twists conventional expectations. The voice of this subject resists the unitary notion of the *self* and offers models of poetic, irreverent expression. French feminism especially, has argued for the value of nonlinear forms of narrative and narrative in which a nonunified voice

prevails. The power of French feminism's theories and examples helps explain and expand the field of women's autobiography.

Postcolonial feminist theory foregrounds cultural diversity and complicates the idea of difference; it insists on the multiple analysis of cultural forces shaping identity. Categories of subject formation, such as race, class, gender, sexual orientation, and so on, form the basis for this analysis, which is ideologically aware and calls for activism within a multicultural politics. During the second wave particularly, postcolonial feminist theorists rightly criticized white feminists for their exclusionary, racist attitudes toward women of color, especially those white feminists who reduce diverse women to an essentialized "Woman"—assumed to be white, heterosexual, and middle-class. **Alice Walker**'s *womanist* criticism, Gayatri Chakravorty Spivak's treatment of the concept of "the Subaltern," and **bell hooks**' revolutionary theory and practice exemplify this feminism's complexity.

For postcolonial feminism, autobiography has been especially important because of the power of personal testimony. As women write about the oppressive conditions they face as women of the underclass and women of color, they lay the groundwork for oppression's recognition and for social action. In the United States, figures such as **Audre Lorde**, bell hooks, **Leslie Marmon Silko**, and **Maya Angelou** serve as writing exemplars of postcolonial autobiographies. But the global nature of this feminism brings in autobiographers from all over the world.

Postmodern feminist theory shares some important common ground with postcolonial feminist theory. Both are engaged in the analysis of the subject at the defining intersection of identity and culture. At this intersection, histories and economies of race, class, gender, sexual preference, and other determining forces socially construct the subject. The individual voice of autobiography is important here. Through these acts of self-representation, women seek to map out an identity and to testify to individual agency, diminished as it may be. These autobiographical acts provide crucial clues about how women might negotiate language and culture to alleviate the damage of oppressive molds of contemporary identity. Because postcolonial feminisms have taught us not to set up representative figures who "speak for" whole constituencies, women autobiographers are careful to speak for themselves. However, constituencies develop around such speaking: autobiographical expression has the potential to demonstrate in vivid detail how occupying a particular subject position feels to an individual. For instance, Audre Lorde in *Zami: A New Spelling of My Name* maps the myriad forces that shape an image of being Other: a figure who is either exotic because she is different or erased because she does not fit white, Eurocentric, heterosexual "universals." These autobiographies radically call into question the conventional notion of "woman" and trouble its designations. As the postmodern/postcolonial subject performs autobiographically, she replaces the unified, humanist self with an identity that demonstrates intersections of social designations and rehearsals of forced scripts.

All feminisms emphasize cultural critique and the concepts of agency and identity. Recently, feminisms have highlighted the centrality of language as a site of struggle. These feminisms have opened the narrative possibilities for feminist writers with their critiques of the hegemony. In the academic arena, for instance, Linda Nicholson, in her introduction to *Feminism/Postmodernism* (1990), describes conventional academic voice as an oppressive omniscience, very different from the particularity of identity groups seeking to describe their own struggles and points of view. Postmodern theorists such as Judith Butler analyze and critique this masculineist perspective and its genres, forms that delimit the world and employ a unitary neutrality, which pretends to be universal but in fact speaks for already ensconced power.

For women's autobiography, feminisms have helped explain the experiences of women, their sense of who they are, what limits them, and what is possible for them. Feminist theory has defined and explained categories of identity, the center of the autobiographical genre. Among feminists, debates will continue about the nature of identity, agency, experience, and power. And these theoretical conflicts among feminisms will continue to be productive for the understanding of women's autobiography. *See also* **African Women's Autobiography**; **Australian Women's Autobiography**; **Diary**.

Further Reading: Butler, Judith. *Bodies That Matter* (New York: Routledge, 1993); Fuss, Diana. *Essentially Speaking* (New York: Routledge, 1989); Gilmore, Leigh. *Autobiographics: A Feminist Theory of Women's Self-Representation* (Ithaca, NY: Cornell University Press, 1994); Holmstrom, Nancy. *The Socialist Feminist Project: A Contemporary Reader in Theory and Politics* (New York: Monthly Review Press, 2002); hooks, bell. *Talking Back* (Boston: South End Press, 1989); Mohanty, Chandra T. *Feminism Without Borders: Decolonizing Theory, Practicing Solidarity* (Durham: Duke University Press, 2003); Nicholson, Linda, ed. *Feminism/Postmod-ernism* (New York: Routledge, 1990); Nicholson, Linda, ed. *The Second Wave: A Reader in Feminist Theories* (New York: Routledge, 1997); Riley, Denise. *Am I That Name? Feminism and the Category of "Women" in History* (Minneapolis: University of Minneapolis Press, 1988); Smith, Sidonie, and Julia Watson, eds. *Women, Autobiography, Theory: A Reader* (Madison: University of Wisconsin Press, 1998); Warhol, Robyn, and Diane Price, eds. *Feminisms: An Anthology of Literary Theory and Criticism.* 2nd ed. (Rutgers University Press, 1997).

Victoria Boynton and Kathryn Russell

FISHER, M.F.K. (MARY FRANCES KENNEDY) (1908–1992) M.F.K. Fisher inaugurated a literary style that so smoothly blends autobiography with discussions of the planting, harvesting, cooking, and eating of food that the stuff of life becomes the essence of life. Thus, it is impossible to single out one book as Fisher's significant or quintessential autobiography: her books are inextricable fusions of the life and the food that sustains it. She explains, in her foreword to *The Gastronomical Me* (1943), that she has chosen her subject because "Our three basic needs, for food and security and love, are so . . . entwined. . . . [When] there is food in the bowl . . . there is nourishment in the heart, to feed the wilder, more insistent hungers" (353). Most of her works, such as *The Gastronomical Me, Among Friends* (1971), and *Sister Age* (1983), are compilations of previously published essays, her characteristic literary genre.

Fisher's writing—elegant and eloquently understated—captures the essence of a lifetime, a universe of the rare, best hours of life, bursting like meteors to illuminate the rest of the cosmos, difficult and dark. Although her own life was full of joy, disappointment, early sorrows, and later delights, it is these precious hours that prevail in her writing. For Fisher, one paradigmatic moment involves peas. In *With Bold Knife and Fork* (1968), which has more recipes than many of her writings, she writes of peas: "The best way to eat fresh ones is to be alive on the right day, with the men picking and the women shelling, and everybody capering in the sweet early summer weather, and the big pot of water boiling, and the table set with little cool roasted chickens and pitchers of white wine" (189). In fact, she has unpacked this perfect picnic twice before, in *The Gastronomical Me* and *An Alphabet for Gourmets* (1949), where we learn that with her on their small farm in Vevey, France, in June 1938 are her parents, several friends, and Dillwyn Parrish, whom she would marry in 1940: "There sat most of the people in the world I loved, in a thin light that was pink with Alpen glow, blue with a veil of pine smoke from the hearth. . . . [A] cow . . . moved her head among the meadow flowers and shook her bell in a slow, melodious rhythm, a kind of hymn. My father lifted up his face at the sound and, his fists all stained with green-

pea juice, said passionately, 'God, but I feel good!' I felt near to tears" (666).

Fisher, the daughter of a fourth-generation newspaper reporter and editor, was born in Albion, Michigan, on July 3, 1908. Three years later, the family moved to Whittier, California, where she grew up amidst a family whom she considered "all-beautiful" (*Among Friends* 1990, 56). "I still feel embarrassed," she wrote, "that I was not born a native Californian because I truly think I am one. I really started to be me somewhere there. . . . And I do feel 'native'" (*Welcoming Life* 6). Throughout her life she lived either in California or in France, and from 1971 until her death in 1992 on the Glen Ellen Ranch in Sonoma Valley. There she befriended and influenced a parade of cooks and cookbook authors, including Alice Waters, James Beard, Julia and Paul Child, Betty Fussell, and Michael Field, her collaborator on *The Cooking of Provincial France*.

She was educated at Illinois College, Occidental College, UCLA, the University of Dijon, and in many kitchens and open hearths. Her first marriage, to Al Fisher, with whom she spent three years in Dijon while he earned his doctorate in English, was an awakening: "It was there," wrote Fisher, "that I started to grow up, to study, to make love, to eat and drink, to be me and not what I was expected to be" (*Welcoming* 1997). On their return to California, where Al began teaching at Occidental College, Mary Frances began studying old cookbooks and writing short essays, a form in which she soon excelled. She showed them to Dillwyn ("Tim") Parrish, a painter (and relative of Maxfield Parrish)—"a man destined to draw out anything creative in other people" who became the love of her life. During an attempted ménage à trois in Vevey, Tim and Mary Frances drew closer together; the Fisher marriage broke up in 1937 (though the divorce was not final until 1939), and her writing career—enhanced by her fresh California beauty—began in earnest. The brief, bright hours her writing captures so well—"I eat, sleep, listen, even cook and read with an intensity and a fullness that I have never felt until now"— punctuated the darkness of Mary Frances' and Tim's life together. Parrish developed Buerger's disease, a fatal, excruciatingly painful circulatory illness (now known to be a consequence of heavy smoking), which required the amputation of his leg. He committed suicide in 1941.

Two years later, Fisher bore a daughter, Anna, but never identified the father. Her second daughter, Kennedy, was born in 1946 when she was in a brief (1946–1951), distressing marriage to editor Donald Friede, during which time she burned twenty-five years' worth of notes and journals, to her everlasting regret. Then she rebuilt her life from the ashes, lived as a devoted mother, ardent friend, and lover. She solidified the literary reputation that had begun in the 1940s with the publication of *Consider the Oyster* (1941), followed by *How to Cook a Wolf* (1942), then a well-received translation of Brillat-Savarin's *The Physiology of Taste* (1949), and frequent articles in *The New Yorker*. Throughout three succeeding decades her devotion to culinary literature never waned, reinforcing her unsentimental but ardent commitment to feed deep human "needs for love and happiness" (*The Gastronomical Me* 353). This communion pervades the distinguished writing of her passionate life.

Further Reading: Ferratry, Jeannette. *Between Friends: M.F.K. Fisher and Me* (New York: Atlantic Monthly Press, 1991); Fisher, M.F.K. *M.F.K. Fisher: A Life in Letters, Correspondence 1929–1991.* Selected and compiled by Norah K. Barr, Marsha Moran, and Patrick Moran (Washington, DC: Counterpoint, 1997); Gioia, Dominique. Compiled and annotated *A Welcoming Life: The M.F.K. Fisher Scrapbook* (Washington, DC: Counterpoint, 1997); Lazar, David, ed. *Conversations with M.F.K. Fisher* (Jackson: University Press of Mississippi, 1992); Reardon, Joan. *M.F.K. Fisher, Julia Child, and Alice Waters: Celebrating the Plea-sures of the Table* (New York: Harmony/Crown, 1994).

Lynn Z. Bloom

FOOTE, JULIA A. J. (1823–1901) A noted evangelist and the first woman to be ordained a deacon by the African Methodist Episcopal (AME) Zion Church, Julia Foote wrote her autobiography "A Brand Plucked from the Fire" in 1879. Focusing on her conversion, faith, and initial struggles to preach, the narrative is seeped in the rhetoric of the Holiness revivals of the 1870s and walks a fine line between ultraconservative Christianity and, for the times, a radical form of nascent **feminism**.

Foote's autobiography opens with her birth, in 1823, to parents who were former slaves, in Schenectady, New York. Raised within the African Methodist Episcopal Zion tradition, Foote was sent in childhood to live and work for an influential white family, the Primes, but returned to live with her family at age twelve because she was needed as a caretaker for her younger siblings and due to her uneven relationship with the Primes. Though several critics have described her parents simply as fervent Christians, Foote actually shows a more conflicted picture, censuring them especially for intemperance. Nonetheless, she credits her mother as a central figure in turning her away from the temptations of adolescence (she speaks of both the theater and dancing). Foote joined the church in 1838, and gradually grew convinced that she should testify and perhaps even preach about her sanctification. Though she could not yet bring herself to challenge nineteenth-century norms, her fervor distanced her from her parents.

She married George Foote, a sailor, in 1841, and moved to Boston with him. The marriage seems to have been rocky, though, because her husband lacked her level of religious commitment. She says little of him in her narrative, though she notes his death around 1848.

The height of her struggle with the dominant antebellum sense of women and preaching came soon after her marriage, when she defied her pastor, the Reverend Jehiel Beman (who was a member of the prominent family of ministers and black activists), and, in a move that echoes Anne Hutchinson, began testifying and holding meetings of church members in a variety of settings. Beman censured her for preaching in her home and engineered her excommunication from his church.

If anything, her fight with Beman, coupled with a stay in Philadelphia (during which she and other women preached), and a visit to her family (now living in Binghamton, New York), convinced Foote that she needed to devote her life to preaching—ironically, still within the framework of the AME Zion church. In 1845, she embarked on her first tour of New York state, visiting Owego, Onondaga, Ithaca, Geneva, Rochester, and Binghamton; she then returned to Philadelphia before attending the General Conference of the AME Zion Church in Pittsburgh. The rest of the decade saw more preaching in New York, Pennsylvania, Ohio, and probably Massachusetts. During this period, she made a powerful friend and ally in Daniel A. Paine of Baltimore, who would later rise to the rank of bishop. This connection, in addition to her growing relationships with other black church leaders, and a friendship with Thomas Doty (who ran the *Christian Harvester* and later, somewhat patronizingly, introduced Foote's narrative) secured a place for her, albeit somewhat marginal, in church activities, and she spent much of the 1850s and 1860s in the Cleveland area. The Holiness movement that swept the Midwest in the late 1860s and 1870s saw her return to active preaching. Deeply tied to these events, her narrative was initially published in 1879 and then reissued in 1886.

All scholarly accounts published to date claim that nothing is known about Foote's activities during the 1880s and 1890s—other than that she was ordained a deacon in 1894 and did missionary work. The autobiography of Alexander Walters, a bishop in the AME Zion Church, though, fills in this gap in Foote's **biography**. Walters notes that when he was called to San Francisco in 1883—work that also involved trips to Portland, San Jose, and Los Angeles—Foote was already well established on the West Coast and "rendered me valuable services" (1893, 46). Foote and Walters formed a tight bond, and Walters notes that "from 1884 until the year she died, 1901, she made my house her home" and that his family was "greatly indebted to this godly woman for her gracious influence" (46). Walters' "home" shifted to Tennessee in 1886, and in 1888, to New York City, where Foote aided him in a massive revival at the beginning of 1889. Walters was elected bishop in 1892, and his power in the church undoubtedly aided in Foote's ordination as a deacon and later, in 1900, as an elder. Based on her earlier practice, it is safe to assume that much of these final two decades of her life was spent preaching.

Arguably, her contributions in the AME Zion Church's history are even more important than her narrative, though church histories all but ignore her. Still, in recent years, Foote's autobiography has been recognized as a key text among nineteenth-century African American women's spiritual autobiographies—one which, in the words of Joycelyn Moody, "transforms defiant verbality into a matrifocal theology that teaches how to honor the sacred through sass" (2001, 128). Critics have noted several similarities between Foote's narrative and that of earlier African American women preachers—Jarena Lee, Maria Stewart, **Zilpha Elaw**, and so forth—but her text is just as much a product of the revivals of the 1870s. She clearly saw the narrative as an extension of her testimony, and thus, as Moody notes, Foote's "autobiography becomes increasingly less chronological and more directive and didactic as it progresses" (151).

Further Reading: Foote, Julia. "A Brand Plucked from the Fire." In *Spiritual Narratives*, edited by Susan Houchins (New York: Oxford University Press, 1988), online from the New York Public Library, Digital Schomburg at: http://www.digilib.nypl.org:80/dynaweb/digs-t/wwm978/@Generic_BookView; Grammar, Elizabeth Elkin. *Some Wild Visions: Autobiographies by Female Itinerant Evangelists in Nineteenth-Century America* (New York: Oxford University Press, 2003); Hine, Darlene Clark, ed. *Black Women in America* (Bloomington: Indiana University Press, 1993); Moody, Joycelyn. *Sentimental Confessions: Spiritual Narratives of Nineteenth-Century African American Women* (Athens: University of Georgia Press, 2001).

Eric Gardner

FRAME, JANET PATERSON [CLUTHA] (1924–2004)

If some phenomena in the Southern Hemisphere are inverted from those in the Northern Hemisphere, then an appropriate term for New Zealand author Janet Frame's writing might be "bioautography." Throughout her writing, and especially in her autobiographical work, it is not easy to differentiate between the self and others, past and present, fact and myth. Frame wrote not only of her own self, but autographed life in all its diversity. Biographer Michael King remarks in *Wrestling with the Angel: A Life of Janet Frame*, "Talking *and* writing, she conveyed a vivid sense that reality is itself a fiction, and one's grasp of it no more than preposterous pretense and pretension" (2000, 518).

Janet Paterson Frame was born to George Samuel Frame and Lottie Clarice Godfrey on August 28, 1924. She was born bereaved; her twin did not develop fully in the womb. The Frames had five living children in all; Janet was the third. Her siblings were oldest sister Myrtle, older brother George (Geordie), and younger sisters Isabel and June.

Frame's *To the Is-Land* (1982) the first volume of her autobiography, describes a childhood and adolescence marked by transience and upheaval. Her father's job as a railway worker meant that the Frame family moved frequently. Even when the family was granted some stability by a transfer to Oamaru in 1931—where they would live for thirteen years—the Frames remained unsettled financially and socially. Frame's reflections in *To the Is-Land* integrate competing perceptions: the adventures, pleasures, and confidences of childhood are woven with memories of ridicule at school, lost friendships, and shunning by neighbors who were appalled by the family's living conditions and "uncivilized" nature. As Frame gets older, the feeling of not quite "fitting" in grows stronger too.

Further upheavals within the family occurred when Geordie was diagnosed with epilepsy; the death by drowning of Myrtle in 1936, followed a decade later in 1947 by Isabel's death from drowning, too (which figures in her second volume, *An Angel at My Table* 1984). One constant, however, was Frame's love of language and literature, nurtured by her mother. She cites as early influences the Brothers Grimm, Shakespeare, Whitman, and Coleridge. Frame's writing in *To the Is-Land* marks her growing, maturing intellect and imagination. She excelled in academics, and received encouragement from those who recognized her talent.

For Frame, however, there seemed to be an inverse relationship between the expansion of her intellect and the alienation she felt toward others. This was unwittingly endorsed by teachers and mentors who praised her "originality," a judgment that would weigh heavily on her all her life. Frame writes, "I came to accept the difference, although in our world of school, to be different was to be peculiar, a little 'mad'" (*An Autobiography* 1991, 109). In retrospect, this judgment foreshadows Frame's most profound period of upheaval: a slow unraveling that led to the (mis)diagnosis of schizophrenia after a suicide attempt in 1945. At the time she was in Dunedin, taking classes at the university and working toward a career in teaching. That career was abandoned abruptly, however, when she walked out of the classroom on the day she was to have her teaching observation.

From 1945 to 1959, Frame was in and out of mental hospitals, for varying lengths of time. However, she also had early literary achievements, as well as periods of growth and travel. *An Angel at My Table*, the second volume, reflects the shifts of these years: 200 electroconvulsive therapy (ECT) "treatments"; insulin-shock therapy; the threat of prefrontal leucotomy (lobotomy); the death of her sister Isabel; publication of her first book, *The Lagoon and Other Stories* (1951) and the writing of her second book, *Owls Do Cry* (1957); the death of her mother; opportunity to travel abroad. In 1957, while in living in London (written about in Part II of *The Envoy from Mirror City*, the autobiography's third volume), Frame received a shock of a different sort: a doctor's verdict that she never suffered from schizophrenia. This announcement was jarring and Frame's ambivalence was profound: she "had longed to be rid of the opinion [diagnosis of illness] but was unwilling to part with it" (*An Autobiography* 375).

During the next three decades, Frame (she changed her name legally in 1958 to Nene Janet Paterson Clutha) came to be known as "New Zealand's most distinguished writer," and a remarkably productive one: In all, eleven novels, four collections of short stories, one book of poetry, a children's book, several articles, and her three-volume autobiography. She was annoyed when readers mistook her fiction for autobiography. Her autobiography was fictionalized, however, in Jane Campion's 1989 film *An Angel at My Table*, which in turn exposed Frame's writing to a larger audience, especially in the United States.

Janet Clutha died of leukemia on January 29, 2004. Janet Frame, envoy through fiction and autobiography, remains.

Further Reading: Ash, Susan. "'The Absolute, Distanced Image': Janet Frame's Autobiography." *Journal of New Zealand Literature* 11 (1993): 21–40; Blowers, Tonya. "To the Is-Land:

Self and Place in Autobiography." *Australian-Canadian Studies: A Journal for the Humanities & Social Sciences* 18, no. 1–2 (2000): 51–64; Blowers, Tonya. "The Textual Contract: Distinguishing Autobiography from the Novel." In *Representing Lives: Women and Auto/Biography*, edited by Alison Donnell and Pauline Polkey, 105–116 (New York: St. Martin's Press, 2000); Frame, Janet. *An Autobiography*. 3 vols. (New York: George Braziller, 1991); Frame, Janet. *An Angel at My Table* (Vol. 2) (New York: George Braziller, 1984); Frame, Janet. *The Envoy from Mirror City* (Vol. 3) (Auckland, NZ: Hutchinson, 1984); Frame, Janet. *To the Is-Land*. Vol. 1. (New York: George Braziller, 1982); King, Michael. *Wrestling with the Angel: A Life of Janet Frame* (Washington, DC: Counterpoint, 2000); Petch, Simon. "Speaking for Herselves: The Autobiographical Voices of Janet Frame." *Southerly: A Review of Australian Literature* 54, no. 4 (Summer 1994–1995): 44–58 Schwartz, Susan. "Dancing in the Asylum: The Uncanny Truth of the Madwoman in Janet Frame's Autobiographical Fiction." *ARIEL: A Review of International English Literature* 27, no. 4 (October 1996): 113–127.

Amy L. Burtner

FRANK, ANNELIES (ANNE) (1929–1945)

Arguably one of the most famous female autobiographers of the twentieth century, Anne Frank kept a **diary** for the last few years of her life, most of which was spent hiding from the Nazis in a secret apartment in Amsterdam. Her work, titled *The Diary of a Young Girl*, was first published posthumously in 1947. It has been translated into more than fifty different languages and is currently available in three different editions: the original edition by Anne's father, Otto Frank; the Definitive Edition, reinstating the material that Otto Frank deleted; and the Critical Edition, which places the two previous editions side by side and provides supplemental materials that prove the authenticity of both editions.

Frank's diary is an intriguing text for a number of reasons. It is not only a text that chronicles the trials and tribulations of an adolescence spent in hiding, it is an examination of lives spent in hiding by all Jews in occupied Holland. Frank's tale is not the most horrific of Holocaust narratives, and it is in part for that reason it has become a story that can be shared with young children. It is not, however, a pure autobiography, and as Frank fully intended her work to be published at a later date; she rewrote and edited select passages. For Frank, writing in her diary was akin to a form of therapy. As she said in her entry of April 5, 1944, "When I write, I can shake off all my cares." (Frank, *The Definitive Edition* 1997, 247)

Anne Frank was a young German Jewish girl growing up in Holland, who went into hiding with her family and four others on July 5, 1942, to escape the horrors of the Nazi regime. Her story would likely be unknown save for the fact that her parents gave her a diary as a birthday present on June 12, 1942, and that she planned a career as a writer. She took to writing in her diary regularly, and within two weeks began writing epistolary entries to a young friend she named Kitty. Her **letters** to Kitty explained all the events going on in her life and also avoided shorthand responses that later she (or others) may have had trouble understanding. Every detail of life in the secret rooms hidden in her father's former business office was described, providing a remarkable resource for future scholars and general readers. The unedited diary shows a blunt examination of life from an animated and stifled young woman. Nothing was beyond the scope of her examination, from philosophical essays on the differences of thought brought on by adolescence to candid discourses on her physical development.

Frank's life in hiding was markedly different from the one she had led previously. The gregarious young girl was confined to interaction only with her family (her father Otto, mother Edith, and sister Margot); a select number of workers from her father's company who aided them from the outside; the van Pels family, Hermann

and Auguste, with their son Peter (in the diary renamed the van Dan family, Hermann and Petronella, with their son also named Peter); and Fritz Pfeffer (renamed Alfred Daan). Often scolded for her animated behavior, particularly in view of the need for absolute silence in the secret annex, Frank took to discussing many of her interests and desires in the pages of her diary. In a little more than two years of entries, the reader can see Frank's growth into a highly articulate young woman, who likely would have made her mark on the world in some fashion, given the chance.

Anne and her family were discovered and arrested by the SS on the morning of August 4, 1944. She died of typhus in the early months of 1945 in the Bergen-Belsen concentration camp.

The focus of Frank's work is her relationship with the other inhabitants of the secret annex. We see a young woman growing and maturing in a physically stifling **space**, but whose outlook is unconfined. Although painted as a perfect and pure martyr by many commentators, Frank reveals her own conflicts and frustrations, petty jealousies, growing pains, and attendant difficulties. In consideration of the fact that she intended her diary to be eventually published, her discourse is surprisingly open. Readers who wish to gain a full sense of this should read the Definitive Edition or the Critical Edition, as Otto Frank excised various entries and portions of entries from the initial publication. The majority of the deleted or censored entries dealt with sexual matters, or unflattering portrayals of the other people also hiding in the annex.

Frank's influence has been incredibly widespread, due in no small part to her father's focus on the universal aspects of her story by editing his daughter's words. Her books are required reading in many schools and have become a mainstay of tolerance-education programs. The reasons can easily be seen in the following often-quoted lines from Frank's entry of July 15, 1944: "It's difficult in times like these: ideals, dreams and cherished hopes rise within us, only to be crushed by grim reality. It's a wonder I haven't abandoned all my ideals, they seem so absurd and impractical. Yet I cling to them because I still believe, in spite of everything, that people are truly good at heart" (Frank, *The Definitive Edition* 1997, 328).

The idea that someone could live through the horrors of the Holocaust and still believe in the goodness of all people may be hard to believe, but it must be noted that Frank herself did not know much about the horrors of the Nazi regime. It should also be noted that while those words were among the last she wrote, her final comments on August 1, 1944, focused on the clash she felt between the way she behaved, the way others wanted to her behave, and the way she felt she should behave, a more common theme in her writings:

> If I'm quiet and serious, everyone thinks I'm putting on a new act and I have to save myself with a joke, and then I'm not even talking about my own family, who assume I must be sick, stuff me with aspirins and sedatives, feel my neck and forehead to see if I have a temperature, ask about my bowel movements and berate me for being in a bad mood, until I just can't keep it up anymore, because when everybody starts hovering over me, I get cross, then sad, and finally end up turning my heart inside out, the bad part on the outside and the good part on the inside, and keep trying to find a way to become what I'd like to be and what I could be if . . . if only there were no other people in the world. (Frank 2003, 241)

Frank's work has been a tremendous influence on the lives of people around the world, primarily as an example of the indomitable spirit of mankind. In Eleanor Roosevelt's introduction to *The Diary of a Young Girl*, she wrote, "Anne's diary is an appropriate monument to her fine spirit and to the spirits of those who have worked and are working still for peace" (Frank ix–

x). But the truth of Frank's words is found in her final entry, as young people struggle to find their true selves and from that realization come to know the truth of all that she said. The validity of her growing pains lends credence to all that she writes.

While her diary is Frank's best-known work, there is another collection of her writings, titled *Anne Frank's Tales from The Secret Annex*. This volume is an edited collection of fiction that Frank wrote in the annex, as well as personal material that was not included in the first edition of *The Diary*. This material is divided into two sections, "Fables and Short Stories" and "Personal Reminiscences and Essays." These stories show the budding author, whose burgeoning talent is clear to see.

Further Reading: Enzer, Hyman A, and Sandra Solotaroff-Enzer. *Anne Frank: Reflections on Her Life and Legacy* (Urbana: University of Illinois Press, 2000); Frank, Anne. *Anne Frank: The Diary of a Young Girl* (New York: Doubleday, 1972); Frank, Anne. *Anne Frank's Tales from the Secret Annex* (New York: Bantam Books, 1994); Frank, Anne. *Diary of a Young Girl: The Critical Edition* (New York: Doubleday, 2003); Frank, Anne. *Diary of a Young Girl: The Definitive Edition* (New York: Bantam Books, 1997); Gies, Miep. *Anne Frank Remembered: The Story of the Woman Who Helped to Hide the Frank Family* (New York: Touchstone, 1987); Lee, Carol Ann. *The Hidden Life of Otto Frank* (New York: William Morrow, 2003); Muller, Melissa. *Anne Frank: The Biography* (New York: Owl Books, 1998).

Solomon Davidoff

FRENCH WOMEN'S AUTOBIOGRAPHY Until approximately the time of the French Revolution (1789), French women wrote none of what are traditionally described as "autobiographical texts." Critics (e.g., Philippe Lejeune) point to the industrial revolution, the rise (and fall) of the bourgeoisie, and the romanticism of the end of the eighteenth century as the principal factors in the emergence of autobiography as a genre. Lejeune points to Jean-Jacques Rousseau's *Confessions* (1781) as the model of the "first" autobiographical text, one that fulfills Lejeune's "autobiographical pact," a definition given to autobiography wherein the author, the narrator, and the protagonist must all be identical.

Such a narrow definition of "traditional autobiography" leaves out the vast majority of French women writers, and certainly all of those who wrote before the second half of the nineteenth century. In addition, it would have been unusual in France for non-nobles to write about themselves. Those outside the nobility would more likely have written about those inside the nobility, giving biographical information, describing their relationship to the nobility and in so doing, often giving insight into their own lives. It would seem more appropriate, then, to expand our definition of autobiography to include as autobiographers those writing personal narratives in the form of poetry, **letters**, **memoir**, and so on. Briefly, and for the purposes of this essay, "autobiography" is understood broadly as the creation of a female **subjectivity** through a variety of types of personal writing, that is, the production of a discourse of **identity** in the personal narrative text.

Early French Women Autobiographers

Modern scholars most often point to Christine de Pizan (c. 1365–c. 1430) as the earliest example of feminist and "personal" writing by a woman. Pizan was among the first writers in what is now France to write in the vernacular (Early French), and was definitely France's and almost certainly Europe's first female author to earn her living by writing. Her work, including her autobiography *Avision-Christine* (also sometimes called *L'Avision*) [1405 Christine's Vision], deals with feminist themes as they present themselves in both the public and the private sphere: education, religion, politics, women's roles in society, and courtly love, to name but a few. Her work was well received during her lifetime and continues to receive considerable critical attention today.

Among other French women Renaissance writers are Marguerite d'Angoulême (also known as Marguerite de Navarre) (1492–1549) and her daughter, Jeanne d'Albret, Queen of Navarre (also known as Jehanne de Navarre) (1528–1572). Both women wrote numerous political and religious texts, including Marguerite's "Le Miroir de l'âme pecheresse" (1531), a long and highly personal poem, which expresses her views on religion and religious reform. The work was condemned by Sorbonne theologians after its first publication, but was later reprinted in *Marguerites de la Marguerite des princesses* (1547). Marguerite's daughter, Jeanne, published during nearly all of her political career (1563–1571). Beyond her religious and political writings, she published numerous personal letters including those written to the royal family during an 1568 trip from Bearn to La Rochelle and one written later to Elizabeth I of England. These were published as *Lettres de tres haute tres vertueuse & tres chrestienne Princess Jane Royne de Navarre*. In 1570, she published the *Ample declaration sur la jonction de ses armes des Reformes en 1568*, a justification of her having left Bearn to join the army at La Rochelle. Throughout her *Mémoires*, a composite of her life and a harangue against her enemies for their treachery and their injustice, one sees the conscience of a queen, the responsibility of a mother for the rearing of a future king (Henri IV), and the determination of a woman faithful to a cause that she considered just.

Marguerite de Valois (also known as Marguerite de Navarre and as la reine Margot) (1553–1615) was the youngest daughter of Catherine de Medici and Henry II. A Catholic, she was married to the Protestant Henri of Bourbon (who would become Henri IV) in 1572 for political convenience and in hopes of resolving religious conflicts in France at the time. But with Marguerite childless, and considered "treacherous" because of her opposition to Henri's succession to the throne, their marriage was finally annulled in 1599. Her treasonous actions landed her in prison in the castle of Usson, in Auvergne, and it is while she was there that her husband became king and she began to write her memoirs. What remains of *Les memoires de la roine Marguerite* [Memoirs of Queen Marguerite] was published in 1628; we don't know if the original narrative went past 1582, although we do know that more was planned. Marguerite's other writing has not yet been translated: it includes letters, poetry, and *La Ruelle mal assortie* (a brief comic dialogue between an educated woman and her uneducated lover).

Marie de Rabutin-Chantal, Marquise de Sévigné (1626–1696), born in Paris, married to Breton nobleman Henri, Marquis de Sévigné, widowed by age twenty-six, was an admired member of the literary salons and the royal court. The Marquise de Sévigné wrote numerous letters to various family members describing her life, feelings, and thoughts, some of which were so detailed they have now become part of the historical record of the period. Sévigné was disappointed when both her son (a military officer) and her daughter, Françoise (married to the Count de Grignan) left Paris (and her), but their departure prompted her to write lengthy correspondences to them. Her more than 1,000 surviving letters not only report events at court, but give deeply moving expressions of love, fear, and pride about the lives of her children:

> [My] son has gone to Candia. . . . He consulted M. de Turenne, Cardinal de Retz, and M. de La Rochefoucauld upon this: most important personages! and they all approved it so highly, that it was fixed upon, and rumoured abroad, before I knew anything of the matter. In short, he is gone. I have wept bitterly, for it is a source of great grief to me. I shall not have a moment's rest during his voyage. I see all its dangers, and terrify myself to death: but, alas, I am wholly out of the question; for, in things of this nature, mothers have no voice. (July 1668)

Madame de Sévigné was aware that her letters were being made public during her lifetime and almost certainly adjusted her words to "suit" a larger audience. To this day, there is no full translation of her letters from the French to English.

Elisabeth Charlotte, duchesse d'Orléans (also known as Liselotte von der Pfalz) (1652–1722) was born in Germany, but became the second wife of Philippe, duc d'Orléans (who was eighteen years her senior and the brother of Louis XIV) in 1671. When her husband died in 1701, the duchesse d'Orléans was left alone with their two children. She wrote an immense volume of letters (more than 7,000 of which survive today), extracts from which have been arranged to form a memoir of her life and her descriptions of life at court, published under the title *The Entire Memoirs of Louis XIV and the Regency* (2001). These letters, although lesser known than some of the others mentioned above, are still important documents and give us great insight into this woman's life.

Writers during the French Revolution and Nineteenth Century

With the French Revolution and the turn to the nineteenth century, French women writers began to write specifically about their own lives in forms other than memoir—ostensibly about other people but with a good deal of their own autobiography included—and personal correspondence. As in prior epochs, however, these autobiographical documents were rarely published during their author's lifetime. The vast majority of autobiographical writings are published posthumously, and sometimes not until a great many years after the writer's death.

The French-Swiss woman of letters, Anne Louise Germaine Necker, baronne de Staël-Holstein (known as **Madame de Staël**) (1766–1817) wrote her autobiographical *Dix Années d'exil* [Ten Years of Exile], published posthumously in 1821, during her time in forced exile from France. She was banished from Paris as early as 1795 and again on a number of occasions in part because of her opposition to Napoleon's government. *Delphine* (1802), which earned her a near-fifteen-year exile from Napoleon's Paris, is about a young woman whose relationship with a married man leads to the ruin of both. After leaving Paris, Staël made a home base of her estate in Coppet (on Geneva Lake) writing and holding literary salons when at her home but also traveling extensively to Germany, and later to Italy, Russia, Finland, Sweden, and England. *Corinne* (1807), a tragic love story based on her travels in Italy and Germany, was an immediate success. *De l'Allemagne*, a study of German culture, appeared in 1810. Although the work passed the censors, it was banned by the police and nearly all 10,000 copies of the French edition were seized and destroyed. A few copies escaped the police and were published in another edition in England. There are English translations of most of her works. See, for example, her correspondence (translated 1970) and her memoirs (new edition 1968).

George Sand (born Aurore Dupin, 1804–1876) began work on *Histoire de ma vie* [The Story of My Life] in 1854 after a whirlwind of love affairs. Married to François-Casimir Dudevant in 1822 and later (more or less) amicably separated (divorce was illegal at the time), Sand moved to Paris with her two children in 1830. Her first books were collaborative efforts with her lover at the time, Jules Sandeau (from whom she took inspiration for her nom de plume), *Le Commissionnaire* (September 1830) and *Rose Blanche* (December 1830). Among her most notable relationships were those with composer Frédéric Chopin and author and poet Alfred de Musset. Her split from Musset caused a tremendous "he said"/"she said" war of words resulting in the publication of several volumes for each author, each recounting in minute detail how s/he had been wronged by the other. Sand's autobiographical works (nineteen volumes) were published as a collection in the prestigious

Pléiade edition in 1970 under the title *Oeuvres autobiographiques* [Autobiographical Works].

Marie-Catherine-Sophie de Flavigny, comtesse d'Agoult (1805–1876) was married to the Comte Charles d'Agoult in 1827. She left him in 1833 and became Hungarian composer Franz Liszt's mistress for the following ten years. The couple had three children together, only one of whom survived (Marie had two other daughters with Charles, the eldest of whom died at age six). Her daughter with Liszt, Cosima, later married the composer Richard Wagner (it is of note that Cosima Wagner kept diaries of their life together, which were later published as *Cosima Wagner's Diaries*). Marie de Flavigny published her semiautobiographical novel *Nélida*—a thinly disguised account of her relationship with Liszt—under the pen name Daniel Stern in 1846 (note that "Nélida" is an anagram of "Daniel"). Her two volumes of autobiography, *Mes souvenirs* (1877) and *Mémoires* (1927), were both published posthumously.

Maria Konstantinova Bashkirtseff was born in Ukraine in 1858, but traveled in Europe with her mother before arriving at their destination of Nice, France, at age twelve. An artist educated in Paris, Bashkirtseff began keeping personal journals in early adolescence which, on her early death from tuberculosis at age twenty-six in 1884, numbered nearly 20,000 pages. Her *Journal de Marie Bashkirtseff* was severely edited for content and published posthumously by her family. It was received with such success that it continued to be published until 1980, at which point, it, along with all of her correspondence, was "reedited" to include all of the passages that had previously been removed (so not to sully her good name). The entire work is currently available to the public and continues to be well received.

The Twentieth and Twenty-First Centuries

The twentieth century brings with it a relative explosion of writing by women, and personal (or autobiographical) writing in particular. Nearly all of the most well-known women intellectuals in France published autobiographies during their lifetimes or left personal writings, journals, correspondence, and so forth that have been made public since their deaths. The list of writers is long: Colette, **Simone de Beauvoir**, **Marguerite Duras**, Nathalie Sarraute, **Annie Ernaux**, Marie Cardinal, Julia Kristeva, Marguerite Yourcenar, Clara Malraux, **Anaïs Nin**, Benoît Groult, and Violette Leduc, among others.

Sidonie Gabrielle Colette (best known simply as Colette, 1873–1954) wrote more than fifty novels and scores of short stories. Colette blurs the line between autobiography and true fiction in her work: her characters' adventures and names mirror her own and her family's. Her husband (Henri Gauthier-Villars, "Monsieur Willy," fifteen years her senior) "encouraged" her to start a career as a writer (as the story goes) by locking her in her room until she had written a significant number of pages. In a very short time, Colette published four Claudine novels (1900–1903) under the name "Willy," which was in fact her husband's pen name. The series became a huge success and inspired all kinds of commercial products—a musical stage play, a Claudine uniform, Claudine soap, cigars, and perfume. In 1906, Colette divorced Willy and became a music hall performer, a chosen life of scandal. A chevalier and later grand officer in the French Légion d'Honneur, and a member of the Belgian Royal Academy, Colette was the first woman to be admitted to the prestigious Goncourt Academy. Her work, nearly all of which is autobiographical to some degree, treats two broad themes: her own childhood and women's sexual **identity**. *Gigi* (1945), which treats the development of sexual identity, was published when the author was seventy-two; the novel was made into a film in 1948, and in 1958 Vincente Minnelli directed the musical, version of the film with Leslie Caron, Maurice Chevalier, and Eva Gabor.

Marguerite Duras (born Donnadieu) was born in Gia Dinh, in French Indochina (now Vietnam), near Saigon in 1914 and died in 1995 in Paris. Duras left Indochina at age seventeen (she was sent to school in Paris by her widowed mother), and, although she studied math and law at the Sorbonne (the University of Paris), always dreamed of writing. Dozens of novels, plays, and films later, Duras, elected as a member of France's prestigious literary Académie, left us with several autobiographical accounts: *Un barrage contre le pacifique* (1950 [The Sea Wall]), *L'amant de la Chine du nord* (1991 [The North China Lover] 1993), *La Douleur* (1985 [The War: A Memoir 1986]), and *L'amant* (1984 [The Lover]) for which Duras was awarded the Prix Goncourt, France's highest literary prize.

Simone de Beauvoir, France's most well-known female philosopher, feminist, and author, left us with eight volumes of autobiography, containing nearly 4,000 pages of text. Born in Paris in 1908 (she died there in 1986), Beauvoir is best known for her feminist/philosophical work *Le Deuxième Sexe* (1949 [The Second Sex]), an exploration of the ways in which society shapes women to be "feminine." In addition to her extensive "official" autobiography (in which she treats everything from her childhood, her relationships with her mother and lifelong partner Jean-Paul Sartre, her fear of old age and death, accounts of her travels, and her final goodbyes to the loved ones in her life), several of her fictional works are semiautobiographical. Her first novel, *L'invitée* (1943; [She Came to Stay 1949]) and *Les Mandarins* (1954; [The Mandarins 1956]), for which she won the prestigious Prix Goncourt, are both quasi autobiographical. The first examines the philosophical problem of the Other and the second is about left-wing intellectuals in post–World War II France. Beauvoir's work was not without controversy, but won her worldwide fame. Her books have been translated into more than fifty languages, and, during her life, Beauvoir traveled to every continent signing her work for fans worldwide. In 1999, her adopted daughter, Sylvie le bon de Beauvoir, published volumes of her mother's correspondence, most notably hundreds of letters written from 1947 to 1964 between Beauvoir and her American lover, playwright Nelson Algren. Her letters to him contain a rich history of French intellectual life of the time and many of the stereotypes of this philosopher are broken when we read about "the woman in love": "Je suis heureuse d'être si malheureuse parce que je sais que vous l'êtes aussi, et qu'il est doux de partager cette tristesse-là" (*Lettres à Nelson Algren* 1997). ["I am happy to be so miserable because I know that you are also and that it is beautiful to share this sort of sadness."]

Finally, this brief overview of France's women autobiographers would not be complete without mention of Annie Ernaux (1940–). Ernaux has published thirteen books to date. Hers is a vast *projet autobiographique*—an autobiographical project— telling essentially the same story over and over again from varying points of view. While her first autobiographical novels were more or less ignored, her fourth, *La place* (1983) won France's second literary prize, the Prix Renaudot. Since that time, this humanities professor living near Paris frequently finds herself on the best-seller list and her works are widely read around the world (author's translation):

I've always had the feeling that there is an abyss between the world of literature and the lives of oppressed people . . . I'm aware of the unheard of luck I've had to be able to appropriate a language which is not my own, and which, in an echo of the words of [Jean] Genet, is "the language of the enemy," that of the oppressors. This creates a feeling of responsibility. This power of language, I wouldn't be able to use it to publish "pretty" books, that doesn't interest me . . . In order to unveil the inner workings of injustice in our society, I instead try to restore my own sen-

sations in the most honest way possible, and, in so doing, to maybe even provoke the feelings of the reader.

In conclusion, French women's autobiography can perhaps be summed up as follows: an enormously rich history of women's stories containing their pain, their love, their social and physical burdens, and, importantly, their contributions to society, both political and social. Their personal writings stem from their standpoint of being women—a classification which, depending on the politics or the religion of their time, often rendered them as "inhuman" or legally "incompetent." In all cases, these women were never allowed a legitimate voice with which to "testify" to the vastness and importance of their individual lives, and yet, that they defied laws and mores to do so anyway is indeed the truest "testimony" that they could have given us of the importance of their existence.

Further Reading: Bair, Deirdre. *Simone de Beauvoir: A Biography* (New York: Simon and Schuster, 1990); Beauvoir, Simone de. *La Cérémonie des adieux* (Paris: Gallimard, 1981); Beauvoir, Simone de. *Le Deuxième Sexe* (Paris: Gallimard, 1949); Beauvoir, Simone de. *La Force des choses I, II* (Paris: Gallimard, 1963); Beauvoir, Simone de *L'invitée* (Paris: Gallimard, 1943); Beauvoir, Simone de. *Lettres à Nelson Algren* (Paris: Gallimard, 1997); Beauvoir, Simone de. *Les Mandarins* (Paris: Gallimard, 1954); Beauvoir, Simone de. *Mémoires d'une jeune fille rangée* (Paris: Gallimard, 1958); Beauvoir, Simone de. *Une mort si douce* (Paris: Gallimard, 1964); Bolster, Richard. *Marie d'Agoult: The Rebel Countess* (New Haven: Yale University Press, 2000); Brée, Germaine. "Autogynography." *The Southern Review* 22 (1986): 223–230; Bruss, Elizabeth. *Autobiographical Acts: The Changing Situation of a Literary Genre* (Baltimore: John Hopkins University Press, 1976); Burr, Anna Robinson. *The Autobiography: A Critical and Comparative Study* (Cambridge: The Riverside Press, 1909); Butler, Judith. *Gender Trouble: Feminism and the Subversion of Identity* (New York: Routledge, 1990); Coe, Richard. *When the Grass Was Taller: Autobiography and* the Experience of Childhood (New Haven: Yale University Press, 1984); Colette. Le Pur et L'impur (Paris: Hachette, 1941); Duras, Marguerite. L'Amant (Paris: Les Editions de minuit, 1984); Eakin, Paul John. Fictions in Autobiography: Studies in the Art of Self-Invention (Princeton, NJ: Princeton University Press, 1985); Ernaux, Annie. Les armoires vides (Paris: Gallimard, 1974); Ernaux, Annie. Ce qu'ils disent ou rien (Paris: Gallimard, 1977); Ernaux, Annie. La femme gêlée (Paris: Gallimard, 1981); Ernaux, Annie. La Place (Paris: Gallimard, 1984); Ernaux, Annie. Une Femme (Paris: Gallimard, 1987); Groult, Benoîte. Il était deux fois (Paris: Denoeel, 1968); Groult, Benoîte. Les trois quarts du temps (Paris: Livre de Poche, 1984); Gunn, Janet Varner. Autobiography: Toward a Poetics of Experience (Philadelphia: University of Pennsylvania Press, 1982); Gusdorf, Georges. Auto-bio-graphie (Paris: Editions Odile Jacob, 1991); Hewitt, Leigh D. Autobiographics: A Feminist Theory of Self-Representation (Ithaca, NY: Cornell University Press, 1994); Jelinek, Estelle C. The Tradition of Women's Autobiography: From Antiquity to Present (Boston: Twayne Publishers, 1986); Jelinek, Estelle C., ed. Women's Autobiography: Essays in Criticism (Bloomington: Indiana University Press, 1980); Leduc, Violette. La Bâtarde. Translated by Serek Coltman (New York: Farrar, Straus and Giroux, 1964; Misch, Georg. A History of Autobiography in Antiquity (Cambridge: Harvard University Press, 1951); Moi, Toril. Simone de Beauvoir: The Making of an Intellectual Woman (Oxford, UK: Blackwell, 1994); Morgan, Janice, and Colette T. Hall, eds. Redefining Autobiography in Twentieth-Century Women's Fiction: An Essay Collection. Gender and Genre in Literature (New York: Garland Publishing, 1991); Neuman, Shirley. "Inventing the Self." The Southern Review 22, no. 2 (1986): 407–416; Olney, James. "(Auto)biography." The Southern Review 22, no. 2 (1986): 428–441; Olney, James, ed. Autobiography: Essays Theoretical and Critical (Princeton, NJ: Princeton University Press, 1980); Sarraute, Nathalie. Enfance (Paris: Gallimard, 1983); Sand, George. Oeuvres autobiographiques (Paris: Editions de la Pléiade, 1970); Sheringham, Michael. French Autobiography: Devices and Desires, Rousseau to Perec (Oxford: Clarendon Press, 1993); Smith, Sidonie. Subject-

ivity, Identity, and the Body: Women's Autobiographical Practices in the Twentieth Century (Bloomington: Indiana University Press, 1993); Spacks, Patricia Meyer. "Selves in Hiding." Women's Autobiography: Essays in Criticism, 112–132. Edited by Estelle Jelinek (Bloomington: Indiana University Press, 1980); Staël-Holstein, Germaine de. Corinne ou l'Italie Edited by Simone Balayé (Paris: Gallimard, 1985); Staël-Holstein, Germaine de. Delphine (Geneva: Librairie Droz, 1990); Stanley, Liz. The Autobiographical "I": Theory and Practice of Feminist Autobiography (Manchester: Manchester University Press, 1992); Stanton, Domna, ed. The Female Autograph. 1984. Reprint (Chicago: University of Chicago Press, 1987); Wagner, Cosima. Cosima Wagner's Diaries. Edited by Geoffrey Skelton (New Haven: Yale University Press, 1997); Willard, Charity Cannon. Christine de Pizan: Her Life and Her Works (New York: Persea Books, 1984); Wilson, Katharina M. Medieval Women Writers (Athens: University of Georgia Press, 1984); Yourcenar, Marguerite. Souvenirs Pieux (Paris: Gallimard, 1974); Zimmerman, Margarete, and Dina De Rentiis, eds. The City of Scholars: New Approaches to Christine de Pizan (New York: W. de Gruyter, 1994).

Kimberly K. Carter-Cram

FULLER, (SARAH) MARGARET (1810–1850) A key figure in the nineteenth-century transcendentalist movement, and a pioneering advocate of woman's rights, Margaret Fuller is the author of the seminal Woman in the Nineteenth Century (1845), and the travelogue Summer on the Lakes (1843), as well as some two hundred articles for Horace Greeley's New York Daily Tribune. Educated by her father, Timothy Fuller, a congressman and Harvard graduate, Fuller had the unique privilege of being tutored early on in Latin and Greek. Her exceptional intellect, mediated and influenced by the likes of Ralph Waldo Emerson, Nathaniel Hawthorne, and Henry David Thoreau, increasingly engaged social and political issues and sought alternative views to the masculine terms of her nation's dominant patriarchal ideologies. Fuller's venture into autobiography—from her first journal sketches, poems, and essays—enabled her to **voice** a self, gradually empowered, apart from the domestic confines of nineteenth-century gendered behavior.

As nineteenth-century America's most prominent woman of letters, Fuller worked to more inclusively define the social implications of American democratic ideals. From her famous Boston "Conversations" (1839–1844) for women in which she conducted discussions from Greek mythology to woman's rights, to her final *New York Tribune* dispatches from Italy that described the struggle of the Italian people to establish a republic, Fuller wrote, and spoke, with the authority of her own lived experiences.

Woman in the Nineteenth Century (1845), which established her fame, grew out of "The Great Lawsuit: Man versus Men, Woman versus Women" (1843), published in *The Dial*, the transcendental journal she edited. Building on her early "Autobiographical Sketch" (1842), Fuller broadens her discussion of the influence of her father's education by interrogating its gendered assumptions and biases: "[T]he time has come for Eurydice to call for an Orpheus, rather than Orpheus for Eurydice" (Steele 1992, 252) she notes, suggesting the prejudices of her times.

With its collage of biographical facts, its references to the classics, mythology, the Declaration of Independence, the Bible, the poetry of Ben Jonson, Sappho, Mary Wollstonecraft's *Vindication of the Rights of Woman* (1792), and quotes from the U.S. Constitution, among other sources, *Woman in the Nineteenth Century* defies containment in any one genre and articulates the autobiography of an inclusive female creative principle. For example, Fuller empowers mythologized female personas like the Goddess Ceres and the Scandinavian goddess Iduna to demonstrate alternative models to dominant nineteenth-century paradigms of women's passivity and dependence on men. The childhood **memory** of her mother's garden also came to represent a creative fecundity kept in bounds by the norms of a nineteenth-century domestic ideology that Fuller would dismantle by privileging organic nature as the source of a feminized language of transcendence.

The expansive autobiographical style of *Woman in the Nineteenth Century* exemplifies a refusal to work within the binary, mutually exclusive categories of inherited behavior patterns: The "heart" (woman) and "mind" (man) that gendered and dichotomized nineteenth-century Victorian society, are brought together in her famous dictum that, "There is no wholly masculine man, no purely feminine woman" (Steele 1992, 310). Fuller argued that gendered values were shared and not relegated to fixed social categories: the public and domestic spheres, like the spaces of her mother's garden and her father's study, were necessarily interdependent.

An adherent of the nineteenth-century transcendental belief in the divinity of the individual advocated in Emerson's doctrine of "Self Reliance," Fuller nevertheless questioned the degree of independence that women and other underprivileged groups (slaves, the American Indian, the poor) could achieve within the social structures that oppressed them. By interrogating the failures of democratic policy, Fuller came to be considered one of the most radical democratic thinkers of her time. From her intellectual beginnings, stimulated and formed by the great minds of European thought and the myths of ancient Greece and Rome, Fuller evolved a transnational vision and respect for otherness that exceptional for her age. In *Summer on the Lakes*, the travelogue of her journey westward to the Great Lakes region, she describes her brief stay with Native Americans. Her insights allow her to understand that Native Americans, like women, have been appropriated by cultural prejudices that have denied them the ability to live equally. Finally, in Italy, where Fuller spent the last years of her life documenting the Italian revolution, the political and personal spheres that Fuller grappled with to combine for her whole life, come together. As she daily immerses herself in Italy's struggle for democracy, she meets Giovanni Ossoli, a man fighting for the cause, and with whom she has a child.

The inward, private life Fuller only intuited in her childhood love of her mother's garden comes to symbolize a discourse of the domestic possibilities of a more empathetic public world. The Italian revolutionary cause documented in Fuller's *New York Tribune* column, *Things and Thoughts of Europe*, becomes a model of the democratic idealism she felt disappointed by in her own country. Tragically, at the age of forty, on her way back to America she drowned with Ossoli, and their two-year-old son Angelo, just off Fire Island, New York, when the *Elizabeth* was shipwrecked. Controversial for her resistance to the gendered and racial constructions of her time, Fuller remains prophetic in her assessment of the self's fluid multiplicity and its potential for overcoming cultural biases; it was a potential she articulated first to herself and then to her nation as she recorded her experiences in worlds that expanded and reinvented the hope of a democratic ideal that would transcend its fallibilities.

Further Reading: Chevigny, Bell Gale. *Woman and the Myth: Margaret Fuller's Life and Writings*. 1976. (Boston: Northeastern University Press, 1994); Fuller, Margaret. *Dispatches: Margaret Fuller. These Sad But Glorious Days: Dispatches from Europe, 1846–1850*. Edited by Larry J. Reynolds and Susan Belasco Smith (New Haven: Yale University Press, 1992); Fuller, Margaret. *The Letters of Margaret Fuller*. Edited by Robert N. Hudspeth. 5 vols. (Ithaca, NY: Cornell University Press, 1983); Fuller, Margaret. *Summer on the Lakes* (Urbana: University of Illinois Press, 1991); Fuller, Margaret. *Woman in the Nineteenth Century* (New York: Greeley and McElrath, 1845); Steele, Jeffrey, ed. *The Essential Margaret Fuller* (New Brunswick, NJ: Rutgers University Press, 1992).

Adrianne Kalfopoulou

G

GAGNIER, REGENIA (1953–) Currently professor of English at Exeter University, Regenia Gagnier is the author of *Subjectivities: A History of Self-Representation in Britain, 1832–1920* (1991). Gagnier's book analyzes nineteenth-century working-class women's autobiography, a **class** of women who have traditionally received very little academic attention. In her analysis of women's nineteenth-century working-class autobiographies, Gagnier pays careful attention to situating their texts within the social, political, and economic backgrounds from which these women write and work.

Gagnier's analysis runs counter to the way that many literary critics view autobiography. Typically, when literary critics write about autobiography they think of it in terms of what Gagnier calls "abstract individualism" (*Subjectivities* 39). When critics look at people through the lens of abstract individualism, they in effect see the individual as independent from the economic and social circumstances that make up a person's life. Those material matters are less important than the understanding of one's individual self. The emphasis instead is on the individual as a unique being who makes sense of her life by writing about it. In effect, middle-class autobiography offers the individual an opportunity to reflect on her life as a person. In the eyes of

the literary critic, this person is a fully autonomous, creative human being, with the capacity to determine the direction of her future. Such is the material of which "good" literary autobiographies are made.

In contrast to middle-class autobiographies, women's working-class autobiographies tend to serve a different function. Rather than focus on their individual concerns and self-development, these women's autobiographies, according to Gagnier, are more pragmatic. They communicate specific ideas and give information to their audience. In other words, nineteenth-century working-class women wrote their autobiographies with specific rhetorical purposes; they were interested, for example, in giving information about their own labor history in order to help other workers. Regardless of their topic, for the most part, these women seemingly had little interest in discovering themselves through writing. They wrote because they had a reason to do so that had less to do with themselves as individuals than with informing their audience about the oppressive circumstances of their lives.

In her book, Gagnier explains that typical working-class autobiographies are quite different in form from their middle-class counterparts. Usually, middle-class autobiographers discuss their family background, their childhood, and education. Such is not the case with working-class autobiographers who typically begin their narratives by offering an apology because of their class. Working-class autobiographers do not include such family information because individuals rarely had childhoods since they were forced to begin working at any early age in order to provide financial help to their families. Likewise, working for these women usually precluded going to school. Gagnier explains that middle-class narratives include the problems that individuals encounter and eventually overcome successfully, resulting in a life well lived. Such is not the case, however, in working-class autobiographies. Individuals do not master the many obstacles in their lives. Instead, their autobiographies document lives of constant work. Because their narratives are not oriented toward a successful outcome, working-class women's autobiographies usually stop in the middle of their lives.

While many working-class autobiographies followed a different form from their middle-class counterparts, Gagnier does include a discussion of those working-class autobiographies that looked to middle-class models as a way to structure their own narratives. But as she explains, these writers do so at a cost to their own psychological well-being. When working-class writers tried to write about and understand their lives using a middle-class model, they had to come face-to-face with how circumstances in their lives were determined by economics and other factors beyond their control. Adhering to a middle-class ideology in turn caused them to blame themselves for their so-called failures. Thus, trying to understand their lives through writing came at a great psychological cost and only helped to underscore what they did not have and could never hope to have.

Gagnier's book, *Subjectivities*, helps the student of autobiography to understand the differences that exist between middle-class and working-class autobiography. By looking at nineteenth-century, working women in the context of their social, historical, and economic circumstances, one comes to learn how such forces help to define a person's life. Moreover, these autobiographies demonstrate different rhetorical functions than one usually presumes for the autobiographical genre. Finally, by reading the works of middle-class women alongside working-class ones, it becomes more apparent how much power and control that the middle class had over their lives and how they were able to construct themselves as individual subjects with unique qualities. Working women's autobiographies, on the other hand, demonstrate that class does help to shape life experiences in ways quite unimaginable to the middle class.

Further Reading: Corbett, Mary Jean. *Representing Femininity: Middle-Class Subjectivity in Victorian and Edwardian Women's Autobiographies* (New York: Oxford University Press, 1992); Gagnier, Regenia. *Subjectivities: A History of Self-Representation in Britain, 1832–1920* (1991).

Phoebe S. Jackson

GENDER   While it is possible to consider the concept of the individual through a variety of discourses (religious, economic, legal, or philosophical, to name a few), to define a field of study as "women's autobiography" indicates that the primary category at work here is that of either biological sex or of gender. The separation of, or connection between, these two terms has historically been problematic. Twentieth-century Anglo-American **feminism** initially found it useful to define sex and gender against one another in order to contradict the idea that women had certain innate behavioral traits. The sex-gender binary implies the existence of a body that is unalterably sexed as male or female, according to anatomical difference. Gender is supposedly "inscribed" by culture onto this already determined body, and the cultural associations that come with one's masculine or feminine gender are figured as the source of one's sexualized **subjectivity**. The division can be seen as liberating in that it suggests that what has historically been perceived as the difference between the sexes is actually a set of meanings ascribed by the cultural concept of masculine or feminine gender, and which can therefore be altered through cultural change. Such meanings might include the association of women with passivity and irrationality, with the domestic, private realm rather than with the public, with the body and the material rather than with the mental, spiritual, or transcendent.

However, anthropologists such as Sherry Ortner have attempted to demonstrate a greater interplay between nature (sex) and culture (gender) than this model might imply. It is suggested that as women's participation in, for example, the reproductive process, is more lengthy than men's, women are seen as having closer ties to the natural, biological aspects of the life of the species. Women's cultural roles then reflect this perception, denying them access to the highest cultural forms on the grounds that they can never be truly transcendent. Psychoanalytic theories of femininity also explore questions of gendered **identity** as emanating from the cultural symbolism attached to the body. The work of Hélène Cixous and Luce Irigaray focuses on the role of language as symbolic of cultural structures and are commonly linked through a specific concept of women's writing, *écriture feminine*. Both work within the framework of post-structural psychoanalysis, which maintains that women are associated with the Other, the nonsubject against which the masculine subject constitutes itself in its phallocentric system. Cixous depicts the nature-culture interplay she sees as specifically feminine through the image of "writing the body." She views such writing as expressing women's position in culture through poetic imagery, an alliance of rhythm with sense, and irreverence, all escapes from rational discourse. The imagery of the body is important in this context as it symbolizes that which has

traditionally been excluded from culture. Irigaray also invokes female body imagery in order to demonstrate feminine multiplicity, which she opposes to masculine logic of the positive and the negative, presence and absence. This binary logic is seen to be sexualized through its phallocentrism: it is derived from the presence or absence of the penis, a single term that can give rise only to two oppositional states. Women's genitals are instead conceived as a single organ, which is simultaneously made up of two parts, two lips, not subject to binary logic. Again, the biology of sexual difference is shown to affect the cultural symbolism that makes up gender, but biology is still being used as the basis, the given, with gender as its cultural development.

The Concept of the Sexed Body

The last thirty years, however, have seen a proliferation of histories of the concept of the sexed body. Thomas Laqueur has traced the ways in which the Enlightenment discourse of rights effected a change in the concept of sexual difference, from woman as anatomically inverted, inferior man, to woman as a biologically different being with an equal, but separate, social role to play. Biology is thus shown to be a subjective, historical discourse rather than an objective science; it engineers and conceives the boundaries of the body in order to correspond with the desired social limits.

Recent work in gender studies has destabilized these concepts still further. First, if gender is to be thought of as merely a set of cultural meanings, it is separate from biological sex. There is thus no reason to suppose a direct, univocal link between a biological sex and a cultural gender. It is therefore unnecessary to restrict gender options to only two possibilities (masculine and feminine) as gender does not need to follow the sexual binary. If we assume two sexes, there is still **space** for many gender identifications, opening up a space for non-heterosexual gender identities. Second, sex has also been redefined as a fluctuating concept, as culturally dictated as is gender. Michel Foucault has suggested that sex is in fact a grouping together "in an artificial unity, anatomical elements, biological functions, conducts, sensations, and pleasures" that "enabled one to make use of this fictitious unity as a causal principle, an omnipresent meaning, a secret to be discovered everywhere" (*The History of Sexuality: I* 1976, 154). Following Foucault, Judith Butler proposes that it is meaningless to refer to a precultural body, because the only knowledge that we have of that body is through culture, society, and discourse. Sexual differences merely masquerade as having been created before the advent of discourse; sex and gender, instead of being separate categories, elide into one another. The historical and repressive use of sex is in justifying a gender-binarized culture, which prescribes that one must belong to one of two fixed gender roles.

In this model, the sexed body is merely another signifier within culture, creating the illusion of an internal, coherent identity. When conceived as an autonomous unity, it suggests a similarly autonomous, fixed identity. It sustains the illusion through a series of acts that are assigned a meaning by the discourse of gender: the teleological process of cultural regulation retrospectively reascribes these acts to an identity. If the cause is located in the self, the regulatory discourse through which the acts are seen disappears. The body corporeally "stylizes" this discourse through its acts; it cannot be taken as a fixed absolute as all statements of or regarding the body must be read, interpreted, seen as part of a socially produced text. The fact that it is constructed through this series of acts leads Butler to coin the term "performative" to describe the operations of gendered identity. Because these acts can only be performed or known through discourse, it is impossible to escape being implicated through this discourse, which is arranged around the two rigidly constructed genders of reproductive heterosexuality; it is impossible to avoid being in some way im-

plicated in the process of normalizing this binary opposition.

Butler, however, argues that realizing that one is constructed through discourse is the beginning of any strategy for subverting that discourse. Although it is impossible to step outside the received codes that govern society, one can recognize that, as a social being, one sustains these codes and, through this recognition, shifts that sustenance. She uses the idea of iteration and re-iteration to describe the process by which acts are performed, repeated, and become the norm. If one examines these acts, it is possible to choose not whether to repeat, but how to repeat them, and, by assuming various, perhaps contradictory aspects of "masculinity" and "femininity," create a "gender" that cannot be subsumed into either category. This may, she suggests, enable the displacement of gender norms. The category "women" is thus shown to be potentially unstable; something in process, capable of being remade; the idea of categorization is itself rendered problematic.

The concept of women's autobiography rests first on the possibility of categorizing the autobiographical, then on the categorization of women. It would thus appear to rely on a prediscursive concept of biological sex. The nature of autobiographical content, however, creates additional complexities. Autobiography itself complicates the distinction between the textual and the "real," as it depends on some level of referentiality or comparison between a life as portrayed in the text and the existence of that life outside the text. This does not, however, necessarily imply a reference to something nontextualized. The text could, instead, be seen to be referring to a life in the sense of something constructed through other texts, other discourses. Instead of defining "women's autobiography" in reference to an objective biological sex, one could define it as a conjunction between the discursive construction of gender within the autobiographical text and the reader's discursively constituted understanding of gender.

Domna C. Stanton observes that women's writing, when so defined, is always read autobiographically, with reference to the sex of the author. She explores this process of reference through the figure of the "female autograph," which introduces the idea of an autobiographical text "signed" by the author not only as an individual, but as a woman. Autobiography—self life writing—is reconceptualized as autogynography, or writing the self as a woman, thus maintaining its categorical specificity. Stanton views the graphing of the auto as an act of self-assertion, a constitution of the female subject within and against a phallocentric system that always defines woman as an object. Because women are defined as objects, their potential existence as subjects makes manifest the idea of the subject as fundamentally split, existing in both states simultaneously. Stanton thus theorizes the understanding of women's autobiography in a gendered framework as both necessary and contingent: necessary in the sense that subjectivity is gendered; contingent in the sense that that framework is historically and culturally situated. She leaves this contradictory position open, positing the understanding of autobiography through gender as a transitional stage in which women can claim an authority of the signature which, within autobiographical theory, they have so far been denied.

Stanton's framework also incorporates considerations of how women have been seen to "contaminate" the purity of autobiography: while masculine transcendence is seen to record the details of a life in order to produce a text that surpasses those details, feminine attention to detail is used to demonstrate that women remain embedded in the bathetic. Autobiography criticism has, historically, been a particularly strong manifestation of how generic qualities are interpreted differently according to the gender of the author. Jacques Derrida's work on genre has been particularly influential in opening this question. In French, the word genre carries a triple meaning: a

genus or type in the taxonomical or biological sense; a literary genre; and a gender, particularly grammatical gender. The word thus sets up a relationship between a (nominally) objective scientific categorization, a mode of writing, and a sexualized classification that itself carries linguistic and textual resonances. Derrida's subsequent discussion of literary genres is thus inflected by these other connotations. Destabilizing the "law of genre" in a literary sense also destabilizes gender classifications.

Derrida observes that the point at which a text "marks" itself as belonging to a particular genre cannot itself be part of that genre. This follows from his suggestion that every system "grounds" itself at a supposed point of origin, which defines the laws or rules that govern all the other elements in the system. Yet if this point is that which defines the other elements, it cannot itself obey only the same rules as the other elements: it must have an extra quality, that which allows it to define. The origin, as classificatory function, is therefore inside the system, as it defines itself to be, but also outside the system. Thus, whether or not an autobiographical text is subtitled "an autobiography," the designation "autobiography" is not itself a piece of autobiographical material like the others in the text: it has a different function. Genre classifications run somewhere along the boundaries of a text; they subvert the very purpose they attempt to fulfill, that of closing the text, sectioning it off from the rest of literature. As in Butler's framework, both taxonomically defined sex, and gender, by the same logic, subvert their own classificatory objectives.

Categorization thus becomes difficult in defining women, in defining a genre called autobiography, in separating women from their texts whether those texts are explicitly deemed autobiographical, and particularly in the elision between women's selves and their autobiographies. This elision is often couched in terms of **embodiment**, partly relating back to the question of whether women can transcend the material in their extratextual lives, and partly suggesting that even their texts remain in some way "embodied." In this context, an emphasis on physical or bodily metaphors within an autobiography is seen as a metatextual "incorporation" of the author into it, commenting on the confusion between life and text that women's specific situation seems to engender.

Classification is further complicated by the association between women and the irrational or uncategorizable. If autobiography is characterized by the attempt to apply a narrative to and find meaning in a life, the unity and coherence that this implies automatically excludes women. To some extent, this exclusion comes about through nineteenth-century autobiographical criticism, rooted in the historical period during which the model of bourgeois career advancement was seen as the "natural" narrative for a life. Women's exclusion from the public sphere also excluded them from an uncomplicated relationship with this model. The bildungsroman form, or narrative of personal development leading to a moment of self-realization, is also complicated for women in this period, as autonomous feminine development was seen to culminate in marriage, leaving only the early part of the life for independent scrutiny.

Attempts to resolve these difficulties are obvious in women's engagement with the *Künstlerroman*, or narrative of artistic development. Authorship is itself often seen as a form gendered as masculine: models range from Harold Bloom's Oedipal framework, which sees writers engaged in a struggle to differentiate themselves from their literary "fathers," to Sandra Gilbert and Susan Gubar's suggestion that the pen is traditionally figured as a metaphorical penis, giving birth to texts through a paradoxical exclusion of the feminine. Thus, women's autobiographies not only negotiate the integration of private and public realms, but in creating a written commentary on this process also query their exclusion from artistry and authorship. The nineteenth century sees this practice develop from the 1820s,

when the most well-known British women's autobiographies were those of Mary Robinson and **Charlotte Charke**; the former a scandal **memoir** written by the mistress of the Prince of Wales, the latter that of an actress notorious for cross-dressing both onstage and off. From this point, a progression can be traced through the domestic to the artistic, as descriptions of women's lives are "made safe" by a focus on the private, familial realm, by means of which the generation of texts is linked to the generation of children. The flowering of women's autobiographies thus both builds on and reconfigures the gendered characteristics ascribed to their authors, in a manner both liberating and proscriptive. On the one hand, the nineteenth-century concept of the exemplary, thus public, life, meant that the unification of women's traditional sphere with authorship could serve as a model for future women's writing: on the other, the contested nature of the idea that women authors could be exemplary increases the sense in which the female author's person went on trial along with the quality of her text. Nonetheless, the public nature of this enactment of gendered characteristics suggests a refiguring of the boundaries analogous to Butler's notion of performative acts.

To categorize texts as "women's autobiographies" depends, as we have seen, on a double movement of classification: the text is demarcated after the fact of its writing through its author's gender, but this recognition also depends on the author (whether consciously or unconsciously) having assumed her gender prior to the act of writing. Feminist writing of or about autobiography requires a more specific act of classification: it is an intentional act based on recognizing one's identity as being primarily defined by gender. Feminist criticism thus seeks to isolate and emphasize the gendered features of a work. However, feminist, autobiographical criticism emphasizes the publicizing of private experience—that the (feminine) personal is political—and as a result, counters the masculinist bias of traditional autobiography criticism by incorporating autobiographical elements into the critical text. This is partly an attempt to avoid remasculinizing the perceived disruption of gender boundaries by using only traditional, abstract critical tools, but is also itself a refiguring of gendered norms: the concept of the critic as rationalizing, dominating, and pinning down the text is remade as a more fluid model of interaction, which can itself be seen as more appropriate to the theories developed about the nature of women's autobiography. Thus Liz Stanley views the use of autobiographical material in critical practice as an opportunity to metatextually interrogate the impact that criticism can have on "life," as well as its effects on views of "past" lives, on whether readings can ever really uncover the "truth" about a life.

Further, her insistence on the use of autobiographical material as a way to emphasize the "personal," whose presence in supposedly abstract or scientific writing renders that writing inevitably subjective, problematizes the power relationships that place the critic as superior to the audience, as well as to the text. Similarly, **Nancy Miller** writes of the "risk" involved in writing what she terms **personal criticism**, where the critic puts herself forward to be judged in the hope of further engaging the audience to believe that what is being written about matters: guaranteed by the investment of the self into the text. Such voluntary ceding of power is linked to gender norms in that all questions of power are inflected by the historical dominance of masculine over feminine.

The focus on a nonoppositional concept of gender has suggested two other possibilities for reconfiguring traditional norms. The first is a focus on all-female relationships such as those between mother and daughter. All-female relationships are often seen as part of a continuum of experience that can be envisioned as a positive, specifically feminine trait. This idea not only offers a counter to the feminine as universal

negative, but also suggests a model of femininity revolving around the self as experienced primarily in relation to others. This concept has been useful in theorizing Renaissance women's autobiographies, where it is also placed in the context of a patriarchal society that defined women only in relation to their husbands or fathers and also in recent **postcolonial women's autobiographies** where the exploration of a strong sense of **place** and community ally with the feminine. The **mother/daughter relationship** also defines women more strongly than the maternal relationship defines the son: because mother and daughter mirror one another in femininity, various psychoanalytic and ontological theories have suggested that it is more difficult for a daughter to break the bond and become a fully autonomous individual.

Second, lesbian sexualities have offered a model, for a gender does not exist only in opposition to the masculine. Theorists such as Monique Wittig have suggested that lesbians are not, in fact, women, as the term "woman" is inevitably defined by a sexual relationship with men. Further, Butler's concept of assuming an identity through a theoretically limitless combination of performative acts offers the possibility of a multiplicity of genders, all in some sense "queer," as they do not conform to a simple binary opposition between masculine and feminine. However, this model also contains the possibility of subverting its own aims, as it replaces the masculine-feminine binary with an opposition between heterosexual and homosexual identities, however these may be combined in practice.

Henrietta Moore, a feminist and social anthropologist, provides an alternative argument for conceiving sexual and gender differences. She provides a survey of ethnographic material, which shows a broad and varied range of conceptions: for example, a Nepalese model where masculine and feminine are thought of as, respectively, bone and flesh, locating the moment of difference, in a literally physical sense, within each individual's body. Cultural gender is thus given a biological grounding within all bodies, collapsing the boundaries between internal and external, as well as those between cultural gender and biological sex. Both masculinity and femininity are construed as necessary features for a body to exist. This thesis seeks to connect macrocultural models to the experience of individuals or small groups within a society, trying to find a common ground in an existence divided by a vast number of different social, historical, and cultural discourses. It suggests that the answer may lie in a practice which, rather than using the concepts of sex and gender as starting points, works back toward them from different directions in an effort to realize that they are not privileged over and above all the other forms of identification that we are somehow required to incorporate.

Rosi Braidotti's notion of "nomadic subjectivity" is one attempt at this type of practice. She writes of the body as holding a unique position in its ability to epitomize both individual specificity and the sense of a material interrelation with the world. The nomadic subject is figured on a number of levels of identification that can coexist chronologically, and between which the subject is able to flow. In gendered terms, the first level of identification is figured as the realization of the difference between men and women; the historical universalization of male subjectivity at the expense of the female, represented only by her absence in culture. The second includes the differences between women as a gendered group; this level is rooted in everyday experience. This is the place of the various feminist theories of cultural woman. The third level refers to the differences within each individual woman: between the first two levels of experience, between **memory** and genealogy, and between the conscious and the unconscious. The idea of a subjectivity that is able to migrate between, and combine, these different levels of analysis allows the coexistence of any number of different concepts of sexual and gender difference. This concept, which retains the body as the incorporation of all these levels of subjectivity, is valuable in that it reinstates the body as living matter, however construed and whatever features are imparted to it, enabling the individual to be situated not only in the context of gender politics but of rights, of relations to others, and of all other human discourses. Each concept of gender difference is thus rehistoricized and placed in a position where it can interact with other modes of differentiation, preventing it from becoming absolutist or prescriptive.

To return this theory to a textual context, one might consider Nancy Miller's assertion in "Women's Autobiography In France: For a Dialectics of Identification" (1980):

> The difference of gender as genre is there to be read only if one accepts the terms of another sort of "pact"; the pact of commitment to decipher what women have said (or, more important, left unsaid) about the pattern of their lives over and above what any person might say about his, through genre. I say "his" deliberately, not because men in fact lead genderless lives, but because the fact of their gender is given and received literarily as a mere donnée of personhood, because the canon of the autobiographical text, like the literary canon, self-defined as it is by the notion of a human universal, in general fails to interrogate gender as a meaningful category of reference or interpretation. (267)

Here, gender becomes a genre in the sense that it implies a set of conditions given by the text and through which it is read: it is contingent not only on the individual text but on the individual reading moment, avoiding recourse to a universal or prescriptive norm. As autobiographical texts are themselves seen to break down the differences between genres, and to operate under a number of different categorizations, the category "gender" can be related to the other discourses whose interaction forms not only the text but the reader. This double process of historicization allows the gendered female subject to speak as such, without her gender either becoming fixed and normalized, or dominating her textualized life.

Further Reading: Butler, Judith. *Gender Trouble: Feminism and the Subversion of Identity* (New York and London: Routledge, 1990); Grosz, Elizabeth A. *Volatile Bodies: Toward a Corporeal Feminism* (Bloomington: Indiana University Press, 1994); Laqueur, Thomas. "Orgasm, Generation, and the Politics of Reproductive Biology." In *The Making of the Modern Body: Sexuality and Society in the Nineteenth Century*, edited by Gallagher, Catherine and Thomas Laqueur, 1–41 (Berkeley: University of California Press, 1987); Foucault, Michael. *The History of Sexuality*. 1976. Translated by Robert Hurley (New York: Penguin, 1998); Marcus, Laura. *Auto/Biographical Discourses: Theory, Criticism, Practice* (Manchester: Manchester University Press, 1994); Stanton, Domna C. "Autogynography: Is the Subject Different?" In *The Female Autograph: Theory and Practice of Autobiography from the Tenth to the Twentieth Century*, edited by Domna C. Stanton, 3–20 (Chicago and London: Chicago University Press, 1984).

Elissa Rospigliosi

GERMAN WOMEN'S AUTOBIOGRAPHY Any attempt to clearly define "German women's autobiography" is problematic, since German can be understood as "German-national" or "German-speaking." Germany, historically split into various kingdoms and principalities, has rarely been a singular entity. Barely unified in 1870, it was again divided into West and East Germany after 1945, leading to ongoing political debates about what constitutes "Germanness." For the purpose of this discussion, German means "German-speaking," which includes Austria and Switzerland, and Germans in exile. Similarly, autobiography is an ambiguous term, and it is used here in the broader sense of life writing: family chronicles, diaries, **letters**, and novels with a strong autobiographical element. This approach ac-

knowledges the fact that women's autobiographical writings often remained unpublished. Until recently, women writers did not have access to the literary and publishing world and did not lead lives that could compare with the typical autobiographer: male, successful, and in tune with the public life and spirit of the time.

As in other European countries, German autobiographical writing begins as religious and confessional writing. Religious mystics like the eleventh-century **Hildegard von Bingen** or the thirteenth-century Gertrude the Great relate their visions and personal lives, which they perceive as inextricably connected to God, who speaks to them and through them. These narratives are also characterized by attempts to evade accusations of heresy through aligning themselves with the authority of church doctrine and male theologians and confessors. Religious testimonies continued to be an important part of women's autobiographical writing: the seventeenth century Jewish woman Glückel of Hamelin records Hamburg Jewish life as well as a personal, ongoing dialogue with God. In the eighteenth century, leading Pietist women Johanna Petersen and Dorothea Zinzendorf related their religious experiences in an emotionally charged style, while devotee of the Herrnhut community Susanna Katharina von Klettenberg wrote a spiritual autobiography. Her life is also famously narrated in the first person by Johann Wolfgang von Goethe as "Confessions of a Beautiful Soul" in *Wilhelm Meister's Apprenticeship* (1795).

The most popular secular autobiographical account in a female **voice** from the seventeenth century, the outrageously bawdy Thirty Years War adventures of the settler and petty crook "Courage," is a fiction by the male writer Grimmelshausen. However, secular autobiographical texts written by women also begin to emerge at this time. They are primarily unpublished family chronicles, diaries, and entries into pre-printed almanac-cum-diaries (*Schreib-*

Kalender) written by women from the aristocracy or merchant **class** who relate their lives as connected to family history. In the eighteenth century, letters written by women both aristocratic and bourgeois were posthumously published, as were correspondences between spouses-to-be. There is also a wealth of memoirs and autobiographical, short-prose pieces written by women, although the majority were published anonymously or posthumously. Very few eighteenth-century women published autobiographical writings under their own name; exceptions are an autobiographical essay by the writer Sophie von La Roche or the adventurous **travel narrative** of Swiss army wife Regula Engel. Since bourgeois women were completely dependent on their families or spouses for their livelihoods, these writings do not express protofeminist sentiments. Feminist critics suggest that one needs to search carefully for "blind spots" and "silences" in the text in order to detect suppressed criticisms of husbands and families.

The early nineteenth century saw the publication of the archetypal German autobiography, Johann Wolfgang von Goethe's *Dichtung und Wahrheit* (1811 [Poetry and Truth]), which draws together life events into a teleological narrative of the writer's development as an artist, simultaneously acknowledging the blurred boundaries between fact and fiction. While it was impossible for women to similarly proclaim their public achievements and significance as artists, female writers associated with the Romantic movement wrote letters and diaries that formed part of the literary and artistic culture of the time (most famously the literary salon host Rahel Varnhagen). Bettina von Arnim uses the female forms of letters and diaries to create semifictional narratives. In *Goethes Briefwechsel mit einem Kinde* (1835 [Goethe's Correspondence with a Child]), she latches on to the renowned writer's authority, contrasting his classical serenity with her self-portrayal as a chaotic and inspired "wild child." In *Die Günderode* (1940 [*Miss Gunderode*]), adapted from her correspondence with the five-years-older poet Karoline von Günderode, Arnim reconstructs their tempestuous friendship, contrasting her "wild" persona with her friend's calm demeanor and classical poetry. She also critically explores the marginalized situation of women poets in Romantic literary circles, ending on a sombre note by relating Karoline's suicide in 1806.

During the second half of the nineteenth and the first half of the twentieth century, published women autobiographers tend to connect their own lives to the political movements of the time, responding to the revolutionary fervor of the *Vormärz* era (the years before the failed bourgeois revolution in 1848) and the first-wave **feminism** of the *Allgemeine Deutscher Frauenverein* (German Women's Public League, the first national women's rights group in Germany) founded in 1865 by Louise Otto-Peters. Louise Aston's autobiographical novel *Aus dem Leben einer Frau* (1846 [From a Woman's Life]) reflects her experience of leaving the rich industrialist she was forced to marry at age seventeen. Strongly influenced by George Sand (she took to wearing trousers and smoking cigars as well), Aston scathingly portrays the situation of women compelled to stay married for financial reasons and condemns the shocking discrepancy between the lives of factory owners and workers in early capitalist Germany. Fanny Lewald, in *Meine Lebensgeschichte* (1863 [The Education of Fanny Lewald: An Autobiography]), describes her precarious situation as a Jew and professional woman writer in a literary world dominated by men and strongly agitates for women to be given the opportunity to work and live independently. The Moravian aristocrat Marie von Ebner-Eschenbach, whose work critically depicts social relations in rural Austria, describes the early influences that led her to rebel against her conventional mother and become a writer in *Meine Kinderjahre* (1906 [My Childhood Years]). Around the turn of the twentieth century, women more directly connected to the **women's movement** publish autobiographies outlining their struggles for the rights of women: for example, feminist writer Hedwig Dohm, Viennese factory worker turned socialist politician Adelheid Popp, and impoverished aristocrat and bohemian Lu Märten. In 1944, Anita Augspurg, suffragist and first female law graduate in Germany, and her work and life partner Lida Gustava Heymann publish their joint autobiography, *Erlebtes, Erschautes* [Things We Have Seen] from their exile in Switzerland.

Women authors who were part of bohemian circles from approximately 1900 to 1933 also published autobiographical works. Franziska von Reventlov's autobiographical novel *Ellen Olestjerne* (1903) blends extracts from diaries with a third-person narrative that recounts Ellen's transformation from rebellious daughter of provincial parents to bohemian who expresses her liberated **sexuality** in a "free love" relationship with a fellow artist and then decides to bring up her child without a father. The Jewish poet Else Lasker-Schüler begins a unique experiment of fusing life and art by creating the fantastic autobiographical "I," "Prince Jussuf of Thebes," who is sometimes Jewish and sometimes Arabic. The author "stages" her transformation into Prince Jussuf in poems and prose texts, especially *Der Malik* (1917 [The Malik]), *Mein Herz—Ein Liebesroman mit Bildern und wirklich lebenden Menschen* (1920 [My Heart—A Romance with Pictures and Real People]). She undertakes this transformation more literally through her own performance in fantastical, androgynous costumes in her poetry readings. This alter ego enables Lasker-Schüler to create a mythical autobiography that, for her, is more real than real life could ever be. She begins a short autobiographical note: "I was born in Thebes (Egypt), though I came into this world in Elberfeld, in the Rhineland." The expressionist poet Claire Goll recounts the bohemian life of the 1920s and her numerous affairs with male artists in her polemic "scandalous memoir" *La Poursuite de vent* (1976 [Chasing the Wind]).

The time of experimentation with new literary and relationship forms evident in these texts came to an abrupt end when the National Socialist Party came to power in 1933. National Socialist ideology saw women first and foremost as mothers and helpers of heroic men. However, the experience of the Third Reich—opportunism or exile, or surviving a concentration camp—dominates German women's autobiographies until the present day. The most iconic female autobiographical account of persecution by the National Socialists is the Diary of Anne Frank, published in 1947 in an edition collated by her father that documented her life in hiding with her family until their capture and her death in 1945. Cordelia Edvardson, however, in her 1986 autobiography of the Theresienstadt concentration camp, *Gebranntes Kind sucht das Feuer* [Burned Child Seeks the Fire], sharply criticizes the use of Anne Frank's diary by postwar readers to indulge in sentimentality and cathartically rid itself of memories of the Holocaust. Ruth Klüger likewise recounts surviving Auschwitz-Birkenau as a teenager in *Weiter leben* (1995 [Still Alive: A Holocaust Girlhood Remembered]), offering a scathing feminist reading of the **gender** politics of *Vergangenheitsbewältigung* or coming to terms with the Third Reich past that categorize war and fascism as strictly men's business.

On the other side of the divide between victims and perpetrators, there are some self-justificatory autobiographies by women who were part of the National Socialist Party hierarchy or the German army, for example, Hitler Youth leader Melitta Maschmann or the aviation pioneer and test pilot Hanna Reitsch. The GDR writer **Christa Wolf** eschews self-justification in her searching 1976 autobiographical novel *Kindheitsmuster* [Patterns of Childhood] that explores how she turned from a bright but difficult child into a good little Nazi and ardent Hitler Youth girl. Stories from childhood are interwoven with the adult narrator retracing her childhood steps in her hometown, now part of Poland. On yet another level of time, the narrator reflects on the difficulties of her autobiographical project: her quest for the meaning of her childhood is dogged by the haunting sense that if only she could understand herself as a child, she could understand the collective psyche of the whole of Germany and the origins of the Third Reich, an impossible task that must end in failure. Other autobiographies from this period, for example Ruth Rehmann's 1979 *Der Mann auf der Kanzel* [The Man in the Pulpit] work through the postwar generation's realization of their fathers' complicity in the National Socialist regime.

Second-wave feminism has also inspired autobiographical writing in German. Two iconic examples are Verena Stefan's *Häutungen* (1975 [Shedding]) and Karin Struck's *Klassenliebe* (1973 [Class and Love]). Stefan's text combines a narrative of sexual transformation from painful heterosexuality to fulfilled lesbianism with an experimental form that combines a variety of styles and strives to create a new, woman-centerd language. In contrast to Stefan's highly personal journey of discovery, Struck's autobiographical novel connects the working-class protagonist's painful relationship with a leftist man to the ways in which women are neglected in Marxist thought. Another form of leftist feminist life writing is the *Protokoll*, relating life stories of "ordinary women" as told to the author/compiler. This form was pioneered by Erika Runge in her 1974 work, *Frauen: Versuche zur Emanzipation* [Women: Fragments on Emancipation]. In the GDR, Maxie Wander challenged socialist gender ideologies in her 1979 collection, *Guten Morgen, Du Schöne: Frauen in der DDR* [Good Morning, Gorgeous: Women in the GDR], where the narrators reflect discontent with sexual hierarchies, dogmatism, and conformism in GDR society. A later collection of letters and diary entries written while Wander was dying of cancer, *Leben wär eine prima Alternative* (1980 [To live Would Be a Splendid Alternative]), frankly confronts the fears, hopes, and feelings of powerlessness. Recent autobiographies by women include the popular 1984 autobiography by Bavar-

ian farmer Anna Wimschneider, *Herbstmilch* [Autumn Milk], who depicts hard times in rural Germany during the war and postwar periods, while in the 1990s autobiographers like Freya Klier and Daniela Dahn note the difficulties of coming to terms with German reunification. The specific difficulties of German history and its impact on women's lives remain salient topics for autobiographers. *See also* **Confession; Memoir.**

Further Reading: Davies, Mererid, Beth Linklater, and Gisela Shaw, eds. *Autobiography by Women in German* (Oxford: Peter Lang, 2000); Edvardson, Cordelia. *Burned Child Seeks the Fire: A Memoir.* Translated by Joel Agee (Boston: Beacon Press, 1997); Klüger, Ruth. *Still Alive: A Holocaust Girlhood Remembered* (New York: Feminist Press at the City University of New York, 2001); Kosta, Barbara. *Recasting Autobiography: Women's Counterfictions in Contemporary German Literature and Film* (Ithaca, NY, and London: Cornell University Press, 1994); Lewald, Fanny. *The Education of Fanny Lewald: An Autobiography.* Translated, edited, and annotated by Hanna Ballin Lewis (Albany: State University of New York Press, 1992); Rehmann, Ruth. *The Man in the Pulpit: Questions for a Father.* Translated by Christoph Lohmann and Pamela Lohmann (Lincoln: University of Nebraska Press, 1997); Stefan, Verena. *Shedding.* Translated by Johanna Steigleder Moore and Beth E. Weckmueller (New York: Feminist Press at the City University of New York, 1994); Wolf, Christa. *Patterns of Childhood.* Translated by Ursule Molinaro and Hedwig Rappolt (New York: Farrar, Straus and Giroux, 1984).

Antje Lindenmeyer

GIOVANNI, NIKKI (YOLANDE CORNELIA JR.) (1943–) One of the most prominent African American poets to achieve national attention during the 1960s, Giovanni is a political activist who expresses strong racial pride and the necessity for an active revolutionary posture for African Americans to throw off the yoke of white oppression. Her autobiography, *Gemini: An Extended Autobiographical Statement on My First Twenty-Five Years of Being a Black Poet* (1976), has received little critical attention, perhaps because it is not a traditional autobiography. Rather than trace the events of her life from early childhood to the time of her writing (1971), Giovanni's autobiography covers only a few selected events in her first twenty-five years. In addition, Giovanni interweaves autobiographical events with political and social commentary. As a result, while her autobiography gives the reader a portrait of this contradictory and remarkable poet, the book can also be read as a portrait of a people.

Gemini begins with Giovanni's personal reflections on Knoxville, Tennessee. Although it jumps around in time, in this section of the book Giovanni includes stories about her family, showing the roles various people played in shaping her beliefs and allowing a glimpse into her personal life. She shared a deep bond with her grandmother, Louvenia, the person who first influenced and inspired her toward activist ideals and who taught her to value intergenerational relationships. Giovanni goes into some detail in describing her close relationship with her sister, Gary, whom she hero-worshipped to the point of fighting her sister's battles on the playground, sometimes to her sister's dismay. Giovanni tells us about her first unsuccessful attempt at Fisk University, her grandfather's alma mater (she was not considered a "Fisk woman" in part because she left school without permission to have Thanksgiving dinner with her grandfather who was gravely ill (he died shortly thereafter) and her later successful completion of her degree under a different dean's supervision. She shares the birth of her son, her fear of labor, and of being a mother. These memories portray a loving, close-knit family and show her connection to them and her community, as well as her growth as an artist.

From this point forward, the book becomes a personal philosophical text, combining social and political commentary and is less a true autobiography. Personal events are still included—Giovanni recounts her trip to California during which she passed up the chance to meet **Angela Davis**, and her subsequent trip to the Caribbean. And while Giovanni certainly discussed her political agenda in the first half of the book, it is developed more fully in this section. Here, her mind is at work, explaining, exploring, lecturing, questioning. In Haiti, she realizes that being black will not keep her from being taken advantage of because she is considered a "foreigner," an experience that leads her to question the way immigrants are treated in the United States. She thinks about Angela Davis and her treatment due to her radical political agenda, and urges black Americans to get involved in eradicating racism and defending antiracist activists.

There are also critical pieces on black literature and music, with an essay on Lena Horne, a discussion of the novels of Charles Chesnutt, and a book review of *The Sound of Soul*. She ends her autobiography with a long chapter explaining her reasons for becoming a writer—to tell her truth—which, like the rest of the autobiography is entertaining, captivating, insightful, and at times frustrating.

Giovanni's autobiography may be offensive to some readers. As in her poetry, Giovanni's positions are radical. She frequently refers to whites as "crackers" and challenges her audiences, both black and white to take **race** issues seriously. Her tone may be angry, but her intention is to awaken her readers to the realities of racism. While the Right might consider her remarks and statements racist, she would argue that such an accusation is impossible: "The facts show that Black people by the definition of racism cannot be racist. Racism is the subjugation of one people by another because of their race, and everything I do to white people will be based on what they did to me" (44).

Ultimately, it does not matter whether Giovanni's autobiography is traditional. Its value lies in its mere existence. Giovanni spends the first chapter reminiscing about the Knoxville of her youth, the people, and the **place** that shaped her into the woman she was at the time of writing. She wrote her autobiography for her son: "And I thought Tommy, my son, must know about this. He must know we come from somewhere. That we belong" (21). In tying together her personal life and social/political views, the richness of Giovanni's text indeed lets readers know that she does come from somewhere. That she belongs. Giovanni's introspection serves to sharpen her own creative and mental powers while giving her audience insights into what and how she thinks. Herein lies the true power of *Gemini. See also* **Memory**.

Further Reading: Fowler, Virginia C. *Nikki Giovanni: An Introduction to Her Life and Work* (New York: Twayne, 1992); Fox-Genovese, Elizabeth. "Writings of Afro-American Women." In *The Private Self: Theory and Practice of Women's Autobiographical Writings*, edited by Shari Benstock, 61–89 (Chapel Hill: University of North Carolina Press, 1988); Giovanni, Nikki. "Gemini: An Extended Autobiographical Statement on My First Twenty-Five Years of Being a Black Poet." In *The Prosaic Soul of Nikki Giovanni*, 1–190 (New York: HarperCollins, 2003); McDonald, Kathleen. "Nikki Giovanni." In *African American Autobiographers*, edited by Emmanuel S. Nelson, 150–155 (Westport, CT: Greenwood, 2002); Tate, Claudia, ed. *Black Women Writers at Work* (New York: Continuum, 1983).

Althea E. Rhodes

GOLDMAN, EMMA (1869–1940) An outspoken anarchist and feminist, Emma Goldman was once known as "the most dangerous woman in America." Goldman's two-volume autobiography, *Living My Life* (1931), relates in detail her participation in countless political struggles, her advocacy of anarchism, free speech, pacifism, and women's equality, as well as the more intimate aspects of her life including her numerous love affairs. *Living My Life* blends the personal and the political, attempting to demonstrate a life lived in harmony with the tenets of anarchism, defined by Goldman as "the philosophy of a new social order based on liberty unrestricted by man-made law; the theory that all forms of government rest on violence, and are therefore wrong and harmful, as well as unnecessary" (Goldman, "Anarchism" 1917, 50). Unlike her essays, however, Goldman's autobiography does not systematically explicate her theories of anarchism; instead, these are revealed through her experiences with police and other government authorities, as well as with various well-known activists, artists, writers, and thinkers, including Margaret Sanger, Peggy Guggenheim, and Peter Kropotkin.

Goldman was born on June 27, 1869, in what is now Lithuania. She moved to the United States in 1885 with her sister, settling in Rochester, New York. There, she worked in a textile factory. In 1887, she married Jacob Kershner, thus gaining U.S. citizenship. One year later, she divorced him, left Rochester, and moved to New York City where she quickly became involved in the anarchist movement. She undertook her first lecture tour in 1890, soon realizing her strength as an orator.

In August 1893, she addressed more than one thousand workers in New York's Union Square, urging them to "demonstrate before the palaces of the rich; demand work. If they do not give you work, demand bread. If they deny you both, take bread" (*Living My Life* 123). The press described her speech as "incendiary"; she was arrested for inciting a riot and sentenced to a year in prison, marking the beginning of her lifelong struggle for freedom of speech. In 1901, when an unknown anarchist shot President McKinley, authorities claimed the man had been inspired by one of Goldman's lectures, generating further antianarchist hysteria.

From 1906 to 1917, Goldman published the anarchist magazine *Mother Earth*, combining her interests in both political and literary writing and providing her with an outlet to promote her views. The government frequently confiscated the magazine for printing "obscene" and "subversive" material, including contraception and anti-conscription information.

When the United States entered World War I in 1917, Goldman began organizing and lecturing about pacifism. In June 1917, Goldman was indicted for conspiracy to violate the Draft Act. In February of that year, the government had passed the Immigration Act, allowing the deportation of "undesirable" immigrants; authorities had denaturalized Goldman's ex-husband in 1908, so she was no longer considered a citizen. In December 1919, she was deported to Russia, along with 248 other radicals. Goldman quickly found herself at odds with the new communist government, but despite her misgivings refrained from speaking out publicly. However, after the violent suppression of anarchists deemed "counter-revolutionary" by Lenin, she felt she could no longer remain in Russia. She left in 1921 and two years later published *My Disillusionment with Russia*, recounting her experiences under the Bolsheviks. Her criticisms angered communists throughout the world, and Goldman found herself under attack from the Left and the Right.

Goldman began writing her autobiography in 1927, hoping its publication would facilitate her readmission to the United States. The book was published in 1931 and generated neither the sympathy nor the sales she needed, quickly going out of print. Other than a ninety-day lecture tour in 1934, Goldman was never permitted to return to the United States. She died in Toronto, Canada, on May 14, 1940, and is buried in Waldheim Cemetery in Chicago, near the Haymarket Memorial.

Like many of her contemporaries, the death of the Haymarket martyrs greatly inspired Goldman. The event figures prominently in her autobiography, which begins with her arrival in New York in 1889; on her first day there she met fellow anarchists Alexander Berkman and Johann Most, two men who greatly influenced her politics and her life. That evening, she attended a lecture by Most commemorating the third anniversary of the Haymarket Affair. On May 4, 1886, in Chicago's Haymarket Square, a bomb was thrown into the crowd at a meeting of striking workers, killing seven police officers. Although no evidence proved who threw it, the eight speakers at the meeting were arrested and convicted for murder, almost solely because of their anarchist beliefs. The execution of four of the men on November 11, 1887, caused an enormous public outcry. In beginning her life story with these events—the anarchists' deaths and Most's speech that first evening in New York—Goldman posits her conversion to anarchism as her "birth."

"The Anarchist Queen" had faded into near obscurity when feminists revived interest in her in the early 1970s. A quotation incorrectly attributed to her—"If I can't dance, it's not my revolution"—frequently appeared on T-shirts and banners. Several of Goldman's books were subsequently reprinted, including *Living My Life*, and feminist scholars published new research about her.

Candace Falk's *Love, Anarchy, and Emma Goldman* (1984) examines Goldman's struggle to write her autobiography. Falk points to a disjuncture between the personal Goldman and her self-portrayal in *Living My Life* (1931), specifically her treatment of her relationship with Ben Reitman. Her love affair with Reitman was painful, for although she was passionately attracted to him, he was openly unfaithful to her. While she found it difficult to cope with Reitman's infidelities, Goldman publicly espoused "free love" and rejected marriage and therefore sought to downplay their relationship in her autobiography in order to present a life more in line with her ideology. Falk's book draws on Goldman's **letters** and personal correspondence, which are now housed, under Falk's direction, in the Emma Goldman Papers Project at the University of California, Berkeley.

Goldman's other works include *Anarch-*

ism and Other Essays, The Social Significance of the Modern Drama (1914), and numerous essays and pamphlets.

Further Reading: Falk, Candace. *Love, Anarchy, and Emma Goldman.* 1984 (New Brunswick, NJ: Rutgers University Press, 1990); Goldman, Emma. "Anarchism: What It Really Stands For." 1917. In *Anarchism and Other Essays,* 49–67 (New York: Dover Publications, 1969); Goldman, Emma. *Living My Life.* 1931. Vols. 1 and 2 (New York: Dover Publications, 1970).

Audrey Vanderford

GORDON, MARY (1949–) Best known for her engagement with moral and political issues surrounding the Catholic Church, novelist and critic Mary Gordon's most prominent autobiographical work is a set of memoirs titled, *The Shadow Man: A Daughter's Search for Her Father* (1996). Other shorter autobiographical pieces have been collected in *Good Boys and Dead Girls: And Other Essays* (1991), and more recently, in *Seeing Through Places: Reflections on Geography and Identity* (2000). In these essays, Gordon foregrounds her childhood, religious upbringing, and feminist politics, focusing on their intersections and the conflicts they may produce—subject matter on which she also draws heavily in her fiction.

That Gordon writes extensively about her own family and the culture of Catholicism is unsurprising given the insular Catholic community in which she was brought up, her father's singular and (to her) dynamic personality, and the dramas she witnessed played out among her mother's family during her childhood and adolescence. Like her relationship with the Catholic Church, Mary Gordon's relationship with her father is at the heart of much of her fiction and autobiographical writing and is a deeply conflicted one.

Gordon's earliest years were spent with her parents in Queens, New York. When she was seven, her father died and she and her mother moved back to her grandmother's house on Long Island. As she re-

counts in *The Shadow Man*, Gordon idolized her father, who had led his family to believe that he attended Harvard and led a bohemian life as a youth in Europe. In actuality, David Gordon (originally named Israel) was a Lithuanian immigrant to Lorain, Ohio, who spoke Yiddish, lived with other immigrants in a segregated area in town, and did not attend high school, presumably due to poverty. As Mary Gordon discovered in the process of researching her memoirs, her father had spent several years in the 1920s and early 1930s publishing his own pornographic humor magazine, *The Hot Dog Annual,* under the pseudonym "Jack Dinnsmore." A convert to Catholicism, David Gordon went on to publish poetry and cultural criticism expressing xenophobic and anti-Semitic political positions. Gordon's mother, the offspring of Irish-Catholic immigrants, supported the family and later deteriorated into alcoholism when Mary was an adolescent. Mary Gordon attended Barnard College and was propelled to literary fame with the publication of her best-selling first novel *Final Payments,* which appeared in 1978 when she was just twenty-nine. In *Final Payments,* Gordon created a heroine, Isabel Moore, who was raised in a small Catholic community in Queens and whose father is at the center of her emotional life—though at the novel's beginning he has died and is alive only in her **memory** and imagination.

Significantly and a bit surprisingly, Gordon attributes her **feminism** to her Catholic education, pointing to female role models such as the Virgin Mary, whom she describes as having a creative power that operates independently of man, and Teresa of Avila, who initiated the reform of the Carmelite Order by opening a convent and writing advice on how to pray. Along the same lines, Gordon also attributes her feminism to the social justice espoused by the Catholic Church. Gordon was an adolescent when the Second Vatican Council was convened by Pope John XXIII from 1962 to 1965. Though she claims that at the time she had little opinion about "Vatican II," Gordon's desire for greater inclusiveness and social justice within Catholicism coincides with the newfound openness that emerged in the contemporary Catholic Church. Coming of age in the late 1960s and early 1970s, Gordon was also influenced by the American civil rights and feminist movements in her literary treatment of religion, politics, and **gender**. In both *The Shadow Man* and *Good Boys and Dead Girls*, Gordon raises questions about women's secondary roles in the hierarchical structure of the Catholic Church and positions herself in opposition to the Vatican's antigay and antiabortion stances. The heightened atmosphere of experimentation and change that pervaded the social movements of the 1960s likewise influences the more experimental form Gordon's writing takes.

The Shadow Man in particular is compelling because it mixes different narrative techniques, an experiment with form that has gained much ground in autobiographical writing of the postwar period. Much of Gordon's **memoir** is spent narrating her own desire and attempt to investigate and imagine her father's life, rather than recounting a detailed and chronologically linear description of her childhood. Her book instead weaves together such disparate forms as the literary analysis of her father's writing, photographs, and **letters**; the recording and analysis of dreams; and "impersonation," that is, her own fictionalizing of her father's story through first-person narration. Gordon's reliance on imagination and fictionalization serves two purposes in the text: one is to fill in the many gaps in the record of his life; the other is to explain and justify much of what she does uncover, namely David Gordon's abandonment of his native religion and family and reinvention of his own **identity** and background. As Gordon explains, "I wrote my father's history as one of the Lives of the Saints" and compares her enshrining of him to the sacred containers used by the Church: "chalice, ciborium, monstrance, pyx; . . . containers to enclose, keep safe, keep intact, keep protected from the world's contamination the sacred matter" (*The Shadow Man* 10). Thus, her process of research and writing her father's life with all its flaws and failures, leads her to perceive how the ecclesiastical rituals embedded in her way of seeing the world have allowed her to reshape a life she herself refers to as "ordinary" into an elevated and tragic form. Gordon's significance lies in her location as a feminist writer who draws deep meaning from the Catholic religion, rather than simply rejecting it as fostering repression and guilt.

Gordon frequently cites Catholic writers Mary McCarthy, best known for her autobiography, *Memories of a Catholic Girlhood* (1957), and Flannery O'Connor. These two women may be viewed as Gordon's natural precursors. In addition to *Final Payments*, Gordon's novels, *The Company of Women* (1980), *Men and Angels* (1985), *The Other Side* (1989) and *Spending* (1998) have been highly acclaimed national bestsellers. She has received the Lila Acheson Wallace-Reader's Digest Writer's Award and a Guggenheim Fellowship. Gordon teaches at Barnard and lives with her family in Manhattan.

Further Reading: Gordon, Mary. *Good Boys and Dead Girls: And Other Essays* (New York: Viking, 1991); Gordon, Mary. *Seeing through Places: Reflections on Geography and Identity* (New York: Scribner, 2000); Gordon, Mary. *The Shadow Man: A Daughter's Search for Her Father* (New York: Random House, 1996); Labrie, Ross. *The Catholic Imagination in American Literature* (Columbia and London: University Missouri Press, 1997); Pearlman, Mickey, ed. *American Women Writing Fiction: Memory, Identity, Family, Space* (Lexington: University Press of Kentucky, 1989).

Elizabeth J. Toohey

H

HALKETT, ANNE, LADY (1623–1699) A lively and engaging autobiographer, Anne, Lady Halkett offers modern readers a unique insight into the events and disruptions of the English civil wars from the perspective of a deeply religious aristocratic woman, loyal to the monarchy. These memoirs also provide evidence of the pitfalls of courtship in the mid-seventeenth century, the difficulty for women to maintain a reputation for virtue, and the frustrations of securing property in wartime.

Born in London on January 4, 1623, Anne Murray (later Lady Halkett) was the daughter of Thomas Murray, Provost of Eton College and former tutor to Charles I, and Jane Drummond Murray, governess to the duke of Gloucester and Princess Elizabeth. Anne's father died the year she was born, and she spent much of her early life at the Kent estate of her brother-in-law, Sir Henry Newton. Her first suitor was Thomas Howard, but her mother forbade her to marry him. After her mother's death, she went to live with her eldest brother, Henry, and there met Colonel Joseph Bampfield, a spy for Charles I. In 1648 (the year before the regicide), Anne helped Bampfield perform one of the more celebrated events narrated in her memoirs: assisting in the Duke of York's escape from England disguised in women's clothing.

Telling her his wife was dead (he may have believed this himself), Bampfield pressed Anne to marry him, and she consented once arrangements could be made to secure their property from confiscation by the Parliamentarians. In 1650, Anne traveled to Edinburgh to recover part of her mother's inheritance and was welcomed by the Royalists gathered in Scotland, including Charles II. She attended wounded soldiers at Kinross and stayed with the countess of Dunfermline in Aberdeenshire. On a trip to Edinburgh in 1652 to sue for her inheritance, she met Sir James Halkett, a widower. Periodically, Anne heard rumors that Bampfield's wife was still alive, but she maintained her faith in him and allowed his visits until one of the rumors was confirmed in 1653.

In 1656, Anne married Halkett and remained at his estate in Scotland until his death in 1670, when she took up residence in Dunfermline for the remainder of her life. There she wrote her memoirs and, having failed to gain appropriate compensation for her lost property, supplemented her income by teaching. At his succession to the throne in 1685, James II awarded her a pension of £100 per year for her service to him when he was Duke of York. Only one of her children, Robert, survived infancy, but she outlived him by seven years, dying in 1699 at age seventy-six.

The original manuscript of Halkett's autobiography is tainted: a few pages are missing at pivotal points in her life, leading to modern critical speculation about whether Halkett was in fact Bampfield's mistress before her marriage to Sir James Halkett; certainly, she takes great pains to establish her innocence of any wrongdoing. Her memoirs testify to the public nature of her life; her friends and family are always intimately aware of all of her activities, which leads to occasional outbursts of conscience and attempts to vindicate herself from what must have been a terrible blot on her reputation:

> Itt is nott to bee imagined by any pious, vertuous person (whose charity leads them to judge others by themselves) butt that I looked upon itt as unparaleld misfortune (how inocentt so ever I was) to have such an odium cast upon mee as that I designed to marry a man that had a wife, and I am sure none could detest mee so much as I abhored the thought of such a crime. (Loftis 35)

The most authoritative support for her virtue comes straight from heaven: Halkett interprets instances of being saved from personal danger as evidence of divine support and approval. These moments, in which she describes the divine will at work, usually involve her recovery from serious illness, which she looks back on as a series of personal spiritual trials imposed by God. Her difficulties in securing and reclaiming family property are also mentioned throughout the narrative and form additional trials she must endure.

Autobiographical writing became increasingly popular throughout the seventeenth century, particularly as it provided an outlet for the kind of religious self-examination encouraged by Protestantism. Halkett was probably aware of such writing either as a developing trend or at least a commonly practiced discipline, like the devotional meditations that makeup the bulk of her writing. Certainly she had no immediate intention that her memoirs would be published, and though a mysterious version of her life appeared in 1701, it cannot be assumed that Halkett's autobiography acted as an influence on eighteenth-century life writings. A more authoritative edition did not appear until 1875.

Halkett has left us with many writings, but only two genres of work: fourteen extant volumes of *Meditations*, which consist of prayers and religious meditations, and her autobiography, which covers the years 1623–1656 and was written in 1677–1778, twenty years before her death. *See also* **Memoir**.

Further Reading: *The Autobiography of Anne, Lady Halkett*. Edited by J. G. Nicholls (London: Camden Society, 1875); Ottway, Sheila. "They Only Lived Twice: Public and Private Selfhood in the Autobiographies of Anne, Lady Halkett and Colonel Joseph Bampfield." In *Betraying Ourselves: Forms of Self-Representation in Early Modern English Texts*, edited by Henk Dagstra, Sheila Ottway, and Helen Wilcox (New York and Basingstoke: St. Martin's Press, 2000); Wiseman, Susan. "'The Most Considerable of My Troubles': Anne Halkett and the Writing of Civil War Conspiracy." In *Women Writing 1550–1750*, edited by Jo Wallwork and Paul Salzman, 25–46 (Bundoora, Victoria, Australia: Meridian, 2001).

Nancy Weitz

HARRIET MARTINEAU'S AUTOBIOGRAPHY Harriet Martineau (1802–1876), famous journalist, historian, novelist, and travel writer wrote her autobiography in 1855 in the very short time of three months, as she believed she was about to die. Since she recovered, however, her work was published posthumously in 1877. The published text consists of two volumes by Martineau and one volume of "Memorials" by Maria Weston Chapman, the American abolitionist and feminist and a close friend of Martineau's.

The first volume spans Martineau's childhood and covers her life until age thirty-seven. The second volume deals with her life until age fifty-three. Her autobiography is divided into six periods, each of which is arranged into sections, thus yielding a sense of linear development and progression. Maria Weston Chapman's biographical "Memorials" complete Martineau's life story and underline Martineau's importance as a female philosopher and writer. The **letters** and **diary** entries supplement Martineau's own story of her personal and professional development and complete the missing years from the first writing of the autobiography (1855) until Martineau's death in 1876.

The text presents a candid, psychologically detailed account of Harriet Martineau's development from a difficult childhood through to a self-sufficient womanhood, in which she is self-confident and has achieved professional success. She sees herself as a model for human development and thus presents a didactic success story: discipline and hard work lead to her importance and popularity as an educator, author, and journalist. Her autobiography can also be regarded as the story of a female philosopher's emancipation from **gender** restraints. She participates in the discourse on individualism traditionally regarded as a masculine prerogative. She speaks directly and strongly about herself and therefore violates the ideology of female propriety, self-effacement, and modesty, instead opening up new spheres for women. She shows great awareness of her status as an influential personality, stating that, "My business in life has been to think and learn, and to speak out with absolute freedom what I have thought and learned" (I, 133). Although she self-confidently publishes her works, she takes great care to partly conform to gender roles by emphasizing women's "natural" enjoyment of housework and professing her own liking for feminine duties. In addition, she avoids associating herself with well-known radical feminists, such as Mary Wollstonecraft, whom she condemns as a "poor victim of passion" (I, 400).

Her personal story is stylized as a step-by-step human development out of theological and metaphysical obscurity into the light of positivist Enlightenment. Throughout, morally driven plans and schedules for her life as well as personal restrictions and suffering are important for her. She is proud to lead a rational, regulated life without love or passion and thus demonstrates that she is able to fully control herself. She presents herself both as a patient sufferer from various illnesses and as a disciplined worker and ambitious thinker. Her purpose in writing her autobiography is clearly to help others by sharing her experience, which she considers her moral duty; her aim is to impart the whole truth of her life, and even leaves her private papers and personal documents to Weston Chapman.

Martineau's text is marked by a pronounced split between experiencing "I" and narrating "I": she attempts to recreate her feelings and experiences as a child, but her older and wiser self evaluates, criticizes, and interprets actions in retrospect and already hints at the future, which reveals her belief in the linear development of her mind and life. Emotions and events are refocused in the light of the happy ending.

In the first volume, Martineau describes her childhood as unhappy and as "the winter" of her life. Although her education and the intellectual atmosphere around her were egalitarian (Harriet was educated in the same way as her brothers), the emotional climate was repressive and austere. The lack of love, her sufferings and constant fears play a central role in her account. Having felt threatened by the world around her as a child and having experienced various grave illnesses during her life, Martineau regards her body as unreliable—this may underlie her denial of passion and **sexuality**. Apart from her fears and illnesses, these experiences lead her to intellectual endeavor at a very early age (she starts to read Milton's *Paradise Lost* at age seven, which provides her with "moral relief through intellectual resource" (I, 43). As an adult, she remarks that she must have been an intolerable child, but emphasizes that she could have been otherwise had she received more love and understanding from her parents.

Her view of childhood as a formative influence on human life leads Martineau to structure the story of her childhood in terms of its influence on her later intellectual achievements and personal growth. A child's experiences of suffering are important for her later tenacity in dealing with adversity and illnesses and her wish to control both her life and her body.

Religious fantasies about martyrdom become her refuge during her childhood. Later, however, she criticizes her religious fervor and also comes to regard her Unitarianism only as the starting point of her development, which would later have to be overcome. Her later faith is marked by a radical optimism and the belief in necessity (the universe is governed by laws that cannot be influenced by the human will). Her selfish concern for personal salvation is replaced by a confident altruism. Philosophy, in her case Positivism, frees her from restrictions into harmonious contact with the world.

Several events promote her literary career and the transgression of the feminine sphere: her family's financial fortunes steadily decline, making it necessary for her to earn money by writing. In addition, her fiancé becomes insane and soon dies, leaving her unmarried from that time forward. Later, she describes herself as "probably the happiest single woman in England" (I, 133). Furthermore, her deafness, which later forces her to use an ear trumpet, provides another occasion to turn away from the conventional social life expected of women and instead spend her time reading and writing.

After dwelling on her unhappy childhood, Martineau describes the start of her public career as an author and the circumstances surrounding the writing of her greatest success, *Illustrations of Political Economy* (1832–1834). After her first appearance in print, she feels that her brother's approval finally makes her an author: " 'Now, dear, leave it to other women to make shirts and darn stockings; and you devote yourself to this.' " (I, 120). In spite of having said this, however, during her entire life she takes great pains to present herself as feminine, emphasizing the pleasure she takes in housework.

Martineau repeatedly shows that her own tenacity leads to her success. The price she has to pay for success is high: her whole life is marked by long-lasting, serious illnesses, which she herself attributes to overwork, stress, and additional trouble with her mother, who tries to meddle in her affairs and does not approve of her daughter's success.

In London, Martineau's work becomes fashionable. However, she makes it clear that she will never again write for money or fame, but that she regards it as her duty toward others. She describes her motivation for writing on special topics (such as birth control and political reforms), her business deals with publishers, her disciplined method of writing, as well as her acquaintances with famous contemporaries (e.g., Malthus, Dickens, Charlotte Brontë, Wordsworth, Godwin). The first volume thus is composed of Martineau's development from a childhood of suffering to literary success and self-confidence: "I had now, by thirty years of age, ascertained my career, found occupation, and achieved independence" (I, 181).

The second volume continues to focus on Martineau's commitment to her career, her political interests, her various travels, and her illnesses. Once she has established herself as a famous writer and thinker, she rarely alludes to her personal position as a woman and becomes increasingly interested in the general development of humankind and society instead of her own life.

Martineau describes her travels in America at great length, which for her are part of a campaign against slavery as well as against the oppression of women. Her abolitionist opinions and critical political views are at the center of her interest. Her travels to continental Europe, Malta, Egypt, and Jerusalem and the writing of her subsequent political travel accounts are time and again interrupted by physical breakdowns, which she bears with great patience. One illness (probably a uterine tumor) confines her to bed for five years, during which she continues to write (among which is her essay, "Life in the Sick-room") and readjusts her view on life and death. She criticizes Christianity for its negative view of the body and argues that due to her "necessarianism" (the philosophy of necessity developed by John Priestley and David Hartley), she is no longer afraid of death. When conventional medical methods fail to cure her disease, she causes a sensation by undergoing treatment by mesmerism and pronounces herself to be cured in her *Letters on Mesmerism* (1845) and in her autobiography.

The second volume of her autobiography focuses on her philosophical development (she studies and translates Comte's *Positivism*), as well as on human development and the future of humankind in general. In her reflections on her life, Martineau interprets her development as a movement away from **subjectivity** (childhood's agonizing egotism and religious self-centeredness) and toward truth, which connects her to the larger world and provides contentment.

She describes the final period of her life as the most satisfying: she fulfills her dream of independence by purchasing land and having her own house built at Ambleside. Although famous and respected, at Ambleside she manages her own small farm and is cared for by her niece. She describes this period as the happiest one of her life: "My life began with winter, burst suddenly into summer, and is now ending with autumn;—mild and sunny" (I, 180). She ends her autobiography with serene reflections on life and death, believing that she would

soon die of heart troubles; however, she lived for another twenty-one years.

The third volume contains Maria Weston Chapman's biographical "Memorials," the aim of which is primarily to chronicle how Martineau influenced politics and people around her: "*Harriet Martineau's Autobiography* gives the impression the world made upon her: a memoir ought to give the impression she made on the world" (III, 81). Weston's "Memorials" also supplement Martineau's own autobiography in supplying personal details from her journals and correspondence with literary celebrities, family, and friends. The chapter headings introduce Weston's aim, which is to capture both Martineau's private and public selves, her home and her philosophical interests.

Chapman discusses Martineau's achievements, as her aim is to present Martineau not only as a remarkable person, but especially as an influential female intellectual. As in her own autobiographical account, Martineau emerges again as a model of discipline and patience and as a paragon of intelligence and success: her hard work and plans for her life are highlighted. Chapman also quotes Martineau's "rules" that she set up in her journal at age twenty-seven as guidelines for her future. The "Memorials" also contain Martineau's own obituary, which is entitled "An Autobiographic Memoir," in which she very briefly gives her family background and presents herself as a modest writer who is driven by a sense of duty. Her statement that "Her stimulus in all she wrote, from first to last, was simply the need of utterance" (III, 461) cannot obscure her importance and great influence as a writer, educator, philosopher, and feminist, which is so forcibly expressed in her autobiography and Chapman's "Memorials."

Further Reading: Martineau, Harriet. *Harriet Martineau's Autobiography*. 3 vols. (London: Smith, Elder and Company, 1877); Myers, Mitzi. "*Harriet Martineau's Autobiography*: The Making of a Female Philosopher." In *Women's Autobiography: Essays in Criticism*, edited by Estelle C. Jelinek, 53–70 (Bloomington: Indiana University Press, 1980); Smith, Sidonie. "Harriet Martineau's *Autobiography*: The Repressed Desire of a Life Like a Man's." In *A Poetics of Women's Autobiography: Marginality and the Fictions of Self-Representation*, edited by Sidonie Smith, 123–149 (Bloomington: Indiana University Press, 1987); Thomas, Gillian. *Harriet Martineau* (Boston: Twayne, 1985).

Miriam Wallraven

HEILBRUN, CAROLYN (1926–2003) Carolyn Heilbrun is a major figure in women's autobiography; her life and work represent an unusual and valuable combination of circumstance and intent: she was an early feminist and woman academic, facts which work in concert with her career-long interest in women's **biography** and autobiography. Her works that would be classed as autobiography, *The Last Gift of Time: Life Beyond Sixty* (1997) and *When Men Were the Only Models We Had: My Teachers Barzun, Fadiman, Trilling* (2002), were published late in her career, but elements of autobiography appear in nearly all of her published work. The works are organized thematically rather than chronologically. In fact, Heilbrun has never written a traditional autobiography, one that would seek to explain her life from childhood to adulthood, but has produced a body of theoretical work and practical example that is unequalled.

Born in 1926, a married woman and mother of three during her graduate school years, Heilbrun has always been aware of her generation's relation to third-wave **feminism**. She was educated at Wellesley and Columbia, and became a tenured professor at Columbia University. As president of the Modern Language Association (MLA) in 1984, she gave her convention address highlighting the fact of her gender. She has a distinguished record of speaking as a woman about issues that concern women, both as the academic Carolyn Heilbrun and the crime novelist Amanda Cross.

Heilbrun puts autobiographical example and analysis to use in her explorations of women's lives, fiction, and biography. In *Reinventing Womanhood* (1979), a classic of feminist criticism, Heilbrun uses autobiography to illustrate key points. She writes frankly of herself at age fifty and of her family background. Years later, in *The Last Gift of Time*, she tells readers of the courage it took to write about herself, of how much it went against the grain of her training as a scholar to include that type of material. Autobiographical material also figures prominently in *Writing a Woman's Life* (1988), particularly in the context of crime fiction, where her activities as Amanda Cross, the mystery writer, constitute a feminist practice to accompany the more theoretical work of Carolyn Heilbrun. She tells a story that suggests the centrality of biography and autobiography in her intellectual life: in the late 1930s and early 1940s, she read methodically though the shelves of the biography section at the public library, where nearly all of the biographies were about men. *Women's Lives: The View from the Threshold* (1999), incorporates autobiographical material in the context of a 1990s flurry of academic women's autobiographies. Taken together, the references throughout these works show a development in Heilbrun's use of autobiographical material, and her self-assessments contribute to the reader's understanding of feminist issues (particularly as they relate to educated women). The autobiographical elements, in tandem with the literary analysis, keep the ideas firmly connected to concrete examples.

In the first of her two distinctly autobiographical works, *The Last Gift of Time*, she structures her discussion around various issues relevant to women's lives after age sixty, including such diverse topics as e-mail, her lifelong Anglophilia, family relationships, and women's clothing. She writes at length about her relationship with **May Sarton**, who made Heilbrun her literary executor, and about the profound and personal interest she finds in the work of Maxine Kumin that makes Kumin "an unmet friend." She also describes her work in researching and writing *The Education of* *a Woman: The Life of Gloria Steinem* (1995), providing another useful analysis of how women's lives have been lived and written about, and inviting comparison with the reviews that biography received on publication. Heilbrun's biography of Steinem, Susan Kress (1997) notes, provides Heilbrun opportunities for "extracting the revelatory lesson from the particulars" a skill demonstrated throughout her work.

In *When Men Were the Only Models We Had*, Heilbrun organizes the autobiographical material around her ideological and/or personal relationships with three male figures important to her professional development. While she never met Clifton Fadiman, Jacques Barzun and Lionel Tilling were men she knew personally. The three men served as models for her of the intellectual/professional life she wanted for herself. In analyzing their work, their lives, and their significance to her, Heilbrun constructs not only a loose sort of intellectual autobiography but also a portrait of society and, more specifically, the culture of Columbia University. As always with Heilbrun, the autobiographical material provides concrete examples for larger feminist analysis instead of a comprehensive picture of her life.

Heilbrun's influence has been substantial, particularly for feminist academics in the United States. What she has written, and what she has done, reinforce each other: in a collection of work like *Hamlet's Mother and Other Women*, for example, readers see not only Heilbrun's ideas, but can also note that she was reclaiming "The Character of Hamlet's Mother" from misogynistic assumptions in *Shakespeare Quarterly* as early as 1957. She has worked with graduate students, mentored junior faculty, and tirelessly put feminist issues before the sometimes reluctant eyes of the MLA membership and a broad general readership. Her relationship with **Nancy K. Miller** has been especially productive professionally, and Miller captures Heilbrun's influence in her foreword to *Hamlet's Mother and Other*

Women: "[F]or feminists of my generation . . . it has always seemed that Carolyn Heilbrun was already there, there for us, and yet still somehow ahead."

Further Reading: Heilbrun, Carolyn. *The Education of a Woman: The Life of Gloria Steinem* (New York: Dial Press, 1995); Heilbrun, Carolyn. *The Last Gift of Time: Life Beyond Sixty* (New York: Dial Press, 1997); Heilbrun, Carolyn. *Reinventing Womanhood* (New York: Norton, 1979); Heilbrun, Carolyn. *When Men Were the Only Models We Had: My Teachers Barzun, Fadiman, Trilling* (Philadelphia: University of Pennsylvania Press, 2002); Heilbrun, Carolyn. *Women's Lives: The View from the Threshold* (Toronto: University of Toronto Press, 1999); Heilbrun, Carolyn. *Writing a Woman's Life* (New York: Norton, 1988); Klingenstein, Susanne. "'But My Daughters Can Read the Torah': Careers of Jewish Women in Literary Academe." *American Jewish History* 83 (1995): 247–286; Kress, Susan. *Carolyn G. Heilbrun: Feminist in a Tenured Position* (Charlottesville: University of Virginia Press, 1997); Matthews, Anne. "Rage in a Tenured Position." *New York Times Magazine.* November 8, 1992.

Rosemary Erickson Johnsen

HILDEGARD VON BINGEN (1098–1179) was one of the most important women authors of the Middle Ages. At a time when few women wrote or were recognized as contributing members of society, Hildegard von Bingen was active as a major author of theological and visionary writings and artwork, and she served as a counselor to popes and kings. She is the first known woman composer for whom a **biography** survives. Sickly from birth and plagued by health problems all of her life, Hildegard experienced visions from God that were recorded into manuscripts that survive to the present day. Her writings and visions interested the political and religious leaders of her time, and she often consulted with and even reprimanded male leaders at a time when women had few opportunities or rights in society.

Hildegard was born in Bockelheim on the Nahe River in 1098. She may have belonged to the illustrious Stein family, whose descendants are the present-day princes of Salm. Her father was a soldier in the service of Meginhard, Count of Spanheim. At age eight, due to her sickly nature and her parent's promise to give a child to God, Hildegard was placed under the care of Meginhard's sister, Jutta, who lived as a religious recluse at the church of St. Disibod on the Disenberg River. Hildegard had little instruction, given that she could hardly walk nor even see very well. She was taught to read and sing the Psalms, but never learned to write. She eventually was invested with the Benedictine habit. When Jutta died in 1136, Hildegard was appointed superior of the community of women.

Experiencing visions from God for most of her life, she received a command at around age forty, to begin writing down what she was seeing and hearing. A male monk was provided to write down her visions, which were submitted to Pope Eugene III (1145–1153) for approval. Her popularity and requests for her counsel began to put a strain on the religious community, and in 1147 she established a convent at Rupertsberg near the town of Bingen. Her nunnery was completely independent, and Hildegard oversaw its construction, which included such features as water pumped in through pipes (a rarity during this time period).

Hildegard was actively sought as a counselor and religious figure of her time, and despite her physical infirmities she traveled widely throughout southern Germany and Switzerland, and as far as Paris. As a composer of music, her monophonic chant was very different from the music of her time. Her secretary and nuns consistently recorded her visions, music, and even the art related to her visions in the manuscripts that they produced in their scriptorium. As a result, much of her work survives, despite the fact that few manuscripts survive from this time period. In her later life, she came under severe discipline by the church for burying an excommunicated young man in her convent's cemetery. Her community was placed under interdict, which meant that they could not conduct the services of the church or receive communion. Hildegard staunchly defended her decision, and eventually the interdict was removed, but not without much worry and correspondence on Hildegard's part. She died in her convent at Rupertsburg on September 17, 1179.

Hildegard's literary output consists of some seventy poems and nine books. Two of the books are on medical and pharmaceutical advice, dealing with the workings of the human body and the properties of various herbs. (These books are not based on her visions, but on her observations and those of others.) She wrote three books on theology: *Scivias* (Know the paths!), *Liber vitae meritorum* (on ethics), and *De operatione Dei*. Except for the second book, they deal mainly with the content of her visions that were dictated to her secretary. *Scivias* was written from 1141–1151 and is divided into three sections containing twenty-six visions. She also directed the production of this manuscript from her scriptorium in Rupertsburg and had artistic reproductions of what she saw in her visions placed directly into the manuscript. The *Liber vitae meritorum* was written between 1158 and 1163 and is a description of a Christian's life of virtue. *De operatione Dei* (also called *Liber divinorum operum*) was written between 1163 and 1174 and is a contemplation of all nature in light of the Christian faith. Things like the sun, moon, stars, planets, animals, and humans are all expressive of something supernatural and spiritual, and Hildegard writes about all of these things in relation to her visions.

More than 300 of Hildegard's **letters** survive. They were written to bishops, abbots, popes, and kings and urged them to live moral lives and to be upright and spiritual. She wrote hagiographical lives for St. Rupert and St. Disibod (patron saints of her convent), fifty allegorical sermons, a morality play (*Ordo virtutum*), and an invented language consisting of 900 words and an alphabet of twenty-three letters. As a music composer, Hildegard composed more than seventy chants with music that survive to the present, many of them contained in her *Symphonia armoniae celstium revelationum*, composed in the 1150s.

According to Hildegard, her visions often appeared as images of brilliant white light and symphonies of sound from which colorful images and figures emerged. Recent medical commentators on these visions relate them to experiences that people with intense and sustained migraines often have, while others believe that her visions are genuine revelations from God. Hildegard's visions provided her with a vista to expound in her writings and letters on issues such as social justice, political and religious accountability, and the plight of women in the medieval world. Her life and writings speak to many modern-day themes and concerns and have produced a renaissance of interest in her in the last thirty years.

Further Reading: Bowie, Fiona, and Oliver Davies. *Hildegard of Bingen: An Anthology* (London: Society for the Propagation of Christian Knowledge, 1990); Flanagan, Sabina. *Hildegard of Bingen: A Visionary Life* (London: Routledge, 1989); Newman, Barbara. *Sister of Wisdom: St. Hildegard's Theology of the Feminine* (Berkeley: University of California Press, 1987); *Vision: The Life and Music of Hildegard von Bingen.* Compiled and edited by Jane Bobko (New York: Penguin, 1995) (with accompanying music CD).

Bradford Lee Eden

HOFFMAN, EVA (1945–) Hoffman's evocative **memoir**, *Lost in Translation: A Life in a New Language* (1989), gives her a special role in women's autobiography, voicing as it does the loss, pain, and difficulty facing immigrants who are forced to translate themselves into a new language. In doing so, Hoffman helped launch a new subgenre in women's autobiography, the language memoir.

Eva Hoffman (born Ewa Wydra) emigrated from Poland to Vancouver, Canada, with her parents when she was thirteen years old, in 1959. She went on to earn a Ph.D. in American and English literature, teaching at a number of universities in the United States. She moved to New York and began working for the *New York Times* in 1979, later becoming editor of the *New York Times Book Review* (she left the *Times* in 1990). To date, Hoffman has published four books. She has won a number of literary awards and fellowships and has lectured at numerous universities in both the United States and England, teaching literature and creative writing. She currently lives in London. As *Lost in Translation* makes clear, however, her experience of immigration has not been a simple story of cosmopolitan travel and success.

For Hoffman's parents, the decision to emigrate was made against a background of what appeared to be a rising tide of anti-Semitism in Poland. Hoffman's parents (who were Jewish) had already lost many family members in the Holocaust. For the adolescent Hoffman, however, the move meant the loss of a beloved childhood homeland, the loss of a living language, a language that had connected her to the world (in contrast, English seemed alien and abstract, not fully real) and a forced translation into a new Canadian mold.

In English, the word commonly used for a longing for one's childhood home is "nostalgia," but in Polish it is *tesknota*, a word that "adds to nostalgia the tonalities of sadness and longing" (*Lost in Translation* 1989, 4). Each word embodies cultural assumptions, as Hoffman is keenly aware: in the English-speaking community that Eva enters, the past is something to be discarded, memories are not seen as valuable. Hoffman evokes her own memories against these assumptions: "How absurd our childish attachments are, how small and without significance. Why did that one, particular, willow tree arouse in me a sense of beauty almost too acute for pleasure, why did I want to throw myself on the grassy hill with an upwelling of joy that seemed overwhelming, oceanic, absolute? Because they were the first things, the incomparable things, the only things" (*Lost in Translation* 74). Hoffman suggests that it is this incomparable nature of our childhood attachments that makes them so absolute. In contrast, the shift to another language brings emptiness, precisely because of its nonabsolute nature:

> The words I learn now don't stand for things in the same unquestioned way they did in my native tongue. "River" in Polish was a vital sound, energized with the essence of riverhood, of my rivers, of my being immersed in rivers. "River" in English is cold— a word without an aura. . . . It does not evoke. . . . [T]his radical disjoining of word and thing is a dessicating alchemy, draining the world not only of significance but of its colors, striations, nuances—its very existence. It is the loss of a living connection. (*Lost in Translation* 106–107)

The language migrant's experience of this disjunction, Hoffman suggests, is far from the playful freedom promised by the structuralist theorists of language, rejoicing in the idea of words as arbitrary labels.

The new Canadian mold also included a different style of **gender**: As Hoffman notes at various points in her memoir, both the feminine body and gender distinctions were seen differently in Canada than in Poland. Hoffman registers the teenage Eva's discomfort with the gender polarization. She discusses the issue further in an interview with Mary Zournazi, noting that a migrant's translated self can find itself in what is literally a foreign body.

Hoffman acknowledges a particular affection for an autobiography by an earlier female immigrant, Mary Antin (*The Promised Land* 1912). As Hoffman notes, each autobiography is a product of its time. Antin (who emigrated to America from Russia in the early twentieth century) writes her story as a success story, the success of becoming an American. Hoffman, however, remains aware of what is lost, as well as what is gained, in translating one's self.

If a single book can be said to have launched the new genre of "language memoir," it is *Lost in Translation*. Some major language memoirs by women that followed Hoffman's include Alice Kaplan's *French Lessons* (1993); Susan Varga's *Heddy and Me* (1994); **Shirley Geok-lin Lim**'s *Among the White Moon Faces* (1996); Kyoko Mori's *Polite Lies* (1997); Natasha Lvovich's *The Multilingual Self* (1997); Lisa Appignanesi's *Losing the Dead* (1999) and Anca Vlasopolos's *No Return Address* (2000).

Hoffman's other works include *Exit into History: A Journey through the New Eastern Europe* (1993), *Shtetl: The Life and Death of a Small Town and the World of Polish Jews* (1997), and a science fiction novel, *The Secret* (2002). *See also* **Memory**.

Further Reading: Bammer, Angelika, ed. *Displacements: Cultural Indentities in Question* (Bloomington: Indiana University Press, 1994); Besemeres, Mary. *Translating One's Self: Language and Selfhood in Cross-Cultural Autobiography* (Bern: Peter Lang, 2002); Hoffman, Eva. *Exit into History: A Journey through the New Eastern Europe* (London: Heinemann, 1993); Hoffman, Eva. *Lost in Translation: A Life in a New Language* (London: Heinemann, 1989); Hoffman, Eva. *Shtetl: The Life and Death of a Small Town and the World of Polish Jews* (Boston: Houghton Mifflin, 1997); Zournazi, Mary, ed. *Foreign Dialogues: Memories, Translations, Conversations* (Annandale, New South Wales: Pluto Press, 1998).

Mary Besemeres and Susan Tridgell

HOOKS, BELL [GLORIA WATKINS] (1952–) Hooks draws on her matrilineal heritage for her pen name so that, as she puts it, "[W]hen the name bell hooks is called, the spirit of my great-grandmother rises" (*Talking Back* 1989, 166). Well known for her contributions to accessible critical **race** theory, she has also published two autobiographies that pursue similar themes to those presented in her academic writings. Although *Bone Black: Memories of Girlhood*

(1996) and *Wounds of Passion: A Writing Life* (1997) are not yet as widely known or read, hooks' ability to draw on autobiographical experiences to simplify difficult theoretical concepts makes her an important figure in the study of women's autobiography.

Hooks was born in Hopkinsville, Kentucky, and moved from her segregated childhood community to Stanford University in California, where she completed a B.A. After completing an M.A. at the University of Wisconsin and a Ph.D. at University of California, Santa Cruz, hooks worked her way up academic ranks to become Distinguished Professor of English at City College in New York. She is a respected teacher, scholar, and activist who has written on the place of black women within **feminism**, the representation of African Americans in film and popular culture, racism more broadly, and quite recently, love. Her early scholarly work concentrated on Toni Morrison and her depiction of her own girlhood in *Bone Black* is clearly influenced by Morrison's sketches of growing up poor and black.

Bone Black draws on quilting as a dominant metaphor and presents a "crazy quilt" of young Gloria Watkins' childhood struggles to understand herself as a racialized and gendered being. In the preface, hooks describes the book as "an autobiography of perceptions and ideas." Throughout the autobiography, she constructs herself as a childhood narrator in two separate voices, first person and third person. The narrative fragments are linked by repeated returns to matrilineal relationships, a precocious understanding of racialization, a deeply unhappy childhood sense of not belonging, a related awareness of the continuously unfair treatment of women and a persistent idealization of elderly people. In telling of the poverty in which she was raised, hooks paints a negative portrait of her parents' generation, idealistically situating in her grandparents' generation the power and love to which she has recently turned in her theoretical writings. Whether feeling ugly in her hair, shameful about her masturbation, or confused by her mother's choice to stay with an abusive man, the child narrator consistently writes of finding solace in church scenes and situates the strength of elderly relatives and friends either in the church or in secular traditions such as canning food, storytelling, and witchcraft. Hooks portrays herself as an avid reader of whatever she is given or comes across, whether it is literature, biographies, religious stories, popular romances, or pornographic magazines. Overall, *Bone Black* is an intense portrait of a sense of solitude with poignant vignettes of many of the painful aspects of coming-of-age mixed with some celebration of knowledge and the potential of old age.

Wounds of Passion for the most part concerns the competing desires for a major love relationship and for a writing career. In part, it narrates her long relationship with Mack, the man seven years her senior whom she first met at a Gary Snyder poetry reading. But it also covers the period during which hooks wrote *Ain't I a Woman: Black Women and Feminism* (1981) and engages with her lover's effect on that process. While tackling the difficulty that many women have balancing the gendered constraints of heterosexual love with the life of the mind, hooks continues to be engaged with the power and difficulty of living through the body in the alternating first- and third-person voices of *Bone Black*. Its experimental format is equally effective in a narrative that evokes the difficulties of writing as a woman. The racialized constraints placed on hooks and her partner bring them together at the same time as the gendered constraints placed on hooks separates her from him. The book gives insight into the struggles of a black woman to have a separate **identity** as a writer, and, in the process, examines many intersections, between love and work, men and women, artistic communities and academia. *See also* **Voice**.

Further Reading: hooks, bell. *Bone Black: Memories of Girlhood* (New York: Henry Holt and Company, 1996); hooks, bell. *Breaking Bread: Insurgent Black Intellectual Life* (Boston: South End Press, 1991); hooks, bell. *Happy to Be Nappy* (New York: Jump at the Sun, 1999); hooks, bell. *Homemade Love* (New York: Jump at the Sun, 2002); hooks, bell. *Outlaw Culture: Resisting Representation* (New York: Routledge, 1994); hooks, bell. *Remembered Rapture: The Writer at Work* (New York: Henry Holt and Company, 1999); hooks, bell. *Wounds of Passion: A Writing Life* (New York: Henry Holt and Company, 1997); "Voices from the Gaps: Women Writers of Color." http://www.voices.cla.umn.edu/authors/HOOKSbell.html.

Sally Chivers

HURSTON, ZORA NEALE (1891–1960)

Zora Neale Hurston was born January 7, 1891 (the year is sometimes given as 1901 or 1903, since Hurston was notorious for being unclear about her birthday), in Notasulga, Alabama, a small community near Tuskegee. Hurston was the fifth of eight children born to Lucy and John Hurston. Her mother died in 1904, after which Hurston was sent to school in Jacksonville, Florida, where she went from being the pampered daughter of a preacher who was the mayor of an all-black community (Eatonville, Florida), to living with relatives and working as a domestic servant, and moving from place to place in several states of the deep South. Eatonville would become an important setting for her influential novel, *Their Eyes Were Watching God* (1937), evidence of the importance of autobiography on her work.

Hurston later attended school in Baltimore, Maryland, at Morgan Preparatory High School (she arrived in Baltimore in 1917 while working as a maid with a Gilbert and Sullivan touring company); at Howard University in Washington, DC, from 1918 to 1919; and intermittently until 1924. Hurston's first short story, "John Redding Goes to Sea," was published in the Howard University literary magazine

while she was at school there. Two of her poems were published in *Negro World*, and another short story, "Drenched in Light," was published in *Opportunity* in 1924. Hurston attended Columbia University in 1925, Barnard College in 1926, and graduated from Barnard in 1928. She was the only black student at the college at that time.

Hurston wrote plays, essays, poetry, short stories, and novels, but all of her writing was based on folklore: her "Negro" characterizations are so true to life that Hurston is noted as an excellent anthropologist; she also studied anthropology at Columbia University. Hurston's short story, "Spunk," was selected by editor Alain Locke for publication in the important anthology *The New Negro* (1925). It won second prize in a literary contest later in 1925, and at the award dinner, Hurston met Langston Hughes and Countee Cullen.

"Spunk" is typical of Hurston's writing: the story has a very literate narrative, but the dialogue is in heavy black English dialect. Hurston's choice of subject matter provided inspiration for many later black writers, such as **Alice Walker** and Toni Morrison.

Hurston belonged to the Depression-era group of black writers that also included Ralph Ellison and Richard Wright. Some critics include Hurston in the Harlem Renaissance with writers such as Langston Hughes. Hughes and Hurston attempted to collaborate on a play, first called *The Bone of Contention*, and later *Mule Bone: A Comedy of Negro Life* (1931). Hurston had gathered some of the folklore used in *Mule Bone* in Florida, Alabama, and Louisiana beginning in 1927. In May 1929, she moved to New Jersey, where she and Hughes were supported by the same rich white patron of the arts, Charlotte (Mrs. R. Osgood) van der Veer Quick Mason. Hughes and Hurston fell into disagreement, and the play was not completed at that time. Hurston later copyrighted *Mule Bone* as her own independent work, claiming to have completely rewritten it after the collaboration failed. Hughes at first insisted he was coauthor, but eventually ceded all rights to the play to Hurston. Even though white Harlem Renaissance patron Carl van Vechten had sent *Mule Bone* to more than one theater group in an attempt to get it into production, the play was never performed while either of the collaborators was still living.

Hurston's longer works include *Mules and Men* (1935), the first collection of black American folklore published by a black writer, and a second collection, *Tell My Horse* (1938), gathered in Hurston's trips to the Bahamas, Tahiti, and Jamaica; her novels *Jonah's Gourd Vine* (1934) (based partially on Hurston's parents), *Their Eyes Were Watching God* (1937) (a novel based in oral tradition, and with an unusually strong female hero), *Moses, Man of the Mountain* (1939) (a history of black Americans), and *Seraph on the Suwanee* (1948) (about white life in Florida); as well as Hurston's autobiography/**memoir** *Dust Tracks on a Road* (1942, reprinted in 1985 with restored material and a new introduction).

Like Richard Wright, Hurston was a writer who used autobiography to show the living conditions of blacks not only to black readers, but also to white readers, although Wright criticized Hurston for what he seems to have regarded as her falsification of black life. Hurston presented social problems in her writing, but there were also good and happy elements among her recollections. One thing Hurston and Wright held in common was the importance of the search for self and self-identity in their autobiographies. Wright's works, however, were filled with hostility toward whites, but Hurston writes in *Dust Tracks* that she grew up feeling different from *everyone*, not just from whites or authority figures. Her written work all seems to grow out of dislocation and disorientation and from the search for self. Some critics point out that the inaccuracies and omissions in *Dust Tracks* make it more fiction than autobiography, but not all of the difficulties in the first published version were Hurston's. It

was heavily edited because it was sexually explicit for the time. Hurston does say in *Dust Tracks*: "This is . . . hear-say," but what autobiography isn't?

Zora Neale Hurston wrote and published more than fifty essays, short stories, and plays, and her work appeared in magazines such as *American Mercury* and *The Saturday Evening Post*. She later taught drama at the North Carolina College for Negroes in Durham, North Carolina. Her writing declined in popularity toward the end of her life, partly because her work was not the type of obvious "literature of protest" that was becoming increasingly popular at that time. (Hurston had been criticized for not writing protest literature since the 1930s.) She separated herself from other black writers and activists of the 1950s because she had been raised in an all black town and argued the benefits of segregation.

Hurston died on January 28, 1960, poor, in a charity home, and largely forgotten, in Fort Pierce, Florida. None of her books was still in print at the time of her death. It was Alice Walker who was one of those largely responsible for the rediscovery of the works of Zora Neale Hurston. Walker had become interested in Hurston in the early 1970s while teaching a university course on the novel; and she edited the important work, *I Love Myself When I Am Laughing . . . And Then Again When I Am Looking Mean and Impressive: A Zora Neale Hurston Reader* (1979). Walker and other writers and university professors were also responsible for the renaissance in Hurston scholarship and publication and for her secure place in today's literary canon. Walker also wrote an article for *Ms.* magazine about having gone to Florida in an attempt to locate Hurston's unmarked grave.

Many other texts have been written and published about Hurston since the Hurston renaissance began in the late 1970s; one of the most read is Robert Hemenway's *Zora Neale Hurston: A Literary Biography* (1977). Mary Helen Washington, who wrote a new foreword to *Their Eyes Were Watching God* in a series edited by Henry Louis Gates, Jr., dates the resurgence of interest in Zora Neale Hurston to two papers presented at the December 1979 Modern Language Association (MLA) conference in San Francisco, and to the ensuing discussion. Alice Walker was present at that session, and gave what Mary Helen Washington calls "the earliest feminist reading" of Hurston's work, a view now shared by many other writers and critics. *See also* **Identity**.

Further Reading: Andrews, William L., et al., eds. *The Oxford Companion to African American Literature* (New York: Oxford University Press, 1997); Bernard, Emily, ed. *Remember Me to Harlem: The Letters of Langston Hughes and Carl van Vechten* (New York: Vintage Books, 2002); Hurston, Zora Neale. *Their Eyes Were Watching God: A Novel.* With a foreword by Mary Helen Washington, 1937. Reprint (New York: Harper and Row, 1990); Locke, Alain, ed. *The New Negro: Voices of the Harlem Renaissance* (New York: Touchstone, 1997); Meisenhelder, Susan E. *Hitting a Straight Lick with a Crooked Stick: Race and Gender in the Work of Zora Neale Hurston* (Tuscaloosa, AL: University of Alabama Press, 1999).

Freda J. Fuller-Coursey

HUTCHINSON, LUCY (NÉE APSLEY) (1620–1681)

While Lucy Hutchinson's autobiographical "Life of Mrs. Lucy Hutchinson, Written by Herself" exists in print only as a fragment and as an addendum to her *Memoirs of the Life of Colonel Hutchinson*, she remains significant to an understanding of a Puritan woman's relationship to the English civil war and to politics in general. Her writings also give an insight into the education and regulation of women's lives in the seventeenth century.

Lucy Apsley was born July 29, 1620, in the Tower of London to Lucy St. John and Sir Allen Apsley, lieutenant of the Tower. Her father died when she was ten years old, and she lived with various relatives after her mother remarried. While the education of women was far from widespread, women in upper-class households were often given a formal education, though not equal to men's. Even so, Lucy's education was unusual in that she had greater exposure to and learning in the classics—Latin and Greek—than most upper-class women, in part because of her father's influence. By age seventeen, in addition to her scholarly pursuits, Lucy also began composing songs that were admired by members of the court. John Hutchinson was attracted to her because of her studiousness; Lucy married him in 1638 when she was age eighteen and eventually bore ten children, including twin sons. At least two of their children died young. During the Civil War years and up through the Restoration, Lucy supported her husband's involvement in the Council of State and in his role as a signatory of Charles I's death warrant. Lucy also tended the wounded during the civil war as she continued to write and translate texts. In 1663, following the 1660 Restoration of Charles II to the throne, John Hutchinson was arrested and imprisoned, though not tried formally, for allegedly participating in an uprising against Charles II; he died in prison in 1664 at age forty-nine. In the years between 1663 and 1678, Lucy Hutchinson was involved in dealing with her husband's debts and trying to protect her husband's estates at Owthorpe. Eventually she sold his estates to John Hutchinson's half-brother, Charles Hutchinson; she was buried at Owthorpe in October 1681.

Lucy Hutchinson gained a reputation after her death as a memoirist and literary figure, and more recently, scholars have come to view her as a kind of political historian. In particular, Lucy Hutchinson's autobiographical fragment, in concert with her *Memoirs of the Life of Colonel Hutchinson*, gives a sense of her religious, national, political, and familial **identity** through anecdotal descriptions of her upbringing and adult life. Framing her life in relation to "The Almighty Author," and viewing her own authorship in conventionally humble terms, she asserts that her autobiography is written to express her thanks to God and her parents. Yet in her autobiography she also links herself to a national identity through her connection to the Normans on her mother's side, and the Saxons on her father's side. In this way, she sees herself as deeply English as well as deeply Puritan. We see these same moves toward establishing a national identity in her depiction of England's geographic and political landscape and in her description of the once Edenic government as an ideal mixture of monarchy, aristocracy, and democracy. Lucy Hutchinson's Puritan identity also emboldened her to make explicit criticisms of England's contemporary political state.

Lucy Hutchinson composed *Memoirs of the Life of Colonel Hutchinson*, the work for which she has come to be most famous, during the years 1664–1670 as a kind of defense of her husband after his arrest, imprisonment, and subsequent death in prison for the alleged rebellion against Charles II. Many have come to see this work not only as a defense of a postwar Puritan dissenter, but also as an account of the religious and political conflicts that took place during the period prior to and during the civil war and Commonwealth periods. The full manuscript of Lucy Hutchinson's autobiography, attached to the published *Memoirs* as an autobiographical fragment, is now lost. While the exact date of the autobiography's composition is unknown, it is believed that she wrote it sometime between 1668 and 1674. While *Memoirs* was not published until 1806 by Julius Hutchinson (the great-grandson of Colonel John Hutchinson's half brother), it was likely circulated and read in its manuscript form during her lifetime, as were her other manuscript texts. Her other works include a new translation of Lucretius' scientific and ethical treatise *De rerum natura* from Latin into English, which shows Lucy Hutchinson's extensive knowledge of Latin. She also composed a biblical epic, *Order and Disorder*, which was the only of her works printed in her lifetime and is noted as one of the first long poems composed and published by an English woman writer. Her works taken together give a picture of the complicated relationship between her political and religious identity and her intellectual desires. While her deep commitment to Puritan doctrine reinforced her inferiority as a female and essentially denied her the right to publish, her relationship to the politics of the time and her deep desire for intellectual pursuits supported her drive to produce religious, political, literary, and even scientific works. *See also* **Class**.

Further Reading: Hutchinson, Lucy. *Lucy Hutchinson's Translation of Lucretius: De rerum natura*. Edited by Hugh de Quehen (Ann Arbor: University of Michigan Press, 1996); Hutchinson, Lucy. *Memoirs of the Life of Colonel Hutchinson* (London: H.G. Bohn, 1863); Hutchinson, Lucy. *Memoirs of the Life of Colonel Hutchinson, with the Fragment of an Autobiography of Mrs. Hutchinson*. Edited by James Sutherland (London and New York: Oxford University Press, 1973); Hutchinson, Lucy. *Order and Disorder*. Edited by David Norbrook (Oxford: Blackwell Publishers, 2001).

Jennifer Wynne Hellwarth

IDENTITY Identity would appear to be a simple and logical proposition of autobiography: the identity written about within the pages of the text is the self-description of the author and her life. Such an assumption arises naturally from the component parts of the word "autobiography": auto—self; bio—life; graph—writing. However, identity proves to be a far more elusive subject than such a basic equation. The issue of identity becomes complicated because of the nature of humanity as well as the nature of textualizing a life. Theorists of life writing grapple with such questions as these: Is the written self the same as the self who lived the life? Is memory accurate? What is left unsaid? How do we know if "truth" is really being told? Is "truth" available to be told? As these questions imply, the problem of identity in autobiography centers on the complexity involved when the living self creates a written self.

Identity—who the person is, or who the person represents herself to be—is not merely a set of characteristics, behaviors, and biological traits encoded through genetics; identity may also be learned, created, manipulated, or compelled. Women's identity is a particularly troublesome notion, in any event. Throughout the centuries, women's lives have been marginalized, misrepresented, and misinterpreted, and their socially constructed identities bear the marks of these oppressive experiences. Autobiography in the Western tradition was often understood to be the "great man" writing from a "strong" sense of identity about the active, dynamic life he had lived. Women's identities, in contrast, have been cast as ordinary and thus unworthy of book-length reflection; their lives were perceived to be fragmentary and ultimately unimportant.

Furthermore, names are the surface contact point of identity. Women's identities, as suggested by their names, are far more volatile than are men's because women have commonly taken their fathers' names. A married woman's surname is in itself a problem: some may decry a woman assuming her husband's last name, but even the maiden name is a patriarchal construct. More so than men, women's lives may shift to the point that they acquire many different names throughout their lives. Thus, a female author's name is problematic when examining life writing through the filter of Philippe Lejeune's paradigm, *On Autobiography*, because he argues that the name on the cover initiates a contractual agreement with the reader who expects the story contained within the pages to match that of the author's name. To complicate matters further, name changes may occur when an autobiographer moves from one culture or one language to a different culture or different language.

Identity is also heavily involved with the past and thus with memory. Writing the life—or, more accurately, writing *a* life—requires memory, which proves to be as slippery a concept as identity. We know, we think we know; we remember, we think we remember, but eyewitness testimony demonstrates that one event provides multiple interpretations. Does the adult self accurately remember the child self? Does the writing self wish to revise events, behaviors, or reactions of the lived self? In cases of trauma, the validity of memory becomes even more problematic. Some scholars of memory assert that a trauma etches itself deeply into the brain and so that memory is more reliable than the memory of everyday life, whereas other scholars argue that a trauma causes some victims to forget the event. Women's memory of trauma, then, exemplifies the difficulty of theorizing it.

If autobiography is the presentation of a writer's identity, then she has control over how she puts forth that presentation. The life writer must make conscious, literary decisions about where to begin her text and where to end it. Does the story begin in infancy, in childhood, or at the first significant event of her life? Does it focus on only one aspect of her life—a career, say, or the involvement in a historical event? Does the author cast herself as the star of her text, a supporting character, or a victim? Each authorial act creates the identity portrayed within the text.

To complicate matters even further, some life writers write and assess their lives through different voices, thereby challenging the solidity of the life writer's "I." For instance, Mary McCarthy, Nathalie Sarraute, and **Christa Wolf** have each written an autobiography wherein multiple selves interact with each other or reflect on divergent memories.

Early literary critics of autobiography focus on men's life writings, accepting attendant cultural assumptions about the reality and autonomy of the self. The rise of feminist theory saw greater questioning of those assumptions as well as new ways to interpret the life writer's "I" and women's reality. Critics writing in English who have advanced such thinking include **Mary G. Mason**, **Shari Benstock**, **Julia Watson**, and **Sidonie Smith**. Paul John Eakin, among others, has asked if the concept of the independent self of autobiography is a myth.

Questioning whether women's identities are socially constructed according to **gender** conventions is useful when studying women's autobiographies. For instance, whereas the traditional white-male model of autobiography emphasized the author as a singular person engaging the world, life writings by women has been examined in terms of relationships, as have women's identities. Women, as well as other marginalized people, find their identities shaped by cultural dynamics; many women define themselves by relational roles, such as mother, wife, daughter, friend.

Women autobiographers textualize their identities, selecting and configuring important aspects of their life stories. Events may be imperfectly remembered, and the story may be fragmentary and disrupted. Identity shifts as circumstances and relationships change and as the author composes her life. In the hands of a woman autobiographer, identity is often revealed as a construction, a product of social forces. *See also* **Voice**.

Further Reading: Eakin, Paul John. *How Our Lives Become Stories: Making Selves* (Ithaca, NY: Cornell University Press, 1999); Lejeune, Philippe. *On Autobiography*. Edited by Paul John Eakin. Translated by Katherine Leary (Minneapolis: University of Minneapolis Press, 1989); Smith, Sidonie. *Subjectivity, Identity, and the Body: Women's Autobiographical Practices in the Twentieth Century* (Bloomington: Indiana University Press, 1993); Smith, Sidonie, and Julia Watson. *Reading Autobiography: A Guide for Interpreting Life Narratives* (Minneapolis: University of Minneapolis Press, 2001).

Deborah Lee Ames

I KNOW WHY THE CAGED BIRD SINGS

Best known as a poet and prolific autobiographer, **Maya Angelou** chronicles her life story in a series of six memoirs, beginning in 1969 with the publication of *I Know Why The Caged Bird Sings* and concluding most recently with *All God's Children Need Traveling Shoes* (1986). During the 1960s, highly visible writers like Malcolm X and Eldridge Cleaver used the autobiographical form to heighten the consciousness of white Americans, resulting in a surge of interest in black autobiographies. *Caged Bird* grew out of this literary climate and is often considered one of the most significant black female autobiographies of the post–Civil Rights era. It is one of the first black female autobiographies to detail the deeply personal struggles that accompanied one woman's attempts to challenge the racist social structures that ignore and diminish her at every turn.

Angelou's first autobiography focuses on her turbulent childhood and adolescence and details her emotional, physical, and spiritual development as she struggles to overcome parental abandonment, racism, poverty, social displacement, and the trauma of rape at the hands of her mother's boyfriend. *Caged Bird* is often considered a classic bildungsroman or coming-of-age saga, in which the protagonist, Marguerite or "Ritie" (Angelou's given name is Marguerite Johnson), gradually finds the inner strength to do battle with a series of dramatic personal challenges.

The autobiography begins with Angelou's earliest memories, shortly after she and her older brother Bailey are sent away by their parents to live in the small segregated community of Stamps, Arkansas, under the watchful eye of her paternal grandmother whom she calls "Momma." Her young life in Stamps is portrayed as a series of harsh encounters with the racist social structures relieved only by the strict but kind ministrations of her grandmother and the close relationships she developed with her brother and a few friends and neighbors. In the brief time that Angelou and her brother are sent back to live with their mother in St. Louis, her mother's boyfriend rapes the eight-year-old girl. In response to this traumatic event, eight-year-old Marguerite becomes mute and turns her feelings of violation and guilt inward. After she returns to her grandmother, literature and education become Angelou's only escape from the silence and denial of her self-imposed isolation.

As a teenager, Angelou heads to California to live with her parents. The **memoir** relates the difficult period in which she attempts at first to live with her passive father and his jealous girlfriend. Feeling misunderstood and fearful, she runs away to live with a group of other teenagers in a junkyard. It is in this environment of independence and equality where she secures for herself a new found autonomy and self-worth. This period encourages her to seek out her mother in San Francisco where Angelou experiences an important political awakening. Defying the unspoken yet blatant discrimination that threatens her prospective job conducting a streetcar, Angelou persists in pursuing the position until she is given the job. It is during her persistence in reaching for this job that Angelou comes to a new understanding of the bigotry she has suffered her whole life. *Caged Bird* concludes on an ambivalent note, however, as Angelou becomes pregnant after an awkward sexual encounter and gives birth to a son whom she decides to raise with her mother's support. As a teenage mother, Angelou feels vulnerable and uncertain but has clearly made progress from her beginnings as a young black "ugly duckling" whose primary fantasy was to become a beautiful white girl.

Although over the course of her life Angelou has been active as an educator, historian, author, actress, playwright, civil rights activist, producer, and director, it is her accomplishment as a writer that has made her an important **voice** in contemporary literature. Two works of poetry, *Just Give Me a Cool Drink of Water 'fore I Diiie* (1971) and

And Still I Rise (1976), were nominated for a Pulitzer Prize. In 1993, President Bill Clinton commissioned Angelou to compose and deliver a poem for his 1993 presidential inauguration. Her poem, "On the Pulse of the Morning," employs many of the recurring themes that are woven throughout all of Angelou's writings and her professional work, namely, the struggles and triumphs of human beings in the face of oppression, social injustice, and personal doubt.

Of all her works, *Caged Bird* is considered a groundbreaking and controversial text because of its brutal honesty in dealing with topics such as **race**, rape, and teenage pregnancy. It is a classic American autobiography about a black woman's struggle against the forces, both internal and external, that threaten to silence her and ignore her personhood. Many literary critics analyze the text in terms of its autobiographical content and literary style. It is frequently described as a contemporary text with roots in the African American slave narrative. Slave narratives were largely nineteenth-century autobiographies that followed the arduous journey of a slave as he or she moved northward. In this genre, the physical journey becomes a metaphor for the enslaved individual's psychological movement into a new state of awareness as a "free self." Angelou's memoir traces her movement from the South (Stamps) to the North (San Francisco) and uses dozens of incidents to reveal the evils of segregation, oppression, and racism as she journeys toward personal liberation. This pattern suggests that while writing this first autobiography, Angelou was also clearly influenced by the political context of the Civil Rights era.

In *Caged Bird*, Angelou appears to be clearly and consciously presenting life events in a style that favors literary and historical interests above complex emotional truths. The "doubled" authorial voice in *Caged Bird* is the most prominent source of tension in the text and has received some important scholarly attention. This dual voice is made up of the child who relates the poignant incidents of her childhood and adolescence and the adult narrator who comments on and analyzes the importance of these incidents from her past.

The "adult" Angelou's ironic or wry narrative observations—such as when she suggests that she does not blame her mother for sending her away after the rape because "There is nothing more appalling than a constantly morose child" (74)—seem intended to distance her reader and herself from the painful event she is recalling. The adult narrator's comments often take a painful experience from Angelou's childhood and place it in a larger context of black experience, making the autobiography feel more political than personal. Angelou describes in her autobiography how she felt shame and anger when her eighth-grade graduation ceremony was undermined by the white speaker's implication that the black graduates are destined to be "maids and farmers, handymen and washerwomen" (152). Angelou, as narrator, refuses to let this painful **memory** linger on the page. When the black graduation audience joins in singing "Lift Ev'ry Voice and Sing," which Angelou calls the "Negro national anthem," the adult author shifts her perspective and observes: "We were on top again. As always, again. We survived" (156).

These types of literary maneuvers are found throughout the text. Angelou's shifting tone in *Caged Bird* expresses an ambivalent attitude toward her youthful self-image, her complicated family relationships, the isolated black communities she lived in, and the larger white world. In one instance, she describes this ambivalence as "fear-admiration-contempt" about "white 'things'" that she felt were out of her reach (40).

Yet it is Angelou's honest portrayal of her internal battle with these contradictory feelings that makes the autobiography a revolutionary example of the genre. In the last part of the memoir, she expertly portrays pivotal moments of self-awareness that finally allow her to escape the emotional traps of ambivalence and denial that kept her silent and confused for much of her early life. She has an epiphany when she realizes that her silence at the discrimination she faced day after day when seeking her first streetcar job and the silence of the white clerk who allowed her to fill out an application but refused to do anything else, was a "charade" that made them both victims of the "same puppeteer"—a bigoted social structure that was built on hollow, meaningless stereotypes and "comfortable lies" (227). Angelou comes to perceive the utter illogic of white hate while also accepting her own ability to either perpetuate or defy discriminatory practices. She comes to believe she is an individual with agency, not a victim of circumstance who has no choice but to obediently conform to the social roles offered to blacks.

Angelou's title, *I Know Why the Caged Bird Sings*, was inspired by a Paul Laurence Dunbar poem called "Sympathy." Dunbar concludes his poem by admitting why the caged bird sings: "It is not a carol of joy or glee, / But a prayer that he sends from his heart's deep core / But a plea, that upward to Heaven he flings— / I know why the caged bird sings!" The song is therefore an expression of longing—to be heard, to escape from the many limitations, both societal and self-imposed—that imprison the individual. It is this quest to express the self's deepest truths that imbues Angelou's first autobiography and persists as a compelling theme throughout all of her work.

Further Reading: Angelou, Maya. *The Complete Collected Poems of Maya Angelou* (New York: Random House, 1994); Angelou, Maya. *I Know Why the Caged Bird Sings.* (New York: Bantam, 1970); Braxton, Joanne. *Maya Angelou's I Know Why the Caged Bird Sings: A Casebook* (New York: Oxford University Press, 1994); Elliot, Jeffrey M. "Maya Raps." In *Conversations with Maya Angelou*, edited by Jeffrey M. Elliot, 86–96 (Jackson: University of Mississippi Press, 1989); Hagen, Lyman B. *Heart of a Woman, Mind of a Writer, and*

Soul of a Poet: A Critical Analysis of the Writings of Maya Angelou (Lanham, MD: University Press of America, 1997); Smith, Sidonie. *Where I'm Bound: Patterns of Slavery and Freedom in Black American Autobiography* (Westport, CT: Greenwood, 1974).

Patricia R. Payette

INCIDENTS IN THE LIFE OF A SLAVE GIRL Written by **Harriet Jacobs** in the 1850s, *Incidents in the Life of a Slave Girl* was published in 1861 and describes the life of Harriet Jacobs, who uses the pseudonym Linda Brent. The original narrative was edited by Lydia Maria Child and includes an appendix by Amy Post. The most comprehensive present-day edition of *Incidents* is edited by Jean Fagan Yellin and was published in 1987.

Jacobs was born a slave in Edenton, North Carolina, in 1813. In her autobiography, Jacobs selects, describes, and analyzes events in her life and in the historical life of the United States. She does so to convince her main audience of Northern white women that slavery must be abolished and that they must begin to work in the public realm to advocate abolition. The majority of Jacobs' narration of her personal life centers around her struggle with her owner's father, Dr. Flint. From the time Jacobs was fifteen years old, Flint pursued her sexually, making Jacobs' life miserable. In order to thwart him, Jacobs learns that she would have to be very cunning in order to stay out of his clutches. Her strategies from that point include staying in the presence of other people, psychologically manipulating Flint and taking a powerful white man as her lover.

Jacobs reacts to Dr. Flint's sexual advances as a woman protecting her honor. She treats his whispering of "foul words" (Yellin 1987, 27) in her ear and his notes about what he would like to do with her with "indifference and contempt" (27):

What he could not find opportunity to say in words he manifested in signs. He invented more than were ever thought of in a deaf and dumb asylum. I let them pass, as if I did not understand what he meant; and many were the curses and threats bestowed on me for my stupidity. (31)

Not only does Jacobs understand Flint's written and verbal cues to attempt to force her into the role of "slave mistress," but she also comprehends his "made-up" language of "signs." She employs psychological and linguistic strategies to protect herself from Flint's words and actions: she shows him indifference and contempt, a strategy that a white woman might have adopted if placed in a similar circumstance. She can treat him in this way because she knows that, as a man of standing in the community, he has to "keep up some outward show of decency" (29).

She uses this response because she knows that the response of a "virtuous woman" will unbalance Flint, who expects all slave women to behave as if they had no choice. Flint responds to Jacobs' contempt and indifference not by raping or beating her, as he could. Instead, he redoubles his efforts to dominate her sexually and eventually claim her as his "property." This incident is a good example of how Jacobs shows her sexual and racial oppression and her strategies for self-preservation.

As part of this psychological-sexual game, Flint cannot allow Jacobs to have any other man, for to permit her to do so negates his status as her "master." Jacobs recognizes Flint's fear and uses his jealousy to protect herself. She knows, for instance, that Flint will not send her out of the town to his plantation, as he had threatened, because he was jealous of his son. She can also reassure herself that she will not be punished with agricultural labor, for "jealousy of the overseer had kept him from punishing [her] by sending [her] into the fields to work" (41). Thus, by capitalizing on Flint's fear that she will give some other man the privilege of defining her as "mistress," "slave," or "other," Jacobs manages to keep her body safe.

Jacobs enters into a relationship with Mr. Sands, a powerful white man, as part of her plan to outwit Flint. Because of Sands' power and social standing, Flint would be unable to control Sands or make his life unbearable in the community. Flint can browbeat an African American man into staying away from Jacobs; he may also be able to force a non-property-owning, non-status-holding white man to abandon her, but a man of Sands' stature is out of Flint's reach. Jacobs, understanding the sphere Flint moves in, knows that in order to assert her autonomous self over Flint and his wishes, she must link herself with Sands—or a man of the same social **class** as Sands.

When Jacobs confesses her loss of virtue to her readers, she shows chagrin over her entrance into a sexual affair without the benefit of marriage. She claims, however, that slave women are wrongly put in a position where they are not allowed the protection of marriage. While Jacobs realizes that her situation places her outside the realm of "white" morality, she also knows that she cannot be defined by the slave system either. She is not a slave who does not "care about character," and she will not allow herself to be defined as such.

In relating her story, Jacobs appears to confess that she was immoral, that she "knew what [she] did and [she] did it with deliberate calculation" (54). She then informs the reader that "the slave woman ought not to be judged by the same standard as others" (56). Jacobs has to enter into an "illicit" sexual relationship with Sands in order to protect herself. Flint cannot hurt Jacobs, or the children she produces, without having to answer to Sands. Moreover, Sands has a greater claim on Jacobs' emotions and affections than he does on her body. In that sense, the favors he gains from her must be earned by kindness, rather than taken as "right of ownership." This type of relationship positions Jacobs as a person with more agency and **subjectivity**.

Jacobs also states her feelings of guilt about the birth of her children. When she indicates that she feels guilty, Jacobs stands to win the support of those Northern women that she hopes will work for abolition. Jacobs' ability to manipulate Flint, and her white readers, comes from her understanding that she is considered to be outside the white system of morality. On being informed that her second child is a girl, Jacobs mourns: "Slavery is terrible for men; but it is far more terrible for women. Superadded to the burden common to all, *they* have wrongs, and sufferings, and mortifications peculiarly their own" (77). With this plea, Jacobs forces her white female audience to confront the sisterhood of women.

As she narrates certain events in her life, Jacobs also comments on events that were happening in the United States. In her commentary on public events, Jacobs sets up connections between herself as a poor black slave woman and various other nondominant groups. For instance, Jacobs articulates the relationship between poor whites and blacks when she discusses the time, after Nat Turner's rebellion in 1821, when the middle-class town whites allowed the lower-class whites from the country to come and search the homes of the town's black residents. According to Jacobs, the majority of "low whites" in the South were eager "to exercise a little brief authority" over free blacks and slaves whenever the opportunity should arise (64). Jacobs maintains that this desire was a direct result of those whites "not reflecting that the power which trampled on the colored people also kept themselves in poverty, ignorance, and moral degradation" (64). In addition to denouncing the racial terrorist tactics that allowed groups of these "low whites" to rush "in every direction" (64) and inflict "shocking outrages" (64) on black people, Jacobs links the "poverty, ignorance, and moral degradation" of poor whites to that of free blacks and slaves.

By linking poor whites and free blacks and slaves in this way, she exposes the institution of slavery as a social construct, "a power," and an institution that "trampled

on the colored people." Harriet Jacobs comments on the consternation that news of Nat Turner's rebellion caused within the Southern slaveholding community, declaring that it was strange that the slaveholders "should be so alarmed, when their slaves were so 'contented and happy'" (63). Jacobs understands that white slave owners have produced a myth in the United States, a myth that slaves are content with their bondage and that plantations are like a family, with the white slaveholding man at its head.

She knows that searching the local black population's homes was to be done by poor whites from the country, who would take this "grand opportunity" to ingratiate themselves with the holders of power and who would also assert their dominance over the blacks (64). Jacobs declares of these lower-class whites: "I knew nothing annoyed them so much as to see colored people living in comfort and respectability; so I made arrangements for them with especial care. I arranged every thing in my grandmother's house as neatly as possible" (64). She knows the whites will be angry at seeing a black family "living in comfort and respectability." Therefore she takes "especial care" to make the house tidy and comfortable in order to arouse their ire. The slaves and free blacks in Jacobs' town are obviously not the mythical "contented" slaves; otherwise there would be no need for such searching. With her exposure of that myth as a fiction, she also dismantles the paternalistic notion of the contented slave.

By using "white" domestic and female seduction novelistic techniques with alternative outcomes, Jacobs questions the significance and efficacy of white women's acculturation. Because of her use of such fictive techniques, *Incidents* was considered for a time to be a false slave narrative. Jacobs and her text, however, function as literary forerunners to other African American women authors. Jacobs' influence can be seen on Frances E. W. Harper, who in turn influenced **Zora Neale Hurston**, a literary foremother to **Alice Walker**. The resurgence of interest in Jacobs' narrative since the 1980s has helped develop various literary fields of inquiry, including African American women's subjectivity, the use of verbal tactics as protection for the body, methods of resistance, and the development of cultural myths about black people and women.

Further Reading: Andrews, William L. "The Changing Moral Discourse of Nineteenth-Century African American Women's Autobiography: Harriet Jacobs and Elizabeth Keckley. In *De/Colonizing the Subject: The Politics of Gender in Women's Autobiography*, edited by Sidonie Smith and Julia Watson, 225–241 (Minneapolis: University of Minnesota Press, 1992); Braxton, Joanne M., and Sharon Zuber. "Silences in Harriet 'Linda Brent' Jacobs's *Incidents in the Life of a Slave Girl*." In *Listening to Silences: New Essays in Feminist Criticism*, edited by Elaine Hedges and Shelley Fisher Fishkin, 146–155 (New York: Oxford University Press, 1994); Carby, Hazel. *Reconstructing Womanhood: The Emergence of the Afro-American Woman Novelist* (New York: Oxford University Press, 1987); Ernest, John. *Resistance and Reformation in Nineteenth-Century African-American Literature: Brown, Wilson, Jacobs, Delany, Douglass, and Harper* (Jackson: University Press of Mississippi, 1995); Garfield, Deborah M., and Rafia Zafar. *Harriet Jacobs and Incidents in the Life of a Slave Girl: New Critical Essays* (Cambridge: Cambridge University Press, 1996); Jacobs, Harriet. *Incidents in the Life of a Slave Girl, Written by Herself* [1861]. Edited by Jean Fagan Yellin (Cambridge: Harvard University Press, 1987); Yellin, Jean Fagan. "Text and Contexts of Harriet Jacobs' *Incidents in the Life of a Slave Girl, Written by Herself*." In *The Slave's Narrative*, edited by Charles T. Davis and Henry Louis Gates, Jr., 262–282 (Oxford: Oxford University Press, 1985); Yellin, Jean Fagan. *Women and Sisters: The Antislavery Feminists in American Culture* (New Haven: Yale University Press, 1989).

Samantha Manchester Earley

INDIAN (EASTERN INDIAN) WOMEN'S AUTOBIOGRAPHY. *SEE* SOUTH ASIAN WOMEN'S AUTOBIOGRAPHY.

IRISH WOMEN'S AUTOBIOGRAPHY

Irish women have a strong autobiographical tradition in a nation renowned for its storytelling. Their texts are important contributions to Irish literature and valuable indicators of the lives of Irish women. The fact that Ireland, as Edna O'Brien puts it in *Mother Ireland*, "has always been a woman, a womb, a cave, a cow, a Rosaleen, a sow, a bride, a harlot, and, of course, the gaunt Hag of Beare" (11) has made it difficult for women to define their own lives. Life stories represent one means for Irish women to break the silence.

Several forces have oppressed Irish women. The Catholic Church's focus on marriage and motherhood and its denial of female **sexuality** were augmented by the state's denial of women's legal rights. These forces were reinforced by the profound changes in the Irish economy produced by the great famine that made Ireland an increasingly male-dominated society.

Despite the historical subordination of Irish women, however, individual women have managed to claim political and literary **identity** even in the most difficult times, but they have tended to be those with privilege. The following autobiographies—a representative, not inclusive group—demonstrate that the women who could write their life stories had the advantages of education, money, or higher social status. Thus, almost all of them are Anglo-Irish women, who have had much more privilege than native Irish women. The exception is Peig Sayers; however, Sayers did not write her autobiography, but told it to her son.

It is no accident that almost no women's autobiographies were published in the nineteenth century because of the famines in Ireland. The clustering of autobiographies in the early twentieth century is connected to the Irish literary revival (or renaissance), characterized by nationalism and interest in Ireland's Gaelic heritage. The "Big House" theme in some of these texts (e.g., those of

Lady Gregory and Elizabeth Bowen) refers to the country manors of the wealthy Anglo-Irish, a dominant subject of Irish fiction.

The cultural repression of female sexuality has resulted in heavy censorship of writing that addressed women's emotional and sexual lives. Both Kate O'Brien and Edna O'Brien (not related) left Ireland partly because of this censorship. Several others, including Mary Colum, Maud Gonne, and Eavan Boland, have lived for large periods of time out of Ireland, so that their life stories are written partly from the perspective of the outsider.

Typical characteristics of these life stories include losing their mothers at an early age, doing voracious reading as girls, and developing as writers partly through membership in groups of writers and artists. Many of these autobiographies are silent about their authors' private lives, focusing instead on the people they met and the activities in which they participated. However, Nuala O'Faolain's 1998 autobiography blatantly reverses that trend. Finally, although they range from a poor storyteller to a countess, Irish women autobiographers are adamant about their love for Ireland.

Autobiographies of the Eighteenth and Nineteenth Centuries

The Memoirs of Mrs. Leeson, Madam: 1727–1797 are significant as one of the first life stories by an Irish woman and the only one by a prostitute. Leeson was one of the wealthiest women of Dublin as owner of a first-class brothel. When she died, however, her friends had to pay for her burial. Leeson's money problems began when she decided to retire and could not collect on her IOU's. When she announced that she was writing her memoirs, some of the IOU's were paid, but she continued to write for the royalties. She published the first two volumes of *The Memoirs of Mrs. Leeson* in 1795, finished the third just before her death, and had promised a fourth, even more explicit volume. "The text still reads

well," states Mary Lyons, who edited the 1995 edition (xvii).

Leeson explains how she was driven "on the rocks" (29), even though she was born into a wealthy family. When her mother and eldest brother died of spotted fever, her father, stricken by grief, put his son in charge of the family's affairs. The son, however, squandered the family's money and beat his siblings so terribly that Leeson fled to Dublin. When she became pregnant, she had to sell her clothes to buy food, so was easy prey to a man who offered to support her. He was the first in a series of wealthy lovers.

Leeson's success in attracting rich lovers led to a small fortune and great admiration from "the ladies of the sisterhood" (92). So, in 1784, she purchased a large Dublin house, furnished it elegantly, and personally selected a staff of prostitutes. Her brothel became known for elaborate masquerades; in one, Leeson acted the role of Diana, goddess of chastity.

Her second volume features ex-lovers' **letters**. The third includes anecdotes of amusing events placed between the story of her career as a madam and that of her retirement. Leeson's last passage complains of how ill and disheartened she is—even her fingers refuse to write. Her final words are a prayer for compassion.

The autobiography of Dorothea Herbert, eldest daughter of an affluent churchman, is important as a window into life in eighteenth-century rural Ireland of a single woman in an upper-middle-class Anglo-Irish family.

Herbert's text does exhibit what **Felicity A. Nussbaum** has noted in "Eighteenth-Century Women's Autobiographical Commonplaces," of other eighteenth-century women's life writing: the mimicking of male definitions of women (1988, 19). Thus, Herbert faints during emotional moments and weeps copiously at slight rebuffs from her suitor. But, her control as a writer—the cleverness of her literary strategies, the keenness of her social observations, and the sharpness of her wit—contradicts the image of helpless wench.

Edited by distant relatives and published in 1929 and 1930 in two volumes as *The Retrospections of Dorothea Herbert, 1739–1770 and 1770–1806* more than 100 years after its composition, Herbert's text had the original title of *Retrospections Of An Outcast Or the Life of Dorothea Herbert Authoress Of The Orphan Plays And Various Poems And Novels In Four Volumes Written in Retirement*. Scholars were delighted with how much Herbert reveals about life in eighteenth-century Ireland when the autobiography finally was published.

The question is this: why did Herbert label herself an outcast? Her father's status and income as the rector of three churches and her parents' kinship to gentry gave the family access to the social circles of both prosperous gentleman farmers and local gentry. At the Cashel Races of 1789, Dorothea and her sisters were "the Gaze and Astonishment of the Whole Race Course" (Herbert *Retrospections of Dorothea Herbert, 1770–1806*, 218). She attracted so much romantic attention from the neighboring farmer's son that both she and their friends assumed that they would marry. Inexplicably, his ardor cooled and Herbert was devastated. She writes, "The perjured Wretch has since married another—Joined himself in execrable Union with a Common Drab of the City" (335).

The news of her lover's marriage provoked Herbert, full of grief and despair, to retreat to solitude and writing in 1805. In 1800, her favorite brother had died in a fall from a horse, and in 1803, her father died. She alleges that at this time, her family locked her in her room and beat her, a claim that made Louis M. Cullen, in his historical note to the 1988 edition, conclude that Herbert must have been deranged (*Retrospections* 451). Herbert's claim, however, deserves to be taken seriously. Her father's estate was relatively small, but it had to support his widow, a young son, and three unmarried daughters, including Herbert, who had received a slightly larger inheri-

tance than the others (*Retrospections* 447). Her claims that her family abused her in order to secure her inheritance are not totally implausible. Unprepared by her social **class** for any vocation, she was an economic and social liability for her family.

Another early Irish autobiography, *The Nun of Kenmare*, published in 1889, is a public disclosure of a cloistered life. Although the courage of its author is notable, this is a minor addition to the autobiographical canon because of its narrow focus. Sister Mary Francis Clare Cusack writes to defend herself against accusations by priests and bishops that led to her resigning her vocation. She had become known as the nun of Kenmare both in Ireland and in America, first as a writer and then for her fundraising to help victims of famine. She wrote biographies of St. Patrick, the Irish patriot O'Connell, and Pope Pius IX; *Women's Work in Modern Society*, and a highly praised *Illustrated History of Ireland*.

Sister Mary Francis Clare Cusack's achievements are reflected in the authoritative tone of her autobiography. It was written four years after its author had come to America to provide an education to Irish emigrant girls in America. The author focuses exclusively on her life as a nun. Despite the letter to the pope at the beginning, the book seems to have been designed for an audience of general readers because it includes explanations of convent life and different religious orders. She explains what it is like to be a nun: "I was not long an inmate of the convent before I discovered that life there was very much like life anywhere else. It had its sorrows and its joys. Differences of temper often broke out and made unpleasantnesses" (31). The author's tone is primarily one of moral outrage. This text does have great value for what it reveals about an exceptional woman unafraid of battling male authority.

One of the most prolific Irish autobiographers is Lady Augusta (Persse) Gregory (1852–1932), whose three autobiographies are considered valuable historical documents about the Irish literary revival, the founding of the Irish theater, and the Irish folklore movement, as well as the life of one of the key figures in early-twentieth-century Ireland: William Butler Yeats. They are central texts in women's autobiography.

Our Irish Theatre: A Chapter of Autobiography (1913) describes the first years of the Irish literary theatre, including the riots and censorship battles. It also reveals how Lady Gregory came to write plays in response to an invitation from William Butler Yeats. *Seventy Years: Being the Autobiography of Lady Gregory* (1974) was written late in her life and not published for fifty years. It shows how Lady Gregory was able to be fully involved in both her public and private lives and to persevere in the midst of civil war and radical changes in Ireland's political and social structures. Both texts are framed with addresses to her grandchildren. She tells in *Seventy Years* how when she was born, her parents were disappointed that she was not a boy. However, just when "this little-welcomed girl had nearly gone out with but a breath of the world's air" (1), her mother saved her because the other children were looking forward to a new baby. Lady Gregory concludes with a chapter dedicated to memories of her son Robert, killed in World War I.

Coole is a semiautobiographical text about the Gregory estate, Coole Park, which Lady Gregory made a center of literary activity and folklore research at a time when other Irish Big Houses were increasingly isolated. *Coole* documents the house's history and what it meant to her. Although Coole Park was not burned during the war (Lady Gregory's childhood home *was*), it was razed the year after she died in 1932. Because the subject of the Anglo-Irish "Big House" is so salient to Irish history, *Coole* is a particularly important text.

Isabella Augusta Persse grew up on her family's estate near Galway, only seven miles from Coole Park. When she married Sir Gregory, she was age twenty-seven, and Sir William was age sixty-two, and had re-

cently retired from being governor of Ceylon. When he died twelve years later, Lady Gregory began her writing career. First, she edited and published Sir William's autobiography and made a solo trip to the Aran Islands, where the inhabitants spoke an ancient dialect of Irish. The trip would lead to her learning Irish and becoming a national leader in collecting Irish folklore. She found the correspondence of Sir William's grandfather and published it as *Mr. Gregory's Letter-Box* in 1886, the year she met the Irish poet William Butler Yeats. Yeats would become a close friend who would stay for extended periods of time at Coole Park.

The cut-and-paste method of composition that Lady Gregory developed served her well, as Mary Fitzgerald notes in " 'Perfection of the Life': Lady Gregory's Autobiographical Writings," included in *Lady Gregory: Fifty Years After* (48). She drew extensively from her daily journal to write her autobiographies, although they include relatively little private or personal information.

Early-Twentieth-Century Writing

Katharine Tynan (1861–1931) wrote more than 100 novels and twenty-five books of poetry and was a founding member of the Irish Literary Revival. She is regarded as a minor poet and writer of potboilers, but her six autobiographies have met critical acclaim both when they first appeared and in recent reappraisals of early-twentieth-century Irish writing. Tynan occupied a liminal **space** between the Catholic middle class, traditional Victorian values, and England (where she lived for twenty years) on the one hand, and Irish nationalists, the aesthetic avant garde, and Ireland, on the other. Her autobiographies are valuable cultural bridges between these polarities, says Taura Napier in *Seeking a Country: Literary Autobiographies of Twentieth-Century Irishwomen* (2001, 56). They are marked by a precision not typical of her poetry or fiction (62), particularly about the personalities of her friends and associates. They are important texts in women's autobiography.

Tynan's six autobiographies are as follows: *Twenty-Five Years: Reminiscences* (1913), *The Middle Years* (1916), *The Years of the Shadow* (1919), *The Wandering Years* (1922), *Memories* (1924), and *Life in the Occupied Area* (1925).

Twenty-Five Years is particularly important as the story of her childhood and how she came to be a writer. Tynan grew up when good Irish Catholics were not supposed to read novels, go to the theater, or dance, and her mother tried to enforce those rules. But her daughter found a village shop that kept butter and eggs on one side and stationery, books, and magazines on the other. She remembers, "Even now I can feel the ecstasy of touching those green and scarlet and blue backs of books and knowing that I might read what I would" (1913, 43). Her father bought her books and took her to the theater.

When Tynan published her first poem in the *Irish Monthly*, she met the first of her literary friends: "Everybody who wrote was a wonder to me; an editor, even a Dublin one, was of the Olympians"(105). She met more people after 1885 when she published her first book, *Louise de la Valliere* (1885), an instant critical and popular success. In 1886, her father built a room where she could write and entertain her literary friends. William Butler Yeats often walked the five miles from Dublin to her home even in winter, "so long as he found at the end a fire, a meal, bed, and talk about poetry" (256). She states, "We were all writing like the poets of a country newspaper" until Yeats came along (255).

Tynan became an active member of the Land League and a follower of Charles Stuart Parnell, and ends *Twenty-Five Years* with Parnell's funeral. She married a fellow writer, Henry Hinkson, in 1893, and they moved to England, where they had five children. *The Middle Years* discusses her journalistic work, and *The Years of the Shadow* covers the years of World War I. Although her husband died in 1919, she does not mention his death explicitly (Napier speculates

that Tynan practiced "a certain ruthlessness of privacy" [2001, 63]). *Memories* is devoted almost exclusively to individual portraits. Most of Tynan's self-writing, however, centers on her self, unlike many other Irish women, although she is not self-analytical. She does return to certain themes, such as her father's role in her life, and often includes **letters** from friends (Napier 2001, 68).

Maud Gonne (1866–1953) is legendary in Ireland. She worked indefatigably on behalf of Irish freedom and its people; she was the inspiration for William Butler Yeats' greatest love poems and was seen as Ireland's Joan of Arc and the very image of Cathleen ni Houlihan, the female symbol of Ireland. Her autobiography, *Servant of the Queen: Reminiscences* (1938), is a classic in women's autobiography for her historical significance as a female leader and its literary merit.

Born in England into a wealthy family of merchants, Gonne moved to Ireland in 1868 with her family when her father, who had Irish heritage, was stationed there with the British army. Although the family left for Italy in 1871, when her mother became ill with tuberculosis (she died during the trip), she returned to Ireland with her father Thomas when he won a permanent post in Dublin in 1884. He died in 1886, and Maud ultimately went to live in Paris, where she met and fell in love with a well-known French political activist, Lucien Millevoye. The couple had two children, but because he was already married, their relationship was kept secret. Their first daughter died at age three, but Iseult, whom Gonne referred to as her adopted daughter, survived. Gonne and Millevoye had a pact that lasted much of their lives: to work together against England on behalf of Ireland and France.

The title of *Servant of the Queen* alludes to a vision Gonne had on a train as she returned from western Ireland, where she had helped to stop a famine. As she looked out the window, she saw a beautiful tall woman, whom she knew to be Cathleen ni Houlihan, the spirit of Ireland, leaping from one stone to the next across the bog. "I heard a voice say: 'You are one of the little stones on which the feet of the Queen have rested on her way to Freedom'" (1938, vii). Gonne interpreted the vision as a sign that she must dedicate her life to serving Ireland. She would become identified with Cathleen ni Houlihan when she played the title role in the play written by Yeats and Lady Gregory. (Gonne was a remarkable beauty: six feet tall with red, wavy hair.) She was also a charismatic leader. For example, when she learned that a thousand people were to be evicted from their homes in Donegal, she arranged for the building of Land League huts. She obtained seed potatoes and more money for famine victims working at relief jobs.

She did lecture tours in America and France to raise money for Irish causes and to get other countries to condemn England's continued rule of Ireland. It was on one of these tours that she met John MacBride, an Irish soldier. Their marriage in 1903 is the final event of Gonne's autobiography. Although the marriage lasted only two years, it did produce a son, Sean. Gonne was awarded custody, but she still feared that MacBride would take him, so she avoided Ireland for eleven years. MacBride was executed for his role in the Easter Rising of 1916; after his death Gonne returned to Ireland, where she resumed her activist work. She had been arrested and imprisoned for several months in England, although no charges were filed. When she became very ill in prison, the English authorities let her go because they did not want to make her a martyr. Gonne then spent the next decade working to improve prison conditions for Irish political prisoners. The Irish Free State honored her in 1932.

Gonne met Yeats in 1889, and they became lifelong friends, but, although he asked her to marry him several times, she always refused. *A Servant of the Queen* avoids specific reference to Gonne's private life, partly at the request of her family.

The autobiography of Elizabeth Plunket, *Seventy Years Young: Memories of Elizabeth, Countess of Fingall, Told to Pamela Hinkson* (1937), is as much a portrait of the upper-class Anglo-Irish as it is of the countess. It thus has historical value; that and the quality of the writing makes it an important text for women's autobiography. Moreover, the Countess of Fingall understands that an autobiography is a fiction: she acknowledges that the person of whom she writes is not herself, but someone else whom she can see from a distance as if she'd never even met her (9).

Her life story is an Irish version of the aristocratic memoirs written by prominent late Victorian and Edwardian women in England, writes Julia Bush in "Ladylike Lives? Upper Class Women's Autobiographies and the Politics of Late Victorian and Edwardian Britain" (43). The countess describes the famous people she met and the volunteer work she did. Unlike *Seventy Years Young*, however, English upper-class women's autobiographies were considered to be of "slight" literary value (43).

Elizabeth Plunket was born into a family to whom English King Henry II "gave" a large section of western Ireland. Her ancestors built much of Galway, including the wall to "keep the wild Irish at bay" (*Seventy Years Young* 18). She recounts childhood memories of visiting peasant cottages with her siblings when the residents "received us like kings and queens" (25). She refers to her husband as a true Irish gentleman, but makes little reference to their domestic life. The fact that this book was written in the late 1930s is significant because by then the Protestant ascendancy had lost not only its land, but also its power and status. The countess' purpose is to "present . . . a picture of a life that is now quite done with, a world that is ended" (9).

Killeen, the home of her marriage, and Danesfield, the home of her childhood, were classic Anglo-Irish "Big Houses."

Plunket refers to "a look that the windows of Irish country houses often have, as though indeed that was the spirit inside them, the spirit of the colonists and conquerors, looking out across the country which they possessed, but never owned" (29). The conclusion of her autobiography tells the story of the night that she and her husband were told that a neighbor's house was burning and that theirs was next. The Countess of Fingall sat in her fur coat with her jewels in her lap, waiting for the rebels to arrive. They never did. Elizabeth knew, nonetheless, that the glittering world of castle balls and hunt breakfasts had vanished.

The Oral Tradition: Peig Sayers

An old woman telling stories in front of the hearth, the place usually reserved for the man of the house, is the subject of the most unusual autobiography by an Irish woman, the only one written originally in Irish. She is Peig Sayers, a famous storyteller from the Great Blasket Island, who dictated her life story to her son, Micheal O'Gaoithin. It was published in two versions in Irish in 1936 and 1939, then translated into English and published as *Peig: The Autobiography of Peig Sayers of the Great Blasket Island* (1974), and *An Old Woman's Reflections* (1962). These texts are critically important to women's autobiography because they record a nearly vanished oral tradition and the life of a native Irish woman.

Sayers was one of Ireland's last Gaelic storytellers, and the Great Blasket Island, where she lived for forty years after marrying one of the island's fishermen, was part of the region where Irish was spoken. Sayers knew that her story was not simply about her life, but also about the ancient oral culture of western Ireland that was dying: "I did my best to give an accurate account of the people I knew, so that we'd be remembered when we had moved on into eternity . . . We'll be stretched out quietly—and the old world will have vanished" (212).

Soon after her books appeared in Irish,

Peig Sayers became an emblem of the Irish revival movement and the teaching of Irish in the schools. Even in translation, her texts display colorful idioms. For instance, all the property her parents owned was "the grass of two cows" (13), and her people were so poorly nourished that they "weren't too hot in their skins" (176).

Although Sayers' autobiographies are valuable for what they reveal about the Irish oral tradition and the Irish language, they also chronicle how one woman survived acute poverty and painful loss by using her wits and working hard. Like her mother, Sayers had ten children, of whom only one survived into adulthood. As a young girl of twelve, she was placed in domestic service in a town twelve miles away from her home. She decided to marry rather than go back into service when her father proposed a match. The Great Blasket Island is a rocky, forbidding place that is no longer inhabited, but in Sayers' time, some two hundred people lived there. Because of the terrain and terrified that her children would drown, she smashed their toy boats. In 1920, when the islanders had to use heather for fuel, her son Tomas fell to his death while pulling a heather bush on top of a cliff.

Mid-Twentieth-Century Autobiographies

Mary Maguire Colum (1885–1957) was a celebrated literary critic who fought **gender** stereotypes all her life, but achieved great prominence as a critical writer. Eugene O'Neill called her "one of the few true critics of literature writing in English" ("Our Rostrum" 1935, 5). Her autobiography, *Life and the Dream,* first published in 1947, won rave critical reviews. Edmund Wilson declared it the best chronicle of the Irish literary renaissance ("The Memoirs of Mary Colum" 1947, 111). The quality of the writing, Colum's centrality to Irish and American letters in the twentieth century, and her early **feminism** make this a crucial text in women's autobiography.

Colum was the oldest of five children born to a middle-class Catholic family in County Sligo. Because her father often had to travel for his work as a constable and her mother was in ill health (she died when Colum was ten), Colum spent much of her early childhood with her grandmother. Even as a child, Colum read frequently from poetry and novels to essays and history. When a relative discovered what she had been reading, all of the questionable books were put beyond her reach. But then the twelve-year-old read Kant and Locke. After the death of her grandmother, she was sent to other relatives, then to boarding school at the Convent of St. Louis in Monaghan, where she loved the exposure to art and music. She was such an outstanding student there that she was sent to a girls' school in Germany.

Although her female relatives disapproved, her male relatives urged her to go to the National University in Dublin. It was there that Colum realized that she wanted to be a writer. On her first day, she saw an advertisement for the Abbey Theatre. She and her friends were so excited on opening nights that they would stay up all night talking about the play. After graduation, Colum took a job teaching at a school where she met Padraic Colum. She accepted his marriage proposal to get rid of other suitors. When they could not find work in Ireland, they sailed to America, planning to stay only several weeks, but never returned to Ireland except for visits. Colum became good friends with many writers, including James Joyce, and wrote a **biography** about him. She published her critical writing in America's leading magazines and journals. In 1937, she published *From These Roots: The Ideas That Have Made Modern Literature*, a groundbreaking discussion of modernism.

In *Life and the Dream*, dream refers to Colum's hope of a world of human equality. She wrote, "I think there is no superior race or superior sex; there are only superior or inferior individuals" (1937, 375).

Another Irish renaissance writer was Kate O'Brien (1897–1974), a best-selling author in the 1930s and 1940s. O'Brien wrote nine novels, six plays, a travelogue/autobiographical essay, *My Ireland* (1962), and her autobiographical text, *Presentation Parlor* (1963). In her novels she focused on the emotional struggles of middle-class Irish Catholics. She was the first Irish fiction writer to address questions of female autonomy and sexual freedom (Dalsimer 1990, xi). Her autobiographical works deserve attention for her attempt to write a new kind of autobiography, focused not so much on the writer as on her reflections about the world.

O'Brien was born in Limerick into a prosperous family of nine children. Her father was a horse breeder. Her mother died of cancer when she was five, and her father died ten years later. O'Brien received a degree from University College, Dublin, and worked as a governess in Spain during the winter of 1922–1923. She married a Dutch journalist and moved to London in 1923, but the marriage lasted only a few months. She lived in England until 1949, and then moved to Galway, Ireland, for fifteen years. The last nine years of her life were spent in England.

O'Brien lived outside of Ireland partly because her writing stirred such controversy. Two of her novels were banned by the Irish Censorship Board. When she died, she was buried in the grounds of a Carmelite convent in Faversham, England, where her grave has the inscription "Pray for the Wanderer." There has been a revival of critical interest in her work in recent years.

My Ireland and *Presentation Parlor* were her last published works. O'Brien insisted that *My Ireland* was not autobiographical, even though it contained her personal reflections on the Irish landscape and her experience of it. Her style of autobiography is to deflect everything about her self onto the landscape, events, or other people (Napier 2001, 137). The emphasis in *My Ireland* is on images, not knowledge, explains Michael Cronin in "Moving Pictures: Kate O'Brien's Travel Writing" (1993, 144).

Presentation Parlor focuses on the aunts who helped to raise her and her siblings when her mother died. "We would have been a lost and queer bundle of orphans without them" (1963, 3), she writes. The title of her autobiography comes from the name of the parlor in the convent of the Presentation order where two of her aunts were nuns and where the family met with all of them. O'Brien concludes that even though she wrote this book "to try to find in their modest lives the essence of them," she felt that she had failed (138). The book does provide remarkable portraits of these five very different women, along with valuable information about the biographical basis of much of O'Brien's fiction.

The autobiographical texts of Elizabeth Bowen (1899–1973), a prominent mid-twentieth-century novelist, are important as tools for analyzing her fiction; moreover, her family history, *Bowen's Court* (1943), is a key document in understanding the symbolic role of the "Big House" in Ireland. But the texts themselves are not key to the canon of women's autobiography, except as they demonstrate a deflected approach to the genre.

The crimson glow of a big house burning to the ground is the luminous moment that ends Bowen's autographically inspired novel, *The Last September* (1929). (It was published ten years after such a scene was common in the Irish countryside.) It was almost inevitable that Bowen would write a "Big House" novel since she so loved her family's home, Bowen's Court, and struggled to hold onto it despite the huge financial drain. Her passionate feelings about the house led her to understand the significance of **place** for anchoring the self. She claimed that the story of her early childhood, *Seven Winters and Afterthoughts* (1962), was her only autobiography, but scholars agree that at least three other texts are autobiographical: *Bowen's*

Court (1979), *Pictures and Conversations* (1950), and *A Time in Rome* (1960).

All of Bowen's autobiographical texts are centered on place. *Seven Winters* demonstrates how, as a child, Bowen came to know her world on walks in Dublin with her governess and parents. When they went beyond her family's wealthy neighborhood, she was intimidated: "I had heard of poverty-rotted houses that might at any moment crumble over one's head. Only on familiar pavements did sunshine fall" (1962, 17). A spatial metaphor describes her perceptions of Roman Catholics, "whose world lay alongside ours but never touched" (50).

Bowen's Court in County Cork was the family's summer and holiday home. It represented the past and family for Bowen: "With the end of each generation, the lives that submerged here were absorbed again. With each death, the air of the place had thickened" (*Bowen's Court* 451). Bowen researched family history to write *Bowen's Court*. By writing this book, she discovered what that continuity was for her: not the physical place, but its survival in Bowen's imagination as a vision of peace (457).

A Time in Rome describes her feelings about Rome as a place—its architecture, physical sites, and history. *Pictures and Conversations* begins with a telling essay titled "Origins" that describes a time period in England, where she and her mother had gone to live when her father had a bout of mental illness. Bowen and another girl had come upon the corpse of a sheep, "its body hideously torn open" (6). The intrusion of violent death into her Edenic landscape amounted to a loss of innocence, which would become the theme of her fiction. Similarly, her adult realization that Bowen's Court and other Anglo-Irish "Big Houses" would not last forever and that they also symbolized violence and injustice for others, set the stage for another departure from paradise. Bowen sold and razed Bowen's Court in 1960. However, her loss—both of the physical house and of Bowen's Court as an "innocent" symbol—enabled her to live in a world of which the Anglo-Irish were no longer in possession, but in which they were exposed to "risk and growth," argues Declan Kiberd in "Elizabeth Bowen: The Dandy in Revolt" (143).

Current Autobiographical Women Writers in Ireland

Edna O'Brien (1932–) is an internationally renowned, extremely prolific novelist and short story writer, playwright, and screenwriter. Her autobiographical essay *Mother Ireland* has been applauded by critics as one of her best pieces. As an example of a new way of writing autobiography in conjunction with the history and myth of one's nation, *Mother Ireland* deserves to be a prominent text in women's autobiography.

O'Brien was born in a small village in County Clare in western Ireland. She attended a pharmaceutical college in Dublin, worked briefly as a pharmacist, eloped at age sixteen with writer Ernest Gebler, and moved to County Wicklow. Their sons were born in 1952 and 1954; the marriage ended in 1964. In 1959, she moved with her sons to London, where publishers offered her an advance to write a novel. The result was *The Country Girls* (1986). O'Brien writes explicitly about women's lives and loves, and as a result, her work has been heavily subjected to censorship in her homeland. Her local priest and the residents of her childhood home burned her first novel.

Mother Ireland, with photographs by Fergus Bourke (1976) is illustrated with photographs of the Irish landscape and people. Her tone is often sardonic as O'Brien details the failed insurrections, degradations of poverty and famine, and deprivations imposed by religion. She critiques the tradition of engendering Ireland as female and satirizes the tourist stereotypes of Ireland: the superficial infatuation with quaint cottages, holy wells, and peasant food (33).

O'Brien juxtaposes remembered scenes and stories with mythical and historical references and personal reflections. For example, she remarks how amazing it is that literature is so loved in a country that bans so many books (39). But the heart of the autobiography begins with the memories of her hometown. She relates how Catholicism thoroughly infused her childhood, but sex—forbidden but tantalizing—colored even religious practices so that even kissing the cross on Good Friday was a sensual experience (97). She tells what it was like to go to convent school, where she became infatuated with a nun. As a young girl, O'Brien fell in love with books, torrid stories of thwarted love, and betrayal. Then she discovered film and the theater.

O'Brien, like so many Irish writers, has lived all of her adult life away from Ireland. She writes in *Mother Ireland* how, after her "escape," she felt pity for the land and the people, but had to leave because she saw too much that was wrong in Irish society. At the end, however, she reveals that it is love, not hate, for Ireland that keeps her away: "I live out of Ireland because something in me warns me that . . . if I lived there I might cease to feel what it has meant to have such a heritage" (144).

Nuala O'Faolain (1942) is a columnist for the *Irish Times*, whose autobiography, *Are You Somebody? The Accidental Memoir of a Dublin Woman* (1997) was a best seller and "an emotional episode . . . in public life in Ireland" (211). The public reaction to this work justifies its importance in the canon of women's autobiography. In his "Letters after the Fact: Responses to Nuala O'Faolain's *Are You Somebody?*" critic Eibhlin Evans calls it a "publication sensation and . . . a work of unusual courage and frankness" (*Critical Survey* 2002, 52).

Are You Somebody? is significant for what it says about contemporary Irish life and for its relationship to earlier autobiographies by Irish women. The same conditions, including the oppressive mandates of religion, attitudes toward female **sexuality**, and **gender** stereotypes also figure here. But unlike most of the earlier autobiographical texts, personal revelation is at the heart of O'Faolain's work. Her message is that despite her career achievements as a journalist and filmmaker, she still had low self-esteem.

O'Faolain describes how her mother's marriage and too many children made her into "a shy animal on the outskirts of the human settlement" (26). She tells about her own seductions by alcohol, barbiturates, and sex. She shows how the Irish love for storytelling and drink correlate with psychological emptiness. Her autobiography is seen as emblematic of a generation of Irish people (Evans 61).

Eavan Aisling Boland (1944–), one of the foremost Irish writers today, addresses the tension between the life of a poet and that of a woman in Ireland in *Object Lessons: The Life of the Woman and the Poet in Our Time* (1995), which has received international attention and praise.

Boland begins with the story of her grandmother's death in a Dublin hospital in 1909. She has to imagine her grandmother's life because, like other Irish women, so little is known about her: she cannot even find her headstone in the cemetery. Her point is that in a society where wife and mother are subsidiary roles, a woman is forced to exist on the margins of that society if she chooses to have a personal life. If she is a writer, she will be faced with "unacceptable conflict" (248). Boland acknowledges that Irish women have gone from being the objects of poems to authors in a very short time (236). But she contends that nothing will change if women do not challenge the factors that oppress Irish women.

Boland put her autobiography together as a poem might be written, "in turnings and returnings" (xiii). Thus, the story of her grandmother comes up again and again. The text is both anecdotal and reflective, as Boland enters and reenters the story of her life to try to understand "the mystery of being a poet in the puzzle of time and sexuality and nationhood" (xiii).

Boland was born in Ireland, but at age five moved to London, where her father was Irish ambassador to England. Her mother as a painter. Returning to Dublin at age fifteen, Boland had to learn what it means to be Irish. She is still engaged in that process, even as she helps to redefine the ethos of Ireland. She went to Trinity University, where she joined other young writers trying to emulate the model of Irish poetry they had inherited. But it was not a model that Boland could accept. When she married and moved to the suburbs and had a child, she discovered that the poems she had been writing no longer had even tangential connections to her life. However, there was no tradition of writing poetry about being married, living in the suburbs, and raising children. *Object Lessons* concludes with Boland's call to Irish women poets to revolutionize poetry so that it can address women's lives.

Bernadette Devlin (1947–) has followed in Maud Gonne's footsteps. This leader of Northern Ireland's civil rights activities was the youngest woman ever elected to the British Parliament. She is fearless and totally dedicated to her cause. She wrote *The Price of My Soul* (1969) to refocus public attention from her and to Ireland's social and economic problems. The book won praise for its objectivity, clarity, wit, passion, and outrage.

The title refers to the cost of preserving one's own integrity. It begins with Devlin's account of how her family was ostracized by her mother's relatives because her mother had married a road sweeper. Both her parents died early, and Devlin and her older siblings took care of the younger children. The sense of unfairness she felt about her mother's relatives would spur her political sentiments about the unfairness of British rule.

At Queen's University, she helped found the People's Democracy, which sought equal opportunity for all citizens. Devlin organized sit-ins and picket lines and helped plan the January 1969 march from

Belfast to Londonderry through hostile towns and villages. At one point, she led efforts to build a barricade against the police, by helping to stack trash and furniture in the streets. When the People's Democracy ran eight candidates for Parliament in the general election of 1969, Devlin won one-third of the vote in her district. Then, when the minister of Parliament for mid-Ulster died that March, Devlin opposed his widow's candidacy and won. She became the British House of Commons' most vocal member, denouncing her colleagues and advocating reform. She also continued her civil rights activities and was arrested several times and was finally sentenced to six months in prison for "riotous behavior." She lost her seat in Parliament to a fellow civil rights activist in 1974.

The Price of My Soul documents the theoretical and political struggles in the movement, as well as Devlin's experience in London as a member of the British Parliament. It affords insight into political and social events and the life of a courageous young woman. *See also* **Memoir**.

Further Reading: Adams, Hazard. *Lady Gregory.* The Irish Writers Series (Lewisburg, PA: Bucknell University Press, 1973); Benstock, Shari. *The Private Self: Theory and Practice of Women's Autobiographical Writings* (Chapel Hill: University of North Carolina Press, 1988); Biuso, Thomas N. "Looking into Blasket Island Photographs." *Eire-Ireland: Journal of Irish Studies* (Winter 1984): 16–34; Bloom, Harold, ed. *Elizabeth Bowen* (New York: Chelsea House, 1987); Bowen, Elizabeth. *The Last September* (New York: Knopf, 1952); Colum, Mary. *From These Roots: The Ideas That Have Made Modern Literature* (New York: Scribner's, 1937); Colum, Mary. *Our Friend James Joyce* (Garden City, NY: Doubleday, 1958); Dalsimer, Adele. *Kate O'Brien: A Critical Study* (Boston: Twayne Publishers, 1990); Daniels, Kate. "Ireland's Best." *The Southern Review* 35, no. 2 (Spring 1999): 387–402; Eckley, Grace. *Edna O'Brien* (Lewisburg, PA: Bucknell University Press, 1974); Fallon, Ann Connerton. *Katharine Tynan* (Boston: Twayne, 1979); Greer, Mary K. *Women of the Golden Dawn: Rebels and Priestesses* (Rochester, VT: Park Street Books, 1995); Haberstroh, Patricia Boyle. *Women Creating Women: Contemporary Irish Women Poets* (Syracuse, NY: Syracuse University Press, 1995); Hoogland, Renee C. *Elizabeth Bowen: A Reputation in Writing* (New York: New York University Press, 1994); Jordan, Heather Bryant. "Rifling the Past: Elizabeth Bowen's Wartime Autobiography." *Notes on Modern Irish Literature* 2 (1990): 52–57; Kenneally, Michael, ed. *Cultural Contexts and Literary Idioms in Contemporary Irish Literature* (Totowa, NJ: Barnes & Noble, 1988); Kohfeldt, Mary Lou. *Lady Gregory: The Woman behind the Irish Renaissance* (New York: Atheneum, 1985); Kopper, Edward. *Lady Isabella Persse Gregory* (Boston: Twayne Publishers, 1976); Kulkin, Mary-Ellen. *Her Way* (New York: American Library Association, 1976); Lassner, Phyllis. *Elizabeth Bowen* (Savage, MD: Barnes and Noble, 1989); Londraville, Janis, and Richard Londraville. *Too Long a Sacrifice: The Letters of Maud Gonne and John Quinn.* Foreword by Anna MacBride White (Selinsgrove, PA: Susquehanna University Press, 1999); Napier, Taura S. *Seeking a Country: Literary Autobiographies of Twentieth-Century Irishwomen* (Lanham, MD: University Press of America, 2000); O'Brien, Darcy. "Edna O'Brien: A Kind of Irish Childhood." In *Twentieth-Century Women Novelists*, edited by Thomas F. Staley (Totowa, NJ: Barnes and Noble, 1982); O'Brien, Edna. *The Country Girls Trilogy and Epilogue* (New York: New American Library, 1987); O'Neill, Eugene. "Our Rostrum." *Forum* (December 1935): 5; Pethica, James, ed. *Lady Gregory's Diaries* (New York: Oxford University Press, 1996); Reynolds, Lorna. "*The Last September*—Elizabeth Bowen's Paradise Lost." In *Ancestral Voices: The Big House in Anglo-Irish Literature*, edited by Otto Rauchbauer, 149–158 (New York: Olms, 1992); Rose, Marilyn Gaddis. *Katharine Tynan* (Lewisburg, PA: Bucknell University Press, 1974); Saddlemyer, Ann, and Colin Smythe, eds. *Lady Gregory: Fifty Years After* (Totowa, NJ: Barnes and Noble, 1987); Target, George William. *Bernadette: The Story of Bernadette Devlin* (London: Hodder and Stoughton, 1975); Ward, Margaret. *Maud Gonne: Ireland's Joan of Arc* (London: Pandora, 1990); Wills, Clair. "Contemporary Irish Women Poets: The Privatization of Myth." In *Diverse Voices*, edited by Harriet Devine Jump (New York: St. Martin's Press,

1991); Wilson, Edmund. "The Memoirs of Mary Colum." Review. *The New Yorker*, March 27, 1947, 111.

Susan R. Bowers

ITALIAN WOMEN'S AUTOBIOGRAPHY

One can hardly speak of "Italian women' autobiography" if autobiography is to be defined according to the commonly accepted meaning. Despite Philippe Lejeune's and other critics' objections, he defined autobiography as a retrospective narrative account of the writer's own existence, in which s/he emphasizes his or her individual life, and particularly the story of his or her own personality. The inscription of any self-reflective literary work into a circumscribed canon of autobiography is always problematic, due to the intrinsically heterogeneous and transgeneric nature of autobiographical oeuvres, especially in relation to Italian women's autobiography. Within the Italian literary context, the female subject finds its way into the literary work through unconventional, oblique paths, by playing with those elements that make autobiography a highly ambiguous genre, such as hybridity and generic contamination. Italian women's self-reflective narratives are constructed across genres, thus creatively challenging generic conventions. The heterogeneity of their works is nurtured by the crossing and combination of autobiography with **biography**, in the works of A. Banti, *Artemisia* (1947); L. Romano, *Le parole tra noi leggere* (1969); and G. Manzini, *Ritratto in piedi* (1971). We see heterogeneity in the overlap between the theoretical and the ideological essay about childhood remembrances, for example in D. Prato, *Giù la piazza non c'è nessuno* (1980), *Le ore I* (1987–1988), and *Le ore II. Parole* (1994); A. Guiducci, *La mela e il serpente* (1974); G. Pistoso, *Le confessioni di una piccola italiana* (1983); R. Tumiati, *La pace del mondo gelatina* (1984); R. Rossanda, *Anche per me. Donna, persona, memoria dal 1973 al 1986* (1987); L. Passerini, *Autoritratto di gruppo* (1988); C.

Cerati, *La cattiva figlia* (1990); D. Maraini, *Bagheria* (1993) and *Un clandestino a bordo* (1996); L. Levi, *Una bambina e basta* (1994); R. Loy, *La parola ebreo* (1997); and D. Calamari, *Tutta colpa di Fidel* (1998). Heterogeniety appears in the cross of portrait with self-portrait, for instance in G. Manzini, "Autoritratto involontario" (1969), in *Sulla soglia* (1973), self-referential with metanarrative writing (i.e., S. Aleramo, *Il passaggio* [1932] and *Andando e stando* [1942]; G. Manzini, *Lettera all'editore* [1945]; and N. Ginzburg, *Mai devi domandarmi* [1970]). The combination of epistolary with **diary** forms provides another set of examples: S. Aleramo, *Amo dunque sono* (1927) and *Diario di una donna* (1978); E. Morante, *Diario 1938* and *Paragone* (both 1989). Mixing self-reflective with novelistic modes also results in heterogenious texts, for instance in S. Aleramo's, *Una donna* (1906); E. Robert, *Un ventre di donna: romanzo chirurgico* (1919); G. B. Rigatti-Luchini, *La notte insonne* (1972); F. Cialente, *Le quattro ragazze Wieselberger* (1976); F. Duranti, *La bambina* (1976) and *Piazza mia bella piazza* (1978); F. Sanvitale, *Madre e figlia* (1980); and A. Banti, *Un grido lacerante* (1981). Finally poetic and narrative modes mix in S. Aleramo, *Il frustino* (1932); A. Merini, *Reato di vita: Autobiografia e poesia* (1994). It is indeed by virtue of this wide variety of autobiographical narratives that the term "autobiography" seems to be inappropriate in relation to Italian women's literary tradition and that the more flexible notions of S. Doubrovsky's and A. Battistini's **autobiographics** is more useful.

Views of Recent Italian Women's Autobiographies

The deficiency of women's autobiographies within the Italian context is not fortuitous. Italian mainstream culture has always viewed autobiography with suspicion: It is only since the late 1980s and the early 1990s that this attitude has changed, thus acknowledging the genre's right to be included into the literary canon. Benedetto Croce's and Antonio Gramsci's criticism of autobiography's literary value is not foreign to this attitude, considering the dominant influence these two intellectuals have had on the national culture. In *Autobiography as History and History as Autobiography*, Croce only justifies the existence of autobiography as a documentary source for historians, while he dismisses other forms of the genre as motivated by pride and vanity. The only form of autobiography that he accepts he calls "historically imperfect," by virtue of its imaginative elements and because events are only viewed and interpreted by the narrator's subjective perspective, which is a principle that is contrary to the historian's objectivity. Ironically, these considerations did not prevent him from including his own autobiographical sketch in the same volume, using the same justifications that Jean-Jacques Rousseau, the father of modern autobiography, employed for writing his *Confessions*.

Similarly, Antonio Gramsci, while insisting on the sins of pride and vanity as the primary motivation of the autobiographical enterprise, only admits autobiography when it is inspired by an ideological aim, that is, when one's own life exemplifies a political theory. Interestingly, in the thoughts of two of the most influential twentieth-century Italian philosophers, autobiography, among all other literary genres, is the one that needs a justification to be written.

Despite the distrustful attitude toward autobiography, a tradition of men's autobiography exists as the critical works of Andrea Battistini, among others, prove. Going as far back as the seventeenth century, which he identifies as the historical period when the codification of the autobiographical genre was effected, Battistini retrieves a tradition of men's autobiographies going from Cellini to Cardano, Vico, Da Ponte, Casanova, Alfieri, Goldoni, and Gozzi. Others have then studied the autobiographical works of the nineteenth century such as those by Pellico, D'Azeglio, and the Risorgimento autobiographers, as well as Settembrini and De Sanctis; and of the twentieth century, such as those by D'Annunzio, the autobiographical "fragments" by the Vociani group, Bonaiuti, Montale, Vittorini, Ungaretti, Saba, Bertolucci, Bontempelli, De Chirico. Nonetheless, at the beginning of the twentieth century, G. Verga confesses that autobiography is repugnant to the Italian taste, while L. Pirandello writes in one of his rare autobiographical sketches, "I'm not talking about me" (1933) in sheer denial, as its title well illustrates. If this has been the prejudice surrounding autobiography up to the first half of the twentieth century, it is not surprising that Italian women writers have experienced resistance to a genre that assumes the subject's self-centeredness and a profound awareness of the relevance of one's life within a historical and cultural context. There is hardly any need to recall how difficult and meandering women's path toward self-awareness has been throughout history. It has been nearly impossible historically for Italian women to expose themselves directly in writing and to think of their lives an important. Besides, the pervasiveness of Catholic moral values in the deepest strata of Italian society has further relegated women to the private sphere, thus excluding them from any powerful public position. Subliminally, this has deprived them of the right to public visibility and, consequently, to self-expression.

Consequently, Italian women writers have often opted for the oblique mode of self-referentiality through a male relative's biography—father, husband, son—those life histories is perceived as more acceptable by the patriarchal establishment than their own. In this sense, the case of Italian women writers is one of the best to illustrate M. Mason's theory about the relational nature of women's personal narratives. In some cases, women's lack of confidence is sufficient to explain this phenomenon. In others, this tortuous means of self-referentiality through the biography of the male relative serves the opposite aim, that is, as the founding principle of one's own birth through writing, despite the figure in the foreground. In fact, it would be diminishing to view these oeuvres as the sole product of compliance and submission to the normative cultural discourses. Instead, what emerges from the studies of Italian women's autobiographical narratives is their attempt—in some cases very obvious, in others more cryptic—at disseminating their voices as a form of transgression and resistance against the main (male) culture. In this sense, Italian women's contravention to the generally acknowledged laws of the genre operates not only as a challenge to the conventional means of self-definition but also, and more significantly, as a choice of literary experimentation in search of alternative routes of self-analysis. This latter line of action takes shape mainly throughout the twentieth century, whose opening sees the publication of a number of female-authored autobiographical texts such as S. Aleramo's *Una donna* (1906), A. Guglielminetti's "Aridità sentimentale" (1911), Neera's *Una giovinezza del secolo XIX* (posthumously published in 1919), A. Negri's *Le solitarie* (1917) and *Stella mattutina* (1921), and C. Tartufari's *Il gomitolo d'oro* (1924), P. Drigo's *Fine d'anno* (1936), G. Deledda's "La Grazia," published in *Sole d'estate* (1933), and *Cosima, quasi Grazia* (1937). According to R. Pickering-Iazzi, some critics' assessment of such a proliferation as a deplorable "epidemic" among women writers corresponds to a defensive response among men who are threatened by women's power and self expression. In challenging the very tenets of autobiography, Italian women autobiographers also challenge the way of preserving patriarchal relations of power throughout the literary tradition by recounting the process of masculine **identity** building. This political as well as literary awareness does not take place before the mid-nineteenth century, due to the absence of women's voices within the national literary context, and is effectively launched with *Una donna* (1906) by S. Aleramo. Its publication represents a breakthrough: it acknowledges women's right to self-exposure and self-expression and encourages women writers to approach the writing of the self as a means of deconstructing **patriarchy** and inventing new models of visibility for the female subject. *See also* **Voice.**

Further Reading: Aricò, S., ed. *Contemporary Women Writers in Italy: A Modern Renaissance* (Amherst: The University of Massachussetts Press, 1990); Guerra, E. "Memory and Representation of Fascism: Female Autobiographical Narratives." In *Italian Fascism: History, Memory, and Representation*, edited by R.J.B. Bosworth and P. Dogliani, 178–194 (Basingstoke and London: Macmillan Press, 1999); Mason, M. "The Other Voice: Autobiographies of Women Writers." In *Autobiography: Essays Theoretical and Critical*, edited by James Olney, 207–235 (Princeton: Princeton University Press, 1980); Parati, G. *Public History, Private Stories: Italian Women's Autobiography* (Minneapolis and London: University of Minnesota Press, 1996); Parsani, M.A., and N. De Giovanni. *Femminile a confronto. Tre realtà della narrativa contemporanea: Alba De Cespedes, Fausta Cialente, Gianna Manzini* (Manduria, Bari and Roma: Lacaita, 1984); Pickering-Iazzi, R. "The Politics of Gender and Genre in Italian Women's Autobiography in the Interwar Years." *Italica* 71, no. 2 (1994): 176–197.

Alberta Gallus

J

JACOBS, HARRIET ANN (1813–1897)
"Slavery is terrible for men; but is far more terrible for women." This statement from Jacobs' work *Incidents in the Life of a Slave Girl* (1861) encapsulates its central argument and explains its singular importance among the more than one hundred American slave narratives published between 1831 and 1865. Furthermore, **letters** and other authentic nineteenth-century documents prove that Harriet Jacobs, after her escape from slavery, wrote the original manuscript herself while working as a house servant for a family in New York. Hence, *Incidents in the Life of a Slave Girl*, though adhering to the plot structure and veiled character identities required by white abolitionist editors, attests to the narrative force of a black woman's creativity and intellect.

Born a slave in Edenton, North Carolina, in 1813, Harriet Jacobs labored twenty-seven years as a house slave for a prominent doctor and his family. This close proximity to her master and mistress meant that she was subjected to his sexual harassment and the subsequent jealous rage of his wife. As a slave, Jacobs was forced to understand that she was expected to obey her master's demands. She was not entitled to choices or to make any decisions about the directions of her life. Yet, Jacobs reveals in her narra-tive two ways she succeeded in undermin-ing the institution of slavery and her master. First, she determined to take control of her own body by choosing to bear two children by a local white lawyer. This lawyer eventually purchased the two children and Harriet's brother from Jacobs' master. He took Jacobs' daughter north to freedom, and her son eventually traveled there as well. Second, Jacobs evaded her master's wrath by hiding in the garret above her grandmother's house for seven years until she was able to escape north. Once there, Jacobs was eventually reunited with her two children.

Literacy and writing as a means of self-expression, freedom, and resistance are significant themes in Jacobs' work. Jacobs was taught to read and write by an unusually kind mistress. Literacy enabled Jacobs to withstand her seven-year confinement because she read the Bible and manipulated her slave master by writing him letters that he believed were sent from the north. Once she did escape, Jacobs met and befriended Amy Post, one of the leading white abolitionists. After hearing about her life in slavery, Post encouraged Jacobs to write a narrative for use in their antislavery cause. Though hesitant to try publishing her story because of her limited education, Jacobs began writing in 1853. The demanding work as a house servant to the Willis family left little time for writing, so it took Jacobs eight years to complete the manuscript's first draft. Jacobs' daughter, Louisa, who had been educated as a teacher copied the manuscript, presumably standardizing the spelling and punctuation. Harriet Jacobs then procured the assistance of another prominent abolitionist, Lydia Maria Child, to edit the manuscript for publication.

In the introduction to *Incidents in the Life of a Slave Girl*, Child insists that she made few editorial changes. However, letters written by Child to various acquaintances attest to the extent of the changes she made in the manuscript. She altered the names of Harriet Jacobs (to Linda Brent), her children, and other family members and friends to protect them from social and political repercussions. She also deleted and rearranged a few of the original chapters and gathered scenes describing the "savage treatment" of slaves on neighboring Southern plantations that Jacobs had witnessed into one chapter. All of this, and the authenticating letters, prefaces, and appendix attached to the text of Jacobs' narrative, was in keeping with the formulaic pattern for slave narratives that the abolitionists had developed over the course of thirty years.

Editorial intrusions aside, Harriet Jacobs achieved her goal to tell the world what she and thousands of other slave mothers suffered in American bondage.

Further Reading: Deck, Alice A. " 'Whose Book Is This?': Authorial vs. Editorial Control of Harriet Brent Jacobs' *Incidents in the Life of a Slave Girl: Written By Herself*." *Women's Studies International Forum* 10, no. 1 (1987): 33–40; Foster, Frances Smith. *Witnessing Slavery: The Development of Antebellum Slave Narratives* (Westport, CT: Greenwood, 1979); Goldsby, Jacqueline. " 'I Disguised My Hand': Writing Versions of the Truth in Harriet Jacobs's *Incidents in the Life of a Slave Girl* and John Jacobs's 'A True Tale of Slavery.' " In *Harriet Jacobs and Incidents in the Life of a Slave Girl*, edited by Deborah Garfield and Rafia Zafar, 11–43 (Cambridge: Cambridge University Press, 1996); Niemtzow, Annette. "The

Problematic Self in Autobiography: The Example of the Slave Narrative." In *The Art of the Slave Narrative: Original Essays in Criticism and Theory*, edited by John S. Sekora and Darwin T. Turner, 105–106 (Macomb, IL: Western Illinois University Press, 1982); Olney, James. " 'I Was Born': Slave Narratives, Their Status as Autobiography and as Literature." In *The Slave's Narrative*, edited by Charles T. Davis and Henry Louis Gates, Jr., 148–175 (New York: Oxford University Press, 1985); Smith, Valerie. Introduction to *Incidents in the Life of a Slave Girl*, by Harriet Jacobs (New York: Oxford University Press, 1988); Smith, Valerie. *Self Discovery and Authority in Afro American Narrative* (Cambridge, MA: Harvard University Press, 1987), 9–28; Stepto, Robert. *From behind the Veil: A Study of Afro American Narrative* (Urbana: University of Illinois Press, 1979); Yellin, Jean. "Texts and Contexts of Harriet Jacobs' *Incidents in the Life of a Slave Girl: Written By Herself*. In *The Slave's Narrative*, edited by Charles T. Davis and Henry Louis Gates, Jr., 262–282 (New York: Oxford University Press, 1985); Yellin, Jean, ed. Introduction to *Incidents in the Life of a Slave Girl: Written By Herself*, by Harriet Jacobs (Cambridge, MA: Harvard University Press, 1987).

Alice A. Deck

JAPANESE WOMEN'S AUTOBIOGRAPHY Japanese women's writings have a long history dating from the twelfth century, and women's autobiography can be counted among the oldest genres in Japanese literature. The growth of women's autobiography is paradoxical in the sense that, had women's status equaled that of men's, these texts would not have been created. Indeed, the creativity/productivity of women reflect the status of women in general. Japanese society was male-centered until the mid-twentieth century. Women were considered socially inferior, but they played important roles as educators for court ladies of high rank, some of whom bore future emperors. Perhaps because of their status, they turned their interests and energies to literature, a kind of **confession** literature.

Women's Autobiography in Early Japan

There are two categories of Japanese women's autobiography in terms of historical periods of time. The first appeared during the Heian period (794–1191), during feudalism, when aristocrats established a prominent court culture in the Middle Ages. Educated middle-class women, many of whom served at court, took up a part of producing court culture through writing. Employing the form of **diary** writing, educated middle-class women articulated their inner feelings. The genre of *Nikki Bungaku* or diary writing is seen until the earlier Kamakura period, around the thirteenth century. The second category consists of autobiographies written after the Meiji period (1868–1912). As seen in Western and other parts of the world, women's autobiographical works in this historical period are those of the personal history of an individual (such as a social reformer) as well as fictional forms of autobiography. Taking these types of works in the early twentieth century as a starting point, women's autobiography as a part of women's literature began to thrive in the twentieth century.

During the Heian period, women's writing flourished as educated middle-class women were allowed to express their feelings through writing. As a result, there were several distinguished women writers in the fields of fiction and autobiographical writing. In this period, women of the middle-class, such as the daughters of provincial governors (minor officials) or scholars, were often well educated. Many served at court which was thought to be a successful path for women in that period. They were familiar with reading and writing *waka* poems. In their world at court, they kept journals and wrote poetry through love **letters**. As the means of correspondence in the Heian period, *waka* poems are put together in prose-style autobiographies.

One of the most well-known women's autobiographies is *Kagerō Nikki*, translated as *The Gossamer Years*, written by "the mother of Fujiwara Michitsuna" in the late tenth century, the mid-Heian period. Categorized as an autobiography/diary, *Kagerō Nikki* records the unhappy marriage of a wife of an eminent man at court. The second wife of Kaneie Fujiwara discloses her disturbed state of mind during her married life. In this autobiographical work, she reminisces about her younger days, between the ages of nineteen (in the year 954) and thirty-nine. The work displays the author's jealousy toward her husband's other wives and mistresses and her excessive affection for her only son. Although *Kagerō Nikki* does not explicitly refer to the social and political situations of the Heian period, readers observe women's status within the social system through the recording of the author's private life and her feelings.

Another celebrated autobiography from the Heian period is *Sarashina Nikki* written by the daughter of Sugawara Takasue in around 1060. This autobiography is also about the married life of an educated middle-class woman during a forty-year period between the ages of ten (in the year 1017) and fifty-one. The work begins with the description of the author's life in an eastern province where her father took up his governorship. The author's detailed description of her feelings and lifestyle gives readers insight into a woman's life and the way of thinking in the Heian period, in contrast to the author's depiction of women's status in *Kagerō Nikki*. In her teens, the author of *Sarashina Nikki*, adored the novel, *The Tale of Genji*, and wished for a comparable, dramatic love. However, she marries an ordinary man of no distinguished rank. She is disappointed at first, but during her marriage comes to realize that personality is more important than appearances.

An important autobiography of the Kamakura period (1192–1332) is *Utatane* [Fitful Slumbers] and *Izayoi Nikki* [The Diary of the Waning Moon]. Written by a nun named Abutsu (1222?–1283), it consists of two sequential works. In the first, *Utatane*, the author records her life around age twenty, and describes her heartbreaking experiences as an innocent girl seduced by a married man of the noble class. She ends up becoming a nun. In the second, *Izayoi Nikki*, the author is in her fifties and records her petition to the Kamakura Shogunate (1279). Because she has been the second wife of a man in the Fujiwara clan, the author tries to justify her right to inherit her late husband's assets instead of the first wife's son. Later readers and critics often see the author as manipulative for her allegation in *Izayoi Nikki*, but readers see the author's transition from *Utatane* to *Izayoi Nikki*.

The literary works of the Japanese Middle Ages were made public through their circulation among court ladies or other educated middle-class women. The author's manuscript was circulated and sometimes several copies of the original manuscript were made to satisfy eager readers. *Kagerō Nikki*, written in the Heian period and *Sarashina Nikki* from the Kamakura period, are still familiar to modern readers. They illustrate the lives of middle-class women, particularly with respect to the marriage system. The study of Heian literature has been done by several Western scholars, among them Donald Keene and Edward Seidensticker. Keene's thorough study of Japanese literature *Appreciations of Japanese Culture* (1971) has a section on "Feminine Sensibility in the Heian Era," which includes his discussion on the *Kagerō Nikki* and the *Sarashina Nikki*. Seidensticker translated several Heian literary works into English, including the *Kagerō Nikki* as *The Gossamer Years* (1964). *See also* **Class**.

The Twentieth Century and the Present

After a long, unproductive period, women's autobiographical works reemerged as women's status improved in the early twentieth century. Until the mid-twentieth century, women had been denied many civil rights. One social reformer, Raicho Hi-ratsuka (1886–1971), wrote a personal history, focusing on her contribution to the improvement of women's social status. A precursor of Japan's modern **feminism**, Hiratsuka wrote *Genshi josei wa taiyō de atta* (1971 [Women Were Originally the Sun]), which encouraged Japanese women in the mid-twentieth century to agitate for civil rights.

Japanese women's literature since the early twentieth century has seen remarkable growth, though Western scholar and critic Donald Keene sees its growth as "modest" (1971, 26). Much of this literature, however, contains autobiographical elements. Yuriko Miyamoto (1899–1951), Fumiko Hayashi (1903–1951), and Chiyo Uno (1897–1994) are among the authors who have written a fictional form of personal history. Miyamoto's *Nobuko* (1924–1926), *Banshū Heiya* [The Banshū Plain], and *Fūchisō* [The Weathervane Plant], the latter two published in 1946, are considered **autobiographical fiction**. Written from a communist perspective, *Banshū Heiya* describes the lifestyle of the nation and its belief in the Japanese emperor at the time of World War II. Hayashi's *Hōrō-ki* [A Vagabond's Story], published in 1930, has enjoyed popularity because of its lively portrayal of her wandering life. Uno published many autobiographical novels that vividly describe her liberated lifestyle. These autobiographical works of the early twentieth century are significant not only because they seek to improve women's social status in modern Japan, but also because they demonstrate diverse women's lives.

Further Reading: Abutsu. *The Izayoi Nikki*. Edited by Ichinose Sachiko (Tokyo: Shinten-sha, 1975); Buckley, Sandra, ed. *Encyclopedia of Contemporary Japanese Culture* (London: Routledge, 2002); Hayashi, Fumiko. *Hōrō-ki* 1930 (Tokyo: Shincho-sha, 1979); Hiratsuka, Raicho. *Watakushi no Aruita Michi*. Writer's Autobiography series. Vol. 8 (Tokyo: Japan Library Center, 1994); Hiratsuka, Raicho. *Genshi josei wa taiyō de atta: Hiratsuka Raicho Jiden*. 4 vols. (Tokyo: Otsuki Shoten, 1971); Keene, Donald. *Appreciations of Japanese Culture* (Tokyo: Kodansha International,

1971); Keene, Donald. *Anthology of Japanese Literature* (New York: Grove, 1955); Keene, Donald. *Seeds in the Heart: Japanese Literature from Earliest Times to the Late Sixteenth Century*. Vol. 1 of *A History of Japanese Literature*. 1993 (New York: Columbia University Press, 1999); Keene, Donald. *Dawn to the West: Japanese Literature in the Modern Era, Fiction*. Vol. 3 of *A History of Japanese Literature*. 1984. Reprint (New York: Columbia University Press, 1998); Keene, Donald. *Modern Japanese Diaries: The Japanese at Home and Abroad as Revealed through Their Diaries* (New York: Columbia University Press, 1999); Miyamoto, Yuriko. *Banshū Heiya*. 1946. Reprint (Tokyo: Shinippon Publisher, 2000); Omori, Annie Shepley, and Kochi Doi, trans. *Diaries of Court Ladies of Old Japan*. 1920 (Boston: Houghton Mifflin, 1920) Seidensticker, Edward, trans. *The Gossamer Years: The Diary of a Noblewoman of Heian Japan* (Tokyo: Charles E. Tuttle, 1964); Uno, Chiyo. *Uno Chiyo: Anthology*. 12 vols. (Tokyo: Chuo Koronsha, 1977–1978).

Ayako Mizuo

JONG, ERICA (1942–) Erica Jong's autobiographical writing poses a problem because she is compulsively autobiographical. Autobiographical elements feature in all her writing, from her novels, to her **biography** of Henry Miller, to her other prose, which includes her only explicitly autobiographical work, *Fear of Fifty* (1994). Clearly untroubled by transgressing literary boundaries, Jong underlines the convergence between her autobiographical and her fictional writing by using the same alliteration, the same phrasing, and two of the same words in the title of her **memoir** as she used in the title of her first, best-known, and commercially most successful novel, *Fear of Flying* (1973). What the similarity in the titles indicates, the contents confirm. Between the autobiographical and the novelistic, there is significant overlapping of characters and events.

Jong's autobiographical impulse derives from her attitude toward writing. As she notes in her biography of Henry Miller, "you can't hide behind words. What and

who you are shines forth on every page—whether you pretend objectivity or not" (*Devil* 1993, 25). In short, for Jong, objectivity is something of a fraud; all writing is inherently self-reflexive. The implication is that autobiography ought not to be privileged as the exclusive means of self-representation. Jong goes even further. In a letter to Miller, Jong acknowledges "the impossibility of ever telling the truth about one's life, the impossibility of literal autobiography" (*Devil* 17). Indeed, Jong suggests that autobiography may well be another form of fiction (*Devil* 26).

Thus, there are two difficulties in dealing with Jong's autobiographical writing. The first is that her ostensibly nonautobiographical prose contains so much autobiographical detail. The second is that her explicitly autobiographical memoir may well contain fictional enhancements. Before dealing with the explicitly autobiographical *Fear of Fifty*, it is useful to comment briefly on the autobiographical components of Jong's other prose.

In varying degrees, Jong incorporates into her novels her sexual exploits, her literary preoccupations, and her family relationships. Of all Jong's fictional personae, none is closer to Jong than Isadora Wing, the central character in the trilogy, *Fear of Flying, How to Save Your Own Life* (1977), and *Parachutes & Kisses* (1984). From Isadora's first failed marriage to a brilliant psychotic, to her second failed marriage to an emotionally unresponsive Chinese American psychiatrist (*Flying*), to her passionate affair with a younger writer from an old left-wing family (*How to Save*), to her third divorce and search for stability and love as a single mother (*Parachutes*), the trajectory of these novels is as much about Jong's life as it is about Isadora's. Jong's family, friends, and miscellaneous lovers are given only thin fictional cover. It would be difficult, for example, not to find the aging Henry Miller in Jong's fictional creation Kurt Hammer, whose underground reputation rests "on tattered copies of his reputed-to-be pornographic novels smuggled in through customs in the days when sex was considered unfit for print" (*How to Save* 187). There are many other characters in the trilogy who are easily identifiable as members of Jong's family and entourage.

Despite such correlations, Jong insists that the parallels between her own life and her mythic lives in her novels do not make her identical with her fictional creations (*Devil* 46). Her practice when writing fiction may be summarized as telling the same story differently in every novel. Thus, Jong has it both ways: her novels are autobiographical, yes, but they are also transformations, modifications, and even improvements of her life. Whatever their distortions, the novels are an important if imperfect map of Jong's life, even if some of the small roads are left out or renamed.

Like her novels, Jong's biography of Henry Miller, *The Devil at Large* (1993), tellingly subtitled, *Erica Jong on Henry Miller*, is autobiographical. The work is less a sequential narrative of Miller's life than a record of Jong's friendship with Miller, begun at the time of the publication of *Fear of Flying*. Jong sees in Miller's writing a desire for "abundance" and liberation, with its concomitant rejection of compartmentalization (*Devil* 48). According to Jong, Miller's work, like her own, obliterates the distinctions between fact and fiction and between physical and spiritual, so that, for Miller as for Jong, sexual experience prepares the way for transcendence. Because of these literary and philosophical affinities, Jong's discussion of Miller's literary career and her critical assessment of what his **place** ought to be in the American literary canon is also Jong's assessment of her own literary career and her potential canonicity. *The Devil at Large* is, in fact, almost as much about Erica Jong as it is about Henry Miller.

Jong is also a strong presence in her essays, twenty-four of which are collected in *What Do Women Want?* (1998). Taken together, these essays provide Jong's perspective on the status and sexual needs of late-twentieth-century women as well as a commentary on the life, loves, and opinions of Erica Jong. The essays mix personal experience (i.e., "Coming Home to Connecticut" 299–302) with political and social commentary (i.e., "The President's Penis" 149–157). The disparateness of the essays is more apparent than real, however. There are important congruencies between the private and the public. For example, in the first essay of the collection, "My Mother, My Daughter and Me" (1–10), Jong analyzes the dynamics of domestic power reflected in the interactions of the women of her family. That analysis establishes the parameters of the second essay, "Curst Lady: The Vicissitudes of Being Hillary Rodham Clinton" (11–28), in which Jong examines Hillary Rodham Clinton's desire to wield power in the political world and the compromises she strikes with her president/husband to achieve that goal. In these and the other essays in the collection, Jong shows that private and public life are interrelated, interactive, and highly political. As in her novels and in her biography, Jong favors an inclusive, multigenre approach to individual and social understanding.

This same expansiveness is at work in *Fear of Fifty*, her only explicitly autobiographical work to date. In part, *Fear of Fifty*, like *Fear of Flying* and Jong's other prose, articulates the Zeitgeist of Jong's generation. However contradictorily, Jong's "I" is also the socially representative "we." As she says in the preface, "I make the assumption that I am not so different from you or you" (*Fifty* xxvi). So this autobiographical memoir is, like Jong's other writing, a composite form that includes social commentary. In part, *Fear of Fifty* is a meditative personal inquiry into the meaning of Jong's life. In it, she records her developing awareness of herself as a woman and an author, an interdependent, even inseparable process of coming to terms with a multiplicity of confusing and often contradictory roles. In the course of her self-examination, Jong considers herself as daughter, wife, mother, friend, feminist, poet, novelist, sex object, secular Jew, spiritual seeker, unashamed devotee of the literary canon, celebrator of writers (especially women) left out of the canon, and a patron of psychoanalysis.

Despite such efforts at comprehensiveness, Jong's self-awareness proves partial and imperfect. In Chapter 2 of *Fear of Fifty*, Jong attempts to dispose of "all that David Copperfield crap" (17), yet in the penultimate chapter, she is still excavating the details of the past. There she describes an interview with her mother intended to illuminate certain troubling childhood experiences, but these efforts prove inconclusive and unsatisfactory. For Jong, retrieving the personal past is an unreliable and discontinuous process, full of lacunae, subject to intermittent reinterpretation in light of later disclosures, yet always and inevitably incomplete. *Fear of Fifty* is less a chronicle of Jong's life than a testament to the impossibility of writing literal autobiography. *Fear of Fifty* is clearly not conventional autobiography. Even when Jong knows the names, dates, and places, she frequently suppresses authenticating details. Indeed, for full coverage of such events as Jong's lesbian affair, her novels provide more graphic elaboration than this memoir. The looseness of the memoir form, moreover, releases Jong from the bondage of sequence. The narrative does not unfold in strict chronological order, but by a series of tentative revelations that are governed by the associative logic of **memory**. What distinguishes *Fear of Fifty* from Jong's other prose work is not its autobiographical bent, which is present in all her prose, but its sense of urgency. Mid-life, for Jong, is that "time when time itself begins to seems short" (xxvi). In place of the youthful buoyancy of Jong's earlier fictional personae is an older Jong who worries about the approach of death.

In *Fear of Fifty*, Jong finds hope and solace in her protean assertions of self, the autobiographical impulse that is at the heart of all her writing. Jong's sexual and imaginative fecundity allow her to be mother, daughter, lover, wife, writer, and spokesperson for her generation. The multiple roles Jong embraces, and the continuities of blood and word they create, provide Jong with a form of secular transcendence. In essence, Jong's autobiographical writing is her way of affirming life and thwarting the finality of death.

Further Reading: Fishkin, Shelly Fisher. "Erica Jong." April 1, 2003. http://www.erica jong.com/fishkinessay.htm; Jong, Erica. *Any Woman's Blues: A Novel of Obsession* (New York: Harper and Row, 1990); Jong, Erica. *At the Edge of the Body* (New York: Holt, Rinehart and Winston, 1979); Jong, Erica. *Becoming Light: New and Selected Poems* (New York: Harper, 1991); Jong, Erica. *The Devil at Large: Erica Jong on Henry Miller* (New York: Random House, 1993); Jong, Erica. *Fanny, Being the True History of the Adventures of Fanny Hackabout-Jones* (New American Library, 1980); Jong, Erica. *Fear of Fifty: A Midlife Memoir* (New York: HarperCollins, 1994); Jong, Erica. *Fear of Flying* (New York: Holt, Rinehart and Winston, 1973); Jong, Erica. *Fruits and Vegetables* (New York: Holt, Rinehart and Winston, 1971); Jong, Erica. *Half-Lives* (New York: Holt, Rinehart and Winston, 1973); Jong, Erica. *Here Comes and Other Poems* (New York: Signet, 1975); Jong, Erica. *How to Save Your Own Life* (New York: Holt, Rinehart and Winston, 1977); Jong, Erica. *Inventing Memory: A Novel of Mothers and Daughters* (New York: HarperCollins, 1997); Jong, Erica. *Loveroot* (New York: Holt, Rinehart and Winston, 1975); Jong, Erica. *Megan's Two Houses: A Story of Adjustment*. Illustrated by Freya Tanz (Los Angeles, CA: Dove Kids, 1996). A reissue of *Megan's Book of Divorce: A Kid's Book for Adults as Told to Erica Jong* (New York: New American Library, 1984); Jong, Erica. *Ordinary Miracles* (New York: New American Library, 1983); Jong, Erica. *Parachutes and Kisses* (New York: New American Library, 1984); Jong, Erica. *Shylock's Daughter: A Novel of Love in Venice* (New York: HarperCollins, 1995). Paperback reissue of *Serenissima: A Novel of Venice* (Boston: Houghton Mifflin, 1987); Jong, Erica. *What Do Women Want? Bread Roses Sex Power* (New York: HarperCollins, 1998); Jong, Erica. *Witches* (New York: Harry N. Abrams, 1981); Templin, Charlotte. *Feminism and the Politics of Literary Reputation: The Example of Erica Jong* (Lawrence: University Press of Kansas, 1995).

Bernice Schrank

JORDAN, JUNE (1936–2002) June Jordan wrote poems, essays, plays, librettos, and children's books, and she wrote for one reason: she believed it was her best weapon against injustice. Best known for her political poetry and essays, Jordan was also a highly accomplished teacher, playwright, composer, and urban planner.

All of Jordan's writing emanates from the autobiographical. She writes her personal story into the historical and social context in which she lives. For instance, *His Own Where* (1971), her first book for children and young adults, was written to oppose her son's initial encounters with racism. It is written completely in the black vernacular. Her second work for younger readers is a **biography** of *Fannie Lou Hamer* (1972), which came about after Jordan met Hamer while participating in a voter registration drive in the South and Hamer became a sort of surrogate mother to her. Jordan's essays commonly begin with a personal anecdote and her poems explore her relationships with family, friends, lovers, and **place**. Her **memoir**, *Soldier: A Poet's Childhood* (2000), documents growing up poor and black in New York City, with a tyrannical father who often beat her for no reason and a mother who was so depressed that she was incapable of intervening. Regardless of the genre, woven into all of her writing are accounts of the intersections of **race**, economics, and **identity** as they played out in the United States during her lifetime.

According to her memoir, June Jordan was born in New York on the "hottest day in July," July 9, 1936, to Granville and Mildred Jordan, two immigrants from the West Indies who met and married in New York (3). Jordan's father worked diligently as a postal employee, but he was never able to pull his family out of poverty and into the kind of life he had imagined would be available to him in America. Frustrated by what he saw as his personal failings, Granville was dictatorial and cruel. He often beat his daughter and his wife for no apparent reason, and he would force June

to march around the neighborhood military style for hours. Determined to raise his daughter so that she might realize the American dream that he found elusive, Granville tried to remake Jordan into a boy, a white boy. He taught her to box, speak "correct" English, and forced her to memorize Shakespeare's sonnets, the poems of Paul Laurence Dunbar, Langston Hughes, Edgar Allan Poe, and others. Yet, in spite of his extreme behavior, it was her father's hard-driving personality and love for justice that led Jordan to a life of activism and to her success as a writer. In addition to introducing her to the great writers and poets, he was the one who arranged for her to attend the best all-girls schools in the city, and he was the one who developed her appreciation of beauty and truth.

Jordan began attending Barnard College in 1953, but then dropped out in 1955 to marry a fellow graduate student, Michael Meyer. Their only child, Christopher David, was born in 1958. By 1963, in addition to the strains of racist attitudes toward mixed couples, Jordan and Meyer were also dealing with the difficulties of living separately. These additional stresses were exacerbated by Jordan's increased activism in the Civil Rights movement and Michael's involvement with another woman. By 1965, the marriage had collapsed.

Around the same time as her divorce from Meyer, Jordan began collaborating with the world renowned architect R. Buckminster Fuller. Their work to redesign East Harlem was published in *Life Magazine* and led Jordan to receive the Prix de Rome prize in environmental design.

In 1969, Jordan published her first book, *Who Look at Me?* an ekphrastic poem about race and representation. She also published many collections of poems including *New Days: Poems of Exile and Return* (1974), *Things That I Do in the Dark* (1977), *Passion* (1980), and collections of occasional essays including *Civil Wars* (1981) and *On Call* (1985).

From February 1989 to November 2001 Jordan wrote a regular column for *The Pro-*

gressive, a magazine known for its work to champion peace and social justice, and as always, her writings originated in response to social or economic injustices that she had witnessed. According to Jordan, if she wasn't writing to elicit change or awareness, then she was writing for the wrong reason.

Jordan's poems have appeared in more than thirty major anthologies, including *The Norton Anthology of Modern Poetry, The Norton Anthology of African American Literature, Homegirls: An Anthology of Black Feminism* and *The Village Voice Anthology*. In January 1994, *The Library Journal* hailed Jordan as "one of the most important poets writing today." In September 2000, *Black Issues Book Review* described Jordan as "an a-bomb" and "the consummate tough girl." She has received numerous awards including a Rockefeller Foundation grant for creative writing, the National Association of black Journalists Award, and fellowships from the National Endowment for the Arts and the New York Foundation for the Arts.

Jordan's last book, *Some of Us Did Not Die* (2002), published posthumously, brings together her writing of more than fifty years of activism on the frontlines of the major political movements of her time while documenting her final battle against breast cancer. As was Jordan's way in any situation, she did not let despair overcome her as she faced her own death. Instead, she took her place among the many women around the world who know that the cancer that causes the maiming and killing of thousands of women every month is more than just a coincidence, and in her essays and poems, she made that her final fight.

Further Reading: Mullaney, Janet Palmer, ed. *Truthtellers of the Times: Interviews with Contemporary Women Poets* (Ann Arbor: University of Michigan Press, 1998); Guy-Sheftall, Beverly, ed. *Words of Fire: An Anthology of African-American Feminist Thought* (New York: New Press, 1995).

Adrienne Cassel

JOURNAL OF A SOLITUDE May Sarton's *Journal of a Solitude* (1973) has been praised as a "watershed in women's autobiography" for its deliberate recounting of a woman's anger and desire for control (Heilbrun 13). Because of its depth and honesty, *Journal of a Solitude* has become one of the most read and admired of Sarton's many works. Written when she was age fifty-eight, the journal chronicles a year of Sarton's life in the small village of Nelson, New Hampshire and addresses the emotional upheavals that followed her decision twelve years earlier to live a life of solitude. Sarton began the work in part to revise the false impressions that she believed her earlier **memoir**, *Plant Dreaming Deep* (1968), had left with readers. Many had come away from that work with the impression that Sarton's solitude was idyllic and that as a solitary woman and artist, she was fully in control of her internal and external circumstances. The truth, however, was more complex. "The anguish of my life here—its rages—is hardly mentioned," she notes in reference to the earlier account. "Now I hope to break through into the rough rocky depths, to the matrix itself. There is violence there and anger never resolved" (12).

Sarton regarded the journal as the best vehicle for capturing the unstructured immediacy, or pulse, of the moment. She distinguished the form from the more consciously shaped distillations of the past found in her earlier and later memoirs such as *I Knew a Phoenix* (1959), *Plant Dreaming Deep*, and *A World of Light* (1976). Written in the spirit of the moment, *Journal of a Solitude* provides a record of Sarton's daily activities, thoughts, challenges, and epiphanies about the value of solitude in her life; her work as a poet and writer; and her evolving sense of self as she entered her later years. The dated entries vary greatly in length. Some read like informal essays, while others consist of a single, attenuated paragraph. Topics range widely, from her writing process and the work of poets and writers she admires to seasonal changes in the weather and visits with friends. Other topics include the burden of keeping up with household chores, the condition of her garden, and contemporary political developments and social unrest. Despite the broad and disparate scope, several key themes emerge to provide an overall coherence to the work. These include the continuing struggle to maintain emotional self-control, the desire to achieve balance between an often-precarious solitude and the need for human attachment, writing as a means to clarify experience, the joy found in the natural world, the process of growing into old age, and the value of solitude for women as a spiritual and creative necessity.

Sarton argued that so long as the dilemmas one experiences privately are examined attentively and honestly in writing, the results should have universal value and appeal. Accordingly, she felt that her decision to live alone as a middle-aged, single woman responsible only to her self would prove meaningful to others. By "describing what the pilgrimage is like," she felt her experience could be a comfort to others (*Journal of a Solitude* 40). Much of the work addresses her bouts with depression and periods of deep loneliness, anger, and self-doubt. She notes, for instance, that her decision to start the journal was an effort to come to terms with the pain and loss that followed a failing love affair. The details of the affair are omitted to protect the **identity** of the person involved. The lover, in fact, is referred to only as "X," a decision that reflects Sarton's professed need to be honest on the one hand, yet detached and self-restrained on the other.

Sarton's anger and frustration arise from a number of causes, including frustration with the intrusions made on her time and **space** by outside commitments like lecture engagements and trips to visit friends, the feeling of despair when she is without time to analyze experience, and the fatigue and increasing sense of boredom she feels with her life in Nelson. Often, the frustration she feels is with herself. She admits in the journal of being a difficult and at times absurd character unable to control her temperament. She mentions, for instance, an emotional outburst in response to a close friend's innocent comment about some faded flowers in a vase. The pleasure of the friend's visit is regrettably cut short, Sarton explains, by what she irrationally felt was a criticism. She then ponders whether such destructive explosions might serve as safety valves for preserving an overall inner sanity. The episode reflects the tension Sarton generally experiences in relationships. At times, they feel like collisions, and yet she admits, they are what challenge her and give her strength.

In addition to frustration with her own mood swings, Sarton was also still reeling from the negative reaction her novel, *Mrs. Stevens Hears the Mermaids Singing* (1965), had received from some critics who disapproved of the novel's lesbian protagonist. The novel, now considered her most important, had in fact been a vehicle for Sarton's own coming out, an event for which she paid a heavy price in the loss of two teaching jobs, a dispute with her publisher, and ambivalence from critics about her work.

If depression sometimes exerted its hold over her, Sarton found a means to control it in the routine discipline she applied to her writing and daily life. Indeed, establishing order is Sarton's way of keeping anxieties and emotional chaos in check. Her need for order and beauty is voiced often in entries devoted to the household circumstances conducive to her work—the placement of a vase of flowers, for instance, or the satisfaction of a weeded garden and a tidy desk. She also steadies herself by finding joy in the world around her house. Throughout the journal, Sarton reveals the aesthetic pleasure she derives from events of the moment: the changing play of light in a room, the look of ice-covered trees after a winter storm, the sight of a scarlet tanager outside her window. While these events may ordinarily be considered too mundane for traditional autobiographical accounts, Sarton makes them sacred. Together with the writing, especially of poetry, they provide her with a sense of continuity, stability, and unity with the universe.

As it does in *Plant Dreaming Deep*, Sarton's house becomes a strong and signifying presence. As an empowering metaphor for solitude and self-creation, the house reinforces the domestic sphere as a nurturing influence on the female artist. While it sometimes reinforces the isolation that comes with solitude, it also reflects Sarton's openness to others. Solitude, she maintains, is a path toward communion. By making the house a place of poetry in which she can grasp the essence of things, it becomes a beacon of hope and welcome to others. Photographs of the house appear throughout the book and convey a sense of hope and safety that parallel Sarton's image of herself as a lighthouse keeper, someone who guides others away from the hazards of a rocky shore and promises refuge and human warmth.

As a single woman, Sarton understood that her life of solitude differed greatly from that of many women whose energies were absorbed by the needs of spouses and children. "The house *is* open in a way that no house where a family lives and interacts can be," Sarton declares in the journal. "My life, often frightfully lonely, interacts with a whole lot of people I do not know and will never know" (*Journal of a Solitude* 115). Sarton did not wish to be labeled a feminist writer, but she was sympathetic to the challenges and sacrifices of women whose needs for autonomy and wholeness were often sacrificed in the care of others. While she believed marriage could be a positive union between two people, she knew that many marriages failed to achieve this ideal. Several statements in the journal reveal her support of the women's liberation movement. She called on men, for example, to assume the nurturing responsibilities she felt were taken for granted in women. Espe-

cially for women artists, Sarton felt marriage could be a compromise that made securing the necessary solitary time and space a difficult if not impossible task. Nevertheless, she believed that close relationships instigate growth. Ideally, one strives for the difficult balance between relationship and solitude. Sarton felt uniquely qualified to communicate this message to readers who, having read her work, opened up to her about their lives in **letters** to her. Her drive to answer all these queries often taxed her solitude and led her to feel exhausted and resentful. At no time, however, did she give any indication of ceasing her correspondence with her readership.

The journal closes with references to new beginnings. Sarton notes the decision to end her relationship with "X" and to move into a new house by the ocean in York, Maine, the setting for her next journal, *The House by the Sea* (1977), and the six that followed. Where the need for beauty and order predominates in *Journal of a Solitude*, her move to the sea suggests a new direction, this time toward wildness and greater openness. Sarton senses that the move will restore the inner calm that was too often compromised in Nelson. In the later journals, including *Recovering: A Journal* (1980) and *At Seventy* (1984), Sarton addresses her growth into old age, illness, and the loss of friends. In writing about these changes, she would continue to display a courage that was characteristic of her never-ending journey of self-examination and self-renewal.

Though generally positive, the critical reception of *Journal of a Solitude* was less enthusiastic than that of the earlier memoir, *Plant Dreaming Deep*. Nonetheless, the lukewarm critical reception has been more than offset by an attentive general public and the work continues to enjoy a wide and sustained readership in the United States. The volume of fan letters Sarton received throughout her life from admiring, predominantly female readers, attested to the honesty and courage found in her work. In the

1970s and 1980s, feminist scholars increasingly recognized a voice of strength and openness in Sarton, not only about a woman's creative process, but also about the significance of women's love for women. An often-cited quote from *Journal of a Solitude* provides a useful summary of the work Sarton hoped her journals, and indeed all her work, could perform: "On the surface my work has not looked radical, but perhaps it will be seen eventually that in a 'nice, quiet, noisy way' I have been trying to say radical things gently so that they may penetrate without shock" (90). Perhaps what is most radical about this journal is the depth to which it ascribes and restores spiritual meaning to the everyday "mundane" events and emotional struggles experienced by both Sarton and her readers. *See also* **Feminism**.

Further Reading: Braham, Jeanne. " 'Seeing with Fresh Eyes': A Study of May Sarton's Journals." In *That Great Sanity: Critical Essays on May Sarton*, edited by Susan Schwartzlander and Marilyn R. Mumford, 153–165 (Ann Arbor: University of Michigan Press, 1995); Hunting, Constance, ed. *May Sarton: Woman and Poet* (Orono: The National Poetry Foundation, University of Maine, 1982); Sarton, May. *Journal of a Solitude* (New York: Norton, 1973); Schillig, Lisette. "With Sure and Uncertain Footing: Negotiating the Terrain of a Solitude in May Sarton's Journals." In *Herspace: Women, Writing, and Solitude*, edited by Jo Malin and Victoria Boynton, 39–71 (Binghamton, NY: The Haworth Press, 2003).

Lisette T. Schillig

JULIAN OF NORWICH (1342–1343–c. 1420?) The medieval English mystic known as Julian of Norwich has left little evidence of her everyday life; in fact, even her name is unknown, and she probably assumed the name Julian from the church (St. Julian's) in Norwich, England, in which she chose to live in seclusion. Yet the autobiographical dimension of this contemporary of Geoffrey Chaucer is fundamental to her **identity** as a literary figure who de-

scribes the spiritual revelation she experienced in her thirty-first year. This revelation is the subject of a Middle English prose text, which exists in two distinct forms, a short version composed soon after the event, and a longer version written a number of years later. As Julian formulated her narration, she was aware that as a woman she was subject to criticism by those who disapproved of women teaching theology, so in order to clarify her purpose, she described certain incidental autobiographical details associated with her experience. These details consist mainly of the specific time at which her revelations occurred and of the persons present and the physical symptoms that preceded her experience. Yet the main autobiographical subject of her work is her description of the life-changing religious events, which, as she argues, justify and even require her narration.

Although very little is known about Julian's personal history, aside from what she relates of her revelations, much is known of the history of England in her day, and certainly the background of what historian Barbara W. Tuchman has called "the calamitous 14th century" is relevant. Since the Black Plague struck England in 1348 when Julian was a child, she was intensely familiar with the presence of widespread death, and two more great waves of the plague were to devastate the nation before she reached age thirty. Although she probably spent most of her adult life in religious seclusion, she could not have been entirely unaware that England was at war with France (the Hundred Years' War, 1337–1453) throughout her lifetime. She would also have heard ominous rumors about political developments such as those associated with the mental decline of the aging King Edward III, the relatively early death of Edward's son the Black Prince, the accession to the throne of Edward's ten-year-old grandson Richard, and the turbulent events resulting from the power struggles that occupied the entire reign of Richard II. Though the bloody Peasants' Revolt of 1381 occurred years after Julian's religious visions, the social tensions that were to lead to the revolt must have been building perceptibly during her early life.

Julian herself says nothing of contemporary events except insofar as her decision to flee the world reflects a rejection of them. For her, the definitive moment of her autobiography occurred when, in May 1373, having wished for illness and suffering in order to emulate Christ, she became severely ill and drew near to death. As she prepared to die, with her mother at her side, she experienced a sequence of "showings" (Middle English, "shewings") or revelations accompanied by a kind of spiritual dialogue with Christ. In the course of the first fifteen showings, Julian's physical pain and weakness were relieved, and she awakened the next day much recovered but so confused about her intense experience that she told an attending priest that she had raved. She immediately realized, however, that her visions were more than mere raving, and, deeply ashamed of having spoken so carelessly, she fell asleep only to have a sixteenth revelation validating the first fifteen.

It was clear to Julian that the revelations made to her were divinely intended for her fellow Christians, so she duly recorded them despite her awareness that her motives might be misunderstood. She stipulates that she is not educated, which may only mean that she is not a Latin scholar, but she firmly if modestly maintains that her transmission of her spiritual experiences is a fulfillment of divine will.

Another remarkable feature of the autobiographical aspect of Julian's writings is that the two versions of the *Showings* or *Revelations of Divine Love* are separated in time by nearly twenty years. The effect of this interval indicates two things. First, Julian remained devoted to the truths revealed to her and meditated at length on

them for many years. Also, she developed over time a more elaborate sense of the implications of her visions. For example, one famous passage in the long text (Chapter 60) discusses Christ as mother, explaining that the nature, intensity, and comfort of Christ's love are those of a mother.

Although Julian became an anchorite or religious recluse (probably after her revelations), she did enjoy a certain local fame, since some of the few facts we have about her life include records of money left to her in wills, and the writings of **Margery Kempe** document a visit to her at Norwich. Yet, in the turbulence of the fourteenth and fifteenth centuries her existence was never known outside of her small community, and with the English Reformation of the sixteenth century, the traditional establishments and often the documents of the Roman Church were widely destroyed. It was in the seventeenth century that a few surviving manuscripts of Julian's *Showings* began to appear, and the first printed version of the work (the long version) was published by Serenus Cressy in 1670, which was titled *XVI Revelations of Divine Love. Shewed to a Devout Servant of our Lord, called Mother Juliana, An Anchorete of Norwich.*

Julian of Norwich had little influence on literature until the twentieth century, but, as her works became better known during that period, interest in them grew, and her writing began to receive recognition from such distinguished figures as T. S. Eliot, who alludes to her in his poetry. In an age that celebrated individualism, it was finally possible to acknowledge the quiet but monumental individualism of a medieval anchorite.

Further Reading: Baker, Denise Nowakowski. *Julian of Norwich's Showings: From Vision to Book* (Princeton, NJ: Princeton University Press, 1994); Julian of Norwich. *A Book of Showings to the Anchoress Julian of Norwich.* 2 vols. Edited by Edmund Colledge and James Walsh (Toronto: Pontifical Institute of Medieval Studies, 1978);

Julian of Norwich. *The Shewings of Julian of Norwich*. Edited by Georgia Ronan Crampton (Kalamazoo: Western Michigan University Press, 1994); Krantz, M. Diane F. *The Life and Text of Julian of Norwich: The Poetics of Enclosure* (New York: Peter Lang, 1997); Lagorio, Valerie Marie, and Ritamary Bradley. *The Fourteenth-Century English Mystics: A Comprehensive Annotated Bibliography* (New York: Garland, 1981); McEntire, Sandra J., ed. *Julian of Norwich: A Book of Essays* (New York: Garland, 1998).

Robert W. Haynes